EMMELINE B. WELLS

EMMELINE B. WELLS

AN INTIMATE HISTORY

Carol Cornwall Madsen

The University of Utah Press
Salt Lake City

The Defiance House Man colophon is a registered trademark of The University of Utah Press. It is based on a four-foot-tall Ancient Puebloan pictograph (late PIII) near Glen Canyon, Utah.

21 20 19 18 17 1 2 3 4 5

LIBRARY OF CONGRESS CATALOGING-IN-PUBLICATION DATA

Names: Madsen, Carol Cornwall, 1930– author.
Title: Emmeline B. Wells : an intimate history / Carol Cornwall Madsen.
Description: Salt Lake City : The University of Utah Press, [2016] | Includes bibliographical references and index.
Identifiers: LCCN 2016049355| ISBN 9781607815235 (cloth : alk. paper) | ISBN 9781607815242 (ebook)
Subjects: LCSH: Wells, Emmeline B. (Emmeline Blanche), 1828–1921. | Mormons—United States—Biography. | Mormon women—United States—Biography.
Classification: LCC BX8695.W45 M335 2016 | DDC 289.3092 [B]—dc23
LC record available at https://lccn.loc.gov/2016049355

Printed and bound in the United States of America.

Contents

Photographs follow page 242 and page 358.

Acknowledgments

Though I have been retired from Brigham Young University (BYU) for a number of years, much of the research and most of the encouragement and help in preparing this volume came from my association with the Joseph Fielding Smith Institute for Latter-day Saint (LDS) History. Shortly after retirement in 2006, I produced the first volume on the life of Emmeline B. Wells entitled *An Advocate for Women: The Public Life of Emmeline B. Wells, 1870–1920*. This current volume, focusing on her private life, is a companion piece to the earlier one.

Leaving a paper trail of thousands of pages from diaries, letters, newspaper articles and editorials, and a volume of poetry, Emmeline Wells challenged any biographer to reduce such an abundance of resource material into a comprehensive but concise history of her life. In order to do justice to this reservoir of information, I made the decision to write two volumes, the public and the private lives of Emmeline B. Wells, following her example of dichotomizing her life in that way.

The fountainhead of source material for both of these volumes is her forty-seven diaries, written between 1844 and 1920. A great swath of time—1846 to 1872—is missing, although the compulsory nature of her writing suggests those diaries are lost, not unwritten. Some years are incomplete, and the last few were written for her by her daughter Annie Cannon. Numerous biographical sketches, published in LDS Church magazines and newspapers, and written by or for her for many purposes, contain the general contour of her life. Most of them correspond, although facts in some accounts are enhanced, exaggerated, and sometimes altered. Many have been the researchers on this project, mainly students at Brigham Young University, who have helped to pare away the colorful but mythical wrappings of the facts, which are fanciful enough without embellishment.

That stream of willing helpers at BYU has been augmented over the years by others who have graciously accepted invitations to do further research, to read and respond to the various drafts, to comment, instruct, suggest, revise, and in myriad ways improve early attempts of this biography. Maureen (Maura) Ursenbach Beecher and Jill Mulvay Derr, my colleagues at BYU, have lent me great encouragement along with historical tidbits that have enhanced my understanding of Emmeline and her friends. From the beginning they have been my models of exemplary historians. For this volume I also owe great appreciation to Lavina Fielding Anderson and Cherry Bushman Silver for their meticulous reading of the manuscript and their insightful comments and suggestions.

Cherry Silver and Sheree Bench are currently finishing the editing of the diaries of Emmeline B. Wells, and their help in discerning words as well as meanings from the diary entries has been invaluable. When published, the diaries will enlarge our understanding of many of the references and experiences alluded to in this volume. The Wells diaries easily take their place among the great diaries of Mormon history.

I appreciate the cooperation of the curators and staff of Mormon history at the L. Tom Perry Special Collections at the Harold B. Lee Library at Brigham Young University, where the diaries are housed. Information has also been gleaned from the LDS Church History Library, the Utah State Historical Society, Special Collections at the University of Utah Library, the Pioneer Memorial Museum of the Daughters of Utah Pioneers, the library of the Relief Society General Board, the British Library, and the Fawcett Library of Women's History in London. Pictures have come from a variety of sources, as indicated. All these repositories have been forthcoming and helpful over the years in making available the materials that have been essential to the making of this book. I am especially grateful to John Alley of the University of Utah Press for all he has done to bring this volume to fruition. His patience, cooperation, suggestions, and understanding will never be forgotten. Most of all, no one has been more at my side throughout all these years than Jennifer Reeder, an astute researcher, a great scholar of Mormon women's history, an adviser and mentor, and a dear friend. Truly, this book could not have come into being without her enduring interest, help, and encouragement. Whatever merits the book might have are in large measure due to her close association with it. I take full responsibility for whatever lapses might be detected.

As Emmeline expressed her own wonder at the power of place, I quickly learned from my visits to New England why it held her so tenaciously in its thrall. With the gracious help and amazing knowledge of the late Carolyn Chouinard, New Salem's local historian, I traveled to all the sites that were part of Emmeline's early life. I felt the strong attachment Carolyn felt for these places, since she was a longtime admirer of Emmeline Wells and had studied her New England years. Through Carolyn I came to feel the mystique about this place that Emmeline so vibrantly conveyed in her reminiscences. I also followed the trail of her diary as she visited Europe in 1899, seeing it as she saw it, through her written descriptions. With the assistance of the holdings of the Fawcett Library of Women's History in London and the British Library, this pinnacle experience of Emmeline's working life was opened up to me. I have tried as far as possible to inhabit her world and experience it in the places where her life unfolded.

For the patience and encouragement of my husband, Gordon, and my ever-loyal children, I am eternally grateful, and to them this book is dedicated.

To the Reader

Could mortal lip divine
The undeveloped freight
Of a delivered syllable,
'Twould crumble with the weight.

—Emily Dickinson

Emily Dickinson was a master of the economy of syllables, the words they created in her hands often heavy with "undeveloped freight." Emmeline Wells also understood the impact of each delivered syllable, but unlike Emily, she used them unsparingly. She drew them together in words that filled thousands of pages of letters, poems and stories, editorials and articles, and most significantly her diaries. She began writing in her youth and never stopped until shortly before her death. It is from this multitude of words, crowding the story of her life to its very margins, from which this narrative unfolds. What follows is an attempt to explore Emmeline's interior landscape with enough context to situate it in time and place. This is one woman's story told, as far as possible, in her own words. It follows the chronological trajectory of her diary, written within a narrative framework to provide coherence, interpretation, and understanding. In making her diary the cynosure of all her writing and by privileging it as the primary source from which I have constructed this narrative, I have focused the story on *her* perception of herself and the people and events that made up her world. Her life experiences plucked every emotional string, movingly replayed in her diary, the friend to whom she could be wholly honest. It received the wounding shards that continually penetrated her life but also celebrated the bright clearings in her hedged-up world. I think of her as a woman triumphant because despite the unyielding grip with which a plethora of challenges seized her throughout her life and her strong penchant for entertaining sorrow, she moved forward with equally extraordinary determination to resist these disabling forces.

While history and even biography are often a matter of finding and then linking enough pieces of information and relevant events to create a convincing and thorough study, the problem in assembling the pieces of Emmeline's life was that there were so many. Besides her own writings, newspapers, magazines, and other publications are replete with life sketches and information about her. Much of her life was lived in public, which, in itself, is remarkable for a woman in the nineteenth century. Minutes of meetings, conventions, and conferences note her participation. Histories of organizations—religious, social, and political—record her extraordinary range of public involvement, while her diary entries are powerful evocations of a life whose mind and heart are often in tension. That she was the most widely known Mormon woman of her time, in and outside the Mormon Church, was undisputed among her contemporaries. She was self-created in that respect. From a child of obscure New England beginnings, she drew herself upward to become a woman of ambition, ability, and achievement. Those qualities are more specifically addressed in a prior volume focusing on Emmeline's public life.[1] Together these volumes show the dichotomies but also the connections between the public and private woman.

As far as she was able, she did not let her public activities intrude on her family life, and she succeeded to a remarkable extent, as her daughter Annie noted.[2] Similarly, she protected the introspective, emotional reflections of her inner world from the curious minds and quick judgments of her peers, the public, and her rivals. She carefully constructed a facade of willed pleasantry to hide the mercurial life within.

Even her published writings are examples of this pattern of contrasts. Her forceful, opinionated, and analytical editorials on women's rights and other issues of her time diverge dramatically from the sentimental poetry and nostalgic sketches of New England life that she usually wrote under the folksy signature "Aunt Em," the name by which she was best known. Her infatuation with nature, born of her New England beginnings, did not produce great poetry, just deeply felt visual images, openly expressed emotions, and prayerful utterances in simple rhythmic, rhyming prose.

Emmeline would not have considered herself a feminist, even if the term had been used in the nineteenth century, but she happily, consistently, and determinedly acknowledged that she was progressive in her thinking and actions. She favored equal rights for women and believed that when Joseph Smith "turned the key" to women through the organization of the

1. Carol Cornwall Madsen, *An Advocate for Women: The Public Life of Emmeline B. Wells, 1870–1920*.

2. Annie Wells Cannon, "Mothers in Israel," 66.

Relief Society, he opened long-closed doors for them and the possibility of untold opportunities.[3] For Emmeline, this symbolic gesture was a talisman for the future.

A faithful member of the Church of Jesus Christ of Latter-day Saints (Mormon), she was not self-righteous or insular in her beliefs. But she never equivocated on them. She was a bridge builder, reaching beyond Mormon borders to make connections with both local and national individuals not of her faith while never pretending to be anything but a loyal Mormon. She valued the perspectives of other women, particularly those in the national suffrage movement and the National Council of Women, on the social and political issues of the time and firmly believed that members of her church could revise Gentile perceptions of Mormons and their beliefs through more interaction. She herself made lasting personal friendships among Mormon detractors while dispelling misconceptions about her people. She concurred with Joseph Smith's conviction that "it is necessary to hold an influence in the world and thus spare ourselves an extermination; and also accomplish our end in spreading the gospel or holiness in the earth."[4]

Though she came to love her western home, Emmeline was a New Englander until the day she died. Many trips to Massachusetts and the rural area where she had once lived enabled me to see and feel the land that so pervaded her life and memories. I have visited the rural Massachusetts villages that formed the physical boundaries of her childhood—Petersham, New Salem, and North New Salem. The events occurring in each place were so embedded in her consciousness that they found repeated reference in her writings and conversation. Seeing the church, the school, the baptismal brook, the spot on which her home once stood, and the groves of trees brought into reality the descriptions in so many of her poems and essays. Basking in the natural world of tall pines, languid streams, and verdant meadows that surrounded these quaint mill towns enabled me to understand why the sense of place had so beguiled her and held such power in her mind and memories. Her nature resonated the natural world's many moods, from the hope and expectancy of spring to the shadowed cold and dark of winter.

During those early years, Emmeline's friends and instructors concluded that her precocity and ambition bespoke a life apart from the ordinary. That she would find fulfillment of that prophetic assumption in the world of

3. "A Book of Records Containing the Proceedings of the Female Relief Society of Nauvoo," April 28, 1842, LDS Church History Library, Salt Lake City. See also "A Wonderful Age," *Woman's Exponent* 27 (February 1, 1899): 100.

4. "Book of Records," May 26, 1842.

poetry was the hope that kept pen to paper throughout her productive life. She wanted to achieve, indeed, to excel in that artistic realm. But her embrace of Mormonism at age fourteen put her on a course whose destination she did not then see. The unexpected turns and detours she encountered as she pursued that path led her to find solace and purpose through her lifelong faith in an overruling power that guided her throughout the journey. Along the way she learned that personal ambition could be combined with public service. "To be" might also mean "to do." The ponderings of her youth among her beloved hemlock groves spawned a yearning "for a field of true usefulness," and time taught her that "if there is a determination to succeed no obstacles however opposing in their nature can hinder one."[5] And so she fashioned her life.

Her certitude of a providential world arose from her Congregational background and meshed well with her Mormon convictions. This trust bore the weight of her trials and framed her response to them. In every experience, she found, there was always a lesson to be learned, a nature to be refined, a submission to be tested, or a faith to be strengthened.

Her long life could be seen as triumph against the reverses that might have felled her along the way. She never underplayed her losses or disappointments, but neither did she allow them to stifle her spirit or undermine her commitments. Only halfway through her long life, she had already found the strength that would take her all the way. "I have risen triumphant," she exclaimed to her diary. This declaration accompanied her throughout her life and paved the way for that long journey.

5. Emmeline B. Wells, Diary, July 8, 1875.

EMMELINE B. WELLS

CHAPTER 1

A New England Heritage
(1828–1832)

"IS NOT MY LIFE A ROMANCE indeed it is a novel strange and marvellous."[1] Dramatic words for a sixteen-year-old girl. But teenage Emmeline was already a deserted wife and bereft mother when she wrote them, and dramatic as her words were, they were only introductory to the literary romance by which she defined her life. Others agreed. "Probably no story in fiction compares more of romance, pathos, courage, and devotion than does hers," one admirer wrote shortly before her death.[2] Another observed that "the narrative of her life is as interesting as any romance and full of rich and tender lessons."[3] In later years, Emmeline transcribed some of that narrative into a fanciful autobiography, rendering her early life story as a personal roman à clef, only slightly disguising real places, events, and individuals with fictitious names. She warned the reader in "Hephzibah," the title she gave to this early life history, that if the tale she told were "true to life, there would be some heavy dark shading." Yet amid these dark corners of her life, she promised there would be "touches of pathetic sweetness" and the "holy calm of summer twilight."[4] This undulating path of joy and sorrow, exultation and disappointment, triumph and tragedy etched the contours of her life. "When I look back," she wrote in September 1874, "it seems incredible that I should have passed through such hard and thorny places,"

1. E. Wells, Diary, February 20, 1845.

2. Mrs. F. B. Robinson (Eliza Deseretta Baldwin), "Emmeline B. Wells, Lit.D.," paper given at Ladies Relief Society at Beaver, UT, ca. 1920, Utah State Historical Society, Salt Lake City.

3. "Aunt Em," 139–42.

4. "Hephzibah," *Woman's Exponent* 18 (June 1, 1889): 1–2, serialized from vol. 18 (June 1, 1889) through vol. 19 (September 15, 1890). Many of the details of her early life are scattered throughout her diaries and New England articles, most of which corroborate the factual basis of this long, serialized sketch of her life through 1846.

but "I have always [been]... hopeful believing in the light after darkness."[5] And that was her saving grace. Her ability to rationalize disappointment, surmount failure, and spiritualize loss sustained her determination to excel and to serve.

Large in ambition, and hoping to fulfill the expectations of her teachers and schoolmates that she was "a child of destiny," Emmeline became a prominent actor in nineteenth-century politics in Utah, her adopted state after conversion to the Church of Jesus Christ of Latter-day Saints, and a formidable participant in the national women's rights movement of that century. The political and social issues that engaged her considerable talents ensured a public presence and an impressive measure of public acclaim.[6]

Though her passion for public service and desire for distinction took her into a broad realm of human experience, they did not embrace the whole of her identity. As "Aunt Em," the familiar sobriquet by which her friends knew her, she presented a very different persona from the self-assured, resolute public woman. This alter ego was energized by poetic aspirations and consumed by pensive meditations. Aunt Em lived in a world peopled by her large extended family and a host of friends, fueled by ever-increasing church assignments, and embellished by her strong attachment to the natural world. It was a life thinly curtained from the public stage she entered in midlife. However, she seldom publicly exposed the emotional heights and depths her roller-coaster life evoked and attributed all to "God's will." Her daughter Annie, the one most like her, found it was not "an easy task to draw aside the curtain and disclose home pictures" of her mother, when asked to describe Emmeline's home life. "Especially do I think this true," Annie explained, "because there has been so marked a difference between her public and her private life." Those qualities that motivated her public activism, Annie continued, shielded "with equal zeal the innermost thoughts and activities of the home."[7]

This distinction between the public and the private was evident in Emmeline's modes of writing as well. She used the pages of the LDS woman's newspaper, the *Woman's Exponent* (1872–1914), which she edited for thirty-seven years, to support the emancipation of women from the customs and traditions that restricted their social usefulness and individual potential. In concert with national leaders and organizations, she supported woman suffrage and equal opportunity for women. At a time when some of the

5. E. Wells, Diary, September 1, 1874.

6. For the story of her public life and contributions, see C. Madsen, *Advocate for Women.*

7. A. W. Cannon, "Mothers in Israel."

principles of the religion she had adopted were under siege, she also became an articulate and persuasive defender of her faith.[8]

While her pen brought her prominence in this public career, producing innumerable letters, editorials, newspaper articles, and reports to national conventions, she also gave voice to a more intimate expression of her thoughts and feelings in private letters and notes, in her volumes of poetry, in reflective articles for her paper, and especially in her diaries. Recognizing Emmeline's penchant to read and her early propensity to write, her mother cautioned her about "getting strange notions into [her] head" and warned her against becoming a "wishy-washy novel writer." She wisely advised her daughter to study and submit her compositions for correction in order to learn how to write something worthy of reading.[9] Emmeline would herself come to realize that "there is no excellence without labor."[10]

Despite her mother's wishes, in midlife Emmeline did dabble in fiction, veering dangerously close to writing the sentimental novels and stories her mother disdained. However, a contemporary of Emmeline declared that she had written "more than any other Latter-day Saint writer of her sex, and has done it in a sane, dignified way," certainly comforting words had her mother lived to hear them.[11]

Her Puritan background taught her to rely on a providential ordering of her life. This strong conviction of an overruling power led her to accept "God's will" in the "heavy dark shadings" that clouded her life as well as in the moments of "pathetic sweetness." She carried her sorrows "silently, loath to burden another with anything she [could] herself endure," one friend noted.[12] She thus met life with remarkable self-discipline, accepting the bitter and the sweet with equanimity. In her nearly century-long life, her New England roots continually defined her character even as they nourished her memory and imagination.

Slender and delicate, even fragile looking, Emmeline never measured more than five feet tall. Her hair was black until it took on the gray and then white of age. Her features were considered by some as "aristocratic," which in later years her bearing came to match. She was fashionable in her dress, as long as fashion dictated the style she early chose for herself, but in time her apparel could be described only as quaint. She was fastidious about her

8. Polygamy, along with Mormonism's monolithic economic and political systems, was the source of most of the antagonism toward and censure of Mormonism.

9. Aunt Em, "The Old Garrett," *Woman's Exponent* 17 (October 1, 1888): 67.

10. Aunt Em, "Midnight Soliloquy," *Woman's Exponent* 8 (April 15, 1880): 175–76.

11. Susa Young Gates, "Emmeline B. Wells," 50–51.

12. "Aunt Em."

appearance, disdaining the "elderly" purple in favor of gray and blue for her silk dresses. She even removed purple flowers from her bonnets, replacing them with blue forget-me-nots, the color of her eyes and reminder of the dainty New England flowers she loved to gather. Her daughter Melvina made the delicate petticoats that gave shape to her long skirts, and a quarter yard of pastel tulle or some other diaphanous fabric tied in a bow around her neck completed her usual attire. Her disdain for purple did not extend to her jewelry, however. She chose to wear a ring of deep-purple amethyst, her birthstone, on her first finger and amethyst earrings in her pierced ears.[13] Besides a small string of gold beads that often adorned her neck, she wore a long chain holding a gold pocket watch.[14] As she aged, she appeared as a quaint apparition from the long ago.

Her personality did not always match this physical description, however. Within her lay an inner force that when tapped gave her an aura and demeanor of "commanding power," as one friend observed. Others commented that she was "exceedingly frank," "outspoken almost to bluntness," "sarcastic at times, not to say caustic," but "generous to a fault." A counterbalance to her singular earnestness was "her keen sense of humor," which, according to one witness, "prolonged her life and preserved her reason, in the midst of crushing trials."[15] She was noted as being the "most observed" in social settings, both at home in Utah and in the social gatherings at eastern women's conferences. When a relative accompanied her to an important woman's meeting in New York, she noted that despite being so small and "oddly attired," before the meeting was over, "Aunt Em was the figure of attention.... [S]he was the one who knew all the Rules of Order and the proper procedures."[16] Her encyclopedic memory, her knowledge of current events, and her exhilarating conversation were legendary and ensured a ready invitation to public and private gatherings.

She began life as Emmeline Blanche Woodward, the fifth daughter and seventh child of David and Diadama Hare Woodward. She was born in

13. Emmeline occasionally used "Amethyst" as a pseudonym for some of her writings.

14. Jean Cannon King, a great-granddaughter, "Daughters of Utah Pioneers History of Emmeline Blanche Woodward Wells," files of Daughters of Utah Pioneers History Department, Salt Lake City, typescript copy in my possession.

15. "Emmeline B. Wells," in "The Five General Presidents of the Relief Society," 135–37; Augusta Joyce Crocheron, "Emeline [*sic*] B. Wells," in *Representative Women of Deseret*, by Crocheron, 62–71; Gates, "Emmeline B. Wells," 45–53; Whitney, "Emmeline B. Woodward Wells."

16. Abbie H. Wells, letter to Judith R. Dushku, March 27, 1975, as quoted in Patricia Rasmussen Eaton-Gadsby and Judith Rasmussen Dushku, "Emmeline B. Wells," in *Sister Saints*, edited by Vicky Burgess-Olson, 457–78.

Petersham, Franklin County (later Worcester), Massachusetts, in 1828, at a time when the country was moving into what historians have called the "Age of Democracy" with the election of Andrew Jackson to the US presidency. She was destined to spend her adult life in a monumental effort to extend the democratic vision of that optimistic time to all of America's citizens, men and women alike. She brought a host of capabilities to aid her in this pursuit. Her leap-year birthday, February 29, commemorated only every four years, was an aberration that seemed to foretell a life that would similarly skirt the conventions of her sex, time, and place.

Petersham was a picture-perfect New England village. Though Emmeline spent only fifteen years of her long life in New England, it held her in a lifelong thrall. Settled in the mid-eighteenth century, Petersham was one of a cluster of mill towns in central Massachusetts that were situated in an idyllic part of the state. The area was fed by several streams, edged by thickly wooded hills, and graced by flower-laden meadows. Oak, chestnut, and walnut trees marked the upper ridges of the hills that surrounded the villages, while the hemlock, beech, and softwoods sheltered the streams and ponds and lined the roads that led from village to village.[17] The stone walls that demarcated the farmland and the meadows were built from the rocks that emerged when the plow tilled the thin and rocky soil. Several generations of use depleted much of its fertility, and the commercial farms were eventually abandoned, leaving only the stone walls to mark a once-thriving agricultural industry. But the numerous streams that flowed into ponds of varying sizes not only added to the region's beauty but also facilitated the development of several industries. Factories and mills—woolen, cotton, and cider—flourished along the streams. Old Factory Village was so named because of the numerous mills flanking the village's section of the Swift River, the principal stream flowing through Petersham. Made of stone and heavy timber, the mills were spartan in design and furnishings but sturdy enough to perform their function.[18] Typically, Emmeline commemorated her birthplace, the Old Factory Village, three miles south of Petersham Center, in verse:

17. Details about this period of Petersham's history come from Mabel Cook Coolidge, *The History of Petersham, Massachusetts*; and John Fiske, "An Historical Address: 200th Anniversary Celebration of the Town of Petersham, Massachusetts, July 4, 5, 1954," copy in my possession. I am also indebted to Delight Haines, director of the Petersham Historical Society, and Carolyn Chouinard of New Salem for copies of early maps and other contemporary data relating to the period in which Emmeline Wells lived in the area, including information taken from cemetery records and other historical documents.

18. Michael J. Tougias, *Quiet Places of Massachusetts*, 58–59.

A village nestled down among the hills,
With quaint old fashion'd houses low and brown:
And picture-like some old neglected mills,
In days gone by, the pride of all the town.[19]

Emmeline's grandfather Elisha Woodward owned a cider and a woolen mill near the town. Emmeline remembered the old woolen mill "situated in the centre of the little cluster of dwellings, on a clear placid stream of water that bounds over its rocky bed, on through the town." A carding machine adjoined the mill, "turning out in great abundance the soft, white rolls that were spun on the great wheels in all the country houses" by the women of those households.[20] Mill towns prospered through this practical division of labor. Most of the mill owners also cultivated the usable farmland, providing self-sufficiency for the townspeople. The major female commercial occupation was braiding hats from bleached and dyed palm leaves, a technique introduced in 1820 when town resident Ruel Farrar studied the construction of an imported French palm-leaf hat and taught the skill to the women of the village. This cottage industry later expanded to include basket weaving and other homemade novelties that were popular with the "summer people."[21] During a visit to New England in 1885, Emmeline observed that the craft was still practiced.[22]

Petersham and most of the surrounding mill towns reached their population and industrial zenith between 1820 and 1850. Petersham numbered 1,794 residents in 1800,[23] and by 1840 it had grown into a bustling commercial and trade center.[24] Like most rural villages, the Petersham town common was the center of civic life and drew the residents together in shared

19. "Hephzibah," *Woman's Exponent* 18 (June 1, 1889): 1–2.

20. Ibid., 2.

21. Charles K. Wilder, "Charles K. Wilder Wrote of the Industries in Petersham in 1855," in *History of Petersham*, by Coolidge, 158–62.

22. Emmeline B. Wells, "My Trip East," December 28, 1885, 47. This is a separate diary and reminiscence written between December 1885 and January 1886 during her first visit to New Salem after a forty-year absence.

23. The population rose slightly in 1840 but thereafter continued its decline. By the time Emmeline's daughters Belle and Louie visited, in 1883, the old country homes had been turned into boardinghouses, and small hotels were built to accommodate the "summer people" who had made the area a summer retreat from the heat of Boston. Population data from Charles K. Wilder, comp., *Sketches of Petersham Natives and Adopted Citizens by J. B. Howe*, 219. See also Louie Wells, "Letter IV," *Woman's Exponent* 12 (September 15, 1883): 61–62.

24. "Petersham History."

cultural and social activities. Petersham's town common was situated on a small rise surrounded by wooded hills and farms and easily spotted from a distance. On a return trip to the town she had left many years before, Emmeline's sister Lucy spied "the church on Petersham Hill" well before reaching the town of her birth. Its dome glowed, on that October morning, "like fire 'neath the sun's golden rays...presenting a living picture transparently beautiful!" In October, Lucy noted, New England was wrapped in an autumnal haze. It was the town's peaceful beauty that made it a summer retreat for city dwellers.[25]

The old Congregational church, which dominated the view of Petersham's common, was the "center of the town and society," elevated, in both function and location, above the other buildings on the common. For many years, it was also the town hall. Over time, religious dissension among the townspeople led to the erection of several other churches claiming a spot on the town common and interspersed by stately country homes and the schoolhouse.[26] Just off of the common was the cemetery, where Adaline, the oldest child of David and Diadama, who died in 1829, was buried.

It was to Petersham that Benajah Woodward migrated from Taunton, Massachusetts, in 1777. The economic possibilities opening up in central Massachusetts gradually drew Benajah's branch of the Woodward family to Petersham, which included his five sons and two daughters, not all of whom remained permanent residents. Benajah acquired a twenty-acre parcel of land on which his son Seth built the family home in which Benajah lived.

The Woodwards had a long history of military service reaching back to 912 and the Norman invasion of England. Emmeline's ancestors fought with such valor and renown at the battles of Hastings, Agincourt, and Edgehill "as to be given by the king a shield of pure gold with the motto 'Gentle but brave.'"[27] Benajah, his father, Israel, and his grandfather John had all been

25. L[ucy]. M. Hewlings, "Back to the Long Ago," *Woman's Exponent* 23 (April 15, 1895): 252–53.

26. "Reminiscences of C. Frederick Bosworth, Locating Houses as Early as 1836," in *History of Petersham*, by Coolidge, 205. The schoolhouse was of an "antiquated" design, square with a roof that slanted on each side from a point in the center. It had high windows and a porch on the front. The seats were on elevated tiers situated on opposite sides of the room.

27. Information taken from "Biography of Emmeline B. Wells," written by herself in the third person. In the sketch she noted that "these historical facts are from Woodward letters and records examined, attested, signed and sealed by the Rector of Old Crusaders' Church, Astor Manor, Warwickshire." This explanation was abbreviated in Whitney's account of her life (586). Appreciation to Mary Hamblin, a great-granddaughter of Emmeline, for a photocopy of the original typescript.

colonial soldiers in Taunton, and later all five of Benajah's sons fought in the Revolutionary War.[28] Benajah's descendants, including Emmeline, were proud of their Revolutionary heritage and looked back with equal pride on the accomplishments of the first American Woodward, Nathaniel, a mathematician, surveyor, and carpenter, who arrived in Boston in 1630.

In 1778 Benajah's son and Emmeline's paternal grandfather, Elisha Woodward, married Lucy Manson, the daughter of a British officer, in Taunton, and soon afterward followed his father to Petersham, having acquired a piece of land near Old Factory Village, where he established several mills and a prosperous farm.[29] The educated and cultured Lucy brought refinement to the rural village. She and Elisha raised a family of four sons and a daughter, who was named after her mother, but lived only a day after her birth in 1790. Lucy died six months later. Within another half year, Elisha married Desiré King and three more children were added to his family. Desiré died a year after Emmeline's birth, and so all of Emmeline's happy recollections of her grandfather were as a widower.

The second son born to Elisha and Lucy Manson Woodward was David, Emmeline's father. Unlike his father and some of his uncles, David seemed to have achieved little prominence in Petersham, but he married well. Perhaps because of his family's status in the community, he successfully won the hand of Diadama Hare, daughter of James and Sarah Morgan Hare (also Hair), who were descendants of the earliest settlers of Brookfield, a village a few miles southeast of Petersham. In later years Emmeline was pleased to learn that Lucy Stone, a noted woman suffragist of Boston, whom she greatly admired, was also born in Brookfield.[30]

Like the Woodwards, the Hares were early patriots.[31] Diadama Hare was born in 1794 (or 1795) in Brookfield, located on one of the main Massachusetts Bay paths that connected various towns throughout the

28. Harold Edward Woodward, comp., *Some Descendants of Nathaniel Woodward Who Came from England to Boston about 1630*.

29. Family records differ on his acquisition of the land. Some indicate he bought it from his son Seth, who had migrated to Petersham before Benajah, and other records indicate he inherited a parcel from his father. See ibid., 18.

30. More on Emmeline's relationship with Lucy Stone is in C. Madsen, *Advocate for Women*, 219.

31. Josiah Howard Temple, *History of North Brookfield, Massachusetts*; Thomas Snell, *A Sermon Containing a Brief History of the Town, and Especially of the Church and Parish of North Brookfield, from 1798 to the Present Time*. Demographic data can be found in *Heads of Families, First Census of the U.S., 1790, State of Massachusetts*. Family genealogy comes from Woodward family genealogical records, copies in my possession, courtesy of various family members.

colony and later state.[32] Colonial New England had a history to tell, and the towns and villages outside of Boston provided the scenic settings.

After the death of each of her parents, nineteen-year-old Diadama left North Brookfield, met thirty-three-year-old David Woodward, and married him the next year, 1814, in Petersham. Family stories describe Diadama as a handsome woman with long, beautiful hair, who attracted the attention of General Lafayette (Gilbert du Mentier), a Frenchman on the staff of George Washington. Her descendants were fond of describing the time Lafayette chose her to dance with him.[33] Of more importance to Emmeline was her discovery that Diadama's British ancestors displayed both musical and literary talent, which remained strong traits in the family line.

Over the next twenty-five years, Diadama gave birth to ten children, seven daughters and three sons.[34] The oldest, Adaline Emily, born in 1816, died in 1829, a year after Emmeline's birth. Diadama's second daughter, Lucy, born in 1817, was the first to inherit her mother's love of learning, her interest in literature, and her cultured demeanor. She and Emmeline were most similar to their mother and to each other than they were to other family members. Both aspired to be teachers and poets. Lucy married Henry H. Granger in 1837, and the couple settled in Hardwick, close by Petersham, where they parented six children. Henry and their son Corydon were both killed in the Civil War.[35]

Pallas and Cordelia (Delia), Emmeline's other two older sisters, made their permanent homes in Massachusetts. Pallas and her husband, William Clark, settled in Orange, a village north of Petersham, and Delia, thrice married, followed the fortunes of each of her husbands as they moved throughout Massachusetts, eventually settling in Swampscott, just outside of Boston. Emmeline's older brother James also remained in Massachusetts and died in Springfield at age fifty-seven. Her other older brother, Manson,

32. Nathaniel Hawthorne mentions the path in *Twice-Told Tales* (Boston: American Stationers, 1837), and George Francis Marlowe features it in *The Old Bay Paths: Their Villages and Byways and Their Stories*. See also J. G. Holland, *The Bay Path: A Tale of New England Colonial Life*.

33. From the family records of Glenys Harris, descendant of Emmeline's sister Pallas, copy in my possession.

34. All of the Woodward children were born in the same Petersham house in the same room, described as the southeast front room across from the parlor on the northeast side of their home. E. Wells, Diary, February 16, 1901. Hiram Clark, a step-brother, was born in North New Salem.

35. E. B. W., "Lucy M. Hewlings," *Woman's Exponent* 29 (May 15, 1901): 105; also noted in Woodward family history in possession of Glenys Harris of Orange, MA. Used by permission. Of Lucy's six children, only Louis lived beyond the age of thirty.

and his family lived for a short time in Concord, Massachusetts, moving to Aspinwall and Nemaha City, Nebraska, and finally settling in Kansas, where he died in 1897.[36] Emmeline and Manson met just once, in 1882, after her move to Utah.[37] Emmeline's two younger sisters were baptized into the LDS Church, and like Emmeline they also settled in the West. Adeline Marie was born in December 1829, married Justice Earl in Salt Lake City, and some years after his death moved to California. She died at age ninety in 1919. Ellen Celeste, born in 1831, married Elijah Knapp Fuller in Salt Lake City as his fourth wife, raised eleven children, and then moved to Arizona, where she died in 1916. Hiram, the son of Diadama's second husband, Samuel Clark, traveled to Utah with Emmeline but eventually returned to New England. He died in 1923.

Preeminent among Emmeline's memories of Petersham was her association with her grandfather Elisha Woodward. He lived in a large, red-painted, gambrel-roofed farmhouse, with several types of outer buildings. Besides the kitchen garden, Elisha's property included rows of apple trees and beehives where the honey, gathered from his numerous flower gardens, accumulated each season. A favorite playhouse for the children was the barn, which sat amid saddle and dairy houses, a cider mill, and long sheds housing farm equipment.[38]

Emmeline found her grandfather's house to be "roomy, home-like and commodious," despite the heavy oak furniture and large antique fireplaces that dominated the public rooms. The bedrooms had small corner fireplaces and corner cupboards with brass handles, their contents always a mystery to Emmeline. The attic was redolent with the enticing aromas of the medicinal herbs drying on the large beams across the ceiling, as well as from the barrels of nuts, cider, and corn. In the parlor, the old grandfather enchanted his youthful audience with stories and fairy tales while his eager listeners warmed themselves before the fire. The candles threw their shadows on the walls of the long, low rooms and dark furniture, making a perfect setting for the stories of his own adventures that Elisha also told his grandchildren. He brought out his old colonel's uniform, complete with sword and musket, for

36. "F. L. Woodward Tells of Aspinwall and Nemaha City." F. L. Woodward was Manson's son. See also US Census, Illinois, Ogle County, Flagg; and US Census, Nebraska, Nemaha County, Aspinwall.

37. In October 1882, after attending the National Council of Women Executive Meeting in Omaha, Emmeline visited Atchison, Kansas, where she indicated that she visited relatives and friends but made no mention in her diary of the names of those relatives. See "From Omaha to Atchison," *Woman's Exponent* 11 (October 15, 1882): 79.

38. Hewlings, "Back to the Long Ago," 252–53.

them to see as he regaled them with tales of his Revolutionary War years. To the children, Elisha was a fount of historical incidents, humorous anecdotes, and fanciful stories, and their influence on Emmeline was notable at an early age. But of all the tales he told his grandchildren, they liked best his recital of meeting, courting, and marrying his wife Lucy Manson, who, he delighted in repeating, was the daughter of a British officer. She played the harp and dressed in "costly silks and creamy laces," he told them, and he was always proud to add that she gave them all up as well as her British loyalty to adapt to the manners and customs of the people among whom she lived until her death thirteen years after her marriage to Elisha.[39]

It was in her grandfather's garret, which held his wife's beautiful silks and laces, that Emmeline's fanciful nature first revealed itself. There she played school by herself, using her rag dolls as pupils. Dressing up in her grandmother's silks, she composed verses and fairy tales, which she sometimes recited to the family as well as to her rag dolls.[40] It was also in that attic that Emmeline discovered letters written by her grandmother, which encouraged her to one day put her own thoughts on paper.[41]

Emmeline always felt herself a favorite of her grandfather's and was devastated at his death when she was thirteen. No longer would she roam through the rooms of the old farmhouse, imagining the mysteries that they held. Nor would she be able to sit beside the corner fireplace in her grandfather's upstairs room, alone with him, and listen to his stories or tell him stories of her own. In her written reminiscences, she idealized her early childhood, and her grandfather was a compelling presence in her memories.

But most of all Petersham launched Emmeline's love affair with nature. "I have had a passionate love for the great out-spread book of nature," she wrote many years later, when Utah had become her home.[42] Her effusive and numerous evocations of nature's beauty and wisdom attest to that infatuation.[43] On the rare days she was alone in her *Woman's Exponent* office, her mind reached back to that halcyon childhood. "All day long my mind has been there among those hills and vales and by the shady brooks and the blue sky only overhead," she wrote one hot day in July 1893. Confined to her

39. Ibid.; "Hephzibah," *Woman's Exponent* 18 (June 15, 1889): 9, 10. See also H. Woodward, *Some Descendants of Nathaniel Woodward*, 33.

40. "Aunt Em," 140–42.

41. Aunt Em, "The Old Garrett," 67.

42. "Emmeline B. Woodward Wells." Orson F. Whitney was the grandson of Newel K. and Elizabeth Ann Whitney.

43. For a long narrative showing the intensity of her love of the natural world, see Aunt Em, "Love of the Beautiful in Nature," *Woman's Exponent* 5 (October 1, 1876): 65.

"pentup office with only dull uninteresting people coming and going," she longed "to be out among the hills.... in the scenes of girlhood." Such memories, she wrote, come "over me like a vision and wrap me in a mystic cloud of enchantment." These summons of idyllic childhood scenes gave Emmeline a brief surcease from "the real world of sorrow and suffering," an escape from the "cold dreary world" to "dreams of Elysium."[44] Throughout her life, her emotional retreat into nature and into the intimate world of memory served as a safety valve, diffusing the pressure of her kinetic activities.

Emmeline's first real birthday was celebrated on February 29, 1832, four years after her birth. The leap-year celebration was a happy and memorable time for Emmeline, with all of the family around her to share the long-awaited day. She had the pleasure of collecting her grandfather and leading him along the path in the woods to her dinner party. He was given a place of honor on the old-fashioned "settle," or bench, that could seat six or seven people, where he could see the large sputtering turkey on the rotating spit. With both mother and father, brothers and sisters, and a beloved grandfather gathered around the table, Emmeline's first birthday was stamped indelibly on her memory.[45]

But her Elysian life in Petersham came abruptly to an end just nine months later. As her father was driving a load of logs up a wooded hill, the wagon tipped and pinned him beneath the load. Although he was immediately extricated and taken to a nearby home, he died within hours. Thus, at age four, Emmeline experienced her first emotional trauma. Woodward family life changed in an instant, and Diadama was forced to confront all of the challenges that a nineteenth-century widow with eight children still at home inexorably faced.

How is it that when joy is at its height
A shadow broodeth o'er the gayest scene;
When every pulse is throbbing with delight,
Dark clouds like omens come and intervene.[46]

44. E. Wells, Diary, July 14, 15, 1893.
45. "Aunt Em," 139.
46. E. Wells, "A Glance Backward," in her *Musings and Memories*, 167–71, esp. 168.

CHAPTER 2

A New England Childhood
(1828–1844)

David Woodward's untimely death introduced his wife, Diadama, to the forbidding world of single parenthood in early nineteenth-century America. Maintaining eight children, ranging in age from one to fifteen, presented a formidable challenge to the thirty-seven-year-old widow. Few vocations were available to women beyond household or factory work, midwifery, or perhaps turning their homes into boardinghouses. Public school teaching by women was still in its infancy, requiring more education than many widows had, and public nursing, beyond the level of midwife, was considered a male profession until midcentury. No record remains of how Diadama supported her large family, but Emmeline later cited her mother as her inspiration to work for women's rights, as Diadama had learned firsthand the "injustice of the laws in regard to women, their property rights, and guardianship of their children."[1]

Emmeline remembered her mother as "a woman of strong characteristics, tall and dignified in figure, though gentle and womanly in manner and bearing."[2] In Emmeline's estimation, she had the qualities she would need in adapting to the new role that David's death imposed on her and was capable of "managing an estate as well as most men." Then, in 1834, a more hopeful future emerged with Diadama's marriage that October to Samuel Clark Jr., a house painter.[3] Their marriage required the family to leave their beloved Petersham and move ten miles away to North New Salem, one of several small communities making up the town of New Salem. Samuel's greatest contribution to the family appears to have been his siring of Hiram, born

1. Crocheron, "Emeline [*sic*] B. Wells," in *Representative Women of Deseret*, by Crocheron. See also Kate B. Carter, "Emmeline B. Wells."

2. "Hephzibah," *Woman's Exponent* 18 (July 15, 1889): 25–26.

3. Upon his marriage to Diadama, Samuel Clark became the legal guardian of her minor children, and his permission was necessary for their actions until they became of legal age (eighteen).

on April 15, 1835, who became a favorite of his older sisters.[4] Besides the notice of their marriage and two other legal documents relating to property transactions, the only evidence relating to Samuel Clark Jr. is his name, occupation, and the date, December 29, 1836, painted on an inner closet door off the vestibule of the Second Parish meetinghouse in North New Salem. Samuel Clark fades from Woodward history and from the statistical records of New Salem and surrounding towns. Had he died shortly after marrying Diadama, it is likely that Emmeline or other family members would have noted this second widowhood of their mother. The fact that he is so completely absent, except for a reference in Emmeline's diary to her "cruel guardian," suggests some kind of marital separation. Diadama is the dominant figure in Emmeline's diary during her years in New Salem.

North New Salem was home to Emmeline from ages six to sixteen. The Clark home was situated amid several broad acres of meadowland, pastures, hillsides, and woods, offering Emmeline all of the natural beauty and wonders that had so entranced her in Petersham.[5] The town common, located high on New Salem hill, was dominated by the First Parish Church and the New Salem Academy at which many of the ministers of the Congregational church had been educated or served on the board of trustees (or both).[6] North New Salem, sometimes referred to as North Village, had its own grammar school, church, Haskell's store (sometimes Hascall), and the home and office of Dr. Andrews. In the center of the village were the typical trade shops, all situated around the Middle Branch of the Swift River, amid a forest of hemlocks and mountain laurel.

Time—or her idealistic nature—may have enhanced Emmeline's memories of her childhood home, situated on a small rise above the Moose Horn Brook. The nearby "moss-covered well," the apple orchard whose aroma wafted into Emmeline's bedroom in the spring, the brook that flowed below the homestead, and the purple violets, lilacs, and pink roses Diadama carefully nurtured all vividly found their way into poems and reminiscences. It was the larger natural setting surrounding the home, however, that Emmeline most relished. Scattered among the thick green meadowland like pendants of blue glass were numbers of ponds, their smooth surface broken only by the scalloped leaves of white and pink water lilies. Created by beaver dams, the ponds attracted a variety of waterfowl, especially the beautiful blue herons, who built their nests in the tops of the trees, and wood ducks,

4. Hiram's birth date is noted as 1836 in some records. Emmeline cites both dates in her diary entries.

5. Mark W. Harris, *Among the Dry Bones: Liberal Religion in New Salem, Massachusetts*, 97.

6. Elizabeth Peirce, "New Salem Revisited"; Tougias, *Quiet Places of Massachusetts*, 47–51.

who built theirs in the trees' protected cavities. Moose Horn Brook teemed with speckled trout, one of which Emmeline proudly caught using just two sticks, as her brothers had taught her.

The brook was also where Emmeline remembered, "I rambled up and down, hour after hour," hearing the rippling sound of the brook as it "wound its way through and out of the hemlock grove, one of the most romantic spots that I have ever seen."[7] Though she rhapsodized on the beauty of flowers, streams, and meadows, nothing gave her more pleasure than the trees that surrounded the villages. "Trees are almost companions to me," she wrote. "Trees appeal to me with a power and significance so wonderful that I can find no words to give expression to the sentiment."[8] But she did—often—in both poetry and prose. Hemlocks, her favorite of all trees, enchanted Emmeline with their graceful boughs, sweet aroma, and whispering sounds and inspired the feelings that she wove into summer reveries and poetic verses. The hemlock grove was "perhaps the dearest spot of all and where I let my fancies run wild most uncontrollably," she wrote.[9] Under those boughs, "I have pondered over many a difficult lesson too ambitious to give up and to[o] young to solve all the questions that were given me to answer."[10] No child, she asserted, "ever could have enjoyed more the secluded haunts of the woods than I did.... [M]y heart swells with tenderness for them."[11]

In her adult pen sketches, Emmeline luxuriated in her memory of the symbiosis she felt with the natural world, but from her solitary moments in the woods as a child she also learned "many a hard lesson" that helped give form to her lofty goals. "Was it under the hemlock boughs or the hardy oak tree," Emmeline tried to recall, that she sat as a child

> with proud ambition burning in my soul, ambition to be great and known to fame, when a gentle whisper came, I used to think it was a fairy, and whispered so strangely I scarcely comprehended, but I know its purport: "There is no excellence without labor you must work, toil, not sit idly indulging in fruitless day-dreams, but active work must be done if you would attain to any degree of honor, or be useful to yourself or others."...These mysterious whisperings were cautions, they awakened higher thoughts and nobler ambitions. I yearned for a field of usefulness.[12]

7. Aunt Em, "Reminiscences," *Woman's Exponent* 16 (October 1, 1887): 67.
8. Aunt Em, "Dear Old New England," *Woman's Exponent* 29 (June 1, 1900): 1–2.
9. Aunt Em, "Maytime Memories," *Woman's Exponent* 20 (May 1, 1892): 153–54.
10. E. Wells, "My Trip East," December 28, 1885, 46.
11. Aunt Em, "Maytime Memories," 153–54.
12. Aunt Em, "Midnight Soliloquy," *Woman's Exponent* 8 (April 15, 1880): 175–76.

These were indeed cautionary words to a young, ambitious child, but for a while, at least, Emmeline was free of those demands. Her life was a round of family, make-believe, and the mysteries of the natural world. Her "nymph-like ways," as her neighbors described them, did not worry her family, though they caused those neighbors to wonder. What were they to make of "this weird little thing," as they called her, who "loved pasture and rocks and trees and mosses better than sofas, or easy chairs, or soft carpets and who preferred the songs of birds, to parlor music however proper?"[13]

But there were other pleasures besides the long, solitary hours she spent in the hemlock grove. She also shared in the fun the countryside offered to adventurous youth, especially "nutting," or the gathering of chestnuts. Several times during the season, the young teenage boys and girls of the town, baskets and lunches in tow, set out for a day of fun while filling their baskets with the fallen chestnuts. Taking advantage of their unsupervised outing, the boys teased the girls "unmercifully" by refusing to climb the trees and shake the branches to loosen the nuts unless the girls consented to a kiss, "which, of course, the girls wouldn't do for anything," Emmeline insisted. Undaunted, the boys chased the girls among the trees "until they could corner them, when submitting gracefully was the wisest course to pursue; and besides," she reasoned, "how could we go home with empty baskets? And the boys were [so] obstinate." By the end of the day, with buckets full, the boys and girls, "almost unwittingly," divided into groups of two or three, and sometimes the "attachment of a lifetime" began in such outings.[14] Afterward, love letters were often left in lilac bushes throughout the village, "to wait the coming of the ardent sweet-heart to read his true-love's words by starlight."[15]

Emmeline was not outside such friendly pairings. John Smith seemed to be her first beau. "John always got me the best seat everywhere," she remembered, "and brought me candy nuts and raisins, helped me fill my basket when we went berrying or nutting and drove away all the other little boys who sought my society at school or play." In fact, she wrote, he "appropriated me when I was in the village and when I went away out of town to other schools he was quite jealous." John eventually married her friend Louise Thompson and died years before Emmeline visited New Salem in 1885.[16]

For the village people of rural Massachusetts, the grand event of the year was Thanksgiving, the quintessential New England tradition, since

13. Ibid. See also "Hephzibah," *Woman's Exponent* 18 (July 15, 1889): 25.

14. Aunt Em, "Chestnut Time," *Woman's Exponent* 14 (November 1, 1885): 83; Aunt Em, "Suggestive Days," *Woman's Exponent* 9 (November 15, 1880): 93.

15. Aunt Em, "Souvenirs of Lilac-Time," *Woman's Exponent* 11 (June 1, 1882): 2.

16. E. Wells, "My Trip East," December 28, 1885, 42.

orthodox Congregationalists did not celebrate Christmas because it was associated with "Piscopals or Church of England people or worst of all *Roman Catholics*," Emmeline explained.[17] It was both a community and a family holiday. While a fixed date was not set for observing the holiday until 1863, it was usually celebrated in late November or early December.[18]

Preparations began long before the day arrived, including decorating the meetinghouse with pine branches, hemlock boughs, long trailing vines, and red berries to provide a festive setting for the annual Thanksgiving sermon. Choir members were also decorated for the occasion, the women in white dresses enhanced by pale-green ribbon and white chrysanthemums, while the basses and tenors placed a knot of green ribbon in the buttonhole of the vests of their Sunday suits.[19]

Solemnities ended at the conclusion of the service, and then the family celebrations began. Roast turkey, chicken pies, and sometimes a roasted pig, all surrounded by platters of vegetables and dishes of baked beans, teased the appetites of the most avid celebrant. New England also offered an abundance of ingredients for the requisite Thanksgiving pie: pumpkin, mincemeat, apples, currants, raisins, and all types of berries.[20]

For Emmeline, the most delightful aspect of the holiday was the return of her married brothers and sisters to the old homestead. How often she described its low-slung ceilings and great open fireplace with its high mantelpieces. On that day, the home gave way to children, "breathless with playing games—and with calling to one another, from garret to cellar—running about with ginger-bread and maple sugar, eating all day long, and

17. Aunt Em, "New England Thanksgiving," *Woman's Exponent* 22 (January 15, 1894): 82. Emmeline did not reminisce about other holidays except to describe family dinner at Christmastime.

18. Sarah Josepha Hale, popular author and editor, described the holiday in her novel *Northwood: A Tale of New England* and used the periodical she edited, *Godey's Lady's Book*, to campaign for a national Thanksgiving holiday. Jane C. Nylander details early New England Thanksgiving celebrations in *Our Own Snug Fireside: Images of the New England Home, 1760–1860*, 263–82.

19. Aunt Em, "Thanksgiving Half a Century Ago," *Woman's Exponent* 24 (December 1, 1895): 83 (written November 28, 1885). Warren Parish, minister of the First Parish Church of New Salem, had added a choir to the worship services in 1804, and choirs had evidently become customary in both parish churches during Emmeline's time of membership. See M. Harris, *Among the Dry Bones*, 101–2.

20. "Thanksgiving Day," *Woman's Exponent* 31 (December 1–15, 1902): 49–50. Harriet Beecher Stowe also describes the preparation and celebration of a New England Thanksgiving in *Oldtown Folks*, 338, as quoted in Nylander, *Our Own Snug Fireside*, 271. Reprinting earlier articles or using the same themes and descriptions of her childhood experiences over her entire editorship of the *Woman's Exponent* reveals the enduring grasp of her early years in New England.

upsetting the whole house." The gathering eventually included several generations, the loving grandmother greeting her grandchildren, and siblings and cousins resuming their family association. It was a time of rejoicing for the adults and a day of fun for the children, with sledding and snowballing outside and games and storytelling inside. Nuts, apples, sweetmeats, and Emmeline's favorites, molasses candy, maple sugar, and popcorn, ended the day of plenty.[21]

In every reminiscence of those early days, Emmeline singled out her mother for special notice, a woman who served as an imposing matriarch of her large family, "presiding in her home with the dignity and grace of a queen...tall and majestic in figure." Emmeline remembered her on special occasions dressed in a "heavy grey pongee dress" with a "snowy white apron, and a small magnificent crepe shawl" covering "her beautiful shoulders." A string of amber beads was her only other adornment. All was crowned by her "abundant wavy and glossy" auburn hair, which she wore "coiled up and fastened at the back with a very high tortoise-shell comb." In later years, Emmeline noted, "her mother would be designated at once, from her outward appearance, as being a strong-minded woman," an epithet usually ascribed to female public activists, though Diadama was not one of them.[22] From all her reminiscences of these years, it is clear that Diadama Hare was Emmeline's model and inspiration for her own life.

The free-spirited Emmeline roamed the town at will. As happy in her solitary walks as with her friends, she absorbed her New England surroundings. Being one of the younger members of her large family, she had more leisure than the others. Often, her brother Hiram reminded her, he had to fetch her from "[her] hiding place in the Hemlock grove" when she was needed at home.[23] But her very precociousness declared an end to such liberty, as her mother recognized the need to channel her talents and intellect by educating them.

Emmeline attended the common schools in Petersham and North New Salem. The terms were usually eight weeks in the summer and ten weeks in the winter, the students all meeting together in a single room. When Emmeline turned seven, her mother decided to send her to Hardwick

21. "Thanksgiving Day," 49; Aunt Em, "New England Thanksgiving," 82. See also Aunt Em, "Thanksgiving Half a Century Ago," 83.

22. See especially Aunt Em, "Holiday Pictures," *Woman's Exponent* 9 (December 15, 1880): 107. Evidently, her mother did not wear the typical homespun clothes and simple hairstyles of most women of her social status, preferring "pongee," or Indian silk, for her best attire, expressing the individuality that suggested a more independent nature. From Emmeline's various descriptions of her mother, Diadama exuded confidence and control.

23. E. Wells, Diary, February 27, 1896.

to live with her sister Lucy and her husband, Henry Granger, for better schooling than North New Salem then offered. Emmeline passed a delightful summer going to school and playing "with or without companions." She was very pleased to find that the old gambrel-roofed house where she lived with her sister and brother-in-law had a garret, much like her grandfather's in Petersham. "Often my sister would come and listen to my conversation with my scholars as I termed the beams in the wooden building," she remembered.[24]

When the Grangers moved to New Braintree the following January 1836, they sent for Emmeline to stay with them again. Once more Emmeline packed her small, antiquated hair trunk and rode alone in "a great lumbering old-fashioned stage coach" to New Braintree. After enrolling her in school, the Grangers unexpectedly decided to move back to Hardwick. Lucy made arrangements for Emmeline to stay in New Braintree in a boardinghouse "in the care of a most wise and prudent woman." Her home was "one of the kind calculated to inspire in a romantic and poetical nature like mine, a sentiment of the most enthusiastic character and indeed it did," Emmeline remembered. "Here I flourished like a plant in its native soil without cultivation or attention." The proprietors of this large Victorian home, Eunice and James Barr, looked upon Emmeline as "a sort of notional or whimsical child who always wanted to do out of the way things." The disabled Mr. Barr left the management of the house and the care of their boarders to his wife. Overworked, she had little time to supervise the wayward Emmeline and so devised a quick means of bringing some "wholesome discipline" into the life of the spirited girl, which included such harsh measures as "getting up early and taking cold baths and going up to bed in the dark," to all of which Emmeline emphatically objected but obligingly obeyed.[25] The unending pleasures offered by this enticing multistoried home outweighed the discomforts of the rigid routine.

Seemingly addicted to the hidden delights of attics and garrets, Emmeline explored the Barrs' long attics under the eaves and found old newspapers, letters, and manuscripts, which, she claimed, so fervently fed her "creative imaginations that I dwelt as 'twere in another sphere." Her romantic nature turned every setting, even the wide window seat of the Barrs' parlor overlooking the garden, into a place of "wild and fanciful dreams of future promise held out to me by the good angels of my destiny." Throughout her life, her challenge would be to allow destiny's good angels to balance her desire for acclaim with her equal desire to serve.[26]

24. E. Wells, "My Trip East," January 23, 1886, 136.

25. Ibid., 137–40.

26. Ibid., 140, 141.

After several school terms in New Braintree, Emmeline returned to school in North New Salem, this time attending a school in the heart of the village, across the street from the church. There she continued to study the required subjects, which, for good measure, included manners, as specified by Massachusetts law. At the end of each term, students received a Reward of Merit, a printed certificate that served the student "as an honorable testimony of approbation for industry, punctuality and good conduct."[27]

Visiting the North Village in 1880, Emmeline's daughter Melvina saw the old village schoolhouse, pleased that it was furnished with all of its original furniture. "I wanted to see the very seat you occupied," Melvina wrote to her mother, "when you formed those ambitious projects to become a literary lady." She noted that the old-fashioned desks were "notched thick with names" and wondered if her mother would recognize any of them. All of her mother's stories of her school days flooded Melvina's mind during the visit. "It seemed to me," she concluded, "a sacred spot."[28]

Finally, in 1841, when Emmeline was thirteen, her mother found the means to send her daughter to the New Salem Academy, a private school, where she would join her friend Irene Hascall, already a student there.[29] Her terms at the academy would end her years of formal education. Founded in 1795, it was designed to bring a higher level of learning to New Salem students, which included the inculcation of piety, religion, and morality in each student and instruction in those languages and those aspects of the liberal arts and sciences as the trustees directed.[30] Emmeline left no record of how her schooling was financed, but it may have come from the estate of her grandfather, who died the year she entered the academy. His death marked Emmeline's second encounter with irreparable loss, and though their visits had diminished after she moved to New Salem, his influence remained strong, and her experiences with him and the memory of times spent in the Woodward homestead never left her.

The establishment of such academies enabled women to pursue schooling in ever-increasing numbers. Usually established by the leading men of these communities, who served as trustees, as was the case of the New Salem

27. A copy of such a certificate is in my possession, courtesy of Carolyn Chouinard of North New Salem.

28. Mell [nickname of daughter Melvina Whitney], "Letter from Massachusetts," *Woman's Exponent* 9 (August 15, 1880): 46.

29. Emmeline sometimes used the term *high school* to refer to her post–grammar school education, but there were no public high schools in the area until later in the nineteenth century. The academy was established to provide that level of education to the area's students.

30. Dorothy Waldo, "Story of the Academy from Its Earliest Days," 47.

Academy, and first taught only by male preceptors, they offered more than an "ornamental" education, instructing their students in a variety of academic subjects.[31]

With this advance in female education, women began to claim a large share of the teaching profession. In 1832, the *Greenfield Gazette and Franklin Herald*, the major paper in Franklin County, showed its support of this progressive outlook by running an article entitled "Notice to Female Teachers," which quoted from the *Journal of Education*: "The female mind seems happily adapted to the business of superintending the early cultivation of the disposition of children; and it is one of the most promising features of our time that female talent is asserting its right and taking an active part in the business of Education."[32]

When Emmeline's mother enrolled her daughter at the academy, she gave her daughter a gift of inestimable value. It would become the vehicle that carried her along the winding road of her life and enabled her to reach what she believed her "angels of destiny" had in store for her. Education at the academy and her natural talents lifted Emmeline's sights above the limitations of her social origins and eventually made her one of the growing number of female literary and educated women who were her models of achievement.

Emmeline's attendance at the academy fell within its brightest and most successful period, 1836–48. A year after Emmeline completed her studies in 1843, its enrollment had risen to 147, drawing students not only from New Salem but also from surrounding towns.

Emmeline boarded at the school and attended several of the eleven-week terms. She became part of a clique of seven friends, calling themselves the "club of seven," who often met together for late-night conversations. In one of them they shared their secrets and dreams for the future. All vowed that "none of us will marry a man who has not a professional title" such as "eminence, Rev., Prof., D.D., M.D., or A.M. [Master of Arts]," though on close observation of the relationship of their minister Alpheus Harding and his wife, they all decided against marrying a minister. For most of

31. Benjamin Rush, an educator and signer of the Declaration of Independence, was an early advocate of "higher education" for women and instigated the Philadelphia Academy for Women that became a model for others. Information about these academies, and especially the controversy surrounding women's education, can be found in Nancy Woloch, *Women and the American Experience*, 91–96, 109–10, 130–35. For a bibliography of the subject, see ibid., 101–2; and Ann D. Gordon, "The Young Ladies Academy of Philadelphia."

32. "Notice to Teachers," *Greenfield (MA) Gazette and Franklin Herald*, September 11, 1832. Photocopy of original in my possession.

them, reality shattered their resolves.[33] Only two of the seven schoolmates "gained a crown worth wearing," Emmeline later recounted, and "these two girls [Emmeline and Irene Hascall] became members of the Church of Jesus Christ of Latter-day Saints."[34] In the meantime, her small world rested atop New Salem Hill, with the academy, the First Parish Church, and the boardinghouse its compass points for Emmeline. She was also atop her highest hopes and unexpected good fortune.

But Emmeline was fashioned by more than education. Religion was an equal partner in molding the woman she was to be. In the small villages of New England during Emmeline's early years, the church was the center of community life and offered the villagers sociability as well as spirituality. It provided them a ready-made community network that offered mutual support and a sense of belonging. As the social and political as well as spiritual center of the town, the village church symbolized the unity and shared values of the community.[35]

Being close-knit and comfortable with their common patterns of worship, these rural communities of believers were measurably disconcerted by schisms within Congregationalism and inroads by other sects. The revivalist movement of the early nineteenth century thus loomed as a threat to the unity that had been their religious anchor. Moreover, many of the denominations and sects that began breaking into the tight Congregational circle often appealed more to the common person and less to affluent members of the community, creating a measure of social stratification. A clear distinction was apparent between the educators of the New Salem Academy, along with the minister and the influential trustees and contributors, and the farm, mill, and factory workers of North New Salem.

The growing religious divisiveness within Congregationalism was exemplified in religious developments in New Salem and the North Village. At first, it was a matter of practicality. The journey from North New Salem to

33. In "Hephzibah," Emmeline describes the club of seven and explains her distaste for the clergymen she met at school, who were always asking her to make a "change of heart" and telling her she was a "sinner" when "Grandpa always thought her good enough." See "Hephzibah," *Woman's Exponent* 18 (August 15, 1889): 42.

34. Aunt Em, "A Reverie," *Woman's Exponent* 13 (December 15, 1884): 110.

35. Karen V. Hansen, *A Very Social Time: Crafting Community in Antebellum New England*, 7–11, 138–39, 146–47. In some instances, parishioners did not wholly agree with the religious orientation of the minister but attended as a matter of convenience. The North Village church was mainly Trinitarian in its religious persuasion, setting it apart from the First Parish of New Salem, which was decidedly Unitarian. The differing religious philosophies of the two churches as preached by their ministers also reflected the different social strata of their members. M. Harris, *Among the Dry Bones*, 54–69.

the First Parish Church on the New Salem Common became wearisome to many villagers, and in 1807, they purchased a building of their own closer to their village. Alpheus Harding, the minister of the First Parish, preached in the North Village one Sunday each month, maintaining the tie between the two congregations. As Trinitarians, the North Village congregation resented paying tax to support Harding, who was a strict Unitarian. A petition to exempt the new society from financially supporting the First Parish proved successful with passage of an 1823 amendment to the 1811 Religious Liberties Act in Massachusetts, which firmly established the right of dissent and the right to pay to the denomination of one's choice.[36] The two congregations reflected just one of the many "shades of religious belief among its members."[37]

Adding to the division among Trinitarians and Unitarians was the appearance in New Salem of the Baptists and Universalists, two dissenting sects that began drawing away members and revenue from the Congregationalists. Later, the Methodists settled in the southern part of Franklin County, appealing to the villagers in that area. With exemption of a state-imposed religious tax and the addition of several denominations now contending for members, "competition between churches reached a pitched battle in antebellum New England," observed one historian. This "sea of sectarian rivalries," as a Congregational minister described the conflict, resulted from the spread of doctrinal controversy and the introduction of differing methods of religious worship.[38] Community division, ostracism, and even hostility resulted from the growing religious dissension.

The Second Parish, as the North Village church was designated, first employed Levi French (1824–30) and then Erastus Curtis as pastor, the latter serving from 1832 to 1843, approximately the same time that Diadama and her family lived in New Salem.[39] Emmeline and her friends called him "Priest Curtis," certainly at that time a term of derision. His wife, Deborah Grosvenor, was the daughter of a minister who had thought his daughter suitable to be a minister's wife and had encouraged the marriage. But

36. M. Harris, *Among the Dry Bones*, 117–18. These theological differences were major influences in the gradual decline of a unified theology within Congregationalism in the New Salem area.

37. The establishment of a Trinitarian society gave those parishioners who were not Unitarian an opportunity to leave the First Parish Church. These alterations and the overall drift into liberalism, exemplified in New Salem by the Unitarians, are examined and explained in ibid., 124–25.

38. Hansen, *Very Social Time*, 146–47.

39. Eugene Bullard, "Historical Address," 44. See also Rev. Theophilus Packard Jr., *A History of the Churches & Ministers, and of Franklin Association in Franklin County, Mass.*, 2.

Emmeline recalled that it turned out to be an unhappy one, for "she was far superior to him," and the neighbors were convinced that she was "the real author of his sermons." Emmeline remembered hearing Priest Curtis call Deborah from her work to his study to read, revise, and make suggestions for his sermons, and his loud and "oft-repeated calls for Deborah became quite proverbial in the village." She also remembered his being very absent-minded, often leaving his sermon on the study table when he left for church, to be sent after by a parishioner. Emmeline was sensitive to the secondary and unheralded role of the bright and talented Deborah and was even more determined that she would never be a minister's wife.[40] Alpheus Harding and Erastus Curtis remained blots on the ministerial profession, as far as Emmeline was concerned.

Preparations for the Sabbath were done with a keen eye to the Eighth Commandment. "We had all our work put away on Saturday afternoon," Emmeline remembered, "to prepare for the Sabbath."[41] The steepled, white meetinghouse, trimmed in green, dominated the North New Salem Village. Church buildings were usually unheated, although this one had a long box stove that, unfortunately, did little to offset the winter chill. Sermons often lasted two hours in the morning, with another sermon in the afternoon, and often an hour of standing prayer. At the front of the church stood the high, old-style pulpit, looming menacingly with the minister's fiery sermons emanating from its lofty position. Looking down on the secluded, high-backed wooden pews, it marked not only the physical but also the spiritual and social distance between the minister and his congregation of mill workers and farmers.

Opposite the pulpit curved a gallery from which the choir sang hymns from the Isaac Watts hymnal, the music providing relief from the often grim nature of the service. In the absence of an organ, the conductor pitched the hymns with a tuning fork.[42] As a member of the choir, Emmeline was obliged to listen each week to "those tiresome preachers." But the sociability that developed among choir members offset the often tedious Sabbath-day services to which the members were subjected.

In 1841, thirteen-year-old Emmeline's life was fulfilling and promising. She was in a school that was prestigious for her time and place, surrounded by friends, devoted to her family, and looking toward a literary future in

40. E. Wells, "My Trip East," December 28, 1885, 46. Emmeline fictionalized the Curtises in "Hephzibah," using Deborah Curtis's maiden name, Grosvenor (spelled "Grovsener" in the novel), as the name of the minister and his wife. See "Hephzibah," *Woman's Exponent* 18 (September 15, 1889): 57.

41. E. Wells, Diary, June 6, 191.

42. Aunt Em, "Dear Old New England," 1.

her beloved New England. But events were already transpiring that would irrevocably alter the direction of her life. The growing missionary activity of the recently organized Church of Jesus Christ of Latter-day Saints, more commonly known as the Mormon Church because of its newly revealed book of scripture, the Book of Mormon, spread throughout New England in the 1840s. The region had already experienced intense religious dissension and competition when the Baptists, Methodists, and Presbyterians arrived during the 1830s and especially from the divisions within Congregationalism. Traditional New Englanders thus found the arrival and success of the Mormons one more disturbing piece of evidence of religious unrest. New Salem had already accommodated itself to five newly built or remodeled Protestant church buildings, with four more in adjoining towns. But unlike the appearance of other denominations, the advent of the Mormons into Franklin County drew suspicion and acrimony. To many churchgoers, Mormonism fell far outside the dogma of traditional Christianity. Those who converted needed large doses of their New England stubbornness to hold fast to their new faith.

CHAPTER 3

A Trying Ordeal

(1842–1844)

THE LATTER-DAY SAINTS preached a gospel of restoration. They proclaimed that church founder and prophet Joseph Smith had been commissioned by God to restore the original Christian Church, which had fallen into apostasy. They offered an additional book of scripture, the Book of Mormon, revealed and translated by the hand of God, as a second testament to the biblical account of Christ's divine mission. They claimed the restoration of priesthood authority and the reality of continuing revelation. Mormonism also acknowledged the efficacy of good works in this life and happiness and reward in the next. "Men are that they might have joy," its scriptures declared (2 Ne. 2:25). The Mormon message resonated with many, and the concept of a supreme being who continued to speak to his children and to direct their affairs had great appeal.[1]

Mormon beginnings were clouded, however, by opposing voices claiming that Joseph Smith was a deluded visionary, the Book of Mormon was a fabrication, Mormons rejected the Bible, and some church members, including their prophet, had indulged in gold digging and "divining." The rumors preceded the missionaries and effectively deterred the skeptical. Only those for whom the message transcended the rumors and brought them to a more satisfying spiritual understanding than they had yet experienced braved the ridicule and defamation that followed their affiliation.

The LDS mission in Massachusetts was opened in June 1832 by Orson Hyde and Samuel H. Smith, and additional missionaries spread their

1. Included in the Mormon message was Joseph Smith's translation of the Book of Mormon from a set of gold plates inscribed by record keepers among the ancestors of the American Indians, who came to the American continent six hundred years before the birth of Christ. The plates were bestowed on Joseph Smith by a heavenly being and witnessed by eleven persons before being returned to the hill where they were deposited. The book reinforces the Bible as the Word of God to his people.

message throughout the state.[2] In November 1833, two missionaries traveled to Wendell, a small town in the eastern part of Franklin County and a few miles west of New Salem. One of their contacts in Wendell was Jonathan Crosby Jr. Crosby was impressed with their message, but to be certain of its truth, he invited the two missionaries to meet with a Methodist friend who, in Crosby's estimation, was "great in argument on Theological questions." If anyone could "whip them out," Crosby believed, Elias Harris could. Upon meeting the missionaries, however, Harris asked questions about "the Mormon book" and some of the gospel ordinances but did not enter into any argument with them. "I brought these men here for you to whip them out," Crosby protested, to which Harris responded, "They have the truth. I can't do it, neither can anyone." Crosby admitted he didn't think Harris could, but just "wanted them tested."[3] Within the month, Crosby and five others, including Lucy Harris, Elias Harris's wife, were baptized. The missionaries organized a small branch of the six new members and appointed David Nielson and later Elias Harris as the president of the branch, following his baptism.[4]

Harris engaged in vigorous proselytizing himself, visiting New Salem in October 1840. He was instrumental in several faith healings and soon became well known among church members in the New Salem area.[5]

Eli P. Maginn, a young convert from Canada, joined the New England missionaries in 1839, traveling to Peterborough, New Hampshire, for his first field of labor. At age twenty-four and six feet tall, he had a commanding demeanor and appeared older than his years, attributed by one observer to "the many hardships, privations, persecutions and mobbings which he has passed through for the gospel's sake." A committed biblical scholar, he was instrumental in the conversion of hundreds of New Englanders.[6] When the Peterborough churches were closed to him, he preached in a hall so crowded that "the people were obliged to stand in the street to hear him," many of them coming from outlying towns.[7] In November 1841, Elder Maginn visited Wendell and New Salem with much success, noting that in New

2. Eastern States Mission History, 1830–1870.

3. Jonathan and Caroline Crosby Papers, ca. December 1833.

4. Ibid. The other four converts were Theresa Merchants, David Nelson or Nielson, and Mary and Sarah E. Harris. Journal History of the Church of Jesus Christ of Latter-day Saints, October 14, 1833, 4 (hereafter cited as Journal History).

5. For examples, see Samuel Ruggles Aiken, "A Life's Sketch," and Samuel L. Aiken (son), "Memory Sketch," in Samuel R. Aiken Papers, typescript copies.

6. Reported in "Mormonism," reprinting "A Seeker after Truth," letter to the editor, *Boston Weekly Bee*, n.d. "Seeker" noted Maginn's facility in quoting scripture from memory "with the greatest ease and correctness" and detailed the text of his sermons.

7. Quoted by James F. Brennan in "Talk on Mormonism."

Salem alone thirty-five to forty had "obeyed" since the previous August. "I have preached from one to three times almost every day," he reported, "and cannot fill one to twenty of the calls for preaching; there is the greatest excitement in this country that I ever beheld during my travels, since I left Nauvoo; a period of near three years in which I have traveled through eighteen States and British Provinces."[8] Maginn's success in all the villages where he preached proved the effectiveness of his persuasive oratory.[9]

No doubt aware of the success of the Mormon missionaries in nearby villages, Erastus Curtis, the minister in the North Village, did not open his church for their preaching. However, the sympathetic postmaster, who was the first to meet the missionaries and was interested in hearing them speak, arranged for their use of the schoolhouse. The missionaries preached to an enthralled audience, and numerous baptisms followed. Erastus Curtis used all his power to thwart the influence of the missionaries, calling on his parishioners one by one to dissuade them from listening to the elders, but many could not resist the persuasive appeal of the Mormon message.[10] Moreover, gifts of the spirit were manifest on numerous occasions.[11] Elizabeth Woodbury was one of the recipients of the gift of healing. Paralyzed for many years, she was administered to by the missionaries and was able to walk to her own baptism.[12] "There had never been at any time in the history of the oldest inhabitant of that little village such an exciting time," Emmeline remembered.[13]

Emmeline's mother was one of the first believers. Despite the cajoling, threats, and derision of the minister, she was baptized along with her two youngest daughters, Adeline Maria, twelve, and Ellen Celeste, ten.[14] Hiram,

8. E. P. Maginn to President Smith Sr., March 22, 1842, *Times and Seasons* 3 (May 2, 1842): 779.

9. For the Salem missionary conferences, see Journal History, May 18, 3, and September 11, 1842, 1.

10. Emmeline transferred some of these details to "Hephzibah," *Woman's Exponent* 18 (October 15, 1889): 73–74; and 18 (November 1, 1889): 81–82. An account also appears in Zula R. Cole, "How Firm a Foundation: Haskell-Pomeroy Pioneers," 2, typescript 1952, rev. ed. 1965, photocopy in my possession, used by permission.

11. For scriptural passages on spiritual gifts, see 1 Cor. 12:4–11, Moro. 10:8–7, and D&C 46:11–26.

12. Cole, "How Firm a Foundation," 3. See also "Hephzibah," *Woman's Exponent* 18 (November 1, 1889): 82.

13. "Hephzibah," *Woman's Exponent* 18 (November 1, 1889): 82.

14. Hiram was not yet eight years old, the minimal age for baptism. For the statistical report on baptisms in Massachusetts, see Journal History, May 18, 1842, 3. Adeline Maria was named after her oldest sister, Adaline (with an *a*) Emily, who died at age fourteen.

at five, had not yet reached the minimum age for baptism into the church, age eight. Her older children, all married or living away from home, disdained the missionaries and joined the townspeople in coaxing their mother to reconsider. But she would not be dissuaded and was anxious about their influence on Emmeline. She urged her daughter to return home from school to hear the missionaries, and Emmeline reluctantly did so, always dutiful to her mother's bidding, though far more interested in her studies. She was surprised, however, to find that she enjoyed the manner of singing and praying in their meetings, so different from the services of her own church.[15] Though studious and thoughtful, Emmeline was just thirteen and paid only scant attention to the preacher. To her mother's disappointment, she returned to school without baptism, perplexed over the change in her mother, who seemed so certain of the choice she had made.

When Elder Maginn returned to North New Salem in late February 1842, Emmeline was again among the crowd to hear him preach. Ashbel Green Hascall, well known in the village but less so in the parish, attended the Sunday meeting and announced to his wife afterward, "I've been to a Mormon meeting. The preacher, Elder Maginn, spoke more good sense than all the ministers I ever heard."[16] Several asked for baptism, including Ashbel's wife, Ursulia, and daughter Irene, one of Emmeline's best friends. But Emmeline was still uncertain. Resolving the dilemma that now confronted her was not easy for the young teenager. Having done well in school, she was flattered by the attention of her instructors and their anticipation of a bright literary future for her. On the other hand, Emmeline had always trusted her mother and obeyed her counsel throughout her young life, and Diadama had won the respect of her neighbors as well. Thus, Emmeline was puzzled that so many, including Diadama's own older children, now doubted her judgment and questioned her new religious enthusiasm.

Baptisms were scheduled for the next morning, and Emmeline struggled through a sleepless night. "Two powers seemed to be warring with [me]," she recalled. "One said, 'Obey your mother, go down into the waters of baptism in the little brook that always seemed a sanctuary.' The other voice said, 'Do not heed the sayings of your mother or the Elders, a brilliant future awaits you, you must not make this sacrifice.'"[17]

The morning of March 1, 1842, the day Emmeline would celebrate her fourteenth birthday, arrived cold and gray. For the baptisms, ice had to be

15. "Hephzibah," *Woman's Exponent* 18 (January 15, 1890): 121–22.

16. Cole, "How Firm a Foundation," 2.

17. In her diary Emmeline frequently alluded to the soul-searching that preceded her baptism, but the most detailed account is in her autobiographical "Hephzibah," *Woman's Exponent* 18 (February 1, 1890): 131–32.

cut away in the brook that ran past Emmeline's home. With the morning also came Emmeline's decision to follow her mother's counsel. Children were told to heed the advice of their parents, she concluded, and should follow their example.[18] Her respect for and confidence in her mother overrode the enticements offered by her teachers and school friends.

The scene at the baptismal site was anything but sacred or even peaceful. Fifty years later, Emmeline recalled the commotion the baptisms evoked among the townspeople. "Such a scene...we had with the congregational minister and other notables," trying to the last to dissuade her.[19] But Emmeline, her friends Irene and Catherine Hascall, and Irene's mother, Ursulia, were among the seven to be baptized and were not deterred by the jeering of the gathering crowd. Their determination fortified Emmeline, who was the last to receive the ordinance that morning. When her name was called, she felt on her shoulder the hand of one of the prominent townspeople, father of one of her schoolmates. "Think of the sacrifice you are making," he pleaded, and even at fourteen she felt the portent of his words and the significance of this life-changing decision. "It was a trying ordeal," she admitted, but promised her mother that having made her decision she would thenceforth "dedicate her life to the work of the Church," a vow whose ultimate consequences she could not then have fully envisioned.[20] The event warranted a brief accounting in verse as she recalled the band of seven receiving the "holy ordinance" that day:

By one ordain'd to ministry divine;
Proving their faith in that, which they believe,
Though friends and kindred they must then resign.[21]

With "the crisis over," she saw that "the path was dark but clearer to my duty to my Mother, and her instructions to me were strict in lessons of obedience to parental authority."[22] Not yet wholly knowledgeable in the religion that would direct her life from then on, she felt secure in accepting her mother's guidance.[23]

18. Ibid. See also E. Wells, "My Trip East," December 28, 1885, 44.

19. E. Wells, Diary, March 1, 1892.

20. Cole, "How Firm a Foundation," 3.

21. Emmeline B. Wells, "Baptism in Midwinter," in her *Musings and Memories*, 237.

22. E. Wells, "My Trip East," December 18, 1885, 45.

23. Ibid. In her reminiscent account "My Trip East," Emmeline wrote, "A miracle was wrought too on that occasion [of her baptism] on the person of Miss Sophia Wickes, afterwards Weeks. She was healed of lameness and we gave God the glory." A more detailed account of this healing is Aunt Em, "Faith," *Woman's Exponent* 8 (April 1, 1880): 163. The name of the healed woman, however, is different in Joseph

Mormonism upset the placid life of the villagers because it not only drew members away from the local Congregational church but also encouraged their migration out of New Salem to "gather" with the other Latter-day Saints in Nauvoo, Illinois, headquarters of the church at that time. North New Salem, like most of the other nearby villages, "never became afterwards what it had been in other days," Emmeline observed years later, "for many of the very best and brightest men and women went with that little band of Pilgrims and their places were not filled."[24]

After the turmoil surrounding her baptism, Emmeline returned to the academy for another term. As she completed her studies, Emmeline personally experienced for the first time the deep disdain for Mormons held by those who had denounced the course she had taken. She nonetheless successfully completed this final term at the academy, which ended her only formal schooling. Now fifteen, she had in hand the certificate indicating her qualification to teach, and she was ready to test her ability as an educator.[25]

Emmeline applied to the Beechwoods School in Orange, a few miles from her home. As required by Massachusetts law, she needed now to pass a district examination and acquire a certificate of good moral standing from her minister. "Going through an examination," she admitted, "was a perfect terror for a bashful girl of fifteen," and she "trembled like a frightened bird."[26] At its conclusion, the school trustee asked her to give an example of her handwriting. She called to mind a phrase from Hamlet she had learned at school and quickly wrote, "A man may smile and smile and yet be a villain."[27] The words surprised the examiner. Her handwriting was

---

Sudweeks, "Concerning Myself: The Life of Laban Morrill," typescript copy in Mountain Meadows Massacre Research File, LDS Church History Library, Salt Lake City, which identifies the healed woman as Permelia Drury, the wife of Laban Morrill. In a letter to Permelia's granddaughter Sarah D. Syrett, July 21, 1937, included in the Morrill biography, Annie Wells Cannon notes that Emmeline often recounted the miraculous healing and that Emmeline had also identified the woman as Permelia Drury in her verbal recitals of the event. See http://www.hirf.org/history_bio_Morrill_G.asp. The healing of Sophia Wickes may have occurred at a different time, or Emmeline may have confused the names.

24. "Hephzibah," *Woman's Exponent* 18 (March 1, 1890): 146.

25. The certificate from the principal or preceptor read: "This may certify that Miss Emmeline Blanche Woodward has been a member of the New Salem Academy. She sustains a good moral character and made good proficiency in English studies, and in my opinion she is qualified to instruct youth in the elementary branches of science." Courtesy of Carolyn Chouinard, North New Salem.

26. Aunt Em, "Reminiscences," *Woman's Exponent* 16 (October 1, 1887): 67.

27. The exact quote, which comes from Shakespeare's *Hamlet*, reads, "Meet it is I set it down / That one may smile, and smile, and be a villain" (1.5.107–8).

clearly acceptable, but the words seemed hardly compatible with a young and inexperienced fifteen-year-old girl, he told her.[28]

Obtaining a certificate of good character from the minister was the second hurdle confronting Emmeline. It was, if anything, more challenging than the examination. Erastus Curtis was the community minister to vouch for Emmeline, and he bore little goodwill toward the Mormons. He resented them for drawing away half of his parishioners (nearly eighty had left by then) and blamed her mother for influencing them. It seemed unlikely that he would be disposed to certify Emmeline's good moral standing under these circumstances. The minister's reaction to Emmeline's request gave truth to her concern. He felt her too young and, more important, too prone to promulgate Mormon teachings, which, in reality, she hardly knew after her year's membership away from home or church meetings. He prolonged the interview, constantly repeating his objections. But with no reason to question her exemplary life and with the intercession of his sympathetic wife, Deborah, "Priest Curtis" was obliged to give her the coveted certificate.[29]

Her next challenge was to transform her appearance from a schoolgirl to a schoolmarm, to create a visible distinction between the teacher and her students. At fifteen and scarcely taller than the oldest students, Emmeline shifted from short to long dresses and from long curls to a short bob. But she had no need to enhance her intellectual abilities with any assumed airs. Her terms at the academy had honed her natural talents and given her the tools and the credentials, as well as the confidence, for intellectual pursuits.

She was posted in Orange, about ten miles from her home in North New Salem. Her salary was a dollar and a half a week, and she was able to make arrangements to permanently board with the Pearces, an older couple, who lived in a "low, brown farm house" across the way from the school. The furniture was plain, and her room gave her a place of quiet after the rambunctious actions of her students.[30] Her months in Orange as a teacher were among her happiest times, she recalled, days when "life seemed so bright and joyous and no shadow fell across my pathway."[31] The trials of

28. "Hephzibah," *Woman's Exponent* 18 (April 1, 1890): 163.

29. In her writings Emmeline occasionally alluded to her difficulties with Erastus Curtis and dramatizes this exchange in "Hephzibah," *Woman's Exponent* 18 (March 15, 1890): 156.

30. Emmeline details her room's furnishings, the surrounding land, and the farm hands when she revisits the area in 1885. See E. Wells, "My Trip East," December 28, 1885, 58–61. Bits of description come from a variety of other references in articles in the *Woman's Exponent* and other publications.

31. Aunt Em, "Reminiscences," 67.

becoming a Mormon faded in the bright light that seemed to once again shine on her future in New England.

While Emmeline was developing teaching skills and exploring the land around the school and the Pearce home, plans of another kind were being made that would end the idyllic life from which she obtained such pleasure and once again demonstrate what commitment to the church entailed. A second group of Mormon converts was preparing to leave for Nauvoo after the school term in the fall, and Emmeline's mother wanted her daughter to be numbered among them. The group included President Elias Harris; his wife, Lucy; and their two sons, James Harvey Harris, a young man Emmeline's age, and younger brother Oleander.[32] Worried that her precocious daughter Emmeline might be swayed from her new religion, Diadama proposed that Emmeline go with them. With three younger children and a home to dismantle along with the intense opposition of her older children, Diadama would need more time to prepare for the journey herself.[33] At some point in the negotiations, the idea was proposed that the two young fifteen-year-olds marry. James had already shown interest in Emmeline, and Diadama felt certain that Emmeline would accede to her wishes, as she had done before. Lucy was less enthusiastic and had doubts about Emmeline's suitability as a wife to her son. But she reluctantly agreed to the marriage.

Evidently not knowing of the prearranged nuptials, Emmeline was surprised when James visited her at the Pearces' home and began wooing the unsuspecting girl. But she was not entirely averse to his attentions. In both poetry and fiction, she romanticized their brief courtship, particularly remembering when he boldly kissed her as he quietly proposed. "The fountains within were deeply stirred," she wrote,

By a strange, sweet music, exquisitely rare,
. . . For someone had whispered, "Wilt thou be mine?"
And a kiss as delicious as honey-dew.[34]

Her expectations were all romance at the time, as she recalled "the fascination of love's young dream—the country fields, the meadows, the haying

32. Lucy and her sister Sally, daughters of Nymphas and Sarah Gibbs Stacy, were the only members of the large and prominent Stacy family to join the LDS Church. Sally married John Murdoch and remained a loyal member of the church after her husband's untimely death in 1844.

33. Diadama's marital status at that time is unknown. Though Emmeline mentioned the "cruel guardian" who might have halted her baptism, a possible reference to Clark, she never mentions him in any of her reminiscences about her last years in New Salem and refers to her mother as the "matriarch" of the family.

34. From Emmeline B. Wells, "The Happy Maiden," in her *Musings and Memories*, 58–59.

time, the...dancing in the old kitchens and on the sanded floors, the brooks the birds the swaying hemlocks the sighing pines and O so many sweet & tender memories."[35] She had anticipated a continuing euphoria in marriage, writing, "O love keep singing with joy o'er laden, In the heart of the wife as well as the maiden."[36] Experiencing at the time what she called "the buoyancy of youth and full assurance of innocent physical life, and with consciousness of good mental endowments," she agreed to join her "fortunes with one in whom my mother at least placed implicit faith and trust."[37]

She later noted that the marriage offered her an advantage she had not fully anticipated. When Mormonism began to succeed in the area, she wrote, her classmates and teachers harassed her on every side, trying to "tear me from my beloved home and the arms of a tender parent to keep me from Mormonism." But then, she wrote, "the Good Spirit interposed and provided a way for me to be released from the hands of a cruel guardian who pretended so much respect for me that he did not wish me to associate with my own mother and sister because they were Saints of the Most High God or as he called them Mormons." Her marriage and removal to Nauvoo would relieve her of these attacks on her conversion. "I adopted this method of escape not merely for escape," she explained, "but he with whom I was to be connected was my lover in truth. I loved him and I believed his professions to be true."[38]

The two fifteen-year-olds were married by a justice of the peace in Vernon, Vermont, in a short and solemn ceremony.[39] There was little about the restrained celebration the next day that left Emmeline with pleasant memories. She remembered it as "a horrible ordeal...with relatives and

35. E. Wells, Diary, July 14, 1892.

36. E. Wells, "The Happy Maiden," in her *Musings and Memories*, 59. See also "Hephzibah," *Woman's Exponent* 18 (April 15, 1890): 171–72. She would find other occasions to which the sentiment was applicable.

37. E. Wells, Diary, July 29, 1895.

38. Ibid., February 20, 1845. The reference to "cruel guardian" may be a reference to her stepfather, who evidently prevented neither her baptism nor her marriage.

39. A notice in the *Franklin Democrat* of Greenfield, MA, August 22, 1842, under "Marriages," states, "In Vernon, Vt. by Lorenzo Brown, Esq., Mr. James H. Harris of South Orange to Miss Emeline B. Woodward of New Salem." The New Salem Vital Records up to 1850 records the marriage of "Emeline Woodward to James Harris" as occurring on "July 29, 1843 in South Orange" (a town near New Salem). Emmeline always noted July 29 as the date of this marriage, but Annie Wells Cannon's handwritten copy of the marriage certificate gives the date as July 28. Emmeline B. Wells Papers, L. Tom Perry Special Collections, Harold B. Lee Library, Brigham Young University, Provo, UT.

guardian attending."[40] Especially did she remember the disappointment exhibited so clearly by Mrs. Harris, her new mother-in-law. Lucy Harris did not feel the fanciful Emmeline to be an appropriate wife for her son, and the abrupt decision for them to marry was disconcerting to her. With more remorse than joy, Emmeline often recalled the "blue waters of the Connecticut [River] as it flowed on that evening past the windows of the house so close." This was the Harris home that would also be her home for the next nine months.[41]

The haste in which the marriage was arranged prevented the usually thoughtful Emmeline from recognizing what became obvious to her in later years. She was too young to judge of men herself, she realized, and her emotions were stronger than her judgment. "I know now," she wrote years later, "that the sentiment I felt was not one strong enough to live upon air—I had indeed made a sacrifice and a very great one, but I knew it not at that time." Hindsight brought only regret. "Since [then] how severely have I felt it & yet it was unavoidable—Fate decided it for me."[42]

A half century later, she still mused over that early marriage, which "affected my whole after life. I cannot tell it here not even after all these years. My destiny changed or the course of my life drifted into an entirely different channel from that heretofore anticipated by me or any of mine. This was as completely a turning point as one could possibly have." A fifty-year hindsight generated in her a feeling that "I was mysteriously guided and my way marked out."[43] Indeed, throughout her life she demonstrated a fatalistic view of life, a sign of obeisance to the power of Providence, but without becoming its slave. The marriage took her to Nauvoo and the world of Mormonism that would embrace her throughout her life in ways not accorded to many other converts.

And so it was that circumstances deriving from events in her early life caused her later to cloak them with more grim portent than she had actually felt while experiencing them. She might even admit that doing so gave voice to her penchant to see her life as "a romance," evident in her long story of "Hephzibah" and in the imagery of her nostalgic poetry. Noting the

40. E. Wells, Diary, July 2, 1902. In her poem "A Glance Backward," Emmeline describes the celebrants as "Old friends and true" and notes that "The song, and jest, and merry tale went round." Yet the young couple, she added, "even then… felt some potent sway / Of dread, the very atmosphere pervade." E. Wells, *Musings and Memories*, 167–71.

41. E. Wells, Diary, July 29, 1900.

42. Ibid., July 29, 1895.

43. Ibid., July 28, 1894.

anniversary of this early marriage year after year in her diary, she expressed the memory in bittersweet terms. "This is an anniversary of mine that will not bear thinking of scarcely," she wrote on July 28, 1890. "Jim came for me to the Pea[r]ce farm and tried to get me away in the night but I would not go, not even to please my mother.... I was being persuaded to renounce my ambitious aspirations & to go to Nauvoo, where I would see Joseph the Prophet and learn more than in the highest schools of the day," she recounted. "I yielded at last, after much persuasion and cast my lot with the saints in the centre Stake of Zion." "Men scarcely realize when a young girl marries what a sacrifice she makes. It is indeed a new and trying ordeal," she concluded. "How my heart longed for something entirely different." As time enabled Emmeline to confront the reality of these early life-changing events, she was on the cusp of a maturing process that would one day define the foundation of her character—resilience, self-confidence, and self-direction within the framework of what she discerned as "God's will."[44]

While living with the Harrises, Emmeline was obliged to face the daily disapproval of her mother-in-law. Lucy seemed unable to countenance Emmeline's imaginative, carefree personality, which disturbed her structured domestic pattern. Allowing no leeway for youth or inexperience, nor especially for intellectual or literary proclivities, Lucy scorned Emmeline's bookish and meditative temperament as shiftless and irresponsible. Emmeline's indifferent mastery of housekeeping skills particularly irritated Lucy, and the two were destined for misunderstanding and distrust.

Emmeline wrote a long description of the Woodwards' final family gathering at Christmas that year, lingering lovingly over the details of the rustic country house with its plainly furnished parlor and the large square table that accommodated the family members gathered together to share one last meal as a family. Her descriptive pen brought the day to life, and it became the stuff of numerous stories and articles about Christmas.[45] Plans were made for selling the family homestead when Diadama was ready to move to Nauvoo, which would create an inevitable rift in this close-knit family.[46]

Being wrenched from the New England world that had so lovingly cradled her for nearly sixteen years infused Emmeline's memories of her

44. Ibid., July 28, 29, 1890.

45. Elements of that last Christmas and other holidays celebrated by the family are found in Aunt Em, "A Little Chat about Christmas," *Woman's Exponent* 4 (December 15, 1875): 109; Aunt Em, "Something about Holidays," *Woman's Exponent* 5 (December 15, 1876): 111; "Holiday Picture," *Woman's Exponent* 9 (December 15, 1880): 107; Aunt Em, "Christmas Tableaux," *Woman's Exponent* 15 (December 15, 1886): 105–6; Aunt Em, "A Happy New Year," *Woman's Exponent* 19 (January 1, 1891): 105–6.

46. Aunt Em, "One Christmas Eve," *Woman's Exponent* 41 (December 1912): 29–32.

childhood with an idealism and rosy haze that the passing of years only intensified. "Leaving her New England home," she wrote in the third person for a publication in 1895, "was to her sensitive nature almost heart-rending, so dear were all the associations and so emotional and poetic her temperament." But she tapped into what would prove to be a deep well of Yankee stoicism and resolution, "and the parting over she bravely faced the West resolved to make the change without regret."[47]

The small group of converts left North New Salem on April 24, 1844. At the same time, Emmeline began what would become a lifelong obsession—diary writing. On the top of the first page of her first diary, she wrote: "Emeline B. Woodward No. New Salem Frank. Co. Mass." Directly below her name, she added, "James H. Harris & Emeline B. Harris So. Orange Franklin Co. Mass." These identifications were followed by a single page that reads: "On the 24th of April 1844 I left my mothers house at North New Salem Franklin Co. Mass and started for the west. The next day we took the cars at Springfield and at 4 of the clock we were in Albany we stayed there all night and the 25 we took a canal boat going to Buffalo we journeyed it in 8 days we had no stormy weather we arrived in Buffalo the 2nd day of May."[48] She did not write again until February 1845 in Nauvoo. It was an inauspicious beginning for a career diarist and might have ended with that single entry, yet it grew into a rich personal accounting of a long and multifaceted life.

New England had nourished many of the qualities that Emmeline fully employed in the days ahead. Perhaps unrecognized even by herself, she took with her a strong sense of community along with a commitment to discover and fulfill whatever life as a Latter-day Saint had in store for her. Even as she had internalized the strictures of Calvinism, she also had opportunity to exercise the spontaneity of a free soul, a dichotomy that in many ways framed her life. She was also beginning to develop a nature "full to overflowing of emotions[,] of ambition[,] of faith[,] ever stirring for advancement." She added to this self-appraisal, however, that it would not be "for self alone but for all mankind," an unbounded goal that revealed much about the future of this young New England girl.[49]

47. From a photocopy of a three-page handwritten autobiographical sketch (in the third person) entitled "Emmeline B. Wells," on stationery from the Hotel Aragon in Atlanta, where Emmeline attended a suffrage convention in January 1895. It may have been requested by a local newspaper, but I have not found a published copy. Photocopy obtained from the personal files of Emmeline's great-granddaughter Helen Clayton Shurtliff, used by permission.

48. E. Wells, Diary, April 24, 1844.

49. Ibid.

CHAPTER 4

Great Expectations

(1844–1845)

WHATEVER EMMELINE'S dreams of the future might have been as she left her childhood home and traveled toward Nauvoo, Illinois, in the spring of 1844, it is not likely that they bore much resemblance to the realities that awaited her. She clearly hoped for a satisfying and purposeful life within the fold of her new faith and in the security of her young husband. Even more immediate was the eagerly anticipated birth of her first child.

Emmeline and James traveled with a company of about twenty-six Latter-day Saints to Albany, New York, where they were joined by a group of LDS missionaries returning from their labors in the eastern states. Among the returning missionaries who boarded the canal boat to Buffalo were Jacob Gates and his wife, Mary Snow Gates. They spoke enthusiastically about the Prophet Joseph, and Emmeline found their conversation to be "a continuous revelation." Mary Gates took Emmeline under her wing and promised to introduce her to the prophet when they reached Nauvoo.[1] Inexplicably, Emmeline wrote nothing more about the trip after leaving Albany. The group arrived in Nauvoo sometime in mid-May.[2]

The small settlement of Commerce, Illinois, situated on a promontory of land jutting into the Mississippi river in southern Illinois, held promise of becoming a bustling trade center. But the panic of 1837 sent many of the early town promoters away, and only a few remained, including Daniel H.

1. Gates, "Emmeline B. Wells," 45–53; E. Wells, Diary, June 8, 1890. See also E. Wells, Diary, May 14, 1910.

2. It is surprising that Emmeline did not record the events of the journey, especially since she had rarely ventured beyond a short radius of her home and this was such a new adventure for her. Only in later accounts does she make brief references to it.

Wells, who had migrated to Commerce in 1834, and Hiram Kimball, who arrived in 1835.[3] This area would become the fourth gathering place of the Saints.[4] Though the members of the church had only recently settled in Missouri, dissension between the growing Mormon population and other residents led to the imprisonment of their leader, Joseph Smith, and an extermination order by the governor, Lilburn W. Boggs, sending the Mormons to seek refuge elsewhere. Plodding through the winter snows of 1838–39, they found temporary refuge in Quincy, Illinois, while Joseph Smith, his brother Hyrum, and four of their associates languished in prison. It was imperative that the church find a permanent home as soon as possible to accommodate the thousands of members vacating Missouri and the converts coming from abroad. At the Prophet Joseph's direction, Commerce, Illinois, became their destination. Fifty miles north of Quincy, the small settlement beckoned the Saints with a paucity of residents and an offer of cheap land. While land was readily available for purchase, much of it was a swampy breeding ground for mosquitoes and so inhospitable for settlement that prominent LDS poet Eliza R. Snow claimed that no one "but Saints full of faith, and trusting in the power of God could have established that city."[5] The newcomers, like the earliest settlers, battled malaria and a host of other ailments, and many died or were disabled for weeks at a time. After losing two sons in Nauvoo, Nancy Naomi Alexander Tracy despairingly noted that "it seemed almost impossible to raise a child there."[6]

3. In a series of letters to family members in Trenton, New York, Daniel H. Wells and his sister, Catherine Wells Woods, early settlers of Commerce with their mother, wrote optimistic letters about their life in the small community and their hopes for its growth and development. The letters were edited by Maureen Ursenbach Beecher, and a selection appeared as "Letters from the Frontier: Commerce, Nauvoo, and Salt Lake City."

4. Intending to make Independence, Missouri, its central headquarters and gathering place for members, the Church of Jesus Christ of Latter-day Saints had moved from its beginnings in 1830 in New York to Ohio and thence to Missouri. There Joseph Smith had been charged with "treason," a nonbailable offense, and held in Liberty Jail with six others as hostage until all the Saints had left pursuant to an "Extermination Order" by the governor. Joseph Smith joined the Saints in Quincy in 1839 before moving to Commerce.

5. Eliza R. Snow, "Sketch of My Life," microfilm of holograph, LDS Church History Library, Salt Lake City, original in Bancroft Library.

6. "Life History of Nancy Naomi Alexander Tracy Written by Herself," typescript copy, L. Tom Perry Special Collections, Harold B. Lee Library, Brigham Young University, Provo, UT.

All of the church's forced relocations from New York, Ohio, and Missouri had been occasioned not only by the unorthodox teachings of this upstart religion, but also by the church's history of "gathering." This principle brought church members to a central location where they could contribute to the church's mission to establish a righteous environment for the return of Jesus Christ and to build a temple wherein they could make sacred covenants and receive instruction and ordinances relating to their eternal state. Such a large and constantly growing covenant community of single-minded and cohesive residents unnerved many of the residents of the sites where the Saints had gathered. Nauvoo, they hoped, would be different. How much Emmeline knew at that time of this early portion of LDS history or the principle of gathering, which had brought church members to this frontier region on the banks of the Mississippi, she never mentioned. In time, however, her natural curiosity, her penchant for study, and her remarkable memory would turn her into a ready resource of detailed information about the church and its history.

Mary Gates knew that Emmeline's greatest desire upon reaching the sainted city was to meet Joseph Smith. Hoping to help Emmeline fulfill this desire and also to "realize the greatness and wonderful power of the Prophet," Mary offered to introduce them.[7] The time was now at hand. As the steamboat neared the bend of the Mississippi and gradually edged toward the city's upper landing, Emmeline was surprised at the number of people who crowded the riverbank to greet the passengers as they disembarked. She hoped that the prophet would have time to meet their boat and depended on Mary Gates's promise to identify him. As she stepped ashore, however, she noticed one tall figure clearly distinctive from the others. Though she did not know so at that moment, this was her first view of the Prophet Joseph, and the impact of that meeting evolved into a testimonial that she regularly rehearsed at church gatherings and committed to writing when she became one of the last to have personally known him:

> His majestic bearing, so entirely different from any one I had ever seen...was more than a surprise. It was as if I beheld a vision.... Before I was aware of it he came to me, and when he took my hand, I was simply electrified—thrilled through and through to the tips of my fingers, and every part of my body, as if some magic elixir had given me new life and vitality.... The one thought that filled my soul was, I have seen the prophet of God, he has taken me by the hand.[8]

7. Mary Gates quoted in "Joseph Smith, the Prophet," esp. 554–56.

8. Emmeline B. Wells quoted in ibid., 554–56; Emmeline B. Wells, "The Prophet Joseph." Another version is included in "Emmeline Blanche Wells."

When Mary Gates caught up with her, intending to take her to meet Joseph, Emmeline declined her invitation, still savoring the moment she first saw him on her own and felt the power of his touch. She now looked forward to hearing him deliver the sermons that so inspired his followers.

By 1844, the environmental ravages that had plagued Nauvoo had lessened their grip, and the city proffered a healthier place to these newcomers. This was to be home to the young James and Emmeline, their own city of promise where together they would see their lives and dreams unfold.

When the New England Saints arrived in Nauvoo, its population had grown close to twelve thousand inhabitants, with between a fourth and a third of its residents emigrant converts from Great Britain. Mills and factories stood amid the stately brick homes that were gradually replacing log cabins. All were surrounded by green fields and fruitful gardens.[9] Wide right-angled streets separated the lots, presenting a vista of spaciousness and light. Numerous public buildings were planned or under construction, and two newspapers, the *Nauvoo Neighbor* and the *Times and Seasons*, kept residents informed. The Nauvoo House, a hotel under construction, was slowly taking form on a small rise above the Mississippi River. Nearby was the Mansion House, built for the residence of Joseph Smith and his family. Large enough to both entertain and lodge guests, it was one of the finest buildings yet constructed in the city and was frequently used as a social center.

The Seventies Hall, nearing completion on Parley Street, served as a training school for missionaries as well as a meeting hall.[10] To Emmeline's great pleasure, a music hall was also under construction. Having sung in her church choir in North New Salem, Emmeline was an early applicant for the Nauvoo choir. She had found that such an association gave her entrée to a group of like-minded friends while satisfying a lifelong love of music.[11] Gustavus Hills organized the Nauvoo Music Association, whose fund-raising helped to stage musical and choir performances under director Stephen Goddard. The Nauvoo Brass Band, organized by Britisher William Pitt just two years before Emmeline arrived, and a martial band, under the

9. Leonard J. Arrington and Davis Bitton, *The Mormon Experience: A History of the Latter-day Saints*, 68–69.

10. Glen M. Leonard, "Nauvoo" and *Nauvoo: A Place of Peace, a People of Promise*. See also Milton V. Backman Jr., *People and Power of Nauvoo*; Carol Cornwall Madsen, ed., *In Their Own Words: Women and the Story of Nauvoo*; and Robert Bruce Flanders, *Nauvoo: Kingdom on the Mississippi*. Numerous other studies on Nauvoo are listed in James B. Allen, Ronald W. Walker, and David J. Whittaker, eds., *Studies in Mormon History, 1830–1997: An Indexed Bibliography*, 807–14.

11. Her friendship with Eunice Billings Snow, daughter of Titus and Diantha Morley Billings, began when they were both members of the Nauvoo choir.

direction of Levi W. Hancock and Dimick B. Huntington, enlivened many civic occasions. There was no want of musical offerings and community dances during the Saints' brief stay in Nauvoo.[12]

Nor was there a lack of dramatic offerings. Theatricals under the direction of Thomas A. Lyne and George J. Adams were performed in the newly constructed Masonic Hall, an imposing three-story structure on Main Street.[13] The Nauvoo Dramatic Association sponsored some of the first plays presented in Nauvoo, providing another form of entertainment with a strong emphasis on moral content.[14]

The educational offerings of the city were progressive and extensively pursued. In 1841, in accordance with the city's charter, the municipal council developed a common school system, certifying teachers (including Emmeline), providing them a modest wage, and determining the texts to be used, all with the goal of giving every child a uniform education.[15] Besides providing for young students, the city council also gave higher education a priority when a university was established in 1841. Without a formal campus, classes were held in various city locations. Students took courses in literature, foreign languages, philosophy, astronomy, and chemistry as well as math, from arithmetic to integral calculus.[16]

The city militia, known as the Nauvoo Legion, attracted many young men, including Emmeline's husband, James. Established by the city charter, with Joseph Smith commissioned as lieutenant general by Governor Thomas Carlin, the militia became one of the largest city militias in the state.[17] With a military band and more than fourteen hundred members

12. Jeni Broberg Holzapfel and Richard Neitzel Holzapfel, eds., *A Woman's View: Helen Mar Whitney's Reminiscences of Early Church History*, 225. Helen Mar Whitney remembered that William Cahoon, John Pack, Stephen Hale, and their wives were members of the choir along with William Pitt, William Clayton, Jacob Hutchinson, and James Standing, who were members of the band as well.

13. Ibid., 226.

14. For detailed information about drama in Mormon Nauvoo, see Nola Diane Smith, "Reading across the Lines: Mormon Theatrical Formations in Nineteenth Century Nauvoo."

15. Hiram Clawson, director of the Salt Lake Theatre, and Seymour B. Young, Emmeline's doctor and member of the Quorum of the Seventy, were two of her students who remained close friends. E. Wells, Diary, July 18, 1894, and March 8, 1912.

16. David E. Miller and Della S. Miller, *Nauvoo: The City of Joseph*, 91–92, 89–90. Parley P. Pratt, Orson Spencer, and Sydney Rigdon were among the earliest faculty of the university. See also Leonard, *Nauvoo*, 192–98; and Holzapfel and Holzapfel, *Woman's View*, 148–49.

17. Arrington and Bitton, *Mormon Experience*, 68–69; Philip M. Flammer, "Nauvoo Legion"; Miller and Miller, *Nauvoo*, 95–101. A more current study of the Nauvoo Legion is Richard E. Bennett, Susan Easton Black, and Don Q. Cannon, *The Nauvoo Legion: A History of the Mormon Militia in Illinois, 1841–1846*.

in its first year, growing to two thousand by its second, the Nauvoo Militia held its thrice-yearly "musters," which became grand military parades attracting the whole community. Few occasions matched its performance at the laying of the cornerstone of the temple on April 6, 1841.[18] It was a gala introduction to the solemn services that followed and the first of many such displays of pageantry under the command of Joseph Smith.[19]

By 1844 the foundation and lower walls of the temple were completed, and its location on a prominent bluff above the city provided a clear view of the ambitious structure from the river below. When Emmeline first saw it, the temple had been under construction for three years but was still unfinished, nor would it be for another year.

Thus, what Emmeline saw as she arrived on that spring day in May 1844 was a city of promise, housing a people of vision and hope. They melded well with the earlier residents, and the future for the community was bright. The energy and sense of mission of the inhabitants were palpable, and the swampy land they had settled five years earlier was now yielding to well-drained, fertile fields. The sharp reduction in the malaria-bearing mosquitoes, along with better and more abundant food, water wells, and shelter, greatly improved the health of the community. In the years that the Saints had claimed this portion of Illinois as their own, they had effected an amazing metamorphosis. From a few inhabitants, there were now thousands joined by a steady stream of immigrants. Just a year after the Saints' arrival from Missouri, Joseph Smith presciently changed the name of the city from Commerce to Nauvoo, a Hebrew word signifying a beautiful location and "carrying with it also the idea of rest," he explained, certainly more in anticipation of what it might yet become.[20]

James and Emmeline were fortunate to have a place to live upon arrival and with the Harrises moved into Alphonso Green's home, a new brick house on Parley Street and a place "where the Prophet Joseph was almost idolized."[21] There Emmeline was able to feel even more of that "wonderful power that characterized all his utterances."[22] For the next few weeks, the young couple took every opportunity to hear him speak and had additional occasions to shake his hand.[23] Those experiences firmly secured in Emmeline

18. This was the second temple the Saints had built. They had abandoned the first in Kirtland, Ohio, when they moved their headquarters to Missouri.

19. Miller and Miller, *Nauvoo*, 98; Holzapfel and Holzapfel, *Woman's View*, 120–21.

20. Joseph Smith, quoted in Miller and Miller, *Nauvoo*, 35.

21. "Joseph Smith, the Prophet," 555.

22. E. Wells, "Biography of Emmeline B. Wells," 3, typescript copy in my possession, courtesy of Helen Clayton Shurtliff, a great-granddaughter. A variation appears in Orson F. Whitney, ed., *History of Utah*, 4:586–90.

23. "Joseph Smith, the Prophet," 555.

"the abiding faith that helped her through the unexpected reversals just then unfolding in her history."[24] Even as James and Emmeline anticipated the birth of their baby and made plans for a home of their own, undertones of impending turmoil were crescendoing.

The steady flow of converts gathering to Nauvoo and its satellite communities foretold a strong and unified political threat to Nauvoo's neighbors. Even more alarming to them was what this population growth portended: the development of a self-governing, armed—by virtue of having its own militia—Mormon city-state. Converging with these worrisome developments were some of the new doctrines that unfolded in Nauvoo during the tumultuous years of 1843 and 1844. The concept of "a plurality of Gods" and the doctrine that all men might become gods in the same manner that God himself had reached that station, explained by Joseph Smith in a public discourse in 1844, seemed blasphemous, even to some members.[25] But to others, hints of a plurality of wives were more immediate and even more scandalous.

Though unknown to most of the Saints in Nauvoo but rumored in the city as well as among outsiders, Joseph Smith's private introduction of polygamy as a divine commandment became a major cause of dissension within and hostility outside the church. Anticipating the furor that a public announcement of the practice would evoke, Joseph taught the principle privately to some of his closest associates. Though only those men to whom the prophet taught the new doctrine had authority to practice it, some others, learning of the practice, assumed such authority and attempted to induce unsuspecting women to accept their proposals.[26] Confusion, suspicion, and misrepresentation understandably followed. The clandestine nature of its introduction, the euphemisms employed in the public denial of its practice, and the unauthorized implementation of the principle for personal gain, as well as its repugnance to most individual sensibilities, made polygamy a menacing synonym of Mormonism and helped to ignite the public outcry toward the church and its leaders in Nauvoo and in the years that followed. Against all standards of acceptable Victorian marriage and morals, and

24. E. Wells, "Biography of Emmeline B. Wells," 3.

25. Joseph Smith enunciated this doctrine in a sermon in honor of King Follett, who had died in an accident while building a well near the temple. Integrated reports of the various note takers of the sermon, including Thomas Bullock and Wilford Woodruff, can be found in Andrew F. Ehat and Lyndon W. Cook, eds., *The Words of Joseph Smith*, 340–62; and Stan Larson, ed., "The King Follett Discourse: A Newly Amalgamated Text." For an explication of the sermon, see Richard Lyman Bushman, *Joseph Smith: Rough Stone Rolling*, 534–37. See also Joann Follett Mortensen, *The Man behind the Discourse: A Biography of King Follett*.

26. See Bushman, *Rough Stone Rolling*, 526–50.

seemingly reinforcing the practice of arranged marriages at a time when personal choice and romance were establishing a foothold in the formation of marital relationships, polygamy became the object of a long campaign by moral crusaders and the federal government to quell its practice. However, during the fifty years it was authorized by the church for its members, its faithful adherents—about a third of the membership at different periods, according to scholars of the subject—accepted it only after consultation with their own consciences and then defended it as they had accepted it, as a true religious principle, their right to practice it guaranteed by the First Amendment. For them, plural marriage was not a social experiment or a response to perceived social disorder in those volatile years of the nation's history, as it has sometimes been rationalized. Nor was it simply a "character building" experience for those within the system. And they certainly did not view Mormonism as an institutional framework conceived to nourish and propagate the controversial practice, as some critics of the church avowed. Not until polygamy came under repressive public attack in Utah in the 1860s and '70s did the Mormons develop a consistent sociological and constitutional public rationale for living the principle. While abuses of the practice naturally ensued, most of those involved attempted to live it as an essential element of the restoration, to which the church was committed.

Those to whom Joseph first revealed the commandment, both men and women, were admonished to ponder and pray about it in recognition of the impact such an assault would be on their own moral beliefs and the criticism that would follow. While a variety of motives can always be ascribed to human behavior, the personal literature of the women who entered the practice attests that for the majority, it was indeed an affront to their standards of sexual behavior and a frightening threat to the most basic of Victorian institutions, the family. Their acceptance of the new doctrine, therefore, necessitated an inviolate belief that it was indeed of God and that whatever the personal sacrifice, which was enormous, it would be more than compensated by eternal rewards.[27] Without this depth of conviction by the women of the church, the practice could never have taken hold or survived. As Elizabeth Ann Whitney observed when her husband took additional wives, "I am more favorably disposed to women as a class, learning more of the true nature of woman-kind than I ever could without this peculiar experience."[28]

27. A comprehensive study of polygamy is Kathryn M. Daynes, *More Wives than One: Transformation of the Mormon Marriage System, 1840–1910*. See also Andrew H. Hedges, Alex D. Smith, and Richard Lloyd Anderson, eds., *Journals*.

28. Elizabeth Ann Whitney, "A Leaf from an Autobiography," *Woman's Exponent* 7 (January 1, 1879): 115.

Though the practice was not publicly acknowledged until 1852, it was well established within the church before then. Yet there were few guidelines for its implementation beyond the approval (ofttimes neglected) of the first wife and presiding church authority. Each family developed its own system, attempting to accommodate a plethora of variables, all of which resulted in widely varying household arrangements. The ostensible preeminence of the father in his plural families sustained prevailing Victorian prescriptions of family organization. But the position of the wife and mother underwent a subtle but significant redefinition in plural marriage. While polygamy was denigrated by its critics as demeaning to women, robbing them of their singular position within the family, their actual status in terms of authority and function rose. In many instances, plural wives had far more latitude in controlling the dynamics of their family life, in the absence of consistent partnering, than monogamous wives and often experienced far more autonomy and independence.[29]

Polygamy, however, added one more aberration to what non-Mormons considered acceptable social behavior and traditional Christian doctrine, and Joseph Smith became the target of their scorn. Just weeks after the Harrises arrived in Nauvoo in May 1844, the smoldering embers of dissent were finally ignited with a publication issued by an opposition press operated by Mormon dissidents. In early June 1844, they published the first and only edition of the *Nauvoo Expositor*, which denounced Joseph Smith for teaching "heretical doctrine" and profiteering from land sales. It advocated the revocation of the city charter and objected to the indeterminate boundaries between religious and temporal matters. Declaring the press a "public nuisance," the city council, under Joseph Smith as mayor, ordered its destruction. Though not without precedent elsewhere, this act of suppression incensed anti-Mormons and kindled fears in the city of an imminent attack by Nauvoo's hostile neighbors. In anticipation of the escalation of such unrest and with the consent of Illinois governor Thomas Ford, Joseph Smith called on the city militia to arm itself and prepare to defend the city if necessary.

In the meantime, Joseph Smith and members of the city council were charged with "riot" for destroying the press, and though twice acquitted in

29. Joan Smyth Iversen argues this point in "Feminist Implications of Mormon Polygyny." Wives and children in plural marriages also bonded, as a rule, more tightly with each other than with their husband or father. Independence was achieved by the availability of other wives to share household and child-care responsibilities or through possession of a home of one's own. The downside, besides the emotional pain of sharing a husband and lack of marital companionship, was the need for some plural wives to share or take full responsibility for the economic well-being of their families as well as finding themselves in legal limbo.

Nauvoo, they were ordered by Governor Ford to stand trial a third time in nearby Carthage, the county seat. All of the defendants were released on bail, but then Joseph and Hyrum were rearrested on the charge of treason, presumably for calling up the militia. Treason was a nonbailable offense, and so the two of them, as in Missouri, were incarcerated, this time in Carthage Jail. Apostles John Taylor and Willard Richards, who had accompanied the Smiths to Carthage, remained with them. Though the prisoners had been promised the governor's protection in anticipation of hostile action, on the afternoon of June 27, an unrestrained mob rushed into the jail, killing both Joseph and Hyrum and wounding John Taylor. Only Willard Richards escaped injury.[30]

"In one day," Zina Huntington Jacobs [Young], lamented, "fell the Prophet and Patr[i]arch of the church of the Lat[t]erday Saints, the kind husbands, the affectionate Father, the venerable statesman, the Friends of man kinde, by the hand of a ruthless Mob mixed with desenters."[31] "Every heart is filled with sorrow," Vilate Kimball wrote to her absent husband, Heber, an apostle, three days after the martyrdom. "The very streets of Nauvoo seem to mo[u]rn."[32] Brigham Young's wife Mary Ann also wrote to her husband to tell him of the "great affliction" that had befallen them in the death of Joseph and Hyrum by a "verocious mob. The great God of the creation only knows whithe [whether] the rest shall be preserved in safety or not."[33] Years later Emmeline added her voice to theirs. "How well I remember that day and time," she wrote in 1891. "How dark the clouds seemed to hang over the city of Nauvoo, it was as though the sun could not shine."[34] She remembered "the terrible sorrow and the darkness which seemed to cover the city like a funeral pall. It is utterly impossible," she declared, "to describe it to anyone who was not there to feel it."[35]

Could the church survive the loss of its murdered prophet, many wondered, and if so, who should now govern it? It was not long before several made claim to that position, while others left the church to develop their own form of Mormonism. Some, disillusioned and apprehensive, simply left Mormonism altogether. But the majority stayed the course, and in

30. The details of this final episode in Joseph Smith's life can be found in numerous studies, including Bushman, *Rough Stone Rolling*, 544–50; and Leonard, *Nauvoo*, 362–417.

31. Zina Huntington Jacobs, Diary, June 27, 1844, Zina Diantha Huntington Young Collection.

32. Vilate Kimball to Heber C. Kimball, June 30, 1844, photocopy of original, Vilate Kimball Papers.

33. Mary Ann Angell Young to Brigham Young, Brigham Young Papers.

34. E. Wells, Diary, June 17, 1891.

35. Ibid., June 27, 1897.

August, when Brigham Young, as president of the Quorum of the Twelve Apostles, gathered the Saints together in the grove near the uncompleted temple, Emmeline and James were among the many who "were present at the memorable meeting of August 8, 1844, when the mantle of Joseph Smith fell upon Brigham Young," as he accepted leadership of the church.[36] "When Brigham Young rose in the midst of the people," Emmeline recalled, "most of them rose to their feet," and those who had known the prophet, she continued, "declared in a loud voice, as loud as they could almost, that it was the prophet Joseph himself risen again.... It was a transfiguration real and convincing." As a memory only, either Emmeline may have absorbed others' testimonies of the event, or she was indeed one of the claimants of its authenticity. Years later, she remembered it (writing in the third person) as "another abiding testimony for the young girl who was passing through such fiery ordeals."[37]

Joseph's death left in its wake individual confusion that had a profound effect on her life. Sometime during that summer of uncertainty and social disarray, Elias and Lucy Harris, demoralized by the sudden alteration of their expectations, were among those who chose not to cling to what appeared to be a nebulous future with a new leader. They made plans to move to the nearby community of La Harpe with their son Oleander, James's younger brother, and assumed that James and Emmeline would leave with them and continue under their parental and financial wing. But this was not to be. The younger Harrises decided to remain in Nauvoo, determined to make it on their own.[38] "Those were queer days," Emmeline wrote, "so new and strange and mysterious to me and to many others. Joseph was gone and the people were always telling of him and longing to

36. "Emmeline Blanche Wells," esp. 5:150–51; E. Wells, "Biography of Emmeline B. Wells," 4. The event took place before thousands who assembled at the grove, near the temple, but no contemporary account exists. A collection of postevent accounts is Lynne Watkins Jorgensen and *BYU Studies* Staff, "The Mantle of the Prophet Joseph Passes to Brother Brigham: A Collective Spiritual Witness." Jorgensen published an update of that article with accounts taken from family histories rather than firsthand memories: "The Mantle of the Prophet Joseph Passes to Brother Brigham: One Hundred Twenty-One Testimonies of a Collective Spiritual Witness." Problems relating to the lack of firsthand accounts are noted in Richard S. Van Wagoner, "The Making of a Mormon Myth: The 1844 Transfiguration of Brigham Young"; and Reid L. Harper, "The Mantle of Joseph: Creation of a Mormon Miracle."

37. E. Wells, "Biography of Emmeline B. Wells," 4. More details about her response to this event, as she recalled them, are noted in Thomas C. Pomeroy, "Emmeline B. Wells."

38. E. Wells, "Biography of Emmeline B. Wells," 3–4; O. Whitney, "Emmeline B. Wells," 4:587.

hear his voice again. Brigham and Heber were the Apostles to whom the Saints seemed to turn."[39]

Left to themselves, the two young Harrises were indeed completely on their own. Emmeline realized that her early life, "always petted and indulged to the very extreme," had not prepared her for "the stern realities of life.... [W]e two so unsophisticated alone in a strange place where all were strangers to us.... [H]ow hard it was how severely we were put to the test."[40] There she began to apply her conviction that "somehow it was all for the best," that God's mercy brought light after darkness. They were invited to make their home with Aaron Johnson and his family, then living on Water Street near Joseph Smith's store, which proved to be a step toward that light. Aaron Johnson was a prominent Nauvoo resident. He served as a justice of the peace, a member of the High Council, and a lieutenant in the Nauvoo Legion. He and his wife, Polly Zerviah Kelsey, had four children, the youngest eight years old. Faithful Latter-day Saints, they willingly offered shelter to the young couple in their two-story brick home.[41]

While enjoying the hospitality and friendship of the Johnsons, Emmeline had an attack of the ague, and for fifty-three days, according to her recollection, she suffered the dreaded chills and fever that accompanied the ailment.[42] Her husband was "kind, tender and solicitous," but also "young and inexperienced," and she depended on the help of the Johnsons. They were especially caring on the quiet summer Sunday morning of September 1, 1844, when Emmeline, not yet recovered from her illness, gave birth to a son.[43] Besides the Johnsons, she was assisted in his birth by Diantha Morley Billings, a midwife.[44]

With a baby to care for, Emmeline was determined to rally and urged her husband to summon Brigham Young for a healing blessing. He came to their aid, and through his administrations by the laying on of hands, she recovered enough to witness the christening and blessing of her baby when

39. E. Wells, Diary, September 24, 1891.

40. Ibid., September 1, 1874.

41. Aaron Johnson was a bishop in Garden Grove, Iowa, a way station for the Saints when they exited Nauvoo; founder, first bishop, and first postmaster of Springville, Utah; missionary; twenty-year member and first Speaker of the Utah Legislature; and major general of the Nauvoo Legion in Utah. Information compiled by Susan Easton Black, comp., *Membership of the Church of Jesus Christ of Latter-day Saints, 1830–1848*, 25:503–12.

42. E. Wells, Diary, November 24, 1898.

43. E. Wells, "Biography of Emmeline B. Wells," 4; O. Whitney, "Emmeline B. Wells," 4:587.

44. E. Wells, Diary, April 10, 1908.

he was just eight days old. The name she gave him was Eugene Henri. But her joy was short-lived. Unfortunately, the baby contracted the same chills and fever as his mother, and after just six weeks of life, he died on October 6. He was buried in the cemetery just outside the city.[45] Of their families, only James was there to mourn with her.[46] His parents did not acknowledge this tragedy in their son's life, nor were any of Emmeline's family near to comfort her. "It seems such a sad thing to bury your only *son* as I did so young, so inexperienced," she recalled. "No one can imagine my condition of mind. I cannot express it myself.... I recall in detail what transpired on that day. Away from all who loved me—save one [double underline] my husband, among strangers though they were Latter day Saints, the agony, the suspense, the loss of consciousness, the trust I had in God was my strongest support."[47] Her sorrow was compounded by her continued illness, and she still felt its effects fifty years later. "Sick with ague and delicate in the extreme," she recalled, "I cannot help feeling it sorely and so many years ago." In time, Emmeline came to recognize how imperative sons were to plural wives. "If he were living how much happiness he might bring to me; what a rock to lean upon; what a shelter and protection his strong arm might be for his nervous and delicate mother," she wrote in 1874. "I feel sure he would have grown up pure and true."[48] Eugene Henri would be her only son.[49]

45. From "Eugene Henri Harris" under "Deaths," *Nauvoo (IL) Neighbor*, October 9, 1844: "Eugene Henri Harris died 6 October 1844 from chills and fever." The mortality rate was high in Nauvoo during these years. Statistics show that in 1844, out of a population of approximately 11,000, 25.9 deaths occurred per 1,000 persons, translating to 285 deaths in 1844, 80 of them children under the age of five, by far the most vulnerable age group. Eugene Henri was one of them. On average, 23 deaths occurred every month that year. M. Guy Bishop, Vincent Lacey, and Richard Wixon, "Death at Mormon Nauvoo."

46. She wrote only one brief, rather prosaic poem of Eugene Henri's death entitled "Eugene Henri," which begins, "Life's sweetest flower seems gone, / Faded from earth away, / Yes our sweet babe has from us fled, / To turn again to clay." E. Wells, *Musings and Memories*, 273.

47. E. Wells, Diary, September 1, 1894.

48. Ibid., September 1, 1874.

49. O. Whitney, "Emmeline B. Wells," 4:587; "Emmeline Blanche Wells," 5:151. The general facts of her life are rehearsed in the many biographical sketches written of her. She noted on several occasions in her diary how much she needed a son. On one occasion she fretted about the necessity of sending messages to her husband when she was in need of household goods. "I wish I had any other resources," she lamented. "In this I regret as I have ever done not having a son" (E. Wells, Diary, September 16, 1874). When financial arrangements were being made following the sale of her house, she again expressed her sorrow, but also her resignation, at losing her son. "I regret I have not a son to speak for me, as all the others have," she wrote on March 4, 1890, "but I must submit to divine guidance and destiny that has overshadowed my life."

By November, James was restless, jobless, and overburdened with responsibility for his young wife, particularly in the absence of any financial help from his parents. He decided to follow the example of others who had found steady work in the bustling river town of St. Louis, enabling them to obtain necessities for their families. On November 16, he left his young wife in the care of the Johnsons and took a river boat downstream, promising to return in two weeks. But instead of his return, he sent Emmeline a letter, asking her to join his parents and brother at La Harpe, and in time, he would return to her there. But Emmeline did not feel comfortable with the Harrises. Her initial unhappy experience with her mother-in-law still smoldered, and their antagonism toward the church was offensive to her. Before the baby's birth, Lucy had pressed Emmeline to let her take the baby, once born, to La Harpe, where she felt he would have better care than the youthful, inexperienced parents could give, a proposal Emmeline resolutely rejected. Their absence during the challenging weeks of Emmeline's illness and Eugene Henri's birth and death only added to Emmeline's antipathy toward her mother-in-law, although she always retained a love for James's younger brother, Oleander, and he for her. Though James wrote again, repeating his wish for Emmeline to join his parents, Emmeline was determined to wait for him in Nauvoo. It was a decision that forever estranged Lucy and Emmeline.[50]

After James left, Emmeline sank into an emotional abyss. As days and weeks slipped into months without his return, she felt only an overwhelming sense of abandonment and despair. With no additional word from him, it was three months after he left before she could formulate her feelings into words and return to her diary. "Here was I," she wrote, "brought to this great city by one to whom I ever expected to look for protection and left dependent on the mercy and friendship of strangers." Those months of empty waiting had left her morbidly reflective. "My life has been one continual round of troubles & afflictions it seems sometimes as if death would be a comfort and then again when I think of the Gospel I feel resigned to the lot God has assigned me but what has life ever been to me from the days of my childhood almost ever since I left my mothers arms I have been afflicted and troubled yes in school I had enjoyment to be sure but how often was I crossed." She remembered how recent was the pull of her schoolmates, her teachers, even her older siblings to remove her from the influence of the church.[51]

Now she felt rejected by her husband. With all the anguish of her sixteen-year-old heart, she begged for an end to her woes. "Merciful Providence,"

50. Lucy blamed this decision of Emmeline's for James's failure to return to his family. See Emmeline's elaborate account in "Hephzibah," *Woman's Exponent* 19 (June 1, 1890): 1–2; and 19 (June 15, 1890); 9–10.

51. E. Wells, Diary, February 20, 1845.

she pleaded, "wilt thou long suffer this must I forever be unhappy wilt the time never come when happiness and enjoyment will be the lot of this lump of clay when thraldom and oppression will be cast off." She could bear no more affliction but longed for the promised "days of joy and gladness." Indeed, in the inflated rhetoric of youth, she could see her life as nothing more than "one continual round of troubles and afflictions."[52] The lesson on submission to unalterable circumstances came to her unbidden and stark in its initial teaching and took its place beside the other gratuitous lessons her life was slowly accumulating.

52. Ibid.

CHAPTER 5

Changing Directions
(1844–1845)

NOW ON HER OWN, sixteen-year-old Emmeline left the Johnson household and took up residence with Olive Bishop, a thirty-seven-year-old convert from Connecticut who had traveled to Nauvoo in the same company as Emmeline the previous April. Olive Bishop was a cousin to Elizabeth Ann Smith Whitney, whose husband, Newel K. Whitney, was presiding bishop in Nauvoo. Through this association, Emmeline came into close contact with the Whitney family and was employed to teach their younger children.[1]

Three months after James's departure, the abandoned Emmeline confronted another life-changing event. It began on February 7, 1845, when Patriarch John Smith, uncle to Joseph Smith, gave Emmeline a patriarchal blessing.[2] Aware of the abandonment of both her husband and his parents, Patriarch Smith promised her that "the eye of the Lord is upon thee for good & he will give thee a companion that shall hold the keys of the priesthood." With the completion of the temple, this companion would be able to give her "an inheritance in the house of the Lord which will unfold unto thee the mysteries which have been kept hid from the foundation of the world & reveal unto thee the way & manner to redeem thy dead friends & give thee power to bring [them up] in the first resurrection clear back to Noah or so far that there shall not be a broken link in the chain & thy

1. O. Whitney, "Emmeline B. Wells," 4:587; *Chronicles of Courage*, 8:151. Almost all of the biographical sketches include reference to this introduction to the Whitney family.

2. The role of a patriarch is to give a father's blessing, as in ancient times, to church members. These blessings announced their lineage as descended from one of the twelve tribes of Israel, pronounced future events, and promised blessings.

companion shall assist thee to accomplish all these things."[3] The meaning of such lofty thoughts may have escaped the young Emmeline at the time, but she would eventually understand the significance of such promises in her life and the lives of her Woodward family.[4]

That understanding came from the kindly bishop who had provided a home for her with his wife's cousin and a livelihood as the teacher of his children. He now offered her an eternal family. Uncertain, confronted with this startling new information about the faith she had accepted, and longing for the absent James, Emmeline wrote a letter to the bishop. She did not date it, so its timing is not exactly known. But Bishop Whitney had evidently interpreted the words of her recent patriarchal blessing for her, explaining the principle of plural marriage and the sealing of couples and families to one another. She learned the plan in which all families could be linked by connection to a priesthood line and the importance therefore of temple marriages or sealings by priesthood authority. Vulnerable, lonely, and confused—what was she to think about this new concept of marriage, or even of another marriage, and to one thirty-three years her senior who had been happily married for years? Exposing the perplexity and uncertainty with which she struggled, the letter also reveals a mind and heart that were striving to find truth and comprehension in all the bidden and unbidden events that had so dramatically entered her path:

> When the heart is sick and the soul faint and we feel we have no friend on Earth to whom we can go with feelings of perfect confidence and trust the very mind seems ready to burst. Could I go to the Lord and tell him all but I do not know what to say. Since Friday night I have been thinking of some things which makes my heart ache. What shall I do or what shall I say can I ever be the same happy girl again at this time feeling as I do I answer never no never. When my friends are grieved on my account what can be worse? Nothing. And yet I must keep up appearances of happiness because if I do not

3. Excerpts from "A Blessing by John Smith, Patriarch, upon the head of Emeline B. Harris, Daughter of David and [Diadama] Woodward, born Feb. 29th 1828, Worcester Co., Massachusetts," Nauvoo, February 7, 1845, typescript copy in my possession.

4. In the temple, which was then under construction in Nauvoo, ordinances considered essential for salvation were performed for the living and also for the dead by proxy. By serving as proxy for her deceased progenitors and unconverted family members, Emmeline would act as "a savior on Mount Zion," redeem them from their unsanctified state, and bring them into the family of Christ. Genealogical work has long been an essential aspect of Mormonism by which living members can identify their progenitors and perform for them these ordinances, which, if accepted, will bring them salvation and weld generations together through patriarchal or family lines.

> I shall be questioned. O I almost despise myself and if I had one single soul to rest on to whom I could tell my feelings I should feel relieved. O I could wish life were a dream a vain delusive dream but no O no it is an awful reality. I have been happy but I fear I shall never be again. You have represented things to me strangely. I do not know what to think or what you think of me I am afraid you have lost to[o] much confidence [in me] to ever be restored and yet I could wish for it pray for it and I believe live for it. I feel that I could resign the world for peace of mind and live alone in seclusion were it possible. If I only knew what the Lord required of me I feel almost humble enough to do anything and I pray that I may be made so. A few of my [the first four words crossed out] contemplations.[5]

On February 14, 1845, just a week after receiving her patriarchal blessing, two weeks before her seventeenth birthday, and three months after James's departure, in an upstairs room of the Whitney home, with Elizabeth Ann Whitney as witness, Brigham Young married Emmeline to Newel K. Whitney as a plural wife. Unknown to Emmeline, Olive Bishop had been his plural wife for more than a year.[6] Emmeline was now married to a man who possessed priesthood keys, as her patriarchal blessing pronounced, and could assure her of all the spiritual blessings that such a union could provide. Like all other plural marriages in Nauvoo, it was a private sealing and known only to those persons involved. She expressed her feelings about this event in a long autobiographical poem: "Ah, little one," the kind man said, "you sadly need a friend," Emmeline wrote of the beginning of their relationship. "Nor can you longer sorrow bear alone," the poem continued. "He took her in his arms, as her own father might," the verse went on,

> *This stranger patriarch, and comforted and blest*
> *Her aching heart, and showed her greater truth and light,*
> *Even where to seek a haven of sweet rest.*"[7]

That day did indeed initiate a secure interval for Emmeline in the midst of such personally harrowing times. Years later, she reflected on that mercurial season and the unexpected source of security after losing James and her baby. "His [Eugene Henri's] father left me alone in a strange city and

5. Emmeline Wells, letter to Newel K. Whitney, photocopy of original handwritten letter, Newel K. Whitney Papers.

6. Though slow to enter the practice, Newel K. Whitney was sealed to a number of deceased women as well as seven living women before leaving Nauvoo.

7. E. Wells, "Faith and Fidelity," in her *Musings and Memories*, 207–28. This long autobiographical poem relates her loss of James, her meeting and marriage to Newel K. Whitney, and his death.

wandered away and never returned," she wrote. "Broken hearted, young and desolate," she never saw him again. Though she was now alone, homeless, and friendless, still a stranger to the new city, she yet felt that "the hand of Providence was over me and must have guided me to the safe haven I found."[8]

Emmeline never commented on the age disparity in her marriage to Whitney. At the time, it is likely that the promise of security overruled any reluctance to marry him. Because most states and territories put the age of consent for a woman to marry, with a parent's permission, at age fourteen, including Illinois (and later Utah), youthful marriages were not unusual. Though legally Emmeline needed a parent's approval until she was eighteen, there was none available to give that approval. However, her marriage to Whitney was a religious, not a civil, ceremony, so legal age requirements were not a factor.

In Emmeline's case, Whitney was an able provider, a respected church leader, and a priesthood bearer, holding keys necessary for salvation. Emmeline was a lone woman, already a member of his extended household, and in need of someone to care for her. She expressed only gratitude for her marriage to Newel K. Whitney. In fact, a second letter to him, written three years after their marriage, indicates that she could love him as well as she loved the teenage boy to whom she once gave her heart.

Although she was no longer adrift and alone, her heartfelt soliloquies continued. "When will sorrow leave my bosom," she cried out to her diary a week after marrying Whitney. "All my days have I experienced it. Oppression has been my lot."[9] Four days later, her lamentation continued. "This day like all others is full of trouble sorrow and affliction are my attendants. O my God how long wilt Thou suffer this... have mercy and forgive and grant me the desire of my heart and I will forever praise thee." Afraid to "unbosom her heart" except to those whom she had learned to trust, Emmeline used the mute pages of her diary as a welcome confidant during that uncertain period.[10]

She allowed her dreams to become false reality, and she thought she would awake to find herself actually at the side of James. She was certain her dreams were real when, a few days later, a steamboat came upriver. She was so anxious to meet the passengers that she "was obliged to lay aside my work," certain that James was among them. Though others had doubted his return, none of their words were able to shake her "confidence in the

8. E. Wells, "My Trip East," January 18, 1886, 100.

9. E. Wells, Diary, February 20, 1845.

10. Ibid., February 24, 1845.

only man I ever loved." When she stepped out into the yard on the way to the landing, she saw a man approaching from the dock. He walked like James, and she was sure he had returned at last. Then, just as she was about to cry out his name, he spoke, and she found that the dusk had deceived her. How long she had dreamed of his return! How much she remembered their time together! How often she had looked for him with every steamer that docked at the riverside in Nauvoo! Surely, she thought, he cannot have forgotten all his promises and vows. "No never," she believed. "They must sting him to the very soul and I pray God that they may and that remorse of conscience will bring him back to the path of duty." Anger had now crept into her anguish. "God knows that I have ever been true to him and if he would be as true to me I could not complain." No longer pleading only for his return, she was willing to settle for even a letter that she might know something of his whereabouts.[11]

A month later, in March 1845, Emmeline indirectly learned that James had gone to sea for three years. Despite her dismay at his prolonged absence, the depth of her gratitude for this secondhand information matched the intensity of her earlier pleas for his return. "O God," she exclaimed, "I bless Thee that in thy mercy Thou has this day permitted me to hear news from a distant shore and that thou art kind and tender O God forgive my unbelief and save him from the wave give him dreams and visions of the night that he may know Thy will O Lord and do it and grant that he may return to me and not forget his first love."[12]

What exactly Emmeline believed was the nature of her relationship with Whitney is not clear. Years later, speculating on that connection, Emmeline's sister Adeline Maria Earl and Emmeline's granddaughter Margaret Cannon Clayton opined that Emmeline had originally believed that her "sealing" to Bishop Whitney was an adoption, not a marriage.[13] Her continuing expectation that James would return would seem to confirm this idea. But the words of the marriage ceremony, clearly denoting what it was, would preclude this assertion. Moreover, Emmeline recognized the necessity of marriage to a priesthood holder in order to receive all the blessings of the Gospel, as evident in a second letter to Whitney. Adoption had a specific ecclesiastical meaning in early Mormonism. It was a practice by which individuals and families could be "adopted" into a specific priesthood line, often

11. Ibid., February 28, 1845.

12. Ibid., March 24, 1845.

13. Sealing here means a permanent connection applicable in the next life as well as in mortality—that which is sealed on earth is sealed in heaven. A couple married by appropriate priesthood authority are thus sealed in an eternal relationship.

headed by a general authority of the church. That priesthood connection had significant meaning in Mormon theology. It was not a prevalent practice, however, and faded by the end of the nineteenth century. That either of these two relatives of Emmeline understood this meaning of "adoption" is also unclear.[14] Adeline Maria also noted that Emmeline made no mention of a marriage to Whitney when Diadama and Emmeline's younger siblings arrived in Nauvoo later that year.[15] But some version of the story evidently stayed in the family for several generations. Though Emmeline never provided details of this marriage, she always noted February 14 as the day of her *marriage* to Bishop Whitney. One thing was certain. With that marriage, Emmeline entered a higher strata of Mormon society than she might ever have expected, one where she would remain throughout her life.

After March 1845, Emmeline did not write in her diary for several months. In the meantime, she greeted her two friends from North New Salem, who had migrated to Nauvoo with their husbands: Catherine Hascall and her husband, Thomas H. Woodbury, and Catherine's cousin Irene

14. An explanation of the "law of adoption" as practiced in the early church is Gordon Irving, "The Law of Adoption: One Phase of the Development of the Mormon Concept of Salvation, 1830–1900." A succinct explanation is given in Richard E. Bennett, "Adoption, Law of," 9–10. See also Wilford Woodruff, "The Law of Adoption"; Richard E. Bennett, *Mormons at the Missouri, 1846–1852: "And Should We Die,"* 187–94; Samuel M. Brown, "Early Mormon Adoption Theology and the Mechanics of Salvation," 3–52; and Jonathan A. Stapley, "Adoptive Sealing Ritual in Mormonism."

15. This silence is understandable since Emmeline was still reconciling herself to the new principle of marriage and plural marriages were still not disclosed. Adeline Maria's speculation is in a letter to her niece Lillian Clark Ramsey, dated March 9, 1916, which states: "My husband's sister, Elinor Earl, told me that Emeline told her that she did not know she was sealed to Bishop Whitney until '47. They told her she was sealed as an adopted daughter. Mind you she never told me for she knew what I would say, for I never did believe in polygamy...but Emeline has proved she did believe it, or she did not have the moral courage to do different." Original holograph in my possession. Margaret Clayton stated in an interview conducted by Dennis Rowley and John Bluth, November 17, 1977, in Salt Lake City that "Bishop Whitney (Newell [*sic*] K. Whitney) took her into his family and had her sealed to him. And she didn't understand the sealing business, I don't think anybody does. But she didn't understand it and she didn't know that sealing meant the same as marriage. And she was a young girl, only 16. But she wouldn't go back. She believed in the gospel and believed in Joseph Smith. And she wouldn't go back to Nauvoo [did Clayton mean New Salem?]. So Bishop Whitney took her into his family and had her sealed to him. And she told me, herself, that she just nearly died when she found out that sealing meant the same thing as marriage and that she was expected to live with this old man as his wife" (6, 7). L. Tom Perry Special Collections, Harold B. Lee Library, Brigham Young University, Provo, UT.

Hascall and her husband, Francis Pomeroy, whose earlier seafaring adventures may have influenced James's decision to go to sea. By May 1845, the Samuel Aiken family, the Jeremiah Woodbury family, and Lorin Farr had all made homes in Nauvoo. Arriving a year after Emmeline, this group of New Salem Saints found the city to be even more comfortably established than she did, with goods, food, and entertainment in ready supply. "The corn is so high we can [look] out upon the city and see [only] the tops of the houses," Irene Pomeroy effused to her parents back in New England. She measured a stalk that was actually eleven feet tall, and she was sure she could find one measuring twelve. Even housing was more accessible, she discovered.[16] Irene found Emmeline to be "quite fleshy" and busy teaching school in a private family (the Whitneys), who "appeared to like her very much."[17]

More than just surviving the trauma of the prophet's and his brother's murders, the community of Joseph's followers found new impetus to carry on the work and to create a unified and committed society of Latter-day Saints. "The Church is in prosperous circumstances for there appears to be the most union that has ever be[e]n," observed one longtime resident, Zina Huntington Jacobs, in March of that year.[18] The neatly spaced homes and buildings, separated by cultivated land, gave the town an appearance of "a perfect garden," Irene explained to her parents back in New Salem. The top stone of the temple was laid just a day before she arrived, she noted, and had been put in place with "Praises and Hosannas."[19] In July, Irene reported to her parents that Emmeline was in "tolerable health" along with the Ponds, but Emmeline's spirits were lifted, Irene noted, when she received letters from her sisters Pallas and Lucy. Irene also mentioned that she had seen none of Elder Harris's family.[20] If she knew any of the facts about James's departure or Emmeline's marriage to Whitney, she did not disclose these details in her letters.

When the Harrises confirmed to Emmeline the news that James had gone to sea for three years, Francis Pomeroy's mother urged Emmeline not to feel despondent. As a former seaman, Francis "had always come back,"

16. Irene Hascall Pomeroy, letter to Mr. Ashbel G. Hascall, North New Salem, Franklin Co., Mass. Postmarked: Nauvoo Ills. July 13 [1845], written July 6, 12 [1845], in "Letters of a Proselyte: The Hascall-Pomeroy Correspondence," *Utah Historical Quarterly* 25 (January 1957): 64.

17. Ibid., 62.

18. Z. Young, Diary, March 10, 1845.

19. Irene Hascall Pomeroy, letter to Mr. Ashbel G. Hascall [Irene's father], North New Salem, Franklin Co., Mass., Postmarked: Nauvoo Ill., June 4 [1845], in "Letters of a Proselyte," *Utah Historical Quarterly* 25 (January 1957): 60, 61.

20. Ibid., July 13 [1845], 64.

she explained, "and she thought he [James] would now."[21] Her words may have given hope to Emmeline.

In the meantime, Emmeline's school had increased to thirty or forty children, and she was paid a dollar and a half per week, Irene informed her cousin. "She is the same as she used to be," she added, "though not quite," an ambiguous comment at best. Then, in September, Irene explained, Emmeline had to leave her school so that the schoolhouse could be "occupied as a tenement," but she secured a position "in a common school for nine shillings per week."[22] While making new friends who would remain her friends for life, Emmeline was also learning the self-dependence that became the constant in her toccata life.

When Emmeline picked up her pen again in June 1845, a month after her New England friends arrived, it was not to record her joy at once again being reunited with them but to release more waves of longing for James. Perhaps their presence as well as their questions triggered her return to the pain of James's absence. "Wilt thou, O God forever separate me from one to whom I gave my whole and undivided affection in all the honesty and truthfulness of my heart and with all the simplicity and virtue of a youthful girl," she wrote. Worried that others, particularly her New England friends, believed that somehow she had been the cause of his abandonment, she asserted her innocence and her confidence that he could never "rise up and say I neglected him or reproached him." "No," she continued, "even when he has left me to the mercy of a cold unfeeling world am I ready to receive him to my heart again whenever he returns and I want O how much I desire to have him come." He, only, she declared, could calm her in her distress or soothe her in affliction or make her happy in his society. "O that thou couldst hear my voice and thou wouldst return."[23] Now, however, more secure than she had expected to be when James left, Emmeline was occupied primarily with school teaching and the pleasure of singing with the Nauvoo choir at concerts and building dedications. She was also getting to know the large Whitney family.

Of most importance to Emmeline that summer of 1845 was the arrival of her mother and her three young siblings, Adeline Maria, sixteen; Ellen, fourteen; and Hiram, just nine. What they talked about during this first meeting after more than a year of separation can only be surmised, but Diadama undoubtedly told her about the difficulties in leaving North New

21. Ibid., 67.

22. Irene Hascall Pomeroy, letter to Miss Ophelia M. Andrews [cousin], North New Salem, Franklin Co., Mass. Postmarked: Nauvoo, Ills. July 30 [1845], written July 26, [1845] in ibid. A shilling was worth twenty-four cents.

23. E. Wells, Diary, June 6, 1845.

Salem and the strenuous journey to Nauvoo. It had not been an easy trip for them. Diadama's son James had sold the home, some of its proceeds providing travel supplies for Diadama. The rest of the money, designated for her use, he put in the care of Joseph Woodbury, who was traveling to Nauvoo in the same company as Diadama. Woodbury, unfortunately, decided to return to Massachusetts halfway through the journey, taking Diadama's money with him. Later, an accident rendered Diadama unconscious for several hours in the care of some kindly strangers. But upon regaining consciousness, she insisted on continuing the journey. "O what faith she had," Adeline Maria wrote about that incident. "She was bound to see Emmeline if possible."[24] Emmeline owed much to her mother for her own perseverance and unshakable commitment to her pursuits.

That Emmeline remained with Olive Bishop rather than joining her family was not questioned, since her mother had few means to acquire housing herself. The tight-knit North New Salem community, however, looked after its own, and Samuel Aiken's wife, Nancy, invited Diadama and her three young children to live with them. They settled in amid the warmth and welcome of their New England friends, Diadama finally fulfilling the dream she had held on to since her baptism four years earlier. To the pleadings of her older children to return home, having now seen Emmeline again, Diadama responded that "she would not go back for 'all the world.'" In fact, wanting to share the conviction she had in her new religion with her older children, she told them "to prepare to come and get all they can to bring with them."[25] She promised that they would have "a sumptuous feast and merry time yet together, kill the fatted calf—at any rate, when my children come I will make merry for them."[26] But they did not come.

When Diadama learned of Emmeline's strained relationship with the Harris family, she urged her daughter to visit them to try to make amends. Always obedient to her mother's wishes, Emmeline relented and traveled to La Harpe, staying with the Harrises for two weeks. They were confident, she learned, that James would return from his sailing voyage "to be an husband

24. Adeline Maria Woodward Earl, letter to [her niece] Lillian Clark Ramsey, March 9, 1916, copy of original in my possession.

25. Irene Hascall Pomeroy, letter to Ursulia B. Hascall, North New Salem, Franklin Co., Mass., Postmarked: Nauvoo Ills Jan 23 [1846] in "Letters of a Proselyte," *Utah Historical Quarterly* 25 (April 1957): 142.

26. The letter was written by Diadama on August 4, 5, 6, 1846, to Lucy and Henry Granger and signed "Mother and Grandmother." Emmeline published it as "An Old Letter," *Woman's Exponent* 15 (December 1, 1886): 98, several months after her return from her first visit to New England, perhaps making a copy of her mother's letter at that time. The only extant copy is its publication in the *Woman's Exponent*.

and be steady."[27] But that eventuality was now far beyond the horizon. Emmeline was consumed with her teaching while savoring the presence of her mother and younger siblings. She was also quietly finding her niche within the large Whitney family. In becoming a Whitney, Emmeline's grandniece exclaimed, she had taken a step that "set the stage for her to become one of the luminaries of the Mormon women of her time."[28] But for Emmeline at that time, there was little expectation of such a notion, for once again, the saints would be forced to find a new Zion far away in the west.

27. Ursulia B. Hascall, letter to Col. Wilson Andrews, North New Salem, Franklin Co., Mass. Postmarked: Nauvoo Ills. May 3 [1846], written May 2d, 1846, in "Letters of a Proselyte," *Utah Historical Quarterly* 25 (April 1957): 145.

28. Letter from Marjorie Bland (Emmeline's grandniece) to Kay and Ted Bezzerides, March 22, 1982, copy of typescript in my possession, courtesy of Marjorie Bland.

CHAPTER 6

Nauvoo

(1844–1846)

Newel Kimball Whitney and his wife Elizabeth Ann Smith, to whom Emmeline's life would be permanently connected, were early converts to Mormonism. Their association with the Mormon Church began in Kirtland, Ohio, where both had migrated. Newel was born in Marlborough, Vermont, in 1795, the eldest son of Samuel and Susanna Kimball Whitney. During the War of 1812, seventeen-year-old Whitney became an army sutler, selling goods to the military. Afterward, he tried merchandising in several areas before settling in Mentor, Ohio, in 1821. There he rented a small cabin on the property of Elijah Smith, a resident of Kirtland for three years. Smith had traveled with his wife, Rachel Webster, from Connecticut, following the lead of his fifty-one-year-old unmarried sister, Sarah, and her traveling companion and niece, Elizabeth Ann Smith.[1] Newel and Elizabeth Ann met during his business travels through Kirtland and married on November 6, 1822. Elizabeth Ann noted that her husband was "proverbial as being lucky in all his undertakings" and "accumulated property faster than most of his companions and associates."[2]

1. Gertrude Van Rensselaer Wickham, *Memorial to the Pioneer Women of the Western Reserve*, 782; Janet Lisonbee, *Obituaries and Life Sketches of the Early Saints Who Died in the Kirtland, Ohio, Area*, 18. Sarah Smith seemed to be financially independent and eager to invest in land in the newly settled Connecticut Western Reserve. See also Elizabeth Ann Whitney, "A Leaf from an Autobiography," *Woman's Exponent* 7 (August 15, 1878): 33, serialized in vol. 7 between August 1, 1878, and February 15, 1879.

2. E. Whitney, "Leaf from an Autobiography," *Woman's Exponent* 7 (August 15, 1878): 41. See also Mark Lyman Staker, "Thou Art the Man: Newel K. Whitney in Ohio." See also Staker, *Hearken, O Ye People: The Historical Setting of Joseph Smith's Ohio Revelations*, 195–256.

Elizabeth Ann, called Ann during her Kirtland days, was born December 26, 1800, the eldest child of Gibson and Polly Smith. Despite the indifference of her parents toward religion, Elizabeth Ann expressed a natural inclination toward things spiritual at an early age and convinced Newel to be a seeker with her after "true religion." They both became interested in the doctrine taught by Sidney Rigdon, a local minister in the Reformed Baptist Church. Rigdon taught a return to primitive Christianity, as promulgated by Alexander Campbell and the Disciples of Christ. After becoming Campbellites, the Whitneys regretted the fact that the church made no claim of authority to administer the gift of the Holy Ghost, an essential element of true Christianity in Elizabeth Ann's mind. They were adrift once more, but in the fall of 1830, they experienced an extraordinary epiphany during a midnight prayer when both Newel and Elizabeth Ann felt an overwhelming spiritual manifestation. "The spirit rested upon us," Elizabeth remembered, "and a *cloud* overshadowed the house" from which a voice declared: "Prepare to receive the word of the Lord, for it is coming."[3] Indeed, the word did come—in the form of four Mormon missionaries whose preaching in the vicinity of Kirtland drew large crowds. Among the many converts were members from Sidney Rigdon's Kirtland congregation and Rigdon himself, and in November 1830, the Whitneys were baptized.[4]

Fayette, New York, where the church had been organized in April 1830, had proved hostile toward its early converts, and Joseph Smith looked to a friendlier environment as mooring for the fledgling church. Nearby Kirtland, Ohio, gave promise of being that place. Three months after the Whitneys became Latter-day Saints, they felt privileged to host the Mormon prophet and his pregnant wife, Emma, when they first arrived in Kirtland.[5] Their meeting initiated in the Whitneys a lifetime of total devotion, consecration, and service to their new faith that inscribed the names of

3. Edward W. Tullidge, *The Women of Mormondom*, 41–42 (emphasis Elizabeth Ann's). Reprinted in Orson F. Whitney, "Newel K. Whitney," 125; and Carol Cornwall Madsen, "A Legacy of Faith."

4. The four missionaries were Oliver Cowdery, Parley P. Pratt, Peter Whitmer Jr., and Ziba Peterson. James B. Allen and Glen M. Leonard, *The Story of the Latter-day Saints*, 54. See also E. Whitney, "Leaf from an Autobiography," *Woman's Exponent* 7 (September 1, 1878): 51.

5. Elizabeth Ann noted the unexpected arrival of Joseph at their home, who said, "You have prayed me here, now what do you want of me?" Elizabeth Ann remembered that Joseph's presence in their home "was the fulfillment of the vision we had seen of a cloud as of glory resting upon our house." E. Whitney, "Leaf from an Autobiography," *Woman's Exponent* 7 (September 1, 1878): 51. Other references are O. Whitney, "Newel K. Whitney," 125; and Tullidge, *The Women of Mormondom*, 42.

Newel and Elizabeth Ann Whitney among those of Joseph Smith's most enduring and loyal followers. After years of close companionship in the work of building the church, Joseph was moved to say to his friend, "Thou art a faithful friend in whom the afflicted sons of men can confide, with the most perfect safety.... [H]ow warm that heart! how anxious that soul! for the welfare of one who has been cast out, and hated of almost all men. Brother Whitney, thou knowest not how strong those ties are, that bind my soul and heart to thee."[6]

Whitney's single-minded attention to the details of his commercial enterprises had made him a prosperous merchant. But as a Latter-day Saint, his talents and aims had to be redirected to building a spiritual kingdom. "Thou art a strange man," declared Joseph Smith Sr. in Newel's patriarchal blessing, "and thy ways have been unlike the ways of other men." But the patriarch recognized that Whitney had nevertheless sought to be "a man of God" and counseled him "to do away all thy unbelief and doubts, and in this the Lord has given thee strength."[7] Even Emmeline alluded to his peculiar ways. Remembering his birthday years after his death, she noted that he was "aristocratic and reserved" but "eccentric surpassing any one I have ever seen." But he also evoked reverential feelings in Emmeline. "I looked to him almost as if he had been a God; my youth, my inexperience of life and its realities caused me to trust most implicitly in one who had power and integrity always at his command."[8] Though the transition from profit making to prophet serving was gradual, Joseph Smith prophesied that "the time cometh that he [Whitney] shall overcome all the narrow mindedness of his heart, and all his covetous desires that so easily besetteth him; and he shall deal with a liberal hand to the poor and the needy, the sick and the afflicted, the widow and the fatherless: and marvelously and miraculously shall the Lord his God provide for him even that he shall be blessed with all the fulness of the good things of this earth, and his seed after him from generation to generation." Whatever Whitney's eccentricities or materialistic penchants were, Joseph declared that his name "shall be on high and his rest among the sanctified."[9] These blessings, along with

6. Hedges, Smith, and Anderson, *Journals*, 94.

7. Newel K. Whitney, Patriarchal Blessing bestowed in Kirtland, OH, September 14, 1835, by Patriarch Joseph Smith Sen. [Sr.], Oliver Cowdery, clerk, N. Whitney Papers.

8. E. Wells, Diary, February 5, 1891, and September 23, 1874.

9. N. Whitney, blessing bestowed by the Prophet Joseph Smith "through the Urim and Thummin, according to the spirit of prophecy and revelation," October 7, 1835, Frederick G. Williams, clerk, N. Whitney Papers.

specific admonitions appearing in the Doctrine and Covenants directed to Whitney, are the clearest insights into the personality of Newel K. Whitney as he adapted to a spiritually oriented life.[10]

At the first patriarchal blessing meeting, held several months before the 1836 dedication of the Kirtland Temple,[11] Elizabeth Ann "received the gift of singing inspirationally," and she sang "the first Song of Zion ever given in the pure language," identified as the Adamic tongue.[12] She used that gift frequently throughout her life for the spiritual edification of her friends and family. While Newel and Elizabeth exulted in their newfound religion, Elizabeth's aunt Sarah Smith's early animosity to Mormonism remained unabated. This created a constant dilemma for Elizabeth Ann, whose love for her aunt and her commitment to the church were in perpetual conflict. As close as they were, Sarah nevertheless went so far as to write Elizabeth out of her will, leaving her possessions to her non-Mormon relatives, most of them still living in Kirtland at her death.

Because Joseph Smith had declared Independence, Missouri, to be "the center stake of Zion," some members had already settled there, but others had hoped to remain in Kirtland. As with other communities where the Saints had settled, however, their neighbors became wary and then hostile as great numbers of converts swelled the Mormon population. Internal dissent over the failure of the Kirtland Safety Society, established by Joseph Smith and other church leaders as a monetary institution for church

10. E. Whitney, "Leaf from an Autobiography," *Woman's Exponent* 7 (November 1, 1878): 83; and (November 15, 1878): 91. For other accounts, see "The Aaronic Priesthood"; and Joseph B. Wirthlin, "Newel K. Whitney: Faithful Steward, Steadfast Saint," 204. See also "History of Joseph Smith." Revelations recorded in the Doctrine and Covenants relating to Newel K. Whitney are sections 64:26; 42–46; 72:8 (his call to be bishop in Kirtland), 84:112; 114; 93:50; 96:2; 104:39–42; 117:1; 4; 11 (his call to be bishop in Adam-ondi-Ahman [Spring Hill], a Mormon community in Missouri).

11. In the Kirtland temple, special ordinances were performed particularly for those called to spread the message of the newly restored gospel, a primary mission of the church. It was also used for Sabbath-day services, for instruction, for blessing and testimony meetings, and for receiving revelation. Patriarchal blessings were often administered there. E. Whitney, "Leaf from an Autobiography," *Woman's Exponent* 7 (November 1, 1878): 83.

12. Ibid. The "pure language" was usually understood to be the language spoken by Adam before the corruptions of Babel. Parley P. Pratt interpreted her song, which, according to Elizabeth Ann, "describes the manner in which the ancient patriarchs blessed their families, and gives some account of 'Adam-ondi-Ahman,'" an area in Missouri where Adam is to return and receive keys from prophets of the various dispensations. Lamar C. Berrett, "Adam-ondi-Ahman."

members, also threatened the unity of the Saints and their loyalty to the prophet.[13] By 1838 most of the remaining Saints had made the journey to what they hoped would be their longed-for permanent settlement in Independence, Missouri. Kirtland had been a winnowing stage in the church's development.

Once again, however, in 1838–39, the Saints were driven from their homes. Fleeing Missouri, they were welcomed by the hospitable city of Quincy, Illinois, and from there they moved upriver to the sparsely inhabited Mississippi river town of Commerce. Having lost virtually everything in their flight from Kirtland, the Whitneys, who did not make it all the way to Missouri, joined the Saints in Commerce. When Joseph Smith and Emma finally reached Commerce themselves, after Joseph's six-month incarceration in Liberty Jail, they secured a log house for their family, and Joseph provided the Whitneys with a small cottage nearby. After completion of his store, Joseph hired Newel to manage it and offered the Whitneys lodging in the store's spacious upper floor. The Whitneys were residing there when the Relief Society was organized in 1842.[14]

All of these events transpired before Emmeline became a member, but they were chapters in the institutional history of the church that would one day be fixed in her retentive mind. She learned much, according to one biographer, from her intimate companionship with Elizabeth Ann Whitney, "and she absorbed into her very soul the spirit and genius of Mormonism" as well as its history.[15]

Emmeline arrived in Nauvoo too late to join the Relief Society, which had been disbanded in March 1844, but from the teachings of Elizabeth Ann, who was counselor to Emma Smith, the president, she became a "vicarious" member, learning of its origins, of Joseph Smith's talks to the women, and of its significance in the organizational pattern of the church. The Nauvoo Relief Society had tremendous impact on her conviction of the personal and community value of such a society. Its organization, she was convinced, was one of the most significant ecclesiastical features of women's

13. The governing board of the Kirtland Safety Society included Joseph Smith, Sydney Rigdon, Frederick G. Williams (the First Presidency), Newel K. Whitney, Joseph Kingsbury, and Warren Parrish. See Staker, *Hearken, O Ye People*, chap. 33.

14. E. Whitney, "Leaf from an Autobiography," *Woman's Exponent* 7 (November 15, 1878): 91. Both of Emma Smith's counselors had given her refuge when she needed it, Elizabeth Ann in Kirtland and Sarah Cleveland in Quincy, Illinois, after the Saints had been driven from Missouri. In 1843 Elizabeth Ann conducted the Relief Society meetings during the yearlong absence of Emma Smith and without the aid of Sarah Cleveland, who moved from Nauvoo that year.

15. Gates, "Emmeline B. Wells," 4.

experience in Nauvoo.[16] Besides its spiritual and benevolent features, she regarded the society as a liberating force in women's lives and as a training ground for personal advancement and leadership.[17] Such opportunity, she believed, directly correlated with one of Joseph Smith's statements to the women at the April 28, 1842, meeting: "I now turn the key to you in the name of God, and this Society shall rejoice and knowledge and intelligence shall flow down from this time—this is the beginning of better days to this Society."[18] This symbolic gesture announced a bright new horizon through the temple ordinances and also infused members of the society with a sense of mission and worth that energized their service and broadened their perspective of the wisdom in utilizing women's talents and insights in both religious and civic settings. In fact, Emmeline believed, the proximity of the 1842 organization of the Relief Society with its spiritual and ecclesiastical empowerment of women and the 1848 organization of the first US women's rights movement, which set in motion a crusade to expand women's political, legal, and educational rights, was not coincidental. Joseph Smith, she believed, had turned the key of knowledge and intelligence that empowered women to overcome their social disabilities, opening doors long closed to them in civic life.

Also of special importance to Emmeline was Joseph Smith's organizational structure of the Relief Society, which was similar to the governance pattern of the church. The minutes and precedents, he said, would serve as a constitution and by-laws, and of particular interest to Emmeline was his announcement that the officers were to serve as long as they properly and faithfully exercised their duties.[19] A foundation of her work for women was her certitude that the Relief Society gave Mormon women not only an ecclesiastical position as partners with members of priesthood quorums in "building the kingdom," but also a sisterhood that helped unite their diverse backgrounds and expectations into a union of mutual concerns and purpose. In her public life, Emmeline depended on this female support and association. Her family was her primary anchor in her private life.

When Newel K. Whitney addressed the Relief Society at its tenth

16. See Jill Mulvay Derr and Carol Cornwall Madsen, "'Something Better' for the Sisters: Joseph Smith and the Female Relief Society of Nauvoo"; Jill Mulvay Derr, Janath Russell Cannon, and Maureen Ursenbach Beecher, *Women of Covenant: The Story of Relief Society*, 1–58.

17. For Emmeline's view of the qualities that the Relief Society nourished in its members, see "Women's Organizations," *Woman's Exponent* 8 (January 15, 1880): 122.

18. "A Book of Records Containing the Proceedings of the Female Relief Society of Nauvoo," April 28, 1842, LDS Church History Library, Salt Lake City.

19. Ibid., March 17, 1842.

meeting, on May 27, 1842, he affirmed the connection of women to priesthood through the binding elements of the temple endowment. Having just received the temple ordinances from Joseph Smith, he was consumed with the knowledge and promises that awaited. "Without the female," he said, "all things cannot be restor'd to earth—it takes all to restore the Priesthood.... I rejoice in the prospect of what lays before." As a bishop and as husband of counselor Elizabeth Ann, he was particularly sympathetic to the concerns of the women of the church as well as their needs. Through the ministration of temple ordinances, he assured them, "there are great blessings before [you], that would astonish you if you could behold them." He closed by affirming that "you have my heart's desire for the prosperity of the Society" and the hope that they might "go on and glorify your profession."

As the only extant document containing the words of Joseph Smith exclusively addressed to the women of the church, along with the sermons of other church leaders, the Nauvoo Relief Society minutes were carefully preserved by Eliza R. Snow, the first secretary, and revered as a sacred record. Years later, Emmeline made her own copy of the minutes, with her comments in the margins.[20] Through her study of the minutes and her conversations with Elizabeth Ann Whitney, she became as familiar with the original Relief Society as most of the women who attended its meetings. Thereafter, for Emmeline, the Nauvoo Relief Society served as the measuring rod for the proceedings of the Relief Society after its reorganization in Utah in 1867.

Joseph and his brother were murdered in Carthage Jail, while being held there on the charge of treason.[21] Though outsiders expected that the leaderless church would soon fragment and disperse, members rallied with a determination to complete the temple as a monument to their slain leader and to receive the saving ordinances of the gospel. For a brief period, the Nauvoo community enjoyed a time of peace, erecting new buildings and transforming log cabins into solid brick homes. The once environmentally hostile village was actually blossoming into Nauvoo the beautiful. Emmeline's association with the Whitneys was similarly blossoming, bringing her into a circle of new acquaintances, including several church leaders whose names appear throughout her later diaries as longtime friends.

By December 1845, the temple was sufficiently completed to be utilized, and before the city was vacated the next year, nearly six thousand men

20. E. Wells Papers, Perry Special Collections.

21. A brief explanation of the use of the charge of treason in both Missouri and Illinois can be found in Gordon A. Madsen, "Austin King's Court of Inquiry," in *Sustaining the Law: Joseph Smith's Legal Encounters*, by Gordon A. Madsen, Jeffrey N. Walker, and John W. Welch, 294–95.

and women received their endowments. Emmeline and her mother were among the number and also served as proxies for the vicarious baptism and endowment of Emmeline's oldest sister, Adaline, who died in Petersham as a young girl.[22]

Marriages, both monogamous and plural, were solemnized in the temple and both witnessed and recorded. In addition to Elizabeth Ann, Whitney was sealed on January 7 and 26, 1846, to Olive Bishop, Emmeline, Elizabeth and Abigail Pond (who were Emmeline's New Salem friends), Elizabeth Mahala Moore, Henrietta Keys (or Keyes), and Ann Houston.[23] All had been left to their own resources for various reasons, and Whitney provided a priesthood connection for them. Not all remained in the Whitney family, however. Later that year, death took Abigail Pond, and Ann Houston died shortly after arriving in the Salt Lake Valley in November 1848. Of his plural wives, only Emmeline and Ann Houston bore him children: Emmeline, two daughters, Isabel and Melvina, and Ann, her only child, Jethro, who was raised by Olive Bishop after Ann's death. Elizabeth Ann was agreeable to these additional marriages, declaring, "I am willing and ready to defend enthusiastically those of my sisters who have been genuine enough and who possessed sufficient sublimity of character, to practically live the principles of divine faith, which have been revealed in these the last days, in the establishing of the kingdom of God upon the earth. It has required sterling qualities indeed to battle with the opposition on every hand, and not be overcome."[24]

In February 1846, when Emmeline left Nauvoo with the Whitney family, traveling in the Heber C. Kimball company, she had been able to spend only a few months with her mother and younger siblings.[25] It was another tearful parting from her mother, but Emmeline expected Diadama to follow with

22. Nauvoo Temple Endowment Register, January 31, 1846. Newel K. Whitney and Elizabeth Ann, along with about sixty or so others, had already received the temple ordinances at the hand of Joseph Smith and now took their places as officiators, repeating the ordinances for each other in the temple before administering them to others. See Andrew F. Ehat, "Joseph Smith's Introduction of Temple Ordinances and the 1844 Mormon Succession Question."

23. Nauvoo Temple Endowment Register, "Records of Early Church Families"; "Newel K. Whitney," Newel K. Whitney File.

24. E. Whitney, "Leaf from an Autobiography," *Woman's Exponent* 7 (January 1, 1879): 115.

25. This vanguard company was meant to include only the available apostles and their families and several other church officials, but many other church members, not all properly prepared, chose to leave at the same time. See "Scenes in Nauvoo, and Incidents from H. C. Kimball's Journal," *Woman's Exponent* 12 (July 1, 1883): 18, reprinted in Holzapfel and Holzapfel, *Woman's View*, 294.

the younger children in the spring, when most of the Saints were planning to leave the city. Emmeline was just two days short of being eighteen when she began that long westward journey and once again had little knowledge of what lay ahead for her. She was still known to everyone, including her mother and New England friends, as Emeline Harris. But she was now a Whitney, and her link with the Harris family was irrevocably broken.

The Harrises never returned to the church. They made homes in several Illinois towns where Elias farmed. After his death, Lucy married Jesse Blackinton (sometimes Blackington), a native New Englander, who lived near the Harrises in Roscoe, Illinois. The two eventually returned to New England, making their home in New Salem. Jesse died in 1878 at the age of eighty, and Lucy lived on as a widow for eleven more years.[26] She was cared for by a niece, who inherited the Blackinton home at Lucy's death.[27] Emmeline visited Lucy several times before Lucy died.

Nauvoo opened a new chapter in Emmeline's self-characterized "romance." Her association with her mother, her older sisters and brothers, her first husband, her only son, and her beloved New England lay behind her. She was now a Whitney, married to Newel for "time and all eternity," and living among the highest echelons of church leadership. Moreover, she was now under the mothering care of her sister-wife Elizabeth Ann Whitney and her unflinching example of devotion to Mormonism. Emmeline was young but already well seasoned in life's ambiguities and troubles. "All things are changed for her, whom we knew long ago," she wrote of herself during this time of transition.

She lives within a wall of human love;
A barrier so strong, stronger than she can know,
Encircles her with strength as from above.[28]

Though unable to be a complete barrier against the challenges she would meet, the Whitneys were bulwarks of love, encouragement, and confidence that gave her both stability and security as she faced a future far from her native New England.

26. Illinois Public Domain Land Tract Sales; Federal Census Records for 1840, 1850, and 1860 for Illinois; *The History of Winnebago County, Illinois*, 618; Deaths Registered in New Salem for 1878 and 1889, LDS Church Genealogical Record for Lucy S. Blackinton, LDS Church History Library, Salt Lake City.

27. From an article, "Lost and Found," *Orange (MA) Journal*, August 3, 1883, which recounts the discovery of the eighty-seven-year-old Lucy Blackinton, lying in an old swamp but miraculously alive after she had been missing for more than a week.

28. E. Wells, "Faith and Fidelity," in her *Musings and Memories*, 221.

CHAPTER 7

Winter Quarters

(1846–1848)

As Nauvoo's Mormon population continued to grow and the city took on the characteristics of a city-state with its own armed militia, Mormonism's adversaries were determined to drive the Mormons out of Illinois. Knowing there would be no peaceful settlement, church leaders negotiated a plan in which the members would abandon the city to avoid escalating harassment and possible violence and bloodshed. The evacuation of Nauvoo began in February 1846 when the first company of Saints crossed the Mississippi, led by members of the Quorum of the Twelve Apostles who were in Nauvoo at that time. Prepared or not for the journey, hundreds of families elected to leave in this first exodus from Nauvoo.[1] Emmeline recalled that there were many murmurings among the people when they left, and "Brigham Young preached telling those who were dissatisfied to take their teams and go back," but "none who did ever prospered," she observed.[2]

February and March were not good months for Midwest travel. The temperature was often freezing or below, snowstorms were frequent, and no roadways led from Nauvoo to the Missouri, which was the planned way station three hundred miles west. The storms facing the Camp of Israel, as this first company was designated, turned the soil into a dark, greasy mud until the cold temperatures froze it into solid ruts.[3] Days of travel were lost

1. William G. Hartley has identified three major evacuations. The first consisted primarily of church leaders and their families, who hoped their removal from the city would provide more time for the members to prepare for the trek. The largest group left in May, and in September those needing more time to outfit themselves were forced from the city, many at gunpoint. See Hartley, "Winter Exodus from Nauvoo: Brigham Young's Camp of Israel, 1846" and "Spring Exodus from Nauvoo: Act Two in the 1846 Mormon Evacuation Drama"; and Richard E. Bennett, "'Dadda, I Wish We Were Out of This Country': The Nauvoo Poor Camps in Iowa, Fall 1846."

2. E. Wells, Diary, August 19, 1917.

3. Eliza R. Snow capitalized on this titular association with the Israelite exodus

while rain or snow beat down on the tents and wagon covers, and inevitable repairs had to be made. Jean Rio Baker, a later traveler across Iowa, described the challenges Iowa presented: "a perfect succession of hills, vallies, bogs, mud-holes, log bridges, quagmires, with stumps, a foot above the surface of the watery mud, so that without the utmost care, the wagons would be overturned, 10 times a day."[4]

To succeed, the whole enterprise had to be a cooperative venture. The interdependence of the Saints created a large, cohesive body of migrants, single-mindedly marching westward to an undisclosed destination, pulled forward by the hope of living their religion unmolested and pushed ever westward by the inevitable conflicts with their Gentile neighbors. In the Heber C. Kimball company, in which Emmeline traveled, were a number of his wives and their children, as well as several other families, including the Whitneys.[5] Emmeline's immediate traveling companions were Elizabeth Ann Whitney and Elizabeth Ann's daughter Sarah Whitney Kimball, one of Heber C. Kimball's wives. Whitney's other wives traveled with their respective families. Having no birth family with whom to travel during this early exodus, Emmeline accompanied Newel and his wife Elizabeth Ann. As part of the Kimball entourage, Emmeline was thrust into close proximity to the highest leadership of the church. Brigham Young, president of the Quorum of the Twelve Apostles, and several members of the Quorum and their families constituted their own companies traveling together with the Kimballs. The addition of those Saints who elected to travel in February rather than in the spring swelled the number of refugees to nearly three thousand, with five hundred wagons and hundreds of sheep and cattle accompanying them.[6] The Whitney family joined this early exodus not only because Bishop Whitney was part of Heber C. Kimball's extended family but also because Brigham Young had specifically invited him.[7]

---

from Egypt in several poems: "The Camp of Israel," "Song for the Camp of Israel," "Song for the Camp of Israel, Let Us Go," and "A Journeying Song for the Camp of Israel," in *Eliza R. Snow: The Complete Poetry*, compiled and edited by Jill Mulvay Derr and Karen Lynn Davidson, 319, 321, 323, 344.

4. Jean Rio Griffiths Baker Pearce, Journal, May 2, 1851.

5. There were about sixty-six individuals in Kimball's entourage. See Stanley B. Kimball, *Heber C. Kimball: Mormon Patriarch and Pioneer*, 181. In Nauvoo, Newel Whitney had been "adopted" into the priesthood line of Heber C. Kimball.

6. Stanley B. Kimball, *Historic Resource Study: Mormon Pioneer National Historic Trail*, 36–37.

7. Joseph Smith Jr. et al., *History of the Church of Jesus Christ of Latter-day Saints*, 7:573. Bishop George Miller had also been requested to travel with this first group. Their responsibility as bishops was to supervise the temporal affairs of church members.

Joseph Kingsbury accompanied the Whitneys and took over responsibility for the family during Whitney's long absences to procure equipment and supplies for the fleeing Saints. One of Kingsbury's plural wives, Loenza Alcena Pond, the younger sister of Whitney's two Pond wives, was also one of Emmeline's companions during the journey across Iowa.

Though brief, like her Nauvoo diary, Emmeline's partial travel diary nonetheless fully displays her fine command of language as well as her poetic temperament. Her love of the scenic is clearly evident. When she reached the first encampment, about seven miles west of the Mississippi, for instance, she described the scene as similar to pictures she had seen "of the ancients pitching their tents and journeying from place to place with their cattle and their goods."[8] On another occasion, she used her keen observation to describe a prairie fire that "ran like lightening through the grass making a crackling among the bushes resembling the noise of burning crackers."[9] She was intrigued with the tent cities that sprang up at various encampments, "houseless villages" she called them, and often detailed their layouts. Sleeping on the ground for the first time, in "Mr. H. C. Kimball's tent," with thirty-one others who shared her first night "in the wilderness," she noted the peaceful and calm interior of the tent despite the snow whirling about outside.[10] Throughout the journey, she usually slept either in a tent or in the wagon, but occasionally the hard and often uncomfortably wet open ground was her night chamber. Little inconvenience or discomfort, however, seemed to dampen her wonder at this new experience.

For most of those who had left so precipitously in the midst of winter, the three-hundred-mile journey across Iowa raised more challenges than the later one-thousand-mile journey from the Missouri to the Great Salt Lake. The weather, the unmarked trails, and the trips to Missouri border towns for supplies lengthened the journey to nearly four months of constant, arduous labor.

Initially, Emmeline attended to Sarah Ann, Elizabeth Ann's daughter, who gave birth less than two weeks after leaving Nauvoo. Emmeline also served as a "faithful nurse and companion to Mother Whitney in those troublous times," according to Elizabeth Ann's daughter-in-law Helen Mar Kimball Whitney.[11] She assisted in setting up and dismantling the camps each day and dealt with unexpected exigencies, yet she still found free

8. E. Wells, Diary, February 27, 1846.

9. Ibid., April 17, 1846.

10. Ibid., February 27, 1846. See also Aunt Em, "A Morning in Camp," *Woman's Exponent* 29 (July 15–August 1, 1900): 17.

11. Helen Mar Kimball Whitney, "Our Travels beyond the Mississippi," *Woman's Exponent* 12 (February 15, 1884): 138, reprinted in Holzapfel and Holzapfel, *Woman's*

moments to scribble in her diary.[12] Though the eighteen-year-old Emmeline often wrote of the dancing and game playing of the "young people," she did not seem to be part of the fun. Her position as a plural wife to an important church official may have been a deterrent. But she enjoyed the cheerfulness displayed by members of the camp, particularly "a good old fashioned Welsh woman whom we all designated 'grandma'; and she kept us in almost perpetual good humor with her comical jokes and fun," all expressed in her lilting Welsh accent.[13]

Despite the miserable conditions, Emmeline found this new adventure exciting. But by April 6, a tenuous spring reverted briefly to violent weather. "This is a new era the most trying time we have had," she wrote.[14] "A morning in camp is not very amusing," she recalled years later, especially when tents blew over in the night and belongings were scattered. Preparing breakfast and then packing up the cooking and sleeping equipment, gathering and hitching the animals, and hunting for strays became repeated annoyances. All had to be done in a hurry, for no one wanted to be left behind to the mercy of Indians and wild animals. "Looking back upon it," Emmeline wrote more than fifty years later, "the wonder is how we had the courage, the perseverance, the endurance to accomplish it."[15]

After a bruising week, a gentle spring followed, and Emmeline's first sight of the budding spring prairie flowers, particularly the blue violets, reminded her of the flowers that grew around her New England home. From then on, she continually picked bunches of wildflowers in the woods and fields, all reminders of the life she had left behind. She enjoyed her first taste of honey made from wildflowers and relished hearing the "melodious" sounds of the flute in the evening, played by Horace Whitney, the eldest Whitney son and husband to Helen Mar Kimball.[16]

Emmeline noted the Sabbath meetings when instructions were given along with the call for "union patience meekness forbearance, etc. in order to make us happy."[17] She joined in the celebration at the Locust Creek encampment when William Clayton celebrated the birth of a son to his

---

View, 366. Elizabeth Ann had injured her arm and was often unwell during the journey. Helen Mar Kimball was married to Horace Whitney.

12. E. Wells, Diary, March 3, 1846.

13. Blanche Beechwood [Emmeline B. Wells], "Witty People," *Woman's Exponent* 8 (March 15, 1880): 153. The woman, known as "Grandma Wilson," was Catherine Davis Wilson, a close friend of the Whitney family. She later assisted Emmeline at the birth of her daughters.

14. E. Wells, Diary, April 6, 1846.

15. Aunt Em, "A Morning in Camp," 17–18.

16. E. Wells, Diary, April 16, March 25, 1846.

17. Ibid., April 6, 1846.

wife back in Nauvoo by writing a new hymn, "All Is Well." "The band gave a christening," Emmeline wrote, "giving music first with the brass band and then with drums and violins." She sang with others at this happy event that commenced "soon after dark" and "was kept up until after twelve o'clock."[18]

In late April, this first company of exiles reached a place that Emmeline described as "the most beautiful spot I ever saw viewing it from the opposite bank [of the river]."[19] She was thrilled to see that "the ground was covered with a carpet of green and interspersed with flowers which might have done honor to the Elysian bower." There, the companies learned, they were to establish a way station for the Saints who would follow. Cabins were built, seeds planted, fences erected, and a small group of men and women left to direct the affairs of what would be known as Garden Grove, about halfway across Iowa. With this pleasing and hopeful entry, Emmeline ended her trail diary.[20]

The Kimball company finally arrived at the Missouri River the middle of June. Brigham Young had hoped to send a vanguard company all the way to the Rocky Mountain region that year, but the unexpectedly long crossing of Iowa and lack of provisions scuttled that possibility.[21] They would stay in their winter quarters until spring, and by the end of 1846, the Saints had established small encampments on both sides of the river. The following spring, a pioneering company was scheduled to mark out the trail to the Rocky Mountains that thousands would follow for years afterward.

Along with the small settlements that grew up on both sides of the Missouri River's banks, church leaders had gained "permission" to settle temporarily on the west side, in Pottawatomie Indian territory. They called their encampment Winter Quarters. By the end of their first year of exile, nearly ten thousand refugees were living in tents, wagons, sod houses, and log cabins, almost four thousand of them in Winter Quarters.[22] Others

18. Ibid., April 15, 1846. Also noted in Paul E. Dahl, "'All Is Well . . .': The Story of 'the Hymn That Went around the World'"; and Carol Cornwall Madsen, *Journey to Zion: Voices from the Mormon Trail*, 28.

19. This spot was probably the headwaters of the Weldon Fork of the Grand River, according to Hartley, "Winter Exodus from Nauvoo," xxi.

20. E. Wells, Diary, April 26, 1846.

21. In Nauvoo, Joseph Smith had noted the possibility of eventually moving westward to the Rocky Mountains. See Ronald K. Esplin, "'A Place Prepared': Joseph, Brigham and the Quest for Promised Refuge in the West." A larger study is Lewis Clark Christian, "A Study of Mormon Knowledge of the American Far West prior to the Exodus (1830–February 1846)"; a short version is Christian, "Mormon Foreknowledge of the West."

22. Richard E. Bennett, "Eastward to Eden: The Nauvoo Rescue Missions," *Mormons at the Missouri, 1846–1852*, and "Winter Quarters"; Maureen U. Beecher, "Women at

were scattered in temporary camp sites all across Iowa, including Garden Grove and at a second way station, which Parley P. Pratt named Mount Pisgah.[23] Many Saints terminated their travel there until properly equipped to continue on to the Salt Lake Valley.

As a member of the Whitney family, Emmeline was well provided for during her two-year stay at the Missouri. Heber C. Kimball built a long series of one- or two-room dwellings for his large extended family, including the Whitneys, providing better accommodations than available to many of the other exiles. Emmeline resumed teaching, mainly the youngsters in the extended Kimball family. But that first winter was hard for everyone. Poor housing, inadequate food, and pervasive disease took infants, the elderly, and even the young and strong to their deaths.[24] Having few resources, the Saints were vulnerable to all of these life-threatening challenges. But with a harvest of vegetables and grain the next year, more adequate housing, and the return of sunshine and warmth, life became easier. As Helen Mar Whitney recalled, there were "many happy seasons after the mighty struggle with the destroyer was over."[25]

After three years as a Whitney, Emmeline had carved a place for herself in the family and rapidly developed a special kind of camaraderie with forty-eight-year-old Elizabeth Ann and Elizabeth Ann's daughter-in-law Helen Mar, just a few months younger than Emmeline. What would later become a well-established service to Elizabeth Ann, Emmeline became her scribe, writing letters for her in addition to attending to her personal needs.[26]

Winter Quarters"; Maureen C. Ward, ed., *Winter Quarters: The 1846–48 Life Writings of Mary Parker Haskins Richards*; Holzapfel and Holzapfel, *Woman's View*, 411–65.

23. In Hebrew, *Pisgah* refers to a "high place," usually a mountain. Moses saw the Promised Land for the first time from Mount Nebo, usually considered to be Mount Pisgah. "And Moses went up from the plains of Moab to Mount Nebo, the top of Pisgah, which is opposite Jericho" (Deut. 34:1). Parley P. Pratt scouted the area and determined the location of this second way station, thirty-six miles from Garden Grove. An interesting account of the settlement is included in "Life of George Whitaker, a Pioneer," as written by himself, typescript, Utah State Historical Society and LDS Church History Library, Salt Lake City.

24. Extant records indicate that the death rate for the first year at Winter Quarters was 82.1 per 1,000, extremely high even for a frontier community. Infants and young children accounted for a third of these fatalities. US mortality rates were not available until the 1850 census. The personal accounts indicate that nearly every family felt the devastating effects of this high toll of sickness and death.

25. Helen Mar Whitney, "Scenes and Incidents at Winter Quarters," *Woman's Exponent* 14 (February 15, 1886): 138. See also Holzapfel and Holzapfel, *Woman's View*, 411–79.

26. Reference to surrogate letter writing is in Holzapfel and Holzapfel, *Woman's View*, 440.

Her teaching occupied much of her time but also reignited her literary interests, and she found the time to indulge her fondness for writing poetry, compiling the poems into a small handwritten volume. An acquaintance of Emmeline's, Mary Parker Richards, also a would-be poet, remembered the Sunday afternoon when she visited "Emaline Haris at Bishop Whitneys and got a 'Book of Poetry' her own Composition to read. with permission to write off a piece on true freindship [*sic*]."[27] Two days later, she "got Bro Camball to write off the lines on True Frendship for me," and the next day, she returned the book to Emmeline. Easily lending itself to a musical setting and distributed among many of her friends, this poem quickly became attached to a familiar tune and was sung on a variety of occasions. Under the title "Lines, on True Friendship," the poem was published in 1851 in the Salt Lake City *Deseret News*, becoming Emmeline's first published poem.[28] The first verse reads:

A friend that's often changing is not the friend for me,
Affections always ranging, I care not e'e n to see;
I want a friend who's fixed and firm,
Whose heart is tender, true and warm,
And scorns to use deception, O, that's the friend for me,
O, that's the friend for me.

In the meantime, Emmeline anxiously awaited the arrival of her mother and younger siblings. But Diadama did not have the means to properly equip herself and children to leave Nauvoo in the spring of 1846 with the large company of Saints. "I must tell you something new (under the sun) that has happened to me," Diadama wrote to her children in Massachusetts in August 1846. "Your industrious, busy mother has been out of work; had nothing particular to do—I bought a skein of cotton yarn, and am knitting for myself."[29] While written with a hint of humor, her lack of employment

27. Incident noted in Ward, *Winter Quarters*, 191. A handwritten copy of the poem under the name of Emeline B. Harris appears on pages 14–15 in an unidentified personal book of handwritten poems dating to ca. 1848 in the LDS Church History Library, Salt Lake City.

28. Emeline B. Whitney, "Lines, on True Friendship," *Deseret News*, March 8, 1851, 1. It is also included under the title "True Friendship" in her collection of poems, *Musings and Memories*, 165. Hymns and songs were often accompanied by tunes whose meter corresponded with the text. Emmeline's poem would easily fit the meter of many tunes.

29. Mother and Grandmother [Diadama Clark], letter to My Dear Children, Henry and Lucy, August 4, 5, 6, 1845, Nauvoo, IL, printed as "An Old Letter," *Woman's Exponent* 15 (December 1, 1886): 98.

was serious. Help came when a Mrs. Foster in Montrose, Iowa hired Ellen to work for her. "The mob is fussing," Ellen wrote to her sister Pallas in August 1846, "but we do not mind much about them let them come if thay [*sic*] want to. Thay have threatened it long enough, [but] thay will not make out much," she believed.[30] Diadama was less confident than Ellen about their situation. "The mobocrat spirit is influenced anew," she reported in her letter. The old settlers who had bought property from the exiled Saints, she observed, were taking newcomers into their plot to drive out the remaining Mormons. "All their talk is of whipping, hauling and driving them [the Mormons] from place to place until worn out—burning houses, fields, fences, wheat, corn, and everything, to make the people leave the city, so that they can come in and plunder." But, she emphatically assured her children back home, she "was not sorry, nor never have been," for leaving New England, and in her last heartfelt plea she implored her children to join her in her new religious life. Her willingness to undo her tightly knit family by joining the church and leaving New England with four of her children denoted the strength of her conviction, but it took a heavy toll on the entire family. This was Diadama's final known plea to her children.

To the despair of Diadama, the "fussing" that Ellen noted quickly turned into armed attacks, and by the end of September, Diadama and her children were forced out of Nauvoo with the other remaining Saints, most of them without means to travel and thus totally unprepared for the long trek to Winter Quarters. Diadama had been offered a chance to stay in Nauvoo unmolested if she would denounce Mormonism, but the Aiken family, with whom she was living, had no thought of staying, and Diadama was just as determined to leave. Adeline Maria, or Maria, as she was usually called, the eldest of the three children, found two young men willing to ferry the family with their possessions across the river to Iowa, thus allowing them to escape the fighting that became known as the battle of Nauvoo. Ellen and Hiram immediately contracted chills and fever, but Hiram nonetheless helped the two young men build a small bower of tree limbs under which they made one large bed for the family. It provided their only protection against the rapidly deteriorating weather. A large fire kept the area warm, but when the autumn rains began, comfort was simply unattainable. Without either a wagon or a cart, they were obliged to stay where they were until help came their way. Ellen worsened, and Diadama was alarmed to learn from a "gentile doctor" in the area that she had typhoid fever. Finally, rescuers from Winter Quarters arrived, and they loaded their few belongings into the wagon

30. Ellen Woodward to Mrs. William J. [Pallas] Clark, August 28, 1846 (postmarked Nauvoo, Sept. 9), copy of original in my possession.

assigned to their family. Maria remembered that they traveled twenty-five miles into Iowa, where they were able to make a more permanent encampment with some other Saints, using their wagons as temporary housing. But they were little help against the drenching rains, and the cold and damp soon brought Diadama down with the dreaded ague. Seventeen-year-old Maria, the only healthy member of the family, took responsibility for them all. To ease her mother's discomfort, she gathered their quilts together to make a comfortable bed for her under the wagon and carefully nursed her with whatever means she had. But Diadama continued to worsen. Sensing that she would not be able to throw off the fever, she called her children around her, instructed eleven-year-old Hiram to assume responsibility for his sisters, and then spoke her last words to the soon-to-be orphans: "I deliver you dear ones into the hands of the Lord." With the help of some of their friends in the encampment, the children prepared Diadama's body for burial and placed it in an unmarked grave somewhere in Iowa.[31]

Under the protection of Porter Rockwell, the children were taken to Winter Quarters, where they stayed with Emmeline. Maria and Ellen soon found places to live "with first rate families," where they could have board and shelter in exchange for their help. Hiram remained with Emmeline. Maria was less pleased with her situation than the others. Though paid for assisting with the domestic chores of the family, she resented the exhausting work and hard life in Winter Quarters. For Maria, Winter Quarters ignited a latent resentment of her baptism into the church, of her forced relocation to the West, of Emmeline's favored position with the Whitneys, and eventually of the church itself.

It fell to Emmeline to tell the family back home of the death of their mother. Because they had feared that her decision to join the Mormons and move far from home would end unhappily, Diadama's death was grievous confirmation. Emmeline anticipated their reaction and thus waited nearly three months after her younger siblings arrived in Winter Quarters to break the sad news. Her letter circled warily around the most important fact, with a description of life at Winter Quarters and her impression of the Indians she encountered taking the first pages of the lengthy letter. Then she wrote the sorrowful story of their mother's escape from Nauvoo, her

31. Details of their exit from Nauvoo and events following are retold in a letter by Adeline Maria (Woodward) Earl, then eighty-six, to her niece Lillian Ramsay, written March 9, 1916. Photocopy courtesy of Glenys Harris, Orange, MA. Emmeline also describes their plight in a letter to "Dearly beloved brother & sisters" in New England, February 3, 1847, Winter Quarters, NE. It is signed "E. B. Harris," which is crossed out and replaced with "Emeline." Photocopy of original in my possession.

illness, and finally her death.[32] Ursulia Hascall, the mother of Emmeline's friend Irene Pomeroy, when learning of Diadama's death, described her as a woman who "wore her self out with hard work I think, I never saw a female that could live and do as she did."[33] Diadama had been a hardworking and "wise mother," Emmeline noted, and her children "looked up to her with great reverence." "Indeed," Emmeline recalled, "she had actually supplied the father's place so far as that is possible."[34] Diadama had been the cynosure of her family's life.

Her mother's death was only one of several unhappy incidents that occurred while Emmeline resided at Winter Quarters. On February 6, two days after Emmeline wrote the sad news of their mother's passing, Elizabeth Ann Whitney, at age forty-eight, gave birth to her last child, a boy, whom she named Newel Melchizedek. Little Newel, as he was known, was small and feeble at birth, and when he was just a few days old, "he died to all appearances and we all felt he was gone," Emmeline recalled. "But his mother's faith was most wonderful," she wrote, "and she said 'administer to him father' to her husband and he did." To their great amazement and joy, "the child was brought to life by the power of faith and grew strong and comparatively well." Little Newel, however, could never walk and lived only to the age of nine. But before his death, he was baptized and ordained, Emmeline noted.[35] Her care of the boy for much of his short life helped solidify her relationship with Elizabeth Ann, who soon came to fulfill Emmeline's need for the strength and wisdom of her own mother.

As difficult as the two years she spent in Winter Quarters proved to be, the physical deprivations of that time were less traumatic than the emotional distress of the previous two years in Nauvoo. In fact, Ursulia Hascall described Emmeline as being "happy as a queen." She had "everything to eat, drink [and] wear," she wrote, and thought that the Whitneys were "the best people in the world." She "instructs the children has the care of their clothes and does as much or as little as she pleases." Emmeline's life was clearly not

32. Emeline B. Harris, letter to William S. Clark, Brattleboro, MA, postmarked St. Louis, March 20, 1847; it is datelined "Camp of Deseret Winter Quarters West side Mis. River Feb 3, 1847." Copy of original in my possession, courtesy of Glenys Harris.

33. Ursulia B. Hascall, letter to Col. Wilson Andrews, North New Salem, Franklin Co., MA. Postmarked: Boston 5 cts 16 July; written Camp of Israel, Winter Quarters, Indian Territory, April 1847, in "Letters of a Proselyte," *Utah Historical Quarterly* 25 (July 1957): 237–57, esp. 239.

34. "Hephzibah," *Woman's Exponent* 18 (December 1, 1889): 98.

35. E. Wells, Diary, February 6, 1891, also February 6, 1894.

as carefree as Ursulia described, but certainly she had privileges many others did not. Ursulia's next comment, "Where brother Harris is we do not know," seems to confirm Emmeline's reticence to explain the desertion of James, the disaffection of her in-laws, or her plural marriage to Newel Whitney.[36]

With the recruitment of nearly five hundred men to the army to fight the Mexicans in California, the departure of the initial pioneer company in April 1847, and the absence of many husbands and fathers serving missions, the usual female social rituals of visiting, trading and bartering for necessities, arranging social events, and assisting at childbirth, illness, and death took on a new imperative.[37] Female spiritual gatherings offered both emotional and spiritual uplift during the stress-filled days at the Missouri. Many of these meetings consisted of collective prayers for the vanguard company of pioneers, blessings, testimonies, and the exercise of spiritual gifts. Emmeline attended many of these meetings, and among others was "gifted in the interpretation of tongues," according to Helen Mar Whitney, another frequent attendee.[38]

Many of the women who had participated in these gatherings left Winter Quarters for the West with the "big company" in June 1847, two months after the first band of pioneers. The women of the Kimball company, which remained in Winter Quarters for another year, continued to gather in one another's cabins, "singing, praying and prophesying." Helen Mar Kimball Whitney noted that these "little prayer meetings" were held two or three times a week. Sometimes only a few were present; at other times, there

36. Ursulia B. Hascall to Col. Wilson Andrews, in "Letters of a Proselyte," *Utah Historical Quarterly* 25 (July 1957): 239. Just when Emmeline made her marriage to Whitney known is not clear. Ursulia Hascall makes no specific comment about Emmeline's personal relationship to the Whitneys. Emmeline evidently continued to use her Harris name while in Winter Quarters.

37. A social history of life in Winter Quarters is Kenneth W. Godfrey, "Winter Quarters: Glimmering Glimpses into Mormon Religious and Social Life."

38. Examples of these meetings and the pleasure of just visiting can be found in the journals of Eliza R. Snow from late April to June 1847 in Maureen Ursenbach Beecher, ed., *The Personal Writings of Eliza R. Snow*, 166–79. See also Patty Sessions, Diary, May and June 1847; and Donna Toland Smart, ed., *Mormon Midwife: The 1846–1888 Diaries of Patty Bartlett Sessions*, 79–89. Helen Mar Whitney also recounts the meetings in "Scenes and Incidents at Winter Quarters," *Woman's Exponent* 14 (December 15, 1885): 105–6, reprinted in Holzapfel and Holzapfel, *Woman's View*, 455. Joseph Hovey experienced the peace of a comfort blessing given by the gift of tongues, interpreted by Emmeline, in which he learned that "my wife watched over me and my little ones and her heart entwined about me" and that her death was "the trial of my faith." Joseph G. Hovey Journal, July 4, 1847, 41, as cited in Bennett, *Mormons at the Missouri*, 176.

were many. Bishop Whitney visited one of these meetings and spoke to the women, who were trying to console a child whose incessant crying alarmed them. "He was filled with the Holy Spirit the moment he entered the house. His mind was clear and like a fountain, and we only had to ask and receive, for our faith was such that it would take no denial," Helen Mar recalled. When the child finally drifted peacefully to sleep, Bishop Whitney explained that it was the strength of their combined faith that had enabled the child to finally respond. He then admitted that at first he worried about the frequency of their meetings but changed his mind after entering the room and feeling the spirit that filled it. "There were things that he uttered that night," Helen Mar noted, "that he did not know of himself, but by the Spirit some choice truths were revealed through him."[39] "There are those living," Helen Mar asserted in 1885, "E. B. Wells being one of the number—who will readily testify to these statements," relating to the healings, blessings, and teachings that occurred during these "sisters meetings."[40]

These informal gatherings were among those privileges Emmeline experienced that gave her a solid spiritual foundation and conviction of the remarkable spirituality of women, their emotional strength as well as their physical endurance. While always remembering Winter Quarters, like Nauvoo, as a time of great trial, Emmeline also recalled the scenes that promoted her spiritual growth and tempered the unhappy memories. "These seasons of refreshing among the sisters helped them," she realized, "to endure the weary days and almost sleepless nights, while those they so tenderly loved were plodding the sandy plains, wending their way through an unknown country to the then 'promised land.'"[41]

Newel K. Whitney was not among the advance pioneer company because of his responsibilities in Winter Quarters as presiding bishop, after the defection of Bishop George Miller. Heber C. Kimball, in appointing Bishop Whitney to act as head of the family in Kimball's absence, had no hesitation in recommending him to the family "as a worthy, good and exemplary man." "There was 'no person living in the world,'" Kimball told his family, "in whom he placed more confidence."[42] Whitney willingly agreed to assume the position as temporary head of the large Kimball "tribe," as

39. H. Whitney, "Scenes and Incidents at Winter Quarters," *Woman's Exponent* 14 (December 15, 1885): 105–6; Holzapfel and Holzapfel, *Woman's View*, 459.

40. H. Whitney, "Scenes and Incidents at Winter Quarters," *Woman's Exponent* 14 (January 1, 1886): 118; Holzapfel and Holzapfel, *Woman's View*, 461.

41. Emmeline B. Wells, "A Distinguished Woman, Zina D. H. Young," *Woman's Exponent* 10 (December 15, 1881): 107.

42. H. Whitney, "Scenes and Incidents at Winter Quarters," *Woman's Exponent* 14 (September 1, 1885): 53–54; Holzapfel and Holzapfel, *Woman's View*, 440.

Wilford Woodruff characterized Kimball's family, and for the rest of 1847, Newel performed that service for his friend and leader.

In Emmeline's private world, another decision of significance also occurred in Winter Quarters. As the years would prove, Emmeline preferred to use the pen rather than the voice to reveal her private thoughts or feelings to others. Thus, on October 10, 1847, she wrote a long letter to Newel Whitney, announcing her resolution of the perplexity and uncertainties she had revealed to him in her earlier letter. By the date of this letter, she had clearly moved beyond the tragedy of Nauvoo. Her life with the Whitneys and passage of time had given her opportunity to come to terms with the imperatives of the religion she had embraced as a naive country girl. Her experiences had matured her well beyond the innocence of her teenage years. This letter has almost an exultant spirit. She had reached a point in her doctrinal understanding at which she was able to give not only spiritual and intellectual assent to her relationship with Newel Whitney but also emotional and physical consent. She addressed the letter in three carefully chosen appellations, each of which had particular significance in her relationship to him: "Father, Guardian, Husband":

> Whenever I am lonely and feel discouraged my mind dwells upon certain subjects, and certain hopes and fears arise; Then follows a train of reasoning with myself, and inquiring into my own feelings, motives, principles & both for myself and others—in so doing for a week past; I believe I have been enabled to know my own heart [more] than ever before. I have looked on the bright page and also on the dark and I see nothing to make me give up—I will still hope on and if I am at last disappointed, it shall not be my fault—others may be blest before me and perhaps with greater blessings, but I still choose my own humble lot—and that portion of your affection which I enjoy is sweeter to me, than the whole love of another could be now. I am persuaded that I could never again be happy with "the one I once loved," after having known you and shared your affections—I love you because of the noble principles of soul which you possess, and because you have power with God—and for many other reasons—It is not only because I wish to be saved and exalted that I cling to you, (though these to be sure are principles I hold) but if I did not love you purely and freely, I would not cling to you, for I will not look to any man for my exaltation whom I cannot love as well as respect, and that too with my whole soul; for I never love coldly but warmly and tenderly....

> Never did I feel that confidence to go to you that I now do—I no longer have any disposition, to hide my feelings from you, or let them remain smothered in my own bosom—and why should I? If I am not afraid to risk my salvation and exaltation to you, why should I fear to tell you every motive and feeling I have, or every grief or sorrow. It looks so foolish to me now, I think I will always be frank and open hearted to you.
>
> You will permit me to love you as affectionately as I desire when I have no dearer object on earth and I pray that I may never forget to look to my Father in Heaven for every blessing.[43]

Newel was not just her temporal provider. He was also her spiritual mentor and religious anchor. In Mormon doctrine, her exaltation depended on her "sealing," or marriage, to a priesthood holder, a relationship of eternal duration when performed by one holding the sealing keys of the priesthood. This man, "the patriarch," as she poetically referred to him,

> *took her to his home and heart,*
> *Had taught her sacred truths, reveal'd from heaven;*
> *And now she comprehends their purposes in part*
> *For the great mission unto woman given.*[44]

Her conviction of the moral and religious legitimacy of plural marriage took solid root at this time, and despite future challenges and disappointments, she never wavered in her commitment to its divine origin and its certitude.[45]

By the time Emmeline left Winter Quarters eight months later, in May 1848, she was pregnant with her second child.

43. Emeline Whitney, letter to Newel K. Whitney, October 10, 1847, Winter Quarters, NE, N. Whitney Papers.

44. Emmeline B. Wells, "Faith and Fidelity," in her *Musings and Memories*, 221.

45. Massachusetts maritime law declared it legal for a seaman's wife to regain her "feme sole" (single woman) status if three years had elapsed without any contact with her husband. That time expired in November 1847, a month after she wrote this letter, giving herself to Newel as his wife in all senses. The two events were likely only coincidental.

CHAPTER 8

The Nascent Westerner

(1848–1852)

When Emmeline Wells climbed the last hill of her long journey from Winter Quarters, Nebraska, in October 1848, she saw what would be her home for the rest of her life, the Great Salt Lake Valley. What she viewed that day was far different from the deep shaded forests, flower-strewn meadows, and abundant streams and ponds of the New England countryside she had left four years earlier. The valley offered its own kind of beauty, its stark, rugged landscape relieved by canyon rivers that flowed from the sharp, formidable mountains nearly surrounding it. City Creek, flowing from the north, ran through the center of the nascent city, skirting the ten-acre plot of land set aside for a temple. The shimmering surface of the Great Salt Lake, far off in the distance, created a glistening backdrop for the cluster of buildings that claimed the foreground of Emmeline's view. A large, sprawling fort held the dwellings of nearly five thousand new residents of the valley and served as protection from possible attacks from its original settlers, the Northern Ute Indians, though marauding animals were far more threatening. More than four hundred row houses edged the fort, built of logs, sawn timbers, and adobe bricks. Additional cabins filled the center of the fort. Five thousand acres of land were under cultivation, and three saw mills were already in operation, with a gristmill, threshing machine, and flouring and fanning mills soon to be functioning. All of these developments occurred since the pioneer company arrived in the valley just a year earlier. The new emigrants would add mill irons, millstones, a carding machine, printing presses, type, and paper.[1]

As exiles seeking a permanent place of refuge, the Mormons had been living a nomadic life for nearly two decades, and many of them recorded their experiences, especially of this long trek westward, in journals, letters,

1. Hubert Howe Bancroft, *History of Utah*. See also John Taylor, "Address to the Saints"; and Parley P. Pratt, letter to Brigham Young, as quoted in Thomas Bullock, "Glorious News from Salt Lake."

and reminiscences. But Emmeline was silent on her own trail experience. It is difficult to imagine how the great drama of three large companies of Saints, numbering more than two thousand men, women, and children, assembling at the staging area of the Elk Horn River, twenty-seven miles west of Winter Quarters, for the journey west, could have escaped her observant eye and facile pen.[2] It was a scene of unprecedented magnitude, with hundreds of wagons; thousands of oxen, cattle, and other animals; and men and women drivers guiding their oxen, all organized under a system of groups of ten, fifty, and a hundred, each company led by a designated captain. Though the Whitney company of ten was delayed at Winter Quarters awaiting the birth of Ann Houston's baby, Jethro, born on May 8, this great assemblage of people, animals, and wagons constituted a spectacular panorama as they left Winter Quarters.[3] "If any person enquire 'Is Mormonism down?'" Lorenzo Snow cheerfully noted, "he ought to have been in the neighbourhood of the Elk Horn this day, and he would have seen such a host of waggons that would have satisfied him in an instant, that it lives and flourishes like a tree by a fountain of waters; he would have seen merry faces, and heard the song of rejoicing, that the day of deliverance had surely come."[4]

The three large companies began the long trip in April 1848, each headed by a member of the newly organized First Presidency of the church, who had returned from the valley and were sustained as the church's presiding quorum in Winter Quarters the previous December.[5] Emmeline was one of 662 pioneers who traveled in Heber C. Kimball's division.[6] Of Whitney's

2. It is likely that Emmeline did write, and this diary, along with those of the following twenty years, has been lost or unnoticed in someone's store of family mementos. The next extant diary does not begin until 1874, though she occasionally makes reference to diaries written between these years.

3. E. Wells, Diary, May 8, 1914. Some genealogical records indicate that Ann (sometimes Anna) Houston did not leave Winter Quarters and died there on September 23, 1848. Emmeline Wells's diary notes that she died in Salt Lake City in November 1848 and was the first person buried in the private Kimball-Whitney cemetery. A marker at the cemetery noting Ann's burial there validates Emmeline's assertion. The September 23 death date may have been inadvertently assigned to Ann Houston since it was actually the day of Newel K. Whitney's death two years later. See "Private Burial Grounds."

4. Lorenzo Snow quoted in "Letters from the Camp of Israel," 314.

5. The First Presidency consisted of Brigham Young, president; Heber C. Kimball, first counselor; and Willard Richards, second counselor.

6. Thomas Bullock, letter to Levi Richards, July 10, 1848, 400 miles west of Winter Quarters on the north side of the Platte River. Included in "Letters from the Camp of Israel," 313–15; and "Important Letters," in *Heart Throbs of the West*, compiled by Kate B. Carter, 9:464–65. This letter also puts the number of births during the first year at 120, an estimate of "the brethren," Bullock wrote.

wives, Emmeline, Elizabeth Ann, Olive Bishop, and Ann Houston traveled with their husband. Elizabeth Mahala Moore and Henrietta Keys traveled to Utah in company with the Ponds, the Kingsburys, and their own families. The Kimball company fared as well or better than many companies that followed and was guided by men who were already acquainted with the trail and its hazards.[7]

Toward the end of the long journey, assistance teams from the valley met the weary migrants, bringing provisions and, most important, encouragement to face the last leg. On September 22, when those in the first wagons reached the top of Big Mountain and caught their first view of the Salt Lake Valley, Daniel Davis expressed the general feeling. "It made all our hearts swell with joy," he wrote.[8] Finally, on October 8, after nearly four months of travel, the Kimball company made its way into the valley. Emmeline was pregnant throughout the journey, arriving in the valley just a month before the birth of her baby. She wrote only two brief articles in the *Woman's Exponent* relating to this historic western adventure from Winter Quarters, one of them describing the elderly Grandma Wilson, whose unfailing cheerfulness kept the very uncomfortable Emmeline from resorting to tears during trying moments, making hardships easier to bear, and saving Emmeline from "many a nervous head ache."[9] In her later years, it was not her trail stories with which Emmeline entertained her grandchildren, but rather her memories of her carefree days in her much-missed New England.

With 5,133 acres of cultivated land and 875 acres sown in winter wheat in 1848, the Saints anticipated a plentiful harvest. But their hopes turned to despair when the maturing crops were infested by swarms of large black crickets, properly locusts, but more descriptively known as "vindictive little demon[s]," Anson Call noted, which began to systematically devour the crops. With blankets and shovels, clubs and water-filled ditches, the Saints fought back this huge incursion of locusts. But an unexpected cloud of seagulls from the Great Salt Lake appeared and surprisingly ate the huge black insects, thus preserving much of the spring growth.[10] The

7. Some of the incidents of the Kimball company's travels are contained in the trail accounts in the diary of Daniel Davis, 1846–1892, especially May 31–September 22, 1848; Merlin Ross Hovey, "Hovey Family History," ca. 1933, 57; and Alma Helaman Hale, Diaries, 1901, typescript copies in the LDS Church History Library, Salt Lake City.

8. Daniel Davis, Diary, September 22, 1848.

9. Blanche Beechwood [Emmeline B. Wells], "Witty People," *Woman's Exponent* 8 (March 15, 1880): 153. She lived to be ninety-six, no doubt because of her humor.

10. The Saints considered the seagulls' appearance to be an act of divine Providence and, in September 1913, honored the bird with a monument, declaring the

late-summer harvest of wheat and oats was spared this invasion of insects, and many garden vegetables also survived, providing melons, peas, beans, carrots, beets, parsnips, cucumbers, and squash. The uneven production of food from farm to farm, however, left many enduring the harsh effects of the unexpected attack on their harvests. Nevertheless, there was genuine optimism about the soil's productivity, and prospects were good for an abundant crop the following year. One crop, however, was unfailing in its predictability: "Mother Sessions," a popular midwife, "has had a harvest of 248 little cherubs since living in the Valley" (a little over a year), among which were "many cases of twins."[11]

The isolation of the new settlement lifted heavy weights from the minds of the new settlers and produced a feeling of peace the Saints had almost forgotten. "How quiet, how still, how free from excitement we live!" Parley P. Pratt exclaimed. "The legislation of our high council, the decision of some judge or court of the church, a meeting, a dance, a visit, an exploring tour, the arrival of a party of trappers and traders, a Mexican caravan, a party arrived from the Pacific, from the States, from Fort Bridger, a visit of Indians, or perhaps a mail from the distant world once or twice a year, is all that breaks the monotony of our busy and peaceful life," he wrote. Moreover, Pratt added, "Here, too, we all are rich—there is no real poverty; all men have access to the soil, the pasture, the timber, the water power, and all the elements of wealth, without money or price."[12] A poor crop, while creating immediate hardship, could be weathered in anticipation of what the future held with so many available resources all around them. This was indeed the right place, as Brigham Young had declared.

Emmeline's first home upon arrival in the Salt Lake Valley was the wagon that had already sheltered her for four months. It was parked on the northeast corner of Main Street and South Temple, across from the temple block on land on which the Tithing Office and later the Hotel Utah (now the Joseph Smith Memorial Building) were built. It was in that wagon on an icy and blustery second day of November that Emmeline's second child and

---

seagull to be the official bird of the state of Utah. Numerous accounts tell the story of "the miracle of the gulls," especially since 1848 was not the only year the crickets appeared to plague Mormon farmers. See William G. Hartley, "Mormons, Crickets, and Gulls: A New Look at an Old Story"; and Jeffrey Lockwood, *Locust: The Devastating Rise and Mysterious Disappearance of the Insect That Shaped the American Frontier*. See also O. Whitney, *History of Utah*, 1:377; and Bullock, "Glorious News from Salt Lake," 370.

11. Patty Sessions arrived in the valley in September 1847. The report was written in August 1848. She was evidently very busy.

12. Parley P. Pratt, as quoted in Bancroft, *History of Utah*, 282, 284–85.

first daughter, Isabel (Belle) Modalena Whitney, was born.[13] "Our poor wagons and tents were the only homes we had," Emmeline recalled. It was a particularly dreary situation after "such a wearisome journey we had just passed over." She remembered that the witty midwife, Grandma Wilson, "had a serious time trying to make a fire in the big tent," evidently where the necessary hot water and other supplies for childbirth were prepared.[14] After hours of unproductive labor and the unsuccessful efforts of several increasingly anxious midwives, "the Bishop [Whitney] sent Archie Hill to the fort for Dr. Bernhisel and the baby was born 8.15 p.m. in the wagon on Whitney block opposite Temple Block," Emmeline recalled. She rejoiced with the others at the baby's safe arrival and that Grandma Wilson "was very jolly" throughout the long ordeal, keeping Emmeline and the attendants in good spirits.[15] Despite all the challenges, Isabel Modalena survived and lived a long life.

It was not a winter that Emmeline remembered fondly, since she spent it largely in the wagon, caring for Belle. One bright spot, besides the birth of Isabel, was the Christmas celebration hosted by Heber and Vilate Kimball that winter. The Whitneys shared the festivities with the Brigham Young and Willard Richards families, and Emmeline could hardly have been among more distinguished guests. The party, presided over by Heber and Vilate, began with a Christmas dinner, followed by musical entertainment. Her memory, Emmeline admitted, was not very keen because she was too occupied with her baby to take much notice of all the amusements. She did, however, pay attention to the music. With a flute, violin, and bass, everyone eagerly joined in singing familiar songs. Though the instrumentalists were good, Emmeline noted, the singers were better.[16] It was a Christmas like none she had yet known.

By the end of 1849, the Whitney family had a house of their own. It was situated in the same block where their wagon had stood, which came to be

13. When Newel K. Whitney traveled as a sutler with the army during the War of 1812, he sold alcohol to Native Americans. When he refused to sell additional alcohol to one heavily inebriated buyer, the man threatened to kill him. A young Native American girl by the name of Maudalena somehow bested the attacker and saved Newel's life. Emmeline was the only one of Newel's wives to remember this incident by giving her oldest daughter the name of Newel's benefactor, modifying the spelling to the simpler Modalena. See Staker, *Hearken, O Ye People*, 202, 205n13. Staker erroneously states in the note that no Whitney child was christened with this name.

14. E. Wells, Diary, January 17, 1891.

15. Emmeline frequently noted Isabel's birth in her diary each year on her birthday, November 2. See, for example, Diary, November 2, 1874, and November 2, 1908.

16. Aunt Em, "Early Christmas Reminiscences."

known as the Whitney corner. City Creek flowed nearby, and when the city was divided into ecclesiastical wards or congregations, the Whitneys became members of the Eighteenth Ward.[17] Sharing the home with Emmeline and baby Belle were her three younger siblings—Maria, Ellen, and Hiram—along with Elizabeth Ann and seven of her children.[18] Olive Bishop, the foster mother of Ann Houston's boy, Jethro, had a small place of her own. Elizabeth Moore and Henrietta Keys presumably lived with their parental families.

Emmeline was busy with her motherly responsibilities and household tasks, all still new to her. She recalled the difficulty of sewing "rows upon rows of fine tucking for shirt bosoms for Bishop Whitney and the boys, Horace and Orson, and such tucks and ruffles as we used to put in our baby clothes—whipping, overcasting, hemming, and running stitch as with the finest of needles."[19] In 1849, Emmeline satisfied a latent interest in medicine, becoming a member of the newly organized Council of Health, founded by Willard Richards and Priddy Meeks, men trained in the Thompsonian, or herbal, method of medical treatment. With Isabel in her arms, she attended the meetings, where she learned the use of herbal medicines, especially the locally grown herbs.[20] Years later, Emmeline mused that had circumstances been different for her, she would like to have studied medicine, as did her friend Romania Pratt Penrose, who graduated from an eastern medical college and became a respected physician.

At the church's April conference in 1850, Addison Pratt and his wife, Louisa Barnes, were called to serve a mission to the Society Islands (Tahiti), where Addison had already spent five years as one of its first Mormon missionaries in the 1840s. Louisa's mother was from Warwick County, Massachusetts, and was an acquaintance of Emmeline's mother. Emmeline numbered Ellen Pratt, Louisa's daughter, four years younger than herself, as one of her close friends. Because of this connection with the Pratts, Emmeline asked Louisa to take her fifteen-year-old footloose and unruly brother, Hiram, with her to Tahiti to help him find his way in life. Emmeline had full

17. In February 1849, Brigham Young, assisted by Newel K. Whitney, divided the city into ecclesiastical wards. They were named numerically, with the First Ward located on the south edge of the city, what is now 900 South, to 600 South and from Fort Douglas on the East to 600 East on the West. The Eighteenth Ward encompassed the blocks from South Temple to 200 North and from 300 East (and C Street in the Avenues) to Main Street.

18. Though Elizabeth Ann Whitney was known as Ann during Kirtland days, Emmeline always referred to her as Elizabeth Ann.

19. A. W. Cannon, "Mothers in Israel."

20. Susa Young Gates, "President Emmeline B. Wells," esp. 720.

confidence in Louisa's caring nature and wise ways, and Louisa was willing to take responsibility for Hiram, along with the care of her own four daughters.

To Louisa's dismay, however, Hiram found the seaman's life compelling. "Our boy," she wrote some months after arriving in Tahiti, "went with the Captain to learn a little of a sailor's life," and she saw little of him after that. "I am troubled about the boy we brought with us from Salt Lake, gone on the vessel," Louisa lamented to her diary. "I promised his friends I would be a mother to him. I can only pray and warn him of temptation." But Hiram failed to listen to her counsel. As their mission drew to a close in 1852, Louisa was afraid that Hiram would remain in the islands rather than return to Utah with them. "Our boy Hiram is left on Tahiti, exposed to the influences of wicked persons," she confided to her diary. "I sometimes feel that he is lost and undone. Could I know he would go very soon to California where the brethren of the church will watch over him it would relieve my mind of a heavy burden. Oh! the fearful condition of a child left in the world without parents and one not willing to hearken to instruction from those older and wiser!" As it turned out, Hiram left the mission field that year, returning to California before the Pratts. The news she received about him was heartening. "We found...that our boy who occasioned us so much uneasiness, had left for California; and that he gave signs of reformation, which has really relieved my mind. I do sincerely hope he will make the best of his way to the Church."[21]

Hiram did indeed reform his ways, but he did not return to the church. He remained in the West for a period, traveling through California and Arizona, and though he lived in Utah for a brief period, he did not settle there. After the outbreak of the Civil War, he joined the Union army, enlisting in the California Battalion of the Second Massachusetts Cavalry, eventually attaining the rank of captain of the Fifth Massachusetts Cavalry. He was wounded in 1864 at Petersburg, which occasioned a transfer to the Rio Grande in Texas. He married Carrie J. Fuller of Thorndike, Massachusetts, in January 1865 and was mustered out of the army on December 1, 1865.[22] He returned to Massachusetts and lived there for the rest of his life, and Emmeline did not see him again for nearly thirty years. She left no record of what must have been a perpetual heartache at Hiram's decision to leave the church and return to New England.

Emmeline was, however, very much involved in the life of her new community. Besides caring for her daughter and attending the Council of

21. S. George Ellsworth, ed., *The History of Louisa Barnes Pratt, Mormon Missionary Widow and Pioneer*, 149, 154, 174, 180.

22. Obituary, "Hiram E. W. Clark," *Palmer (MA) Journal*, December 13, 1923.

Health lectures, Emmeline joined one of the early Relief Societies organized in the Social Hall by Lydia Knight.[23] It was one of several independent societies that sprang up in the 1850s to provide clothing and food for the Indians living within the territory as well as for the emigrants who flowed into the valley.[24] She also greatly enjoyed renewing her association with her New England friends, some of whom had been in the valley for a year. All of them seemed to be happily situated and enthusiastic about their new life in the West.[25]

On August 18, 1850, Emmeline gave birth once again. Melvina Caroline Blanche Whitney ("Mell" and "Mellie") was born in the more comfortable surroundings of the Whitney home. The day was extremely hot, the sun "ready to broil us all," Emmeline remembered, while also recalling how scarce things still were for the family at that time. But the baby was beautiful, and the family rejoiced at her safe birth.[26] Diantha Morley Billings, who delivered Emmeline's son in Nauvoo, was the midwife for this birth. Zina Huntington Young, a plural wife of Brigham Young, and the ever-jolly Grandma Wilson were also in attendance.

Yet the recollection of the time carried with it a "dark shadow" when Emmeline relived the days that followed. The birth had brought her near death, only to face, just five weeks later, the terrible news of Newel's death. He "seemed well and strong," but within hours, she lamented, he "passed away from earth." "Had I realized it, I could not have recovered so nearly as I had when death came and took the father and husband away and left me with two babies helpless and forlorn."[27] Just three years earlier, in the letter in which she acknowledged her love for him, she had written, "Even as it would tear and rend a vine to disentangle it from the tree, so would it rend my very soul to be separated from thee forever."[28] Now the unthinkable had happened. He who had been so strong and solicitous and comforting during the dark days in Nauvoo was gone without warning. "I was left like

23. Gates, "President Emmeline B. Wells," 720.

24. Richard L. Jensen, "Forgotten Relief Societies, 1844–1867," describes the activities of individual Relief Societies on behalf of the Indian population near Mormon settlements.

25. U. B. Hascall, letter to Col. Wilson Andrews, North New Salem, Franklin County, MA. Postmarked: Kane, IA. October 18, 1848, written in Great Salt Lake City, Aug. 8, 1848 in "Letters of a Proselyte," *Utah Historical Quarterly* 25 (July 1957): 245.

26. E. Wells, Diary, August 18, 1902.

27. Ibid., August 18, 1905.

28. Emeline [*sic*] Whitney, letter to Newel K. Whitney, October 10, 1847. This was the only time I have found her to use the clinging-vine image.

one in a dream," she recalled, "but O, such a sad awakening.... no bright ray to shine on my pathway at all."[29] Once again, she had lost the one to whom she had looked for protection and love, "as good a man as ever lived, a father to all within his reach and more than father to me." In their brief marriage, Whitney had become a spiritual ballast for Emmeline, a fixed anchor that had fastened her fledgling faith to a secure mooring. He was a person whom she could "trust most implicitly" because of the "power of his integrity."[30] Once more, she felt that "life seemed hardly worth struggling for."[31]

Newel's death had indeed come suddenly and painfully at age fifty-five. On a pleasant September afternoon, he returned from his work on the Temple Block with a severe pain in his side, and despite the remedies and medical treatment, he continued to fail, and within thirty-six hours, on September 23, 1850, he was gone. Crowds gathered around his home, anxiously awaiting news of his condition and were visibly distraught when learning of his passing.

Newel had been presiding bishop of the church for eighteen years, endearing many because of his methodical but generous care for their needs. He had also served since Joseph Smith's time as trustee in trust. In Utah, he had been appointed associate justice and treasurer of the state of Deseret, his name being printed on the first currency issued in Deseret, as the Saints designated their new home. He was an officer of the Perpetual Emigrating Fund, and he had assisted in subdividing the city into wards. He had worked closely with Brigham Young, as he had with Joseph Smith, and had traveled with Young in locating and planning various cities, including Ogden, thirty-five miles north of Salt Lake City. Emmeline remembered that sometime after Whitney's death, Brigham Young spoke of his "peculiar distress and grief at Bishop Whitney's death[,] of his sincere friendship for him and the particular respect he had always manifested in refering [*sic*] to him."[32]

The eulogies at his funeral highlighted his contributions. In his office as presiding bishop, the *Deseret News* noted, he was "one of the oldest and most exemplary and useful members of the Church" and able to "receive from the rich and to distribute to the poor, of the goods of this world." He was a "thorough, straight-forward, business man," the article continued, and it was "ever more gratifying to him to pay a debt than to contract one; and when all his debts were paid, he was a happy man." The eulogies spoken of him all concurred that he was "leaving a spotless name behind him, and

29. E. Wells, Diary, August 18, 1891.
30. Ibid., September 23, 1874.
31. Ibid., August 18, 1891.
32. Ibid., October 11, 1874.

thousands to mourn their loss of such a valuable man."[33] He had indeed proved to be a valued asset to the church in his wise implementation of the tasks he was asked to render as a bishop, and his loyalty to Joseph Smith and then to Brigham Young was faultless. Emmeline particularly admired him for his "analytical mind, ready to explain in the finest degree principles and to substantiate truths in the same way." She knew from her own experience with him the importance of such a gift, and she recognized, as did so many others, that there were "few men in the world like him—upright honest and chaste."[34]

As was her wont, Emmeline expressed in poetic form the familiar sense of desolation and loss. "How could she struggle on again, with adverse fate!" she poetically wondered.

Such wounds cannot be heal'd, they are too deep.
O, it was pitiful, too sad e'en to relate!
Her grief was silent, and she could not weep.

And in words that became a patterned response to her repeated losses and disappointments, she wrote:

And so some lives go on in tragedies, each part
To be sustained by human effort grand;
Though 'neath the outward seeming lies the broken heart,
That only One above can understand.[35]

At twenty-two, Emmeline was not the teenage bride she had been six years earlier when left alone in Nauvoo. Then she was a disconsolate sixteen-year-old, unprepared for the traumatic changes that happened in such rapid succession after her conversion: the chaotic baptism, her youthful marriage, the move to Nauvoo, the death of the Prophet Joseph Smith and disaffection of her in-laws, the death of her firstborn, the desertion of her husband, her new experience as a plural wife, and the sad death of her mother. Now she was herself the mother of two and had been sealed in the most enduring of bonds to one of the church's revered leaders. Though widowed, she was a member of a large and loving family and sister-wife to one of the church's most beloved women. She could count among her closest associates members of the leading families of the church. Moreover, her New England friends, already settled in their new environment, welcomed and attended to her. And her education once more served as a literal lifesaver, giving her a vocation whereby she could provide for herself and her two babies.

33. "Died" [obituary of Newel K. Whitney], *Deseret News*, September 28, 1850, 122.
34. E. Wells, Diary, February 5, 1896.
35. Emmeline B. Wells, "Faith and Fidelity," in her *Musings and Memories*, 221.

Her marriage to Whitney had also rooted her firmly within the doctrines and practices of Mormonism. Newel had been a soft-spoken, learned, and patient teacher, and Elizabeth Ann had been a model of wisdom, faith, and compassion. From both, Emmeline acquired the grounding and self-confidence so vital in the years ahead. Moreover, Whitney had promised her that someday she would be able "to devote my whole time to writing and to literary pursuits," sweet words to a budding poet. He also promised her that she would one day "sit and eat and drink and converse with the nobles of the earth and tell them of the Gospel," a more challenging prophecy than the former, but, remarkably, also fulfilled.[36]

Left to her own resources, the twenty-two-year-old widow took steps toward independence. First, she established her residence with Olive Bishop, with whom she had lived in Nauvoo, and two-year-old Jethro, Ann's son. Next, Emmeline opened a school in a small log cabin situated in the Twelfth Ward and commenced teaching, acquiring a class of sixty-five pupils. Despite the lack of desks, charts, or blackboards and only two of any one kind of book, Emmeline enthusiastically taught her pupils each day and prepared her teaching materials in the evening. Sometimes she would cut paper into a variety of patterns and then copy her own poems on them for the students' reading exercises. She also wrote mottoes on small pieces of cardboard that she decorated with bits of colored silk as rewards for her students' diligence. In later years, she was pleased to meet her grown students who recalled "the little pioneer school where they took their first steps in education."[37]

In an environment where plural marriage was accepted and openly lived and would, in 1852, be publicly acknowledged as a principle and practice of the church, few women needed to remain single, whether widowed, divorced, or never married. With two young children to support, and well known through her marriage to Newel K. Whitney, Emmeline did not need to anticipate a long widowhood. Her two younger sisters would soon be married. In 1851, Ellen Celeste, at age twenty, became one of Elijah Knapp Fuller's plural wives. The next year Adeline Maria, at age twenty-three, married Justus (sometimes Justice or Jesse) Earl. Emmeline might have had some suitor, being young, intelligent, talented, and attractive, but she had more opportunity to be discerning and cautious than in her first two marriages. Upon reflection, she perceived that she had had no real choice in either of them. She was too young and inexperienced in the first instance, accepting her mother's arrangement in marrying James Harris. Too emotionally distraught in the second instance to do little more than accede to what was

36. E. Wells, Diary, June 13, 1888.

37. "Early Pioneer Education," *Woman's Exponent* 40 (May 1912): 68.

determined to be in her best interest, she had agreed to marry a man she hardly knew in a marital arrangement of which she had little understanding. She had, however, shown the beginning of her own strength of will in her marriage to Newel when she refused to consummate it until she was herself convinced of the authenticity of the principle of celestial marriage and of a genuine love for Newel.

Despite occasional romantic allusions to her marriage to James, she more often remembered the heartache that accompanied it. If there was to be another marriage, she would be the one to decide when and to whom. Furthermore, having been sealed in a celestial marriage to Newel K. Whitney in the Nauvoo temple, she knew that her third marriage would be for mortality only and that any children born to this union would, in Mormon theology at that time, belong to Newel.

CHAPTER 9

Becoming a Wells
(1852)

AFTER TWO YEARS of widowhood, Emmeline was ready to remarry and Daniel H. Wells was the candidate. None of her writings explain her choice, but he was clearly an outstanding option. He was a man with a promising future, well educated, and well positioned, features that appealed to Emmeline. He was bookish and culturally minded. He was also a tall, well-built, rugged-looking man of thirty-eight, in 1852, when twenty-four-year-old Emmeline set her mind on him. He had a fair complexion that became ruddy over time, fine auburn hair, and penetrating blue eyes.[1] Despite his imposing appearance and chiseled features, he was soft-spoken, his language precise and correct—"laconic," Emmeline called it. Though not eloquent, he had remarkable self-command in his speech and also in his demeanor, but, as one son observed, the "fiery mass of red and wavy silken hair...was clearly indicative of a fiery passion and...served as a warning against any unprovoked aggression." He was as exacting in his dress as in his speech, always neat, clean, and well pressed, whether his clothes were worn or new.[2]

It was his character, however, that endeared him to so many of his associates. "A man of integrity" was the most frequent description by those who knew him well. He was also admired for being steadfast, patient, courageous, and generous.

1. His physique is described by his son Junius F. Wells, quoted in Bryant S. Hinckley, *Daniel Hanmer Wells and Events of His Time*, 23.

2. Bryant S. Hinckley, "Recollections of Rulon S. Wells," in ibid., 391. When he was a teacher in Ohio, Daniel chafed at being called a "redhead" by one of his students, clearly a pejorative epithet to him, and losing his temper on one occasion hit the young man hard enough to send him sprawling to the floor. Fearful that he had actually killed him, which he had not, Daniel vowed never to lose control of his temper again. Ibid., 391–92.

Daniel Hanmer Wells was born October 27, 1814, in Trenton, New York, to Daniel and Catherine Chapin Wells. The elder Wells first married Honoré Francis, with whom he had five daughters. After Honoré's death, he married Catherine Chapin. Daniel Hanmer and Catherine were the offspring of his second marriage. Daniel's father died when Daniel was just twelve. Though little more than a boy, as the only male in the family, he shouldered the responsibility of their hundred-acre farm until his five older stepsisters were married and the property divided.

In 1832, Daniel, his mother, and his younger sister, Catherine, left their home in Trenton to join those seeking better opportunity farther west. They paused in Ohio, where Daniel taught school for a season, but then moved on to Illinois in 1834, settling in the new community of Commerce on the banks of the Mississippi River. Twenty-year-old Daniel purchased some property and built a small house on the bluff some distance from the river. His mother began teaching school with a class of thirty, while Daniel devoted his time to buying land with a view of capitalizing on the thriving real estate boom. Within two years, Daniel was made constable of Hancock County. By that time, Commerce boasted a town council, a debating society, a temperance association, and a church of unspecified denomination.

In 1836, Daniel's sister, Catherine, married James Weston Woods, who later served as a defense attorney for Joseph Smith, and whose son William W. Woods would become Emmeline's son-in-law. Eventually, three of James and Catherine's children moved to Utah, but none became Mormons. On March 12, 1837, Daniel married Eliza Rebecca Robison. Her family, like his, was one of the first hundred settlers in Hancock County. Then, in September 1837, a third wedding knitted the two families together even more closely when Daniel's widowed mother, Catherine, married Eliza's newly widowed father, Charles Robison, making Daniel and Eliza stepsiblings as well as marital partners. Daniel and Eliza's only child, Albert Emory, was born two years later, on March 28, 1839.[3]

With the depression of 1837, Daniel was able to enlarge his holdings at bargain prices. When the Mormons were expelled from Missouri during the winter of 1838–39, they flooded into Illinois and found a warm welcome not only in Quincy, forty-seven miles downriver from Commerce, but in Commerce itself, from the Wells and Chapin families. Daniel found a ready market for his real estate among the land-hungry Mormon exiles,

3. Ibid., 30; "Daniel H. Wells and His Wives," 8:179–80; Orson F. Whitney, "Daniel Hanmer Wells," 4:175–76; Beecher, "Letters from the Frontier." Albert never married, and with no siblings he was overwhelmed to discover upon a visit to Salt Lake City that he had so many stepbrothers and -sisters.

who had to plant that spring or find themselves with no harvest in the fall. Sympathetic to their plight, Daniel subdivided eighty acres of his farm and sold lots to them on easy terms. He was also generous in negotiating with them over a piece of prime real estate as a site for their proposed temple.

After the Illinois Legislature passed a town charter with liberal provisions in 1841, Daniel was appointed an alderman, a member of the Nauvoo town council, and justice of the peace, acquiring the title "squire."[4] When the Nauvoo Legion was formed, with Joseph Smith as lieutenant general, Daniel was appointed commissary general. He was also appointed a regent of the University of the City of Nauvoo and a member of the Nauvoo Agricultural and Manufacturing Association, along with Hyrum Smith, Orson Pratt, and other church leaders.[5] His cordial interactions with church leaders, which included a developing friendship with Newel K. Whitney, also a member of the town council, and particularly Joseph Smith, afforded him opportunity to become intimately acquainted with LDS church matters.

Shortly before Joseph Smith and his brother Hyrum were assassinated in June 1844, Daniel's sympathy for the Mormon people and his association with their leaders had evolved into conversion to the church. His wife, Eliza, however, would have none of it. In deference to her, Daniel postponed his baptism. When the Saints were forced to leave Nauvoo beginning in February 1846, Daniel was faced with a crucial decision. Should he leave with them to wherever their new Zion was to be or remain behind with Eliza, who was adamant in her disapproval of Mormonism?

By August he was still undecided and remained in Nauvoo with those Mormons unable to leave with the earlier migrations. But by the end of the summer, even these impoverished Mormons were being harassed and threatened, though they had already agreed to surrender the city. Daniel could postpone his decision no longer. The matter was settled when he was baptized on August 9 by Almon Babbit, the church's agent overseeing the sale of church property.[6]

4. Emmeline referred to him either as "Esquire" or "General," reflecting his legal and military positions, but never as "Daniel," a reticence typical of nineteenth-century female etiquette.

5. "Daniel H. Wells and His Wives," 8:180; O. Whitney, "Daniel Hanmer Wells," 4:176; Hinckley, *Daniel Hanmer Wells*, 30–34.

6. In her diary, Emmeline gives the date as August 6, 1848, but most biographical sketches give the date as August 9. E. Wells, Diary, March 22, 1914. A postscript to a letter from Joseph Albert Stratton to Elders [Orson] Hyde and [John] Taylor, published in the *Millennial Star*, notes the baptism of Daniel Wells. The postscript is followed by a complimentary paragraph regarding Daniel Wells's activities in Nauvoo on behalf of the church. *Millennial Star* 8 (November 1, 1846): 109.

Within a month of his baptism, Daniel Wells was on the front lines as general in the Nauvoo Legion, commanding a small defensive army to protect the ambushed Saints in what became known as the battle of Nauvoo. By the end of September, it was clear that the outnumbered and outgunned Mormons had no chance to negotiate and fled the city. Daniel H. Wells was among the last to leave Nauvoo.

After helping to settle the refugees in Iowa camps, Wells returned to Nauvoo to remove Eliza and Albert from the lawless condition of the city, taking them to Burlington, Iowa, where his sister and her family were living. He then traveled to Winter Quarters to report the events to Brigham Young, returning to Montrose, Iowa, where some of the refugees had temporarily camped, to help convey them to Winter Quarters. Traveling once again back to Illinois, Wells spent the winters of 1846 and 1847 with Eliza in Galesburg, Illinois, where she had moved. He may have hoped that Eliza's feelings might have moderated once the Nauvoo problem was behind them, but no amount of persuasion altered her feelings toward the church. Like so many others, he had to confront the dilemma so often imposed by conversion. He made the anguished decision to join the Saints and close the curtain on his life with Eliza and Albert.

It had been a long and heartrending process. "I see no prospect short of a complete sacrifice of everything I hold dear on earth as well in a pecuniary point of view, as the kindlier affections of the human heart," Wells wrote to Brigham Young from Illinois shortly before traveling to Winter Quarters in 1848. But he reassured the president of his decision to stay with the church. "Think not that I am despairing or desponding, for although my soul is bowed down under a great weight of affliction, yet my faith is placed upon the Lord of Hosts, and 'come weal, come woe,' I will be with you by the 1st of April, sooner if possible."[7] On March 1 of that year, after promising Wells that he would "in no wise lose your reward in this world" and would receive "eternal life, glory and immortality" in the world to come, Brigham Young gave him ebullient words of encouragement. "Cheer up your heart," he wrote, "and rejoice in the day of your deliverance, and comfort your heart that my prayer is offered up in your behalf, and may the time soon arrive that we shall be able to strike hands and go on our way rejoicing to a land of peace, happiness and holiness, that we may all enjoy health and strength and do the will of Him that sent us."[8]

7. Daniel Wells, letter to Brigham Young, quoted in "Daniel H. Wells and His Wives," 8:181; and Hinckley, *Daniel Hanmer Wells*, 48.

8. Brigham Young, letter to Daniel Wells, March 1, 1848, quoted in Hinckley, *Daniel Hanmer Wells*, 49.

These may have been consoling words to Daniel, but Eliza was crushed. Though Daniel had left her all his property and other material holdings, she dismissed any concern about her material welfare in a poignant plea to him a month after he left for Winter Quarters, expressing what mattered most to her, his companionship, which she had enjoyed for eleven years. An evening stroll in their garden, just coming into springtime flowering, brought memories to her, she wrote, of all they had shared together, when they had "walked happy in each others love and society happy in our friends and enjoying bright satisfactions of peace." These were her thoughts as she traced the familiar scenes they had once shared together. "As some token of love or kindness came to mind," she continued, "so also came the thought that all these things had passed away, that the chances were we should not meet no more." She rued the advent of the Mormons that had unalterably changed their lives and had now drawn them on to different paths. She implored him "to consult your own feelings and return to us soon and think not by so doing you will offend that God who wills not one idle, one useless tear." Even as she pleaded for his return, she was aware that he could have altered his course during their last two years together but did not. Now, she asked only that he "write every chance if only a few lines for there are here many who wish to hear from you but none can feel the deep anxiety felt by your Eliza."[9] But Daniel had made his choice and, like Emmeline, left one life behind and began another totally embraced by the promises of Mormonism. Ironically, Eliza's brother Louis and his wife, Clarissa Duzette, joined the church and traveled to Utah in 1847, a year before Daniel. Like Daniel, Louis had held several civic positions in Nauvoo, making many friends among the Mormons.

Daniel Wells was not only a striking figure wherever he went, but also distinctive for his legal and judicial abilities on behalf of the church in Nauvoo even before he became a member. These efforts for a beleaguered people impressed Brigham Young, and he made Wells his aide-de-camp on his second trek to Utah in 1848.

Upon their arrival in the valley, Young appointed Wells superintendent of public works, an enormous responsibility in the development of Salt Lake City. For the next twenty-two years, Wells served in that position, supervising the construction of most of the public buildings in Salt Lake City, including the Council House and the temple, as well as the various tabernacles, throughout the territory. He held legislative and

9. Eliza Rebecca Robison Wells, letter to Daniel H. Wells, (Council Bluffs), [no day or month] 1848. Daniel H. Wells Papers. Eliza divorced Daniel in 1851, but did not remarry.

educational positions along with military offices during his lifetime, and as early as 1852 he was already a respected, successful community leader and businessman.

He was also a new husband and father. On February 15, 1849, six months after arriving in the valley, Daniel, at age thirty-five, married Louisa Free, ten years his junior. Seven months later, on September 20, 1849, he took another wife, seventeen-year-old Martha Givens Harris. Both Louisa and Martha had traveled west with him in Brigham Young's company. Louisa was accompanied by her two-year-old son, John Brigham, a product of her marriage to John D. Lee, whom she had married in Nauvoo on April 19, 1845, as his third wife. Their marriage unraveled, however, and her sealing to Lee was canceled a month before her marriage to Daniel.[10] Thus, in March 1852, when Emmeline took the courageous and unusual step of proposing herself to be Daniel's wife, his new family included two plural wives, two children with Louisa, and her son by John D. Lee, whom he adopted.[11]

There is little evidence to support the frequency in which women proposed marriage, Mormon or otherwise, although personal documents indicate that there were women who made premarital decisions to marry into polygamy or who encouraged their husbands to take additional wives. Moreover, Emmeline's satisfying experience in polygamy with Newel Whitney only confirmed her decision to enter the practice once again.

All of Emmeline's marriages took place before the evolving notion of romantic love took root as an impetus for marriage rather than economic, family, or proximity considerations, which often decided the partnership. That she found love in all three marriages, only one of which was of her own choice, may well have been unusual at that time. She does not reveal whether she was romantically attracted to Daniel before their marriage, and nothing in Emmeline's extant writings indicate that she and Daniel experienced any prior interaction or demonstrated any shared interest beyond their church membership. Thus, her letter to him on March 4, 1852, was written without a personal context, though it was, along with her letters to Newel K. Whitney, the most important letter of her life. She may well have

10. See Juanita Brooks, *John Doyle Lee: Zealot—Pioneer Builder—Scapegoat*, 65–66, 145. John Brigham was born February 25, 1846, and lived his life under the Wells name. Louisa was considered to have been Lee's favorite wife, and they appeared to have had an amicable parting. They were assigned to different wagon companies within Brigham Young's 1848 large company of five hundred. Ibid., 111, 130–31.

11. Eliza Robison divorced Daniel in 1851 in Illinois. Information on the subsequent marriages of Daniel H. Wells is taken from the *Utah Genealogical and Historical Magazine* 6 (January 1915): 1–16; and "Daniel H. Wells and His Wives," 8:184–201.

tested several revisions to be sure her intent in writing would be subtle but clear to him. The result is a study in obsequious, overwrought prose. She began her letter, "Dear friend:"

> If such I may call thee, would to heaven I could realize in its true character the extent of your friendship; very probably I err in supposing that the friendship I feel for a stranger, would be received by him; but were the secret motives which prompt—nay tested at the shrine of truth and virtue, they would be found pure, as purity and innocent, as innocence; it may be I am to[o] confiding, if so (May Heaven forgive me); and may one act of imprudence, (if such it be) teach me wisdom in future; pardon all my simplicity, overlook it as the weakness of one young in years—and perhaps entertaining to[o] great an idea of the truthfulness of him, whom she addresses thus: yet judging from the short acquaintance, we have had with each other and also, the high estimation people entertain of your worth; you possess in my opinion every quality of mind, calculated to ennoble, dignify & exalt man, in the sphere of life & usefulness.
>
> I esteem your character & principles so far as I know them, or have been informed, far beyond what I can express; but although I am well aware, I possess nothing, which would excite your admiration, or regard, yet it is my sincere desire, you will not betray my friendship; it is entirely my own feelings that cause me to write, as I have written; and should you consider the widow of your <u>departed friend</u> [Newel K. Whitney], worthy the attention of one so noble & dignified as yourself, you will please answer this short epistle, according to your own feelings and sentiments, but should you feel otherwise—judge me not hastily; and remember, that let the result be what it may, I possess for you a strong and unchanging friendship.
>
> Fondly would my imagination picture to me in my lonely musings, dreams of the future, united with a being, noble as thyself, but when from these reflections I call in my scattered thoughts; and view my life in its realities, I feel my lonely situation sensibly; and know how very improbable, would such a change be, to one now so melancholy, so—shall I say unhappy? Believe me not enthusiastic; do not look upon me with contempt because I have addressed you, if your heart receiveth it not, return it to her who hath been so frank and honest-hearted, as to express her own bosom sentiments to you, trusting to your fidelity—conscious that were she thus entrusted, she would never betray even to her most intimate friend, that which

> might wound the pride, or injure the feelings of the betrayed. More I cannot, dare not say, until I am informed of your feelings on the subject.

The letter ends, "A true & faithful friend," followed by a parenthetical statement: "(hastily written for fear of observers)."[12]

It is a letter that required careful composition and confidence, despite the self-abnegating phrases. Emmeline's appeal to Daniel's loyalty to Whitney and to her "lonely situation" placed a burden of responsibility on him that he could not comfortably ignore. Surely, he would have been flattered by such a proposal, even if it startled him. He considered it for a full month while Emmeline endured the torment of waiting. Did she avoid him at public events? Did she remain secluded? Did she disclose her actions or explain her feelings to anyone? Clearly, her daughters were too young to understand. Finally, on April 5, the reply came, as direct and "laconic" as his speech. It began simply "To Emmeline" and ended only with his full name. It is almost as opaque as hers.

> Your letter has been received and favorably considered be assured that it has been no indiferent [*sic*] feelings toward the "Widow of my departed friend" that has hitherto withheld an answer. [T]here are a good many considerations in affairs of this nature in this Kingdom which require the observance of some stipulations which shall prove of mutual benefit to all interested, and as shall subserve the interest of our common cause. If this shall find you still adhering to the same course as indicated in your communication to me I can only say that I will improve an early opportunity of conferring with you upon the subject. In the meantime believe me truly and cordialy [*sic*] your friend
>
> Daniel H. Wells[13]

He wrote this letter the day after he married his third plural wife, Lydia Ann Alley. This marriage was only one of the "considerations in affairs of this nature" that Emmeline soon discovered. In fact, before Daniel acted favorably on her proposal, he married two additional women: Susan Hannah Alley, Lydia Ann's sister, and Hannah Corilla Free, Louisa's sister, both of whom had also been in the Brigham Young company with Daniel. Like

12. Emmeline B. Whitney [Wells], letter to Daniel H. Wells, March 4, 1852, Daniel H. Wells Papers.

13. Daniel H. Wells, letter to Emmeline B. Whitney, April 5, 1852, ibid.

Louisa, Hannah Corilla had been previously married, and she similarly had her sealing to Sterne Hotchkiss canceled a month before her marriage to Daniel. She bore a child from her marriage to Hotchkiss a month after marrying Daniel.[14] Emmeline, as it turned out, was his seventh wife (if Eliza is included), bringing her two Whitney daughters to the family. Daniel thus became a stepfather of four children from his plural marriages. He did not adopt Emmeline's two daughters, however.

Daniel's wives were all close in age to Emmeline. Louisa was the oldest, but only four years older than Emmeline, and Martha Ann was the youngest, just four years younger. The close proximity in both age and marriages drew the wives together, and they retained close relationships with one another throughout their lives.[15]

Emmeline did not record when she and Daniel conferred about their own union, what expectations each communicated (or if they did), and when and how they decided on a marriage date. But haste was not an element. After marrying his first two plural wives seven months apart, Daniel had waited more than three years to enlarge his family, marrying three more wives and then Emmeline within a six-month period. They ultimately selected the last day of the church's general conference, October 10, 1852. The ceremony was performed at six in the evening by Brigham Young in the front room of the Wells home, an old adobe house composed of two adjoining buildings, situated behind a wall on South Temple, near the Tithing Office on the corner of Main Street.

Though not mentioning her former two wedding dresses, Emmeline either cared enough about her wedding dress this time or finally had one worth describing in detail. It was made of a soft, light material patterned with blue and gray stripes and trimmed with fine old lace. It was called a Balzarine dress because of the material, and either Emmeline or perhaps a friend or dressmaker had made it for her in Nauvoo.[16] Around her neck she wore a necklace of gold beads, and she piled her thick black hair high on her head in a style fashionable for that period. Daniel escorted her from the home

14. Sterne Hotchkiss, a "dental surgeon," set up his practice in Salt Lake City in 1850. The reasons for his divorce from Hannah are not known. "S. Hotchkiss, M.D., Dental Surgeon," *Deseret News*, October 5, 1850, 1. Their child was Abby Corilla, born September 20, 1852, who took the Wells name.

15. Margaret Clayton [Emmeline's granddaughter], interviewed by Dennis Rowley and John Bluth, November 17, 1977, L. Tom Perry Special Collections, Harold B. Lee Library, Brigham Young University, Provo, UT. See also "Daniel H. Wells and His Wives."

16. Balzarine was a fabric of mixed cotton and wool used mainly for women's dresses.

she shared with "Auntie" Olive Bishop to his adobe home for the ceremony. Steve Taylor, an employee of Daniel's, drove the large carriage, while she and Daniel sat inside, which gave them protection from the blustery, windy evening. Following the ceremony, the family enjoyed a celebration dinner. Emmeline did not record the names of any other guests. Afterward, Louisa, Daniel's first (plural) wife, and Emmeline, his sixth, left the festivities for a quiet talk together in the orchard behind the home. If Emmeline recorded the words of their conversation, they have not endured in any known record, but their intimate talk bode well for a compatible relationship. Afterward, when the celebration was over, Daniel drove her home and stayed with her for her third bridal night and his seventh.[17]

Looking back at the event twenty years later, Emmeline confessed that she had cherished high expectations for this marriage and that, for the most part, they had not come to pass. "O how happy I was then," she lamented, "how much pleasure I anticipated and how changed alas are all things since that time, how few of the thoughts I had then have ever been realized, and how much sorrow I have known in place of the joy I looked forward to."[18] That this relationship might fulfill the romantic dreams for which she longed, even with only a partial claim on his love, was indeed only a dream.

Reality is seldom a gentle teacher. Expectations so often fall short, and the romantic and idealistic hopes that Emmeline envisioned for this carefully planned marriage tell more about Emmeline's romantic notions of life and marriage than her grasp of what marriage to a man deeply engaged in public duties while also meeting the demands of five families might be. Romance had to yield to reality during those early years. Daniel and Emmeline soon found themselves on different trajectories. Their paths inevitably diverged.

17. Details of the marriage come from several of Emmeline's diary entries: for example, October 11, 1874; October 10, 1889; October 10, 1890; October 10, 1899; and October 10, 1908.

18. Ibid., October 10, 1874. All three of her husbands eventually abandoned their traditional role as provider and protector by desertion, death, or penury.

CHAPTER 10

The Wells Family
(1852–1870)

Sometime after her marriage, Emmeline left Olive's home and moved into the Wells home. By 1856, with the addition of several more children, the adobe house behind the wall could no longer accommodate the growing family. Daniel built a comfortable two-story home on State Street and Third South for Emmeline and her third daughter, Emmeline (Emmie), was born in 1853. That Emmeline did not get along with her sister-wives has been the usual explanation for her separate residence. However, this speculation is repeatedly undercut by Emmeline's own account of the friendship and esteem she felt toward her companions in marriage and the reliance they developed on each other when problems in the family confronted them. Susan and Lydia Ann, especially, filled an important niche in Emmeline's life.

Emmeline's marriage to Daniel was different from his other marriages. Emmeline's appeal to Daniel matched the pattern of a levirate relationship, an ancient Hebrew law by which a man was expected to marry the widow of his brother or kinsman to provide a home for her and to raise up posterity for his brother. Hints of this appeal are evident in Emmeline's letter to Daniel, bringing to mind the story of Ruth and Boaz. In consideration of his friend and brother in the Gospel Newel K. Whitney, Daniel apparently conceded to this biblical practice and married Newel's widow Emmeline for time only, providing a home for her and posterity for Whitney.[1] Why she lived separately from Daniel's eternal mates thus had some logical basis.

Emmeline adored her new home. "I shall never forget the days when we were moving," she wrote in retrospect. "The little sweet things used to run down with things in their hands, they were so overjoyed to have a home, their own home. I recollect so well how delighted Belle was to have a room.

1. The biblical story of Ruth and Boaz is typical of a levirate relationship. Emmeline's justification for Ruth's actions (and by implication her own) is expressed in her article "The Integrity of Ruth," *Woman's Exponent* 7 (November 15, 1878): 89.

We used always to call it Belle's room in those days." Emmeline "put out the trees and shrubs and watched them day by day. Every spot of ground and spear of grass and weed was dear," she fondly recalled. Memories of her girls pattering up and down the staircase remained vivid as she remembered those first days in what was always her most dearly loved home of those in which she lived after leaving New England.[2]

The garden was especially precious to her, as near a replication of the natural setting of New Salem as the dry climate of Utah could produce. There she wrote poems and "quaint stories" as she watched her children play, comparing herself to Margaret Fuller, the noted writer and feminist, who "could not refrain from the desire to read and study even while attending to household duties." Emmeline carefully stored away the scraps of paper on which she wrote ideas that came to her from the books and newspapers she consistently read, ideas that found their way into her own writings.[3] Her fondness for her garden resulted in one of her best-known poems, "The Dear Old Garden," written years later when she nostalgically recalled the early years of her family life in that State Street home.[4]

Furnished the aid of a housekeeper, like the other wives, Emmeline focused her homemaking efforts on sewing and child rearing.[5] Though not by nature attracted to domestic arts, she made most of her daughters' dresses when they were young, and they remember listening to her recite the poems or sing the songs of her youth while she sat sewing and mending. By the dim glow of the "dreadful dip-lights," she sewed the "tucks and ruffles" on her babies' clothes as she had done years earlier for Bishop Whitney and his boys.[6]

Emmeline taught her girls to sew, and Belle and Mell were known for their skill at making gloves and other items of clothing. Though Emmeline could sew, she knew less about cooking. The larger Wells family, however,

2. E. Wells, Diary, May 5, 1888.

3. "Emmeline B. Wells," 2. This is a three-page holograph written by Emmeline in the third person while she was in Atlanta at a suffrage association meeting in February 1895. Photocopy of original in my possession, courtesy of Helen C. Shurtleff, a great-granddaughter. The sketch is written on stationery from the Hotel Aragon in Atlanta.

4. E. Wells, *Musings and Memories*, 190–92.

5. Besides housekeeping assistants, Daniel Wells employed gardeners, teamsters, and a family steward, James Snarr, who acted as a purchasing and distribution agent for the family. He managed the family store, whose supplies came from Daniel's two farms and were available to the family as needed.

6. A.W. Cannon, "Mothers in Israel," esp. 67. Annie remembered her mother sewing by a "dip-light" after giving her last tallow candle to a neighbor who was hosting a party.

counted on her New England baked beans, her doughnuts, and her apple fritters for family parties, but she did not make a name for herself in any aspect of the domestic sphere as her sister-wives did.[7]

Though living apart from the rest of the family, in the early days Emmeline and her children joined them all each evening after dinner for family prayers, always offered by Daniel when he was home. They attended birthdays and other family events and remained well integrated. With the household help Daniel provided, Emmeline also had time to indulge her love of poetry, both reading and writing it. In time, her home became a literary mecca, drawing her own friends as well as those of her children to evenings of stimulating conversation and sociability.

But during the years following Emmie's birth in 1853, Emmeline was obliged to confront the benign neglect of a husband with five other families, all living together with him, and his numerous church and civic responsibilities. Only in her midtwenties, she missed the attention she might more logically have expected in a monogamous relationship. Putting pen to paper, on September 10, 1856, soon after moving to her own home, she expressed her feelings in a letter to Daniel. She began with an invitation for him to visit her. "It's little Em's birthday," she reminded him apologetically, "and as she seldom sees her father I thought there would be no harm in inviting you to supper." Then she ruefully added, "It would not hinder you more than an hour and only 2 blocks and a half to walk[;] it seems a very short distance to me but to you it may be different." After this veiled rebuke, she became inordinately self-effacing in the rest of the letter, perhaps hoping to elicit some measure of guilt for his inattention. Though expressing a strong desire to see him, she explained that if he chose not to come, "it will be no disappointment, as I never expect anything." In fact, she continued, "I should be very sorry if you came merely because I asked you, when you would rather have spent your time else where." In closing, she asked that he would not "tell anybody how simple I am."[8] Such self-deprecation was not a natural trait of Emmeline's, which her later life would prove. No record remains to reveal his response.

In 1862, six years after Emmeline's move to her State Street home, Daniel relocated his other wives into a beautiful, large two-story home, located on the corner of Main Street and South Temple, across the street south from the adobe cottages the Wells family had been occupying. This large, commodious house was his domicile as well. Built by Ezra T. Benson, it became known as the "Wells Mansion" or the "corner house," but the children called

7. Ibid., 69.

8. Emmeline B. Wells, letter to Daniel H. Wells, September 10, [1856], D. Wells Papers.

it the "big house." It was built in a colonial style, with broad porches, wide doors, a spacious entry hall, and a long, artistically designed staircase. The large rooms had high ceilings, and the deep windows, guarded by green shutters, kept the rooms light and airy. It was one of several stately homes that began to rise in the central part of the city. Brigham Young's two homes, the Lion and Beehive Houses, already stood prominently on the north side of South Temple.

The children had ample room to play amid the fruit and mulberry trees that shaded the house, and within the home each wife had her own suite, accommodating a small sitting room, bedrooms, a dining area, and kitchen. Louisa's apartment, on the main floor, included the family parlor, with a large fireplace and, after 1864, a family piano. Family prayers were held in this parlor.[9]

Beyond the material conveniences Daniel provided for his family, he made his home a cultural haven. Reading was a favorite pastime of his, and books were plentiful in the home and available to all the family. He also loved drama, and after the Salt Lake Theatre was completed in 1862, an enterprise under his supervision, he bought tickets to the productions for family members. At the time of Emmeline's marriage to Daniel, Ursulia Hascall wrote a long letter to her sister in Massachusetts describing Emmeline's new husband. "[Emmeline] has married a fine man. He is a perfect gentleman and has a good education, has abundance of books and newspapers for her to read and she is quite happy."[10] Nothing indeed could have been more amenable to Emmeline than the cultural ambience that surrounded her new family, which she replicated in her own home.

Emmeline was not a stranger to Daniel's wives when she married him. She had known Louisa Free for at least a year, and they had much in common. Louisa had been a teacher in Nauvoo, as had Emmeline. Both had experienced previous marriages, and both brought children of other fathers to their marriages to Daniel. In an undated letter written before marrying Daniel, Emmeline invited Louisa to make an informal visit and to "bring some of the other girls" if they were inclined to come. No need to "take time to dress up," Emmeline explained, signing the note "Emeline B. Whitney."[11] Whether the visit transpired or not, this prenuptial contact suggests that

9. Josephine Wells Lyman, "Daniel H. Wells," typescript, photocopy in my possession. See also Annie Wells Cannon, "Home and Family Life," in *Daniel Hanmer Wells*, by Hinckley, 345–46.

10. Ursulia B. Hascall, letter to sister, Great Salt Lake City, August 29, 1853, in "Letters of a Proselyte," *Utah Historical Quarterly* 25: 349–50.

11. Emmeline B. Whitney, letter to Louisa Free Wells, photocopy of handwritten original, n.d., in my possession.

Emmeline's forthcoming marriage to Daniel was indeed a family affair, and Emmeline was eager to befriend at the outset the women who would be so intimately connected with her through Daniel.

As the first plural wife and the oldest, Louisa held a senior position in the family, and she felt a strong responsibility toward all of the children. She conducted "Manner Meetings" each Saturday to teach the children proper etiquette, respect, honesty, and appropriate language. She also served as the family physician. She made a personal study of medicine and nursed the family as well as friends through bouts of measles, whooping cough, and mumps. Junius Wells, Hannah's son, remembered the "family epidemics," especially whooping cough, which resembled "a yelping pet-dog show" when they all "barked together."[12] In 1884, Louisa accompanied Daniel to England on his second assignment as president of the European mission.

Martha Givens Harris of Tennessee was seventeen when she married Daniel in 1852. Regarded as a delightful storyteller, she did little in the public sphere, raising her seven children quietly at home. Though lacking in formal education herself, she desired her children to use proper grammar and diction, useful traits in this literary family. She was noted for her hospitality and especially for her selflessness in caring for eleven of her grandchildren when their mothers died. Her son Heber Manning became the first governor of the state of Utah, and her daughter Emily married future church president Heber J. Grant.[13]

Like Emmeline and Louisa, Lydia Ann Alley was educated and interested in literature. Living a thrifty and unpretentious life with her family before joining the church, she enjoyed the comforts that her marriage brought her that she initially described as "extravagant," but that she came to appreciate. In charge of the Wells library, she urged the children to read and instructed them in good penmanship. She served as a counselor to Rachel Ridgeway Ivins Grant in the Relief Society presidency of the Thirteenth Ward for seventeen years and as a Primary worker for even longer.[14]

Susan Alley, Lydia Ann's sister, married Daniel Wells two weeks after Lydia. Like Martha, her primary focus was her home, where she exhibited her skills as a cook and needlewoman. She and Lydia Ann impressed the family by continuing to use a spinning wheel long after it became obsolete in cloth making.[15] Susan's only daughter, Annette, married H. L. A. Culmer, a noted Utah artist and a fortuitous addition to the cultured Wells family.

12. Junius F. Wells, "A Manner School."

13. Hinckley, *Daniel Hanmer Wells*, 355.

14. "Lydia Ann Alley," in "Woman Suffrage in Pioneer Days," in *Our Pioneer Heritage*, compiled by Carter, 20:334; Hinckley, *Daniel Hanmer Wells*, 382, 383.

15. Hinckley, *Daniel Hanmer Wells*, 356, 348–50.

Hannah Corilla Free, Louisa's sister, married Daniel Wells in August 1852, just two months before Emmeline. Despite the loss of four of her seven children, Hannah was witty and cheerful and a delight to the family. Daniel invited her to join him on his first mission to Europe in 1864 in an effort to console her after two of her children died of diphtheria within a week's time.[16]

This was the family Emmeline joined upon her marriage to Daniel. Close in age and often left without the companionship of their husband, the wives became close in sisterhood. Emmeline praised the friendship that bonded them. These were women, she wrote, "with whom I lived in closest intimacy, closer than sisters, rearing our children in the same household."[17] Living in close proximity to one another, the children, all thirty-seven of them, called the various mothers Aunt and all of their siblings "brother" and "sister." The whole family grieved at the deaths of nine of them before they reached adulthood.[18]

These six wives of Daniel H. Wells soon learned that their talented husband had loyalties beyond the family and was steadily becoming one of the busiest and most indispensable of Mormon leaders. At each general conference during the early 1850s, Daniel was sustained as superintendent of public works and as a member of the Perpetual Emigrating Fund Company, supervising the loan of money to emigrant Saints and their repayment. Brigham Young included him in many of the decision-making meetings relating to the development of the territory. Daniel assisted in organizing the city's wards (ecclesiastical units); he explored the canyons and other areas around the city with Brigham Young for industrial and settlement possibilities; he supervised road building; he was on the committee to compile statutes applicable to Utah; he traveled to Fillmore, the early capital of Utah, as a member of the legislative assembly; and he was instrumental in changing the capital to Salt Lake City. In 1856, he was appointed a regent of the University of Deseret and a decade later its chancellor. He visited settlements throughout the territory with Brigham Young, ascertaining their public building needs. He met at least weekly or more frequently with the First Presidency and members of the Quorum of the Twelve Apostles,

16. Ibid., 347–48.

17. A. W. Cannon, "Mothers in Israel," 68.

18. Of Louisa's six children, her son John, by John D. Lee, died at age ten; Martha's son Hermon Chapin died at nineteen months; Lydia Ann's daughter Lucy Ann died at ten months, and her son Wilford Woodruff died at four months; Susan's son George died at age twelve; and Hannah's daughter Luna died at fifteen months, her son Brigham died at age four, and her son Preston died at one month. Her son Ephraim Willard died at thirteen months, within the same week as her son Brigham.

although not a member of either quorum before 1857. He was in constant communication with Utah's representatives in Washington and later became Brigham Young's official correspondent with them. He helped draft legislation preparatory to Utah's becoming a federal territory in 1850. He wrote the legislative bill regulating the judiciary and counseled with President Young regarding the printing and revising of the laws of the territory. When Utah officially became a territory in 1850, he administered the oath of office to Brigham Young as the territory's first governor.[19]

Along with all of these civic and church responsibilities, Wells served as commander of the Utah Militia as a lieutenant general. He engaged in several Indian skirmishes, developed Indian policies, and participated in negotiations, all of which required meetings, drawing up military orders, and developing systems of regulation.[20] In 1856, he was assigned to travel to Fort Bridger, Wyoming, to acquire provisions for two of the handcart pioneer companies stranded by deadly snowstorms.[21] That same year, at Brigham Young's request, Jedediah M. Grant, Young's second counselor, launched a spiritual reformation. Grant's death in November catapulted Daniel into the highest quorum of the church when Brigham Young called him to replace Grant as his second counselor in the First Presidency.[22] Emmeline's plea in September 1856 for his company amidst these demanding responsibilities may well have struck Daniel as simple self-indulgence.

As one of the highest church officials, President Wells found himself deeply involved in one of the most challenging tests the Saints had yet experienced. Federal territorial officials assigned to Utah interpreted the residents' tenacious loyalty to Brigham Young in both religious and civil

19. Hinckley, *Daniel Hanmer Wells*, 135–53; J. Lyman, "Daniel H. Wells"; "Daniel H. Wells and His Wives," 8:181–82.

20. His various engagements with the Indians for about a twenty-year period are delineated in Daniel H. Wells, "Daniel H. Wells' [first person] Narrative"; and Hinckley, *Daniel Hanmer Wells*, 117–33.

21. Some accounts of the handcart venture are LeRoy R. Hafen and Ann W. Hafen, *Handcarts to Zion: The Story of a Unique Western Migration*; Rebecca Cornwall Bartholomew and Leonard J. Arrington, *Rescue of the 1856 Handcart Companies*; and Howard A. Christy, "Handcart Companies." See also David Roberts, *Devils Gate: Brigham Young and the Great Mormon Handcart Tragedy*; and Will Bagley, "One Long Funeral March: A Revisionist's View of the Mormon Handcart Disasters."

22. Journal History, January 4, 1857, 1. In a brief sketch written for the *American Ancestry*, Wells notes that he was ordained an apostle at the same time he was appointed second counselor in the First Presidency, although this claim has not been verified. According to Deseret News, *2011 LDS Church Almanac*, 92, he was not ordained an apostle but was "sustained as a counselor to the Twelve Apostles" at the October 1877 general conference, a few months after Brigham Young's death. See also Hinckley, *Daniel Hanmer Wells*, 26–27.

matters as disloyalty to the US government. Their complaints reached President James Buchanan's desk soon after he took office in March 1857, and in June, plans were set in motion to send an army escort of twenty-five hundred troops for Alfred Cumming, who agreed to replace Brigham Young as governor and to quell any sign of insurrection. They were sent, President Buchanan explained, for the protection of the newly appointed officials "to act as a *posse comitatus*, in case of need, in the execution of the laws."[23] Despite the number of men involved in its deployment, the posse was dispatched in June 1857 without any public notice. When learning of it, the Saints were understandably alarmed at what appeared to be a territorial invasion.

Church leaders discussed their options and decided to prevent the army from entering the valley by a strategy of harassment and hindrance rather than warfare. If the army still threatened to enter the valley, Brigham Young announced to the Saints that in order to avoid any kind of altercation and to leave nothing for the army's use, they were to abandon their homes and relocate in settlements south of Salt Lake City. A torch would then be laid to commercial and civic buildings as well as to dwellings, leaving only the ashes of a torched city for the army to occupy.[24] It was a dramatic response to an unconfirmed threat.

The Utah War, as the conflict came to be known—technically it was the Utah Expedition—affected the Wells family in two specific ways. As lieutenant general of the Utah Militia, Daniel Wells was significantly involved in the planning and execution of the Mormon resistance. Thus, for much of the fall and early winter of 1857, he was with the militia. When it was learned that the army did not intend to travel on to the valley that winter, only a small contingent of the militia was left to guard the Echo Canyon outposts, and Daniel was able to return to the city.

However, when the army resumed its march toward Salt Lake City the following spring, the Wells family prepared to follow Brigham Young's order to move south. Most of the residents left the city in April 1858. Daniel superintended the move of four of his families at that time, leaving Louisa

23. Quotation from Leonard J. Arrington, *Great Basin Kingdom: An Economic History of the Latter-day Saints, 1830–1900*, 171–74. An early interpretation is Andrew Love Neff, *History of Utah, 1847–1869*, 433–55. See also David L. Bigler, "'A Lion in the Path': Genesis of the Utah War, 1857–1858," esp. 18; and William P. MacKinnon, "'And the War Came': James Buchanan, the Utah Expedition, and the Decision to Intervene" and "At Sword's Point, Part 1: A Documentary History of the Utah War to 1858."

24. L. Arrington, *Great Basin Kingdom*, 175–94; Neff, *History of Utah*, 456–84; J. Allen and Leonard, *Story of the Latter-day Saints*, 298–303. Hinckley, *Daniel Hanmer Wells*, 93–115, focuses on the role taken by Daniel H. Wells.

and Hannah and their children in Salt Lake City until he could find accommodations for all of his family south of the city.

Emmeline, with her daughters, Isabel, Melvina, and Emmie, along with sister-wives Martha, Lydia Ann, and Susan and their children traveled as far as Provo, about forty-five miles south of Salt Lake City. The town, in 1858, was still a fledgling community and hardly prepared to accommodate the thousands who sought refuge in its small environs. There were few permanent dwellings to house the influx of temporary residents, and few were as comfortably situated as the Wells wives, who were fortunate enough to find lodging in the Beauvoir (or Beauvier) house, an existing home.[25] Most of the other transplants were reduced to using tents and hastily constructed shacks for their temporary homes. "We are very pleasantly situated, and very comfortable in every other respect," Emmeline wrote to her sister-wives in Salt Lake City soon after her arrival in Provo. Nonetheless, in the same letter, Emmeline urged Hannah and Louisa to appreciate being in Salt Lake City, "for Provo is nothing like it. Such dismal dark looking houses and dirty streets," she noted. "Our home "is the most neat looking one I have seen in this place." A stroll around the town with Martha one Sunday afternoon yielded "nothing worth looking at."[26]

Emmeline could not resist versifying her thoughts about Provo, which she sent to Hannah and Louisa on April 21 "by way of amusement" and "to make a little fun for you." It begins:

Now girls I'll write you a few lines
Because I want to let you know
How we all do and how we feel
Since we've come to live in Provo.
The dullest place you ever saw
Day after day its always so
Frogs a croaking drums a beating
Charming music here in Provo.

She follows these verses with several more describing her life there, concluding with these lines:

If you don't believe what I've said
Just come and see if it "aint" so
And I will guarantee you'll wish
You'd never seen nor heard of Provo.[27]

25. "Wells Settled His Family," Journal History, April 2, 1858.

26. Emmeline B. Wells (Provo, UT), letter to "Dear absent sisters," April 15, 1858, E. Wells Papers, LDS Church History Library.

27. Emmeline B. Wells, letter to Louisa and Hannah Wells, April 18, 1858, ibid.

After sending the poem, Emmeline worried about the "Esquire's" response to her "nonsense" about Provo, and she asked Louisa and Hannah to reassure him that she was "glad to have come to Provo when he wished me to and nothing could have induced me to do differently." Her excuse for writing the verses was that "we have no amusement nor variety here and one dull lonesome evening I sat and scribbled them and several more but I am very sorry I sent them."[28] Her desire to please Daniel and to avoid offending him created a longtime concern about his attitude toward her writing and later her public activities, though it did not deter her from continuing to do both.

Emmeline apologized to her sister-wives for writing weekly but explained that it was "an inward satisfaction to communicate on paper to absent friends when there is no other way of doing so," a desire that became a lifelong commitment.[29] Complaining in one letter that it felt as though she had been gone three months instead of three weeks, she again explained that she was not "dissatisfied" or sorry that she had agreed to move to Provo when her husband deemed it necessary, but only that she was lonesome for those she had left behind. Indeed, Emmeline's major complaint was the loneliness that all four of Daniel's wives felt without the other two. She especially missed Hannah, who seemed to be a favorite of them all. Hardly able to spell and unacquainted with proper punctuation or capitalization, despite her erudite sister Louisa, Hannah nevertheless wrote letters to her sister-wives. Feeling sensitive about some comments Louisa made relating to her grammatical insufficiencies, Hannah offered a possible solution. "Girls I am not going to write much this time Louisa made so much fun of my pore spelling and leaveing of capituls that I thought if I had time and knew how I would write all the alphabet in capituls and let you place them whare they belong for it is more than I know."[30]

By the middle of May, however, Emmeline admitted to being less lonely, as more of her friends and acquaintances began to arrive in Provo, though she still found the separation from Hannah and Louisa unpleasant. "I think I shall more fully appreciate and enjoy your society than ever," she wrote in anticipation of her return. "It has been <u>one of the greatest comforts</u> to me to have a sociable time with you...for the last 6 years, and to be deprived of it would indeed be an irreparable loss."[31] "One thing I can say truly," she wrote another time, "and that is that is [*sic*] I want to see you all just about

28. Emmeline B. Wells, letter to "Sisters," April 25, 1858, ibid.

29. Emmeline B. Wells, letter to Louisa and Hannah Wells, May 4, 1858, ibid.

30. Hannah C. Wells, letter to "Girls," n.d., Hannah Corilla Free Wells Papers.

31. Emmeline B. Wells, letters to Hannah and Louisa Wells, April 21, 25, 30, and May 4, 1858, E. Wells Papers, LDS Church History Library.

as bad as I ever wanted to see any one in my life."[32] The hope of returning to their normal life in Salt Lake City was reinforced by a conversation she had with Heber C. Kimball, who told her that "we shall go back to Salt Lake City, and we shall go back in triumph."[33]

During the few months she lived in Provo, Emmeline taught school in a tent erected next to the Beauvoir house. Her own daughters and three children of the other wives were old enough to attend her tent school. As a spur to the children in Salt Lake City, she reported to Hannah and Louisa that the three oldest girls had learned "all their letters" and could sing "babes in the woods" by themselves, and she hoped that her pupils at home were not neglecting their lessons.[34]

Because writing poetry was her primary means of passing the time, Emmeline sent additional samples to Hannah and Louisa. Although her first published poem, "Lines, on True Friendship," had appeared in the *Deseret News*, she was reluctant to let Daniel see other poems, not yet confident of their quality.[35] In 1855, when Hannah had accompanied Daniel to Fillmore to attend the one and only session of the legislature held there, Emmeline wrote to Hannah that she was "inclined to give you a specimen of my poetry," but did not want her "to submit it to the criticism of <u>your</u> husband," she explained. "It is all in my mind and has been for 2 or 3 days perhaps I will write it down and let <u>you</u> see it when you come home."[36] It was not long, however, before she was known as the family's poet laureate, and she often wrote long, epic poems for family celebrations, especially Daniel's birthdays.

Daniel remained in the city with other church leaders during that uneasy spring. Finally, after a series of negotiations, the army was permitted to march through Salt Lake City to their proposed encampment forty-five miles southwest of the city.[37] On June 30, after the troops had settled into

32. Emmeline B. Wells, letter to Hannah and Louisa Wells, May 14, 1858, ibid.

33. Emmeline B. Wells, from a Relief Society conference talk, April 3, 4, 1918, General Board Minutes, LDS Church History Library.

34. Emmeline B. Wells, letter to Hannah and Louisa Wells, May 14, 1858, E. Wells Papers, LDS Church History Library.

35. Emmeline B. Whitney, "Lines, on True Friendship," *Deseret News*, March 8, 1851, 1.

36. Emmeline B. Wells, letter to Hannah Wells, December 31, 1855, E. Wells Papers, LDS Church History Library.

37. One correspondent noted that the deserted city in June 1858 was "one of the most extraordinary scenes in American history." Albert G. Browne Jr., "The Utah Expedition," *Atlantic Monthly* 3 (1859): 490, as quoted in L. Arrington, *Great Basin Kingdom*, 192.

Camp Williams, their encampment in Utah County, Brigham Young advised the Saints to return home. Within the next two months, thousands returned to their homes and farms and businesses, which had suffered from months of neglect.

Emmeline returned to her own home and settled into what she thought would be the tranquility of a routine domestic life, caring for her children and enjoying the companionship of the other Wells wives. Her contentment, however, was suddenly shaken a year after her return by a startling message. James Harris was dead. Barely seventeen when he left her, James had followed his desire to become a seaman, and now, after years of silence, Emmeline learned that he had died at sea somewhere near Bombay, India. She was stricken at the news, and years passed before she could describe the scene when she received the news, which she did in verse:

Not thinking of the past, but of the present time,
The sudden news came like a funeral knell;
The message read, "He died on July twenty-nine,"
Nor more nor less of him it did not tell.

The memory of their wedding day with all its hopes for the future came vividly to her mind:

Just sixteen years had past, since on a summer day,
When both were in the bloom of youthful pride,
In a dear garden, old, thousands of miles away
They vowed to stand forever, side by side.[38]

She would cling to the memories, but this news from an unknown source finally brought closure to her brief life with James. Elizabeth Ann (Annie)'s birth on December 7, 1859, six years after Emmie's, brought the year and the decade to a happier conclusion. She gave her new daughter the name Elizabeth Ann, in honor of her beloved Elizabeth Ann Whitney.

Responsibilities flooded Daniel's life as he assumed his duties as counselor to Brigham Young. His territorial duties expanded, and as commander of the Utah militia he was central to overseeing the militia's response to an Indian confrontation in Manti, Utah, which flared into the full-fledged Black Hawk War, lasting from 1865 to 1868.[39] He was involved in nearly all of the skirmishes with Indians until 1870, when the militia was unexpectedly rendered inactive by Governor Wilson Shaffer, a non-Mormon, who

38. Emmeline B. Wells, "Faith and Fidelity," in her *Musings and Memories*, 224–25.
39. See Hinckley, *Daniel Hanmer Wells*, 117–33.

appointed Patrick E. Connor, commander of the army stationed at Camp Douglas in Salt Lake City, in place of Daniel.[40] Despite all of the other church and civic offices he held and the wide-ranging contributions he made to the territory, Daniel Wells was remembered most fondly in newspaper accounts and other biographical writings as General Wells, commander of the Utah Militia and Indian fighter.

While serving with the militia, Daniel was elected third mayor of Salt Lake City, a post he held for ten years. Overlapping the last three years of that office was his appointment as chancellor of the University of Utah in 1869, a position he held for nine years. He had previously been appointed supervisor of the Endowment House, which served, in lieu of a temple, for the administration of Mormonism's sacred rites—the endowment and marriage sealings.[41]

While Daniel was becoming ever more prominent and essential to the Mormon community, Emmeline was finding that her separate home kept her from the more frequent association with Daniel enjoyed by his other wives. Living apart from them gave her immense freedom in developing her own living pattern, which she valued, but she nonetheless missed the pleasure of a more constant presence of her husband. Home for Daniel was the spacious and comfortable "big house," where he could count on well-cooked meals, enjoy the association with sons as well as daughters, and make his choice of apartment for the night. She missed the conjugal relationship available in a more traditional marriage.

So she wrote Daniel another letter in January 1862. Annie was now two, and Emmeline was at once scolding and poignant in her letter, though less self-deprecating than in her earlier one. "Am I presuming to ask you to come to see me?" she began. "It really seems as if I might enjoy the privilege of your society for an hour or so two or three times in the course of a year." But after this rebuke, her tone changed, and she openly professed her love and longing for him. "If you only knew the influence it has over me for good perhaps you would not stay away quite so long.... When in your presence I am completely fascinated, irresistibly drawn toward you, and when deprived of your society for a long time, I seem shut out from the light, and left to

40. J. Allen and Leonard, *Story of the Latter-day Saints*, 345. See also Hinckley, *Daniel Hanmer Wells*, 133. An army division was posted in Salt Lake City in 1862 under Colonel Patrick Edward Connor to provide protection of the mail route (formerly assumed by Mormons) and also to keep them under surveillance. He established his camp east of Salt Lake City and called it Fort Douglas. J. Allen and Leonard, *Story of the Latter-day Saints*, 312.

41. In 1889, after temples became available in Utah, the Endowment House was razed.

grope about in utter darkness." With a tinge of self-pity, she continued, "I would not wish you to think me to[o] free and impassioned in my feelings towards you not least in expressing them—but you who are so loved so idolized by those around you cannot possibly know what it is to have no one to lavish affection upon you, and when my heart yearns toward you, and it seems almost impossible to smother my feelings and hide them—I may not even see you—and so I crush my feelings time after time until I actually become unamiable unsociable untidy and temptations crowd themselves into my mind." With a tone almost of desperation, she pleaded for a visit. "I consider it is very moderate indeed only to ask your company about twice a year—and I have never asked you from any motive of pride or selfishness or vanity—but simply the craving of my own heart, when I have asked you it has been because I felt as if I must see you and you have put me off each time, but do not again." Thinking that she could add nothing to the care and love with which he was surrounded in the big house, she nonetheless wrote of her own need for him. "I feel as if I must sometimes see you if I do have to ask, beg, intercede." Wary of writing too much, she concluded, "I will not say more, give me but a chance to say all that my heart is full of, and I will not tease you again for a long time, I would give more for your society one hour than I can possibly express." The letter is signed simply, "Yours Em."[42]

Whether Daniel responded from his sense of duty invoked by her chastising words or from compassion for the obviously lovesick young woman who needed him can only be guessed. It is likely that a combination of the two appeals touched a tender spot within, and he responded. Louisa Martha (Louie) was born later that year, when Emmeline was thirty-four. Louie would be the last of her children.

Emmeline also wrote a poem to Daniel at the time she wrote the letter. It is doubtful that she sent it along with the letter, but it expresses poetically what she had professed so passionately in her letter:

Wilt thou not condescend to come
Once more and spend an hour with me.
Or has thou quite forsaken one,
Who sues to thee for sympathy.
So lone and dreary is my lot
Thy presence brightens all things near,
Say wilt thou not come once again,
And future hopes and prospects cheer.

42. Emmeline B. Wells, letter to Daniel H. Wells, January 2, 1862, E. Wells Papers, LDS Church History Library.

Or do I ask this boon from one
Who feels no interest for me;
Alas if so how dark and drear
Must be my future destiny.

She signed it only "E."

In the meantime, her two Whitney daughters had grown into talented and attractive young women, and on October 1, 1867, seventeen-year-old Mell married twenty-year-old British convert William Dunford.[43] The Dunfords had settled in Bloomington, Bear Lake Valley, but William and his brother Alma remained in Salt Lake City to work and help provide for the large Dunford family.[44] William did not prove to be a successful employee, however, working only sporadically at a variety of jobs, seemingly unable to hold one for any length of time. The marriage thus worried Emmeline. His publicly known fondness for beer and tobacco was another element of concern. It was not long before her apprehensions materialized. With constant money problems, Mell was concerned about their two young daughters, Daisie Dean, born on June 5, 1868, and Verona May, born on December 11, 1869.

A separation and then reconciliation, the birth of their son, Leslie Alma, nor even Daniel's counsel could mend the marriage.[45] The five-year relationship ended in divorce in September 1872, and Melvina and her three children, for whom she was awarded custody, returned to live with Emmeline.[46] Though unable to care for them, William loved his children and visited them, brought them gifts, and took them on outings or to Bloomington for summer visits. He was keenly aware of the losses his alcoholism caused, but he seemed unable to subdue it. Too often, when William came to see the children, he was drunk, and Emmeline would not allow the children to be with him. She anguished over this failed relationship. Her hopes for a happy

43. E. Wells, Diary, October 1, 1889.

44. Isaac and Leah Dunford, William's parents, and their nine living children struggled during settlement in the Bear Lake area. While William fought the battle against alcohol, Alma took up dentistry, married Brigham Young's daughter Susa, and fathered two children with her before they divorced. See "Final Tribute Is Paid to Pioneer Dentist," *Deseret News*, February 6, 1919, 2; and Leah D. Widtsoe, "Alma Bailey Dunford."

45. Ruth Nelson Baker, "The Story of William Dunford, 1847–1891," photocopy in my possession, courtesy of Ruth Baker. Letters written by William and his brothers to their parents, Isaac and Leah Bailey Dunford, in Bloomington, Idaho, are included in Baker's biography of William Dunford.

46. *Melvina Dunford v. William Dunford*, Probate Court—September Term 1872, County of Salt Lake, Territory of Utah, Hon. E[lias]. Smith, Judge.

marriage "turned to mourning ere long," she wrote many years later, "and our hearts were more sorrowful than as if we had buried our loved one."[47]

Two years after Melvina's disappointing marriage, Isabel became the plural wife of Septimus W. Sears. He was all that William might have been—enterprising, ambitious, and successful. Also a British convert, he became a missionary soon after his conversion as a young teenager, and at age eighteen, he was appointed president of the Liverpool conference. He wrote for the *Millennial Star*, a Mormon periodical published in England, and began his work primarily as a merchandiser after emigrating to Utah.[48]

Sears had married twice before he made Isabel his wife. In 1865, he married Anne Chission, who died soon after their marriage, and in 1866, he married Mary Ann Needham. He and Mary Ann had four children. Isabel became his plural wife on April 11, 1869. This time, Emmeline had no apprehensions about the marriage. She may have realized that Belle would undoubtedly experience the feelings with which she herself struggled as a plural wife, but she had no doubts about the principle itself. On the twenty-fifth anniversary of Belle's wedding, she was grateful for the success of their marriage: "I can but feel how the hand of the Lord has kept watch and ward over her."[49]

As the forty-two-year-old Emmeline approached the threshold of a new decade, she had no way of knowing the path that life would yet take her. Her pleasure in Belle's happy marriage was countered by her worry over Mell's divorce and slow retreat from church activity. Almost debilitated by her unrequited longing for Daniel's affection and attention, she nonetheless kept her feelings close, the diary being her only catharsis. She would have years to perfect her defense for the inner workings of her mind and heart—work and more work—all for causes that became her raisons d'être.

47. E. Wells, Diary, October 1, 1890. Emmeline often reflected on Mell's unhappy marriage, noting that it was "such a sorrowful event to look back upon & yet when it transpired we thought it a grand affair" (October 1, 1888). "Nothing very pleasant about it," she wrote a year later (October 1, 1889), "except the dear girls Daisie and Verona." Leslie Alma had died by that time. This failed marriage brought sorrow to the entire family.

48. As a prominent Utah businessman and longtime secretary of the Deseret Agricultural and Manufacturing Society, Septimus Sears was featured in several newspaper accounts and other publications. Frank Esshom, *Pioneers and Prominent Men of Utah*, 1151. Esshom, "Utah Wheat," featured his business in transporting Utah wheat to England via San Francisco.

49. E. Wells, Diary, April 11, 1894.

CHAPTER 11

The Emerging Journalist
(1870s)

WHILE EMMELINE was privately brooding over Daniel, several events coalesced, adding a dimension to her life she could not have foreseen. Utah was gearing up for the end of its isolation. Passage of the Morrill Act in 1862, making bigamy a crime, put Utah in the congressional spotlight. The act provided a number of sanctions against the church for its support of polygamy, but had little effect at first. In time, however, it would be invoked in the federal campaign to dislodge polygamy as a protected form of marriage and reduce the controlling power of the church in Utah, all of which had tremendous impact on Mormon families.

After twenty years of settlement, Salt Lake City had become an appealing oasis amid the wide stretches of desert land that characterized much of the territory. A population of nearly thirteen thousand gave it the bustling aura of a nascent western urban center, and the russet visage of its earliest adobe dwellings and commercial buildings was interspersed with white plastered structures. Few homes were more impressive than Brigham Young's Beehive House, used primarily for church functions and the entertainment of important visitors. Tree-lined streets were bordered by small streams of water walled by stone casings. Flowers and fruit trees bloomed abundantly.[1] In 1862, the old Social Hall, a longtime venue for lectures, meetings, and socials, though still standing, had been largely replaced for dramatic presentations by the three-thousand-seat Salt Lake Theatre. Emmeline's substantial State Street home was centrally located, and her carefully nurtured garden added to the welcoming aspect of the city.

By the end of the 1860s, however, a more immediate alteration in Mormon life was Brigham Young's economic policies, abetted by completion of the transcontinental railroad in 1869. These policies included the

1. Neff, *History of Utah*, 890–91.

implementation of a cooperative movement in mercantile businesses, a voluntary reduction of prices for consumer goods by Mormon merchants to avoid patronizing Gentile merchants, and a ban on exploiting the mineral resources abundant in the nearby mountains in favor of agricultural development. All were meant to achieve Brigham Young's goal of economic self-sufficiency for the church. Cooperatives were established in various communities, with Zion's Cooperative Mercantile Institution in Salt Lake City as the parent company. Church members were urged to buy stock in their community cooperatives and utilize them as their primary source of retail goods.[2]

To bolster individual compliance with his correlative directive to retrench in material goods and lifestyle, Brigham Young called for the organization of junior and senior retrenchment associations for women in 1869. His daughters constituted the first junior association, and Isabella Horne, mother of fifteen children, presided over the senior association, selecting six women to serve as her counselors. Individual wards organized junior retrenchment societies, and meetings of the officially named Senior and Junior Cooperative Retrenchment Society were held semimonthly in the Fourteenth Ward, where members from all wards could discuss methods of retrenchment. Focusing on home production, the societies encouraged simplicity in dress, entertaining, home decoration, and food preparation.[3] Emmeline's teenage daughter Emmie attended the Junior Society of the Thirteenth Ward, within whose boundaries they lived, and in 1877, at age twenty-four, she became a member of the Young Ladies' Mutual Improvement Association (YLMIA), which evolved from the Junior Retrenchment Society.[4] Utilizing homemade goods was "de rigueur," and those who retrenched in their lifestyle were lauded by church and retrenchment leaders.[5]

To assist in implementing his economic program, President Young also found it prudent to revitalize the dormant Relief Society, which had not functioned on a church-wide basis since 1844 in Nauvoo, Illinois. Although

2. L. Arrington, *Great Basin Kingdom*, 195–256; J. Allen and Leonard, *Story of the Latter-day Saints*, 321–47.

3. See Carol Cornwall Madsen, "Retrenchment Association"; and Susan Arrington Madsen, "Mary Isabella Horne." Susa Young Gates discusses its origins in *History of the Young Ladies Mutual Improvement Association*, 29–41.

4. When the retrenchment movement lost force in the latter part of the century, the Fourteenth Ward meetings continued, their minutes published under the title of "Fourteenth Ward Meetings" in the *Woman's Exponent*.

5. L. Arrington, *Great Basin Kingdom*, 293–322; Leonard J. Arrington, "The Economic Role of Pioneer Mormon Women."

individual societies had formed during the 1850s to assist the ill-fed and ill-clothed Indians living in their midst, not until 1867 did Brigham Young call on bishops to organize Relief Societies in all the wards.[6] When some bishops hesitated, Young appointed Eliza R. Snow to encourage and assist them to follow this important directive.[7] Once organized in the wards, the Relief Society became an important element in fostering home manufacture, and several individual ward Relief Societies organized their own successful cooperatives. Emmeline became an early member of the Thirteenth Ward Relief Society and served as assistant secretary under the presidency of Rachel Ridgeway Ivins Grant for nearly twenty years. Within a decade, she also became a rotating companion, with others, to Eliza R. Snow in visiting Relief Societies throughout the territory, all of which marked the beginning of Emmeline's lifelong passion for the Relief Society.

The last rail completing the construction of the transcontinental railroad was laid at Promontory Summit, Utah, in 1869, bringing many newcomers to Utah.[8] Among them were eastern entrepreneurs eager to find financial success in developing the resources Utah offered, especially in the mining industry. Brigham Young's economic retrenchment program, implemented just as the territory was on the brink of new economic enterprises, seemed unprogressive and backward thinking to some venturous Mormon merchants. These disgruntled business-men formed a loosely knit group whose economic disagreements with Young's policy rapidly developed into theological differences. Known as Godbeites, from William Godbe, one of its leaders, they urged a return to unregulated free enterprise and openly rejected President Young's control over the economy, which brought them excommunication from the church in 1869. The next year, they established the *Mormon Tribune*, later named the *Salt Lake Tribune*, and with Gentile associates they founded the Liberal political party. They also established the Liberal Institute in 1871 that provided a venue for lecturers who brought a diversity of ideas to Salt Lake City audiences. In response, the Mormons established the People's Party, for which the *Deseret News*, founded in 1850, served as its voice. These were the first political parties organized in Utah,

6. Jensen, "Forgotten Relief Societies."

7. Eliza R. Snow, a wife of Brigham Young and a noted poet and probably the most prominent LDS woman at the time, did not officially acquire the title of president of the Relief Society until 1880, but most women viewed her as functioning in that capacity.

8. In 1870, the Utah population was 86,786, of whom 85,000 were Mormons (LDS), or 98.8 percent of the total. By 1884, the general population had grown to 168,600, the LDS constituting just 65.2 percent of the total. Statistics in the appendix included in Richard D. Poll et al., *Utah's History*, 692–93.

differentiated primarily on Mormon-Gentile lines.[9] The activities of these two parties and their competing newspapers characterized Utah politics for more than twenty years.

A polygamist, William Godbe decided that plural marriage was antithetical to his evolving spiritualist beliefs, and so he divested himself of his three plural wives, retaining his first wife, Annie Thompson. Two of his estranged wives, Mary Hampton and Charlotte Ives Cobb, along with Annie, became the first Utah women to join the National Woman Suffrage Association, organized in 1869.[10] Through friends of her mother, a former Bostonian, Charlotte also had ties with the more conservative American Woman Suffrage Association (AWSA), organized in Boston, shortly after the NWSA.[11]

Utah became a major player in the suffrage movement when it granted its women the vote in 1870, without agitation or campaigning from local or national suffragists.[12] The move was a surprise to easterners, given the general non-Mormon assumption that LDS women were pawns of church leaders and tools of a marital system that deluded and subjugated them. However, Utah women had voted on ecclesiastical matters since 1830, and editorials by the LDS Church–owned *Deseret News* had long demonstrated a progressive attitude toward female education and employment. By 1860, woman suffrage had been added to the social changes the editorial page supported.[13] Moreover, Wyoming's passage of a woman suffrage bill in

9. Ronald W. Walker, *Wayward Saints: The Godbeites and Brigham Young*, 212–31.

10. C. Madsen, *Advocate for Women*, 126–28, 144nn57–59.

11. Augusta Cobb abandoned her husband, Henry Cobb, and seven of her children, taking the two youngest, Charlotte and a brother, who died on the way, to Nauvoo in 1842 after meeting Brigham Young and joining the church. She was married to Brigham Young in November 1843 in Nauvoo, four years before her divorce from Henry. Years later, Charlotte's older brother James joined the church and also moved to Utah.

12. Ibid., 119, 120. Suggestions had been made in Congress to "experiment" with woman suffrage in the territories. Only Wyoming and Utah acted on the suggestion.

13. Editors during the 1860s were Judge Elias Smith, Albert Carrington, and publisher and apostle George Q. Cannon, who assumed editorship in 1867. The *News* reflected church leaders' views of fidelity to the ideal of equality, but also their recognition that in granting women the vote, the church would gain approval from national suffragists, double the Mormon electorate, and hopefully offset the notion of Mormon women's subjugation. For a discussion of woman suffrage and other legal rights experienced by Utah women, see Carol Cornwall Madsen, "'At Their Peril': Utah Law and the Case of Plural Wives, 1850–1900"; and Lisa Madsen Pearson and Carol Cornwall Madsen, "Innovation and Accommodation: The Legal Status of Women in Territorial Utah, 1850–1896."

December 1869 created a public mood in neighboring Utah conducive to granting the same privilege to its female citizens.[14]

The major catalyst for action, however, occurred in January 1870 when a group of "leading sisters" of the church met to discuss the antipolygamy Cullom bill, then being debated in Congress.[15] The meeting produced several resolutions: first, to demand suffrage of the federally appointed governor; second, to send two female representatives to Congress to personally present the views of LDS women; and third, to stage a rally to demonstrate women's support of polygamy and their fervent opposition to the Cullom bill. Though the first two resolutions were not acted upon, the third resulted in what was later described as "the great indignation rally," held in the Salt Lake Tabernacle a week after the organizational meeting. With the exception of a few male reporters, only women, numbering three thousand, made up the audience, who listened to twelve representative women express their loyalty to the church and its leaders and their unqualified support of plural marriage.[16] Without Emmeline's own account (no 1870 diary is extant), it could nonetheless be assumed that Emmeline, and perhaps her older daughters, were among those thousands of women, and when the Utah territorial legislature granted the vote to women the following month, she would have been among the first women to vote in the municipal election held shortly afterward.[17] She would also have been as eager as everyone else who thronged to meet Elizabeth Cady Stanton and Susan B. Anthony when they visited Utah the following year.

In 1871 when the two suffragists made their brief visit to Utah, they were acting on the invitation by William Godbe's suffragist wives, Annie, Mary, and especially Charlotte, to speak at the Liberal Institute. With the political and judicial power of the generally anti-Mormon federal appointees and their association with dissident Mormons, the Gentile residents in Utah had been able to establish a stronger presence than their minority status

14. See, for example, "Miss Anna E. Dickinson," *Deseret News Semi-Weekly*, June 23, 1869, 236; "Female Suffrage," *Deseret News Semi-Weekly*, December 5, 1868, 348; "Female Suffrage—Ends to Be Gained by It," *Deseret News Semi-Weekly*, March 24, 1869, 78; and "Female Suffrage in Utah," *Deseret News Semi-Weekly*, March 24, 1869, 78.

15. C. Madsen, *Advocate for Women*, 121–24.

16. O. Whitney, *History of Utah*, 2:391–405, recounts this meeting. Minutes of a meeting held following Utah women's enfranchisement are in Tullidge, *The Women of Mormondom*, 500–505.

17. Although Wyoming women were granted suffrage two months before Utah women, Utah held a municipal election prior to any election in Wyoming, so Utah women could justifiably claim to be the first women to vote. Thomas G. Alexander, "An Experiment in Progressive Legislation: The Granting of Woman Suffrage in Utah in 1870."

would suggest. But the two suffragists were aware of the preponderance of Mormon women in the territory and agreed to address them as well during their July visit.[18] As the only female voters in the nation, except for Wyoming's one thousand, these western women were an object of interest to Anthony and Stanton, who decided to stop in Wyoming and Utah on their campaign visit to the West Coast. Lecturing first in the newly constructed Liberal Institute to a full house, they later drew an audience of a thousand men and women to the old tabernacle on Temple Square.[19] As chief architect of the movement, Stanton formulated the philosophy behind their claims to equal political rights and greater educational and economic opportunity. For many years, she was also the chief orator of the movement. Standing before an audience of enfranchised women and men that hot July evening in the sweltering old building, she hardly needed to expound on the subject of woman suffrage. But, she said, now that Mormon women had the ballot, they were in possession of a political tool of singular importance to them. "If there were henceforth any slavery among [them]," or if "any social institution degrading to women" existed, "they held the power to rid themselves of it," and it would be their fault if they failed. Her audience could hardly have missed her point. Nonetheless, four hundred LDS women turned out a few days later to hear her lecture again. This time, she spoke with equal force about women's inferior status in marriage, the necessity of freer access to divorce, and the right of women to "voluntary motherhood, or the practice of birth control."[20] That she was not invited to return to Salt Lake City, Stanton deduced, was undoubtedly because of the "radical" nature of her lectures.[21] Her coworker Anthony, however, who

18. Carol Cornwall Madsen, "Decade of Detente: The Mormon-Gentile Female Relationship in Nineteenth-Century Utah."

19. Although the current tabernacle has been in use since 1867, the first, or "old," tabernacle, dedicated in 1852, continued to be used for a number of years after the new one was constructed.

20. For details of their lectures, see "Woman Suffrage," *Salt Lake Tribune*, July 1, 1871, 3; "Miss Anthony's Lecture," *Salt Lake Tribune*, July 3, 1871, 3; "Society for the Improvement of Women," *Salt Lake Herald*, July 8, 1871, 3; and "Susan B. Anthony at Salt Lake," *Salt Lake Tribune*, July 19, 1871, 3. Stanton's speech on voluntary motherhood is reviewed in "Woman Suffrage," *Salt Lake Tribune*, July 1, 1871, 3. "Local Items," *Salt Lake Tribune*, July 3, 1871, 3, indicated that a "very small audience" of Gentiles attended Susan B. Anthony's lecture at the Liberal Institute, where she spoke primarily on the value of the vote for working-class women.

21. Introducing a reprint of a *Salt Lake Tribune* article in her paper, *The Revolution*, Anthony noted that she and Stanton had evidently "thrown into the polygamic camp the bombshell of woman's individual sovereignty and direct inspiration from the heart of God equally with that of man." See "The Woman Awakening," *The Revolution*, July 1, 1871. See also Theodore Stanton and Harriot Stanton Blatch,

had confined her address to the necessity of woman suffrage in addressing the disabilities of working women, was welcomed back in 1895 to attend the Rocky Mountain conference of the National American Woman Suffrage Association.

Their visit kindled a nascent feminism within Emmeline. The women's rights message, which they presented in both venues, resonated with her as she remembered her mother's difficulty in providing for her large family when she was widowed. With no educational or economic resources available to her, remarriage was virtually Diadama Woodward's only viable option, and her second marriage, unfortunately, did not bring her the hoped-for stability she needed. None of Emmeline's marriages fulfilled the promise of lasting security, and twice she had faced the same challenge as did her mother. Though her options were broader than her mother's, she also met impediments to self-sufficiency. Twice a participant in plural marriage, she had learned the necessity of developing emotional and psychological self-reliance as well as economic. She realized early on that she had to be "self-supporting in and of myself" and "have the courage to endure" on her own. Yearning for the "strong arm to lean upon" that never seemed to be available, she acknowledged wistfully, "All my life-long this has been one of the principal features of my experience: to discipline myself to bear all things alone." However, she added, "it teaches one to be self-contained and to have strength of character."[22] Life's trials had their compensations, she believed. As the mother of five daughters, with one already touched by life's sudden detours, she was hopeful that they would learn early to develop what life had so dramatically taught her. She was determined, she wrote in her diary, "to train my girls to habits of independence so that they never need to trust blindly but understand for themselves and have sufficient energy of purpose to carry out plans for their own welfare and happiness."[23]

She was buoyed by Stanton's message of equality and the recognition of women's strengths and capabilities. Her editorials suggest she was also familiar with the works of Margaret Fuller, an early American feminist writer and editor of the *Dial*, a publication of the transcendentalists. As a devotee of the romantic tradition and the transcendental philosophy, Fuller enshrined the individual and its self-realization as a preeminent virtue and articulated these concepts in her feminist writings. From Fuller's works,

---

eds., *Elizabeth Cady Stanton as Revealed in Her Letters, Diary, and Reminiscences*, 1:237–40; and Alma Lutz, *Susan B. Anthony: Rebel, Crusader, Humanitarian*, 186–87. Kathleen Barry, *Susan B. Anthony: A Biography of a Singular Feminist*, 237–38, skips any mention of Utah in describing their western trip.

22. E. Wells, Diary, May 21 and June 27, 1876.

23. Ibid., January 7, 1878.

which Emmeline's own writings often evoked, Emmeline seemed to have found inspiration and validation for her own ponderings on women's status and potential.[24]

An even more immediate development that altered the domestic profile of Emmeline's life was the appearance of the first issue of the *Woman's Exponent* a year after the visit of Stanton and Anthony. In April 1872, its first editor, nineteen-year-old Louisa (Lula) Greene, announced its forthcoming publication scheduled for June. Edward Sloan, editor of the *Salt Lake Herald*, originated the idea of a woman's paper and its name. Sloan believed, perhaps in response to the Stanton-Anthony visit or the influence of the Godbeites, that LDS women ought to have a public platform of their own from which to speak for themselves to a censorious national press, pulpit, and public.[25] Ironically, the new publication promised that it would not contend against male privilege, champion any causes, or embroil itself in the woman question, a posture that seemed to controvert the idea behind its founding. This declaration soon slipped away unnoticed, however, as editorials and articles submitted by readers addressed these very issues in ever-increasing number and intensity. Within four years, the paper proudly noted that "Mormon women lead the van in the questions which are being agitated among the sex, whatever the world may think to the contrary."[26]

For Emmeline, the new publication offered a congenial outlet for the multitude of thoughts, interests, and opinions that claimed so much of her attention. It would also eventually be the vehicle that transported her ideologically from the insular outlook of many of her Mormon contempo-

24. Margaret Fuller, an early feminist, served as editor of the *Dial*, a newsletter for New England's largely male transcendentalist writers and poets, and conducted a series of "conversations" with women in Boston about issues of the day. Her major work, *Woman in the Nineteenth Century*, informed much of Wells's philosophy, including the conviction that woman possessed the power to reason, usually considered a male trait, as well as the power of intuition. The "thinking woman" was the ideal of both Wells and Fuller, and women, they advocated, should have all constraints against the development of their innate capabilities removed. See Nancy M. Theriot, "Mary Wollstonecraft and Margaret Fuller: A Theoretical Comparison"; Joel Myerson, ed., *Critical Essays on Margaret Fuller*; Paula Blanchard, *Margaret Fuller: From Transcendentalism to Revolution*; and Margaret Vanderhaar Allen, *The Achievement of Margaret Fuller*.

25. A full-length study of the editorial content of the *Woman's Exponent* is Carol Cornwall Madsen, "Remember the Women of Zion: A Study of the Editorial Content of the *Woman's Exponent*, a Mormon Woman's Journal." See also Lula Greene Richards, "How the *Exponent* Was Started."

26. "Our Position," *Woman's Exponent* 1 (June 1, 1872): 4; "New Volume and Women of Utah," *Woman's Exponent* 6 (June 1, 1877): 4; "Home Affairs: The *Woman's Exponent*," *Woman's Exponent* 6 (June 1, 1877): 4.

raries to a wide-ranging view of women's potential. She began submitting articles under the name Blanche Beechwood and frequently visited the *Exponent* office, then located on the corner of South Temple and First East, across from Brigham Young's Eagle Gate, leading to his property. The new journalistic enterprise intrigued Emmeline, and it is rather ironic that as an aspiring poet she did not use poetry for her earliest contributions to the *Exponent*, nor did she use her own name. Under her pseudonym, Blanche Beechwood, culled from her middle name and the alliterative name of the beech tree, she wrote a series of forty-three essays between 1873 and 1881.[27]

Though her daughters may well have been unaware of their mother's contributions, they did notice the time she spent at the *Exponent* office. Her frequent appearances there, they felt, suggested that she was in need of gainful employment or seeking some public recognition, which seemed inappropriate to them, given her position as the wife of a member of the First Presidency, a complaint that Emmeline commented on in her 1875 diary. Though it appeared "out-of-place to them," she wrote, she explained to her diary that she was "anxious to acquire a thorough knowledge of an Editor's duties."[28] She was indeed rapidly becoming addicted to journalism, and the essay form of prose proved to be a useful literary vehicle in which she could express ideas from her own experience and musings. One of her early Blanche Beechwood essays, "Young Ladies of Society," might possibly have been addressed to her own daughters. In it she chastised "those young ladies of society" who were embarrassed if their mothers took part in public activities or made themselves self-sustaining, elements of Emmeline's life her daughters would soon have to accept.[29]

Inevitably, as she had been drawn into the ideology of the woman movement, her own dissatisfactions as a woman smoothly metamorphosed into the general disabilities that many women faced in marriage and society at that time. Law, religion, and custom dictated a woman's position in both

27. Emmeline's favorite tree, the hemlock, did not lend itself for use as a pen name, and its association with Socrates's poisoned death was likely another deterrent. The use of pseudonyms was popular among women writers and journalists. Jane Cunningham Croly, a well-known journalist and eventual founder of the women's club movement, wrote under the name Jennie June from 1857 until her death. Popular novelist Sara Payson Willis Parton wrote under the name Fannie Fern. Journalist, poet, and author Sara Jane Clarke Lippincott used Grace Greenwood as her pen name. Twenty-three years later, after Emmeline had long abandoned her pen name, she encouraged women writers to use their own names. E. B. W., "Pen Names," *Woman's Exponent* 23 (September 15–October 1, 1894): 190.

28. E. Wells, Diary, March 24, 1875.

29. Blanche Beechwood [Emmeline B. Wells], "Young Ladies of Society," *Woman's Exponent* 5 (October 1, 1876): 70.

private and public realms, and Blanche Beechwood became an earnest spokesperson on behalf of change. For nearly eight years, she served as Emmeline's alter ego and did not disappear until four years after Emmeline became editor of the *Woman's Exponent* in 1877.[30]

The first essay Emmeline wrote under her assumed name was addressed to mothers and entitled "Take Care of the Boys." It confirmed mothers as the primary influence "over the mind of a child," since fathers were often "too much engrossed in business, to be able to attend to these duties; or abroad, preaching the Gospel." She noted that large families played a role in preventing the father from "paying such special attention to every member." A "mother's province is at home," she asserted, while a husband's church, civic, and business obligations, as well as his other families, in the case of polygamists, easily absorbed the majority of his time and attention, she wrote.[31] Two years later, Emmeline privately expressed her own frustration at raising a family virtually alone. "I have all the burden to bear alone," she complained; "no outward help my husband is too much engrossed with public affairs to devote much time or even sympathy to his family, therefore the care and responsibility devolves upon the mother."[32]

Astute readers might also have caught brief reflections of her marital relationship in other essays that became increasingly bold. Even as she wrote admiringly of those women "who have borne neglect in silence and in meekness," she also declared that "when men see that women can exist without their being constantly at hand, that they can learn to be self-reliant or depend upon each other for more or less happiness, it will perhaps take a little of the conceit out of some of them."[33]

In another expression of her marital grievances, Beechwood lamented marriages where the sole motive of women was to please their husbands and in doing so yet failed "to win one word of commendation from the husbands who have promised to love and cherish them."[34] She especially deplored those relationships in which husbands refused to apprise their wives of their financial situations, thus leaving their families vulnerable to unexpected changes in their fortunes. Moreover, she wrote, withholding information on a family's financial status denied husbands and wives a full partnership

30. Her last articles as Blanche Beechwood diverted from the feminist thrust of the early ones and addressed the subjects of manners and poetry.

31. Blanche Beechwood, "Take Care of the Boys," *Woman's Exponent* 2 (November 15, 1873): 94.

32. E. Wells, Diary, October 22, 1875.

33. Blanche Beechwood, "Here and Hereafter," *Woman's Exponent* 3 (January 1, 1875): 114; and "Why, Ah! Why," 3 (October 1, 1874, misdated September 30, 1874): 67.

34. Blanche Beechwood, "Marriage and Wives," *Woman's Exponent* 5 (July 15, 1876): 30.

in what affects them both.[35] That Emmeline was using the new publication as an outlet for her own personal grievances is a curious departure from her determined effort to hide them behind a facade of well-being. But she may have known that she was writing what other women had also experienced and was simply generalizing.

Perhaps intended more for herself than her readers, Emmeline/Blanche also counseled women to avoid lamenting their "cruel fate" if life did not treat them kindly, to control the impulse to go about "sorrowing and mourning," and to avoid heaping their troubles on others—certainly a self-directed cautionary word that she heeded throughout her life.[36]

Perhaps most revealing of these revelatory expressions is the essay "Real Women." Emmeline had often asserted that while she believed it possible that "man is what woman makes him," it is just as likely that "women are what men have made them." She argued that "women often disguise their true feelings because men trample on them." She observed that "it has become general among women to advise each other to disguise their real feelings, afraid to acknowledge them out of policy." She lamented that, too often, "a woman is simply a necessity in his establishment, to manage his house, to cook his dinner, to attend to his wardrobe, always on hand if she is wanted and always out of sight when not needed." Without "acknowledgment of wifely duties," the forty-six-year-old Emmeline concluded, a woman "seeks for happiness through another channel easier of attainment," the impetus for her own search for happiness.[37]

How well her pseudonym protected her anonymity is uncertain. Her submissions were handwritten, and at least the editor, Louisa Greene Richards (who married Levi Richards in 1873), would know the author. Beyond that, it is not known if even her daughters were aware of her submissions. After the publication of thirteen Beechwood essays, she decided to test the effectiveness of her hidden authorship. "If you should find out the veritable name of your weak, confessing scribe," she wrote, "think not the less kindly of her; and while with indefatigable industry and untiring patience, we exercise our powers of mind, and humble judgment in sounding forth our woman's opinion, although strongly enough expressed—judge not hastily or superciliously."[38]

35. Emmeline used a different pseudonym for this article, perhaps to doubly ensure the anonymity of the author: Emile, "A Defense," *Woman's Exponent* 4 (May 15, 1876): 190.

36. Blanche Beechwood, "Make the Best of It," *Woman's Exponent* 3 (September 1, 1874): 55.

37. Blanche Beechwood, "Real Women," *Woman's Exponent* 2 (January 1, 1874): 118.

38. Blanche Beechwood, "Why Some Women Write," *Woman's Exponent* 3 (March 15, 1875): 159.

After reading two guest editorials, which Eliza R. Snow, head of the *Exponent* committee, invited her to write in 1874, and several nostalgic pieces under the name "Aunt Em," Daniel for once in his life complimented Emmeline on her "literary acquirements," she noted. He even "spoke to Br. [George Q.] Cannon [a publisher] of my being a journalist."[39] Emmeline had cleverly written the first requested editorial in a way that required its completion in a second one.[40] She had spent several days writing them, hoping to please Eliza and the committee. "For my own part," she enthusiastically reported, "I would not be at all afraid. I love this kind of work."[41] Blanche Beechwood also appeared in the same issues as the two editorials. "Make the Best of It" advised women to accept circumstances they could not change, and "Our Fashionable Young Ladies" counseled young women to live for something other than the current trends of the day. She identified them as flirting, adopting popular though inappropriate styles of dress and behavior, spending money foolishly, and using slang, while forgetting the more desirable womanly traits of "grace, kindness, self-forgetfulness and true delicacy of behavior."[42] When the *Exponent* issues were delivered, she commented, "The Exponent came and the piece [not identified] I had written rec'd all sorts of comments, not altogether pleasant some of them."[43] Whichever piece evoked the comments, it was at least read.

Like her poetry and diary, Emmeline was discovering that prose could be cathartic to her volatile emotions. When particularly lonely one evening, feeling "the need of a friend to speak to," she consoled herself by writing an article for her paper. "It has been a solace to me in many lonely hours, yet there are times when one feels unfitted and incapaciatated [*sic*] for it."[44] Her *Exponent* articles and editorials, however, belied this self-deprecation. They were products of an informed and fertile mind, and Emmeline was discovering that prose could be as evocative as poetry.

39. E. Wells, Diary, June 3, 1875.

40. Ibid., August 22, 1874.

41. Ibid., August 24, 1874.

42. E.D., "Exhortative," *Woman's Exponent* 3 (September 15, 1874): 60; Blanche Beechwood, "Our Fashionable Young Ladies," *Woman's Exponent* 3 (September 15, 1874): 58. The two editorials she was invited to write are followed by the initials E.D., the only acknowledgments of authorship on any of the editorials in this volume, other than one by ERS (Eliza R. Snow). E.D. indicates that a guest writer wrote the editorial. The Blanche Beechwood pieces were not editorials.

43. E. Wells, Diary, September 19, 1874.

44. Ibid., August 19, 1874.

CHAPTER 12

Recompense
(1874–1875)

As she was taking the first journalistic steps that would lead her to a prominent, eventful future, Emmeline was very much the wife and mother, struggling to adjust to demanding circumstances in both roles. She never appeared to resent her acceptance of plural marriage. Indeed, she wrote that she had "never for a moment doubted the truth of the doctrine."[1] In both of her plural marriages, she loved and admired her husbands and enjoyed close relationships with her sister-wives.

These feelings were evident in her undiminished regard for Daniel. Despite the tone of bitterness in her Blanche Beechwood essays, she did not feel that sharing a husband had to curtail a close, if limited, conjugal companionship. She just wanted her fair share of Daniel. Promised visits did not materialize, and her disappointment was deep and long-lasting, often producing headaches and anxiety. "To see one person who shuns me," she wrote one despondent day, "would be more to me than all the rest who smile upon me and applaud me one word from him would be more satisfactory would yield me more contentment, than all else."[2] Thus, his surprise visit the day after their twenty-second wedding anniversary in 1874 brought a joyful response. "My heart gave one great bound towards him; O how enthusiastically I love him; truly and devotedly."[3] Her fervent wish was that he could—or would—reciprocate those feelings. "No one loves me," she grieved, "as him who has gone," remembering the patient tenderness and love of Newel K. Whitney. She had come to realize that as her child-bearing days began drawing to a close—she was forty-seven in 1875—"the associations of love and its duties" were over as well.[4] Daniel's birthday that

1. E. Wells, Diary, February 14, 1875.
2. Ibid., November 28, 1875.
3. Ibid., October 11, 1874.
4. Ibid., November 2, 1875.

year, however, drew only expressions of gratitude for her marriage to him. "O what a grand life his has been," she wrote. "How proud and thankful I am to have borne his name and to have so noble a father for my children."[5]

As Emmeline gradually shifted into a more public life, she was grateful for the household help that Daniel's financial support provided. She was not entirely relieved of all domestic duties, however. She mentions occasionally cooking for her family and friends, taking meals to the sick, and assisting in the seasonal preservation of the fruits and vegetables from Daniel's farm. It is telling, however, that soon after she became involved with the *Woman's Exponent*, she seldom mentioned to her diary any domestic activities or household chores.

During the decade of the 1870s, while Emmeline was learning the journalistic art, her household buzzed with the social and cultural activities of her daughters. They were all well exposed to the books that Emmeline provided, to piano and guitar lessons, to the study of German and French, and to the instruction of Mary Cook, a well-respected educator who, with her sister Ida, was instrumental in the development of the kindergarten movement in Utah. Both Emmie and Louie at different times assisted in their classes. The Salt Lake Theatre with its dramatic and musical productions and traveling shows formed a large part of their cultural development and entertainment. During the time that Mell and her children lived with Emmeline after her divorce, Emmie came of age, and between the two, Emmeline's home was a popular gathering place for young people. Mell and Emmie and their friends on many occasions "had a gay time singing comic and all that in the empty parlor down stairs," Emmeline wrote one evening. "How gay and joyous they were and how elastic and buoyant their spirits overflowing with wit and humor." When that group left to visit other friends, Louise (Louie), who turned twelve in 1874, arrived with "a crowd of little folks [who] came serenading and we were delighted with their merry voices and gladness."[6]

The casual conversations and informal gatherings took shape when the Wasatch Literary Association (or Club) was organized in Emmeline's parlor in January 1874.[7] The club was the brainchild of Orson Ferguson Whitney, son of Helen Mar Kimball Whitney and future apostle; Rulon S. Wells, son

5. Ibid., October 27, 1874.

6. Ibid., September 3, 1874.

7. The "Twentieth Ward Institute," organized a year earlier by John Nicholson and Septimus Sears, Belle's husband, was its inspiration. Only for men the first year, women joined the second and final year. Its object had been "the intellectual, moral, social and religious improvement of its members." Zina S[moot] Whitney, "Literary Work of the Past," *Woman's Exponent* 22 (September 1, 1893): 31–32.

of Daniel and Louisa and future member of the First Quorum of Seventy; and James Ferguson, a friend of the Whitney and Kimball families, from whose family Orson received his middle name. With the enthusiastic support of Emmie Wells and Mell Dunford who, like their mother, were devoted to literature and music, the Wasatch Literary Association came into being. William Woods, Daniel's non-Mormon nephew, then courting Mell, was an early member along with other scions of well-known LDS families. All were young, single adults, many of whom became not only prominent church authorities but also civic leaders, business and professional men and women, and educators.[8] Orson (Ort), grandson of Newel K. Whitney, was like a member of Emmeline's family, with a special fondness for Emmie. Proficient on the guitar, Emmie often accompanied Orson's vocals at the meetings of the Wasatch club and they performed on Sunday evenings when he joined the crowd of visitors at Emmeline's home. He adored Emmeline as well as Emmie and remained a friend and help to Emmeline throughout her life.

The club was ostensibly a serious endeavor. Its weekly meetings began with a "declamation" or oration and continued with the presentation of essays written by members, the frequent enactment of scenes from Shakespeare plays, the recitation of classical poetry, and the performance of instrumental and vocal numbers. It soon came to be noted, however, more for its aura of wit and good fun; its friendly, if sarcastic, criticism of each other's presentations; and the imposition of fines for a number of imaginative infractions, which clearly outdid the dues in keeping the organization solvent.[9]

Several male members of the association admitted that their main reason for joining was the presence of certain female members, and Mell and Emmie themselves were certainly draws. Some of the young men visited the Wells home without the excuse of a club meeting, and Emmeline was always pleased when the house was filled with young people. The Emmeline Wells home was fast becoming a center for culture, knowledge, conversation, and budding romance. Sleigh-riding parties, buggy rides, balls, parties, association meetings, and the theater often filled a week's schedule, and Sundays, after various ward or tabernacle church services, often found the

8. Orson F. Whitney, in *Through Memory's Halls: The Life Story of Orson F. Whitney*, 55–64, describes the Wasatch Literary Association's organization, dramatic and musical presentations, members and their eventual professions, and some of the witty commentary and repartee, as well as its eventual demise in 1878. See also Ronald W. Walker, "Growing Up in Early Zion: The Wasatch Literary Association, 1874–1878."

9. Orson F. Whitney, "The Wasatch Literary Association," taken from his *Through Memory's Halls*.

Wells home full of visitors, young and old. Along with the young adults, Annie's and Louie's friends also gathered at Emmeline's. With the care that Mell's three children occasioned, visits from Emmeline's sisters Adeline Marie and Ellen, her Relief Society work, and her writing, one might wonder when Emmeline had time to brood. Yet with all this activity swirling about her and her obvious enjoyment of it, only her own clouded mood could deem hers a "dull lonely common-place life."[10] There always seemed to be something missing.

Besides absorbing the festive mood that a crowd of children, grandchildren, and friends brought to her home, Emmeline watched the growing attachment of William Woods to her daughter Melvina. Will had moved to Salt Lake City in 1872 at age thirty-two to begin his law practice, followed by his sister, Eliza, and brother, Park, all three children of Daniel's sister, Catherine. William was eager to succeed in his law practice and made many friends in the city, but when Emmeline realized that Melvina was determined to accept William's proposal of marriage, her "feelings were harrowed up," since he was not a Latter-day Saint. She also continued to grieve over Mell's own distancing from the church. Having sacrificed so much for the Gospel herself, Emmeline could hardly bear to see her child so casually discard it. As their engagement proceeded during the fall of 1874, however, Emmeline struggled to know how to give her daughter "wholesome and timely advice." Though William was Daniel's nephew and Melvina his stepdaughter, this responsibility rested wholly on Emmeline's shoulders.[11]

Despite Emmeline's misgivings, the wedding date was finally set for November 7, 1874, and the family rallied to make it a happy celebration. When the day arrived, the new carpets and drapes, provided by Daniel, along with some new furniture, were all in place, transforming the home into a lovely showplace. Mell's two Dunford daughters, six-year old Daisie and four-year-old Verona, were beguilingly dressed in the white tucked dresses their mother had finished just in time for the wedding. "I never expected to have been so well off in my life," Emmeline noted. "I am pleased with all."[12] William asked his uncle Daniel to officiate at the ceremony, but in the end the Reverend Josiah Welch of the Presbyterian church performed the mar-

10. E. Wells, Diary, September 6, 1874.

11. Ibid., September 17, 1874. See also September 27, 1875. Besides his church and civic responsibilities, Daniel was deeply involved in several business enterprises. He developed the first coal mines in Summit County, managed three lumber mills, and established the gasworks of Salt Lake City in 1872, pledging all of his considerable real estate to launch these enterprises. At this time, they were all very successful. And he was very busy.

12. E. Wells, Diary, November 7, 1874.

riage.[13] Following the evening nuptials, the bridal party greeted the guests at Emmeline's home. When the couple left the party, Emmeline's unexpressed wish was that Will, who "seems in every way qualified to make a good husband," would be "ever tender," but only "time will tell the story truly."[14]

Despite the rhapsodic expressions of love and longing for her husband that dominate her diary during this period, Emmeline was beginning to find "a more easily attained channel of happiness," as she had noted in one of her Beechwood articles. Though she was fearful of being alone, at which time her mind conjured up "all sorts of weird fancies," she found that being alone with "plenty [of] folks within call" was pleasant.[15] Outings with friends sometimes drew her out of herself, and her family and their friends, as well as her own acquaintances, certainly kept her socially active. But the most effective "channel of happiness" during this period of melancholy led to a man named William Hendrie, one of the many entrepreneurs who flocked to Utah after completion of the transcontinental railroad in 1869. He established Hendrie's Bros. Mining Machinery company in Salt Lake City in 1874 to take advantage of the territory's newly opened mines. He was one of a circle of non-Mormon young men befriended by the Wells family through William Woods, Mell's new husband.[16] Woods invited William Hendrie to attend the Wasatch Literary Association, where he met Emmeline and her daughters and found the Wells home and its occupants cordial and welcoming.

Hendrie ostensibly began courting twenty-one-year-old Emmie, but neither Emmeline nor Emmie gave him much encouragement because of his non-Mormon status. In fact, Emmie was more often with her Wasatch Literary friends than with Hendrie, and there were few indications of a traditional courtship. Nevertheless, Emmeline's diary records his consistent presence—usually once a week or more—in the Wells home when he was in Salt Lake City. Emmeline's chronic despondency and sense of "dullness" were noticeably lightened when he was in town. "What pleasure his company always brings, how inspiring and invigorating his conversation is," she

13. The Presbyterian church, located on Second East and Second South, was dedicated just a month before the wedding, on October 13, 1874. "Presbyterian Church: Dedicatory Services," *Salt Lake Tribune*, October 13, 1874, 1. Both Mellie and Will attended the dedication. The proximity of the dedication to their wedding date may have prompted their decision to be married by Welch.

14. E. Wells, Diary, November 7, 1874.

15. Ibid., September 18, 1875.

16. Others in the group included Woods's law partner, W.P. Appleby; Eliza Woods's husband, C.C. (Ned) Wallin; and Ned's partner in the saddlery business, T.O. Tanner.

noted. "He brings a little variety to our monotonous life."[17] The frequency of his visits, his obvious regard and respect for Emmeline and growing fondness for Emmie, along with his fresh and stimulating conversation and fascinating worldliness provided wonderfully effective, if temporary, antidotes to Emmeline's persistent malaise. In fact, he seemed to seek out Emmeline's company as much as Emmie's, though he participated in many of Em's group activities as well as spending time alone with her.

In 1874, when Hendrie became a regular in the Wells daughters' social circle, he was thirty years old, living in the Walker House, a residential hotel popular with businessmen who did not want permanent housing. To gatherings of Mormon friends, he brought a certain sophistication and savoir faire that was particularly irresistible to Emmeline. But accompanying her pleasure in his company was an unquestionable desire to open his eyes to Mormonism. She recorded that the two of them spent an entire evening discussing his feelings regarding the Mormons he had met. "If only he could see the light of the Gospel," she lamented, "I should be so happy."[18] He often called at the Wells home with William (Will) Woods but frequently stayed behind to continue a conversation with Emmeline, "talking of past and present; soberly and earnestly," while Will and Mell left, taking the other callers and sometimes Emmie along.[19] His visits often lasted until midnight or later. "How near he seems to me," Emmeline wrote after one such evening. "I cannot account for it, it is a mystery; can it be that we were acquainted before we came here that our spirits are closely related."[20]

Emmeline convinced herself that Hendrie truly loved Emmie but felt that he spent relatively little time with her because he was "to[o] honorable to manifest more than the most sincere friendship under the circumstances," knowing that "Em. is true to the principles of her religion, and would not think of disobeying."[21] He may have been baffled by the concern over his religious status when Mell was even then engaged to Will, also a nonmember. His friendship with Emmeline was nonetheless genuine, and she was gratified that his pleasure in her company seemed to equal hers in his.

It was William Hendrie with whom Emmeline celebrated her twenty-second wedding anniversary—not Daniel. But Hendrie's attention could not evoke the depth of feeling that Daniel's presence the next evening occasioned. Her disappointment at his absence the day before disappeared, and everyone else was banished to the outskirts of her thoughts. "We never had

17. Ibid., April 24, 1875.
18. Ibid., August 13, 1874.
19. Ibid., September 5, 1874.
20. Ibid., August 9, 1874.
21. Ibid., September 21, 1874.

so striking an interview," she wrote. "It has left an ineffaceable impression upon me." At Daniel's leaving, "he gave me a parting blessing," she wrote, while still wishing that he could feel toward her "in any degree" the love she felt for him. "How happy it would make me," she confessed.[22] Whether she verbally expressed her feelings to him, she does not say, but it would likely be difficult for him to miss the joy she felt in his presence.

In the meantime, she looked forward to her visits with William Hendrie, and unable to accept his invitation to take a ride with him through the park one evening because of a prior assignment, she was inordinately disappointed, but, she rationalized, "perhaps it was all for the best, I pray God to give me wisdom to govern and control and guide all my finest and truest feelings of sacred companionship." But missing this opportunity to be with him gnawed at her. "How sorry I was, how unfortunate it seemed any other time almost I could have gone with him and now it just happened that I could not." She had been waiting for another opportunity to enjoy his company and conversation and "talk over some things that were upon my mind," she lamented, "and now just when everything seemed so desirable and favorable then fate was against me."[23] He always offered a sympathetic ear, and she rejoiced that they could freely talk "a little on every subject" to each other.

Business outside of Utah frequently called Hendrie away. Before one such departure, he tenderly told Emmeline that she "seemed like a mother to him" and that "he loved me as his mother." He explained that "to no living person had he opened his mind and confided the secrets of his heart as he had done to me," which of course brought her thrilling satisfaction and caused her to pray even more fervently that he would embrace the Gospel.[24] Her feelings for him, however, did not seem to be quite so maternally motivated. "What can be the cause of the feeling of nearness which is in my heart for him," she wondered. "It is an enigma to me I have tried every way in the world to put this feeling from me."[25] Were these simply motherly feelings that she was trying so hard to dismiss?

Hendrie's stay in Salt Lake City was only temporary, and he eventually

22. Ibid., October 11, 1874. What Emmeline said to Daniel during their satisfying visits is unknown, but she gradually ceased to write about her constant need for him.

23. Ibid., May 5, 27, 1875.

24. Ibid., October 15, 1874.

25. Ibid., December 11, 1874. Immediately following Emmeline's May 2, 1875, diary entry expressing her desire for Hendrie to convert to Mormonism, her daughter Annie, who took possession of Emmeline's diaries at her death, evidently felt her mother's effusive entries about Mr. Hendrie were unseemly and hastened to provide an acceptable explanation. She explained in the diary that "Hendry [*sic*] so often referred to was very much in love with my sister Emmie. An extremely nice man

returned to his home base in San Francisco before moving permanently to New York in 1878. After a four-year absence with no word, Emmeline was saddened at his silence. She wondered if their brief relationship had been just a transitory friendship, failing the test of time. That one of her earliest poems addressed the subject of friendship suggests how deeply she felt about the relationships she made and how much comfort that her cherished friends' abiding love, "reaching into futurity," was to her.[26] Sometime after Hendrie's last visit to Utah, Emmeline began writing a poignant and revealing set of verses that she called "Mizpah." The inspiration for the poem had come to her from Genesis 31:49.[27] She published the finished piece in the *Woman's Exponent* in 1879, a year after Hendrie's move to New York. The poem is a pledge of remembrance of and fidelity to an absent friend with a prayer that God will watch over the friends in their separation. It begins

> *I had a friend to whom I said farewell!*
> *And then the way seemed lone and dark for me;*
> *The unknown future, none save God could tell;*
> *To me 'twas all one great grand mystery. . . .*
> *And then I said I'll build an altar here,*
> *And "Mizpah" write, e'en as 'twere made of stone,*
> *That God may keep a watch, forever near,*
> *And bless the friendship that we two have known.*[28]

This short interlude in Emmeline's life, rather than becoming another bruising rejection and loss, restored her faith in herself and rallied her energies. "If there is a determination to succeed," she demonstrated once again, "no obstacles however opposing in their nature can hinder one."

---

educated wealthy good family but not a member of the Church. Mother idolized Emmie and desired her happiness but belief caused difficulties."

26. Ibid., December 10, 1874.

27. Ibid., September 12, 1877. Genesis 31:44–45 relates the meeting of Jacob and his father-in-law, Laban, in which they made a covenant of peace. Jacob raised a stone as a symbolic pillar and named it Mispah, meaning "watchtower." The phrase "The Lord watch between me and thee, when we are absent one from another" comes from that biblical incident. It was a theme of some poetic popularity. In 1890, Julia A. Baker's poem "Mispah" was published in *A Little Archive of Poetry* (no other publication data available) and in several other anthologies. In 1912, Baker's poem was also presented in a calendar with paintings depicting each verse. The poem was later included in a 1936 collection of the "country's favorite poems," *The Best Loved Poems of America*. Baker's poem retained its popularity for many years. Florence L. Snow's poem on the same theme, also entitled "Mispah," was published in *Poetry of Kansas* (Topeka: Crane, 1900), 100–101.

28. Emile, "Mizpah," *Woman's Exponent* 8 (September 15, 1879): 57, reprinted in E. Wells's *Musings and Memories*, 56.

CHAPTER 13

A Local Luminary

(1875–1876)

"ANY WOMAN WHO IS A WIFE cannot but regret at times however placidly they may appear outwardly this lack of conjugal affection.... [M]y nervous system is impaired with the trials I have undergone in silence and alone, how long O Lord," Emmeline pleaded in 1875, "must these things be."[1] Not the affectionate attention of a newly acquainted male friend, not the constant and happy swirl of social activities or the popularity of her young daughters, not the appeal of her home as a center of intellectual conversation and cultural expression, nor even her growing prominence and participation in civic and church circles could assuage the heart hunger that permeated every hour and held her so permanently in its thrall. "O my heart aches so. 'tis killing me by inches," she confessed.[2] "O will not God be merciful to me and give me power to overcome this terrible feeling of neglect which is preying upon me more than ever."[3]

Though Daniel was "very demonstrative" during their courtship and early days of marriage, his current indifference to their personal relationship was baffling to Emmeline. Even though they met more frequently than in past years, the meetings were often inadvertent and brief and merely added to her longing for more constancy and interest in her life and the lives of their children. In 1875, she was forty-seven, her Wells daughters were becoming more independent, and she yearned for "conjugal affection." Her life, particularly during this year, was measured by emotional extremes—true ecstasy when she was with Daniel, deep despair when she was not. "What can I do to gain favor in his sight," she wondered. "My home is a pleasant one my children are in every way perfect as mortals

1. E. Wells, Diary, January 7, 1875.
2. Ibid., December 5, 1875.
3. Ibid., December 4, 1875.

can be, I always meet him pleasantly though my heart is breaking."[4] These, however, did not seem to be strong-enough enticements. Even her health followed the waxing and waning of the emotional tides of her daily life. One exhilarating visit brought her rhapsodic pleasure, and her "whole affection went out to him in the strongest torrent of passion.... Nature seemed to have put on her divinest costume to welcome in the new and all absorbing love dawning upon my soul" and provided her "a bridal tribute," she declared.[5] But another visit less than a week later brought a "cooly indifferent" Daniel to her doorstep. "We poor women must not expect aid or succor from our husbands in affairs of the heart," she observed.[6] The next day, however, Daniel dropped by the *Exponent* office where she was working, and their conversation on the walk to her home made the day another "one to be recorded in memory's tablets forever, something entirely unlike any other experience of mine."[7] What was clearly a romantic obsession held her tightly in its grasp, one that "engrosses all my time and attention," she acknowledged, and "takes from me all idea of things which are immediately connected with my everyday life and makes my thoughts most abstracted from what should occupy them."[8] When Daniel visited Emmeline two days after their twenty-third anniversary, he made no mention of it. Nevertheless, Emmeline was clearly aflutter with joy at his belated sign of attentiveness.

This pirouetting relationship created a dizzying turmoil that left her constantly and dismayingly emotionally unbalanced. As she unleashed her feelings to her diary, her confessions seemed to intensify her self-pity and emotional cravings. Instead of relieving them, they seemed to feed on each other and take permanent residence in her heart and mind. Surely, the long soliloquy she wrote near the end of 1875 displayed a mind wholly given to this obsessive desire. "Although one's spirits will revive a little with the weather," she wrote on a sunny winter day,

> yet a depression of such a nature as is calculated to sadden cannot be thrown off in a moment, and one must struggle long before they can overcome such an overwhelming torrent of feelings that master you, as has crushed me, during the last few weeks. When one places implicit confidence in a friendship that has seemed more than heaven, more than the ties of blood or any close connection I say

4. Ibid., January 7, 1875.
5. Ibid., July 13, 1875
6. Ibid., July 29, 1875.
7. Ibid., July 30, 1875.
8. Ibid., October 12, 1875, written two days after their twenty-third wedding anniversary.

> when these hopes are shattered and all the golden chords loosed the silver bowl broken, when we can never again trust to these ties, when we have only ruined hopes to cling to and all is shrouded in darkness, what shall we do, or where shall we re [crossed out] turn, if we have made ourselves an idol and hedged it round with all our loving thoughts, clothed it in bright glowing idealistic costume, created a shrine wherein to worship it, and in all earnestness and sincerity, have made our vows consecrated with a baptism more sad and solemn, than that of any church rite; This it is that crushes the life-blood and fills the soul with despair.[9]

This long peroration of unrequited love marked the apogee of her great store of emotional heartache regarding Daniel. From that point on, she was less at its mercy, more resigned to his absence. Her life with Daniel, she now realized, was to be nothing more than a casual companionship. As her work with the *Woman's Exponent* escalated when she became associate editor in 1876 and editor in 1877, and as her association and correspondence with national figures increased during the next few years, references to Daniel became offhand and uneventful. She noted his visits to the *Exponent* office, his appearances at her home to give blessings of relief to the chronically ill Emmie, and other occasional meetings, but only brief residues of anguish found place in her diaries.[10] While the heart hunger was never sated, her "mind-over-matter" attitude was taking hold and allowing her to sublimate her longings in the events now crowding into her life.

With so much of her life lived internally, and her diary as her most intimate companion, it is little wonder that Emmeline often felt alone and misunderstood. A long day at the *Exponent* office sometimes evoked self-pitying effusions that might well have been part of her prebedtime decompression. "I came home very late," she wrote one weary night, "and with such an aching heart—feeling that my dearest friends did not understand me; and that there was a void in my heart that none of my friends filled though I had so many of them."[11] Even with crowds of people in her home, she felt that there was "no place and no companionship" for her.[12] This frequent complaint stemmed from the chasm between her inner and outer selves. Given that her briskly cheerful self-presentation only masked

9. Ibid., November 27, 1875. Emmeline reversed two words in this quotation from Ecclesiastes 12:6: "or ever the silver cord be loosed, or the golden bowl be broken."

10. Ibid., February 27, March 18, April 4, 12, 30, 1876.

11. Ibid., October 13, 1876.

12. Ibid., November 21, 1875.

but did not alleviate her secret misery and longing for tender affection, it is not surprising that misinterpretation of her motives or her words and actions was almost inevitable.

Her five years as a plural wife to Newel K. Whitney, especially considering the church's unstable status during those years, could hardly have prepared her for the daily exigencies of a long relationship in polygamy. But she certainly knew from her conversations with other oft-complaining plural wives that they also felt the loneliness and neglect that characterized her own experience. Yet the heart-wrenching disclosures of her diary express how profoundly she felt their impact and the intense effort she expended to keep her emotional anguish out of view. "I cannot bear to show any signs of sorrow or feel bad before any one," she exclaimed, despite the fact that she longed "to speak to some one who would comfort me."[13]

Adding to her despair during these years were Emmie's continual spells of an undiagnosed illness. Several times each year, she was immobilized by pain and nausea, often lasting for days. Healing blessings brought temporary relief, and doctors were summoned only occasionally. When Emmie was injured by a falling bookcase one day, Emmeline lamented the fact that she was her only caregiver, with "no strong arm to lean upon only myself and my faith in God my Heavenly Father."[14] She knew that "many women of my temperament have a husband whose affections are at such times comforting," but she had no one. Yet, as she often explained, "I would rather suffer agonies in my feelings than to say even to my husband I am in need of sympathy."[15]

The strain of Emmie's chronic illness was easily exacerbated when any of her other daughters fell ill. Lamenting that she always bore such burdens alone, both physical and emotional, she often felt she could not "endure much more." "O," she exclaimed, when clearly overwrought, "if my younger girls must suffer so I would rather they should die."[16] In more lucid moments, she wondered what she would do without them.[17]

Ironically, the marital bonds that linked Daniel and Emmeline in such loose emotional attachment nonetheless held her in a firm economic grasp. "This is a wearisome kind of life to live," she complained in 1875, "to be no one's particular or special care and yet not be independent." Eighteen years of a separate home from the other families created more than physical distance.

13. Ibid., January 14, May 17, 18, 1875.
14. Ibid., June 27, 1876.
15. Ibid., May 17, 1875.
16. Ibid., October 22, 1875, May 21, 1876.
17. Ibid., September 30, 1874.

She was the manager of her home but did not own it or the household goods, nor did she have any decision-making authority regarding it or the income that supported the families.[18] "If I were a widow or old maid then I could do just as I pleased, but to be bound hand and foot and have no power to act and then to be found fault with" was exasperating for this intelligent and independent woman. Criticized, "according to the notion of my husband's steward," as being "so extravagant, so lazy[,] so everything that is bad," Emmeline felt the weight of another layer of despondency.[19] She chafed under such blind economic dependency.

As her emotional cravings for a love denied turned to resignation, Emmeline redirected her attention to her life outside her marriage. Besides her constant contact with members of both the Whitney and the Wells families, she entered into activities in her ward, which led to even further opportunities and relationships. The Thirteenth Ward, which the Wells family attended, covered a nine-block area, with Third East and Main Street its east and west borders and South Temple and Third South its north and south borders. Both LDS and non-LDS structures stood within its boundaries. Walking along State Street on which her house was located to visit the "big house," Emmeline could look south along the street and see the Seventies Cultural Hall, an important LDS meeting and lecture site, and as she proceeded north toward South Temple, she would pass by the Salt Lake Theatre and the Social Hall. By the 1870s the ward borders encompassed five hotels and three churches that provided religious services for Catholics, Methodists, and Episcopalians. On its inner streets, Emmeline might pass some of the eight saloons and taverns, whose beverages quenched the thirst of Gentiles and more than a few Mormons. The Liberal Institute, a Gentile lecture hall, just a short distance from her house, was probably the most forbidding of the structures in the area. To Mormons it represented the defection of some of the church's brightest intellectuals and successful merchants, members of the Godbeites, who financed its construction. But Emmeline frequently attended the lectures held there, as did many from

18. In 1876 an unsuccessful attempt by the US Land Office to seize the lumber from Daniel's three lumber mills that it claimed were on public land (the sale of the lumber being one of his major sources of income) alerted the family to the volatility of business enterprises in which Daniel had invested. Bryant S. Hinckley, "Building a Commonwealth," in his *Daniel Hanmer Wells*, 309–23, esp. 321–22.

19. E. Wells, Diary, November 6, 1875. In light of her husband's financial difficulties, which would only increase over time, she wondered how she would "get some means to relieve me from embarrassment." Six weeks earlier, she had lamented that it was very hard "to get along with darkness in regard to means of living, etc." Ibid., September 27, November 9, 1875.

the Mormon community, seizing the opportunity to hear some of the country's prominent men and women who made Salt Lake City a stop on their speaking tours.[20]

The Thirteenth Ward meetinghouse, built in 1861, was one of the superior buildings in the city. A major feature was its stained-glass windows. Lighting emanated from two large bronze chandeliers that enhanced the drapes at the windows and pulpit, all in crimson red. A large map of the Western Hemisphere decorated the walls. Some years later an Assembly Room was added, used originally for a ward school but more often rented to various groups for lectures, funerals, dances, and meetings. The building reflected the congregation's appreciation of the artistic attention given to the building's construction and interior design.[21]

In 1867, when Brigham Young called for organization of church-wide Relief Societies, the Thirteenth Ward bishop, Edwin Woolley, selected Rachel Ridgeway Ivins Grant as president, with Annie Godbe and Margaret Mitchell as her counselors.[22] When the Relief Society presidency was reorganized in 1870, Rachel Grant retained her position as president and selected Bathsheba W. Smith, wife of apostle George A. Smith, and Lydia Ann Wells, Daniel's wife, as her new counselors. Elizabeth Goddard was appointed secretary, and Emmeline Wells began her long tenure as Elizabeth's assistant.[23]

Besides substituting for the secretary in her absence, Emmeline regularly contributed fifty cents to the temple fund and goods or money to the poor of the ward. She often spoke at the meetings, encouraging the women to speak themselves, as she learned to do, and to actively pursue participation in the economic programs outlined for the Relief Society, such as saving wheat for emergencies and supporting the associations for young people as they became organized. Over the years, as her suffrage activities and Relief Society responsibilities increased, her attendance at the Thirteenth Ward became less regular, but she retained her secretarial position and continued her donations for nearly twenty years.[24]

20. See Ronald W. Walker, "'Going to Meeting' in Salt Lake City's Thirteenth Ward, 1849–1881: A Microanalysis."

21. Leonard J. Arrington, *From Quaker to Latter-day Saint: Bishop Edwin D. Woolley*, 381, 390–91, 337.

22. Ibid., 425–26.

23. E. H. Goddard, Sec'y, "Letters," *Woman's Exponent* 5 (June 1, 1876): 5. Lydia Ann and Emmeline were both released from their positions in 1890 when they moved from the ward.

24. Relief Society Minutes and Records, Thirteenth Ward, Ensign Stake, 1849–1908, various dates between 1870 and 1890.

The Relief Society gave Emmeline opportunity to learn valuable leadership skills. She had once declined an invitation to speak at the Fourteenth Ward retrenchment meetings because she "did not feel confidence to rise up." But a few months later, when she accepted the invitation to preside at a meeting of the ward Relief Society's visiting teachers' meeting, she noted that it was the first time in her life that she had ever presided but concluded that she "got on excellently well." So well, in fact, that within a month, she was asked to permanently preside over the teachers' meetings. "I feel deeply the great responsibility resting upon me in being called to fill this public office," she wrote, adding that she hoped "to be guided and sustained by the Holy Spirit in this calling and duty" so that she would be humble and "qualified to do all things that are required" of her. Her motivation, she admitted privately, was that she would please Daniel "and gain his good will and favor."[25]

When she spoke at a retrenchment meeting in the Eleventh Ward, she remarked that it was "the first time in my life that I ever spoke in public before men."[26] She may have been inspired by the counsel given at a meeting of the general Retrenchment Society the month before, where the members learned that "it is as essential for the sisters to learn to preach as for the bretheren [*sic*]."[27]

Emmeline's daughter Emmie served as a counselor in her ward's Young Ladies' Retrenchment Society, subsequently the Young Ladies' Mutual Improvement Association (MIA). In the meantime, twenty-one-year-old Junius Wells, son of Hannah Free and newly home from a mission, was asked to organize a Young Men's Mutual Improvement Association in the ward. By 1878, membership in the Young Men's and Young Ladies' MIA exceeded that of the Wasatch Literary Association, which ceased to function that year.[28] Many of its former members continued to frequent the Wells

25. E. Wells, Diary, October 3, 1874, February 4, April 1, 1875.

26. Ibid., March 15, 1875. For most of the nineteenth century, it was deemed improper for women to speak before a mixed audience. In Utah, however, Brigham Young encouraged women to speak in their Relief Society meetings and acquire the ability to address an audience. In earlier days, the teachers who visited ward members monthly constituted a "quorum" with its own slate of officers and meetings, all under the direction of the ward Relief Society presidency. Visiting teachers had the responsibility to visit ward members to collect donations and to dispense goods where needed.

27. Co-operative Retrenchment Society, Minutes of Meetings, February 6, 1875. Eliza R. Snow also encouraged women to learn to express themselves in public. See Derr, Cannon, and Ursenbach, *Women of Covenant*, 92–93.

28. By 1878, with some of its male members on church missions, away at school, or otherwise occupied, including Orson F. Whitney, its leading spirit, who had been absent the previous two years while serving a mission, the association could

household, however, and Emmeline often noted in her diary that "the house is full of boys as usual."[29] If they were not visiting her daughters, her daughters joined them in summer excursions to Brighton Canyon, performances at the Salt Lake Theatre, the warm mineral springs north of the city, or enjoying the wares of the Globe bakery and the ice cream parlor. It was a frenetic time in the Wells household.

Church attendance was not the same measure of orthodoxy during these early years as it came to be in the twentieth century. Sunday services in the Salt Lake City wards were usually sparsely attended, if held at all, since churchgoing members could attend the Sunday-morning or -afternoon service in the tabernacle.[30] Emmeline's attendance at church is indicative of the casual approach to Sunday meetings. The Sabbath was often spent visiting and giving or attending family dinners or other friendship gatherings. One May Sunday, Emmeline "went to have strawberries and cream for the first time this season. [W]e all went together, then Lou. [her daughter] and I went to meeting. Afterwards saw Lula Richards and we called on Mrs. Staines; were pleasantly entertained for a few minutes or half an hour; returned home to find a housefull [*sic*] of young people." To round out the number of visitors, her sister Lucy and several other Woodward relatives came by later that day.[31] On another Sunday, she went to her daughter Mell's home for dinner in honor of Daisie's eighth birthday. "We passed a very pleasant day Belle came down [from Ogden] with her children to give them an out[ing]. In the evening Mr. Andrews [a Chicago acquaintance] called to bid us goodbye. The Wasatch crowd were here most of them. I went up to the Post Office with Frank Kimball and we went and had ice cream."[32]

Before Mell's marriage to Will in 1874, he and his friends spent many Sundays at the house, and there was little cessation of activity afterward. On Sunday, November 8, just days after the wedding, Emmeline wrote, "Stormy and dark Louie went down to show Mellie's servant how to arrange breakfast, Annie took Daisie and Onie [Verona] to Sunday School, it was prize day Lou. Came home and went—Ort, Budd Hebe & Heber Grant called, Ort staid and spent the day, Adeline & Inez were here to dinner, Will. & Mell called on their way up to Lile's to dinner; Ort has been playing and singing nearly all day; this evening Charlie Addie & May [Earl] called

---

not compete with the more inclusive and church-sponsored Young Men's Mutual Improvement Association. Some of the women had married and ceased activity in the association as well.

29. E. Wells, Diary, May 16, 1875.

30. William G. Hartley, "Common People: Church Activity during the Brigham Young Era."

31. E. Wells, Diary, May 7, 1876.

32. Ibid., June 4. 1876.

as they were going to church, Mr. Hendrie arrived today at eleven."[33] These were all typical Sundays, full of visitors, young and old, dinners, sociability, visits with friends and family, and occasionally church services. Sundays in the Wells household were hardly sober, quiet, church-filled Sabbaths during these years of active family life.

Holidays were similar to Sundays. Christmas in 1874 required at least a day of preparation, and gifts were exchanged on Christmas Eve.

> We have been very busy today putting down carpets, and changing things in the upper rooms; in the afternoon while we were all out of the parlor a friend of ours [Mr. Hendrie] left a parcel upon the table; A book for me Elegant Poetical Extracts by [John] Watson; a gold pen with pearl-handle for Em. and candy for the girls; Park [Nehemiah Park Woods, Will's brother] bought hats for Daisie & Onie, Will bought shoes for Mellie and Daisie; and candy nuts etc. for all Mell. had Will a pair of slippers embroidered and made up and Wallin, [Daniel's nephew-in-law], even brought candy for the th [crossed out] children; the Esq. [Daniel] broug[ht] candy & nuts, Belle sent me a very pretty lamp-mat and Inez [Emmeline's niece] gave me a pair of zephyr [fine wool] cuffs of her own crocheting; I gave Em. & Mell a ruffle also Annie & Louie a book mark we passed a very pleasant evening were up until after midnight.[34]

Christmas Day continued the celebration. "We were sewing until three o'clock," Emmeline wrote, and "then we all went to Martha's to dinner; Park Will & Mell Lile and Ned, Hannah Abbie and Junie, and myself—the Esq. dined with us on Turkey plum-pudding mince-pie etc. Lydia Ann invited Em [Emmie]. An [Annie]. Lou. [Louie] came home at dusk Em. went to the party in the fourteenth ward with Harry Emery and Lou. with Parley [Paralee] Kimball."[35]

Though a sometime attendee at Sunday meetings, Emmeline seldom missed the Thursday Fast and Testimony meetings or the ward Relief Society meetings when she was not away. She expanded her range of friends

33. Ibid., November 8, 1874. Prizes were given for attendance at Sunday School, and evidently Daisie and Onie were hoping to win one. The four young men were all members of the Wasatch Club. Adeline Maria and her daughter Inez Earl were Emmeline's sister and niece. Charlie, Addie, and May (or Mary) Earl were Adeline Maria's other children. Lile (Eliza) was William Woods's sister, married to C. E. (Ned) Wallin. Eliza and William were niece and nephew to Daniel Wells. Hendrie was the friend of whom Emmeline was particularly fond.

34. Ibid., December 24, 1874.

35. Ibid., December 25, 1874. Hannah Free Wells was Emmeline's sister-wife, and Abby and Junius Wells were two of her children. The other two were friends.

by attending the semimonthly Retrenchment Association meetings, held in the Fourteenth Ward on Saturdays. The meetings provided a forum for Eliza R. Snow to encourage the sisters in their duties as Relief Society members and elicit their cooperation in supporting Brigham Young's plan of economic self-reliance. Here, also, Emmeline continued to gain confidence in public speaking, as she participated in these "Quaker-style" meetings at which women spoke spontaneously and without advance preparation.[36] From these early associations, Emmeline began to realize the strength of women's collectives in accomplishing goals and influencing policies.

During this bustling time of activity, Emmeline entertained her mother's friend Louisa Barnes Pratt for a month while she was in Salt Lake City negotiating the sale of some property.[37] Louisa found Emmeline to be welcoming and pleasant. "I was quite happy with her," Louisa wrote, "as she ever manifested the greatest interest in my peace and comfort, acting the part of a daughter in every particular.... When my spirits were worn and weary on account of perplexity in my business I felt no where so relieved and comforted as with sister W., in one of her private rooms where I could make my complaints and receive sympathy."[38] With burdens of her own, Emmeline maintained her resolve to cloak her own problems against public perusal.

The unfolding dynamics of Emmeline's strong and engaging personality and the growing breadth of her contacts brought her into membership in the circle of leading sisters in Mormon society, the most notable of whom was Eliza R. Snow.[39] Snow held a unique position among the women of the

36. Gates, *History of the Young Ladies Mutual Improvement Association*, 29–41. See also C. Madsen, "Retrenchment Association." Later, the association became the Ladies Semi-Monthly meetings or Fourteenth Ward meetings, their minutes printed in the *Woman's Exponent* for most of the thirty-five-year history of the association. Relief Society business, parenting, church events, and spiritual experiences and testimonies made up the content of the meetings.

37. E. Wells, Diary, October 7, 1875. Addison and Louisa Barnes Pratt had been temporary guardians of Emmeline's brother Hiram during their mission to Tahiti in the early 1850s. The Barnes family had resided in Warwick, Massachusetts, where Louisa was born in 1802, not far from North New Salem. She lived there until she was eight. The elder Barneses and Woodwards were acquainted during their shared Massachusetts days.

38. Ellsworth, *History of Louisa Barnes Pratt*, 354.

39. Makeup of this select group is noted in Maureen Ursenbach Beecher, "The 'Leading Sisters': A Female Hierarchy in Nineteenth-Century Mormon Society." Though unity and cohesiveness were visible Mormon attributes at that time, a class structure based less on wealth than on church position clearly obtained. The emphasis was somewhat different in the female social system, which recognized family relationships and church position, but also wealth and urban residence.

church. Her approval was sought in almost every venture involving women. She was a counselor to Isabella Horne in the Retrenchment Association, a member of the *Woman's Exponent* committee, "matron" of the Endowment House, and, though not formally installed as general president until 1880, had served as de facto head of the Relief Society since 1868, the highest ecclesiastical position for an LDS woman. While some of those women included in this small coterie of distinguished LDS women gained their prominence through their relationship to church leaders, many paths led to Emmeline's inclusion. Though she was the wife of a member of the First Presidency of the church, none of Daniel Wells's other wives quite achieved the status of "leading sister." Most important of Emmeline's credentials was her association with the *Woman's Exponent* and its expanding value as a communication network for the women of the church and a connection with national women's leaders. Her intelligence and leadership qualities were also becoming well recognized.

Emmeline was not averse to enjoying the reflected eminence that association with the leading sisters gave to all so favored. She occasionally called on Eliza R. Snow, twenty-five years her senior, for advice and visited with her at the semimonthly Retrenchment gatherings and at meetings of the advisory committee for the *Woman's Exponent*. She also traveled with her to Relief Society conferences and participated with her on the planning committee for a women's Centennial Exhibition scheduled for July 1876. Yet she never felt personally close to Eliza. She admired and respected her for her many gifts and dedication to the church, but they differed in personality and in their views of the world outside the boundaries of Mormondom. Whereas Eliza was insular in her feelings, seeing the world outside the church as a misguided and evil Babylon that Mormons had gratefully escaped, Emmeline looked outward, hoping to make friends beyond the Mormon circle, gleaning from them all that could broaden her own worldview and enhance her understanding of the world in which the church functioned. She was in every sense a bridge builder, wanting to create respect and acceptance for the church and especially its women and eschewed those who chose to withdraw into its familiar and comfortable bosom. She welcomed the tourists who began visiting the office of the *Exponent*, and it soon became a magnet for out-of-town visitors by serving as a quasi-information center.[40] In July 1875, forty correspondents and editors from New England and the Eastern Seaboard visited Utah for three days.[41]

40. E. Wells, Diary, March 28, July 13, 1881, March 10, 1889. See also October 14, 1881, May 3, 15, 19, 24, 1883, as samples of her responsibilities and concerns.

41. "Eastern Editorial Excursion," *Salt Lake Tribune*, July 10, 1875, 4; E. Wells, Diary, July 11, 1875.

Many came to the *Exponent* office, where Emmeline made arrangements to exchange papers. In her newsy "Home Affairs" column, she noted that they were persons of "cultivation, polish and refinement" and was pleased that they had found the *Exponent* to be "a very creditable Woman's paper."[42]

She enjoyed meeting the friends of her son-in-law Will and her non-Mormon friend William Hendrie, and her diary is studded with names of the visitors to her home or to the city, as if she did not want to forget those people who brought so much interest and so many new perspectives into her life. Emmeline was remarkably at ease with these non-Mormon visitors and found her hospitality reciprocated.[43]

Expanding her circle of friends both at home and away fed a deep hunger: "I love culture and refinement I never tire talking to those who are intellectual and can impart knowledge to me of things and places, I am not versed in," she wrote in 1875.[44] The appeal of William Hendrie and his friends is self-evident. Bringing new viewpoints and life experiences far different from her own, they all seemed to meld easily into the social ambience of Emmeline's household.[45] Finding too few "congenialities" among some of her local friends, she basked in the company of "literary people," whom she found so much more "inviting and conversational."[46]

One visitor in 1875, Octavia Walton Le Vert, was an original American "socialite," known in the 1850s as the "belle of the South." Well educated and well placed in society, she exhibited a culture and refinement that Emmeline found charming.[47] When they met, Emmeline was taken aback when the distinguished guest kissed her "over and over again," even lifting Emmeline's veil to do so. Her polished manner and refined tone, accompanied by her "abundant treasures of knowledge," stoked Emmeline's pleasure at being "familiarly associated with one who had seen so much of the best society and of the 'literati.'"[48] As prominent visitors continued to make Salt Lake

42. "Home Affairs," *Woman's Exponent* 5 (June 15, 1876): 12.

43. For names of some of these visitors, see E. Wells, Diary, May 14, 23, June 11, 1876.

44. Ibid., December 4, 1875.

45. Ibid., May 8, 9, 14, 19, 27, June 2, 3, 4, 6, 7, 11, 1876.

46. Ibid., September 28, November 21, 1875.

47. Octavia Walton Le Vert (1811–77) in Alabama Women's Hall of Fame. The Alabama Women's Hall of Fame, founded in 1970 and a state agency since 1975, is hosted by Judson College in Marion, Alabama. It celebrates the lives and accomplishments of Alabama's most outstanding women.

48. Ibid., September 17, 1875; "Home Affairs" announced that Le Vert would be giving "readings" from her own writings at the Presbyterian church, and a follow-up "Home Affairs" column gave a brief biographical sketch of her life and accomplishments. See *Woman's Exponent* 4 (September 15, 1875): 61; and 4 (October 1, 1875): 69.

City a travel destination, Emmeline decried her lack of means to entertain them in the manner she wished and lamented the absence of more locally available learned, experienced, and literary people.[49]

As the wife of a counselor in the church's ruling body and mayor of the city, Emmeline had the privilege of meeting two US presidents while Daniel served in those positions. The first, in June 1875, was General James A. Garfield, five years before his election; the second was President Ulysses S. Grant, in October of that same year. For General Garfield's visit, she bought herself a new dress and trimming for her hat in order to be properly attired in his presence. She and Emmie, along with Louisa, her sister-wife, walked together to the train depot to join the Garfield party in taking an excursion to the lake. They "were in a cozy little car with a very select company," she noted with pleasure. "Gen. Garfield came and sat beside me, on the same sofa, and I had an excellent opportunity to converse with this distinguished statesman." She found him to be "most genial in manner, courteous and attentive to ladies" and was thrilled when he gave her his arm to escort her on board the steamer when they arrived at the lake. The boat was renamed for the general, she noted, and "cheers given in favor of Mayor Wells and Gov. [Samuel B.] Axtell."[50] Emmeline attended the tabernacle service the following Sunday, where she had an additional opportunity to visit with General Garfield and the governor. That evening she sent a bouquet of flowers and copies of the *Woman's Exponent* to the future president.[51]

Her meeting with President and Mrs. Ulysses Grant was just as impressive. While the president and his wife were meeting with Governor George W. Emery, newly appointed by President Grant, and other territorial officers, she joined a number of women in decorating their private railcar with flowers and fruit. She was formally introduced to the president and his wife and their entourage at a reception in the Walker House in company with Daniel and other church leaders and their wives. Visibly moved when listening to the organ during a visit to the tabernacle, Julia Dent Grant, the president's wife, said to the women that she had offered up a prayer for "this people," but reminded them that it was "a methodist prayer." The next day, Emmeline was in the party that accompanied President Grant to Ogden in the beautifully decorated train, all of whom "were agreeably entertained" en route. Emmeline was particularly impressed with the graciousness of Julia Grant. "The visit," Emmeline declared, was "one of distinction and in

49. E. Wells, Diary, September 28, 1875.

50. Ibid., June 4, 1875. At the time of General Garfield's visit, he was a prominent Republican member of the House of Representatives.

51. Ibid., June 6, 1875.

many of its characteristics a very singular or remarkable one."[52] These two encounters were the first of six she experienced with US presidents.

While entertaining visitors, attending legislative sessions, and assisting with establishing a woman's commission store stoked Emmeline's ambition to deepen her well of experience, her commitment to the *Woman's Exponent* intensified when she became associate editor and then editor. Louisa Greene's marriage and the death of her first two infants dictated assistance with the publishing demands of the *Exponent*, and in 1875, Emmeline became her associate editor. At midlife, with her children now adults, Emmeline was in the right position to assume partnership in this exciting new journalistic venture. She eagerly accepted this new role, despite a nagging concern that Daniel might disapprove or that some of the family would consider it inappropriate. However, having been asked by many readers why her name was not already listed as an associate of Louisa's, she convinced herself that acceptance would "on many accounts" be better.[53]

But the work as associate editor turned out to be less a pleasurable pastime and more a pressured effort to meet unyielding deadlines with sufficient copy to fill an eight-page, quarto-size, semimonthly publication, a necessary responsibility that only increased when she became editor.[54] Even as Emmeline began writing editorials for the paper, she continued to use Blanche Beechwood for additional articles. As a budding journalist, she reasserted her conviction of the propriety of women as public writers.

She introduced the series on women writers by expressing her regret that the rule of custom declared that clever women, "if they launch out into any field of labor (save that of domestic everyday life)," deserve "criticism, public and private." As a result, only a few women, she lamented, "are willing to produce in writing a witness of their mind's individuality." This was a great loss not only to the public but to women themselves. "I can see no good,

52. Ibid., October 4, 1875. Accounts of this visit are "Visit of President Grant," *Deseret News Weekly*, October 6, 1875, 568; "Home Affairs," *Woman's Exponent* 4 (October 15, 1875): 76; O. Whitney, *History of Utah*, 2:778, 3:116; Edward W. Tullidge, *History of Salt Lake City and Its Founders*, chap. 73; and B. H. Roberts, *A Comprehensive History of the Church of Jesus Christ of Latter-day Saints, Century I*, 5:503–5. Although President Grant had not looked favorably on the Mormons, his visit was a singular event for the city. He is quoted as having said, as he saw the impressive picture of hundreds of children dressed in white bordering the road from the depot to the Walker House, "I have been deceived."

53. E. Wells, Diary, November 28, 1875. More details about the beginnings of the *Woman's Exponent* and Emmeline's role in its publication are in C. Madsen, "Remember the Women of Zion."

54. E. Wells, Diary, March 28, July 13, 1881, March 10, 1889.

sound, wholesome reason against woman's writing upon any of the general topics of the day," she averred. "She may be a profound thinker, but if her ideas never assume any form, what will it avail?"[55]

Writers, she asserted, in an explanation of her own literary challenges, struggle under "a painful pressure constraining to write, perhaps involuntarily; memory, imagination, zeal, perceptions of men and things, a crowd of internal imagery, and we write to be quit of them, and not let the crowd increase." She anticipated improved performance over time. "Your patience," she implored her critics, "may find us better; much to say and well witting how to say it." She felt certain that "at some future time," she would be able "to amplify and perfect and gravitate into something of order these crowding fancies" and promised to do so "in as frank and artless a fashion as heretofore."[56]

Even, perhaps especially, letter writing deserved sympathetic readers. As a lifelong letter writer, Emmeline was particularly fervent about the need for a correspondent who does not judge or criticize the writer for expressing deeply felt thoughts and feelings. "It is a pleasant thing to speak or write frankly and confidentially to those in whom we feel there is safety, and who have souls great enough to sympathize with us in life's ills; we may do this innocently if received in the same spirit."[57] Clearly, this was a plea to the recipients of her own letters to accept her heartfelt messages in the spirit in which they were written. Her extant letters always reflected a deep thought or strong feeling along with the intent of the letters.

In these essays on writing, using Blanche Beechwood's voice, Emmeline asserted women's right to write for the public and, more important, her own need to write, both personally and publicly. She was carefully asserting the legitimacy of woman's claim to the literary field, a profession now open-

55. Blanche Beechwood [Emmeline B. Wells], "A Few Ideas on Writing," *Woman's Exponent* 3 (April 1, 1875): 167.

56. Blanche Beechwood, "An Author's Mind," *Woman's Exponent* 4 (June 15, 1875): 13.

57. Blanche Beechwood, "About Letter Writing," *Woman's Exponent* 4 (July 1, 1875): 24. The quote conveys the same sentiments expressed in a novel of one of Emmeline's favorite authors, Dina Maria Mulock Craik, *A Life for a Life* (1859). Craik writes, "But oh! The blessing it is to have a friend to whom one can speak fearlessly on any subject; with whom one's deepest as well as one's most foolish thoughts come out simply and safely. Oh, the comfort—the inexpressible comfort of feeling safe with a person—having neither to weigh thoughts nor measure words, but pouring them all right out, just as they are, chaff and grain together; certain that a faithful hand will take and sift them, keep what is worth keeping and then with the breath of kindness blow the rest away."

ing to courageous women who did not feel it outside woman's sphere and clearing the path for her own entry.

Even before Blanche Beechwood exited the *Woman's Exponent* in 1881, "Aunt Em" had already made her appearance. Hers would be a longer tenure. In the next thirty-six years, Aunt Em authored 87 sentimental, reminiscent articles idealizing earlier times and romanticizing nature, including a series of ten letters "to the *Exponent*" that she called "After Long Years." Aunt Em also wrote 71 poems for the *Exponent*, sometimes bearing Emmeline's initial or full name and sometimes a pseudonym such as "Emile" or "Amethyst," but always the product of Aunt Em's pen. Before she was through with the *Woman's Exponent*, she wrote 124 essays, usually signed by her initials or full name, and editorials on a variety of subjects. Thus, even in the absence of Blanche Beechwood, Emmeline exhibited two distinct styles—the bold statements of her editorials and articles and the sweet sentiments of Aunt Em.

As editor of the *Woman's Exponent*, Emmeline was soon to know the demands of multitasking when Brigham Young gave her the enormous responsibility to mobilize a grain-saving effort by the women of the church in 1877, soon after she became editor. She recognized the paper as an effective web of communication and the Relief Society as an effective network through which to meet this charge. Utilizing these networks, she enlisted the help of all the women of the church, and grain saving became the church's first welfare project. Eventually taken up as a Relief Society project, it became almost synonymous with the organization itself. Emmeline was always associated with its implementation.

The twelfth celebration of her February 29 birth date occurred in 1876 when Emmeline celebrated her forty-eighth birthday. Her leap-year birthdays were always more elaborately celebrated than the other yearly commemorations. Daniel gave her a bookcase and desk combination, a gift that completely amazed her. "It was the first one I ever had and it came so unexpectedly, I was entirely taken unawares," she exclaimed.[58] By the time her birthday was celebrated again on February 29, her reputation as an editor, a women's rights advocate, and an influential Mormon woman would extend far beyond the borders of her Mormon community.

58. E. Wells, Diary, February 29, 1876.

CHAPTER 14

Successes and Sorrows

(1877–1878)

On New Year's Day, 1877, Emmeline gathered around her all of her five living children and seven grandchildren to welcome the new year. It was a quiet family celebration, but before the day was over, thirty-seven friends dropped by, most of them Emmeline's.[1] Though far from being a "social butterfly," Emmeline was nonetheless accumulating friends as she broke through the cocoon of domestic life into a world of social activity that included visiting, anniversary celebrations, church events, and excursions to the canyons and lake.[2] She marked the new year with a poem, "The New Era," published in the January 1 issue of the *Woman's Exponent*, ascribed to one of her pen names, Emile. In its seven verses, she reflected on one of her signature themes: the nation's need to recognize women's rights and woman's duty in helping to fulfill that need. "Woman, awake!" she wrote,

As mother, daughter, friend,
Thine energies and earnest efforts lend,
To help thy country in her hour of need—
Prove thy integrity by word and deed,
For woman's star is lighting up the dawn
And rosy gleams presage the coming morn.[3]

1. E. Wells, Diary, January 1, 1877. The seven grandchildren were Daisie, Verona, and Leslie Dunford as well as Winifred Woods, Melvina Woods's children; and Isabel, Septimus, and Lucile Sears, Isabel Sears's children.

2. Emmeline often mentioned such happenings in the *Exponent*. On August 9 that year, for example, she noted that a large company of women traveled to the lake, where they ate a picnic lunch in the bowery and then enjoyed bathing in the calm and placid lake, particularly appreciating the cheap rate of the railroad. See "Home Affairs," *Woman's Exponent* 6 (August 15, 1877): 44.

3. "The New Era," *Woman's Exponent* 5 (January 1, 1877): 113.

Although this was her only poem relating to women's rights, she had become a staunch advocate for the advancement of women. Poetry for her, however, was personal, not political. Prose was definitely her preferred medium to wage that battle, and the *Woman's Exponent* was a ready outlet to express her advocacy. In this she was following the pattern of other suffragists around the country who were using journalism as their primary tool of persuasion.

Emmeline missed the high spirits and intellectual curiosity of the Wasatch Literary Association members when they married, served missions, or joined the Young Men's and Young Ladies' Mutual Improvement Associations. However, Annie's and Louie's friends began to take their place. Louie became a center of attraction as a performer in the Salt Lake Theatre productions and as an artist whose paintings were often displayed in many local venues. Aside from her worry over Emmie, Emmeline basked in the company of her daughters and grandchildren, and many family celebrations drew the family together, to her obvious delight. "At evening," she wrote on one wintry day, "when seated around the hearth pleasant feelings spring up in our hearts and a pure affection towards each other," and then longingly added, "if life were all as smooth and serene."[4]

Even as she settled contentedly into her role as grandmother, she was working longer and harder at the office. The year 1877 saw an increase in her correspondence with national women's rights leaders and editors of the most prominent of the woman suffrage papers and other periodicals. She not only sent them copies of the *Exponent*, but also submitted articles and letters for publication in their papers. When the suffrage journal *Woman's Words* (1877–91) was launched, the editor sent Emmeline a copy of its first issue in April, initiating an immediate exchange of the two papers.[5] Founded, published, and edited in Philadelphia by Theresa Juan Lewis, the paper proved to be a comfortable channel through which Emmeline could tell the story of LDS women and hopefully deflect some of the disdain brought on them because of polygamy.[6] It also gave her name recognition among many eastern women's associations.

4. E. Wells, Diary, February 2, 1878.

5. Notice of *Woman's Words* appeared under "Home Affairs" in the *Woman's Exponent* 5 (May 1, 1877): 181. Typically, editors exchanged newspapers with each other to broaden their coverage. Many items in Emmeline's paper were taken from other newspapers, and presumably items from the *Woman's Exponent* were included in papers with which Emmeline exchanged.

6. Emmeline B. Wells, "The Young People of Utah," *Woman's Words* 1 (July 1877): 53; Wells, "Home Industries in Utah," *Woman's Words* 1 (August 1877): 67; Wells, "Retrenchment Associations," *Woman's Words* 1 (October 1877): 101–2.

Emmeline had earlier subscribed to the foremost of these women's periodicals, the *Woman's Journal* (1870–1917), and had developed a correspondence acquaintance with Henry Blackwell, who, with his wife, Lucy Stone, founded the journal as the organ of the American Woman Suffrage Association. With the publication of *Woman's Words*, Emmeline now included Mrs. Lewis, its editor, among her regular correspondents, along with editors of other papers such as the Boston *Watchman*, which regularly berated the Mormons and taunted Emmeline into constant rebuttals. She corresponded with Horatio King of the *Christian Union*, a paper edited by Henry Ward Beecher and Lyman Abbot.[7] She also hosted Eli Perkins, pen name for M. D. Landon, a correspondent for the *New York Sun* and a prominent humorist of the day in the mode of Mark Twain and Artemus Ward.[8] Emmeline never shied away from writing letters to or seeking meetings with influential people in defense of her church and particularly of Mormon women.

Becoming editor of the *Exponent* in 1877 immediately changed Emmeline's routine, as it evolved into a hard task-master but necessary appendage to her life. For thirty-seven years, she was sole editor and publisher, and it would soon become her principal source of livelihood. Altering very little of the original format of the paper, the historically minded new editor told the story of Mormon women in its pages. Through reports, articles, letters, editorials, and minutes of their organizations, the *Exponent* became a record of their thoughts on events of their time, of the clubs they organized, the church meetings they attended, the socials they planned, the legislation they fostered, the political philosophies they supported, and the homes and families they managed. "In its volumes there is much history contained, which is reliable for reference for future historians," Emmeline presciently wrote shortly before the demise of the paper nearly forty years later. In its recording of women's work, "industrial and educational," and of their lives, she could honestly affirm that "there has been no great work during these

7. Emmeline noted the letters she wrote to Abbott: E. Wells, Diary, July 21, July 25, 1877, and mentioned that in return, she received "a large number of letters." Ibid., August 10, 1877.

8. Ibid., May 10, 18, June 13, 1877. She also began a correspondence with Samuel R. Wells and his wife, Charlotte, publishers of the *American Phrenological Journal and Life Illustrated* of New York. Emmeline does not note any relationship between the Utah and New York Wells families, but she maintained an active connection with Samuel and Charlotte, hosting them when they visited Utah and visiting them when she traveled to New York. She had also begun communicating with various members besides the leaders of the National Woman Suffrage Association. Ibid., September 12, 1877.

years commenced by women that has not been considered and helped by this little paper."[9]

Probably the most-read woman's periodical of the time was Sarah Josepha Hale's *Godey's Lady's Book*, much more a typical women's magazine than the suffrage papers with which Emmeline corresponded or indeed than the *Woman's Exponent*. Though Hale promoted education for women, her magazine was less supportive of the legal and political rights for which the *Exponent* advocated. Emmeline seldom makes reference to it. Aside from the articles, letters, and women's rights activities originating in other suffrage periodicals and noted in its pages, the *Woman's Exponent* was explicitly a local paper.

When Emmeline became editor in 1877, Brigham Young gave Emmeline a mission. He commissioned her to write and publish life sketches of the leading women of Zion and to "tell the sisters to take the *Exponent* and keep it, for it will contain the record of their work and a portion of Church history."[10] She began almost immediately to invite women to submit their life stories. Emmeline personally penned biographical sketches of numerous women and wrote lengthy obituaries. In 1889, she renewed her solicitations for life histories. "The columns of this paper are ever open to publish such sketches and incidents," she wrote, urging her readers to submit accounts of their "experiences and testimonies for the benefit of others and to leave them upon record."[11] Included in many of the life stories that followed were valuable personal reminiscences of historical events, providing a female perspective on the organizational period of the church, the western migration, and settlement in Utah, as well as their conversion experiences. In addition, Emmeline, with the help of her daughter Annie, wrote and published numerous collective biographies of LDS women in journalism, medicine, literature, politics, education, philanthropy, and other vocational and volunteer fields. In 1908, she once again solicited her readers' life histories. "I really feel that I can keep their memory before the women of today, and in doing so leave a record of them for the coming generation,"

9. "The Fortieth Volume," *Woman's Exponent* 40 (July 1911): 4. An analysis of the contribution Emmeline Wells made to the Mormon historical record can be found in Carol Cornwall Madsen, "Telling the Untold Story: Emmeline B. Wells as Historian."

10. "The Jubilee Celebration: The Need of Press Representation," *Woman's Exponent* 20 (March 15, 1892): 132.

11. See, for example, "Editorial Thoughts," *Woman's Exponent* 18 (November 15, 1889): 92. She wrote a long "autobiographical" account for Elizabeth Ann Whitney and several about Eliza R. Snow, Zina D. H. Young, Bathsheba W. Smith, and others.

she explained to her diary.[12] As a result of President Young's commission, the *Woman's Exponent* contains nearly eight hundred obituaries and close to two hundred multicolumn biographical sketches of Emmeline's contemporaries. The *Woman's Exponent* is an impressive biographical dictionary of nineteenth-century LDS women.[13]

Emmeline was in a perfect position to write the life histories and obituaries of women because she had long been acquainted with many of them and had met others in her Relief Society travels in later years between towns and villages throughout the territory. She found she had a capacity for making immediate and long-lasting friendships. These visits also enabled her to hone her speaking skills in the conferences and meetings she attended. Though she often spoke on the work of national women leaders and the need for LDS women to be educated in the issues of the day, she also echoed Eliza R. Snow's advocacy of plural marriage, even writing a strong endorsement of the practice in the *Woman's Exponent* the month she became editor.[14] Whatever her personal experience in the practice, she was a reliable public defender.

As head of the grain-saving mission, Emmeline published the enthusiastic reports of women's success in saving grain. Enlisting support of the Relief Society was the key to its success. After a year, Relief Society women had collected more than ten thousand bushels of grain, nearly three hundred bushels gathered through gleaning. Two Relief Society granaries were already erected, and more were under construction, enabling the Relief Society to supervise the storage of grain in its own facilities. Bishop Edwin Hunter, who attended one of the grain committee meetings with church president John Taylor, indicated that "our Relief Societies are doing much good; they have saved much suffering, and have been a great help to the Bishops. They have the Priesthood—a portion of the priesthood rests upon the sisters. They are doing a good work and particularly the storing of grain is commendable."[15]

12. E. Wells, Diary, May 23, 24, 1908.

13. At this same time, Edward W. Tullidge published *The Women of Mormondom*, which also has numerous life sketches of women among the eulogistic appraisals by the author.

14. "Patriarchal Marriage," *Woman's Exponent* 6 (August 15, 1877): 44.

15. "Grain Meeting," *Woman's Exponent* 6 (December 1, 1877): 102. Prior to the meeting in November, Emmeline had written a long paragraph entitled "Storing Grain by Women" under "Home Affairs" in which she commends Brigham Young for giving the sisters "this noble mission" of saving grain. "If we can secure grain by our own industry and economy," she added, it will "be a source of blessing to all within the limit of our sphere of usefulness." *Woman's Exponent* 6 (October 1, 1877): 68–69.

Three events of significance to Emmeline occurred in 1877. The first was the designation of a site in Manti (124 miles south of Salt Lake City) for a temple, shortly after dedication of the St. George temple in southern Utah by Brigham Young.[16] Daniel H. Wells would preside over the Manti temple eleven years later, and it became an important facet in Emmeline's life.

A second event of importance to all the women of the church was the reorganization of stakes (dioceses) throughout the church that included the introduction of stake-level Relief Society officers, a new level of leadership for women.[17] In 1877, Jane Richards of Ogden became the first stake Relief Society president in the church. In President Young's remarks on that occasion was the admonition to the Relief Society to continue holding conferences, for they were "a key to the Society." This directive ushered in a prolific period of meetings that ensured a busy visiting schedule for Eliza R. Snow and her associates to attend stake Relief Society conferences. At many of these conferences, a pattern evolved of giving healing blessings on the heads of ailing children or sick friends by the visitors from Salt Lake, a practice encouraged by Eliza R. Snow. She also admonished the sisters to have faith enough to exercise other gifts of the spirit, many of which were demonstrated in the socials and meetings held in women's homes, including Emmeline's.[18]

Finally, one of Brigham Young's last suggestions before his death on August 29 of that eventful year, spoken in a private conversation with Eliza R. Snow, was to send several of "the sisters," perhaps his daughters Zina Young Williams (Card) and Susa Young (Gates), to the East to lecture on Mormonism. "Well, it's an experiment," he said to Eliza, "but it's an experiment I would like to see tried."[19] The experiment he envisioned was indeed tried less than two years later when Emmeline rather than the recently divorced,

16. Until then, temple ordinances were performed in the Endowment House in Salt Lake City, which placed a hardship on Saints living far distances from the city to receive the ordinances. Generally, vicarious sealings (husband-wife, parents-children) were not performed in the Endowment House, being reserved exclusively for a temple, although there were exceptions, including several in which Emmeline was involved for the Whitney family.

17. Stake leaders were also appointed for the Primary organization and Young Ladies' Mutual Improvement Association, both headed by women.

18. Weber Stake Relief Society, Minutes, October 30, 1877. Emmeline's diary for 1877 had few daily entries. Most of the space contained her notes from this conference and one held earlier in July in Ogden. Spiritual meetings in which these gifts were exercised, especially healing and blessing, were quite common among the women at that time, and Emmeline hosted, attended, and participated in many of them.

19. O. Whitney, *History of Utah*, 2:845.

twenty-three-year-old Susa, then attending the BYU Academy, traveled East with Zina Young Williams. They became the first official representatives of LDS women to a national women's conference, bringing the Relief Society into membership in the National Woman Suffrage Association and beginning a Mormon-Gentile female relationship that brought Mormon women into the national spotlight.

Until the Nineteenth Amendment was passed in 1920, granting suffrage to all women in the United States, Mormon women were active members of the National (later the National American) Woman Suffrage Association through their dues and their representatives at national meetings. This association, and others developing later, kept LDS women connected to the larger society of women. Emmeline, as a continuing representative, dispelled many of the misrepresentations that had clouded the image of Mormon women and helped to bring them into the mainstream of American life, especially after polygamy was discontinued as an official Mormon practice in 1890. Bringing disparate women together in common cause was ever her goal.

At Brigham Young's death in August of that year, Emmeline's private notation was brusque. "President Young died today," she wrote, adding, "He is not so much mourned as one would imagine."[20] But her appraisal was hasty. Six thousand people viewed his remains in the tabernacle on September 1, and the funeral services, scheduled for the next day, were delayed so that many who had traveled from surrounding towns could also view his body, which they did from early morning until after eleven at night. An estimated twenty-five thousand people passed by, bidding a personal farewell to the man who had ruled the LDS Church for thirty-three years.[21] Emmeline published the entire funeral proceedings in the *Woman's Exponent*.[22]

President Young's death marked a significant alteration of Daniel's placement in the church's hierarchy. According to Daniel's own account, Brigham Young had ordained him an apostle when he appointed him counselor in the First Presidency in 1857, but Daniel was not installed as a member of the Quorum of the Twelve Apostles.[23] At Young's death, the First Presidency was dissolved. Daniel was then appointed a counselor to the Quorum of

20. E. Wells, Diary, August 29, 1877.

21. B. Roberts, *Comprehensive History of the Church*, 5:509–18.

22. "In Memoriam, President Brigham Young," *Woman's Exponent* 6 (September 1, 1877): 52; "Funeral Service of President Brigham Young," 6 (September 15, 1877): 60; "Remarks Made at the Funeral of President Brigham Young," 6 (September 15, 1877): 61–63.

23. His statement relating to his ordination as an apostle is in a brief sketch of his achievements that he wrote in October 1890 for *American Ancestry* and is reprinted

the Twelve Apostles rather than a member, a position he held until his death. Although his counsel was often sought by the Quorum, he was never sustained as a member of that body.

With all the changes taking place in Emmeline's life in 1877, her underlying worry was Emmie's health. Despite Daniel's blessings and those of the Relief Society sisters, the undefined malady always returned, and Emmie would be confined to her bed, languishing in pain for days. "Em is my staff and stay now—she is so full of courage," Emmeline observed during one of her sick spells, "and always tender and loving to me."[24] In September 1877, Emmie turned twenty-four, still unmarried, though tremendously popular. She was often paired with Orson F. Whitney, two years her junior, in various socials before he left in 1876 to serve a proselytizing mission for the church. The two had been close friends for many years, and Orson's interest in her was obvious to their associates. Many of them expected a marriage between the two upon his return. During Emmie's illness, Emmeline saw Daniel mainly when he came to her home to bless Emmie. But these visits resurrected her yearning for his steady and comforting presence and for "more and more of some kind hand to care for me, some near and dear friend to sympathize with me in the details of life."[25]

While 1877 slipped uneventfully into 1878, Emmeline pondered many unanswered questions. She recognized that the death of Brigham Young was "to this people something very serious indeed."[26] Almost six months had passed since his death, and a new prophet had not yet been sustained. John Taylor, who succeeded him, functioned for three years as church leader from his position as president of the Quorum of the Twelve Apostles, following the example of Brigham Young after the death of Joseph Smith. Antipolygamy bills were being debated with increasing intensity in Congress, some including proposals to rescind woman suffrage in Utah despite the National Woman Suffrage Association's strong lobbying efforts in opposition. But none had yet passed. These were issues of intense concern to Emmeline. "What will be done in regard to Utah?" she wondered. "What will be the end of Universal Suffrage? What will be done in regulating church matters and are we to have a new prophet? Who will be our leader?" These questions required answers that went beyond immediate church or local resolution. Utah's future was closely tied to congressional scrutiny and

---

in Bryant S. Hinckley, "Tributes and Achievements," in his *Daniel Hanmer Wells*, 19–27, esp. 27.

24. E. Wells, Diary, January 13, February 5, 1878.

25. Ibid., January 9, 1878.

26. Ibid., January 1, 1878.

its subsequent action, and Emmeline wondered how these questions would eventually be "harmonized or settled."[27]

Mormon women were not idle during these threats to their enfranchisement and to the survival of the church. Even as Emmeline contemplated these issues, a bill proposed by senator Isaac Christiancy was being debated in Congress. If passed, it would not only deprive Utah women of the vote, but also impose economic and political sanctions against the church. In 1877, the church responded by preparing a "remonstrance" that Emmeline helped to write.[28] In addition, Emmeline also headed a local petition drive in support of national woman suffrage after reading about the national drive in the *Deseret News*.[29] Emmeline wrote to the *Ballot Box*, volunteering the service of Mormon women whose "ardent" desire was "to be one with the women of America in this grand movement." Moreover, she added, Latter-day Saints "do not believe man has the right to deter women from enjoying the God-given privilege of free agency," which included the right to "act in unison on all subjects and interests to both."[30] Her editorials during this time presented her views on equality of which political parity was only a part.[31]

Knowing Eliza R. Snow's influence with her Mormon sisters, Emmeline invited her to present the plan to circulate petitions. Eliza did so at a special women's meeting and praised the "heroism of the ladies engaged in this movement in the East, and the sisterly feeling they had manifested for the women in Utah."[32] One of them, Sara Andrews Spencer, had been particularly defensive of Mormon women against efforts to deprive them of the vote, and she was frequently commended in the *Exponent* for her unfailing support.[33] As a result of her defense of Mormon women, especially her work

27. Ibid., January 2, 1878.

28. Eliza R. Snow "spoke earnestly about the remonstrance" in a Retrenchment Association meeting, "R. S. Reports," *Woman's Exponent* 6 (January 15, 1878): 122. "Mary," a subscriber to the *Exponent*, also wrote a strong remonstrance of her own against the bill. See Mary, "Remonstrance," *Woman's Exponent* 6 (January 15, 1878): 123; and E. Wells, Diary, January 1 and 2, 1878.

29. "Petitions," Cong. Rec., 45th Cong., 2nd sess., February 11, 1878, 7, pt. 1:916.

30. Emmeline B. Wells, "Convention Letters," *Ballot Box* 2 (July 1877): 1. This periodical became *The National Citizen and Ballot Box* in August of that year. See C. Madsen, *Advocate for Women*, 148–81.

31. See, for example, "Woman's Progression," *Woman's Exponent* 6 (February 15, 1878): 140; and "Special Life Missions," 6 (March 1, 1878): 148.

32. "R. S. Reports," *Woman's Exponent* 6 (January 1, 1878): 114.

33. Emmeline wrote a complimentary biographical sketch about her in her paper, "Sketch of Mrs. Sara J. Andrews Spencer," *Woman's Exponent* 6 (March 15, 1878): 158–59.

to defeat the punitive Christiancy bill, she lost many of her friends and coworkers.[34] Sara was eager to learn all she could about LDS women and wrote to Emmeline for information about them, adding her expression of "sincere friendship" in the letter. Emmeline considered this personal note from such an admired leader "one of the events of my life." "Surely my day-star is rising," she felt certain enough to exclaim.[35]

Emmeline directed the formulation and distribution of the Utah petitions that yielded nearly seven thousand signatures in favor of a woman suffrage amendment to the Constitution.[36] Almost immediately afterward, Emmeline was appointed to the Advisory Board of the National Woman Suffrage Association.[37] The appointment came even before Emmeline had made personal contact with the suffrage association and proved to be a beginning step for her in becoming a national figure.[38]

The *Woman's Exponent* was proving to be an unexpected asset to Emmeline in establishing a public identity. But after only five months of editing the paper, she was finding the pressure daunting. "I've been too busy for anything," she wrote early in January 1878. "I do seem to have so very much to do—it is scarcely possible to do all that is expected."[39] Two weeks later, she lamented, "Work—Work—Work—nursing the sick—looking after the household attending to the office paying bills—mailing papers—answering letters—thinking over all my affairs—trying to look after petitions," and

34. "R.S. Reports," *Woman's Exponent* 6 (March 15, 1878): 154.

35. E. Wells, Diary, February 15, 1878. Emmeline may have meant the term *day spring*, a biblical term meaning dawn, or the rising of a heavenly body such as the sun (sometimes the moon), suggesting the beginning of something. It is used in Luke 1:78 and has other biblical references.

36. Ibid., February 2, 4, 1878.

37. "Home Affairs," *Woman's Exponent* 6 (February 1, 1878): 132. See C. Madsen, *Advocate for Women*, 154–56. A section entitled "Petitions" in the Cong. Rec., 45th Cong., 2nd sess., February 11, 1878, 7, pt. l:916, contains a description of the petition, quoted in Susan Fales and Chad Flake, comps., *Mormons and Mormonism in U.S. Government Documents*, 100: "A statement signed by Emmeline Wells, Eliza R. Snow and 6,979 persons praying for a Constitutional amendment prohibiting states from disfranchising citizens on account of sex." The *Woman's Exponent* notes the number as thirteen thousand in "Home Affairs," 6 (February 1, 1878): 132.

38. From "Petitions" and "Sixteenth Amendment Workers," *National Citizen and Ballot Box* 2 (March 1878): 3; and 3 (April 1878): 2. The articles describe the presentation of the petitions to the Committee on Privileges and Elections and also a list of all the workers from the states and territories. Emmeline Wells and Utah's delegate to Congress George Q. Cannon personally contributed funds to the NWSA. "Treasurer's Report," *National Citizen and Ballot Box* 5 (August 1878): 3. Emmeline continued to offer financial support as she was able.

39. E. Wells, Diary, January 8, 1878.

sadly concluded, "no congenial friend to sympathize with me in my heart-hunger."[40] Even her stint as associate editor did not prepare Emmeline for the responsibilities as editor of an independent paper. "I never supposed when I commenced working on the paper that I should have to do everything for myself," she complained. "I feel sometimes my burden is heavy."[41] The burden never eased. As late as 1898, with shorthand and typewriters readily available, she never had the luxury of using either. "It seems dreadful for us who have written so much," she mused, "to still continue on the old lines."[42]

Although the *Exponent* consumed most of her time, she attended the legislature, supported the grain-saving program, and also promoted the silk industry, headed by her friend Zina D. H. Young and established to provide the manufacture of silk in Utah rather than buying it from Gentile merchants.[43] "Many duties press heavily upon me," she acknowledged. Yet this was the time in which she made a resolution that guided her decisions and actions throughout the rest of her long life. "I desire to do all in my power to help elevate the condition of my own people especially wom[e]n."[44] She struggled to reconcile the self-aggrandizing nature of personal ambition with the self-denying quality of altruism. Whether consciously or not, by that reconciliation she created and thus controlled to a large extent her public image. Her private complaints of overwork revealed the price she paid for doing so.

As if time were not already a fleeting commodity, Emmeline was intent on educating herself to be culturally equal to the many visitors she entertained. She took French lessons and read voraciously on varied subjects. In fiction she turned primarily to contemporary writers, having studied the classics in school. She read most of the novels of Maria Corelli (pen name for Mary Mackay), one of the most popular British novelists of her day. George Eliot (Mary Ann Evans) was another favorite, and some of the novels of George Sand found their way into her library. She also attended

40. Ibid., January 18, 1878.

41. Ibid.

42. Ibid., March 4, 1898.

43. Because of Emmeline's interest in developing silk manufacture in Utah, the *Exponent* noted meetings of the Deseret Silk Association and suggested making Relief Society presidents local vice presidents of the association to promote the industry. See, for example, "Home Affairs," *Woman's Exponent* 6 (February 1, 1878): 132–33. She was also very much interested in a bill before the legislature permitting enfranchised women to hold certain public offices. It was vetoed, however, by Governor George W. Emery. "Home Affairs," *Woman's Exponent* 6 (March 1, 1878): 149.

44. E. Wells, Diary, January 4, 1878.

lectures by Romania Pratt and Ellen Brooke Ferguson, local doctors, for whom she had great admiration. "I would love to have her superior knowledge," she wrote of Dr. Ferguson, "but then she has not had my experience. I do not envy her I only desire to obtain knowledge and wisdom." Later, when Emmie had one of her painful episodes, Emmeline revealed that "if I were young I would certainly devote my life to the causes of disease and the necessary & effectual remedies."[45] Medicine was not only a field of interest to her but also a profession that she thought was "one of the noblest occupations woman can choose for a life-work." Yet with all of these extracurricular activities and heartfelt complaints of too much work, she still managed to write two or more long editorials each month, notices for the "Home Affairs" column, a report of the semimonthly Retrenchment Association meetings, sometimes a poem or two, as many as ten letters a day, and at least one "Aunt Em" article.[46]

Complaining of lack of time to write, however, meant only that she did not have time to write as carefully and thoughtfully as she would have liked because of the persistent deadlines imposed by her paper. In 1878, a year after becoming editor, she wistfully lamented at the end of a frustrating day, "If I could only gratify my own aspirations by acts of benevolence, and travel and write purely for love of writing having plenty of time for each article instead of hurrying them off half-finished to the press it would seem as if there was some pleasure in it."[47]

Adding to her disquietude was the state of the Wells family finances. Daniel had led in many business enterprises in the valley, including coal mining, stock raising, the manufacture of nails and brooms, and the establishment of a gas works company to provide gas for both domestic and commercial lighting. He also operated three sawmills at the base of Cottonwood Canyon. Troubles began when the government claimed his mills were trespassing on federal land and all his lumber was confiscated. Later, as electricity became more popular, his gas works company began to fail, and Daniel carried its financial burden. According to his son Rulon,

45. Ibid., January 12, 14, February 12, 1878. These two women were among several LDS women who had medical degrees. Dr. Pratt had answered the call of Brigham Young for women to attend medical schools in the East in order to assist in the medical needs of their communities in Utah. Dr. Ferguson had received her medical training before her conversion to Mormonism and her residence in Utah.

46. In an article entitled "What We Women Do with Our Time," Emmeline suggested that women should take an hour's walk in the sunshine each day and allow an hour for "personal culture in reading, music, or whatever pursuit is most to her taste," an ideal never realized in her case. *Woman's Exponent* 6 (February 1, 1878): 132.

47. E. Wells, Diary, January 9, 1878.

he had invested heavily in the gas works company with the understanding that the church and community would support it as a communal venture. With Brigham Young's death in 1877, that support failed him. Unwilling to declare bankruptcy, Daniel worked for years to settle the debts on this investment, which eventually included the sale of his city property and some of his other business interests. Though he finally paid his debts and regained some of his holdings, he never returned to the comfortable solvency he had once enjoyed.[48] This state of affairs, which was finally resolved in 1888 after a decade of uncertainty, meant a major displacement for his wives. At first, this meant only that the family was advised to "practise the most rigid economy."[49] More changes were ahead. Emmeline, especially, regretted her dependency on someone else but felt encouraged that her "business" seemed relatively prosperous.[50]

And then the heaviest blow struck. On a beautiful spring day in April 1878, Emmie finally succumbed to her lingering illness. "My heart is nearly broken," Emmeline lamented, "all the world is dark and I know not what to do—where shall I turn for comfort we are all of us overcome with grief—what can we do to relieve our overburdened hearts."[51] Despite her chronic illness, Emmie had been the center of the group of young people her age. She had been the magnet that had drawn them to Emmeline's home and kept the house so full of vibrant promise. At this time, she was a favorite of the twenty-four-year-old son of Sarah and Hiram Kimball, Frank, who visited her often during this last illness. She also had a final visit from her longtime friend Ort Whitney, who returned from his mission just days before her death and went quickly to her bedside. Though she was delirious, he bade her a long farewell to which she was able to answer, "Oh, Ort, I'm so glad you have come." After her death a few days later, Ort wrote a brief verse to her and placed it on her bier among the canopy of flowers that covered it.[52]

Just days after Emmie's death, the stricken Emmeline poured her grief into an editorial tribute to her daughter that she signed "A Friend." She introduced the piece with a short verse using her pseudonym "Emile." Other poetic fragments interspersed throughout the editorial testify to Emmeline's inimitable hand. The tribute provides a poignant recital of Emmie's final hour and then describes the funeral, held, as many were at the time, at

48. Clara Hedges Anderson, "Daniel H. Wells' Experience"; Hinckley, *Daniel Hanmer Wells*, 317–22.

49. E. Wells, Diary, January 7, 1878.

50. Ibid., February 3, 5, 1878.

51. Ibid., April 8, 1878. Emmeline gives no indication of the nature of Emmie's long illness or the final cause of her death.

52. O. Whitney, *Through Memory's Halls*, 101.

home. Apostle Joseph F. Smith was the sole speaker, with music provided by members of the Tabernacle Choir. In describing the flower-laden casket, Emmeline noted the equally adorned guitar lying below it, remembering how often Emmie accompanied Orson as he sang the songs they both loved.[53] Acknowledging the human need for grieving, Emmeline wondered, "Can there be any sin in mourning for one whose compassion for the poor had become proverbial?...Whose charity was such that, 'E'en her failings leaned to virtue's side'...? No! We cannot think so."[54] Emmeline's grief found its release in this last loving homage to her beloved daughter.

It was July before Emmeline could pick up her pen and write again in her diary. The occasion was a trip with Eliza R. Snow to attend a Relief Society conference in Farmington, a community seventeen miles north of Salt Lake City. Still emotionally reeling, Emmeline longed for comforting words from Eliza, who, uncharacteristically, had not honored Emmeline with a consoling poem, as she so often did with others. "I cannot say much to Aunt Eliza," Emmeline sadly acknowledged. "She does not think I ought to give way to emotions not in the least."[55] Eliza's withholding of any personal response, written or verbal, to Emmeline's bereavement seemed to belie her sympathetic response to other bereaved parents. Emmeline was perplexed. It was only a comforting word from Eliza for which Emmeline yearned. The repeated encounters with sorrow and death that Emmeline experienced did not inure her to the flood of emotions that accompanied each one or to the comfort that empathetic friends gave. A month after Emmie's death, Emmeline was moved to express how much the bereaved relished the consolation provided by the "tender ministrations of affection for which instinctively as it were, the heart yearns." "Those who excel in superiority of heart, whose kindly souls are fullest of real sympathy are the best comforters," she wrote. "Heart speaks to heart in the rich eloquence

53. "In Memoriam: A Tribute of Affection," *Woman's Exponent* 6 (April 15, 1878): 172. The brief poem at the beginning of the editorial is included as "A Tribute to Emmie," in her *Musings and Memories*, 229. Another poem, attributed to Emile, appears as "April" in the *Woman's Exponent* 6 (May 1, 1878): 179, and in *Musings and Memories*, 120.

54. "In Memoriam," 172.

55. E. Wells, Diary, July 10, 1878. During this visit to Farmington, Aurelia Rogers approached the two women about the possibility of creating an organization for young boys to help them learn manners and Gospel teachings. Eliza was excited about the idea, and she and Emmeline made plans to visit John Taylor about the matter. See Carol Cornwall Madsen and Susan Staker Oman, *Sisters and Little Saints: One Hundred Years of Primary*, 1–7; and Aurelia Spencer Rogers, *Life Sketches of Orson Spencer and Others and History of Primary Work*, 208.

of tenderness and 'we weep with those who weep,' 'we mourn with those who mourn.'"[56]

Emmeline was now at a crossroads. She had been drawn ineluctably into the national crusade for women's rights through the *Exponent*, through her correspondence with national suffrage papers and leaders, and through her own interest in the affairs of her time. She had also seen her activity as a worker in the Relief Society increase as she traveled with Eliza R. Snow and other Relief Society sisters in their visits to ward and stake societies, totaling more than thirty-four to non–Salt Lake stakes in one single year. She was beginning to meet educated and cultured men and women whose stimulating company she enjoyed and regretted not finding among her own associates. "It is hard to get intelligence into some people—and we do seem to have some of the poorest material for saints or for cultivating up to any high standard," she commented after one meeting. It was strange, she thought, that "we cannot advance more as a people than we do." She noted that some people spent "all their time, and ability in improving the condition of the people mentally morally and religiously and others glide along careless of present or future happiness," a fact that would disconcert her throughout her public life.[57] However, despite her rising prominence in the path she was following, it was not of her choosing. Had circumstances permitted, she would have chosen another way. "If I could only carry out my desires for future improvement and culture how glad I should be—my heart longs inexpressibly for these things and cannot be satisfied because there is no avenue for me to enter to pursue those things that will fill my soul with grace and beauty. O how I long to revel in books in poetry in the haunts of nature."[58]

In happier moments, she thanked God "for all His mercies and blessings in giving me powers and faculties that are a constant source of wealth to my mind." She had an enabling gift of acceptance of the vicissitudes she encountered and welcomed the strengthening of character that followed. "My spirit is usually invigorated and buoyed up" by such gifts, she acknowledged, "and I am able to bear all that devolves upon me."[59] She little anticipated in earlier days that circumstances would unfold as they had. "I know that great things have been developed among this people and with me."[60] And this was just the beginning.

56. "Educate the Heart," *Woman's Exponent* 6 (May 15, 1878): 188.
57. E. Wells, Diary, February 10, 1878.
58. Ibid., January 11, 1878.
59. Ibid., February 5, 1878.
60. Ibid., February 4, 1878.

CHAPTER 15

Wells Goes to Washington

(1878–1879)

UNBEKNOWNST TO HER, in 1878, Emmeline was one year away from personally entering the national scene of women's politics. Her reading and newspaper exchanges involved her more definitively in the women's movement, primarily the drive for woman suffrage. Her talks at Relief Society meetings and conferences began to include references to the rights of women and the drive of national women's leaders for a more equitable distribution of opportunity for participation in civic affairs and for individual advancement. She brought authenticity to her talks, having become acquainted with so many women who wrote, advocated, and preached women's rights through her correspondence with them and their newspaper exchanges. Typical of the topics she covered, expressed in a long sermon at the Weber Stake Relief Society quarterly conference, were the higher cultivation of women's mental powers and spiritual attributes, the mission of woman, her influence in home and society, and the necessity of becoming self-reliant.[1]

As editor of the *Exponent*, Emmeline also began editorializing on women's rights. Many of her ideas were derivative, drawing from the writings of Margaret Fuller and Mary Wollstonecraft, particularly Fuller because of her immersion in American romanticism, which valorized the individual and its self-realization. With romanticism's attention to "imagination, empathy, and intuition," Fuller narrowed the schism between the feminist and the feminine. These essentially feminine qualities, however, were not equated with passivity and dormant intellectuality.[2] Romanticism gave its early

1. "Relief Society Quarterly Conference, Weber Stake of Zion," *Woman's Exponent* 7 (September 1, 1878): 54.

2. Some of the many works on Margaret Fuller are Theriot, "Mary Wollstonecraft and Margaret Fuller"; Blanchard, *Margaret Fuller*; M. Allen, *Achievement of Margaret Fuller*; and John Matteson, *The Lives of Margaret Fuller*.

women adherents impetus to discover their own individuality and identity, to travel through the "country of the mind," as it were, and awaken their intellectual powers as a means of understanding themselves.[3] According to one biographer, Fuller's primary feminist themes were "the value of the individual, the free will, the enlightened intellect, and the awakened sense of moral responsibility." For women, these attributes needed only opportunity to flourish, Emmeline would argue.[4] Romanticism, as expressed by Fuller, also assumed a natural grouping of women as a class because of their exclusive biological characteristics and what she felt was a natural domestic orientation.[5] Ironically, this concept of femaleness allowed for a feminine uniqueness that served, though awkwardly at times, the goals of feminism throughout the nineteenth century.[6] Like other feminists of her time, Emmeline's vision of womanhood combined the natural attributes of the feminine with those features associated with intellectuality.

Latter-day Saint theology shared several philosophical strands with romanticism, perhaps making Emmeline particularly susceptible to Fuller's theories and rendering Mormonism a comfortable matrix out of which Emmeline developed her own feminist philosophy.[7] Both Mormonism and romanticism affirmed the basic goodness of individuals and their common destiny to grow and develop to their highest potential. Their optimistic and hopeful approach to the human condition was a dramatic reversal of the enervating guilt and predestination of Calvinism, Emmeline's earliest religious orientation. Mormonism's assertion of the divine origin of the spirit and the human potential of godhood carried overtones of the transcendental focus on the preeminence of the individual soul, its divine emanation, its susceptibility to an intuitive path to truth, and its worthiness to progress naturally and freely with a concomitant moral accountability. Romanticism's assertion that intuition, or the "divine spark," within all humankind could impart knowledge that transcends the empirical paralleled the Latter-day Saint doctrine of the power of the Holy Spirit to prompt, instruct, and

3. Susan P. Conrad expounds on this idea in *Perish the Thought: Intellectual Women in Romantic America, 1830–1860*, 6–7.

4. Barbara Welter, "Mystical Feminist, Margaret Fuller: A Woman of the Nineteenth Century," 170.

5. Conrad, *Perish the Thought*, 97.

6. Nancy Cott argued that "feminism posits that women perceive themselves not only as a biological sex but perhaps even more important, as a social grouping." This recognition of "shared ground," she claims, "enables the consciousness and the community of action among women to impel change." Cott, *The Grounding of Modern Feminism*, 5, 9.

7. In the late nineteenth century, both Mormonism and feminism were considered outside the norm of religious orthodoxy, as was romanticism.

lead the individual toward understanding and proper action. Moreover, personal agency was fundamental to both Mormonism and romanticism.[8]

Emmeline wrote fifty-seven editorials on woman's need for greater freedom and opportunity and published articles by like-minded women and men, both local and national. Her first objective was to raise women's awareness of their own subjugation. "So long has custom tyrannized over woman to keep her in subjection," she wrote in 1878, "that it will only be by small degrees women themselves can comprehend the advantages arising from the progress of independence of thought and action, and a knowledge for themselves."[9] She asserted her own credo that woman is determined "to attain to an equality with man and to train herself to fill any position and place of trust and honor as appropriately and with as much dignity as her brother man." She deplored any situation in which woman would be "compelled to conditions that are distasteful and objectionable in matrimony" and believed that a woman should have "rights and privileges peculiarly her own" and be able to protect herself in them. Knowing that there was no overt compulsion for women to marry into polygamy and that easy divorce was available to any disaffected wife, legal or plural, she did not need asterisks to make polygamy an exception to her views on marriage. She also abhorred the thought that women were considered in the law almost as "chattel at the mercy or brutality of man." In other words, she wrote, woman's highest motive is that she be "recognized as a responsible being, capable of judging for and maintaining herself, and standing upon just as broad, grand and elevated a platform as man."[10]

Emmeline was well aware of the arguments opposing the expansion of woman's "sphere"—politically, professionally, or even educationally. She deplored the idea that "woman will lose her indefinable charm, designated womanliness, when she can discuss knotty questions, has strong opinions, can match herself with man in force of character and intellectual ability."[11] Similarly, she scoffed at the argument that "woman is more endearing in her dependency, . . . than when she steps out of her sphere and seeks to become

8. Brigham Young asserted that "the actions of men [and women] . . . are left free; they are agents to themselves and must act freely on that agency." This and additional statements by church leaders on agency are in Daniel H. Ludlow, ed., *Latter-day Prophets Speak*, 155–58.

9. "Woman's Progression," *Woman's Exponent* 6 (February 15, 1878): 140. The law in many states at this time still denied married women a legal identity. They were disallowed from owning or conveying their own property, personal or real, or having custodial rights to their children. Nor could they write a will or have control over their own wages.

10. "Woman's Expectations," *Woman's Exponent* 6 (July 1, 1877): 20.

11. "Woman's Progression," *Woman's Exponent* 6 (February 15, 1878): 140.

equal in education and self-reliance to man."[12] No home, she affirmed, "can be really attractive without intelligence, without a broader sympathy than that which confines itself to one's own family." She was convinced that "whatever efforts woman can make, whatever she may do that is not detrimental to home life, that she should be permitted to do without ridicule and without censure."[13]

The image of the sturdy oak and clinging vine, so popular in verse and art, was anathema to her. Rather, she visualized a marital partnership in which each partner granted to the other "all the same freedom of thought, feeling and expression they would grant to one who was not bound to them by indissoluble ties."[14] From her own experience, she came to firmly believe that "as women become conversant with business matters, and step out of the kitchen now and then...these evils which exist to-day may in a great measure be eradicated." The lives women lived almost always depended on their husbands' capacity to provide, and when that support faltered, women had few alternatives, Emmeline knew well. Thus, she felt keenly that "the position of women with relation to money is one which might be discussed by intelligent women advantageously."[15]

That women had an inalienable right to vote was only part of the message on equal rights for women. Women were an essential part of the body politic, and Emmeline envisioned a partnership of men and women working together for the "general welfare" of the people. She had only admiration, not criticism, for those women "who do their own thinking and are not content to sit and dream and wait for the good time coming, but who will themselves open up the way for the advancement of others." She assured her readers that these women would "stand out grandly in the future and be applauded as benefactors of the human race."[16]

Emmeline seemed determined to expand her knowledge about women's rights under the law. She studied the political system and became a delegate to county and territorial conventions in the freer political atmosphere of Utah. In August 1878, at a political meeting of the Mormon People's Party, attended by representatives of five city precincts, she was selected one of four women delegates to the county convention, the other three being Isabella Horne, Sarah Kimball, and Mary B. Freeze. "As this is a new departure from old-fashioned custom," she wrote, "it will of course, call forth criticism and ridicule as all innovations do; but," she continued, "it will be one more ex-

12. "Woman's Expectations."

13. "Woman's Relation to Home," *Woman's Exponent* 8 (September 1, 1879): 52.

14. "Woman's Progression."

15. "Do Women Earn Money?," *Woman's Exponent* 8 (October 1, 1879): 68.

16. "Mrs. Lockwood's Nomination," *Woman's Exponent* 13 (September 15, 1884): 60.

periment bearing upon the question of woman's capabilities." To her critics in the second precinct, Isabella Horne "made some very shrewd allusions to women of the Scriptures... mentioning Deborah who judged Israel for forty years 'and there was peace in the land.'" At Emmeline's suggestion, three women were voted to be members of the Central Committee: Isabella Horne, Sarah Kimball, and Emmeline herself.[17]

At the following county convention, Emmeline was appointed one of two secretaries and later nominated for the office of county treasurer, when a review of the statute granting woman suffrage revealed it did not provide for the right of women to hold office. Emmeline began a quiet campaign to amend the statute, though it would take two years before a bill was presented to the legislature. Though it passed the legislature in 1880, Governor George W. Emery, a non-Mormon, refused to sign it.

Her accelerating participation in politics, along with that of other politically minded friends, drew the attention of Sara Andrews Spencer, secretary of the National Woman Suffrage Association and a sympathetic supporter of Mormon women.[18] As Washington correspondent, Spencer wrote an article in the suffrage paper *Woman's Words*, a portion of which Emmeline printed in the *Woman's Exponent*, in which Spencer suggested, "At our next convention in Washington, let us by all means have one or more of the enterprising, public-spirited women of Utah present. If we mistake not," Spencer continued, "our Gentile sisters have much to learn from these heroic women. What we read of their business ability, courage and patriotism is an inspiration to us."[19] Emmeline's letters and articles published in *Woman's Words* and copies of the *Woman's Exponent* had begun to break down some of the misunderstanding and prejudice of eastern women and had engendered respect for the intelligence and capability of LDS women.

On November 7, 1878, the impetus for joining hands with eastern sympathizers with the antipolygamy movement occurred in Independence Hall

17. "Home Affairs," *Woman's Exponent* 7 (August 1, 1878): 37.

18. In 1878, the forty-one-year-old Sara Spencer had been an active suffragist for seven years, with responsibility as secretary of the NWSA to examine all legislation relating to women and children throughout the country. As a schoolteacher she was an early advocate for equal wages and was a brilliant responder to those who opposed woman suffrage. She was an active journalist and a frequent lobbyist for woman suffrage before various congressional committees. She married Henry Spencer, whose father had developed the "Spencerian" style of penmanship. "Sara Andrews Spencer," pts. 1 and 2, *Woman's Words* 1, no. 11 (February 1878): 161–62; no. 12 (March 1878): 182, reprinted as "Sarah Andrews Spencer," *Woman's Exponent* 6 (March 15, 1878): 158–59.

19. "Our Relief Societies: Similar Organizations Wanted by Christian Ministers," *Woman's Exponent* 7 (October 15, 1878): 76.

in Salt Lake City, the first home of the Congregational Church in Salt Lake City. On that date, two hundred Gentile and dissenting Mormon women assembled to organize an Anti-Polygamy Society. Its purpose was to arouse public opinion against the Mormon practice of polygamy and memorialize Congress to enforce the 1862 antibigamy Morrill Act.[20] It became the base of a strong antipolygamy movement throughout the country destined to last more than two decades. The society enlisted the help of women throughout the nation, writing a letter to the US president's wife, Lucy Hayes, and sending a circular letter to the clergy throughout the country, as well as preparing a memorial for Congress. Emmeline published a report of all of these activities in the *Woman's Exponent*.[21] Attracting such prominent figures as Harriet Beecher Stowe, Julia Ward Howe, Frances Willard, and Lucy Hayes, the society brought the nation's attention to the church's sanction of plural marriage and invited support in pressuring Congress to legislate against it. Proposals to outlaw the practice began appearing before Congress.

Wasting little time after this surprise "uprising" of their Gentile sisters, Zina Young, Isabella Horne, and Emmeline called a mass meeting for November 16 in the Salt Lake Theatre to "protest against the misrepresentation and falsehood now being circulated."[22] Annie Wells read a prepared preamble and resolutions, indicating appreciation for the support of the National Woman Suffrage Association in remonstrating against all efforts to repeal woman suffrage in the territory and noting the intention of the women assembled to memorialize Congress in refutation of the accusations of the Anti-Polygamy Society.[23]

Emmeline was one of the last speakers. "I love woman; it is one of my sentiments," she declared. However, she added, "the time has come when we can no longer be silent, as we are assailed, and that too by our own sex.... We never thought woman could rise up against woman." She was dismayed to witness what she felt was disloyalty to the sex, and though holding no animosity to those who disagreed with "this principle of our faith," she

20. Although Congress had debated such antipolygamy bills for a decade, it did not have the full power of a public outcry against the practice until the women's antipolygamy movement energized it to a crisis level. Enlisting the aid of various denominational women's groups and a budding national social purity association, the movement achieved great success in igniting public opinion against the Mormons. For many years, polygamy was a divisive factor in the suffrage movement; the American association was unalterably opposed to the membership of Mormon women in its organization, while the national association was eager to affiliate them.

21. "Anti-polygamy Meeting," *Woman's Exponent* 7 (November 15, 1878): 93.

22. "Mass Meeting: Home Affairs," *Woman's Exponent* 7 (November 15, 1878): 92.

23. "Woman's Mass Meeting, Theatre, Salt Lake City," *Woman's Exponent* 7 (December 1, 1878): 97–99, 102–3.

felt that their open opposition required a response. "We intend to meet it with all the energy and fortitude we possess, and it will be 'diamond cut diamond' rest assured."[24]

That Emmeline intended to be one of the diamond cutters became evident six weeks later, on New Year's Day 1879, when she and Zina D. H. Young visited President John Taylor's office to discuss the possibility of sending representatives to the annual convention of the National Woman Suffrage Association, held in January each year. The formation of the Anti-Polygamy Society made representation at the meeting imperative, they argued. Although three of William Godbe's wives had been involved with the movement for a decade, many thought it was time to send "orthodox" Mormons as representatives to fight escalating efforts to rescind women's voting rights in Utah.[25] Moreover, Brigham Young's thoughts two years earlier of sending women east and certainly the recent invitation from Sara Andrews Spencer were tantalizing appeals. The time seemed propitious to send main-line Mormon women east.

On Friday, January 3, 1879, Emmeline, then fifty-one, and twenty-eight-year-old Zina Young Williams packed their bags and boarded the train to Ogden, en route to the national convention of the National Woman Suffrage Association. They took with them a prepared memorial requesting congressional support in the case then being deliberated by the US Supreme Court, brought by polygamist George Reynolds, testing the constitutionality of the practice of plural marriage.[26] This was Emmeline's first transcontinental train ride, traveling eastward for the first time since she had left her New England home thirty-five years earlier, and she was extremely apprehensive about what lay ahead. She and Zina had patiently borne the slanderous barbs the anti-Mormon *Tribune* had leveled against them, calling them "cackling hens," "zion's roosters," and "celestial concubines." Would

24. Ibid., 102–3.

25. Details about Charlotte, Annie, and Mary Godbe's involvement in the suffrage movement are in C. Madsen, *Advocate for Women*, 148–54. Walker discusses the Godbe family in *Wayward Saints*. See also Lola Van Wagenen, "Sister-Wives and Suffragists: Polygamy and the Politics of Woman Suffrage, 1870–1896."

26. George Reynolds had agreed to be the subject of a test case relating to the constitutionality of the practice of plural marriage, prohibited by the 1862 Morrill Act. After two trials, one ending in a mistrial and the other a conviction upheld by the territorial supreme court, the case reached the US Supreme Court and was argued in November 1878. The origin and development of this case are reviewed in O. Whitney, *History of Utah*, 3:45–50. See also Gustive O. Larson, "Government, Politics, and Conflict," in *Utah's History*, edited by Poll et al., 254–55. A more recent study is Sarah Barringer Gordon, *The Mormon Question: Polygamy and Constitutional Conflict in Nineteenth Century America*.

they face similar hostility in Washington? Emmeline tried to distract herself from her worries by meeting her fellow passengers and enjoying the first of many transcontinental rail trips.[27]

Unexpectedly, a more challenging worry presented itself as they traveled eastward. The US Supreme Court issued its decision on the Reynolds case on January 6, 1879, upholding the constitutionality of the Morrill Act and declaring that, while the Supreme Court had no jurisdiction relating to religious *beliefs*, including plural marriage, prohibiting actions relating to those beliefs came within its purview, and the *practice* of polygamy was deemed illegal.[28] The door had been opened for congressional action to penalize those involved in it. The two women would now have to try to minimize the legal sanctions against those in the practice, especially plural wives and their children.

Emmeline believed that the future of Utah and statehood would be deeply implicated in the consequences of the Supreme Court's decision. She also worried that the decision would have an impact on woman suffrage in Utah. Even more, she foresaw confusion and disarray in the families of polygamous marriages. Added to these concerns were persistent issues in her own life. Memories of Emmie's death eight months earlier, dismay over Melvina's drift away from the church (which now seemed final), anxiety over the family's finances, and a persistent ache for the companionship of her husband gave her additional justification in declaring, "No wonder I'm forced to be strong-minded."[29] Now she would join some of the nation's most "strong-minded women" who were battling for the ballot and other civil rights that had been denied to them as women. The strength of her strong-mindedness was on the brink of testing.

Emmeline and Zina made arrangements to stay at the Riggs House, the headquarters of most of the suffrage convention delegates and the home of Susan B. Anthony when in Washington. The proprietor, Jane Spofford, herself an avid women's rights advocate, offered her hostelry for meetings and dinners as well as accommodations.[30] Emmeline and Zina Williams

27. The entire trip is covered in brief daily statements in Emmeline's diary from Friday, January 3 to Tuesday, February 4, 1879.

28. On January 6, 1879, the US Supreme Court declared it was within the jurisdiction of civil government to determine whether polygamy or monogamy should be the law of the land, thus dooming polygamy as a lawful form of marriage.

29. Ibid., January 6, 1878.

30. The Riggs House, a small but elegant hotel, was built in 1856 and owned and managed by Jane Spofford and her husband, Charles, since 1876. Susan B. Anthony often made it her home when she was in Washington, and Jane Spofford usually entertained the annual convention delegates with a reception. In 1891, the Spoffords closed the house, but friends urged them to buy another "hostelry," which they hoped would be called "the Spofford House." These plans never materialized,

were met upon arrival by Elizabeth Cady Stanton, Susan B. Anthony, Jane Spofford, George Q. Cannon (Utah's delegate to Congress), and a little later by Sara Andrews Spencer, whose name, Emmeline asserted, should have a place in Mormon history because of her support of Mormon women, a stance that put her reputation at great risk.[31] "Our heart went forth in great waves of love to her for her courageous defense of the women of Utah here in the Congress of the National Capitol," Emmeline fervently wrote. Both Emmeline and Zina were awed by the presence of these prominent figures in the women's movement, but Emmeline's prior correspondence with them considerably eased their first meeting.[32]

On the morning of January 10, the two Mormon women were invited to ride to the opening session of the conference with Elizabeth Stanton, Susan B. Anthony, and Jane Spofford. Both were seated on the platform and invited to speak. Advance notice filled Lincoln Hall to capacity with delegates and supporters curious to see these two Mormon women and hear what they had to say. Emmeline did not mince words. "Congress had better heed what wrong is contemplated to be done by taking away the only safety they enjoy," she warned. "The women of Utah have never broken any law of that Territory, and it would be unjust as well as impolitic to deprive them of this right [to vote]."[33] Zina Williams reinforced Emmeline's statements in her own brief talk, and Sara Spencer reminded the naysayers in the audience that the two Mormon women had been invited to the convention and added that polygamy was "preferable to the licensed social evil, which is being advocated by many of our bloated public men." She noted that many Gentiles had hoped the women of Utah would use the vote to "discourage the plurality of wives.... Now that these women do not vote to suit these Gentiles, they want to disfranchise them."[34]

---

however. See "The Announcement of the Closing of the Riggs House," *Woman's Exponent* 19 (June 1, 1891): 179.

31. "Over the Hills and Far Away," *Woman's Exponent* 7 (February 1, 1879): 186.

32. George Q. Cannon, Utah's territorial delegate to Congress, noted in a letter to John Taylor on January 28, 1879, that "the correspondence of Emmeline B. Wells had done good for the women's favorable reception." George Q. Cannon, Letterbook.

33. A *Salt Lake Tribune* Washington correspondent ridiculed Emmeline's speech, claiming that people began to leave the hall when the subject of polygamy was mentioned and dismissed her efforts and those of Zina Williams as impertinent and ineffectual. He concluded that their Washington appearance was far more damaging to their cause than had they remained at home. See Pablo, "Washington," *Salt Lake Tribune*, January 18, 1879, 4. See also "Trotting the Utah Roosters Along," *Salt Lake Tribune*, January 8, 1879, 1; "Our Utah Delegates," *Salt Lake Tribune*, January 19, 1879, 2; and "Polygamy and Woman Suffrage," *Salt Lake Tribune*, January 16, 1879, 4.

34. An abridged account of this session of the convention can be found in "The Utah Ladies in Washington," *Deseret News*, January 18, 1879, 2.

Though being "cordially received everywhere," as plural wives Emmeline and Zina were still curiosities, and "their fame and personal appearance became so well known that they are the observed of all observers on the street," attracting more attention even than George Q. Cannon, according to a *Salt Lake Tribune* story.[35] "Dear me," Zina wrote, "what an awful thing to be an Elephant. The ladies all look at me so queer."[36] When the *Woman's Journal*, the newsletter of the more conservative American Woman Suffrage Association, ridiculed the National Woman Suffrage Association for admitting the two Mormon women, Elizabeth Stanton defended their presence and chided Lucy Stone, founder and leader of the AWSA, for the false logic of her statement. "If George Q. Cannon can sit in the Congress of the United States without compromising that body on the question of Polygamy," Stanton retorted, "I should think Mormon women might sit on our platform without making us responsible for their religious faith.... When the women of a whole Territory are threatened with disfranchisement where should they go to make their complaint but to the platform of the National Suffrage Association?"[37] This was a courageous statement and put the nation on notice that LDS women had influential friends in Washington.

Lacking time to linger over her diary, Emmeline made only brief entries, listing the receptions and meetings they attended and the people they met. It was a busy and heady time for the two women, and they found the events throughout their visit to be challenging but also stimulating and very enlightening, as they were able to see the "Mormon question" from a national perspective.[38]

The meetings with President and Lucy Hayes were a major coup for Emmeline and Zina. Accompanying Sara Andrews Spencer and Matilda Joslyn Gage, members of the Resolutions Committee, they presented and

35. "Washington," *Salt Lake Tribune*, January 8, 1879, 4. The paper also reported that Eliza R. Snow, "the chief cackler," had advised the two "hens" to "wear the plainest kind of homespun clothes" to represent the modesty and decorum of Mormon women, but her idea was vetoed by George Q. Cannon, who wanted the women to dress in their "best bib and tucker," which the two women were more inclined to do anyway. "The Hens," *Salt Lake Tribune*, January 16, 1879, 4.

36. Zina Young Williams, Diary, January 26, 1879.

37. "The Brand of the Slave," *National Citizen and Ballot Box* 4 (May 1879): 2. See also "Mrs. Stanton and Mormon Women," *Woman's Exponent* 7 (May 15, 1879): 240. Cannon had been Utah's delegate to Congress since 1874 and served until 1882. In 1880, he was made a counselor to John Taylor in the First Presidency of the church and then, successively, to Wilford Woodruff and Lorenzo Snow.

38. A more detailed report of the convention and the participation of the two women is in C. Madsen, *Advocate for Women*, 148–81.

then read to the president the resolutions expressed in the NWSA Memorial, which the committee had written. One resolution reproved the government for refusing to exercise "federal power to protect women in their citizen's right to vote in the various States and Territories," but employing "federal power to disfranchise the women of Utah."[39] Both Spencer and Gage made it clear to the president that they did not support the plural marriage system but were emphatic about keeping woman suffrage alive in Utah. "The women of Utah have enjoyed the right of suffrage," Spencer argued, "and now Congress proposes to take it from them." The president promised the women that he would consider their complaints and in his next message to the nation would "act according to the dictates of his conscience and the best light."[40] This he clearly did before the year was over.

Afterward, Zina and Emmeline were granted time to present their own memorial relating primarily to the Supreme Court decision, inviting the president "to extend a fatherly care over an oppressed people" and to use his influence to avert legislation that would be injurious to the women and children of Utah. President Hayes listened intently with a slight smile, as they "laid their case before [him]," one report indicated, also noting that the president showed "kindly sympathy with them when they proved what misery would follow from enforcement of the act of 1862 against polygamy." The president's options, however, were clearly limited in view of the Supreme Court decision. Nevertheless, he asked the two women "to put their case in writing and lay it before him" so that he could study it in more detail. Emmeline spent the next few evenings preparing their case for the president and writing additional memorials to be read in Congress. Leaving details of the meeting, as well as of the entire Washington visit, to accounts she wrote for the *Woman's Exponent*, Emmeline simply noted for that occasion, "I said just what I had time to say."[41] Her gift to the president and Lucy was a copy of Edward Tullidge's laudatory volume *The Women of Mormondom*, which she wryly inscribed, "From a Mormon Wife."[42]

39. "Resolutions," *Woman's Exponent* 7 (February 15, 1879): 196–97. Since 1869, proposals had been introduced in Congress to disfranchise Utah women in order to weaken Mormon political dominance. See also Miss Grundy, "Mormon Ladies Calling at the White House," originally published in the *Philadelphia Times*, January 10, 1879, reprinted in *Woman's Exponent* 7 (March 15, 1879): 212.

40. "The Old Hens," *Salt Lake Tribune*, January 14, 1879, 1.

41. E. Wells, Diary, January 13, 1879. See also Miss Grundy, "Mormon Ladies Calling at the White House."

42. E. Wells, Diary, January 18, 1879. Lucy Hayes preserved the book, which resides with her papers in the Hayes Library in Fremont, Ohio. Information courtesy of Patricia Ann Scott.

In addition to their interview with President Hayes, the opportunity to speak before the House Judiciary Committee regarding the Supreme Court ruling was another exceptional moment in their Washington experience. In a letter to church president John Taylor, George Q. Cannon praised the influence of the two women in Washington, as evidenced by their appearances before the House and Senate Judiciary Committees. This was "a mark of respect almost unprecedented," he wrote.[43] It was indeed a challenging moment for the two Mormon women. "We met all their furie [*sic*] with coolness," Zina Williams happily reported, but, in fact their success must be largely attributed to being accompanied by the confident and well-regarded Sara Spencer.[44] In her introduction of the two Mormons, she reminded the committee that it had heard "large numbers of gentlemen upon this question, asking you for legislation, which will work terrible hardships upon women and children. Will you not hear these women in their own behalf?"[45] With little hope that Congress would mitigate the Supreme Court ruling illegalizing polygamy, the Mormon women, perhaps acting on advice from the skilled and experienced Cannon, asked primarily for protection from the family disintegration that would follow enforcement of the Morrill Act. Their counterproposal was that existing plural marriages should be left intact and the children of such marriages considered legitimate, a compromise with which many lawmakers concurred.[46] The response of the Judiciary Committee, which shows that the women had some influence, was to draft a bill "legitimatizing the offspring of plural marriages to a certain date; also authorizing the president to grant amnesty for past offenses against the law of 1862 (Morrill Act)." Some legislators, notably George Edmunds, a Republican senator from Vermont, however, gave them "no particular encouragement," and in three years, he shepherded the stringent Edmunds Act into law, which disfranchised polygamists and included numerous sanctions against the practice and the church.[47] How-

43. G. Cannon to John Taylor, February 7, 1880, George Q. Cannon, Letterbook.

44. Williams, Diary, January 16, 1879.

45. "Mormon Women before the House Judiciary Committee," *National Citizen and Ballot Box* 3 (February 1879): 11.

46. Elizabeth Cady Stanton et al., eds. *History of Woman Suffrage*, 3:130; "Editorial Notes: The Following from the *Mission Mirror*," *Deseret Evening News*, January 24, 1879, 2.

47. The 1882 Edmunds law also prohibited polygamists from serving jury duty and declared all voting registration and election positions vacant, directing that a board of five commissioners perform these duties. The law disenfranchised anyone in polygamy or unlawfully cohabiting and barred them from holding office. It also legitimized children born of polygamous parents before January 1, 1883, and granted

ever, at the time of their visit, Emmeline felt that some of the members, on the surface at least, "were strongly impressed" by their appeal and that "good must result." On the whole, she optimistically concluded, "I felt as if we were accomplishing something."[48]

After a dazzling month, Emmeline and Zina left Washington, arriving on February 4 "safe, safe at home." Belle, Melvina, and Louie were on hand to greet Emmeline at the station, and she was soon ensconced in her own home.

The next morning, she and Zina met with President Taylor and reported their journey to him and the other brethren and found him "specially kind."[49] But after spending a month at the seat of government where laws were being made that would drastically affect the lives of the Saints, Emmeline was uneasily aware that "everything is entirely different here at home." She worried about what seemed to her to be "a lethargy here in regard to affairs now pending."[50] Washington had been all energy and action and decision making, yet those who would be most affected by it all seemed to her to be removed and uninterested.

As expected, the *Salt Lake Tribune* declared the mission of "the roosters who have been strutting around Washington" a complete failure. To Emmeline's great dismay, the paper even attacked her husband, Daniel, the "one-eyed pirate," who, it claimed, was experiencing "the retribution of his descent into polygamy" in the "bankruptcy of his business, discord in his household, profligate sons and betrayed daughters."[51] Charlotte Godbe was even more accusatory. She berated Emmeline for what she felt was a blatant

---

amnesty to those who complied with the law as set by the president. "The Edmunds Law," in *Story of the Latter-day Saints*, by J. Allen and Leonard, 394–400.

48. E. Wells, Diary, January 17, 21, 1879. While in Washington, the two women took advantage of an offer by a professional photographer, Charles M. Bell, to take the pictures of the convention attendees. Emmeline was attired in her best black silk dress and was photographed sitting at a desk with pen in hand for the portrait, perhaps her best-known photograph today.

49. John Taylor had been unsure of the date of their return. As late as January 28, he noted in a letter to Apostle Wilford Woodruff that "our Sisters remain in [Washington], doing all the good they can, and will remain there as long as Bro. Cannon thinks they can be of use to the cause." Taylor to Woodruff, January 28, 1879, John Taylor Family Collection. Both he and they were hopeful that they had indeed done some good in this first appearance on the national scene.

50. E. Wells, Diary, February 5, 1879.

51. "Our Women Delegates," *Salt Lake Tribune*, January 18, 1879, 2. In some respects, the *Tribune* was correct in its appraisal. The "one-eyed pirate" appellation was a discourteous reference to one of Daniel's eyes, which was slightly cast or out of perfect alignment. Daniel's recent losses in his business affairs and a legal dispute over property with one of his sons provided fodder for the newspaper attack on him.

attempt to displace her. Emmeline was surprised by her sharp, unexpected attack, confiding to her diary that "Charlotte Godbe struck at me with a serpent's fangs today. I must pray for strength."[52]

Despite the Saints' apathy, which concerned Emmeline so keenly, she and Zina Williams received plaudits for their courage to stand up for the church and its principles. The always loyal *Deseret News* opined that the Washington visit had definitely been worthwhile: "The ladies are doing a good work in representing their causes in the great political center." To Emmeline's pleasure, a ward Relief Society president wrote to the *Exponent*, saying, "We hold in high esteem our sisters... who have so ably represented us in the Capitol of the Nation."[53] Accolades came from many sources, but none from Daniel. His indifference to her grand adventure made her feel "perhaps not right,"[54] but she nonetheless felt great satisfaction in being able to say, "I thank God I was the first to represent our women in the Halls of Congress."[55]

Emmeline maintained connection with the women she had met at the convention, and sent off letters of appreciation and reports of newsworthy events within days of her return. She had learned the value of correspondence, which strengthened her ties with these eastern women's leaders, despite the lack of constant personal contact. Also, her connection with *Woman's Words*, the *Ballot Box*, and the *Woman's Journal* ensured a continuing awareness of national suffrage activities.[56] Her new relationship with the national suffrage movement prompted Emmeline to add to the masthead of the *Woman's Exponent* this slogan: "The Rights of the Women of Zion, and the Rights of the Women of All Nations."[57]

Although Emmeline felt the trip to Washington had been successful—and it was, in terms of making personal connections of great future value—she did not persuade either Lucy Hayes or the president toward a sympathetic view of the Mormon situation. Lucy continued her support of the Anti-Polygamy Society of Utah, and in his State of the Union address in December 1879 and again in September 1880 during a visit to Utah,

52. E. Wells, Diary, March 8, 1879.

53. "At Washington Still," *Deseret Evening News*, January 28, 1879, 3; "Correspondence," *Woman's Exponent* 7 (May 1, 1879): 235.

54. E. Wells, Diary, February 13, 1879.

55. Ibid., February 19, 20, 1879.

56. Ibid., February 19, 25, 1878.

57. *Woman's Exponent* 8 (November 1, 1879): 81. These words remained until statehood in 1896, when it was replaced with the phrase "The Ballot in the Hands of the Women of Utah Should Be a Power to Better the Home, the State, and the Nation," reflecting the ideological shift in the argument for woman suffrage. On both premises, Utah had granted its women the right to vote.

President Hayes urged that "the right to vote, hold office, and sit on juries in the Territory of Utah be confined to those who neither practice nor uphold polygamy."[58]

Anti-Mormon feeling had definitely accelerated over the past two decades, linking plural marriage and the church to sensationalism and scandal. Ann Eliza Webb's divorce suit against Brigham Young in 1873 and the popularity of her lecture tour that followed had already stirred public antipathy toward polygamy. In 1877, John D. Lee was executed for his role in the Mountain Meadows massacre, bringing more derision of the church. The Supreme Court's decision in the Reynolds case of January 1879, whatever its legal merits, represented the nation's highest judicial action against the Mormons. And in July 1879, only five months after Emmeline and Zina returned from Washington, a mob of men stalked and fatally shot LDS missionary Joseph Standing in the Southern States mission.[59] Even those who disapproved of assassination and mob rule felt that Mormons had brought such violence on themselves because of their unorthodox practices and un-American civic life.

More disconcerting to Emmeline personally was Daniel's arrest in May 1879 for refusing to testify in a polygamy case. As supervisor of temple ordinance work, Daniel had performed scores of plural marriages in the Endowment House, a temporary edifice for that purpose. When he refused to divulge certain elements of these sacred and private rituals in a polygamy case, he was found in contempt of court by the judge, fined one hundred dollars, and imprisoned for two days.[60] His loyalty to church and principle was heralded throughout the territory, and his release, after the two-day incarceration, initiated a celebration of immense magnitude, every detail of which Emmeline noted in the *Woman's Exponent*.[61] A parade of three hundred carriages, seven bands, and ten thousand marchers viewed by fifteen thousand spectators lining the streets and rooftops accompanied Daniel's return to the city from the penitentiary in Sugarhouse. Stores closed, and hundreds of banners floated in the breeze. The procession continued to the tabernacle, which was filled to overflowing with spectators. There President John Taylor spoke to the throng, the bands played, and Daniel responded. When Daniel finally returned to his home that evening, he was serenaded

58. Gustive O. Larson, "The Crusade and the Manifesto," in *Utah's History*, edited by Poll et al., 257–58.

59. "Assassination of a Young Missionary," *Woman's Exponent* 8 (August 1, 1879): 36.

60. The polygamy case related to the marriage of John Miles to two women on the same day, the complainant being the second wife, Carolyn Owens Miles, a British convert. An outline of the case is in O. Whitney, *History of Utah*, 3:56–60.

61. "Public Demonstration," *Woman's Exponent* 8 (May 15, 1879): 242.

by the Tabernacle Choir and the German Vocal Club. Emmeline Wells's editorial tribute was sincerely laudatory. President Wells was imprisoned "for not betraying that which he held more sacred than his life," she affirmed. She printed his response to US Attorney Phillis T. Van Zile's questions that became oft-repeated refrains of loyalty and principle: "It has been and is a principle of my life never to betray a friend, my religion, my country, or my God." Emmeline helped to perpetuate his answer to Van Zile. "His words in the Court Room," she wrote, "will be handed down to posterity, and his name will forever be cherished by all who reverence and honor integrity and principle."[62]

After the glow of her Washington adventure dimmed, Emmeline returned to the pleasures of her family. John Q. Cannon, son of apostle and member of the First Presidency George Q. Cannon, was courting the twenty-year-old Annie, and Louie, irrepressibly lively at seventeen in 1879, continued to indulge her love of drama and music. She attracted swarms of suitors, filling the house with her young friends for jovial evenings. Like her sister Emmie, Louie assisted Mary Cook with her school. She and her mother read novels together and studied French, while Louie also painted, producing pieces that her mother gave as gifts to her friends or kept for her own pleasure. They both served as secretaries of church organizations, Emmeline as secretary of the Thirteenth Ward Relief Society and Louie as secretary of the General Board of the Young Ladies' MIA.

Emmeline reached the end of the year with hope that her time in Washington had been well spent. Her closing editorial for 1879 looked back on her visit with President and Mrs. Hayes and expressed her conviction that his promise to give "careful consideration" to the Mormon situation would result in good for the Mormons. That it did not yield the result she had sought only spurred her efforts to be an earnest participant in the national conversation on Mormonism. Polygamy was destined to curtail Emmeline's desire for a united womanhood whose common goal was to achieve a better, freer life for women. With the help of a determined group of women reformers, who were willing to accept Mormon women on their own terms in the support of woman suffrage and other women's rights, Emmeline and her fellow suffragists waged a battle against long-held institutional constraints on women. She was determined to use the *Woman's Exponent* and her affiliation with the national suffrage movement as platforms for her defense of women and their political and religious rights.

62. Ibid. For a complete account of the trial and events of Daniel Wells's return to the city, see Hinckley, *Daniel Hanmer Wells*, 265–96.

CHAPTER 16

Moving On
(1881–1885)

Two years after her return from Washington, Emmeline continued to enjoy the public attention she and Zina Young Williams had received at the woman suffrage convention as well as for their forthright appeal to President Hayes on behalf of the church. Almost inadvertently thrust into the public realm through her connection to the *Woman's Exponent* and her mission to Washington, Emmeline enjoyed these new public endeavors. In joining the NWSA, Emmeline had personally allied herself—and her Mormon sisters—with a small group of American women who were fomenting change in American society. Already on the outskirts of that society, Mormon women who were sympathetic to the cause had now joined another group of women experiencing the derogation of their fellow Americans. The concept of separate spheres with their respective gendered parameters still characterized American society, and until the end of the century, it was a major stumbling block to the drive for equality.

In Mormon society, however, this age-old tradition had been altered by several factors. In 1870, Mormon women had entered the public domain as voting citizens, among the first American women to do so. In 1872, women were admitted to the bar in Utah, and at the same time, Brigham Young urged women to attend eastern medical schools to improve the level of medical treatment in the territory. Utah's higher educational institutions admitted women as students and faculty members and even appointed them as trustees. Moreover, polygamy redefined the Victorian household, making many plural wives heads of their households, providing wives with more independence, and even enabling them to pursue nondomestic careers. As one visitor said, "They close no career on a woman in Utah by which she can earn a living."[1] Community building required a new definition of

1. Elizabeth Wood Kane, *Twelve Mormon Homes Visited in Succession on a Journey through Utah to Arizona*, 5.

many gendered occupations. Though subscribing to the virtues attendant to nineteenth-century womanhood, Utah women were more liberal in defining "true womanhood" than their American counterparts. Moreover, though polygamy was characterized as detrimental and demeaning to women, reality proved otherwise.[2] Mormon detractors seldom balanced the liberal attitude of Brigham Young and other church leaders toward women's personal advancement and usefulness in the community against the scandalous notions of polygamy during those decades of conflict.

That Mormon women harmonized more agreeably with the "radical" National Woman Suffrage Association than the conservative and restrictive American association was logical considering the liberality of Mormon society at that time, as well as the "radical" practice of polygamy, which was never acceptable to the American association. Emmeline was in effect a prototype of the kind of woman Mormonism fostered at that time, though the dimensions of the world she embraced were always more universal and ecumenical than those of most of her Mormon sisters. Emmeline drew admiration from both her activist cohorts in the East and her friends at home.

She differed from the majority of her fellow activists, however, in that she was obliged to earn her own living. This fact was seldom mentioned in the numerous accolades she won over the years, partly because it drew attention to Daniel's impecunious situation. Without a son who could step in and provide her needs, Emmeline was of necessity thrust on her own resources.

All of her public accomplishments, however, were not her preferred paths to win social acclaim or self-satisfaction. Literary recognition had always been her highest hope. Though by this time she had written nearly a hundred editorials and a copious number of articles and poems, she did not feel they had brought her the kind of public regard she so longed to have for her writing. Thus, in early 1881 she began preparing a compilation of her letters for publication.[3] When the proposed volume was rejected a few weeks later, she was terribly discouraged. "I regret that I am not able to publish my writings," she lamented. "Once before the world in the hands of readers, I feel I should be known for what I am." And in a truly major

2. Iversen, "Feminist Implications of Mormon Polygyny."

3. E. Wells, Diary, February 5, 1881. Such epistolary volumes were common at the time, especially among prominent men. Emmeline was as assiduous in her letter writing as in her diary keeping and would continue to be throughout her long life. Those available show a style somewhere between the very private, personal effusions of her diary and the more ideological pronouncements and descriptions that informed her editorials. The compiled letters are no longer extant.

understatement, she concluded, "Now I am comparatively unknown; perhaps it is best so."[4]

Emmeline's appraisal of herself as being "comparatively" unknown is belied by the realities of her growing prominence. She was already known to eastern readers of the women's papers to which she submitted letters and articles, and she was then corresponding with leaders of the suffrage movement and other prominent women whom she had met in Washington. Through the grain-saving movement, her visits to stake Relief Society conferences, and especially through the *Woman's Exponent*, she was also widely known throughout Utah Territory. Moreover, the January 1881 issue of a local magazine, *Tullidge's Quarterly*, carried a life sketch and long commendation for her literary work.[5] Receiving several compliments, she decided that perhaps "there may be honors yet in store for me."[6] Indeed, her self-professed anonymity was short-lived. When her friend Augusta Joyce Crocheron, a fairly popular local poet, dedicated her volume of poetry to Emmeline that year, Emmeline was immensely pleased. Crocheron gave credit to Emmeline's encouragement and friendship as spurs to its publication and hoped it would prove to be "an acceptable surprise."[7] Upon learning of the dedication, Emmeline felt that there was never a day "more auspicious[,] for fame and friendship are better than riches."[8]

Besides the *Deseret News*, for whom she wrote solicited articles on the Relief Society, visitors, socials, and women's activities, other publications vied for her writings. Many of her poems and stories were published in the *Contributor*, a young men's periodical founded by Junius Wells, one of Daniel's sons, and her writings were later published in the *Young Woman's Journal*, founded in 1889 by Susa Young Gates, as well as the *Juvenile Instructor*, edited by George Q. Cannon.[9]

At the end of 1882, Emmeline joyfully announced that she had finished writing "Hephzibah," a romanticized version of her early life. She was

4. Ibid., February 26, 1881.

5. *Tullidge's Quarterly* 1, no. 2 (January 1881): 250–53. Tullidge also wrote a eulogistic collective biography of Mormon women in 1877, *The Women of Mormondom*, with the help of both Eliza R. Snow and Emmeline Wells, who wrote several of the biographical sketches included in the book. He published *Tullidge's Quarterly* from 1880 to 1885.

6. E. Wells, Diary, March 2, 1881.

7. Augusta Joyce Crocheron, "Dedication."

8. E. Wells, Diary, July 15, 1881.

9. Emmeline often used the pseudonym "Amethyst" for her contributions. Louie joined her in writing for the *Contributor* (1880–96), and Annie began to submit articles for the *Woman's Exponent*, often filling in when her mother was traveling.

Hephzibah, a calculated choice of names, originating in the Old Testament and meaning "my delight is in her" and "a protected one."[10] Though she thought the novella was "far from perfect," she submitted it to the *Salt Lake Herald* to compete in its New Year's story-writing contest. Evidently, the *Herald* agreed with her appraisal, since she did not win the contest, nor was it printed in the paper. She did not abandon the story, however, and returned to it in 1888 when she began revising it for publication in her own paper. It was serialized in twenty-eight chapters for more than a year, from June 1889 to September 1890.[11]

In the meantime, she was deeply immersed in the pressured work of publishing her semimonthly paper. Since becoming editor—and given the publication's very straitened budget—she continued to depend on family members for assistance. May and Emeline Young Wells, two Wells daughters, were available to lend a helping hand.[12] Rob Sloan, an admirer of her daughter Louie and the son of the *Exponent*'s founder, Edward Sloan, served as a writer as well as office aid for a period. Despite the help, Emmeline was still the principal writer for her paper as well as copy editor and mailer, and the pressure mounted between editions.

A huge setback in her work was the accidental flooding of her office in the Council House when the water pipes broke in January 1883. She "mustered all the courage and patience" she could, but very little could be salvaged.[13] Six days after she had reoccupied her rehabilitated office, fire destroyed even more than had the broken water pipes. "Last night," she reported, "there was the most destructive fire which ever occurred in Salt Lake. The Council House was burned and all the adjacent buildings....

10. Isaiah's use of the name is in a promise to Israel that it shall "no more be termed Forsaken; neither shall thy land any more be termed Desolate; but thou shalt be called Hephzi-bah...for the Lord delighteth in thee" (Isa. 62:4). Emmeline had shown her knowledge of the Old Testament in other writings and often used biblical passages where appropriate.

11. The entire story is under the title "Hephzibah," *Woman's Exponent* 18 (June 1, 1889): 1 to 19 (September 15, 1890): 48. When she returned to it in 1888, she found it, six years after its first version, "quite entertaining" and wished she had the means to have it published as a single volume. Unable to raise the funds, she published it in the *Woman's Exponent*. E. Wells, Diary, August 1, 3, 1888.

12. At some point, Emmeline added an extra *m* to her name to distinguish herself from Emeline Young Wells, Louisa's daughter, who never married. Young was merely a middle name. Emeline Young Wells became active in the kindergarten movement and other public affairs, so it was deemed necessary to differentiate their names.

13. E. Wells, Diary, January 25, February 2, 1883.

The Tabernacle took fire twice. I lost in property alone over three hundred dollars."[14] Almost nothing could be salvaged. These enormous disruptions required much of her time to put things back in order even as she tried to issue the paper on time, and the losses were incalculable. Making arrangements to pay her sister-wives Lydia Ann and Susan to bring her dinner every day relieved her of one small task.[15]

The influx of visitors to her office only crescendoed over time. Out-of-town visitors were always welcome, but local people, who came by just to talk, were annoying. "I am so weary," she wrote after one deluge of local visitors, "my brain seems on fire." She was convinced that she would find the work enjoyable "if my surroundings were different. But as it is it is comparatively a life of drudgery."[16] Even Susan and Lydia Ann's prepared dinner did not materially ease the overall pressure. Editing the paper became an unrelenting burden, but despite her complaints she was determined to stay with it. Not only was she becoming increasingly more financially dependent on it, but the paper was also the literary and political channel that carried her words across the country as well as to her fellow Mormons. The more she invested her time and energy in it, the more integral it became to her life. A bright spot in this gloomy landscape was an expression of sympathy from her husband. While unable to ease her financial burden, Daniel recognized her efforts, commiserated with her over the added claims on her time during conference seasons, and to her surprise "was very anxious" about her.[17]

After her extravagantly emotional outpourings of longing for her elusive husband throughout the 1860s and '70s, she had become resigned to the "single" life and freed herself from the emotional indulgences of the past. Thoughts of William Hendrie occasionally found expression in her diary, and she wondered if she would ever "look upon his face again."[18] She and

14. Ibid., June 20, 1883. A cache of stored gunpowder in Hiram Clawson's Wagon Depot exploded and burned nearby buildings, blowing out glass windows in buildings all along Main Street and South Temple. See "Heavy Fire: Corner of a Block Gone at the Head of Main Street; Savage's Art Gallery and the Old Council House: All the Windows of the Co-op Blown to Smash," *Salt Lake Tribune*, June 21, 1883, 4; "The Big Blaze: Further Particulars Regarding Its Ravages in the City: List of the Victims and Extent of Their Loss," *Salt Lake Tribune*, June 22, 1882, 4.

15. E. Wells, Diary, July 3, 7, 1883.

16. Ibid., April 4, 7, December 8, 1881.

17. Ibid., April 8, 1882.

18. Ibid., February 24, 1881, February 24, 1883, birthdays of William Hendrie. She mentioned him only on this day, always wondering where he was and what he was doing. He was clearly still an important item in her life.

Daniel spent occasional hours together, but they were void of the heart hunger so poignantly expressed in the past. On their twenty-ninth wedding anniversary in October 1883, Daniel, as usual, did not visit her, a disappointment that called up "many tender remembrances of bygone days. My husband seemed to love me then," she remembered, but "how is it today? Never has any unpleasant scene taken place between us, in all these years." And with some pride, she concluded, "Through trials that would pierce the inmost recesses of the human heart I have risen triumphant."[19]

Though she felt that she had finally freed herself from the emotional imprisonment her need for Daniel had created, their relationship brought other challenges. That his debts were claiming more and more of his material and emotional resources became evident in 1881 and increased each year. By 1883, some of his visits had become distressingly painful, as Daniel began hinting at the possible sale of her home, along with his other city property, to pay his mounting debts. Emmeline found him to be distressed and "very much engrossed with his own affairs." On another occasion, cognizant of the nature of his concern, she offered him twenty-five dollars in orders from the Tithing Office. "He seemed unwilling to accept it," she reported, "but I insisted knowing his need of something of the kind."[20] As the expected provider for his family, he had hoped to settle these problems without telling or upsetting his families about them, so he could only have been embarrassed and hesitant at her offer. She did not know then, however, how extensive his financial imbroglios would ultimately be and how they would impact her own life, but by 1883, the ominous signs of a dramatic change in her life were hard to miss.

When Daniel actually began selling some of his city property, his wives were apprehensive about the status of their own homes.[21] Emmeline could not bear the thought of losing the home that was not only a fount of precious memories but also a shelter from the tangled world she faced each day. But when Daniel "introduced in the most careful manner" the need to sell it, she could no longer wish away the inevitable. "No one knows how my sympathies and heart's deepest depths were stirred by the very thought of parting with the dear old homestead where my children were born and reared," she lamented. "The very trees and shrubs are my especial friends, they know my heart secrets more than any human soul."[22] She had

19. Ibid., October 10, 1881.

20. Ibid., May 19, December 16, 21, 1881. Having little to spare herself, this was a very generous offer.

21. Ibid., April 27, 28, May 5, 1883.

22. Ibid., May 8, 9, 1883.

always assumed that her home was irretrievably hers, and losing it was impossible to imagine. She had long felt that if she had her "home and means independent" she would feel more secure, but now she was beginning to understand that her future security would be her own responsibility—that she would be independent indeed, but in a way she had not envisioned.[23] Daniel's call to serve as president of the European Mission of the church in 1884, however, delayed action on the sale of any more of his real estate, and his wives enjoyed the reprieve that his assignment gave them. Louisa accompanied him on this mission.[24]

Emmeline's daughters were now making lives of their own. In 1880, Annie was married to John Q. Cannon, but she and her infant son, George Q., returned to live with her mother when John Q. was called as a missionary to Germany. Some years after the death of their first two children, Belle and Septimus moved to Ogden, where Septimus supervised the church's mercantile institution, before moving to San Francisco, where he oversaw shipments of Utah grain to England and Belle tended her four living children. Mell and Will lived only a few blocks away from Emmeline, and once again, they were struggling to accept the death of ten-year-old Leslie Alma, Mell's son with William Dunford, three years after the death of their daughter Winnifred Woods. Leslie had accidentally shot himself with a loaded toy pistol on July 4, 1882, and succumbed several weeks later. Verona and Daisie, daughters of Mell and William Dunford, and Mell and Will's son five-year-old Percival were the only survivors of Mell's children at that time. Percival's untimely death from diphtheria in 1887 at age nine left Mell bereft of three of her five children.[25]

Emmeline mourned the death of another loved one the same year Leslie died. Elizabeth Ann Whitney died on March 17, 1882, perhaps a fitting date for her. Emmeline's moving tribute to her in the *Woman's Exponent* was her last gift to the woman who had been a loving presence in her life. Elizabeth Ann had served for less than two years as Eliza R. Snow's counselor in the general presidency of the Relief Society, finally organized

23. Ibid., December 9, 1881. Even then, she was searching for additional ways to maintain her paper, hoping to sell ads and increase circulation. Marketing her paper had become as essential as publishing it.

24. Daniel had served a shorter term as European Mission president in 1864, at which time Hannah had accompanied him.

25. Winnifred Woods died at age four on Christmas Day 1879. Leslie was ten when he died, and Percival Woods died of diphtheria in October 1887 at age nine. See "In Memoriam," *Woman's Exponent* 8 (January 1, 1880): 117 (Winnifred); "A Sad Event," 11 (August 1, 1882): 37 (Leslie); "He Only Sleeps," 16 (November 1, 1887): 84–85 (Percival).

in 1880, and in the five years before her own death in 1887, Eliza never replaced her.[26]

While Annie was living with Emmeline and Louie, she and Louie maintained a lively social schedule, attending the theater, parties, outings, and other activities. Louie also spent many days with Belle in Ogden before the Sears family moved to California. A mature, sisterly companionship was forged during this time between Belle and Louie, and sometime in 1883, the two sisters announced to their mother that they wanted to go east to visit the places of Emmeline's youth and to attend a reunion of the Dickinson family, since the Wells family were descendants. Melvina had made a similar sentimental journey two years earlier. With Emmeline's blessing, her oldest and youngest daughters left in July of that year. Emmeline was insistent that Louie keep a diary of the journey and presented her two daughters with the names of places to visit and people to see. Rather than keeping a diary, however, Louie wrote letters to her mother and father, describing the people she had met and scenes the girls knew so well from their mother's oft-repeated tales of her childhood. Emmeline printed the letters in the *Exponent*, including Louie's account of the Dickinson reunion.[27] Soon afterward, Annie left her baby son with her mother to join John Q. for the last months of his mission. The *Exponent* was the recipient of Annie's numerous descriptive letters of her travels.[28]

In 1881, before Annie joined him, John Q. visited Orson F. Whitney in London, where Whitney had been sent to assist with the publication of the *Millennial Star*, the church's British periodical. Ort, like John Q., had left a wife behind. He married Zina Smoot of Provo in December 1879 after eliciting an agreement from her that the deceased Emmie Wells had "the right of precedence," probably meaning that she would be on record as his

26. "Elizabeth Ann Whitney," *Woman's Exponent* 10 (March 15, 1882): 153–55. See also Louie Wells, "In Memoriam"; and "Death of Mother Whitney," *Deseret Evening News*, February 16, 1882, 3. Other contemporary accounts of her life are Tullidge, *The Women of Mormondom*, 41–43 (written by Emmeline); "An Incident of the Days of Kirtland," *Woman's Exponent* 20 (January 1, 1892): 100; and "Elizabeth Ann Whitney, a Sketch," *Woman's Exponent* 41 (December 1912): 25.

27. Louie Wells, "Nauvoo the Beautiful," *Woman's Exponent* 12 (August 1, 1883): 37–38; Louie Wells, "Letter Number Two," 12 (August 15, 1883): 44–45; Louie Wells, "The Dickinson Reunion," 12 (September 1, 1883): 53–54; Louie Wells, "Letter IV," 12 (September 15, 1883): 61–62.

28. Annie's letters and articles were published between December 15, 1883, and May 15, 1884, in the *Woman's Exponent*, vol. 12, and in June and July 1884, vol. 13. She and John Q. returned from their mission on June 24, 1884. There are no extant diaries of Emmeline's for the last half of 1883 and for all of 1884. Emmeline's additional care of Annie's baby may well have made diarying more difficult during that period.

first wife through a proxy marriage in the temple. He had asked Emmeline at the time of Emmie's death about having her vicariously sealed (married) to him, but Daniel had evidently deferred his permission. After several months of repeated visits to the Wells home and writing a verse on the "headboard" of Emmie's grave, he finally married Zina.[29] "We sat up talking quite late, and after we went to bed talked two or three hours," John Q. noted in his diary. "Ort opened up to me the story of his life and devotion to my deceased sister-in-law with a minuteness and fervour quite touching." Without explaining what Orson said to him, John wrote, "I thoroughly believe his statement of the case, and hope his desire in the matter will be gratified."[30] It was not until seven years later, in 1888, and ten years after her death, however, that Emmie Wells was finally sealed to Orson F. Whitney in the Manti temple, with Daniel H. Wells officiating.

When Eliza R. Snow was officially set apart as general president of the Relief Society in 1880, Emmeline was appointed assistant secretary to Sarah M. Kimball, the general secretary. She continued to travel to stake Relief Society conferences, which often took three or four days. Her daughters were much opposed to these visits, considering how much their mother had to do, but she felt they were "as much a duty as to edit the paper" and explained that they helped her in her work.[31] On these visits, she often aided Eliza R. Snow in organizing Primaries, explaining that "it is one of my hobbies to organize."[32] Eliza was noted for encouraging women to exercise the spiritual gifts, particularly speaking in tongues and blessing of women in confinement or for healing. These were considered a sacred privilege to women of this era, and Emmeline not only attended to the sick and poor in her ward but also assisted in giving blessings for health and uncomplicated childbirth, and she frequently interpreted testimonies given in tongues. That Mormonism unlocked spiritual opportunities and gifts to women, Emmeline never doubted. In 1877, in a letter to the Gunnison, Utah, Relief Society, she recalled a blessing given to her in Nauvoo by Eliza R. Snow, who prophesied that Emmeline would be called to perform a mission that had never before been asked of a woman. When Brigham Young called her to lead the grain-saving program, "we knew this was the literal fulfilment

29. Orson F. Whitney, Diary, July 28, 29, November 16, December 19, 1879. Mormons believed that deceased individuals could receive the saving ordinances of the Gospel, earthly procedures, vicariously, with relatives or friends serving as proxies for the deceased.

30. "Diary of John Q. Cannon, 1881, Editor 'Deseret News,'" typescript copy dated 1957, LDS Church History Library, Salt Lake City.

31. E. Wells, Diary, November 14, 1881.

32. Ibid., January 4, 1882.

of Sister Eliza's prophecy." She then affirmed that "to those who feel that there are prophetesses as well as prophets, we may speak of these things. To us, they are sacred truths." Knowing, however, that "it is very hard for some people to believe, that women are acknowledged of God as holding any Priesthood power," she felt certain that "time will demonstrate the harmony which exists in sex, and races of people and prove to all that women are not an inferior race of people beings [*sic*], but in many respects superiorly endowed."[33]

While Emmeline did not visibly radiate her spiritual nature in the more definable way it emanated from Zina Young or Elizabeth Whitney, it nonetheless underlay all of her undertakings, convinced as she was of the divinity of the origin of the church, its theological inclusion of women, and its opportunity for leadership, intellectual growth, and spiritual expression. Just a few years before her death, she reminisced on the days in which spiritual gifts were freely exercised. No visits could match "the beautiful little meetings...which the sisters often held in my house," she wrote. She vividly recalled the tender moments listening to "the glorious testimonies borne by Sister [Isabella] Horne, and Sister Eliza Snow, and the rich history told by Sarah M. Kimball, Sarepta Heywood, Elizabeth Howard and others; and the wonderful singing of Mother [Elizabeth Ann] Whitney, with its beautiful interpretation by Aunt Zina [Young]."[34] These women, along with her daughters, were a vital part of the female world Emmeline inhabited wherein she found friendship, spiritual strength, and a sustaining empathy.

In May 1882, the Relief Society decided it was time to open a hospital, as the Catholics and Episcopalians had already done in Utah. Dr. Ellen Ferguson enlisted Emmeline's aid in bringing the subject to the attention of Eliza R. Snow, whose support enabled them to launch the project.[35] When word began circulating that the Relief Society was considering sponsoring a medical facility, Emmeline's office was inundated by people wanting to know about it. "So many inquiring about the Hospital," she complained, "I find it a labor to make the necessary explanations." Their persistence in the

33. Emmeline B. Wells to Mrs. Helena Madsen, February 15, 1877, letter copied into the Minutes of the Gunnison Ward Relief Society, Gunnison Stake, February 1, 1877 (date incorrectly recorded).

34. A. W. Cannon, "Mothers in Israel."

35. E. Wells, Diary, May 4, 6, 1882. Before his death in 1877, Brigham Young had pressed upon Eliza R. Snow the necessity of establishing such a medical facility, and in 1882, Emmeline and Dr. Ferguson, along with Elizabeth Howard, urged her to take action on his directive. Brigham Young had been instrumental in encouraging women to study in the East to obtain medical degrees, and instituting this level of medical care was a natural outgrowth of his interest.

inevitable process of fund-raising brought happy results, however, despite the fact that "some who are very rich have been parsimonous [*sic*] in the extreme toward us," she noted.[36] On July 17, 1882, just two months after the idea was voiced, the Deseret Hospital, a refurbished vacant home, opened its doors.[37] This was to be a center where spiritual ministrations were as freely dispensed as medications, and over its lifetime it provided service to many patients. For more than ten years, Emmeline, as secretary of the Deseret Hospital Association, prepared the annual reports and kept the records of the hospital, requiring hours of consultation with doctors and administrators. It was a laborious responsibility, but she gave her best to its success.[38] In time, however, the logistics of maintaining such a facility proved to be too extensive for the Relief Society, and it closed its doors in 1894.

During this same busy decade, Mormons and the federal government were reaching an inevitable and decisive confrontation. The 1879 Supreme Court decision outlawing polygamy had unleashed a number of punitive antipolygamy bills for consideration by Congress. Some proposed disfranchising all women in the territory, which brought strong resistance from national suffragists through petitioning, lecturing, and lobbying Congress. Several women lawyers along with some congressmen doubted the legality of removing the vote from all women in the territory, but their voices went unheeded. By 1881 these anti-Mormon measures, all designed to enforce the 1862 Morrill Act, culminated in the Edmunds Act, which became law in March 1882. Only the women involved in plural marriage lost their right to vote, which included Emmeline. For twelve years, Utah women had led the nation with the largest number of female voters in the land.

By this time, both local and national politics beckoned Emmeline. One of her concerns related to the 1881 election that should have returned

36. Ibid., May 25, 1882. A planning committee and executive board were created to make the arrangements for the hospital.

37. See ibid., various dates between May 4 and May 26, 1882. Announcement of the new hospital was made in "Deseret Hospital," *Woman's Exponent* 11 (June 15, 1882): 12. Eliza R. Snow headed the ten-member board of directors, with Zina Young as vice president and Emmeline Wells as secretary. A full report of the dedication of the hospital appeared in "Deseret Hospital," *Woman's Exponent* 11 (August 1, 1882): 36. See also "Home Affairs," *Woman's Exponent* 11 (August 1, 1882): 37; and Scott Parker, "Deseret Hospital."

38. E. Wells, Diary, May 5, 1883. The reports were usually printed in the *Woman's Exponent*. For example, see "Deseret Hospital: Report to April Conference, 1883," *Woman's Exponent* 11 (April 15, 1883): 173. At this time, she was preparing to give a verbal report on the "past year's labors" at the first annual meeting of the Deseret Hospital Association held at the Council House. See *Woman's Exponent* 11 (May 15, 1883): 187 for notice of the meeting.

George Q. Cannon to Congress as Utah's delegate in 1881. Though Cannon won the popular vote by an outstanding margin, the governor refused to certify him pending passage of the Edmunds Act, which withdrew voting and office-holding privileges from all polygamists. After the bill's passage, Cannon was thus refused his seat in Congress as Utah's delegate, and the church lost a strong and respected advocate in Washington.[39] At the November election, Mormon John T. Caine, a monogamist, replaced Cannon. It was clear to Mormons that the Edmunds Act would make serious changes in their way of life. Its stringent enforcement allowed crippling prison sentences and fines that sent husbands and sometimes wives into hiding to avoid arrest and prosecution. Because Emmeline did not cohabit with Daniel and he would soon be in Europe presiding over the European Mission of the church, she was generally free from surveillance.[40]

Despite the upheaval of family life in Utah and the unexamined consequences of this widespread federal intervention, the Mormons (with a few Gentiles) mounted a fifth attempt at statehood in 1881 with a meeting of the Central Committee of the People's Party to nominate delegates to a constitutional convention. Emmeline Wells and Sarah M. Kimball, along with a number of other women, served on the preliminary committees, and Emmeline, Sarah, and Elizabeth Howard became delegates to the convention, held the following year. "Although this was a new departure, it caused no friction whatever and was good political discipline for the women, especially in parliamentary law and usage," Emmeline observed.[41] After three days of meetings, she admitted that she enjoyed the work "very

39. The long controversy over his eligibility resulted in a new election in 1883 that sent John T. Caine to Washington as Utah's delegate. For more details about the election, see "The Utah Delegate," *Salt Lake Tribune*, February 14, 1881, 4; "Our Delegate," *Woman's Exponent* 9 (February 15, 1881): 140; Orson F. Whitney, "1880–1881," in his *History of Utah*, 3:130–37, 141; and Davis Bitton, *George Q. Cannon: A Biography*, 239–43. See also E. Wells, Diary, February 11, 1881.

40. Nevertheless, even in his absence, his wives were not totally secure from interrogation. In a letter to Mary Ann Maughan in Logan, dated April 14, 1885, Emmeline indicated that "two Deputy Marshalls" had been after her, but she "happened to be out" when they came to her office, since she had purposely tried to avoid them. "They caught two of my girls however," and she would go before them, she wrote, if she could not avoid doing so. Peter Weston Maughan Family Association Collection.

41. Emmeline noted the election of the three women in her report on woman suffrage in Utah for Susan B. Anthony and Ida Husted Harper's fourth volume of *History of Woman Suffrage* and their part in "framing this constitution." She declared "their work was as satisfactory as that of the male members." Emmeline B. Wells, "Utah." She reported that there were sixty-nine gentlemen and three ladies elected as delegates. More information in "Constitutional Convention," *Woman's Exponent* 10 (April 15, 1882): 172.

much indeed. It suits me admirably and all are quite polite to me."[42] She also reported on the "pretty speech" of a delegate from Nephi, which she found to be "all too poetical to have any bearing upon the subject in question." He argued that "women should not labor but be protected and when they assumed duties which belonged to men they were no longer women," spoken to a bemused Emmeline and her female companions.[43] Once again, this effort at statehood failed to win approval from Congress. But Emmeline happily let her readers know that "the constitution just framed is the only one we have any knowledge of, in which women have had a voice."[44] No victory was too small to be acknowledged, and no failure was too large to be surmounted.

42. E. Wells, Diary, April 12, 1882.

43. Ibid., April 26, 1882.

44. "Constitution of Utah," *Woman's Exponent* 10 (May 1, 1882): 180.

CHAPTER 17

A Return to Her Roots

(1885–1886)

Emmeline's pathbreaking trip to Washington in 1879 was the first time she had traveled to the East since leaving Massachusetts thirty-five years earlier. She had hoped to return often to attend the annual suffrage conventions, but the national mood following that first trip militated against what would undoubtedly have been a publicity-riddled appearance in the nation's capital. Emmeline had long desired to return to her childhood home and revisit the scenes of her youth that had filled so many lonely hours with memory. In 1885, she was seriously contemplating making the trip. She knew that the Woodward family had undergone many changes in forty years. Only Pallas, Cordelia, and Hiram resided in Massachusetts, and Lucy had moved to several different locations when her children married. Manson was presently in Kansas, and James had died four years earlier. Since Ellen and Adeline Maria had journeyed back to New England, and Melvina had visited New Salem in 1880, followed by Belle and Louie in 1883, Emmeline was determined to visit her home state as well.

This would not be an easy reunion for Emmeline, a polygamist's wife, since, unlike her polygamous sister, Ellen, who had long since lived apart from her husband, she was a public figure and a vocal defender of plural marriage. Moreover, all of her siblings whom she would visit were particularly contemptuous of the practice, like most other Americans. Emmeline, their loving sister, who believed and practiced what they so deeply disdained, would soon be on their doorsteps. Despite her misgivings of the welcome she might receive, Emmeline yearned for a reunion.

And so, on a brisk winter day, December 16, 1885, Emmeline, always reluctant to leave her home, "the dearest spot on earth to me," but eager to reunite with her siblings, began her journey eastward to the scenes of her youth and the renewal of the familial ties that had been strained for so long. Orson, Louie, and Annie and her two children accompanied her to the D&RG depot, where Ort gave her an elegant illustrated book entitled *Beauties of Tennyson* as a farewell gift. Taking a southern route to the East Coast, she was happy to have her "dear son-in-law" John Q. Cannon accompany her as far as Provo. He was the last one "to bind me to home affairs," she sadly noted, and remarked to her diary that she could "tell those who think they can live away from Utah that it is indeed very hard to be separated from one's own people or those who believe as we do."[1]

Her natural curiosity and keen eye kept her occupied as she recorded her visual observations in words, and she busily described the sights in her diary. When she reached Chicago and settled herself on the train to New York, she felt more "assured" when the conductor told her there were two ministers and two Bible missionaries on board.[2]

Emmeline was surprised to find so many Mormons living in the East, many of whom eagerly welcomed visitors from Utah. A less welcome Utah resident, whom Emmeline saw when she attended the theater in New York, was one of the Utah commissioners, appointed by the president to supervise voting activities in Utah, as required by the Edmunds Act. He seemed "perfectly at ease with his conscience," Emmeline observed, "and smiled as serenely as if he had not helped to kindle this indignation of the nation against some of the best citizens of this free Republic."[3] She was lavishly entertained by her friends, and with Richard Young as guide, she was the typical tourist enjoying the New York sites of interest, all fondly detailed in her diary and the *Woman's Exponent*.[4] But the highlight of the trip awaited her.

A short train ride the morning of December 23 took her to Palmer, Massachusetts, not many miles from her hometown of North New Salem, where she found her "big handsome well-dressed brother" waiting for her on the platform. He "took me in his arms and kissed me," and then the two of them drove in his carriage to his home in Thorndike, a small community within the boundaries of Palmer. Seeing her beloved brother again, Emmeline was simply "to[o] full for words." Hiram, at fifty, was far more the former captain of the Fifth Massachusetts Cavalry, wounded in Petersburg during the Civil War and mustered out a hero, than the footloose, rebellious teenager she

1. E. Wells, "My Trip East," December 16, 1885. The information relating to this trip is contained in a travel diary written as a long prose narrative or reminiscence with only occasional dates interspersed.

2. Ibid., December 19, 1885, 19. She wrote in greater detail about her train travel to New York under the title "From Salt Lake to New York," *Woman's Exponent* 14 (January 1, 1886): 116.

3. "A Glimpse of New York City," *Woman's Exponent* 14 (January 15, 1886): 124.

4. Emmeline wrote a much more exhaustive account of her days in New York City in her diary as well as in the *Woman's Exponent* above.

had said good-bye to so many years before. Hiram had become postmaster in Thorndike when he first settled there and then entered the retail grocery business in Palmer, rising to become a partner and finally owner of a major meat-cutting business. He left his thriving business when appointed a vice president of the Palmer Savings Bank. Active in local community affairs, he was chairman of the Board of Selectmen, overseer of the poor, and chaplain and commander of the Grand Army Post. To cap his civic participation, he later served two years in the Massachusetts general assembly. Emmeline had every reason to be proud of her youngest brother.

Hiram lived in a home befitting his many achievements. It was a tall, handsome house, with an impressive front door and elegantly furnished rooms. One niece described it as very modern, with an upstairs bathroom, a room next to the pantry just for washing dishes with a window between for convenience, and front and back stairways. A different set of dishes was used for each meal, she remarked, the blue set reserved only for breakfast.[5] Emmeline was equally impressed with the steam heat that warmed every room.

Clouding her joy at being once again with her "long-lost" brother in his beautiful home was Emmeline's apprehension at meeting his wife, Carrie. She greeted them at the door, and Emmeline quickly observed the tasteful elegance of her soft, grayish-brown cashmere dress graced by a cluster of yellow bows at her waist. Emmeline was impressed by the "nice and lady like" appearance of her sister-in-law. But her observant eye noticed more than the details of Carrie's apparel. "I felt from the first moment," Emmeline perceived, "that she had formed a decided opinion concerning me." Noting that Carrie's eyes never left Hiram, Emmeline reserved judgment and did not "fall in love with her at first sight," sensing the begrudging hospitality Carrie was obliged to offer.[6]

Emmeline's timing for this visit was probably injudicious, considering the attention Mormons were receiving following passage of the 1882 anti-polygamy Edmunds Act. By 1885, an even more punitive bill was being debated in Congress that would strike at the financial underpinnings of the church as well as repeal woman suffrage in Utah. One could hardly escape the negative attention leveled against Mormons during this decade. Here now, under her own roof, Carrie was obliged to house one of them for several days. What would the neighbors think? Despite her ladylike qualities, Carrie was unable to cloak her antipathy to Emmeline. At this first meeting,

5. Geneva Ramsey Kingkade, letter to Glenys Harris, June 1, 1967, typescript copy in my possession. The original is in the possession of Glenys Harris, granddaughter of Pallas Woodward Clark, Emmeline's sister.

6. E. Wells, "My Trip East," December 23, 1885, 26.

Emmeline perceived that Carrie would not countenance any reference to Emmeline's belief or principles while under her roof. Though well steeled against the insults and aversion she had experienced from anti-Mormons in Washington and in Utah, especially the slanderous name-calling by the *Salt Lake Tribune*, she did not expect to bear quite the same calumny from her brother's wife. "To insult a guest who has come hundreds of miles to see your husband and one who has cared for him in his tender years, who has loved him with an unbounded affection is it seems to me unpardonable in a wife," Emmeline complained to her diary.[7] Only her concern over her brother's discomfort enabled her to "endure her insult," but the unexpected affront disconcerted Emmeline enough to elicit a desire to leave the next day. But Hiram's obvious embarrassment and the distress that he would feel at Emmeline's hasty departure convinced her to see this uncomfortable situation through to the end.

When at last she was able to take refuge in her room, she gave way to her humiliation with "bitter tears." "I should bear without murmur or complaint such stinging reproaches and such insults to my faith," she chastised herself and concluded that she would try to prove herself "equal if not superior to" the situation.[8]

Gathering the strength to follow her resolve to be gracious, Emmeline breakfasted with the family, no doubt on the blue dishes, on the morning of December 24. Afraid that Carrie would not approve, she resisted an impulse to kiss her brother as he sat in his dressing gown and slippers, reading the morning paper. Charlie, the oldest of Hiram's three children, had already gone off to work, and Geneva, called Neva by the family, and Granger left for school before breakfast was half over. Later, Hiram also set off for Palmer. After unpacking her clothes, Emmeline gave Carrie the gifts she had brought the family, but did not offer her "the carved wooden trifles that were ornamented with The Temple & the Tabernacle," which she held in "such reverence. I felt she should not desecrate them with any scornful words as she had insulted me the night before." At noon, Hiram returned for the midday dinner, "my darling brother with his earnest thoughtful face," and Emmeline felt more at ease. She was surprised, however, when he asked his wife to take Emmeline for a drive through the countryside that afternoon. She first felt "galled" at his suggestion, thinking that her brother seemed "afraid to take me to ride himself."[9] Emmeline felt that it might have been an effort to atone for Carrie's cursory behavior the day before, but Emmeline's "heart was still smarting," and she "had no pleasure in her

7. Ibid., 26, 27.

8. Ibid., 28.

9. Ibid., December 24, 1885, 31.

company." She felt that Carrie held Hiram so much "in her power" that "he did not even dare to mention subjects that lay near to his heart about my family." Time, however, began to close the breach between them, and Emmeline's outgoing manner helped to melt the icy beginning of their first meeting. Like most people who disdained her polygamous status but admired and liked her personally, Carrie began to warm to the geniality of her personality.

When evening came, the children filled the house with their Christmas Eve excitement, which turned Emmeline's thoughts to her loved ones at home, the only moment of homesickness that she records. She pictured the family gathered at Annie's with stories, poems, gifts, and food in abundance. But the domestic scene in Thorndike was equally charming, a setting more befitting the affluent lifestyle of the Clarks and enjoyed by a happy, loving family, its head a pillar of the community and successful provider.[10]

Emmeline woke late on Christmas morning, and when she went downstairs, she found the children had already opened their gifts. Hiram was alone in the parlor, and she was deeply moved by his Merry Christmas greeting and kiss. "My heart was almost to[o] full for words to express and I had to be very careful not to betray the strong emotion that swept over me at this demonstration made so naturally at an opportune time," she happily recounted to her diary.[11] Her feelings for her young brother knew no bounds. He had long been one of the great loves of her life.

Breakfast was eaten in comparative silence. Only Granger, "who tried harder than anyone to entertain me," she commented, "showed me some attention." When their friends called, Neva and Granger went off ice-skating, but Granger soon reappeared "with a chapter of accidents." Since dinner preparations occupied his mother, he laid his woes before Emmeline, who easily responded with the sympathy he wanted. He perked up after their chat, and soon dinner was served. The children showed her their presents, and unlike the unusual silence of the Christmas-morning breakfast, dinnertime "all passed off pleasantly as a summer day." The big event of the day was the program at the church. Hiram was superintendent of the Sunday School and thus supervised the entertainment in which Neva eagerly participated. He also passed out the presents from the two large Christmas trees at the front of the hall. This was hardly the spartan New England Christmas service Emmeline remembered in New Salem.[12]

On the morrow, she would leave Thorndike and travel the few miles to Orange to visit her sisters, though she found herself reluctant to leave.

10. Ibid., 32, 33.

11. Ibid., December 25, 1885, 33.

12. Ibid., 36.

After the rocky beginning, her long-awaited reunion with her much-loved brother came to a pleasant end. She would see him again, but never with quite the same spirit that characterized this first meeting. Even Carrie's initial denigration could not erase the exhilaration Emmeline had enjoyed during her three days with Hiram. The bonds that had once united them in their family and faith had clearly loosened, but their shared memories and genuine love would, she hoped, keep them connected.

A few miles away, in Orange, lived Emmeline's older sister Pallas and her husband, William Clark. Pallas was now sixty-seven, "pale and trembling" and "grown old and feeble," with "shoulders once so straight now stooping." Gone was the slim, graceful, vibrant older sister whose image Emmeline had carried in her mind for forty years. But when they met one another in the hall of Pallas's home, there was no hesitation or stiffness in their greeting. Words of remorse, which seemed to have been stored away until this meeting, came tumbling out as Pallas begged Emmeline to forgive her anger when Emmeline became a Mormon, married James Harris, and left home. "They had built up great hopes for me in a literary career and becoming a convert to the Mormon faith had sorely disappointed them." But Emmeline was not there to regret the past, only to relive its pleasant memories.[13]

For the next few days, Pallas and William drove Emmeline through the countryside as Emmeline re-created a life lived long ago in these familiar places. They visited the family homestead, the schoolhouse, the church, and the homes of her North New Salem neighbors. They drove past the pond, visited the cemetery where her father and older sister Adaline were buried, and passed over the brook where Emmeline was baptized. She was saddened to see that so many of the graceful hemlock groves that had caught her fancy as a young girl had disappeared, but she reveled in seeing the remnants of the trees she still loved. Hiram later reminded her that he was often sent to fetch her from her hiding place among them.[14] Her diary brimmed over with descriptions of the places as they were and had once been as well as of the people she remembered who had once populated the little village of North New Salem.[15]

13. Ibid., 36–39. This reminiscence/diary provided much of the information used in the New England chapters of this book. Thus, details of places and persons visited as well as memories evoked will not be recounted here.

14. E. Wells, Diary, February 27, 1896.

15. E. Wells, "My Trip East," December 26–30, 1885, 41–66. In an article, "Visit to New England," published in the *Woman's Exponent* 14 (February 1, 1886): 132–33, Emmeline also described this New England visit, especially reminiscing over the trauma of her baptismal day and the opposition of her friends and schoolmates. She recalled that forty people had been baptized in the area of North New Salem, nearly all of whom gathered in Nauvoo.

On the last day of the year, she visited Petersham, the town of her birth. In a turn of the road, they found the old red house where James's mother, Lucy Harris, now Blackinton, lived. "She had been very hard and cruel to me in the days that were past," Emmeline remembered, "and I had never quite forgiven her for the unkindness and suffering she had caused me & those dear to me to pass thro'." But Emmeline wanted to visit her and went alone to her house. Lucy did not recognize Emmeline at first, and during their conversation Lucy felt the need to disclaim "stoutly any desire to treat me harshly" back in Nauvoo. Emmeline, however, bitterly recalled that at the time, "she wanted to have taken my baby from me which would have been worse than death to me, it was a part of myself yet dearer still. But that was in that dreadful past when I suffered such untold agonies." At the end of the visit with Lucy, now more than ninety years old, Emmeline gave her a copy of the *Woman's Exponent* and bought her photograph, a common custom in some social circles, of which Emmeline was evidently aware. When she left, Emmeline doubted that she would ever see her again. The visit spawned a page full of pitiful memories, but the continued travelogue of places remembered with joy helped dispel the heavy cloud that settled over Emmeline after the visit. "It had been a day of days a red letter day indeed to me, and one never to be forgotten."[16]

After another round of visits, she and Pallas went together to see their sister Cordelia (Delia). She lived near South Royalston in a "lovely old farm with every comfort possible and her husband a most willing subject," doing all he could to make Delia happy. Emmeline's meeting with this sister was most affecting, as Delia was more demonstrative than the others. She was the last one to see Emmeline as she left for Nauvoo, and she "was as much interested in me as she could be to have me excel in everything." It was a grand reunion for the three sisters, and for three rainy days they spent the time reminiscing, eating, talking, and enjoying being together once again. Finally, on January 5, it was time for Pallas to return home. In the morning, the three sisters climbed a nearby hill that gave them a view of the surrounding countryside, then walked among the "cheekaberry" (chokeberry) bushes, evergreens, and mosses, "jumping from rock to rock," like young girls, before visiting the sugar orchard and barn. What a picture this must have made—Pallas age sixty-seven, Delia age sixty-two, and Emmeline fifty-eight. Pallas returned home, while Delia and Emmeline continued their sightseeing for another day. Then it was time to pack up and return to Thorndike. Emmeline spent only one night at her brother's home before going on to Boston. To her delight, Hiram made the trip with her.

16. E. Wells, "My Trip East," December 31, 1885, 67, 68, 73.

As in New York, Emmeline was treated to many of the cultural offerings of the great city and also the statehouse, where Hiram would soon sit as a representative. They saw the opera *La Traviata* and a cyclorama of *The Battle of Gettysburg*. In the evening, Emmeline found the city charming, all lit up by gaslight. After Hiram returned home, she visited the Tremont Temple, where many woman suffrage meetings were held, but was then in use by a Baptist revival meeting. She resisted her missionary impulse to contravene the "delusions" of both the Episcopalians and the Baptists. "How glad I should be to tell the people the truth," she declared at the end of the day.[17]

One of her goals in Boston was to visit the offices of the *Watchman*, a religious paper with whom she had a running dialogue regarding Mormonism, Emmeline refuting the misrepresentations that filled its columns.[18] She found that her name was well known in the office and was pleased that one of the employees told her that she enjoyed the *Exponent* and often clipped poetry from its pages. From there Emmeline went to the office of the *Woman's Journal*. This was the most prestigious of all of the woman suffrage papers, and Emmeline frequently reprinted its editorials and articles and corresponded with its editor, Henry Blackwell. Serving as the organ of the American Woman Suffrage Association, it expressed the association's opposition to polygamy and articulated its policy to refuse membership of polygamous women and their organizations in the AWSA. Nonetheless, Emmeline had high regard for Lucy Stone, its founder, and often sparred with her husband, Henry Blackwell, through their respective papers. Emmeline was determined to meet at least one of these two giants of the suffrage movement.

Fortunately, Henry Blackwell was in the office and greeted her cordially. To her surprise, he invited her to join him and Lucy for tea the next day, an invitation that she eagerly accepted. The next morning, she busied herself by visiting the New England Hospital for women and children and the New England Conservatory of Music to see Evan Stephens, a young music student from Utah, but her thoughts were on the anticipated visit.[19]

Because the afternoon "was one of some importance to me," wrote Emmeline, she arranged to have her hair coiffed, after which she dressed in her best silk velvet. Henry Blackwell met her at the depot, where the train

17. Ibid., January 8–10, 1886, 82–83.

18. The full name of the paper is the *Christian Watchman and Christian Reflector*. It was published by the Baptist church in Boston under various names (1819 and 1894). It was generally anti-Mormon.

19. Evan Stephens studied music in Boston for ten months. After returning to Utah, he became a popular composer and conductor of the Tabernacle Choir. He led the choir to a second-place award at the Columbian Exposition in Chicago in 1893.

would take them to Neponset, a few miles from Boston. A sleigh drove them up the steep hill to the Stone-Blackwell home, "a very handsome house indeed," Emmeline observed. Lucy Stone was on the piazza to greet them. "Mrs. Wells this is my wife," Henry Blackwell politely said, to which Lucy immediately added, "Lucy Stone." "She is evidently very tenacious of her rights," Emmeline reflected. She also met their daughter, Alice Stone Blackwell, who was eagerly engaged in the work of her parents. The bright fire burning in the grate and the lovely furnishings of the sitting room were in such good taste, Emmeline noted, that they created a beautiful, harmonious scene. The conversation centered on Utah, especially since the US Senate had just passed another antipolygamy bill, the more punitive Edmunds-Tucker Act. Emmeline was surprised and pleased to find that her hosts found the bill "unjust and unconstitutional," especially in the "confiscation of Church property" and "the taking away of suffrage from women," but they said nothing about the purpose for these harsh measures.[20] If polygamy had not been such a barrier, Lucy and Emmeline might have become good friends. They were both single-minded in pursuing what they believed was a just cause, both were self-supporting despite their marriages, both stood firm in their commitment to their unconventional marriages, and both were articulate and persuasive speakers and journalists and commanded the forums of their own newspapers. Moreover, both loved their native New England, and Emmeline was interested to learn that Lucy Stone and Diadama Woodward had both been born in Brookfield, Massachusetts.[21]

Though polygamy was an obstacle to their potential camaraderie, it did not deter Emmeline from writing an admiring tribute to Lucy and the American Woman Suffrage Association in the *Woman's Exponent*. "I fell in love with her the moment I saw her," Emmeline admitted to her readers, "and shall never forget how my heart went out to her."[22] The sentiment was not reciprocated. For Lucy, Emmeline was the public symbol of the detested practice, and her civility to Emmeline was only superficial. In 1888, little more than a year after their visit, when Mormon women representing the Relief Society and the Young Ladies' MIA attended the organizational meeting of the National Council of Women, Lucy Stone did not permit the AWSA to join this new organization of women at that time because of

20. Ibid., January 13, 1886, 93–94.

21. When Lucy Stone married Henry Blackwell, she refused to take his name, and the two of them wrote their own marriage vows, which were a step-by-step protest of the laws relating to married women, which rendered them as virtual legal ciphers at that time.

22. "American Woman Suffrage Association," *Woman's Exponent* 16 (May 1, 1888): 177–78. See also "A Tribute to Lucy Stone," *Woman's Exponent* 22 (November 15, 1893): 60.

the council's favorable attitude toward Mormon membership. Stone was particularly affronted that the council had made "a particular Mormon woman" (a reference to Emmeline) a life member, thus ensuring that her name "stands secured in the [Executive] Committee for the Council."[23]

After a return visit with Hiram and his family, Emmeline traveled to Danvers, the home of John Greenleaf Whittier, whom she greatly admired. Whittier was not only a popular American poet but also a suffragist sympathizer. She was impressed with Oak Knoll, as he named his home, which in the fall, she imagined, "must indeed be glorious: the magnificent old trees, situation of the handsome house the hill or knoll on which it stands all tend to make a picture of beauty & an impression of its grandeur." Whittier was not there, but his three female cousins were, and they graciously entertained Emmeline and let her tour the home, where she observed "the most artistically furnished drawing room I have been in anywhere." Both the setting and its occupants were much to her liking. "I found all these accomplished and intelligent women much more free from prejudice than most of the people one meets here," Emmeline discovered, "and they conversed on the subject of the Edmund's bill and the measures taken to enforce the objectionable law with much feeling and interest in our affairs."[24]

She visited his study with its elegant desk, where she observed "the usual litter of literary people." The hundreds of books that filled the shelves around the room in "library style" contributed to the "attractively furnished and finished" study. Then they went into his bedroom, "a large square chamber" directly above the parlor, with a large and comfortable-looking bed "in the centre of the room with the head to the north." "Everything," she enviously remarked to her diary, "for convenience luxury and comfort was there and one could easily imagine it a fitting place for rest from toil and brain work, and a place suitable for the slumber of the American poet."[25] After refreshments with his hospitable cousins, Emmeline was off to see another literary idol, Elizabeth Stuart Phelps.

Emmeline finally found Phelps in her Andover home after first visiting Ocean View, Massachusetts, where she usually stayed when writing. Elizabeth Stuart Phelps was a popular author of several essays and fifty-seven pieces of poetry and fiction, including *The Gates Ajar*, her most famous

23. Lucy Stone, letter to Frances Willard, president of the National Council of Women, August 23, 1888, in Leslie Wheeler, ed., *Loving Warriors: Selected Letters of Lucy Stone and Henry B. Blackwell, 1853–1893*, 314–15, 393, which identifies Emmeline as the "Mormon woman." Though she did not attend the organizing meeting in 1888, Emmeline became a patron or life member of the National Council of Women by making an initial financial contribution.

24. E. Wells, "My Trip East," January 19, 1886, 105.

25. Ibid., January 19, 1886, 104–9.

work.[26] She found it hard to keep warm in the January weather with its persistent icy rain, but unable to find a carriage for the drive from the depot, Emmeline had no choice but to walk through the pelting rain and make her way on a slippery sidewalk up a steep hill to the Phelps home. When Elizabeth heard the bell, she followed her maid to the door and, at Emmeline's inquiry, abruptly announced that she was the person Emmeline was seeking but did not invite her in from the rain. Elizabeth's unexpected appearance at the door and her brusque response unnerved the surprised Emmeline. Because Emmeline had not made an appointment or brought a letter of introduction, she introduced herself and the purpose of her visit. Phelps's obvious disdain for this unknown and not properly introduced woman embarrassed and humiliated Emmeline. "All the love I had felt for her as an author a writer a woman who desired to help humanity died within me a cruel agonizing death." When Emmeline then explained the esteem in which Phelps was held in Utah, Elizabeth correctly assumed that Emmeline was a Mormon. Acting "like a woman bereft of sense," Phelps exclaimed, "God pity you," "God help you." Before closing the door, Elizabeth hurled a bevy of anti-Mormon epithets at her. Emmeline turned away utterly dejected and disheartened. "O, why do we build up such phantasies, and delusions, and worship that which is afar off, that we know not," Emmeline chided herself. "It was a hard and cruel lesson."[27]

The next day promised better results. She planned to visit Whittier himself at the home where he boarded when in Amesbury. Her anticipation of the visit was fully rewarded. She and the white-haired, courtly gentleman spent the morning in earnest conversation. At his request she explained the practice of plural marriage, and they both talked about the injustice of the Edmunds law. Invited to stay for the noon dinner, Emmeline, Whittier, and two other guests, a judge and his wife, "talked on and on," to Emmeline's delight. How much she liked a lively and intellectual conversation! Then she was off again on her own to Boston, her unfortunate encounter with Phelps overshadowed by the brilliance of her visit to Whittier.[28]

After spending her last few days in New England with Hiram and Carrie, she traveled on to Washington to reinforce her ties with her suffrage friends and confront another US president on behalf of the church.

26. A prolific and popular writer, Phelps devised her fiction around social issues and women's rights. Her book *The Gates Ajar*, offering solace to women who had lost loved ones in the Civil War, sold more than a hundred thousand copies throughout the world. It depicted a heaven where loved ones were reunited in scenes that reflected the warm, comfortable cottages of New England, complete with favorite pets.

27. Ibid., January 20, 1886, 111–14.

28. Ibid., January 21, 1886, 119–22.

CHAPTER 18

A Failed Effort

(1886)

As soon as Emmeline reached Washington in January 1886, she immediately jumped back into the world of congressional politics. She was probably more at home than she had been during her month in New England. Washington was a world she had entered seven years ago and had remained attached to through correspondence, her newspaper, and the friends she had cultivated there. Eager to be apprised of the status of the new Edmunds bill, which became known as the Edmunds-Tucker Act in late 1886, she first visited Utah's delegate, John T. Caine. After discussing what she might be able to do in Washington as a Mormon emissary, he advised her to see Rose Cleveland, President Grover Cleveland's sister, who acted as the president's official hostess until Cleveland's marriage five months later in June 1886.

While waiting to see Miss Cleveland, Emmeline met with Representative Hamilton Willcox, who was one of the first to introduce a bill to Congress granting woman suffrage to the territories twenty years earlier and had remained a fervent supporter. He helped her plan her meeting with the president and gave her a letter of introduction to the president's private secretary. He also wrote a letter to the *Woman's Journal*, expressing his opposition to the new Edmunds bill and urging suffragists in Vermont to see that Senator Edmunds was not reelected.[1] In another letter he advised suffragists who had congressional representatives on the Committee on Territories to write to them and petition them to use their influence to amend the new bill by removing the section repealing woman suffrage in Utah.[2]

1. Hamilton Willcox, "The Utah Women," *Woman's Journal*, January 16, 1886, reprinted in *Woman's Exponent* 14 (February 15, 1886): 138. Senator Edmunds was reelected but resigned his seat in 1891 because of the seating of senators from new western states, which, he felt, changed the character of the Senate.

2. Hamilton Willcox, "Amend the Utah Bill," letter to the *Woman's Journal* (n.d.), reprinted in *Woman's Exponent* 14 (March 1, 1886): 150–51.

As a longtime member of the House, Willcox was aware of the procedure yet to follow in the passage of this bill, a majority vote in both the Senate and the House and the need for a House sponsor, a role Representative John Randolph Tucker assumed, eventually adding his name to the bill. After her fruitful visit with Willcox, Emmeline went to the Riggs House, the Washington headquarters of Susan B. Anthony. There the two long-distance friends enjoyed a warm reunion and Emmeline received assurances that Utah women still had her support in maintaining their membership in the National Woman Suffrage Association, despite the anti-Mormon bias of many new members of the association who sought their expulsion.[3]

Though she had met much anti-Mormon sentiment during her first foray into Washington politics in 1879, Emmeline found the mood far more disheartening in 1886. Not only was a new, stringently punitive anti-polygamy bill soon to be enacted, but anti-Mormon activist Angelia Kilgore Newman, usually referred to as Angie Newman, had successfully petitioned Congress for a forty-thousand-dollar grant to provide a place of refuge and rehabilitation for disgruntled plural wives in Utah.[4] Though recognizing the altruistic aspects of Newman's proposal, Emmeline bristled at the conflict polygamy had created among women. In an editorial, Emmeline asked the question, "Is it not time that woman as a rational being aroused herself to the imperative duties of the age and by every exertion possible maintain the rights of women as a class to self-protection?... Is there not work enough for women to do among their sisters in the world without reaching away over to Utah to hunt out a few plural wives, who have homes and children around them honorably born?"[5] The answer was clearly no when the newly organized Industrial Christian Home Association of Utah procured a residence to house women opting out of their marriages. This served the "purity" women's purpose to "rescue" the enslaved women of polygamous marriages and also allowed Congress to show polygamy's high priority as a

3. E. Wells, "My Trip East," January 28, 1886. The two had met in 1883 in Omaha at the executive meeting of the NWSA, and this was another warm encounter, extremely important to Emmeline. In order to increase membership, Anthony had courted the American Woman Suffrage Association and Frances Willard of the Woman's Christian Temperance Union (WCTU) to strengthen support for woman suffrage. Many members of these conservative groups were adamantly opposed to Mormon membership.

4. Angie Newman worked under the auspices of the Woman's Home Mission Society of the Methodist-Episcopal Church, founded by Lucy Hayes, as well as the "Mormon Department" of the WCTU. These groups viewed Mormon women as objects of pity to be rescued from the enslavement of plural marriage.

5. "Notes from Washington," *Woman's Exponent* 14 (May 1, 1886): 180–81.

congressional issue. It also surely salved the nation's conscience for the havoc wreaked on Mormon families by antipolygamy legislation.[6]

As she had before with President and Mrs. Hayes, Emmeline presented the case for Mormon women before Rose Cleveland when they met. Their shared love of the British woman author George Eliot, the subject of a book Rose Cleveland had authored, gave them some common ground.[7] Emmeline reportedly gave her "the whole theory and principle, lock, stock and barrel, of the Mormon religion, waxing quite eloquent." But Rose Cleveland was unimpressed. "It is very beautiful, the way you regard it," one reporter quoted her as saying, "but of course I do not agree with you or regard it as you do."[8] Emmeline could hardly have been surprised at her response.

Emmeline also attended one of the regular afternoon receptions Miss Cleveland held in the "Red Parlor" of the White House. It was an elegant affair, and Emmeline spared nothing in her description of the social, including the room, the lighting, Rose Cleveland's beautiful attire, and the refreshments.[9] Emmeline's observant eye made fascinating reading for her *Exponent* subscribers. Rumors credited Rose Cleveland as being "the power behind the throne," since she was considered to be "strong-minded, and having great influence with her brother."[10]

6. No first wives were admitted, and other restrictions kept the number of residents low. After an initial flurry of interest, applications dwindled, some women citing the difficulties they had with matron Ruth Woods. Peggy Pascoe treats the genesis and demise of the home in *Relations of Rescue: The Search for Female Moral Authority in the American West, 1874–1939*, 22, 23–26, 28, 29–30, 89–90. A contemporary study is Jeanette Ferry, *Industrial Christian Home Association of Utah*. The home remained under male control but with women matrons to manage its daily business.

7. Rose Cleveland's book *George Eliot's Poetry, and Other Studies* was published in 1885.

8. Emma Janes, "Washington Gossip," *Philadelphia Press*, May 2, 1886, 6. The *Woman's Exponent* carried a brief article about the manner of receiving guests at Rose Cleveland's regular afternoon receptions. "Miss Cleveland's Reception," *Woman's Exponent* 14 (March 1, 1886): 151.

9. "Miss Cleveland's Reception." Emmeline employed her knowledge of French in describing Rose Cleveland's dress, using the French spelling *berthe* rather than the Anglicized *bertha*, referring to a wide, deep collar, usually of lace, that covered the shoulders of her low-necked dress. *Passementerie* is also from the French *passement*, which in this case means any ornamental trimming such as braid, lace, or metallic beads. The half-blown pink tea rose may have been crystal rather than natural. Emmeline's observant eye seemed to catch all the details of what she saw.

10. "Items from Washington," *Woman's Exponent* 14 (February 15, 1886): 140. After her brother's marriage in June, Rose Cleveland moved to Chicago to take up editorship of a magazine, *Literary Life*. "Notes and News," *Woman's Exponent* 15 (July 1, 1886): 24.

Emmeline was just as careful in detailing the appearance of President Cleveland when a chance opportunity to sit next to him at a concert occurred before her private interview with him. She found him "more fleshy" than his pictures indicated, with a bald spot on the back of his head. "One would never judge he was the President from looking at him," she thought, "though he looks quite as *Presidential* as many of his predecessors in office." From the comments she heard as she traveled around Washington, she gathered that he was not a very great favorite, even within his own Democratic Party, and around the villages of New England and New York she found his administration "most severely, and, one might almost say, savagely criticized."[11]

Everywhere she went, she encountered talk of the new Edmunds bill (Edmunds-Tucker Act), which had passed the Senate on January 8, 1886, and which she published in full in the *Woman's Exponent* a month later.[12] Opposition came from lawyers who felt the bill was unconstitutional, while others felt it too stringent in its confiscation of private property, and of course suffragists were angry at its provision to cancel the right of women to vote in the territory.[13] The bill was also denounced because of a clause that disinherited children of plural wives, which was "devilish," according to one writer. "It outrages humanity and justice. What can be more mean and cruel than to cast a stigma upon an innocent child and debar it the rights of inheritance[?]"[14] These objectors, as well as Mormons, hoped that the House of Representatives would reject such a punitive document.

Remarkably, Emmeline was able to write and send off her editorials to Salt Lake City while also writing and mailing newsy letters containing descriptions of events in Washington along with copies of articles and letters from eastern papers, all marked for publication in the *Exponent*. Annie and perhaps Louie were undoubtedly supervising the paper in their mother's absence, with the result that the warm nostalgia of their mother's travels in Massachusetts and her recital of events in Washington contrasted markedly with each other.

Finally, after more than a month in the nation's capital, Emmeline began her journey home, planning to make brief stops in Kirtland, Ohio, and Nauvoo, Illinois, sites important to Mormon history and to her personally

11. "Items from Washington," *Woman's Exponent* 14 (February 15, 1886): 140.

12. "The Latest from Edmunds," *Woman's Exponent* 14 (February 1, 1886): 134–36.

13. "Items from Washington," 140.

14. Reprint from *Our Country*, December 28, 1885, in "Notes and News," *Woman's Exponent* 14 (March 1, 1886): 146. It required numerous laws drawn up by the Utah Legislature to address this aspect of the bill, and concessions were finally made in the interest of the children. See C. Madsen, "'At Their Peril.'"

as well. On March 2, she reached Cleveland, where she wrote letters home, including one to Orson F. Whitney. Well known in church and literary circles, Ort had obligingly written articles for each issue of the *Woman's Exponent* during the months Emmeline was away. "I am beginning to long for home and a sight of the loved ones there more and more," she admitted in her letter to him. "While in Washington (and making an effort at least), to do something for our people, that I might prove loyal to the cause I so devotedly love," she explained, "I felt that I could endure absence from home and even privation, [had it] been necessary, at any rate scorn and ridicule for the sake of vindicating principle, and proclaiming truth."[15] The experience had been sobering to the optimistic Emmeline. The pain of scorn and ridicule she had personally endured during her visit to New England was nothing compared to the ominous threats of the federal government. "Prejudice," she told her readers, "is very much stronger now than seven years ago." Nevertheless, she reminded them that "in the darkest time of deepest trial, the Saints have seen light spring suddenly forth from the midst of darkness, and help has come when most needed."[16] Good had to come from every challenge. This thought was her anchor.

Emmeline had never lived in Kirtland, but it was the home of her husband Newel K. Whitney and his wife Elizabeth Ann, and Whitney and Smith relatives still lived there. She knew the town from Elizabeth Ann's description and happily noted that she instinctively recognized the Whitney store and residence as well as the Johnson hotel. She remembered the story of the first meeting of Joseph Smith and Newel Whitney and the deep friendship that had developed from that time. "All this and a hundred other memories of the dead rushed to mind, as we stood like one entranced gazing upon that historic city." Despite never having lived there, she found its associations so vivid as she visited the historic sites that her "emotions must indeed be under perfect control not to be strongly wrought upon."[17] Walking through the Whitney home touched her in a special way. "I am much attached to places," she reminded her family at home, when she wrote of the visit, "and certainly a house where a prophet of God had lived and received communications from on high, possesses an interest to an ardent believer... so that little chamber in Kirtland, deserted and neglected, had a charm for

15. Emmeline B. Wells, letter to Bishop Orson F. Whitney, March 2, 1886, Orson F. Whitney Collection.

16. "Items from Washington," 140, 141. This is a long editorial in which she describes many of the events that occurred in Washington, noted earlier, and some of her reactions to them. They expand on the more personal reflections she expressed in her letter to Whitney.

17. "Kirtland and Nauvoo," *Woman's Exponent* 14 (March 15, 1886): 156.

me that converted it, for the time being, into a fit place for 'the wise men of the west,' who sat there in council and who knelt there in prayer." Her close knowledge of early Mormon history and relationship with its participants enhanced the visit. "I drank in as much as possible the peculiar situation of Joseph in the Whitney house in Kirtland." Emmeline was intrigued to learn from Elizabeth Ann that Joseph often paced the floor when meeting with his associates as they deliberated together in making decisions affecting the welfare and progress of the church. "O indeed," Emmeline exclaimed, "it was good to be there, knowing what I knew of what had formerly transpired within those walls."[18] She visited the Kirtland temple, observing the architecture and pulpits and recalling the spiritual events that had occurred in that edifice. Kirtland, for Emmeline, was a place noted in history, not in her memory, and she brought a historian's interest in detailed observations and reverence for the sites she visited in that town.

Then she was off to Nauvoo, unlike Kirtland a place that brought back "scenes of sufferings, trials and sorrows" so deeply embedded in her memory. The city had been her home for two perilous years, and walking over the well-known paths evoked a nostalgic description of the changes that had altered the city in the forty years since the Saints' departure. As she strolled along the streets of the city, she opened her heart to "the recollections of the past that sweep like a torrent over the soul, bringing back vividly the remembrance of that which once was, but is now no more." Many of the substantial houses built by Brigham Young, Heber C. Kimball, Bishop Whitney, Parley P. Pratt, John Taylor, Joseph Young, Bishop Hunter, Bishop Woolley, and Esquire (Aaron) Johnson still remained. With permission she went through the Kimball and Brigham Young homes and "several others 'which fond recollection presented to view,' and some of them brought floods of tears that almost blinded us, as we passed from room to room, recalling the incidents that had transpired there...but tongue can never tell it." A few verses that she called forth from memory expressed what she could not compose herself.[19] She had an extraordinary ability to hold phrases, stanzas, and entire poems in her mind and was familiar with biblical passages, to be drawn upon at appropriate moments in her writing and speaking. Emmeline discovered that very few pieces of stone from the

18. "'The Rotunda'—Kirtland—the 'Memorial'" (extracts from a letter written April 16, 1886), *Woman's Exponent* 14 (April 15, 1886): 169–70.

19. "But ah! The tears that are not wept, / The tears that never outward fall, / The tears that grief for years has kept / Within us—they are best of all: / The tears our eyes shall never know, / Are dearer than the tears that flow." "Tears," Charles Wells Moulton, publisher, *Magazine of Poetry and Literary Review* 4 (1892): 382, reprinted as "Nauvoo as It Is Today," *Woman's Exponent* 14 (April 15, 1886): 172–73.

temple remained for souvenir-seeking tourists, so bottles of water from the temple well now sufficed for that purpose. Much of the granite had been made into carriage steps and front-door steps of the homes throughout the town, a practice that greatly offended her. "It seems to us a perfect sacrilege to so deface, destroy and convert to such base uses material consecrated by the prayers and labors of the Saints."[20]

She walked by the river, where she viewed the Riverside Mansion, which had been the home of Emma Smith and Lewis Bidamon, whom Emma married three years after Joseph Smith's death.[21] Although some Mormon visitors to Nauvoo had expressed their disdain of Emma, Emmeline expressed only sorrow and regret. "Here Emma Smith, once the Elect Lady," she wrote, "spent the latter part of her life in comparative quiet—once the honored wife of the great leader of this dispensation, mistress of the Nauvoo Mansion where the Saints congregated around Joseph, the Prophet, sharing the love, affection and confidence not only of her beloved husband, but of the whole body of the people. Sad indeed was her fate, separated from those who were her best and truest friends, without the strong arm of him she had been wont to regard with love and reverence, she was indeed left desolate."[22]

Emmeline's heightened sensitivities enabled her to intuit a widow's sorrow. When she visited Emma's grave site, she was saddened to see that it was unmarked, "and the stranger is not privileged to read upon her tomb the story of her eventful life; no, nor even her name."[23] Perhaps her own Nauvoo experiences, which had wrought such emotional distress and occasioned such spiritual reassessment, enabled Emmeline to see the deeply human toll that Emma's challenging life had exacted from her. The loss of Joseph to other wives, and then to death, created an emotional scar that Emmeline felt could never have healed. Emma's life was unalterably bisected by his death, and she tragically and needlessly lost her honored place in LDS history. Emmeline's own personal losses and the inexorable changes that followed would have given her some ingress into Emma's emotional state. Certainly, Emmeline seemed to say, it was not hers to judge.

She was less reticent to judge Lewis Bidamon, Emma's second husband, whom Emmeline called "that curious specimen of humanity." He

20. "Nauvoo as It Is Today."

21. Emma Smith married Major Lewis C. Bidamon in 1847. Emma died in 1879, seven years prior to Emmeline's visit. There is no record that Emmeline and Emma ever met, but she knew her through the memories of Elizabeth Ann Whitney, Emma's counselor in the Nauvoo Relief Society.

22. Ibid.

23. Ibid. The graveside visit elicited another verse, this time from Tennyson's poem "In Memoriam."

had remarried following Emma's death in 1879, and the couple had taken up residence in the Mansion House. Emmeline felt disheartened when she learned that the young man she met there was the son he had sired with another woman while he was still married to Emma. Fully aware of the liaison, Emma had asked the major to marry the child's mother after Emma's death, which he did. Emmeline found Bidamon's wife to be a very pleasant and hospitable woman, but the knowledge of their illicit liaison made Emmeline even more sympathetic to the indignities Emma faced during so much of her life.[24]

The saddest place Emmeline visited on this journey through an unhappy past was the graveyard east of the city, the resting place of her infant son, Eugene Henri. Like much else of the city, it was neglected, the graves "hidden in grassy beds and mossy hillocks beneath." Only here and there an occasional headstone broke through the overgrown foliage. But the tall, full-grown trees, which Emmeline felt "are the best companions in such a lonely place," were evidence of the graciousness of nature that had provided these stalwart custodians of the unidentified graves.[25]

Finally, after her stops at Kirtland and Nauvoo, a weary Emmeline looked eagerly to her home in Salt Lake City. Even as she began her travels westward, however, some of her friends were petitioning church president John Taylor "to publicly protest against the indignities inflicted on plural wives in the district courts" as a result of the Edmunds law of 1882.[26] On March 6, while Emmeline was visiting Kirtland, a crowded audience of angry women met in the Salt Lake Theatre to do just that. Speaker after speaker rose to denounce incursions of the federal officials into the private lives of Mormon women. A committee on resolutions, elected during the rally collected their complaints and rendered them in nine resolutions: three relating to the vested right of suffrage enjoyed by the women of the territory; three relating to the unconstitutionality of requiring wives, even legal wives, to testify against their husbands; and two expressing appreciation for those senators and suffragists who had condemned the proposed new Edmunds bill. The final resolution reasserted the universal female bond that LDS women had continually invoked, hoping it would bring other

24. From a letter to Helen Mar Kimball Whitney, March 15, 1886, in "Correspondence," *Woman's Exponent* 14 (April 1, 1886): 164. See also Linda King Newell and Valeen Tippetts Avery, *Mormon Enigma: Emma Hale Smith*.

25. "Nauvoo as It Is Today."

26. John Taylor, letter to Mrs. Mary Isabella Horne, Sarah M. Kimball, and Romania B. Pratt, February 20, 1886, Taylor Family Collection. Taylor's letter acknowledged and approved these women's plans for an organized protest.

American women to their aid: "Resolved: That we call upon the wives and mothers of the United States to come to our help in resisting these encroachments upon our liberties and these outrages upon our peaceful homes and family relations."[27]

When Emmeline arrived in Chicago, she learned about the mass indignation meeting and immediately sent home a letter of encouragement and support to Isabella Horne and the others who had planned the rally. "Though absent from your midst on this momentous occasion," she wrote to the sisters, "I am with you in heart and feeling." She explained that she was away only because she was already involved in benefiting their common cause. From all she had learned in Washington, she believed that "the proposition of Senator Edmunds to disfranchise the women of Utah Territory… is simply an act of despotism unworthy a man, and can only be aimed at the mere trifle of political power he would selfishly wrest from those who have been accused of no offense even against the Edmunds law." The last paragraph of her lengthy letter is one long sentence in which she asserts that she is one with them "in indignantly protesting against all the wrongs and cruelties perpetrated upon the people of Utah in the name of, and under the sanction of *law*," and agreed that "Mormon women have some rights that the country is bound to respect, and that as rational beings they are entitled to the protection of the government under which they live, which guarantees to all the rights of conscience."[28]

When Emmeline reached Kansas City, she found a telegram waiting for her from President John Taylor. At the suggestion of Angus Cannon, president of the Salt Lake Stake, he requested Emmeline to return to Washington and, accompanied by Dr. Ellen Ferguson, present to Congress and President Cleveland the memorial that resulted from the women's mass meeting.[29] Tired and eager to be home, Emmeline nonetheless agreed and returned to Washington, where she met Dr. Ferguson, Emily Richards, Franklin S. Richards, and Emily's sister-in-law Josephine West.

Included in the memorial they planned to present to Congress and the president was a series of individual incidents in which wives had been

27. "The Ladies' Mass Meeting," *Woman's Exponent* 14 (March 1, 1886): 148–49. The rally was held on March 6 but reported in this issue. A note indicated that the paper was deliberately delayed in order to report the proceedings of the mass meeting. "Editorial Notes," *Woman's Exponent* 14 (March 1, 1886): 149.

28. "Letter to the Sisters at Home," *Woman's Exponent* 14 (April 1, 1886): 164.

29. John Taylor, letter to Angus M. Cannon, March 17, 1886, Taylor Family Collection. John Taylor hoped that "the presence of two industrious persevering workers of our sisters would be attended with good results."

cavalierly treated by the federal courts and officers, subjected to insulting searches, and even incarcerated for refusing to answer impertinent questions or to testify against their husbands. Essentially, the memorial was a plea for a "suspension of all measures calculated to deprive us of our political rights and privileges, and to harass, annoy and bring our people into bondage and distress." The nine women who composed the memorial committee signed it, with Sarah M. Kimball's name leading the list.[30]

On April 3, Emmeline and Dr. Ferguson were granted an interview with President Cleveland in his library in the Executive Mansion. They waited more than two hours for their turn to meet with him and in their hour meeting were able to present their credentials and the memorial.[31] After listening to the "facts and incidents relating to the abuses and outrages perpetrated in the name of the *law*," explained by the two women, President Cleveland promised "to give the matter serious attention and consideration." Three days later, Senator Henry W. Blair, a republican from New Hampshire, presented the memorial to the Senate and asked that it be read into the *Congressional Record*, an important recognition of their appeal. But Emmeline was under no illusions about the mood of Congress. "The wrongs and grievances have been heard, even in high places," she noted, "but the redress asked for may be very slow in coming. The prejudice is exceedingly strong against the doctrines and institutions of the Saints." Even bad publicity had its bright side, she believed. "The persecution," she optimistically felt, "is spreading the knowledge of truth as nothing else ever could have done. Surely it is 'a marvelous work and a wonder.'"[32]

The next step was the presentation of the memorial to the House of Representatives on April 8, where it was referred to the Committee on the Judiciary. This committee, under the chairmanship of John Randolph Tucker, was in the process of studying the new Edmunds bill, which had passed the Senate in January, in order to make its recommendation to the House. Emmeline found Representative Tucker to be "a very kindly and

30. "Memorial," *Woman's Exponent* 14 (April 1, 1886): 166–67, is a complete reprint. The other eight committee members were Isabella Horne, Elmina S. Taylor, Dr. Romania B. Pratt, Mrs. H. C. Brown, Mrs. Mary Pitchforth, Miss Ida I. Cook, Mrs. Ida Coombs, and Mrs. Mary Jones.

31. "'The Rotunda'—Kirtland—the 'Memorial,'" 169.

32. "Notes from Washington," 180–81. That church leaders invited these women to make a "last-ditch effort" to change the tide in Congress is evidence of their confidence in the effectiveness of these women's ability to explain their grievances and articulate their appeal in rational rather than emotional arguments when called upon. Their presence, alone, gave a human face to those who would experience the effects of the bill.

wise man—a southern gentleman, large hearted and full of that chivalry towards women which seems so thoroughly natural to the 'old Virginians.'" For Emmeline, he was a contemporary model of the chivalric heroes that figured so prominently in the romance tales she often read.[33]

A hearing was scheduled before the Subcommittee of the House Judiciary on May 1, which lasted several days. Those speaking against the proposed Edmunds bill based their arguments on points of law and constitutionality, which Emmeline found "deep, far-reaching, and sound." But one of the strongest voices in opposition to the Mormons was Robert N. Baskin, an Ohio lawyer who had lived in Utah for twenty years and was now an ardent lobbyist for the anti-Mormon Liberal Party in Utah. Baskin wore himself out, according to Emmeline, in presenting a four-hour "startling and bombastic tirade" against the Mormons that she thought was judiciously and logically refuted by Utah delegate John T. Caine. She had also been impressed by the gentlemanly demeanor of Representative Tucker and felt that "he deserves gratitude for the unprejudiced and unbiased spirit he manifested throughout the entire proceedings."[34]

Finally, to Emmeline's undisguised relief, it was time to go home. She had done all that she could do to represent the women of her faith. She had clearly voiced the position of Mormon women and in only two trips to the capital she had learned her way around the halls of Congress and felt no reticence in stating her case before anyone who would listen, including the president of the United States. However, despite the many who spoke against the severity and unconstitutionality of the Edmunds bill and the resounding support of the suffragists who denounced the illegality of repealing women's vote in Utah, Emmeline was sensitive to the futility of their efforts. "All that can be done here in presenting facts and seeking to remove prejudice seems only a drop in the ocean of public sentiment arrayed against a people struggling with the effects of falsehood and misrepresentation," she lamented in her *Exponent* editorial.[35] One bright spot, which she was happy to share with her readers, was the favorable response to the copies of the *Woman's Exponent* she had distributed throughout her trip. "People open their eyes in wonder when one tells them the Mormon women publish a paper." Chiding the sisters at home who "look upon it as too insignificant for them to patronize, or even read," she tried to impress on them "what a power in the hands of the women of this Church a newspaper is." "Our little paper," she continued, "presents the challenging issues facing Mormon

33. Ibid.
34. "Washington Jottings," *Woman's Exponent* 14 (May 15, 1886): 188–89.
35. "Notes from Washington," 180.

women and the Church in clear detail and gives them opportunity to express their own views and to support the Church and their marriages in clear detail."

She was also appalled to discover that few women in the East had any knowledge of the Edmunds Act of 1882 or the proposals contained in the new Edmunds bill.[36] She was even more disappointed that so many of her Mormon sisters lacked a full understanding of the precipice on which the church uneasily rested. The pleas of Mormon women to their eastern sisters for compassion because of their common experiences as women, wives, and mothers, she had come to realize, truly fell on deaf ears. Thus, after returning home as in 1879, a letter from a reader in Provo named M. A. Till praising Emmeline's work was a ray of sunlight in the stormy scene. The flowers and fruit that poured into her office once again were similarly appreciated and validating.

The presence of Mormon women in Washington in defense of Mormonism brought varied reactions from the eastern press. One article, responding to the activities of Emmeline, Ellen Ferguson, and Emily Richards, was particularly vituperative. "Apparently here were the three types of Mormon women," the article explained, "the one so strong-minded that she could not find a husband in the states; the second of the fortune-telling variety, who if they wed at all always wed with cranks or fanatics, and the third an unintelligent being, who could be influenced or led by those with whom she might happen to be associated." The derisive tone and dismissal of their credibility as serious lobbyists were unmistakable.[37]

Two months before leaving on her trip, Emmeline had editorialized that "those who live longest will see in the *finale* of the present controversy and persecution now raging, ostensibly in consequence of the practise of a principle that was taught and practiced by holy men of old, that it will yet appear that officeseeking, political place and power and Mammon were the real motives that caused the raid against the 'Mormons.'"[38] This trip to Washington confirmed her assessment. She was learning the practice of politics. While heretofore arguing from a moral and constitutional position, her growing exposure to the world of politics had shown her the strength of personal and political interests in the campaign against the Mormons.

36. "Our Little Paper," *Woman's Exponent* 14 (May 15, 1886): 188.

37. This brief newspaper article was pasted into a scrapbook collection in possession of a grandniece of Emmeline's, Glenys Harris of Orange, MA. She was gracious enough to allow me to photocopy it. It contained no date or name of publication, but pen notations indicated it referred to Emmeline and her coworkers during this Washington visit.

38. "Thoughts on the Times," *Woman's Exponent* 14 (September 1, 1885): 52.

She was dismayed but hardly surprised when the new Edmunds bill passed the House ten months later in March 1887. She was stunned, however, when it bore the name Edmunds-Tucker Act. John Randolph Tucker, the southern gentleman whom Emmeline had so admired, reversed his position opposing the original Edmunds bill of 1882 and gave strength to the new bill by supporting all of its provisions, giving it his name, and even going so far as to suggest another bill providing for a constitutional amendment outlawing polygamy. According to the harsh provisions, all Utah women, Mormon and Gentile alike, lost the vote; the economic base of the church was severely compromised; and plural marriage was essentially doomed as a religious practice.[39]

But Emmeline would find that family matters would push the church's confrontation with the federal government far to the back of her attention, and once again she would have to marshal all her emotional resources to meet the challenge, without Daniel, who was safely away in England.

39. These and other provisions of the Edmunds-Tucker Act are detailed in Gustive O. Larson, *Outline History of Territorial Utah*, 276–77.

CHAPTER 19

A Family Affair
(1886)

Emmeline Wells was under no illusion that all was well with the Saints when she returned from her long eastern trip. Despite the forceful contention of woman suffragists and the lawmakers who found much of the proposed new Edmunds bill too far-reaching and even unconstitutional, she felt the overwhelming power of the prevailing congressional mood. More than outlawing plural marriage, Congress, through this legislation, hoped to break the strength of the church and its political domination of the territory. Throughout the remainder of 1886, Emmeline's editorials denounced the church's assailants and admonished the faithful to remain true to the principles they had espoused and to endure, in the spirit of their forebears, this latest assault. "It is a time of testing and proving," she averred, "and the Saints have been warned and forewarned that great trials were in store, and that they should be on their guard, and watch every loophole through which an advantage might be taken by the enemy."[1] She repeated her concerns whenever she had opportunity to speak but always with counsel to remain steadfast and accept God's overruling hand in the affairs of the church.[2]

Moreover, Angie Newman's plans were under way to utilize the federal funds she had obtained for a refuge and rehabilitation center for plural wives.[3] Emmeline was certain that no Mormon "women who 'are as true, as loyal and as constant' to the principles they have embraced and in which they steadfastly believe as their brothers" would have use for such a home and that the grant was "a needless appropriation by Congress, for a purpose

1. "Approaching the Narrows," *Woman's Exponent* 15 (November 15, 1886): 92.

2. "Interesting Meetings," *Woman's Exponent* 15 (July 1, 1886): 22.

3. "Home Again," *Woman's Exponent* 15 (June 1, 1886): 4. See Theodore Agnew, "Angelia Louise French Thurston Kilgore Newman."

that has no real existence."[4] However, 150 women, though no more than 20 at any one time, occupied the home at different times during its four years of operation.[5]

More disquieting news, however, for Emmeline, was the death of Louisa, her sister-wife, at age sixty-two. Louisa and her son Melvin joined Daniel in Liverpool in 1885 while he was presiding over the European Mission. Becoming ill, she returned to Utah that same year and died a few months later.[6] As the first of Daniel's wives to die, her death was a keen loss to the Wells family. She had carried the primary responsibility for the family when Daniel was away, and all the family were "deferential to the gentle authority" she exercised and open to the "great-hearted affection" she showed to all. Emmeline would have concurred with Hannah's son Junius in his appraisal of "Aunt" Louisa: "How wonderful she was! Her all-pervading presence and care; her interest and love; her generous hospitality and helpfulness! How smart and keen her perception of our every whim and humor; of every stubborn or willing attitude we took! How lavish her praise for every thought or act of merit, and forgiving and tender when we were wrong!"[7] She would be remembered not only as a gracious wife and conscientious mother, but also as a teacher, friend, and voluntary nurse and caregiver to family, neighbors, and even strangers. Emmeline always remembered Louisa's kindness and assistance to her when she married Daniel.

A somber mood also robbed the usual festive celebration of Pioneer Day, July 24, in 1886. Instead of the daylong merrymaking festivities that usually constituted the commemoration of the entry of the pioneers into Salt Lake Valley, this thirty-ninth anniversary was marked by a mournful restraint. Enforcement of the antipolygamy Edmunds law of 1882 had sent many men into prison or exile, including the leaders of the church. Daniel Wells was himself in England to avoid arrest, as were two of his daughters, Emily Grant, pregnant plural wife of Heber J. Grant, and Abby Young, also expecting and a plural wife of Seymour B. Young, a member of the Council of Seventies.

Fear of the pending Edmunds-Tucker bill added to the subdued celebration. No colorful bunting draped the pillars or hung from the balconies of the tabernacle, where the formal exercises took place. Rather, dark

4. "The Industrial Home," *Woman's Exponent* 15 (December 1, 1886): 100.

5. Pascoe, *Relations of Rescue*, 88–89. The beautiful structure was later used by the Ladies Literary Club for a period and was recommended at one point as headquarters for the LDS women's organizations but without results.

6. "In Memoriam," *Woman's Exponent* 15 (July 1, 1886): 20.

7. J. Wells, "A Manner School."

streamers of gray and black draped the stands. Over the First Presidency's podium was a printed statement that read: "The First Presidency: In Exile for Conscience Sake." Additional epigraphs hung below, one for the Salt Lake Stake Presidency and one for the presiding bishopric. On the side of the organ "in large gilt letters were the words, 'In God we put our Trust,' and below, 'Under the Everlasting Covenant God will and must be glorified.'" Some of Zion's most eloquent orators, Bishop Orson F. Whitney and B. H. Roberts, presented long, serious declamations, and R. R. Irvine read a similarly somber sermon written by Eliza R. Snow. Bands, choirs, and recitations were in harmony with the sedate proceedings. There was little optimism that the federal intrusion into Mormon life would cease, but questions about the outcome of the protracted conflict left the Saints generally perplexed and inwardly defiant.

Though federal officials had sought Emmeline the year before, her husband was safely away in England, and her daughter Belle was residing in San Francisco with her husband, Septimus Sears, while his first wife remained in Salt Lake City.[8] "Trials tend to strengthen and purify," Emmeline editorialized. "The Lord has said He will have a tried people, and those who have set out for 'the prize of the high calling' will have to accept the bitter and the sweet." Latter-day prophets, she reminded her readers, promise "that the severest ordeals will be required to test the Latter-day Saints, that they be as gold tried in the furnace."[9] These words may have been cold comfort to those struggling to maintain family life in the absence of providers and caregivers. They may also have done little to assuage the fears and apprehensions of the future. They may, however, have spread a mantle of martyrdom over those who read her words and felt themselves unjustly singled out for federal censure.

Like the Pioneer Day celebration, the church's semiannual conference in October altered its usual format. The announcement that it would be held in Coalville, Utah, a small farming community east of Salt Lake City, surprised church members. Yet despite the change of venue, members filled the Coalville tabernacle to hear the counsel of four apostles and patriarch

8. In 1885, Septimus Sears, John Clark, Truman O. Angel Jr., and John Daynes were arrested for living polygamously, but all four agreed to pay a fine and to abide the law in the future. Sears had opted to live with Belle and move their residence to San Francisco, where he had business dealings. Their relocation to California also removed them from the opprobrium for their choice to obey the law rather than undergo exile or imprisonment. Abraham H. Cannon, Diary, October 19, 1885. See also "The Status of Former Polygamists," *Deseret News*, October 29, 1889, 2.

9. "Trials Tend to Strengthen and Purify," *Woman's Exponent* 15 (November 1, 1886): 84.

John Smith. Despite the absence of the First Presidency, their written epistle was disseminated to "thousands afar off" that year, Emmeline noted, many of them through reading it in the *Woman's Exponent*.[10] The epistle rehearsed the actions of the federal government against the church and the need to assist one another during this time of trouble.

Emmeline did not attend the general conference in Coalville. That she was in a mind to write about it or even continue her work with the *Exponent* that fall reflects the self-control she had honed to a striking degree over the years. The death of her sister-wife Louisa, her successful evasion of "two deputy marshals" who attempted to interrogate her and her daughters the previous year, together with the palpable worry and forebodings of the future that pervaded the church were all troublesome to her.[11] Disconcerting as all of these disruptive events were, they could not match the cruel happenings that beset her just a month before the general conference and four months after her return from New England and Washington. Understandably, her diary is silent for the last few months of 1886. The emotions she usually recorded in private may have been too raw this time to find expression in mere words.

Life began to unravel for Emmeline on September 5, 1886, at the Sunday-afternoon service in the tabernacle, which she did not attend. Interrupting John Nicholson's sermon was the arrival of stake president Angus Cannon, who had been out of the public eye for more than a year after his imprisonment for plural marriage. Accompanying him was his handsome and popular nephew John Q. Cannon, Annie's husband. After his return from his mission in 1884, John was appointed counselor to the presiding bishop, and as the oldest son of George Q. Cannon of the First Presidency, he was well known in the community. Stepping up to the pulpit, John Q. announced to a stunned audience that he had committed a sin, "next in our belief to the shedding of blood." According to the newspaper report, he offered to "lay down his priesthood" and asked only that he be given opportunity to show

10. "Semi-annual Conference," *Woman's Exponent* 15 (October 1, 1886): 68; "An Epistle of the First Presidency," *Woman's Exponent* 15 (October 15, 1886): 73–76; "October Conference," *Woman's Exponent* 15 (October 15, 1886): 76. President John Taylor and Counselor George Q. Cannon were in hiding, and Joseph F. Smith was in Hawaii. The epistle is attributed to the First Presidency, but Joseph F. Smith could not have been able to sign it. The other two may have had the opportunity to confer with one another.

11. The constant raids by federal marshals attempted to ferret out wives and families of polygamous men. She noted that if it was necessary, she would appear before them. E. B. Wells, letter to Mary A. Maughan, April 14, 1885, in Maughan Family Association Collection.

that "there is still some good in him." His confession was followed by Angus Cannon's announcement that it was his "solemn duty" to excommunicate John Q. Cannon from the church. No further information was forthcoming to the bewildered congregation.[12]

This public confession and excommunication, ordered by his father, George Q. Cannon, followed the confession that a distraught and anxious John Q. made to his younger brother Abraham (Abram), a member of the Council of Seventy, just the day before. Clearly distraught, he explained to Abram that he had "committed himself with Louie Wells" and that "matters had reached such a stage that now he was forced to confess his sin to [Presiding] Bishop [William] Preston and others." That phrase "such a stage" is the only clue that a pregnancy had resulted from their relationship. John Q. had just returned from escorting Annie home from a lengthy visit she had made to Belle in San Francisco, and Louie may have revealed her condition to John upon their return.[13]

Though John accepted the necessity of resigning from the presiding bishopric, he did not foresee a public excommunication. His plan, John told his brother, was for Annie and their three children to live with her mother, for Louie to live with Belle in San Francisco, and for him to leave Salt Lake City because he could not remain "with the sense of shame resting upon him." Both John and Abram deferred to their father, George Q., then in hiding, for guidance.[14]

12. "The hush that followed this avowal it would be impossible to describe," declared the *Deseret Weekly News* in "Sunday Services," September 8, 1886, 533 (reprint of *Deseret Evening News*). An appeal for sympathy for the father and "no unkindness" shown the son ended a long description of the Sunday meeting in "Impressive and Sorrowful," *Deseret Evening News*, September 6, 1886, 2. For a sarcastic review of the proceedings in the tabernacle, see "John Q. Cannon Cut Off," *Salt Lake Daily Tribune*, September 7, 1886, 4; and "The True Inwardness of It," *Salt Lake Daily Tribune*, September 8, 1886, 2. The *Tribune* seized on the event to repeat its disparagement of polygamy, blaming the influence of a polygamous lifestyle instilled in John Q. Cannon by his "promiscuous" father and the religious community in which he was reared: "No Figs from Such Thistles," September 7, 1886, 2. It also mocked sympathetic statements of the *Deseret News* and the clearly dumbfounded tabernacle audience. A public confession of transgression was considered part of the repentance process at that time, but usually in a ward or stake setting after a hearing before the bishop or stake high council.

13. None of the participants' journals make reference to a pregnancy, and the last part of Emmeline's diary for 1886 is missing or unwritten.

14. A. H. Cannon, Diary, September 4, 1886. See Kenneth L. Cannon II, "The Tragic Matter of Louie Wells and John Q. Cannon," for a minutely detailed rehearsal of the sorry affair; and Ronald W. Walker, "Grant's Watershed: Succession in the

While the details of John's indiscretion had been withheld at the time of his public confession, both the Cannon and the Wells families soon learned the disheartening facts. John Q. "suffered a thousand deaths in telling Annie, Louie and Sister Wells...of his fall from the Church," but his agony could have been no worse than theirs. Rumors rushed through the city, and many began to speculate that Louie was the unnamed woman because she and John were often together on family occasions, both with and without Annie.[15] Though never stated, hints of Louie's part in the affair even reached across the ocean to Louie's father and sisters. After hearing the news in Liverpool, Emily Wells Grant wrote to her husband, Heber, that her clearly distressed father, Daniel, exclaimed, "What will we hear next?" He "feels perfectly dreadful" about the scandal, Emily added, and "so do we all of course especially if Louie is mixed up with the affair. We don't believe she is but have heard she is the guilty one. I sincerely hope not." Emily could only imagine the feelings it might cause between Louie and "poor dear Annie." "Aunt Em," she correctly surmised, "I expect is heart broken. It is without exception, I think, the most awful thing I ever heard of. There was no earthly excuse for him and it is certainly too bad."[16]

Annie had actually encouraged John to take Louie as a plural wife as early as 1885.[17] Angus Cannon's plural wife Martha Hughes Cannon, who was in England to avoid testifying against her husband, wrote Angus that she remembered that John had twice asked "for the woman he loved,"

Presidency." The latter article examines the tension that ensued from this problem between George Q. Cannon and Daniel H. Wells.

15. A. H. Cannon, Diary, September 5, 1886. Rumors that John Q. and Louie had married in the Logan temple two years after he and Annie returned from their mission were rampant then and may have reappeared. "On the Quiet," *Salt Lake Daily Tribune*, November 2, 1884, 4. See also "Matter vs. Mind: In the Contest, the Former Comes Off Victorious; The Facts Concerning Cannon's Polygamous Marriage, Cannon's Trial for Assaulting a 'Tribune' Reporter," *Salt Lake Daily Tribune*, November 2, 1884, 4. The *Salt Lake Herald* castigated the *Tribune* for its attack on an innocent woman in "The Tribune's Last Slander," *Salt Lake Herald*, November 4, 1884, 2. Details surrounding this earlier accusation include the name of the informant (Angus M. Cannon Jr.), Emmeline's demand for a retraction, William Woods's assertion of its falsehood, another retraction, and an ensuing altercation between John Q. Cannon and Joseph Lippman, city editor of the *Tribune* and author of the article. For a full account, see K. Cannon, "Tragic Matter," 150–57.

16. Emily Wells Grant, letter to Heber J. Grant, September 25, 1886, typescript copy in my possession. See also O. Whitney, Diary, September 29, 1886.

17. "The Mills of the Gods," *Salt Lake Daily Tribune*, October 9, 1886, 4; "A Curious Case!," *Salt Lake Herald*, October 9, 1886, 8; "The Examination," *Deseret Weekly News*, October 13, 1886, 620.

presumably Louie, but had been unable to gain permission from church leaders.[18] John's brother Abram, who, like many others, was unaware of John's unsuccessful petitions for the marriage, wondered in anguish why the two had not married years earlier, making their union honorable and respected among the Saints.[19] Had John and Louie followed the path of others who had married in Mexico, where polygamy, though illegal, was not prosecuted, they might have avoided the problems they were then facing.[20] But President Taylor had reportedly advised John Q., along with Orson F. Whitney and his own son John W. Taylor, not to enter the practice during this volatile period, and John acquiesced.[21]

If the proceedings of that extraordinary Sunday service had been the extent of public notice of this misadventure, prurient interest may have abated, the unnamed woman perhaps forgotten, and the popular and charismatic John finally forgiven. But the question of the unborn child remained. Thus, only days after the Sunday service, George Q. Cannon, processing the family catastrophe while in hiding, directed Annie to obtain an immediate divorce from John so he could then legally marry Louie and thus avoid arrest for polygamy.[22] Annie obediently sued for divorce, which the judge, Elias Smith, granted within a day, and on September 10, the morning after the divorce was finalized and only five days after his excommunication, John married Louie at the Cannon farm, with Abraham Cannon officiating. President George Q. Cannon may have assumed that the divorce and marriage would also protect John from prosecution for unlawful cohabitation, which was easier to prove than polygamy. Though done quietly and without any public

18. Martha Hughes Cannon, letter to Angus M. Cannon, September 26, 1886, in *Letters from Exile: The Correspondence of Martha Hughes Cannon and Angus M. Cannon, 1886–1888*, edited by Constance L. Lieber and John Sillito, 49.

19. A. H. Cannon, Diary, September 4, 1886.

20. While some church leaders discouraged using Mexico as a sanctuary for plural marriage, many couples felt it was a legitimate, though not legal, alternative for clandestine plural marriages in the United States after passage of the 1882 Edmunds and 1887 Edmunds-Tucker Acts and especially after the 1890 Manifesto.

21. Franklin D. Richards, Diary, January 30, 1888, as noted in Walker, "Grant's Watershed," 203. Like Abraham Cannon, Orson F. Whitney also went to Mexico, where he married his only living plural wife, May Wells, on July 24, 1888, two weeks after being vicariously sealed to Emmie and to another deceased woman, Fannie Ada McBride Cole, in the Manti temple. O. Whitney, Diary, October 11, 1900.

22. All were following President Cannon's directions. He had admitted to his brother Angus that he had given John "counsel as to the course to pursue" and felt that "it is right and from the Lord." George Q. Cannon to Angus Cannon, September 11, 1886, quoted in K. Cannon, "Tragic Matter," 174. Other accounts of this period are O. Whitney, Diary, September 29, 1886; and "Impressive and Sorrowful."

notice (licenses were not required until the 1887 Edmunds-Tucker Act), the precipitate marriage, once it did become known, obviously implicated Louie in John's infidelity.

Despite the shock of his startling revelation and confession, as scion of one of Mormondom's most illustrious families, the well-liked John Q. enjoyed much sympathy and praise for his courage in confessing his sin, promising repentance, and humbly asking for understanding and forgiveness. "Let there be no unkindness toward him personally," the *Deseret News* urged, and reminded the Saints to "remember his pathetic appeal" and assist him to regain his lost privileges.[23] Martha Cannon, his aunt, wept at the news. "The effort required to thus confess, notwithstanding the act that occasioned it," she wrote to her husband, "exhibited a courage that none but those in possession of a high type of manhood could put forth.... Surely," she continued, "if human suffering & sacrifice atones for sin, then he who stood up and confessed not only to thousands, but to the world, will be forgiven." She did not forget Emmeline and Annie. Let us "not fail to extend the same charity and sympathy to mother and daughter," she added. "I am young in experience, but can realize something of a mothers feelings."[24]

Less well known, however, was John's longtime habit of meeting friends at the Walker House, a popular resident hotel usually frequented by Gentile visitors, for a little smoking, drinking, and gambling.[25] To some, his affair with Louie seemed to fit a pattern of skirting the boundaries of appropriate behavior and thus did not seem so inexplicable. Helen Mar Kimball Whitney, Elizabeth Ann's daughter-in-law and Emmeline's friend, evidently knew this penchant of John's. When she learned of events in the tabernacle on that fateful September 5, she wrote that she was at first astonished, but "then I was not—when his conduct has been what it has—having carried a high head & roled [*sic*] in luxury—feeling himself safe in living an easy, & loose life, such as few could do & escape so long."[26] Family connections had likely shielded him in the past, perhaps to the resentment of some, but even his father foresaw negative consequences stemming from

23. "Impressive and Sorrowful."

24. Martha Cannon, letter to Angus Cannon, in *Letters from Exile*, edited by Lieber and Sillito, 49–50. John Q. Cannon's mother, Elizabeth Hoagland Cannon, died in 1882, and thus Emmeline was the only mother to witness this tragedy befalling their children.

25. This weakness was known to some high church officials as well as friends and associates. Louie's brother-in-law Heber J. Grant felt that John Q. had been "careless and indifferent" in his behavior. See Walker, "Grant's Watershed," 203.

26. Charles M. Hatch and Todd M. Compton, eds., *A Widow's Tale: The 1884–1896 Diary of Helen Mar Kimball Whitney*, 188.

the confession. "All John Q's faults will be likely to be made known and accusations may abound," he wrote to his brother Angus. "He must not take refuge in stimulants."[27]

While much sympathy and forgiveness followed John's confession, the women involved drew mainly gossip and disparagement. Drawing within their own tight circle, the Wells women hoped to shield themselves from the criticism and blame they felt from others. One can only imagine the scene in which the three of them, Louie, Annie, and Emmeline, talked together, trying to come to terms with the events that had so shattered their lives. Only they knew the whole of this complicated and sorrowful affair, and only they could explain and give any kind of personal understanding to these extraordinary actions. Only with Annie's and Emmeline's forgiveness of Louie and John's heedless behavior could their family unity be maintained. It was nothing short of a tour de force by these three women, struggling to dispel their individual feelings of resentment, anger, blame, confusion, and regret, that they could find absolution, empathy, and grace from and for one another. Whether they willingly or unwillingly acceded to George Q. Cannon's demands for the divorce and marriage is unknown. What is known is that Annie and Louie, as well as Emmeline, made their peace with one another and eventually with John, and the strength of that bond enabled them to meet the onslaught of public derision that erupted a month later.

For Emmeline, all past sorrows and tragedies lost force in this tragic turn of events. "In the midst of grief and anguish of soul," she wrote to her friend Lillie Freeze the day after Louie's marriage to John, "we Latter-day Saints are obliged to attend to such duties as pertain to our interests, and indeed we <u>feel</u> it a duty to do so, and work while there is yet time and opportunity. It may seem strange," she continued, "that I can go on my regular routine with the overwhelming trial through which I am passing, but I must not sink under it, and if I gave way I should, and true heroism consists in bearing with meekness and humility whatever afflictions the Lord suffers to come upon us; and not in lying down neath the heavy load of care and murmuring, and crying 'it is more than we can endure....'" She ended her letter, "Pray for me that I may not fall short."[28] This is Emmeline at her most reflective. If her own life had not given evidence of her faith in this dictum, it would seem a self-pitying nod to martyrdom. But it was not. As with all of the misfortunes that had beset her, her New England

27. G. Cannon, letter to Angus M. Cannon, September 1886, Angus M. Cannon Collection.

28. Emmeline B. Wells, letter to Lillie Freeze, September 11, 1886, Lillie Tuckett Freeze Papers.

stoicism and her own strength of will enabled her to accept this one, abide by her own counsel, and keep her family intact.

Waiting in the wings was another jolt to her slow return to equilibrium. It began on the morning of October 7 when federal marshals subpoenaed Emmeline and her daughters as witnesses at an arraignment relating to John's unexpected arrest for polygamy.[29] District attorney William H. Dickson served as prosecutor, and attorney Franklin S. Richards represented John. Throughout the hearing, Richards's objections to peripheral questions that intruded too deeply on the private lives of the family were consistently overruled. All who were involved were obliged to testify, including William Woods, who was determined to vindicate Louie and served as a prosecution witness. He testified that John, in a private communication to him, had confessed that he had "committed adultery" against "both his wives" and that his confession should not place any onus on Louie since he had wronged her as well as Annie.[30] The statement was meant to clear Louie's name as that of John's illicit paramour, while affirming the prosecution's charge of polygamy. Commissioner McKay, who adjudicated the proceedings, evidently accepted Woods's testimony as sufficient evidence to convince him that there was "probable cause" to bring the charge of polygamy, especially since there were doubts about the legality of Annie's divorce from John. The judge bound John over for a grand jury to consider an indictment. He was released on a bond of three thousand dollars for the charge of unlawful cohabitation and eight thousand dollars for polygamy.[31]

The *Salt Lake Daily Tribune* showed no restraint in reporting the testimonies given at the hearing, singling out Emmeline Wells for particular ridicule. Continually calling her "Ma Wells" and referring to her as "Zion's feminine curiosity," it depicted her as "giggling" and "bossy" as well as "sarcastic" and "defiant." When she was called to take the stand, the *Tribune* described her as "the over-sensitive, super-refined, oh!-my!-don't-touch-me old lady" who "squatted down in her chair, feeling thoroughly well satisfied with herself and her *entre* act."[32] From the time she had become subject to public scrutiny, as editor of the *Woman's Exponent* and as Utah's representative to the National Woman Suffrage Association in 1879, the *Tribune*

29. "John Q. Cannon Arrested," *Deseret Evening News*, October 7, 1886, 3; "Miss Louie Wells Arrested," *Deseret Evening News*, October 8, 1886, 3.

30. John's reference to "both his wives" was inclusive of Louie, implying it was a third party involved in his transgression. Moreover, Louie's name had never been publicly acknowledged as John's partner in adultery.

31. "The Cannon Case," *Salt Lake Herald*, October 10, 1886, 8; "Held on $11,000 Bail," *Salt Lake Daily Tribune*, October 10, 1886, 6.

32. "A Specimen Case," *Salt Lake Daily Tribune*, October 9, 1886, 2.

had never failed to mock her and her work. Though the newspaper was demeaning and insulting, she shrugged off their barbs. She was far more affronted by her friends' perplexing assumption that she had in some way steered the events that had transpired, and they disapproved of "the course she had taken" in the affair.[33] Helen Mar Whitney, however, was astute enough to know that Emmeline could not and would not have orchestrated John Q.'s public confession and immediate excommunication, especially in the absence of a prior ecclesiastical court hearing. Nor would she have promoted the scandal-producing divorce and marriage of her daughter that followed. "I argue that the course taken by Emmeline—Abram Cannon & the girls, is by advise," Helen Mar confided to her journal, "but this[,] Sol [Solomon Kimball, her brother], nor any of the rest could believe."[34]

Public opinion was quick to judge. But most hurtful, unbeknownst to Emmeline, was Eliza R. Snow's effort to recruit women to support her in relieving Emmeline of her editorship of the *Exponent* and her Relief Society duties. Upon hearing about Snow's efforts, George Q. Cannon immediately instructed Angus to block her plan. "It is not wise," he wrote to his brother. "Injustice may be done by hasty action."[35] Angus, who had visited Eliza the evening before and had already advised that "we deal charitably with E. B. Wells," went again to Eliza and spoke as directed by his brother while also writing a letter to her once more, "suggesting moderation in treatment of Sis. Wells."[36] Why Eliza judged Emmeline so harshly over an incident that she had no part in creating and from which she suffered so intensely is unknown. Where compassion was wanted, only criticism was offered.

With all of the disheartening effects on family and sympathetic friends, ultimately the heaviest weight of this tragedy fell on Louie, Annie, and their

33. Franklin D. Richards, whose wife Jane was a companion to Emmeline in both the Relief Society and suffrage activities, indicated that he had conversed with two other apostles about "the peculiar way it [the Cannon case] is being dealt with," though not suggesting any input on Emmeline's part. Franklin D. Richards, Diary, September 24, 1886.

34. Hatch and Compton, *Widow's Tale*, October 8, 1886, 198. It is strange that Emmeline received criticism rather than sympathy during this time. Helen Mar Whitney was absolutely right in her appraisal of how the events unfolded. Almost a year later, George Q. Cannon "had to defend himself and me [Abraham Cannon] before the Apostles because of what was done in the matter of John Q's divorce and marriage, but Father said he assumed all blame for the part I took in the matter." Abraham H. Cannon, Journal, August 15, 1887, as quoted in *An Apostle's Record: The Journals of Abraham H. Cannon*, edited by Dennis B. Horne, 87.

35. G. Cannon, letter to A. M. Cannon, October 29, 1886, Angus M. Cannon, Diary.

36. A. M. Cannon, Diary, October 28, 29, 1886.

mother, who received no compassionate words from the press or public. Nor could any amount of society's reproach match the burden of Louie's agonizing regrets, Annie's sense of betrayal, and Emmeline's anguish for her daughters.

Her work on the *Exponent* was Emmeline's salvation, and she returned to it as well as to her other commitments in earnest, despite the clouds that hung so heavily above her. How much the public knew about the details of this cause célèbre is hard to fathom, but Louie was never publicly acknowledged as the unnamed woman in the affair, despite the persistent rumors. She was neither excommunicated nor disfellowshipped, nor was she released from her position as general secretary of the Young Ladies' Mutual Improvement Association. She thus tried to conduct her life as before, singing at public events, conducting music at meetings, and attending church services, but Emmeline's and Louie's public activities appeared to be unseemly to some. Apostle Franklin D. Richards felt it necessary to counsel their bishop, Millen Atwood, as to "what course to pursue in relation to Louie Wells, John Q.'s reputed paramour." He was disturbed that she was "leading the singing at funerals and [that] her mother occupies prominent places at meetings."[37] Some still thought that Emmeline had orchestrated events following John's disclosure of the affair, not knowing or willing to believe the extent to which John's father, George Q. Cannon, managed them, particularly his son's excommunication and Annie's divorce.

After the hearing, Louie and Emmeline moved into Annie's home on the Cannon farm, some distance from the heart of the city, to help Annie with her three young children, while John lived in another home on the property, occasionally taking meals with them. No private record from any of the three women reveals how each day was lived during the last three months of that forbidding year. Alone and together, they were obliged to regroup from their own individual Waterloos, searching for the resolve to move forward.

As was feared, on December 8, John was indicted for polygamy. The basis for the indictment was that Annie's divorce decree was invalid and that he and Louie had been previously married. Emmeline, Annie, and Louie, among others, again testified, this time before the grand jury, which bound John Q. over for trial at an undetermined later date.[38] Like so many

37. Richards, Diary, October 30, 1886. That Emmeline is so maligned throughout this affair is not explained in the documents relating to it.

38. The prosecution asserted that John Q. had married Louie before the September wedding that followed his divorce from Annie. The trial went through several continuances before the case was finally dismissed.

other LDS plural wives before her, Louie decided to go into exile rather than testify again in a formal trial. On the last day of the year, she boarded a train for San Francisco to make her home with Belle. The uncertainty of the church's future as it faced the looming sanctions of the Edmunds-Tucker Act absorbed Emmeline's thoughts far less than the uncertainties that now veiled the future of her troubled family.[39]

39. In a brief remembrance of her grandfather John Q. Cannon, written for the family in 1976, Ruth Clayton Kearnes noted that John married "Aunt Louie" in a polygamous marriage, but that "Grandma" (Annie Wells Cannon) divorced John "to prevent his arrest and imprisonment." Ruth Clayton Kearnes, "John Q. Cannon," 1975, copy in my possession. George Q. Cannon surrendered to federal officials the following year, having also been indicted for polygamy.

FIGURE 1. Woodward homestead in Petersham, Massachusetts. Courtesy of Carolyn Chouinard, New Salem, Massachusetts. Author's collection.

FIGURE 2. New Salem Academy, New Salem, Massachusetts. Courtesy of Carolyn Chouinard, New Salem, Massachusetts. Author's collection.

FIGURE 3. Moose Horn Creek, site of Emmeline's baptism, New Salem, Massachusetts. Author's collection.

FIGURE 4. Newel K. Whitney, Emmeline's second husband. LDS Church History Library.

FIGURE 5. Elizabeth Ann Smith Whitney, first wife of Newel K. Whitney. LDS Church History Library.

FIGURE 6. Isabel Modalena Whitney (Sears), eldest daughter of Emmeline and Newel K. Whitney. International Society of Daughters of Utah Pioneers.

FIGURE 7. Melvina Caroline Blanche Whitney (Dunford, Woods), youngest daughter of Emmeline and Newel K. Whitney. Courtesy of Richard Rossing, great-great-grandson of Emmeline B. Wells.

FIGURE 8. Daniel Hanmer Wells, third husband of Emmeline. LDS Church History Library.

FIGURE 9. Daniel Hanmer Wells as an older man. LDS Church History Library.

FIGURE 10. Wives of Daniel Hanmer Wells. LDS Church History Library.

FIGURE 11. Emmeline Wells at various life stages. *Clockwise from the top*: ca. 1850s, ca. 1870s, ca. 1890, ca. 1890s, ca. 1900. Library of Congress, International Society of Daughters of Utah Pioneers, and LDS Church History Library.

FIGURE 12. Emmeline (Emmie) Whitney Wells, eldest daughter of Emmeline and Daniel Hanmer Wells. International Society of Daughters of Utah Pioneers.

FIGURE 13. Elizabeth Ann (Annie) Wells Cannon, second daughter of Emmeline and Daniel Hanmer Wells. Courtesy of Kathleen Cannon Knowlton.

FIGURE 14. Louisa Martha (Louie) Wells Cannon, youngest daughter of Emmeline and Daniel Hanmer Wells. LDS Church History Library.

FIGURE 15. Septimus Wagstaff Sears (*standing*), husband of Isabel Whitney. Author's collection.

FIGURE 16. William Wells Woods, husband of Melvina Whitney, nephew of Daniel Hanmer Wells. Author's collection.

FIGURE 17. Colonel John Q. Cannon, husband of Elizabeth Ann Wells. Courtesy of Kathleen Cannon Knowlton.

FIGURE 18. First home of Daniel Hanmer Wells and his families, "the Adobe House behind the Wall," which was also Emmeline's home and office (1888–93). LDS Church History Library.

FIGURE 19. Emmeline's home (1856–88), 243 State Street. LDS Church History Library.

FIGURE 20. Veronica Dunford Hillard with her grandmother Emmeline Wells. Courtesy of Richard Rossing.

FIGURE 21. Daniel Hanmer Wells family residence (the big house), South Temple and Main Street. LDS Church History Library

CHAPTER 20

Sequel
(1887)

CHRISTMAS IN 1886 was not the joyous family-and-friends celebration the Wells household usually hosted. The shock of the previous months had been absorbed by the community, but the Wells family struggled with its reverberations. No trial date was set in the Cannon polygamy case, but daily reports of fathers imprisoned and wives forced to testify against their husbands kept their own troubles well in mind. One of the consequences that would follow passage of the new antipolygamy bill was the loss of women's voting rights, which eastern suffragists so adamantly opposed.[1] Emmeline kept in contact with her eastern coworkers but wrote few editorials on suffrage during that fall and winter. Uncertainty pervaded the air, with family life disrupted and federal officials unnerving the Mormon community. Though mindful of these challenges, Emmeline's personal turmoil commanded all of her attention. Her great hope was that the scandal that had beset them would fade from public interest in light of the threats facing the church. "In this time of trial to all," she wrote, "individual affairs may possibly be let alone. Gossips may have something to occupy their time and thoughts."[2] To underscore her ire, she took a step to shame them into silence. As one of the speakers at the last quarterly Relief Society conference of Salt Lake Stake in 1886, Emmeline began her remarks with the Savior's injunction "Do unto others as ye would that others should do unto you" and then added, "We should be kind and tender to each other, and never wound the feelings of anyone knowingly."[3]

When Louie left home for San Francisco in December of that year, Emmeline, already emotionally exhausted, could hardly countenance the

1. E. Wells, Diary, January 29, 1887.
2. Ibid., January 13, 1887.
3. "R.S., Y.L.M.I.A. & P.A. Reports," *Woman's Exponent* 15 (December 15, 1886): 110.

separation. "This is a sad beginning for the New Year," she wrote on New Year's Day 1887. "Louie gone and I so desolate."[4] Though fourteen years separated Belle and Louie in age, traveling together to the East three years earlier to view the scenes of their mother's childhood and church history sites had drawn them close. Louie would enjoy the warmth of Belle's love and care, the kind solicitude of her brother-in-law Septimus, and the companionship of Belle's six children: Dot (young Isabel), fourteen; Sep, twelve; Lucile, ten; Emma, six; Eugene, four; and one-year-old Brent (Edward Benton Sears). Learning of her safe arrival, Emmeline hoped that San Francisco would give Louie "free air to breathe without intrusion or any disagreeable gossip reaching her ears."[5] Despite all they had been through, Annie had John Q. and her children as her primary concern, while Emmeline and Louie seemed to cling to each other.

Annie, deeply wounded by this family cataclysm, received sympathy as the injured party and since her little-known divorce from John she had lived apart from him to avoid any suggestion of a plural marriage. Understanding the emotional torment Annie was enduring, Emmeline remained at the Cannon farm after Louie left.[6] In those months together, they had opportunity to work through their feelings and try to find some fragment of routine in their lives. A daily pattern began to emerge when John Q. started driving Emmeline to the city each day where they both worked and back to the Cannon farm in the evenings. John had retained his place on the city council, and during its evening meetings Emmeline continued to work in her office or visited her own home, returning late to the farm with John.

A decision to stay at her own home one stormy night was disastrous. "Such a night as never was for me, no sleep scarcely all alone, and every minute almost cries of sorrow and mourning. The house was like a tomb. I could not bear any one to come to witness my agony and so I stayed alone."[7] Louie's homesickness for her mother, expressed in every letter, merely exacerbated Emmeline's longing for her daughter. "O how sad for us to be separated at a time when she so much needs her mother and those who love her devotedly to comfort her and be around her. Belle is very companionable but her family cares are very heavy."[8]

Emmeline thrived on the daily letters Louie wrote to her and in turn sent her letters and copies of the *Woman's Exponent* and *Daily Herald*. Though

4. E. Wells, Diary, January 1, 1887.
5. Ibid., January 3, 1887.
6. Ibid., January 1, 1887.
7. Ibid., January 11, 1887.
8. Ibid., January 9, 1887.

far removed from the anguish that his family was undergoing, Daniel tried to counsel them from a distance through Emmeline. He did not write to Louie. However, since one long letter he wrote to Emmeline had given her so "much unnecessary pain while I had already almost more than I could bear," she was reluctant to read a second one that he wrote after Louie had moved to San Francisco. She finally collected her courage, "which I begin to think is very great since I have gone through so much and as I read on I found he had modified very much indeed. Altogether I felt comforted."[9] Bearing the burden of the scandal without him made her more sensitive to his accusatory comments. His gentler approach was more effective.

Emmeline's loyal friends continued to frequent her office, impeding her work each day, but causing less resentment from Emmeline, who valued their support the more. She was perplexed at Eliza R. Snow's capricious response to her visits. She was sometimes cordial and sometimes dismissive, causing Emmeline to wonder "whether she is a real friend or only one who does for her own sake," but Eliza was clearly ailing during this last year of her life.[10]

Though her own life was "so changed to me without Louie and my own home," the fifty-nine-year-old Emmeline wrote, with the beginning of the new year, she nevertheless settled back into the same kind of frenetic but now cathartic routine that marked her days before the previous autumn.[11] Editorials and articles for her paper, daily letters to Louie, long letters to Daniel (sometimes twelve pages long), and *Exponent* and Relief Society correspondence, along with occasional poetic verses, flowed from her pen. It is no wonder she lamented the lack of time "to write some thing more creditable than any work I have ever done" and begrudged the fact that "other women with less ability have accomplished more."[12]

She followed the debate over the new antipolygamy bill against which she had testified before the House Judiciary Committee and lobbied individual senators and representatives in person the previous year.[13] Her *Woman's Exponent* editorials berated Congress while admonishing her readers to accept what appeared to be inevitable. She remained current on events in Washington and wrote insightful and well-reasoned editorials on

9. Ibid., January 24, 1887.

10. Ibid., March 29, 1887.

11. Ibid., January 15, 1887. Throughout this difficult period, negotiations to sell her home were in process, adding an additional burden of anxiety. Junius Wells acted as her representative throughout the negotiations.

12. Ibid., January 15, 1887.

13. C. Madsen, *Advocate for Women*, 220–30.

what the Mormons felt was a huge infringement on their constitutional rights.[14] When the House passed the Edmunds-Tucker bill in January 1887, Emmeline noticed that it did so "in a perfect furore [*sic*] under pressure from [John Randolph] Tucker."[15] Besides wrenching families apart and politically neutralizing women's political voice by rescinding their right to vote, it was also financially debilitating to the church. "It is a most cruel & infamous measure," Emmeline asserted, "and contrary to all sense of justice and right."[16]

After reading the memorial to President Cleveland that asked him to veto the proposed antipolygamy bill while also "protesting against the disfranchisement of the legal women voters of Utah," Emmeline sent a telegram, signed by eleven Utah suffragists, thanking the eastern suffragists, particularly Susan B. Anthony, for their support during this stressful time.[17]

Recognizing the inevitable passage of the Edmunds-Tucker bill, Emmeline once again bowed to God's will, which this time took the form of chastisement. "It seems as though every thing had conspired against this people," she wrote. "No doubt the Lord intends to discipline his people."[18]

Her attendance at the territorial convention of the People's Party (where she was elected a delegate at large along with Isabella Horne), meetings of the Deseret Hospital Board, as well as Relief Society trips to outlying areas all kept her in the same dizzying swirl that had long characterized her public life.[19] If Bishop Atwood felt these activities unseemly in view of the September events, there is no evidence he advised Emmeline to desist. Perhaps he sensed that they were accomplished only by great self-discipline. "O how sad is my heart," Emmeline lamented, "and yet I cannot say so, I will

14. See, for example, "Comments," *Woman's Exponent* 15 (January 15, 1887): 124; "Suffrage Women Protest: Comments," 15 (February 1, 1887): 132; "Apostle Lorenzo Snow at Liberty, Comments," 15 (February 15, 1887): 140; "Comments," 15 (March 1, 1887): 148; and "Comments," 15 (March 15, 1887): 156.

15. C. Madsen, *Advocate for Women*, 224.

16. E. Wells, Diary, January 12, 1887. The bill disincorporated the church and the Perpetual Emigrating Fund, escheated to the government all church property in excess of fifty thousand dollars, disinherited wives and children of polygamous marriages (in the case of intestate husbands), abolished the Utah Militia, and prohibited all "sectarian" instruction in the common schools. It also required that all marriages be civilly recorded, whether a religious or civil ceremony. G. Larson, *Outline History*, 276–77.

17. "Suffrage Women Protest," *Woman's Exponent* 15 (February 1, 1887): 132; E. Wells, Diary, January 29, 1887.

18. C. Madsen, *Advocate for Women*, 227–30; E. Wells, Diary, February 17, 1887.

19. "The Territorial Convention," *Woman's Exponent* 15 (November 1, 1886): 85.

not wear my heart upon my sleeve. Died in my own heart, lie buried in my inmost soul; my own little baby my very last one to go away from me where I cannot see her again for so long a time."[20]

When Louie left for California at the end of December, Emmeline gave her a small pocket-size diary, asking her to keep a record of her time away. On the front page, Louie wrote, "322 Pine Street, San Francisco. For mother who wanted me to tell her what I did each day."[21] Louie was faithful to her mother's request. Her entries are daily recitals of each day's activities, usually beginning with a notation of the letters she had written to her mother and husband. She seldom missed a day of letter writing. She made almost daily trips to the post office at 435 Bush Street, near Pine, to mail her letters, while always hoping for letters from home. She "thought a great deal" during these days away, but never specifically mentioned the events that had so changed her life.

Her days in San Francisco soon settled into a pattern. Much time was spent with Belle's children, to whom she read stories and sang songs and with whom she took walks and played games. An additional member of the Sears household was fourteen-year-old Elise Gasser, a Swiss convert of 1884, whose dying mother had given her to Belle.[22] A concert and tour of the conservatory near Belle's home with the two boys Sep and Eugene followed by an evening visit to Tivoli, a playhouse, were the activities of the day after she arrived.[23] Shopping and sightseeing with Belle as well as visits to China Town and to the ocean with Belle and Septimus also filled her days.[24] Of most pleasure to Louie were evenings at the opera house. As a singer herself, she was delighted to see *Il Trovatore*, featuring Emma Abbott, at the Baldwin Theatre, which she "enjoyed more than anything."[25] She relished these musical opportunities. "I have been almost carried away

20. E. Wells, Diary, March 6, 1887.

21. Louie Wells Cannon, Diary, in my possession. The Pine Street house at number 322, where Louie lived during the early part of her stay with Belle and Septimus, is located near the Embarcadero. The post office, no longer standing, was near the entry to China Town. Maps consulted in Special Collections, San Francisco Public Library.

22. When the Sears family returned to Salt Lake City some years later, Elise continued to live with them. She also helped Emmeline with the *Exponent* on occasion. See E. Wells, Diary, April 16, 1892.

23. L. Cannon, Diary, January 2, 1887.

24. Both Belle and Louie often visited China Town. Ibid., January 3, 9, 25, 27, February 2, 1887. Louie occasionally rambled through the neighborhood alone.

25. Ibid., January 18, 1887. Emma Abbott and her troupe traveled to Utah that year and gave several performances in the Salt Lake Theatre.

with the music & have scarcely thought of any thing else it has made me feel bad and yet happy as good music always does," she wrote.[26] When Septimus decided to buy a piano for Belle, he asked Louie to select it, and it became a happy addition to the household, as both women played and Louie often sang.[27] Though her talent in art was highly acclaimed in Salt Lake City, she did not mention visiting any art galleries or exhibits. Without the visual arts, however, concerts and plays satisfied her artistic nature. Clearly, her sister and brother-in-law intended to make her sojourn with them pleasant and peaceful, without reproach.

Louie did not see many hometown visitors and so was pleased when Hiram Clawson, an actor and director of the Salt Lake Theatre and Emmeline's longtime friend, visited with news that round dancing (waltzing) was once again permitted![28] Young Sid Hooper, son of Hiram Clawson's onetime business partner, William Hooper, was attending school in San Francisco and became a regular visitor, mainly to see Dot. Louie corresponded with several friends, and unfortunately the only letter she received from her teaching associate and dear friend Mary Cook "contained more bad news <u>for me</u>."[29] A "friendly letter" from Rob Sloan, her former beau, may have caused her some reflection. However, she declined to answer, thinking it unwise "to write to him under the circumstances," nor did she think "J.Q. would like it though he is very kind and good and I appreciate his friendship." Instead, she sent him a gift of a paper knife.

Though Louie lived for letters, they evoked pain as well as pleasure, exacerbating her homesickness. It persisted like a relentless, gnawing ache that accompanied all her thoughts and activities. After reading letters from home, she often went to bed and "cried myself to sleep." Writing letters to her mother and friends was similarly difficult. "I wrote [a] long letter to mother," she noted on one unhappy day; "felt very sad and cried all the time. I am so miserable and it is such a drag to live." Neither Belle's companionship, Septimus's thoughtful care, the hustle-bustle of the children, nor the musical outings or visits from neighbors could quiet the constant anxiety and apprehension. "Nothing," she wrote on January 18, "can drive the trouble from my mind, hard as I try."[30]

Louie seldom commented on John's letters to her except to remark on the pleasure and surprise she felt at receiving a hundred dollars from him

26. Ibid., January 31, 1887.
27. Ibid., January 28, 1887.
28. Ibid., February 6, 1887.
29. Ibid., February 18, 1887. She does not explain what made the news bad.
30. Ibid., February 13, 1887.

in one of them.[31] The affinity shared by mother and daughter, however, was highly evident in their diaries. After receiving a box of homemade items from Emmeline, Louie wrote that she felt "blue ever since the things came so fresh from dear mother's hand." So vivid a picture they brought to Louie's mind of her mother that "it almost seemed as if I could see her," she wrote.[32] Her mother's unspecified illness in late February deeply distressed Louie.[33] "I feel as if I should die if anything ails ma she seems my only hope and all I have to live for if I can be any comfort to her I will try to live."[34] The future was clouded for Louie; what was her life to be after the baby was born? She wished so much "for what can not be" that she prayed "God may take me soon if he sees fit."[35] Emmeline, more than John, was her anchor throughout these months. "Mother will never know how I have longed for her & for those I love," Louie wrote near the end of her diary, "but if I live," she added, "I shall prove my love & devotion."[36]

In early February, when Louie was well along in her pregnancy, she began to feel a persistent pain in her back and swelling in her legs and feet, symptoms of possible preexisting problems, likely renal failure.[37] The swelling was so extreme, Louie could hardly walk, and Belle bathed her feet frequently to ease the pain.[38] Within days, Louie's entire body had become so swollen she could not fit into her clothes, so Belle made her a loose-fitting garment that eased the discomfort of clothing.[39]

As the days turned into weeks, the pain increased, and though she tried to sew clothes for the baby, she could not do the fine needlework required. "I am so wretched that I can find no pleasure even in making such sweet little things," she confessed on one miserable day.[40] Visits to the doctor were not encouraging, and he offered little relief. Unable to sleep, Louie

31. Ibid., February 18, 1887.

32. Ibid., February 28, 1887.

33. Ibid., January 17, March 1, 3, 1887. See E. Wells, Diary, February 26, March 1, 1887.

34. L. Cannon, Diary, March 1, 1887.

35. Ibid., February 3, 9, 1887.

36. Ibid., March 10, 1887.

37. Louie may have suffered from toxemia or renal failure, as several obstetricians have explained, which can cause the type of symptoms she experienced before and after the birth of her baby. The exact malady, of course, cannot be diagnosed at this point. One of her doctors alluded to the possibility of a preexisting condition as a cause of her extraordinary physical distress. E. Wells, Diary, March 14, 1887. Emmeline's diary makes no mention of any previous or recurring illness of Louie's that might have supported the doctor's diagnosis.

38. L. Cannon, Diary, February 1, 1887. Original document in author's possession.

39. Ibid., February 3, 4, 21, 1887.

40. Ibid., February 10, 11, 1887.

appreciated the attention Belle gave to her, rubbing her back and bathing her feet and legs. When she asked her doctor about returning home to have the baby, he feared she would not survive the journey.[41] Finally, on March 9, the doctor administered morphine to counteract the relentless pain.[42]

Belle's constant care, while sorely needed, concerned Louie. "Belle is so kind and good but I can not bear to have her wait upon me the way she does."[43] Belle even walked with Louie in the moonlight when sleep was elusive and her legs permitted. But all her care gave only momentary relief. By the middle of March, Louie was so weak that she could do little more than lie in bed. "Belle has to lift me as if I were a child," she lamented. "I wish she had some help it is too much for the dear girl to do." Belle, however, tried to do it all, meeting with the doctor, trying new medicines, and administering the hands-on nursing care that helped more than the medications. She even wrote Louie's letters home for her, alarming Emmeline.[44] "So weary, so weary," Louie wrote on one lonely, difficult day. "No one knows how I suffer. I try to be patient and keep up." But her body dictated otherwise. "The skin on my legs seem all broken and red and so so sore."[45] Her misery was so complete that she could not bear to think that she still faced more weeks of pregnancy.[46]

The last entry in this small, slim diary is dated March 26, written in pencil, as are the prior few days' entries. It is a detailed description of a dream. She and her mother were sleeping upstairs in a church or a large hall, she wrote, when Louie had a premonition that something dreadful was going to happen. She dressed and went out into the night to find out what it might be, while her mother waited where they had been sleeping. As Louie walked up a "lovely path" leading from the building, she met Joseph E. Taylor, counselor to Angus Cannon of the Salt Lake Stake, "dressed as a monk." He walked with her a short distance, and when she suddenly looked back she saw the tower of the great hall crash to the ground in a burst of blue light. "I thought of no one but mother being there and screamed when I got back hundreds of people were having their wounds dressed I asked and screamed for mother no one answered me at last Eleanor [Joseph's daughter] said she was crushed the first blow." The dream ended, and Louie awoke in such distress she could not speak about it until morning. Belle,

41. Ibid., February 25, 1887.
42. Ibid., March 9, 1887.
43. Ibid., March 6, 1887.
44. E. Wells, Diary, March 10, 11, 1887.
45. L. Cannon, Diary, March 12, 20, 1887.
46. Ibid., March 9, 1887.

seeing how unnerved she was, stayed by her throughout the day.[47] Emmeline was indeed the focal point of her pain-driven thoughts.

Sometime during this difficult time, the Sears family moved from their Pine Street home two miles away to 21 Glen Park Avenue, near the Laurel Hill Cemetery.[48] Louie's bedroom window offered a slim view of the ocean beyond the green vista of a nearby cemetery, a soothing image when Louie was able to see it.

News of John's pending trial and his statements to the press distressed Louie and angered Emmeline. John had filed an affidavit in early April requesting a continuance of his trial, since Louie was living out of state and could not appear as a witness. He had explained that Louie's "present sickness" was unexpected and would thus prevent her testifying at that time but that her testimony would provide a valid defense to the charge of polygamy.[49] Though his affidavit was successful, Emmeline was appalled at John's statement. "My very soul sickened when I read it." *Sickness*, as John Q. used the term, had long been a euphemism for pregnancy, and Emmeline could hardly have been pleased to have Louie's condition publicly known. In an emotional outburst, she exclaimed to her diary, "I do not know how to endure it along with all the other indignities he has heaped upon us," and she could only pray "for wisdom for grace to know how to act under this and all other circumstances."[50] The specter of a trial haunted them all, knowing that it would resurrect the humiliations and misery of the past year.

In the meantime, Emmeline continued her usual busy routine. On April 5, after a particularly stressful day in her office, Emmeline decided to wait in her own home for John Q. to take her to Annie's after his city council meeting. Alone in the house, she made a fire in Louie's upstairs bedroom fireplace and again gave way to her sorrow as memories flooded over her. "O, the dreadful feelings I had there alone and whenever I went to one of Louie's drawers or touched anything belonging to her it seemed to me as if I should burst with grief." As usual, she turned to poetry to express her feelings. "Sweet Memories" was written that night while she was alone in Louie's room. One verse reads,

47. Ibid., March 26, 1887.

48. The graves in the Laurel Hill Cemetery were removed to an outlying area in the early part of the twentieth century to make room for the growing residential part of the city.

49. Kenneth L. Cannon II elaborates on this legal action and John Q.'s attempts to quash or at least postpone the polygamy indictment in "Tragic Matter," 180–81.

50. E. Wells, Diary, April 19, 1887.

Sweet memories of our busy life a part,
Rifting the clouds that hang around our way,
And gently whispering to the human heart,
Hope on and bear the burden of today.[51]

What might she have written in that lonely hour had she known that Louie was even then in the throes of childbirth? And after weeks of agony, Louie's son came to her stillborn. Almost beside herself when she learned the news, Emmeline said to John more of her feelings "than ever before for I felt it was more than a mother could endure."[52] Emmeline made all haste to travel to San Francisco, arriving the morning of April 11.

The anguish she felt when she first saw her wan and sick daughter was but the beginning of five more weeks of horrendous pain and suffering for both mother and daughter. "Pain and distress beyond anything I have ever seen, so dreadful that I can not tell how to endure it. The groans the moans the piteous pleadings are beyond expression in words," Emmeline wrote.[53] The doctors could neither cure the ailment nor alleviate the terrible pain. Louie's suffering dominated Emmeline's and Belle's thoughts and actions, and there was little time for anything beyond their care of Louie.

Emmeline's only relief from her own suffering was to walk over to the cemetery and gaze at the ocean, while thoughts and feelings competed for her attention. The days and nights soon became a routine of incessant pain, delirium, high fevers, and numbing chills as Emmeline and Belle hovered, helpless to do more than alleviate minor symptoms. There was no relief.[54] Hope and resignation vied for possession of each day.

However trying and wearying the constant nursing was to the caregivers, Louie was overwhelmed with the intensity of her pain. "'I'm so weary, so tired, so weary, weary, weary,'" she cries out, Emmeline despairingly wrote. She calls, "'Mother, Mother, Belle, Belle, Mercy mercy,' and in such pitiful entreating tones."[55] "O it is terrible to see one's own child one's darling suffering so and not be able to even lift them off their pillow or in any way alleviate their pain."[56] Throughout this unbearable time, however, Louie expressed no regrets nor attached any blame. "She has been too lonely too disconsolate & now she has locked up her heart," Emmeline realized. "Such

51. Emile [Emmeline Wells], "Sweet Memories," *Woman's Exponent* 16 (June 1, 1887): 1. It also appears in her *Musings and Memories*, 122.

52. E. Wells, Diary, April 9, 1887.

53. Ibid., April 12, 1887, and following days.

54. Ibid., April 25, 1887.

55. Ibid., May 9, 1887.

56. Ibid., May 12, 1887.

natures are never understood but suffer and bear their cross alone, only God knows what my poor girl has gone thro." "'Nobody knows nobody knows,' Louie herself cries out so pitifully," Emmeline lamented, but she "seldom ever sheds a tear, she dare not give way." Emmeline could not help lashing out at those who had been hurtful and unforgiving. "The hard hearted cruel ones who have caused her untold pain & anguish, O, heaven help me to forgive them."[57] Then, as the end drew near, Louie finally asked for John to come.[58]

On Louie's final night, Emmeline slept near her dying daughter. Louie hardly roused the next morning, but, Emmeline wrote, "she only opened those beautiful eyes upon us, as though she saw someone but not us and passed peacefully to rest at 10 AM."[59]

The next day, Emmeline and her granddaughter Dot went over to the Laurel Hill Cemetery one last time. They visited the grave of Louie's unnamed son, and Emmeline "saw again the beautiful Pacific Ocean lying in the distance & looking so grand & awakening so many thoughts."[60] John arrived two days after Louie's death and spent a night alone watching over Louie's body. If he confided his thoughts to anyone that night, no record appears to have survived. Belle completed sewing Louie's burial clothes and, with Emmeline, dressed her body, Belle's final sisterly act after five months of unceasing care. Little known was the intense burden carried by Belle and Septimus during Louie's stay with them. Belle never flinched from the demands her suffering sister laid upon her. And Emmeline noted that Septimus could not have given Louie more care had he been her father. Their ministrations were unstinting and motivated by Louie's intense need for them.

Before leaving, Emmeline retrieved Louie's small diary. As she turned each page, reading Louie's account of her brief life in San Francisco, she came upon a lock of golden silky baby's hair tied with a pale blue ribbon. By its side Emmeline placed a lock of Louie's fine dark hair, which she had tied with a delicate pink ribbon, and then tucked the precious diary among her other mementos of Louie's last days.

Only Emmeline and John accompanied Louie's body home. The Sears family had no need to observe the formalities of a funeral. They had paid

57. Ibid., April 29, 1887.

58. Belle had evidently led Emmeline to believe that Louie did not want to see John, but Louie may have changed her mind at the end. Ibid., May 15, 1887.

59. Ibid., May 16, 1887.

60. Ibid. Two years later, Emmeline put those thoughts into a poem, "Memories of the Sea," *Woman's Exponent* 18 (July 15, 1889): 25, and included it in *Musings and Memories*, 34.

their respects and given their love to Louie in ways few others could have done. Now the ordeal was over, and John and Emmeline shared the mournful trip back to Utah. "How sad it is to travel with the dead body of one who is dearer than life," Emmeline reflected. The quiet rain they encountered when they arrived served as the tears Emmeline would not shed before her friends.[61]

And many there were to greet them at the Ogden terminal. The arrival of the Salt Lake train brought even more welcomers, mainly members of the Wells family, along with a letter from Daniel requesting that Louie be buried next to Emmie in the Wells burial plot, certainly a relief to Emmeline. All of the local newspapers noted her death, attributing it to "dropsy." The sympathetic *Salt Lake Herald* described the gloom that news of her death had cast over her many friends and stated that she would be remembered "for her graces of mind and manner, her winning disposition, and her varied personal accomplishments."[62] The *Salt Lake Tribune* did not resist giving its own disparaging version of Louie's last moments: "It is a comfort to know that before she died her eyes were opened to the awful fraud of Mormonism," a statement that had no explanation, evidence, or truth. But at least it spared the family a recapitulation of the soul-wrenching events of the previous fall. Helen Kimball Whitney wrote the most perceptive comment about Emmeline during this bleak hour: "We all feel deeply for poor Em. She is in an ocean of sorrow."[63] Indeed, Emmeline could hardly tread water, she was so overwhelmed with grief. Angus Cannon's plural wife Martha Hughes, still in England, though critical of the Wells family, nonetheless expressed sympathy for the bereaved mother in one of her letters to Angus.[64]

The funeral was held at 4:00 PM at the Cannon farm on May 21, the afternoon John and Emmeline arrived home. Brief notices gave only an outline of her service.[65] Members of the Tabernacle Choir provided the music, conducted by Ebeneezer Beesley and accompanied by Joseph J. Daynes. Angus M. Cannon, John's uncle, who was also Emmeline's stake president, conducted and offered remarks, as did the sympathetic Orson F. Whitney.

61. E. Wells, Diary, May 20, 21, 1887.

62. "Startling News Received from San Francisco Yesterday," *Salt Lake Herald*, May 17, 1887, 8.

63. Hatch and Compton, *Widow's Tale*, 236.

64. Lieber and Sillito, *Letters from Exile*, 122.

65. "Louie Wells Cannon Dead," *Salt Lake Daily Tribune*, May 17, 1887, 4. Other brief newspaper accounts included "Louie Wells Cannon Dead," *Deseret Evening News*, May 16, 1887, 5; "The Obsequies," *Deseret Evening News*, May 21, 1887, 5; and "Local Briefs," *Salt Lake Herald*, May 22, 1887, 8. In his journal of May 21, 1887, Franklin D. Richards also noted the funeral but without reference to Angus's sermon.

Hiram Clawson gave the opening prayer. Junius Wells pronounced the benediction, and Abraham Cannon dedicated the grave. Both the Wells and the Cannon families were represented, though neither paterfamilias was in attendance.

Louie had not been forgotten by her friends. Flowers filled the Cannon farmhouse and covered the coffin. An arrangement of white flowers accented with green leaves from the Unity Club, of which she was a member, was designed in the form of an elegant cross and crown. The (George) Careless Opera Company sent an arrangement of purple heliotrope with the name Louie at the top. Also on display was "an exquisite pillow of pure white flowers" with *Louie* inscribed in deep-red geranium blossoms in the center. Many arrangements represented music and art, and others were made of the delicate round snowballs tied in white ribbon. White with spots of color was definitely the color theme of the funeral.[66] The house could not contain all of the friends who came to mourn this beautiful, talented, star-crossed woman. A cortege of thirty-seven carriages followed the family to the graveside, where Louie was buried next to her sister Emmie, who had died nine years earlier at almost the same age.

Emmeline had been meticulous in recording the details of Louie's final weeks, her death, and the funeral and burial services. What she did not record was the shocking and utterly inappropriate statement made by Angus Cannon during his remarks at the funeral. Though not recorded verbatim, he evidently revealed more details about the John Q. Cannon affair than had generally been known and either hinted at or stated the fact that Louie was the woman with whom John had committed adultery. It was reported that Emmeline and a number of women in the congregation fainted at his words while others shouted "Shame!" to silence the speaker, eliciting Angus's explanation that he was simply doing his brother George's bidding.[67] If Emmeline had not already reached her emotional nadir, his words would surely have dragged her to it. In years to come, she continually remembered that day as "one of the most dreadful heart-rending days of my life—the agony, the misery, the tearing asunder of the most delicate fibres of my nature was beyond all that I have ever known."[68] Even writing or speaking about it was distressing. "I cannot talk much about the dreadful experiences of the time eleven years ago," she wrote, "as my heart is too full of pain and anguish. A day and time when the most severe ordeal was

66. "In Memoriam: A Tribute of Love," *Woman's Exponent* 16 (June 1, 1887): 4, 5.

67. Francis M. Lyman, letter to Joseph F. Smith, May 25, 1887, Joseph F. Smith Correspondence, as cited in Walker, "Grant's Watershed," 204.

68. E. Wells, Diary, May 21, 1890.

given me to pass through and the agony was past endurance."[69] Of course, Angus Cannon's remarks at the funeral soon found their way throughout the Salt Lake community. Apostle Franklin D. Richards, who did not attend but heard from his daughter-in-law Emily about Cannon's comments, noted in his diary that "the leading home topic is the death of Louie W. Cannon, on Monday and what occurred at the Funeral at the residence of her husband."[70]

If this were not enough for the Wells family, in September, four months after Louie's funeral, Louie's sister Mell, no longer a church member and having no particular need to show deference to a church leader, happened to meet President Angus Cannon on the street. She exploded in anger with a slap across his face. Still reeling from the death of her third child just two months earlier, Mell could hardly control the emotions that engulfed her. Clearly insensitive to her feelings, President Cannon, ignoring all protocol as a church leader and a gentleman, slapped her back, hard enough to damage her neck. He also threatened to publish a "card," in the newspaper, "giving all the facts in the case of John Q., including his confession charging Louie as being the guilty party with him, should Mell reveal the facts of their encounter to the *Tribune*."[71] When Emmeline heard about the incident from Orson, she was "almost paralyzed." At Ort's advice, she went immediately to Mell's home and there, in discussing the matter and the need to keep it out of the papers, Emmeline reported that she "passed thru a most severely trying ordeal, one that no language can portray." She left the home with her "heart nearly broken."[72]

John and Annie were desperate at the thought that John and Louie's indiscretion might be made public by Angus Cannon's warning. John actually threatened to kill him, and Annie promised to kill herself if he published his card. When hearing of his brother's action, George Q. Cannon asked his son Abram to speak to Angus and counsel him "to avoid resenting anything he may deem an insult from the Wells family."[73] No card was published, and the incident remained as private as far as possible in the close-knit Mormon community.[74]

69. Ibid., May 16, 1898.

70. Richards, Diary, May 22, 1887.

71. A. H. Cannon, Diary, September 14, 1887.

72. E. Wells, Diary, September 14, 15, 1887.

73. A. H. Cannon, Diary, September 14, 1887. George Q. Cannon was still overseeing the actions of his brother and sons, though he was never personally on the scene, being in hiding to avoid arrest.

74. E. Wells, Diary, September 15, 1887.

Emmeline managed to mask her resentment toward her stake president. They continued to meet frequently at church affairs and functioned with apparent cordiality on the Deseret Hospital Board. Emmeline often wrote respectfully of their association. However, at his birthday anniversary in 1898, a decade after these tumultuous events, long-repressed feelings erupted. She acknowledged that he had also experienced sorrow and disappointment in his life, particularly his humiliation when he lost a state senate race in which his wife Martha was among those who ran against him and won. "As he has been unkind and ungenerous to others harsh in his judgment one need not be surprised that it comes back upon him—As ye mete it out to others so shall it be unto you, and therefore he should expect it."[75]

As a final tribute to her daughter, Emmeline wrote a moving, heartfelt piece, "In Memoriam." It included details about the friends and floral tributes, the funeral proceedings (excluding Cannon's remarks), and also her reflections on Louie's life. It was followed a month later with a personal remembrance by Orson F. Whitney, who was like a brother to Louie.[76] Upon receiving copies of the two memorial pieces, Martha Cannon found them shockingly inappropriate. "It is astonishing to note to what a length the vanity of some people will lead them," she wrote to her husband, Angus. "I believe that Aunt Em had genuine true feelings extended towards her, by very many, since her trouble, but if she don't mind will alter it by her own lack of common sense." She also had little use for Orson's tribute, being unable to "hardly account for Bishop Whitney's movement. His better judgment would surely have dictated differently, being conversant with the circumstances of the case. I look upon it as an exhibit of a lack of moral courage on his part, being unable to resist the solicitations of the blinded mother. I would not wish to be thought uncharitable, nor would I wish the time honored custom of speaking of the virtues of the departed reversed," she continued, "but I do dislike to see false impressions foisted upon the public by those professing to be Latter day Saints."[77]

As this tragedy neared its final act, Emmeline demonstrated the self-reliance that had been steadily strengthening in her character. Never once, at least to her diary, did she wish for "a strong arm to lean on" or a partner to

75. Ibid., May 17, 24, 1898.

76. "In Memoriam: A Tribute of Love"; and O. F. W. [Orson F. Whitney], "Louie," *Woman's Exponent* 16 (July 1, 1887): 21. The July 1 issue also contains a poem by Emmeline's sister Lucy Hewlings, entitled "The Dear Departed" (19). Before submitting his piece to Emmeline, Orson F. Whitney read it to his mother, Helen Mar Kimball Whitney. Hatch and Compton, *Widow's Tale*, June 24, 1887, 245.

77. Lieber and Sillito, *Letters from Exile*, 156–57.

share the burden. She had learned to do without Daniel, and in this trying episode she proved that she had mastered her need for him. Nor did she give way, except to her diary, to the overwhelming grief that gripped her so irrepressibly. Some noted the sorrowful mien that could not be totally veiled, but she had vowed never "to wear her heart on her sleeve," and if ever there was a test of this determination, it was Louie's death and all that preceded it. She proved to herself and to any others who may have doubted that she could meet the highest expectations of behavior at such a time, and, even more, she began just a day after the funeral to resume the life she had left a month earlier.

Through it all, Emmeline managed to keep her family together. Though her heart could not release the pain of these past events, her mind turned to the future. Now of principal concern to her was John Q.'s return to full fellowship in the church, his remarriage to Annie, the sealing of John and Louie for an eternal relationship, and a reconciliation of the Cannon and Wells families.[78]

78. Walker, "Grant's Watershed," 195–229, explains the impact of this personal affair on church leadership and the difficulties that arose between the Wells and Cannon families.

CHAPTER 21

Aftermath

(1887–1888)

After Louie's death, Emmeline Wells faced another "annus horribilis." Not the desertion of James, the death of her only son, Eugene, the unexpected death of Newel, the inattention of Daniel, nor even the death of Emmie brought the despair that followed the events of 1886 and '87. "The past is killing me inch by inch," she lamented, the summer after Louie's death. "I shall never be myself again, never; with a broken heart I may live on for a time but the agony of feeling I suffer is beyond expression. May God have mercy upon me and mine and the time soon come when He shall say it is enough."[1] Having taken up her work again, she was able to keep her anguish largely to herself and once again display the composure her friends had come to expect. Returning to work aided her in this effort.

But there was more for her to endure even as she struggled to come to terms with Louie's death—the loss of her home of thirty years. With Daniel's return from England shortly after Louie's funeral, negotiations to sell Emmeline's home were finalized. She began preparing to move just a month later and closed the door for the last time in February 1888. Reluctantly, she distributed many of Louie's possessions to family members, and Septimus took several of Emmeline's household items to Belle in San Francisco. Emmeline's new home was to be the old adobe house behind the stone wall where she had begun her married life with Daniel so many years before. It was old now, small and neglected, and looked depressingly out of place amid the beautiful new structures gradually rising around it. It offered little after the comforts of her State Street home. Moreover, it was to be both her home and her office, which meant she could not find refuge from the relentless pressure of her work and daily stream of visitors, who continued to come by at all hours. Knowing that all of Daniel's other

1. E. Wells, Diary, July 16, 1887.

wives still enjoyed their rooms in the big house just across the street only exacerbated her despair.

She held one last party in her home before moving. All but three of the twenty-six invited guests attended, including Zina D. H. Young, Bathsheba B. Smith, Romania Pratt, Isabella Horne, her sister-wives Lydia Ann and Susan, and others whose names she carefully recorded in her diary.[2] Ice cream and cakes, homemade wine, iced tea, and lemonade made up the refreshments, and bouquets of flowers were given to each guest with an attached card bearing a personalized sentiment of Emmeline's composing. The next day, Emmeline reflected on the "manifestations of power and blessing we had experiemced [*sic*] in the little gathering it was a sweet time."[3] Twenty-nine years after this occasion, she may have been thinking of it and similar events when she noted how the guests were moved by "the glorious testimonies borne by Sister Horne, and Sister Eliza Snow, and the rich history told by Sarah M. Kimball, Sarepta Heywood, Elizabeth Howard, and others; and the wonderful singing of Mother [Elizabeth Ann] Whitney, with its beautiful interpretation by Aunt Zina."[4]

Dismantling her home and preparing the old adobe house for occupation continued slowly throughout the winter. Each time she entered her home on State Street, clouds of nostalgia overshadowed her, and she took great pains not to be recriminatory toward Daniel. When he announced that he was finally out of debt in May 1888, Emmeline was greatly relieved and felt "more assured now that there might be an [crossed out] a way to redeem it, and get a home once more."[5] But that home would not be hers again.

The day she finally moved into the "lonely home behind the wall" happened to be on one of her rare leap-year birthdays, February 29, 1888. All the "girls" of the family furnished the cakes for the party held to celebrate her sixtieth year. The guests feasted on chopped ham sandwiches, ice cream and cake, and oranges, all of which were "handsomely served." They also reminisced about earlier days in the old adobe home, and "music and songs with animated conversation whiled away the hours." The celebration

2. The listing gives an idea of who her close associates were. Besides those mentioned above were Mary Mitchell Pitchforth, Cornelia Horne Clayton, Maria Young Dougall, Matilda Moorhouse Barratt, Priscilla Paul Jennings, Rachel Ridgeway Grant, Elizabeth Coward Ivins, Elizabeth Anderson Howard, Margaret "Maggie" Curtis Shipp, Elizabeth Harrison Goddard, Ellen Spencer Clawson, Dr. Elvira Stevens Barney, Julia Cruse Howe, Sarah M. Kimball, and Elizabeth DuFresne Stevenson. All of their names appear repeatedly over the years in her diary.

3. Ibid., August 5, 6, 1887.

4. A. W. Cannon, "Mothers in Israel."

5. E. Wells, Diary, May 3, 1888.

was bittersweet. As long as Emmeline lived in the adobe house, she never found contentment there. "It is not suitable for me," she declared, missing, among other things, the availability of an upstairs room, away from the bustle of visitors. "This house is not at all like home to me, and never can be." She always reluctantly returned to it after a trip or a day's work away from her office, calling the old adobe structure[6] a "rookery for owls," hardly a welcoming description.[7] She was greatly heartened, however, when her piano was finally moved into the house. "I have been so accustomed to music, that to be without singing or instrumental music seems dreadful."[8]

Even as the Wells family contended with their grief over Louie, it was soon compounded by the death of Mell's nine-year-old son, Percival, from diphtheria.[9] Like her mother, Mell also lost three of her five children, Leslie Dunford, her son from her first marriage, and Winifred and Percival Woods, the only children of her second. The mood that pervaded Emmeline's family was solemn at this second bereavement while also drawing the Whitney family under its shadow. But Mell, like her mother, turned a stoic face to the world, and at her insistence the Wells family carried on with plans to celebrate Daniel's seventy-third birthday just a few days after Percival's funeral.

All of Emmeline's personal challenges played out against a final confrontation of the church with the US government relating to polygamy. A territorial convention was held in July 1887, four months after implementation of the Edmunds-Tucker Act, to make a sixth appeal for statehood, which Emmeline endorsed in the *Exponent*.[10] There was unusual anxiety about this new attempt, however. For the first time, the delegates included in the proposed constitution a clause outlawing plural marriage. Outside

6. Ibid., September 2, 3, 1888.

7. See, for example, ibid., March 20, 1891. Emmeline's acquaintance with the Bible may have brought to mind several biblical passages in which owls and other creatures were associated with places of desolation and destruction. See, for example, Isaiah 14:23 and 34:11.

8. Ibid., August 22, 1888. Emmeline had given the piano to Mell for Daisie to use in practicing her vocal lessons, but when twenty-year-old Daisie went east to study, Mell had the piano moved into Emmeline's new residence.

9. Ibid., July 9, October 18, 19, 20, 1887. Emmeline wrote a column, "He Only Sleeps," about Percival's death in the *Woman's Exponent* 16 (November 1, 1887): 84–85.

10. See "The Constitutional Convention," *Woman's Exponent* 16 (July 1, 1887): 20; "Mass Convention," 16 (July 1, 1887): 21; and "Editorial Thoughts," 16 (July 15, 1887): 28. She felt that statehood would silence the anti-Mormon women who had written such scurrilous novels about the Mormons. She also saw statehood as blocking those public officers who courted fame and fortune "by exposing Mormonism," as if a half century of doing so had not accustomed people to the "stale stories." "Editorial Thoughts," 28.

newspapers weighed in on the issue, and Mormons themselves were "quite up in arms," Emmeline observed. "Many are in doubt about the wisdom of such a course.... [E]ach one asks his neighbor or his friend the meaning of all [crossed out] this political movement, yet no one can explain."[11] Even so, despite the surrender of plural marriage in the new constitution, the federally appointed Utah Commission, which had been set up after passage of the Edmunds Act in 1882 to supervise all elections in the territory, opposed statehood, and Congress followed suit.

Concern over the escalating effects of the Edmunds-Tucker Act informed most local conversations.[12] Emmeline's office was daily deluged with visitors wanting to discuss the ramifications of the act and the future of the church—discussions that kept her at the center of developments but that also meant time spent away from her work. "All the talk is of the Receiver being appointed and what will be done in regard to Church property. Some feel very much worried," Emmeline observed, "and some indifferent and others excited."[13] By November 1887, the receiver had taken possession of the president's office in the Gardo House, suspending all business, and the clerks' desks were locked, with more disconcerting acts to follow. Moreover, the federal attempt to ferret out polygamists continued unabated, and only the death of church president John Taylor, on July 25, 1887, brought Taylor out of hiding. His two counselors, however, remained out of public sight.

Emmeline felt that there was less sadness than at the death of Brigham Young, but "mourning symbols" were visible on city buildings and homes.[14] Next to the announcement of President Taylor's death, appearing on the front page of the *Woman's Exponent*, Emmeline printed Eliza R. Snow's 1844 tribute to President Taylor, who had been seriously wounded at Carthage Jail during the assassination of Joseph and Hyrum Smith. Emmeline also reprinted an account of the murders in Carthage Jail by Willard Richards

11. E. Wells, Diary, July 14, 1887.

12. G. Larson, *Outline History*, 276–77.

13. E. Wells, Diary, October 31, 1887. Franklin S. Richards, the church's attorney, along with two other attorneys, James Overton Broadhead, a former congressman from Missouri, and Joseph Ewing McDonald, a former representative and senator from Indiana, argued the church's position in the case of the *Government v. the Mormon Church Corporation*. Judge Charles S. Zane ruled against the church, and a receiver was appointed to hold church properties over fifty thousand dollars. The church was also obliged to turn over to the receiver money held in the Perpetual Emigrating Fund. US marshal Frank H. Dyer was appointed as receiver. Thomas Alexander, *Utah: The Right Place*, 195–96. The *Tribune* was naturally in favor of the outcome of the case. See "The Receiver Granted," *Salt Lake Daily Tribune*, November 6, 1887, 4; and "Marshal Dyer Receiver," *Salt Lake Daily Tribune*, November 8, 1887, 4.

14. E. Wells, Diary, July 26, 1887.

and her own tribute to President Taylor.[15] His funeral took place in the tabernacle, where the vacant chairs of the First Presidency reminded the crowded congregation of the precarious position in which the church now functioned, with its leadership in hiding, its material resources confiscated, and its families in disarray.[16]

Another much-mourned death occurred later that same year. Though Eliza R. Snow's health had vacillated throughout the year, it was a shock to the church when she died in December, just five months after President Taylor and one month shy of her eighty-fourth birthday.[17] She and President Taylor had been the two most prominent and vocal advocates of plural marriage. Ironically, their deaths coincided with what was clearly the last days of the practice. At the viewing in the Lion House, Eliza's home for nearly forty years, Emmeline noted that she was dressed in "her wedding garment" and looked "like a beautiful bride."[18]

15. George Q. Cannon and Joseph F. Smith, "Announcement of the Death of President John Taylor," *Woman's Exponent* 16 (August 1, 1887): 36–37; "In Memoriam," 16 (August 1, 1887): 37.

16. Counselor Joseph F. Smith returned from Hawaii on July 18, just a week before President Taylor's death, marking the first time the entire First Presidency of the church had been together in the city since 1884, though President Smith and Wilford Woodruff remained in hiding. Details of Taylor's last days and funeral are in B. H. Roberts, *John Taylor, Third President of the Church of Jesus Christ of Latter-day Saints*, 406–63.

17. Like many others who had been close to Eliza, especially during her last year, Emmeline was worried about the officious behavior of Elizabeth Roundy, who had attended Eliza during her months of illness. Emmeline reported that even Eliza's brother Lorenzo did not approve of the course Elizabeth was taking at Eliza's death and had sent his wife, Minerva, to stay at the Lion House, Eliza's residence, and "watch things." E. Wells, Diary, December 6, 1887. The situation caused so much talk that Emmeline felt "over-powered" and hardly knew what to think. "It seems incredible," she wrote, "that one so pure, so devoted in her life & character could be so imposed upon as Sister Eliza has been by this wicked woman." Ibid., December 20, 1887.

18. Ibid., December 7, 1887. Emmeline does not explain what she means by "wedding garment," although it may relate to her temple attire. All of the local newspapers as well as the *New York Times* noted Eliza's passing. Emmeline had already published numerous biographical sketches of Snow in the *Woman's Exponent* and had printed various articles Snow had written for the paper. The December 15 issue of the *Woman's Exponent* carried on its front page a poetic tribute to Eliza R. Snow by Augusta Joyce Crocheron, and Emmeline, in three columns edged in black, wrote a lengthy editorial and added the proceedings of the funeral that was held in the Assembly Hall. See "Eliza Roxie [*sic*] Snow Smith: A Tribute of Affection," *Woman's Exponent* 16 (December 15, 1887): 108–10. Eliza R. Snow was married first to Joseph Smith in Nauvoo and then to Brigham Young. After Emma Smith's death in 1879, Eliza identified herself as Eliza R. Snow Smith.

At Eliza's death in December, the overriding question for the women of the church was who could possibly replace her. She had exerted an influence unlike any other Latter-day Saint woman, and her leadership, zeal, and talents were unmatched. But in reality, an impressive cadre of "leading sisters" had significant capabilities of their own and could assume many of the duties that Eliza had kept in her own capable hands.[19] One was her counselor Zina Diantha Huntington Young, who was appointed by President Woodruff in 1887 to take the reins as Relief Society general president.[20] Zina did not select her counselors at that time but retained Sarah M. Kimball as secretary, Romania B. Pratt as assistant secretary, and Mary Isabella Horne as treasurer.[21] "Sister Zina seems rather elated over being chosen to preside," Emmeline observed and added, "No doubt she expected it as others did for her."[22] Zina left immediately after the conference to attend to her daughter Zina Williams Card in Canada, due to give birth, leaving the presidency incomplete.[23] Sarah Kimball commented to Emmeline that she might be asked to serve as corresponding secretary.[24] This unexpected news was followed by a letter from Zina Young, addressing Emmeline with that title, though no official call had yet been made. When it came, the already burdened Emmeline realized that "evidently my work will be more extensive in the future than it has been.... Responsibilities come thick and fast upon the women of Zion. Those who will must take up the burdens and carry them."[25]

For the next twenty-two years, as corresponding and later general secretary of the Relief Society, she found that the tasks of arranging all of

19. An analysis of these intellectually and spiritually influential women who functioned within the radius of Eliza's life can be found in Beecher, "'Leading Sisters.'"

20. Zina Young had accompanied Eliza since 1868 to aid bishops in organizing ward Relief Societies and became Eliza's counselor when Eliza was elected general president in 1880. Wilford Woodruff succeeded President John Taylor.

21. Sarah Kimball continued to serve as president of the Fifteenth Ward Relief Society and Mary Isabella Horne as president of the Salt Lake Stake Relief Society. Romania Pratt was a physician and surgeon. She had divorced her first husband, Parley P. Pratt Jr., in 1881 and married Charles Penrose as a plural wife in March 1888, but she retained the Pratt name for several years because of the raid against polygamists.

22. E. Wells, Diary, April 12, 1888.

23. Zina Young Williams Card, daughter of Zina Huntington and Brigham Young, had been Emmeline's companion in 1879 on their important mission to Washington, DC. She was then the widow of Thomas Williams but later married Charles Ora Card and moved with him to settle Cardston, Canada.

24. Ibid., April 18, 1888.

25. Ibid., June 12, 1888.

the visits to wards and stakes throughout the territory, representing the Relief Society at national women's conventions, as well as writing all of the correspondence, business transactions, and later the minutes of the Central Board (general board) meetings consumed hours, days, and weeks within an already overcommitted schedule. But for Emmeline, the honor of being a member of the Central Board of the organization she loved fully compensated the labor entailed in the assignment. The new position also raised her stature in a community that lionized church leaders, women as well as men.

With Zina's appointment as president, Emmeline felt that the continuity with Nauvoo remained intact. Zina had been a member of the Nauvoo Relief Society and had served with Eliza R. Snow and Elizabeth Ann Whitney, also veterans of the Nauvoo society, in the reinstituted Relief Society in Utah. They all enjoyed the esteem and love of the sisters of the church. Like Eliza, Zina had been a plural wife of both Joseph Smith and Brigham Young, but unlike the coolly efficient, charismatic Eliza, Zina was warm, approachable, and oriented to personal relationships rather than organizational efficiency. In a long address to the Weber Stake Relief Society in September of that year, Emmeline noted the ascendancy of Zina to the position of "Elect Lady," which Joseph Smith had explained meant "one who presides."[26] "Let the mantle of Sister Eliza fall upon Sister Zina," Emmeline said, "that she may be able to satisfy the people as Sister Eliza did in traveling among the Saints, and assisting in doing good and in performing a great work."[27]

Not until Zina's return to Utah in the fall of 1888 did she select her counselors, after consulting with Emmeline, among others: Jane Snyder Richards, president of the Weber Stake Relief Society and wife of Apostle Franklin D. Richards, and Bathsheba Wilson Bigler Smith, widow of Apostle George A. Smith, both of whom had also been members of the Nauvoo Relief Society.[28] Feeling hesitant about her official duties even a year after her appointment, especially in following the forceful, articulate Eliza, Zina expressed her misgivings to her daughter Zina Card, who replied, "See dear aunt Em, she can help you. She is a natural made General, and can assist you by a few judicious letters and appointments, and give yourself a chance to do your best that you do."[29] The respect and admiration Emmeline had for the

26. "A Record of the Organization and Proceedings of the Female Relief Society of Nauvoo," March 17, 1842, LDS Church History Library, Salt Lake City, photocopy of typescript in my possession.

27. "Memorial Anniversary," *Woman's Exponent* 17 (September 15, 1888): 61.

28. E. Wells, Diary, October 3, 4, 1888.

29. Zina Young Card, letter to Zina D. H. Young, May 25, 1889, Cardston, Canada, Zina Card Brown Papers.

well-loved Zina Young grew into a close bond during the years they served together in the Relief Society. Both revered Joseph Smith, felt honor bound to keep the spirit of the Nauvoo Relief Society ever present, and desired to improve the status of women.

In July 1888, shortly after her elevation to the Relief Society Central Board, Emmeline attended a memorial Relief Society conference in Ogden, where she was asked to speak. It was one of the largest audiences that she had yet addressed. The occasion was the eleventh anniversary of the appointment of Jane Richards as the first Relief Society stake president in the church.[30] At the close of this memorial meeting, Emmeline reflected on the appropriateness of commemorating Jane's appointment, at which women were given a new level of church leadership. "A red letter day for women," Emmeline declared.[31]

Among the many talks was a long sermon that included remarks on the relationship of women and priesthood given by Jane Richards's husband, Apostle Franklin D. Richards. Emmeline intended to print it in the *Exponent*, but because of the sensitivity of the subject the talk went through several readings before publication. Richards first read through the speech and then reviewed it with Emmeline.[32] Once agreed upon, his talk, as well as the entire proceedings of the meeting, was published in the *Woman's Exponent* in four installments. Elder Richards decried the reluctance of women to assert themselves for fear of offending the brethren, he noted the jealousy of many men to share opportunities of personal achievement with women in and outside of church channels, and he affirmed the connection of women to priesthood through the ordinances and endowment of the temple, all of which Emmeline heartily approved. After reading parts of Joseph Smith's words to the Nauvoo Relief Society, Elder Richards declared that other than specific priesthood offices to which men are called, "our sisters share with us any and all of the ordinances of the holy anointing, endowments, sealings, sanctifications and blessings that we have been made partakers of.... Joseph [Smith] desired to confer these keys of power upon them in connection with their husbands."[33] The talk reflected the concept

30. Jane Richard's appointment as first stake Relief Society president in 1877 was followed by the appointment of Isabella Horne as president of the Salt Lake Stake Relief Society. Both women served on the Central Board while also serving in their stake positions.

31. E. Wells, Diary, July 19, 20, 1888.

32. Franklin D. Richards, Journal, July 30, 1888. See also E. Wells, Diary, July 26, 31, August 2, 1888, for comments about preparing the manuscript for publication.

33. The four installments of the Ogden meeting were published under the title "Memorial Anniversary" and appeared in *Woman's Exponent* 17 (August 1, 1888):

of priesthood partnership through the temple ordinances, which was both emphasized and understood in the nineteenth-century church.

As corresponding secretary, Emmeline found her immersion in Relief Society affairs deep and demanding. If making all the arrangements for board members to attend stake Relief Society conferences was difficult, her own visits were pleasurable and stimulating. Over the years, she traveled throughout Utah, Idaho, and Arizona on such visits, meeting new people, making friends, and finding a plethora of platforms on which to proclaim her faith in the church, in women, and in the Relief Society. The church, and specifically the Relief Society, enabled women, she firmly believed, to achieve emancipation from inhibiting customs and to advance in learning and to broaden their contribution to both home and society.

As leaders from Salt Lake City, she and the other board members were often invited by their host stake Relief Society officers to give blessings, both of comfort and of healing and also in preparation for childbirth. The exercise of these and other spiritual gifts was common to both men and women at that time, and Emmeline was frequently called on to interpret a blessing, prayer, or testimony expressed in tongues. Though she often felt timid in thus participating, she relished the meetings and social occasions in which women spiritually refreshed one another by the exercise of such gifts, as they had at Winter Quarters.[34] Though impeding her work and upsetting to her daughters to be away, these trips were invigorating and satisfying to Emmeline. She returned from them tired but spiritually and emotionally nourished.

The first year after Daniel's return from his mission, the Wells family found it difficult to resume their normal life. Because of the surveillance of federal officers, who were acting in compliance with the Edmunds-Tucker Act, Daniel maintained a low visibility in the city. To avoid arrest, he lived with Junius or one of his other sons, an approach that succeeded in keeping him out of the deputies' hands but required frequent, tiring moves. His first private reunion with Emmeline after three years of separation occurred in his son Junius's home. To Emmeline, Daniel appeared weary and in need of comfort from his family, consolations now unavailable to him in his own

37–39; (August 15, 1888): 44–47; (September 1, 1888): 52–54; and (September 15, 1888): 61–62.

34. E. Wells, Diary, December 8–16, 1887. This citation is but one example of her many Relief Society trips. She was consistent in detailing her travels to the ward and stake women's conferences that included meetings of the Primary and Young Ladies' MIA. She met the officers of these organizations as well as many members and priesthood leaders and became friends with the women in whose homes she stayed. Their names are sprinkled throughout her diary.

home. All meetings had to be clandestine, which she felt was an inexcusable imposition.[35] Yet to Emmeline's surprise, Daniel began to ask her to visit him, wherever he was living, much more often than she would ever have expected. Daniel was actually seeking her companionship, and Emmeline's diary records accounts of their furtive meetings. She looked forward to them and enjoyed her time with him, but with a measure of reservation toward this unexpected fervor on his part. Defying the risk of arrest, he also began to visit her at her home/office, where she stopped her work to make tea for him or to prepare a lunch or sometimes breakfast when he risked discovery to stay overnight.[36] As Emmeline gradually warmed to his attention, they eased into this new pattern of companionship as though there had been no resentments or neglect in prior decades of their marriage. It may be that her long, newsy letters to him while he was in England introduced him to a woman he had not taken the occasion to really know before but whom he now found to be a delightful and informed companion. She had a reputation for being a fascinating conversationalist, and this characteristic, as well as her keen observations about current events and the lives of people around her, may have been evident in those long letters.[37] Emmeline often ruminated over this new relationship. Admitting that she had feelings of "unaccountable longing" to see him from time to time, she occasionally was the one to suggest meeting. After one of their visits, she noted that "his statement in reference to last evening confirmed me in the belief that two people separated by distance may have the same longings at the same time, and that there is a connection . . . psychological that is not yet defined by scientists. We are as happy perhaps in our ignorance as if we attained to knowledge."[38]

Her resurgent feelings toward Daniel carried some residual regrets, however. "His manner towards me is most loving and tender," but his loving ways "can never make up for my dear old home which he has taken from me," she was forced to admit. "When I see that others are left in undisturbed possession and know that mine has gone, my heart is too full for utterance."[39] Of

35. Ibid., July 31, 1887. She found that sneaking away in darkness to meet at some "trysting place" put a damper on their meetings. "Such humbug," she declared. Ibid., August 13, 1888.

36. While Emmeline fretted over her new quarters, Daniel was pleased she was there. "He talked of the house and his wish to have me near him so he could venture [to visit her] and feel safe." Ibid., November 9, 1887.

37. She noted in her diary after one of her visits to him that "he always speaks to me of my letters to him in England" (November 10, 1887).

38. Ibid., January 23, 24, 1888.

39. Ibid., April 14, 1888.

course, displacing one person, as opposed to four others, some with children at home, would seem to Daniel a more logical move to ease the financial burden he had been carrying. But this consideration hardly deflated her feelings of discrimination. Ere long, however, even the "big house" was sold in order to make way for the new Templeton Hotel, and Martha, Hannah, Lydia Ann, and Sarah were dispersed to other residences.[40]

In the spring of 1888, just as Daniel and Emmeline were rediscovering each other, Daniel was called to preside over the newly constructed temple in Manti, Utah, 124 miles south of Salt Lake City.[41] This assignment would ostensibly separate him from his families and hopefully prevent arrest, just as his assignment to England was meant to do. The temple was dedicated in May 1888 in a private service with a carefully selected list of guests. Emmeline attended a more public dedication a few days later, along with fifteen hundred others.[42]

Distance did not diminish Daniel's ardor, however, and Emmeline began receiving invitations to visit him in Manti. With virtually no free time, she tried to coordinate her visits with assignments to attend women's conferences in the vicinity of Manti. Their first meeting occurred just weeks after the dedication of the temple.[43] It was leisurely and satisfying. "Last night my husband was very pleased to see me come back," she wrote, "and after an evening pleasantly passed in the Hotel we retired and talked over many matters of special interest to us."[44] Later, after a Relief Society meeting, she walked through the temple with Daniel and then sat with him in his

40. Susan and Lydia Ann lived together with Lydia Ann's daughters Kate and May at 323 Second Avenue; Martha and Hannah at first shared a duplex at 349 East First South before moving into their individual homes, Martha at 182 G Street and Hannah at 140 A Street. Pictures of the homes, which Randall Dixon identified, are included in Hinckley, *Daniel Hanmer Wells*, between pages 382 and 383.

41. His experience as administrator of the Endowment House made him a natural choice to preside over the new temple.

42. E. Wells, Diary, May 15–23. Emmeline and Annie discussed the numerous accounts of spiritual manifestations that had occurred during the dedicatory services. Some had heard a surrounding sound of angelic choirs singing, though no music was then being performed. Others saw halos of light about the speakers, and some heard a soft voice exclaiming, "Hallelujah, hallelujah, the Lord be praised." "Still on at Manti. Continuation of the Temple Dedicatory Services. Some Startling Incidents. The Services Yesterday," *Salt Lake Herald*, May 23, 1888, 8.

43. Emmeline had been invited to attend a women's conference in Gunnison, Utah, at the same time that Daniel was alone in Manti and welcomed a visit from Emmeline.

44. Daniel had an apartment in both the temple and the Temple Hotel, where Emmeline usually visited him.

private office. "We talked of the past and the present and also that night we conversed much together, dwelling upon the joys and sorrows of our lives. Our great struggles and the kindliness that had always diffused itself through our intercourse with each other."[45] Daniel's letter to her a week later was "brim full of loving words and wishes," and she needed sixteen pages in her return letter to express her feelings.[46] They seemed to have rewelded a romantic link that had lain broken for many years. There was a calm serenity about the joy they found in their companionship. Time had leveled Emmeline's emotional upheavals of the past and stiffened her vulnerabilities. She was now sixty and Daniel seventy-four, and time and experience had mellowed them both.

Throughout this period, Emmeline felt the time had come for her to "make a beginning" of temple work. In November 1887, several months after Louie's death, Daniel and Annie had traveled to the Logan temple, about 85 miles north of Salt Lake City, to do sealings and endowments, and after Daniel returned, Emmeline decided to join Annie to continue the work. At that time, Emmeline was rebaptized for the renewal of her covenants, and Annie was baptized as proxy for Louie for the same purpose.[47] Emmeline then proceeded to be baptized as proxy for Helen Maria Fiske Hunt Jackson, the famous writer and defender of Indian rights, and for writers George Eliot (Mary Ann Evans) and Dinah Maria Mulock Craik.[48] She was also proxy for the vicarious baptism of the deceased Fanny Adele McBride Cole, as she had promised Orson F. Whitney. After doing the temple work for the three writers, she stood as proxy for Jackson and Eliot in the ceremony that sealed them to her husband.[49]

45. E. Wells, Diary, June 17, 18, 1888.

46. Ibid., June 29, September 2, 1888.

47. Ibid., November 28, 1887. Rebaptisms of faithful members are not church practice today but were fairly common in the nineteenth century, both in and out of temples. Even then, however, a proxy baptism for "renewal of covenants" was unusual if not unique. This was a stunning gesture of love and forgiveness by Annie and extremely consoling to Emmeline.

48. Helen Hunt Jackson gained renown as the author of the romantic novel *Ramona*, published in 1884, which exposed the treatment of Native Americans. She visited Emmeline, who greatly admired her. George Eliot (Mary Ann Evans) was a famous British writer of classical British novels such as *Middlemarch*, *Adam Bede*, and *The Mill on the Floss*. Eliot was also a favorite of Emmeline's. Dinah Mulock Craik died just two months before Emmeline did her temple work. She was also a popular British poet and story writer and author of children's as well as adult books. Emmeline wrote a brief introduction to a reprint of an article describing her funeral from the *New York Herald*. See "D. M. Mulock Craik," *Woman's Exponent* 16 (November 1, 1887): 83.

49. E. Wells, Diary, November 29–December 3, 1887. The primary purpose of

The following year, on July 13, 1888, shortly after the Manti temple was dedicated, Orson F. Whitney was sealed to Fanny Cole, deceased, and also to Emmie Wells, whom he had loved for years and to whom he had long hoped to be sealed. Emmeline was proxy for the two women. On July 24, less than two weeks after these sealings, Orson married May (Mary) Minerva Wells in Mexico as his second living wife, to the relief of Lydia Ann, May's mother, who had agitated for the marriage for years.[50]

With her family life changed, her removal to the old and uncomfortable adobe house she thought she had left forever, and Daniel once again miles away, Emmeline turned to her new calling in the Relief Society and her work editing the *Woman's Exponent* with vigor and a strong sense of purpose. The church was facing a major reassessment of its place in American society, and the steps in doing so would present Emmeline with new avenues of thought and action and provide a wider scope of influence than she had yet experienced.

---

sealing deceased women to living or deceased priesthood holders was to ensure that they were connected to a priesthood or patriarchal line, essential to entrance into the celestial kingdom. Because marriage is not performed in the next life, it necessarily had to be conducted vicariously in this life for the deceased. The efficacy of these priesthood ordinances, whether baptism or marriage, however, is entirely dependent on their acceptance or rejection in the afterlife by the person for whom the service was performed. The principle of agency is considered by Latter-day Saints an eternal principle.

50. He and May evidently did not live together for some time after their marriage because of the antipolygamy law. She and her sister Kate (Catherine Chapin) lived together with their mother, Lydia Ann Alley Wells, and her sister/sister-wife, Susan Hannah. The two girls were constant visitors to Emmeline.

CHAPTER 22

Changes and Challenges
(1887–1888)

THE SEMIANNUAL CHURCH conference, following the death of John Taylor in July 1887, proceeded for the sixth time without the presence of the First Presidency. The overflowing audience was thus audibly surprised when Wilford Woodruff, president of the Quorum of the Twelve Apostles, entered the tabernacle at the beginning of the last session on Sunday afternoon. "A great deal of emotion was evinced" when the audience saw him walk onto the stand, Emmeline wrote in the *Exponent*. "Never upon any Sabbath day in the Tabernacle was there such an expression made of esteem and reverence as when this aged man [he was eighty-three] and servant of God appeared in the midst of the people, after an absence of almost three years."[1] "His coming in was the event of the Conference," she wrote in her diary, "and the people could scarcely suppress their glad emotions even tho' it was the Sabbath Day and A House of Worship."[2] As president of the Quorum of the Twelve Apostles, Wilford Woodruff was the highest-ranking officer of the church, and thus his risky appearance had particular meaning to the Saints. Conjectures abounded as to who would replace President Taylor. That the president of the Quorum of the Twelve Apostles automatically ascended to the presidency was not yet established procedure.[3] Thus, Wilford Woodruff conducted the affairs of the church "in behalf of The Quorum of the Twelve" until he was sustained as president

1. "October Conference," *Woman's Exponent* 16 (October 15, 1887), 77. Woodruff's sermon appeared (November 1, 1887), 85, 86.

2. E. Wells, Diary, October 9, 1887.

3. Some of the points of deliberation are explained in Walker, "Grant's Watershed." Walker concludes that Wilford Woodruff's succession firmly set the precedent of elevating the president of the Quorum of the Twelve Apostles to the presidency of the church.

of the church at the April 1889 conference, almost two years after President Taylor's death.[4]

In the meantime, to Emmeline's joy, John Q. was rebaptized by his father on May 6, 1888. Five days later, at Emmeline's instigation, Daniel and John Q. met in her parlor to reconcile their thoughts and differences regarding Louie. The success of their meeting helped to clear the path to John's remarriage to Annie. After Apostles Woodruff and Cannon had restored all of John's priesthood blessings, John requested that Daniel perform the marriage, which he did on Sunday evening, May 13, 1888, in the Endowment House. It was followed by a legally required civil ceremony that took place in Emmeline's home. Judge Elias Smith, who had divorced the couple not quite two years earlier, now reunited them. It could be expected that these events conjured up the frightful memories of the past, and Louie's last days of suffering were ever present in Emmeline's mind. But at last her hopes had all been realized, and life for Annie could in some measure resume a normal course.[5]

The following month John Q. moved to Ogden to work as editor of the *Ogden Standard*, a local newspaper that began publishing in January 1888. This required the family's removal to Ogden, forty miles north of Salt Lake City. Having lived with Annie for so many months and enjoyed the companionship of her three children, Emmeline did not greet the news with pleasure. The Cannons returned to Salt Lake City in 1892, however, when John Q.'s father, along with John Q. and Abram, leased the *Deseret News* from the church. John Q. became editor and Abram business manager. John Q. was associated with the *Deseret News* for most of the rest of his life, with a break during the Spanish-American War while he served with the Rough Riders. When the church regained control of the paper, John Q. was once again appointed editor.[6] Salt Lake City continued to be John and Annie's home thereafter.

Even more distressing than Annie's temporary move to Ogden in 1888 was Mell and William's permanent move to Idaho the same year. While heartbreaking to Emmeline, it proved to be an advantageous move for

4. Though First Counselor Joseph F. Smith remained in hiding, George Q. Cannon gave himself up to the federal authorities in September 1888 and was immediately convicted and imprisoned. Emmeline visited him in November and commented that "Br. Cannon did not at all become the striped clothing & indeed it made me feel very bad indeed to see him tho' he was apparently cheerful." E. Wells, Diary, November 28, 1888. Cannon wrote much of his biography of Joseph Smith while imprisoned. See George Q. Cannon, *The Life of Joseph Smith the Prophet.*

5. E. Wells, Diary, May 10–14, 1888.

6. Bitton, *George Q. Cannon*, 152.

William, who eventually became a leading attorney and respected Idaho judge. Since 1884, Will had been making periodic trips to the Coeur d'Alene area of northern Idaho, the site of a mining boom. His two siblings, who had traveled with him to Utah in 1872, Nehemiah Park Woods and Eliza Woods Wallin, were both now dead, so his closest family ties no longer bound him to Utah.[7] Though William had enjoyed a successful law practice with several different attorneys in Salt Lake City, the Wells family events of 1886 and 1887 soured his regard for the Mormon community, and the financial and professional opportunities that Idaho offered prompted a desire for a new beginning there. He joined the rush of attorneys who found their own gold mines in litigating mining claims and formed a legal community whose success paralleled the waxing and waning of the productivity of the mines.[8]

William and Melvina made their first home in Murray, Idaho, the county seat of Shoshone County.[9] Will had painted an appealing picture of the woods and the fine, cool climate of Murray, situated in a narrow mountain valley, but when the time came for Mell to leave Salt Lake City, "the parting was a sad one," Emmeline lamented.[10] Mell left three children in graves, and Verona and Daisie were now making preparations for their own lives, Daisie to study voice in the East and Verona to marry Barry Hillard.

As he had in Utah, Will soon earned an enviable reputation. He was instrumental in overturning a mining claim relating to the famous Bunker Hill mine and winning a satisfactory and totally unexpected judgment for his clients, a case that is still regarded as one of the most famous in Idaho history.[11] He was known for his courtliness, soft-spoken manner, and legal

7. William and his siblings were children of Catherine Wells Woods, Daniel's sister, whose home was Burlington, Iowa. None of them joined the LDS Church.

8. Some of the leading attorneys of the West made their reputations there, including the well-known Clarence Darrow.

9. The history of the area, focusing on Wallace, Idaho, where the Woods family eventually moved, is recounted in numerous publications because of its center place in the history of mining in northern Idaho during the late nineteenth and early twentieth centuries. An anecdotal but useful history is William T. Stoll, *Silver Strike: The True Story of Silver Mining in the Coeur d'Alenes*. See also Richard G. Magnuson, *Coeur d'Alene Diary: The First Ten Years of Hardrock Mining in North Idaho*; and George C. Hobson, ed., *Gems of Thought and History of Shoshone County*, 47–50, 59, 61, 62, 65–67.

10. E. Wells, Diary, August 31, 1888.

11. William Stoll, introduction to 1991 reprint of *Silver Strike*, ix–xix. Details of events leading to the trial and William Woods's interrogation of the major defendant are on 114–56. Without a transcript, Stoll's reminiscent account is an important written record of that eventful trial. See ibid., 87–156. Chapter 14 (114–34) is entitled "Major Woods." The title relates to the position he held in the Union Army during the Civil War.

prowess. His first partner described him as "suave, conciliatory, and kindly," with a "graciousness of manner," a "gentleman of the old school."[12] In later years Woods was noted as one of "that school of lawyers that for many years was the pride of Shoshone County" and a member of "that distinguished bar...that never had any peer in the great northwest for legal learning and acumen."[13] He was an active Democrat and served as a delegate to the Idaho Constitutional Convention in 1889 and as a presidential elector in 1896.[14] He later ran unsuccessfully for the US Senate.

With Belle in San Francisco, Mell in Idaho, and Annie in Ogden, the changes in Emmeline's life accelerated, and nostalgia constantly tugged at her. "How different every thing is from the former days," she wrote at the end of 1888. "How changed we all are—from what we once were.... [I]t is all I can do to keep up my courage."[15] The numerous reminiscent pieces she wrote for her paper emerged from this resistance to a life constantly in flux.

Emmeline's visits to Annie's, however, became a much-anticipated weekly antidote. With two railroad lines connecting Salt Lake City and Ogden and several trains a day, travel between the two cities was easily accomplished, and most weekends found Emmeline basking in Annie's comfortable Ogden home and boisterous family life. She seldom failed to find an acquaintance on her train trips to Ogden, and if none appeared, she would strike up a conversation with a seatmate. These Ogden visits usually included meeting with Jane Richards to discuss Relief Society business, since board meetings had yet to be regularly scheduled.

Emmeline especially relished Sunday nights around the fireplace in the parlor of Annie's eight-room house. Ice cream, popcorn, and candy were always on hand after a delicious noonday dinner or evening "lunch," sometimes served as late as midnight. The Sabbath spent with Annie was indeed a day of rest for Emmeline. The change of pace was always therapeutic both physically and emotionally. She slept late, enjoyed afternoon carriage rides in the countryside, loved Annie's delicious dinners, but most of all looked forward to the late-night conversations with her daughter. Emmeline particularly favored the evenings when John Q. joined them because he was intelligent, witty, and always charming. He was an easy person to like and, ironically, of all Emmeline's sons-in-law, John had the closest bond with Emmeline. At this time, John was thousands of dollars in debt, borrowed from "a gentile to pay his father and other debts," according

12. Ibid., 114, 17.

13. "Taps Sound for Veteran and Jurist," *Wallace (ID) Press Times*, November 13, 1920.

14. Magnuson, *Coeur d'Alene Diary*, 89.

15. Ibid., December 31, 1888.

to his brother Abram, to whom he owed five thousand dollars.[16] John was fortunate that Abram was willing to work with him to find ways to reduce his indebtedness. With his growing family (nine children were added to the three they had before their second marriage), John's financial stresses continued for years, but the gendered division of family responsibilities kept Emmeline and Annie innocent of his spendthrift ways. Nor did his debts dampen John's good humor or diminish his delight in indulging his family.

With so many of her former newspaper helpers away, Emmeline continued the struggle to find voluntary workers for her paper.[17] "If I only had means I might have help to do my work some of it at least and more leisure to write out my thoughts, and study subjects that are deep and difficult to the common mind," she lamented, "but as it is I must drudge on & on without much respite from toil and care."[18] As one fellow journalist noted, the *Woman's Exponent* "has for many years been sustained by her literary enthusiasm and business perseverance."[19] It certainly was not sustained by consistent help or sufficient subscriptions.[20]

Emmeline's lengthy, thoughtful editorials often rolled from her pen after midnight and were finished the next morning, just in time for the edition to go to press. She sorted through exchange newspapers to find articles of interest to her readers and published the minutes of various ward and stake meetings of the Relief Society, the Young Ladies' Mutual Improvement Association, and the Primary Association. In addition to subscriptions, she constantly solicited literary contributions to help fill the eight pages of the paper. Her sister Lucy Hewlings often responded to her pleas by submitting articles and poems. Even those publishers who could afford to pay their contributors were not always successful in getting good copy, Emmeline consoled herself, even while she lamented that she depended "entirely on those who like to get into print."[21]

Typically, desperate for suitable copy for a Christmas issue in 1891, she was obliged to prepare it herself. Besides her editorial, "Christmas Time," she wrote two short articles, "A Green Tea Party" and "Christmas Display"; a poem, "Christmas Eve"; and a short story, "Emily Hamilton's Christmas."[22]

16. A. H. Cannon, Diary, October 1 and November 20, 1887.

17. Office help constantly turned over, as she used some of the daughters of her sister-wives, other young single girls, and later her own granddaughters, besides occasional paid workers. In addition to writing much of the copy, Emmeline did the proofreading and often the folding and mailing.

18. E. Wells, Diary, June 23, 1890.

19. "Emmeline B. Wells," *Tullidge's Quarterly Magazine*.

20. E. Wells, Diary, June 13, 1890, August 31, October 5, 7, 1891.

21. Ibid., October 8, 1890.

22. All were included in *Woman's Exponent* 20 (December 15, 1891): 91–96. Besides

She was nothing if not resourceful. After the final proofreading, folding, and mailing of the paper, the process began all over again. It was grueling work, and the remuneration was pitiable. "Weary, weary, weary" ended many a day's recital of events.

Yet even as she lamented her wearying schedule, she rejoiced in what she felt was fulfillment of a prophecy Newel K. Whitney had given her years before. He had told her she "should have nothing to do but to devote my whole time to writing and to literary pursuits, and that I should sit and eat and drink and converse with the nobles of the earth and tell them of the Gospel."[23] Though she had much more to do than "devote her whole time to writing," at least in the area she most wanted to write, her interest revolved around things literary, and she had, and would yet have, acquaintances among noted people in the world who stimulated her mind and added to her experience and to whom she could talk of Mormonism. She was well aware of the opportunity she had to "travel and speak in the interest of Zion" and considered it a "blessing."[24] It was difficult for her, however, not to succumb to plaints of overwork. "I wish I could accomplish more than I do," she wrote on one busy day, "but my strength is not equal to the desires I have to do good to others. I have been wishing for an opportunity to write a poem of late, but it is very difficult with so many questions to answer daily and so much actual work to do."[25]

Though Emmeline managed to produce poems and even short stories during these busy years, they were never written in the pensive, unhurried manner she envisioned writing should be done. The demanding deadlines of her paper precluded such luxury. "Had I some leisure to sit down and write," she complained one particularly busy day, "to put into... form eloquent and touching the tender pains and sweet sadness that encompasses my life about it might be of some consequence & possess some merit."[26] Her need for the *Woman's Exponent*, which she knew had brought her out of obscurity, was pitted against her intensifying involvement in church activities, politics,

---

these additional pieces of Emmeline's, the paper also printed a poem by Lucy Hewlings, "Trusting," 89.

23. The only account of this prophecy is what Emmeline recorded in her diary on June 13, 1888. She does not give the circumstances or date when Newel pronounced this blessing on her.

24. One such weary day when she desperately wanted to write a poem or story she had been mulling over but could not write because of the interruptions of so many visitors, she found that unless her strength held out "to write at night," she "should have really no time for it," but somehow she managed to find the strength. E. Wells, Diary, July 27, 1888.

25. Ibid., August 7, 1888. See also October 23, November 30, and December 9, 1888.

26. Ibid., February 9, 1888.

suffrage, and the women's movement, all consuming more and more of her interest and time. As counterpoint to these pressures was her chimerical dream of living the insular, focused life of the artist, whose creations defined the circumference of her world. Unable to resolve these warring claims, she just kept working at both, managing to achieve some form of balance.

Meanwhile, Susan B. Anthony and Elizabeth Cady Stanton planned to commemorate in 1888 the fortieth anniversary of the first women's rights convention held in Seneca Falls, New York. The aim of the celebration was to establish an international council of women, dedicated to the advancement of women around the world, that would serve as an umbrella organization for individual national organizations. Mormon women were hopeful that the national and international reach of the Relief Society and Young Ladies' Mutual Improvement Association would make their organizations eligible for membership. Though the Relief Society expected Emmeline to appear as its representative, and she had considered attending the event, the lingering emotional grip of Louie's death precluded her attendance. She did, however, prepare the credentials for the Utah delegates, all of whom were then living in Washington.[27]

Only after sending off the credentials and getting reports of the first day's meetings did Emmeline regret that she had not made the necessary exertion to attend herself. She did, however, report on the event in the *Exponent* and wrote articles about it for Salt Lake City newspapers as well.[28] Out of this

27. The delegates were Emily S. Richards, wife of Franklin S. Richards, the church's attorney; Luella Cobb Young; Margaret Nightingale Caine, wife of Utah's congressional delegate; and Nettie Young Snell. Luella Cobb Young was the wife of John W. Young, a son of Brigham Young, and granddaughter of Augusta Cobb Young, one of Brigham Young's wives, and also a niece of Charlotte Cobb Godbe. Luella eventually left John Young and the church and became a Christian Scientist. Nettie Snell also divorced her husband George Henry Snell and then married Robert Easton, a singer, and settled in New York City with him.

28. Articles on the council in the *Woman's Exponent* began with "Fortieth Anniversary of the Woman Suffrage Movement," 16 (February 15, 1888): 140, and continued in the following issues, all in vol. 16: "Program of the International Council" (March 1, 1888): 150–51; "International Council of Women" (March 15, 1888): 156–57; "The Woman's Council" (April 1, 1888): 164–65; and "Correspondence" (April 15, 1888): 169–70, and "The Woman's Jubilee," 171. Emmeline also wrote a long article on the American Woman Suffrage Association and its founder Lucy Stone, "American Woman Suffrage Association," *Woman's Exponent* 16 (May 1, 1888): 177–78. Stone only reluctantly attended the international meeting in Washington because of the Mormon presence. Despite Stone's visible repugnance of plural marriage, Emmeline had great admiration for her, and their meeting was a highlight in Emmeline's political life.

anniversary celebration came the National and International Councils of Women (NCW and ICW), both of which figured prominently in Emmeline's life and work for women of the church, who felt a certain prestige through membership. Though absent from the organizational convention, she was appointed a member of the NCW Press Committee.[29] These two new organizations encompassed a broader agenda than equal rights for women. Issues such as social welfare, social purity, and peaceful coexistence of nations joined equal rights as objects of concern that broadened the appeal of these organizations to a large segment of women not initially supportive of woman suffrage. Many of their members, however, especially those involved in the social purity movement, disdained membership of LDS women, polygamy being the spur, and began a crusade to prevent their membership.

The Mormon delegates received a warm welcome at the Seneca Falls anniversary celebration. Nevertheless, a question remained concerning not only their membership in the National Council of Women but also their continuing connection with the National Woman Suffrage Association. Its increasing membership of conservative and anti-Mormon organizations did not bode well for the Mormons. Moreover, as the two national suffrage organizations moved ineluctably toward a merger, Lucy Stone's antipathy toward polygamy and the Mormons generally as well as that of the Woman's Christian Temperance Union promised to be strong impediments to Mormon membership in the merged associations.[30] "It is noticeable in almost every instance," Emmeline observed, "that whenever 'Mormons' are to be admitted, a question arises as to the feasibility of the matter."[31]

In June 1888, doubts of their inclusion increased, triggered by the visit to Utah of Julia Ward Howe, famed poet, member of the AWSA, author of the popular "Battle Hymn of the Republic," and stern critic of Mormonism.[32] Howe and her hosts, members of the Grand Army of the Republic, scheduled no meetings with LDS women, so Emmeline wrote a note to her asking for a private interview. To Emmeline's surprise, Howe agreed to see her, perhaps out of curiosity. Accompanied by Dr. Romania Pratt and a basket of flowers, Emmeline visited the celebrated woman in her room at

29. E. Wells, Diary, February 11, 16, 1888. See also C. Madsen, *Advocate for Women*, 241–45.

30. E. Wells, Diary, February 11, 16, 1888; C. Madsen, *Advocate for Women*, 241–45.

31. "Editorial Thoughts," *Woman's Exponent* 16 (May 1, 1888): 180; C. Madsen, *Advocate for Women*, 250–52.

32. Julia Ward Howe assisted in organizing the American Woman Suffrage Association and helped to found the *Woman's Journal*, a popular woman suffrage newspaper, with Lucy Stone. See Paul S. Boyer, "Howe, Julia Ward."

the Continental Hotel. Emmeline declared it a "pleasant call" and hoped they had made "an agreeable impression in favor of our people."[33]

Although Julia Ward Howe hardly disguised her disdain for Mormon polygamists, Emmeline was encouraged by the subsequent visit of two long-time suffragists, Elizabeth Lyle Saxon of Memphis, Tennessee, and Clara Bewick Colby of Beatrice, Nebraska, editor of the *Woman's Tribune*, a popular woman suffrage paper. Their support and advice were useful when a suffrage association was organized in Utah.[34] The two visitors shared the podium in both the Salt Lake Theatre and the LDS Church's Assembly Hall, speaking on social reform and suffrage. A tour of the city with Emmeline included a visit to Angie Newman's Christian Industrial Home, where they were surprised to find only one woman with her five children and three children of another woman, who was at the time incarcerated in the mental hospital in Provo.[35] A reception at the Gardo House followed, attracting five or six hundred people, including the governor.[36] Fruit and olives, sandwiches, and ice cream and cake were served to the guests, and Emmeline and her suffrage coworkers drew on their suggestions for organizing a suffrage association.[37]

The planned merger of the conservative American Woman Suffrage Association and the National Association took place in 1890 under the name National American Woman Suffrage Association (NAWSA).[38] Were it not for the personal friendships and mutual respect that Emmeline, Emily

33. E. Wells, Diary, June 26, 1888. Details about these events can be found in C. Madsen, *Advocate for Women*, 240–47.

34. Plans for their visit are noted in E. Wells, Diary, September 18–26, 1888. Emmeline also included an account of their visit in the *Woman's Exponent*. See "Visit of Mrs. Saxon and Mrs. Colby," 17 (October 1, 1888): 68–69. She summarized their visit in "Utah," esp. 940. See also Carol Cornwall Madsen, ed., *Battle for the Ballot: Essays on Woman Suffrage in Utah, 1870–1896*, 37–38.

35. Emmeline gave her own impressions of the visit in "Comments," *Woman's Exponent* 17 (October 15, 1888): 76–77. See also E. Wells, Diary, September 26, 1888.

36. Many years later, Emmeline gave this estimate in her account of the visit for the *History of Woman Suffrage*, although her diary, written at the time, indicates that two hundred attended the reception. See E. Wells, "Utah"; and C. Madsen, *Battle for the Ballot*, 33–51.

37. E. Wells, Diary, September 25, 1888.

38. Over the years, the "social purity" women gave short shrift to woman suffrage, believing that it was unfeminine and undermined the family values they upheld. Preferring to work through local communities and to influence state legislators to pass legislation conducive to their values, they eventually came to see that with the vote in their own hands, they had more power to accomplish their goals. Susan B. Anthony had undoubtedly influenced Frances Willard, head of the Woman's Christian Temperance Union since 1879, toward this position and was instrumental in bringing the WCTU into membership in 1884, adding 230,000 woman suffrage supporters.

Richards, Zina Young, and other Mormon suffragists had established with NWSA's leaders, efforts to prevent their membership in this and other national women's organizations would likely have been successful.

In the midst of increasing suffrage activity and the attention garnered by the newly organized National Council of Women, Emmeline decided to return to San Francisco to visit her daughter Belle. Withdrawing fifty dollars from her "nest egg," she took Annie's four-year-old daughter, Louise, with her along with Zina (Zine) Whitney, Orson's wife, and their three-year-old daughter, Emily.[39] It could not have been an emotionally easy trip, and Emmeline admitted that the wrenching memories of the previous year rose "like specters before me." She was determined, however, to overlay those haunting memories by pleasant ones and engaged fully in the activities typical of a tourist traveling with a dear friend and two little girls. Belle joined them on trips to Cliff House on the beach, to China Town, to the Golden Gate Park, and to the Presidio. Emmeline shopped for gifts to take back home, and she and Zina and the two children took time from their sightseeing to visit the noted historian Hubert Howe Bancroft, whose *History of Utah* was soon to be published.[40] The trip was an effort to exorcise the grief that had so firmly gripped Emmeline's mind and heart since Louie's death.

Emmeline visited the home on Pine Street where the Sears family lived when Louie first joined them. On another day, accompanied by her fifteen-year-old grandson, Sep, she toured the Laurel Hill Cemetery, walking up and down among the graves, not remembering exactly where her unnamed grandson lay buried.[41] Then they went by the house on Glen Park Avenue, number 21. At Emmeline's request, the present owner, Mrs. Siegel, allowed her to see Louie's room. Emmeline was engulfed by a flood of memories as she entered the room, but these too were held in check.[42]

The travelers left San Francisco for a brief visit to Monterey, stopping in San Jose to visit relatives of Newel K. Whitney. In Monterey they drove along the seashore and stopped to watch the waves afar off, gathering height and momentum as they neared the shore. "I hear, I see it, I feel its grandeur and sublimity in my inmost soul," Emmeline wrote as she saw the waves crashing against the rocks. That scene became the heart of a poem that

39. Ibid., October 14, 22, 29, 30, 1888.

40. Bancroft, *History of Utah*. See also E. Wells, Diary, November 8, 1888. Emmeline was particularly interested in meeting Bancroft since there are at least twenty-two pages relating to Daniel in his history.

41. E. Wells, Diary, November 7, 1888.

42. Ibid., November 19, 20, 1888. Belle and her family had moved from the home after Louie's death. Emmeline and Belle and the others also entertained Dr. Solomon Stambaugh, the doctor who had attended Louie before her death.

captured the emotions she felt as she remembered her loss of James and Louie, both, in her mind, connected to the sea:

> *And the ever constant beating*
> *'Gainst the rocks that hemmed the sea,*
> *Where the winds in fury meeting,*
> *Dashed them backward ruthlessly.*
> *So our human hopes are driven,*
> *Recklessly tossed to and fro,*
> *And our strongest ties are riven—*
> *Rent asunder by a blow.*[43]

Only understanding Emmeline's inadvertent and painful ties to the sea could one be sensitive to the emotional freight this imagery conveyed.

Leaving Belle at the end of their visit was difficult for both Emmeline and Belle. The heartrending crisis of the year before created a deep bond between mother and daughter, drawing them close in shared memory. Before she left, Emmeline spent an afternoon alone with her oldest daughter. They went to the Cliff House and walked along its beach, "picking up shells and pebbles and talking over our past and present." It had been a day of days for Emmeline, telling her diary as evening came, "I shall always remember our day at the seashore."[44]

Though Emmeline may well have seen life through a more romanticized and emotional lens than others, and burdened her diary with woeful thoughts, she did not claim to have suffered more losses than others or more heartache from sharing a husband. She may have been more inclined, perhaps more adept, or even intense than others in describing her feelings about these circumstances in her life. But she did not claim to be unique in these experiences. Though she felt her material status was less advantageous than those of her sister-wives and some of her associates, this comparison did not seem to impinge on her relationship with them or her sense of her own distinct gifts. Rehearsing every day's happenings to her diary perhaps intensified the impact of her feelings and thoughts rather than relieving them, but doing so also allowed her to express them without constraint, something she would never do publicly. She was impelled by that deep-seated sense of destiny so inextricably entwined with the *Exponent*, which extracted all her energy and erected boundaries against so much else of her life, even as it had opened unimagined avenues of experience. This was her compensation.

43. E. Wells, "Memory of the Sea." The poem first appeared in print in the *Woman's Exponent* 18 (July 15, 1889): 26. With James's death at sea and Louie's near the sea, the ocean acquired a palpable poignancy for Emmeline.

44. E. Wells, Diary, November 20, 1888.

Few people knew the extent to which her public stoicism belied the private turmoil that constantly roiled within her. Her enviable sense of the ruling hand of Providence in her life and her irrepressible faith that good would somehow come from the direst of experiences gave some meaning to the disappointments and losses she confronted. The constancy of her rationalizations of these importune events might suggest her use of them as palliatives for what she could not control. It is also possible that her dependence on the ameliorating comfort they brought her rendered them, by repeated instances, as merely formulaic expressions of recognition of a higher power in her life. But her life and writings suggest more. Her rationalizations appeared to be genuine responses to a life that constantly evaded her own desires but offered viable compensations. This conviction enabled her to press on, to rise up when crushed down, and to master self-pity—the hardest challenge of all. It would be easy to read her private writings as cumulative evidence of such self-pity. But she did not succumb to it. She knew that in both her family and her public positions, it was essential that she "keep up for the sake of others."[45] The physical toll of her "unceasing labors" left her almost prostrate by nightfall, frequently faint or sick, and often bedridden with pounding headaches. Yet she saw her work as a challenge she had to meet head-on, a duty to herself and others. Despite feeling unable to cope with all the responsibilities that were thrust on her, she could not let them thwart her in her "career to obtain a subsistence by my own effort."[46]

The events surrounding Louie's death and the calumny they had engendered left deep scars. Yet those whose words or actions that had seemed unforgivable when uttered or written did indeed find forgiveness. All of the Cannons regained their place in Emmeline's and Annie's lives. "No one knows how I have sought to bear up under the pressure," Emmeline confessed. Nor would they. Though she sometimes still wished for someone to confide in, she admitted that it was "not in her nature to do so."[47] By that time, this was so. Through circumstances she could not control, she had become her own source of strength, and she was firmly committed to keep her own counsel. "It is all I can do to keep up my courage," she wrote on the last day of 1888, "but I know I must not give up."[48]

45. Ibid., February 8, 1888.

46. Ibid., August 4, 1888. Though often resentful that she had to provide for herself, she eschewed becoming dependent on the church or other forms of "charity" for her living. The Woods family often sent money, but Emmeline does not indicate that the other two sons-in-law did so, neither of them in a firm-enough financial position to do so. They showed their love and support for her in other ways.

47. Ibid., February 23, 1888. This had not always been the case.

48. Ibid., December 31, 1888.

CHAPTER 23

New Thresholds of Change
(1888–1890)

THE *WOMAN'S EXPONENT* had catapulted Emmeline Wells into public notice while helping her fulfill an ambition to "be someone." But the cost was high. By 1890, the contest for her time was a relentless battle. She found it "such a struggle for existence and so hard to keep above water. I would be glad to have all my time to devote to literature in a very different way instead of being obliged to get my own living," a daily and imperative grind.[1] She was fighting the battle of many artists who resented the imposition of practical concerns on their creative energy. Determined, however, to give voice to the poetry always in her mind, she stretched her working hours, using late nights and early morning, to compose her poems and stories. They actually turned out to be the best hours for writing, she discovered. "I need solitude," she explained. "All fanciful people do. How else could I court favor with the Muses[?]"[2] Those quiet hours opened the store of images that constantly sought expression. She was never at a loss for something to write. "My thoughts go flying so fast and my pen cannot keep pace try as I will."[3]

Though there were many women's publications throughout the country and at least fourteen women editors in Utah before the close of the century, the *Woman's Exponent* was preeminent in Utah during its forty-two-year run.[4] Despite the heavy load of maintaining this semimonthly woman's paper with so little help, Emmeline was wary when she received a letter in 1888 from thirty-two-year-old Susa Young Gates, written in Laie, Hawaii. According to Susa, her husband, Jacob Gates, then serving a mission to

1. E. Wells, Diary, November 13, 1890.
2. Ibid., December 8, 1888.
3. Ibid., January 30, 1892.
4. Martha M. Solomon, *A Voice of Their Own: The Woman Suffrage Press, 1840–1910*. For Utah editors, see Sherilyn Cox Bennion, "Enterprising Ladies: Utah's Nineteenth Century Women Editors."

the islands, suggested that Susa be appointed a "subordinate editor" of the *Woman's Exponent*. Such an association, Susa added, "would exactly meet his wishes," and she found she "burned with longing (inexplicable to me) to the particular place he would have me occupy." She then listed a number of changes to improve the publication: a different quality of paper, a redesign of its cover page, a change in its size, and "many little items" that she would later reveal as "possible improvements."[5] If Emmeline had entertained the thought of Susa's help, especially as offered by her husband rather than Susa, this letter surely squelched it. Susa had also written a letter to Romania Pratt, who adroitly directed Susa away from any designs on the *Woman's Exponent* by suggesting that she edit a journal of her own for the young women of the church.[6] This idea elicited a positive response from Susa. With concurrence from members of the First Presidency and the YLMIA board, Susa launched the *Young Woman's Journal* in October 1889 after Susa and Jacob Gates returned to Utah.[7] Susa served as editor for eleven years.[8] Emmeline felt very much "worked up about the magazine," since, she noted, "so much [is] being said about allowing it to appear." Though she professed not to fear any competition, she was aware that any form of association with a church organization, as the *Young Woman's Journal* had with the YLMIA, could make a difference in the success of a publication, and she may have resented the fact that the *Exponent*'s faithful reporting of YLMIA meetings and conferences was now displaced by summaries and articles in the journal.[9] Emmeline also peevishly noted that the new journal always seemed to be issued on time.[10] Taking advantage of the situation,

5. Susa Young Gates (Laie, Hawaii), letter to Emmeline B. Wells, May 5, 1888, Gates Papers. Annie Wells Cannon returned it to Susa following Emmeline's death in 1921. Making the suggestion Jacob's rather than her own may have been Susa's way of relieving her of responsibility for the bold request.

6. Romania Bunnell Pratt, letter to Susa Young Gates, June 26, 1888, ibid. Romania did not respond to Susa's inquiry until June, a month after Susa's letter to Emmeline. Romania and Emmeline may possibly have discussed the situation and together arrived at a solution for Susa.

7. Emmeline Wells noted its maiden issue in "The Young Woman's Journal," *Woman's Exponent* 18 (October 15, 1889): 77.

8. Susa Gates had enjoyed the help of a large staff of editors for the different departments of the publication as well as the personal proofreading by Elmina Taylor, president of the YLMIA. A younger generation of women eagerly sent their work to the journal, many more voluntarily worked in preparing the copy, and when lesson plans for the young women were included in each issue and the subscription cost lowered, the publication enjoyed a steady growth.

9. E. Wells, Diary, June 6, 1889.

10. Ibid., September 28, 30, 1889.

however, Emmeline utilized the new publication as another outlet for her own poems and stories.

Some of her most popular poetry was produced during this period, despite her time constraints. One of her favorites expressed her feelings about the garden she planted by the house she had so recently lost:

My dear old garden! Still I call it mine,
And mine it is, for in its grateful shade
Of ev'ry tree, and shrub, and flow'ring vine,
My children and my children's children played.
Round these my aching heart instinctive clings,
And they to me are sweet and tender things....
O, would those days but come to me again,
'Twould ease my heart of all this racking pain.[11]

Immediately after publishing "The Dear Old Garden" in June 1889, Emmeline turned her attention to completing the poem she had begun when she visited San Francisco the previous year. Writing "Memory of the Sea" was a pleasure, she found, but "a sad one too." The sea would be forever linked to love and loss.[12] When she read the two poems to Daniel, he praised "Memory of the Sea," but remained silent after her reading of "The Dear Old Garden."[13]

Even as Emmeline finished these two poems within weeks of each other, more were waiting for expression. "I feel these are the children of my brain," she explained, "for each one is a part of my thoughts and fancies and bears a [resemblance] to me or visible impress of myself. I wrestle with them as the mother does in labor, for her offspring."[14]

During this time of frenetic writing, she was justifiably proud to have completed and published numerous biographical sketches, three short stories, and several chapters of "Hephzibah," which she felt would be her crowning achievement. She was clearly enthralled with the story as it slowly unfolded. "Such a wonderful story," she reflected after one day's writing, "so true and so full of imagery and puzzles."[15] The "romance" she claimed her

11. E. Wells, *Musings and Memories*, 190–92. Also printed as "The Dear Old Garden," *Woman's Exponent* 18 (June 1, 1889): 1.

12. *Woman's Exponent* 18 (July 15, 1889): 25. See also E. Wells, *Musings and Memories*, 34–36.

13. E. Wells, Diary, August 1, 1889.

14. Ibid., July 17, 1889.

15. Ibid., March 21, 1890. Without more contemporary evidence, it is sometimes puzzling to determine, in several instances, what is fancy and what is real in the story.

life to be at sixteen was taking literary shape in "Hephzibah." She hoped the story would be published in book form. In fact, she wrote, "I mean it shall be."[16] She was optimistic of its public approval.

The story is actually only a partial biography, focusing on her early life in New England, the upheaval that conversion to the church created in her life's plan, and the trauma of her life-changing experiences in Nauvoo. Emmeline apparently felt compelled to put these admittedly difficult memories of her early life before the public, despite the discomfort and anguish they evoked. "It enters into my very soul to write those things," she revealed after completing one of the chapters. "No one knows save only those whose hearts are interwoven with their themes how much one suffers in writing for the public, the innermost feelings of the soul."[17] Why then she so tortured herself is understood only if one observes the autobiographical nature of her poetry, the constant introspection in her diaries, the deeply personal impact of her reading, and her ceaseless self-appraisal. All marked her as extremely self-referential, literarily at least, an earmark of all diarists who are impelled by some force of self-interest to reincarnate themselves and their lives in words.

That there are several worthy reasons for recording one's history is obvious. Emmeline Wells, however, did not seem to write consciously for the spiritual edification of her descendants or to provide an overview of her life for them, as some early diarists professed to do. Nor did she likely see diary writing as primarily therapeutic. Although her diaries serve these purposes extraordinarily well, the reflective and inward perspective of her writing argues for a more nuanced reading. Her diary was almost her alter ego, the self she could not display to others. Only that silent companion could absorb the superfluity of emotions she so willingly unleashed. One might even read her diaries as the "romance" she felt her life to be, with her exaggerated expressions, self-analysis, and lengthy soliloquies, while the world saw only an efficient and capable woman, up to every task put before her. She was also a chronicler who found outlet in her meticulous record keeping and inerrant eye for detail. At the end of nearly every year's diary is a daily account of money received and spent, items purchased, letters written, names and addresses, and other, often trivial, bookkeeping items. Everything, it seems, deserved a permanent record.

Though Emmeline earnestly cared about the quality of her *Exponent* editorials and articles, she considered them outside the realm of what really

16. Ibid., January 9, 1890. That she was unsuccessful in her determination to extend the story into book form is evident in its serial publication in the *Woman's Exponent*.

17. Ibid., January 17, 1890.

mattered to her. Repeatedly, even tediously, lamenting the lack of time to entertain her "poetic muse," she nonetheless steadily if slowly added poems to her poetic canon and happily sent eleven to the American Publishers Association in Chicago in 1890, four of which were chosen to be included with her picture in a forthcoming compilation of American poetry.[18] She was annoyed by the increasing number of requests to write a poem or verse for some local social occasion and notices or reviews of women's events for the local newspapers. But her ability to "versify" on fairly short notice and her growing reputation as a poet led to these requests, and she never refused an opportunity to be in print. "I do not know where the time is to come from," she despaired when invited to write some songs for a May Day celebration. "Still," she realized, "I am fully aware that a poet lives longest in his songs, and I must make the attempt."

A new genre of poetic expression offered itself to her when Levi Richards, secretary of the Deseret Sunday School Union, requested that she write a sacramental hymn for the Sunday School hymn book. She eventually produced the hymn "'Twas on the Mount of Calvary" and four others. Four of her hymn texts were also included in *The Latter-day Saints' Psalmody: A Collection of Original Tunes*, the first time hymns for the church were given original musical settings.[19] But these poetic diversions were the kind of poetry she hoped would be her legacy. "I have almost given up the dreams of my early life to have the fame the honor of an author, and must not expect more than the hope of living in the memory of some of my dear friends."[20] Though her poetic output did not have enduring quality, it definitely had currency in her own time.

True to her commitment to preserve in writing the lives of early Mormon women, she contributed life histories to the *Juvenile Instructor* and *Young*

18. Ibid., February 4, 1890. See also first page of memoranda at the conclusion of the 1890 diary. She sent a brief biographical sketch and five dollars with her picture to be engraved in the book, a considerable sum for her to raise at the time. Thomas William Herringshaw was the editor of the resulting book, *Local and National Poets of America: With Interesting Biographical Sketches and Choice Selections from over One Thousand Living American Poets.* The poems selected were "At Evening," "The Dear Old Garden," "Memory of the Sea," and an extract from "Beauties of Nature," appearing on 805–6.

19. *Hymns and Sacred Songs, Designed for the Use of the Children of the Latter-day Saints.* Her poem "Our Mountain Home So Dear," with music by Evan Stephens, written for an earlier children's hymnal, is in the current LDS hymnal. John Taylor commissioned first edition of the *Psalmody* in 1888 (Salt Lake City: Deseret News, 1888). The five musicians who composed the music were George Careless, Ebenezer Beesley, Joseph J. Daynes, Evan Stephens, and Thomas C. Griggs.

20. E. Wells, Diary, May 5, 1890.

Woman's Journal.[21] These life sketches, based on interviews with the subject or her descendants and friends (or both) as well as Emmeline's own rich personal relationship with those about whom she wrote are of inestimable historical value. They augment the life stories she published in her own paper, and Emmeline frequently used Brigham Young's directive to publish these histories as a selling point for her paper.[22] By following his counsel, Emmeline made the *Exponent* more than a newspaper reporting current happenings and expressing opinions on contemporary issues. She created a biographical anthology and opened a window to an era that was rapidly passing away. It linked new readers, who had spent their whole lives in Utah, with first-generation Mormon women whose lives provided spiritual and social models for rising generations.[23] Thus, she was drawn away from poetic expression once again by what she perceived as a vital preservation mission of women's presence in Mormon history.

Though she still grumbled at the number of interrupting callers to her office, they were also evidence of her growing reputation as friend and adviser as well as a woman of compassion and ability. She always felt obliged to listen while quietly reporting to her diary, "I am so weary of the confusion of people in whom I have no interest running in and out," but the confusion never ceased.

As her prominence grew, so did the number of outside visitors, whom she welcomed. Well-known Civil War worker Mary Livermore, journalist Fannie B. Ward of the *New York Sun*, Sir Julian Goldschmidt (scion of a large British Anglo-Jewish banking family and member of Parliament), the Dowager Countess of Shrewsbury and the Countess of Selkirk were a few of

21. Ibid., December 14, 26, 1890. She had begun this long series of biographical writings with the publication of Edward W. Tullidge's *The Women of Mormondom*, for which she had written the life story of Elizabeth Ann Whitney and assisted with several others. She wrote sketches on the lives of Martha Jane Horne Tingey (*Young Woman's Journal* 2 [January 1891]: 145–52), Lula Greene Richards and Lucy Bigelow Young (3 [December 1891]: 97–99 and 3 [January 1892]: 145–47), Mary Ann Angell Young (*Juvenile Instructor* 26 [January 1, 1891]: 16–20, 26 and [January 15, 1891]: 94–96, entitled "Heroines of the Church: Biography of Mary Ann Angell Young"), and Vilate Kimball (*Juvenile Instructor* [July 15, 1891]: 447–50, August 15 [506–8], September 1 [540–42], September 15 [561–63], and November 15 [682–85]).

22. "The Jubilee Celebration: The Need of Press Representation," *Woman's Exponent* 20 (March 15, 1892): 132. Tullidge's volume includes references to or short life stories of more than three hundred women. Brigham Young may also have been influenced by a series of biographical stories of early church leaders during Joseph Smith's and Brigham Young's lifetimes, serialized in volumes 25–27 of the *Millennial Star*, between the years 1863 and 1865.

23. E. Wells, Diary, May 23, 24, 1908; C. Madsen, "Telling the Untold Story."

the well-traveled, well-educated men and women of stature who entranced her with their experiences and viewpoints, so different from her own.[24] These she did not resent because they gave her opportunity to indulge in levels of discourse she seldom had with most of her Mormon associates. She often reflected on "the great honor conferred upon me in the opportunity of meeting great people." She was certain that no one could be "all they desire without contact, with older, wiser and perhaps more influential and more cultured people than surrounds them on every hand."[25] It was "quite an event to have them seek me out in such a humble home," she happily shared with her diary.[26]

Emmeline was also impressed with the visit of one of the few ordained women ministers, the Reverend Antoinette Brown Blackwell, sister-in-law to Henry Blackwell (Lucy Stone's husband) and Elizabeth Blackwell, one of the first women to train as a physician. During the reverend's visit, Emmeline presented her with a copy of Parley P. Pratt's *Key to Theology*, *The Voice of Warning*, and *Mormon Doctrine*, a full dose of Mormonism.[27]

Of all the visitors who came during this time, none was more surprising than William Hendrie. Fourteen years had passed since he had left the city, married, and moved to New York. She was stunned one evening, after she had readied herself for bed, to find that "who should come rapping at the door but Mr. Hendrie." They talked "over old times" until "ten or may be a trifle later." She was so emotionally wrought after he left that she could not sleep, having become "excessively nervous on account of old associations being brought up." She recognized that their short acquaintance had been a brief, bright antidote to the constant and unrelieved heartache she had experienced during the 1870s. She did not know that his second visit the following night would be the last time she would ever see him.[28] A little more than a year later, on his birthday, she reflected on that unexpected visit and pondered over "the peculiar attraction that he created in our family.

24. E. Wells, Diary, September 27, October 15, 1889. She occasionally referred to an autograph book she kept of the out-of-town visitors, but if still extant, it has not surfaced.

25. Ibid., September 26, 27, 1889.

26. Emmeline was pleased to receive a complimentary letter from the Countess of Selkirk after her return to London with a request to send her more issues of the *Woman's Exponent*. Emmeline recounts the visit in ibid., October 15, 1889.

27. Ibid., April 11, 13, 14, 1892; see also August 6, 7, 1892. See "Col. and Mrs. Parker: The Tabernacle Lecture," *Woman's Exponent* 21 (August 15, 1892): 30, 31 and (September 1, 1892): 36. A favorite lecturer was Edmund Russell, who originated the Delsarte system, exercises that developed graceful manners of acting and speaking and a style of expressing emotion through voice and gesture.

28. Ibid., May 28–30, 1889.

Emma my darling I fear loved him but she was too good and pure to unite with one not of our faith." She thought about her own birthday, just days away, and admitted that though she was growing older, she did not feel old. "My heart is not a whit older or more unimpassionable."[29] Hendrie had definitely provided a disturbing but welcome counterpoint to the routine of her daily life.

Such bright diversions from her everyday activities not only helped best the fatigue that came from her pressing schedule, but also broadened her outlook and gave her ideas for her own writing and speaking. The *Exponent* and her growing prominence had given her entrée into a new level of society. Lifting her above the prosaic concerns of most of her associates, these excursions into the lofty world of the prominent evoked gratitude for having "some rare chances of that sort."[30]

Emmeline's hosting responsibilities also turned her office into a quasi-official information bureau, and for most visitors she was the primary and often the only contact with the church. She took this unofficial duty seriously, feeling that "some one prepared to answer questions should be on the spot to defend our cause." She felt confident to act as a spokesperson for the church. "I am here to reply to all questions of importance and to defend the principles of our faith to the very last," she declared to her diary. Moreover, she asserted, "I feel that I am needed here that I have a testimony to bear that is of some importance."[31]

As the decade ended and a new one began in 1890, two important events occurred that would have a special impact on LDS women. One was the completed merger of the two suffrage associations, which caused the disaffiliation or dissatisfaction of many members of both associations who were unsympathetic to each other's social and political philosophies and the agitation to exclude Mormon women from the new association.

Shortly before the merger, the NWSA adopted a policy that required the organization of suffrage associations from which to send representatives to the national conventions rather than accepting individual membership. At the 1888 convention, Emily Richards and Isabel Brown, a non-Mormon, were appointed by the NWSA to organize an independent territorial association. Emily and Isabel at first deferred to Jennie Froiseth, who was still NWSA's vice president for Utah, and they had enlisted Emmeline's help in contacting Froiseth for assistance. Froiseth frostily refused to cooperate in any cause with women who supported plural marriage. She agreed, however,

29. Ibid., February 24, 1890.
30. Ibid., September 27, 1889.
31. Ibid., April 26, 1890.

not to oppose their organizational efforts in the territory.[32] Emily and Isabel then turned to the LDS Relief Society, the entity that had previously sent individual delegates to the suffrage conventions. Thus, in early January 1889, general Relief Society president Zina D. H. Young, Jane Richards and her daughter-in-law Emily Richards, Bathsheba W. Smith, Sarah M. Kimball, and Emmeline met with Wilford Woodruff and other church leaders to discuss organizing a territorial suffrage association. These authorities gave the women a unanimously favorable vote, and within weeks, the Utah Territorial Woman Suffrage Association (UTWSA) came into being, with Margaret Nightingale Caine, wife of Utah's territorial delegate John T. Caine, as the first president.

Though Emmeline had been "besieged on all hands to assist in organizing a woman suffrage Association," she was incensed when the executive committee, headed by Emily Richards, decided that "none who have ever been in plural marriage can have any [leadership] position in it."[33] It was clearly a public relations decision, and potentially divisive, but that fear did not materialize and did not disrupt the intent of Utah suffragists to work together to regain the vote. By this time, Emmeline had had so much experience with national leaders that she could not privately help bristling at being relegated to backstage. She had spearheaded a petition drive so successfully that she had amassed thousands of signatures on sixty yards of paper. She had written the articles and bylaws for the UTWSA the morning before its first meeting and prepared credentials for the two delegates to the 1889 national suffrage convention, Emily Richards and Margaret Caine. It is hardly surprising that she "felt very unpleasant about the work."[34] But not for long. She, along with other plural wives, was too invested in the movement to begrudge the slight.[35]

Thus, when the 1889 national suffrage convention opened in Washington, DC, in January, Utah women had a functioning suffrage association

32. "The Sister Suffragists," *Salt Lake Daily Tribune*, January 8, 1889, 4. The newspaper account disparaged the attempt to enlist the support of Jennie Froiseth and referred to Emmeline and Emily Richards as "Mormon Sisteren," "holy matrons," and "celestial queens," while failing to mention the presence of non-Mormon Isabel Brown at the meeting with Froiseth, also a non-Mormon.

33. E. Wells, Diary, January 8, 1889. See also Susa Young Gates, "Woman Suffrage in Utah," Gates Papers; and "Woman Suffrage Meeting," *Woman's Exponent* 17 (January 15, 1889): 121.

34. E. Wells, Diary, January 10, 11, 12, 1889. See also "Woman Suffrage Meeting."

35. Information about the preparatory meeting with church leaders and Relief Society women and the process of organizing and selecting officers is in C. Madsen, *Advocate for Women*, 248–49. More information about the struggle to regain the vote in Utah is in C. Madsen, *Battle for the Ballot*.

that had the full support of church leaders. Their strategy brought them the vote in six years, while the national quest took another thirty. Utah women favored the merger of the two suffrage associations in 1890, despite the tenuousness of their membership, but through the influence of Susan B. Anthony and other NWSA leaders, the Relief Society and YLMIA did in fact become members of the new organization. The following year, 1891, they were also admitted as members of the National Council of Women, again through the good graces of their friends in influential positions. Turning acquaintances into friendships had earned the various Mormon representatives' loyalty and support among the leadership of these organizations and would prove to be of immense help in the future.

Their membership in the National and International Councils of Women, however, would be fraught with controversy and dissension, even as it brought them a wider vision of and alliance with the worldwide effort for the advancement of women. The development of these broadly based women's organizations fulfilled Emmeline's long-held desire to see women united in a common cause. As she wrote a few years later, "This work is bringing women into a nearness of contact that will increase confidence, and a more universal sisterhood will be established by the association and relations of this vast army of workers."[36] And she would be one with them.

But of even more personal impact was the second unexpected event of 1890: Wilford Woodruff's announcement in September prohibiting the continuation of plural marriages. As a precursor to his declaration, a year earlier President Woodruff had ordered the razing of the Endowment House, which had long been a symbol to many Gentiles of polygamy. President Woodruff stated that he intended "to submit to those laws" declared constitutional by the US Supreme Court "and to use my influence with the members of the Church . . . to have them do likewise." He pointedly added, "And I now publicly declare that my advice to the Latter-day Saints is to refrain from contracting any marriage forbidden by the law of the land."[37] After months of deliberation, prayer, consultation with friends who were helping Utah Territory's representative to secure a statehood enabling act in Congress, and faced with the most punitive legislation yet, President Woodruff took the agonizing step of leading the church's capitulation to federal law.

A few days later, on October 6 in the general conference of the church, Bishop Orson F. Whitney read aloud the church's thirteen Articles of Faith, which had been canonized nine years earlier, for a sustaining vote, and then

36. "Women and the World's Fair," *Woman's Exponent* 21 (December 1, 1892): 84.
37. Doctrine and Covenants—Declaration 1, 1981 ed., 291–92.

read the text of Wilford Woodruff's Manifesto.[38] The juxtaposition of these two documents added emphasis to them both.[39]

Utah's chief justice, Charles Zane, whom President Benjamin Harrison had sent to Utah to enforce the antipolygamy laws, believed in the sincerity of the Manifesto, while some anti-Mormons felt it a ploy in order to retrieve the citizens' rights of which Mormons engaged in plural marriage had been deprived since the 1882 Edmunds Act. But this political and institutional bickering and negotiation did not adequately answer the troubling question of how it would affect the personal and domestic lives of LDS women. Emmeline was one of these plural wives. "There are some who will be very much tried over the affair," she observed, "but we must wait and see what the Lord has in store for us—we do not always know what is for our best good here & hereafter."[40] When the Manifesto was read and voted upon at the conference, she was reassured when "many testified of its truth and the inspiration that prompted [it] from the spirit of the meeting."[41] Still, she was curious about the effect of the Manifesto on the relationship of Mormon women and antipolygamists, but even more concerned about the legal and social consequences of this unexpected declaration. She and many other plural wives would discover that discontinuing plural marriage was more difficult than implementing it.

38. The proceedings of the conference are included in O. Whitney, *History of Utah*, 3:743–48. The twelfth Article of Faith states, "We believe in being subject to kings, presidents, rulers, and magistrates, in obeying, honoring, and sustaining the law."

39. "Official Declaration," *Deseret News*, September 25, 1890, 2; "Semi-annual Conference," *Woman's Exponent* 19 (October 15, 1890): 68. The *Deseret News* writer chafed at the report of the meeting sent out by the Associated Press, "a condensed form," he wrote, "which poorly conveys the sentiments of the writer."

40. E. Wells, Diary, September 29, 1890.

41. Ibid., October 6, 1890.

CHAPTER 24

A Leading Sister

(1890–1892)

If Emmeline Wells already felt overwhelmed with the responsibilities warring for her time and attention, organizing the local woman suffrage movement only added to the struggle. Writing a constitution for the Utah Territorial Woman Suffrage Association, traveling throughout the territory to organize local branches, speaking at meetings, and writing editorials supporting the cause increased her workload manyfold.[1] But she was determined to vote again when Utah achieved statehood. She did not attend the convention of the newly merged National American Woman Suffrage Association in January 1890 but wrote the credentials for Maria Dougall and Sarah Kimball, who had assumed the presidency of the territorial association that month following Margaret Caine's resignation.[2] Maria Dougall gave a "glowing description of the visit," Emmeline noted, and also reported to Emmeline how much she was missed by the Washington women.[3] Emmeline's work was drawing support from suffragists locally, and combining Relief Society visits with suffrage meetings as she traveled about the territory evinced the close connection between the two. For this campaign there was little concern over mixing religion and politics. Many Relief Society presidents were also presidents of their county suffrage

1. The new emphasis on woman suffrage provided not only subject matter for Emmeline's *Woman's Exponent* editorials, but also copy in the form of reports and speeches from the various county suffrage organizations and numerous articles and even poems on the topic.

2. Minutes of the first annual meetings of the Territorial Woman Suffrage Association were published as "Utah W.S.A.," *Woman's Exponent* 18 (January 15, 1890): 125–26. Sarah M. Kimball replaced acting president Lydia D. Alder, who had filled in at the resignation of Margaret Caine during the first year. Emmeline was appointed to the Resolutions Committee. Details about the accomplishments of the territorial association can be found in C. Madsen, *Battle for the Ballot* and *Advocate for Women*, 237–92.

3. E. Wells, Diary, March 20, 1890.

associations, and suffrage meetings were often scheduled directly after Relief Society meetings and in the same halls, mainly in deference to the time and travel constraints of the country women.

Remembering her disappointment at being nominated and then declared ineligible to run for county treasurer back in 1878, Emmeline was determined that Utah women should regain the right to vote *and* to hold office when Utah became a state. With so many Mormons—as well as all Utah women—now prohibited from voting because of the Edmunds-Tucker Act, the Liberal (Gentile) Party had the numerical strength to win elections. The loss of Ogden to the Liberal Party was disturbing to church leaders but not devastating, since it was a railroad terminal and had a large Gentile population. However, when the Liberal Party set its sights on winning the February 1890 election for municipal officers in Salt Lake City, church leaders were gravely concerned and employed a variety of measures to increase the Mormon vote. The successful mobilization of women into the local suffrage campaign alerted LDS leaders to the value of their participation in the escalating political drama in Utah. Not only was the effective network of Relief Societies already in place, but there was now a political network of local suffrage units functioning under direction of a territorial association. Not surprisingly, despite her lack of a leadership position, church leaders turned to Emmeline for assistance. "Complications in politics seem to have assumed considerable strength," she wrote in 1889. "It will be a problem, local perhaps and it may be national. I have been advised to speak to the sisters about women taking an active part in the movement and to urge it in the sisters meetings."[4] As editor of the *Exponent*, a veteran of Washington politics, and a recognized organizer and leader, she was a natural catalyst for enlisting women's political interest and support, all they could give since their disfranchisement. At one of the Fourteenth Ward retrenchment meetings, Emmeline made "a speech on the political condition of the City," stirring a latent political interest in many of her listeners.[5]

Both the Liberal and the People's Parties staged massive parades shortly before the election in February. "There has never been so much ado over one as this time," observed Emmeline. Despite a cold and windy snowstorm, the "bands were out and excitement ran high," she noted, but worried that the "Liberals...were so well assured of success that they were making considerable demonstrations and speeches and shouts."[6] Politics had become an all-consuming topic, and while she was deeply absorbed herself, she

4. Ibid., November 8, 1889.
5. Ibid., November 9, 1889.
6. Ibid., February 9, 10, 1890.

felt there were too many who thought "our salvation depended upon the election." Though naturally supportive of her own People's Party, she noted that should the Liberals win, "if they had any justice it would be all right."[7] But her statement might have also implied her skepticism that the Liberals either had or would show justice to the Mormons should they win. If they truly showed any justice, she seemed to imply, then things would be all right. To pervasive Mormon consternation, the Liberals did indeed win all of the city offices. Salt Lake City was no longer wholly in the political hands of the church.

With statehood a possibility since the Manifesto of 1890, one of the first steps was to abandon the local political parties and align voters with the national parties. The First Presidency faced the challenge of breaking up the heretofore unified People's Party to allow members to join either the Democrats or the Republicans. This was a long and complicated process. "Considerable feeling is manifested and some ill will," Emmeline observed. "Dissension is being developed already." Various members of the First Presidency and Quorum of the Twelve vocalized their own party preferences and attempted to draw others to their political views, a measure taken to help steer church members into both parties. But their actions drew controversy.[8] It has caused "much gossip," Emmeline observed, "and almost brings them into disrepute."[9] She hoped that the "bitterness" she felt around her, so openly expressed, would be mitigated if the people would look into both parties "and see what are the fundamental principles."[10] This would indeed be a new experience for the once politically unified Mormons.

Politics continued to rage to Emmeline's dismay, especially since many members of the local Liberal Party refused to join either of the national parties, making a three-way race for local offices. The bonfires, shouting, and hurrahing revived in Emmeline "the old indignation such as we had felt in former persecutions."[11] Martha Wells's son Heber ran for mayor in 1892 as a Republican but lost to the incumbent, Liberal Robert N. Baskin, who was "the most obnoxious to old settlers of any one I think," opined

7. Ibid., January 16, 1890.

8. Edward Leo Lyman, *Political Deliverance: The Mormon Quest for Utah Statehood*, 150–84.

9. E. Wells, Diary, June 2, 3, 1891. She may have been referring to Apostle Moses Thatcher and B. H. Roberts of the Quorum of the Seventy and perhaps Charles W. Penrose of the Salt Lake Stake, who openly campaigned for the Democratic Party, as did several other members of the Quorum of the Twelve for the Republicans. In 1895, Elders Thatcher and Roberts unsuccessfully ran for the US Senate and House, respectively.

10. Ibid., June 2, 3, 9, 1891.

11. Ibid., August 3, 1891.

Emmeline.[12] What Emmeline's political persuasion was at that point, she did not disclose, but she showed interest in the Democratic Party both locally and nationally and seemed agreeable to the candidacy of Grover Cleveland, whom she had met in 1886.[13] She noted the campaigning of the Liberals "to put a stop to all the plans of our people towards any liberty of rights or privileges." She could hardly believe that a "pow wow" they held in the Exposition Building drew Mormons "silly" enough to attend.[14]

In the meantime, Relief Society activities also drew her attention. Emmeline and Isabella Horne proposed the idea of a woman's store, in which individual women could buy a share for five dollars to launch the enterprise. It was hoped that the store would give employment and skill training to many needful young women as dressmakers and clerks. Emmeline agreed to render whatever help was needed but wisely refrained from serving on the board. Making sure the sisters understood the nature and purpose of the new association, the advocates of the proposed store explained that it was strictly a business venture, not a benevolent undertaking, and would be under the direction of reliable women.[15] The new association was to be named the Woman's Cooperative Mercantile & Manufacturing Institution, with Isabella Horne as president.[16] "I am very anxious the enterprise should be a success," Emmeline wrote, "and help women who need to work."[17] She also hoped it would be a means "to promote home industries and help forward the cause of equal rights."[18]

Of particular importance to the women of the church was the long-overdue decision to hold semiannual Relief Society general conferences.

12. Ibid., January 20, 1892. Baskin had assisted in writing the 1869 antipolygamy Cullum bill and was a prominent lobbyist against the Mormons thereafter. He wrote *Reminiscences of Early Utah*, intending to counter "the glaringly false statements" in Orson F. Whitney's admittedly pro-Mormon *History of Utah*. Baskin became Utah chief justice in 1899.

13. See, for example, E. Wells, Diary, June 16, 20, 27, 1892.

14. Ibid., July 20, 22, 1892.

15. "Woman's Store," *Woman's Exponent* 19 (December 1, 1890): 92. The pagination and dates for the December 1 and December 15 issues are incorrect. This editorial is out of order and follows the December 15 editorial. See also E. Wells, Diary, December 12, 1890.

16. E. Wells, Diary, December 12, 19, 1890. A similar organization had functioned years earlier when Louisa Wells was closely associated with it.

17. Ibid., January 9, 1891.

18. "Woman's Store," *Woman's Exponent* 19 (December 15, 1890): 104. The store managed to maintain itself for nearly twenty-five years but gradually lost its momentum and underwent many changes after the death of its president, Isabella Horne, in 1905. The general cooperative movement had actually lost much of its impetus by the 1890s anyway, but Emmeline's purpose in establishing the store was to give women employment opportunity more than to provide homemade goods.

Under the presidency of Isabella Horne, both the semimonthly meetings of the Retrenchment Society in the Fourteenth Ward meeting hall and the Salt Lake Stake Relief Society conferences had been settings for instructions and discussions relating to Relief Society work.[19] Beginning in 1889, churchwide semiannual general Relief Society conferences were scheduled in conjunction with the semiannual general conferences of the church. The meetings were open to all women but geared especially to Relief Society presidents and boards, presided over by general Relief Society president Zina D. H. Young and her successors.

As corresponding secretary, Emmeline's responsibility was to invite all of the Relief Society presidents throughout the territory to the inaugural conference. Thus was initiated a tradition of general Relief Society conferences that brought women to Salt Lake City from all parts of the territory for instruction and fellowship. Scheduled for Saturday evening, April 6, 1889, in the Assembly Hall in Salt Lake City, this first general conference was "quite an event for women," Emmeline noted in her diary. Fifteen stakes were represented, with reports given of the condition of their Relief Societies. The verbal reports augmented the longtime ward and stake Relief Society reports that had been printed in the *Woman's Exponent* over the years. Zina Young presented general instructions and then asked Emmeline to read the maiden address she had written for the occasion, feeling her voice would not carry to the large audience. She emphasized coordinated General Board visits to the various ward and stake societies and endorsed the *Woman's Exponent* as a medium through which the stakes "could speak to each other" and the means "to make the work more uniform."[20] Since ward and stake presidents often held their positions for a decade or more, the semiannual conferences helped to mold a tangible sisterhood, tied to and emanating from the leading sisters in Salt Lake City. Without regularly scheduled board meetings, planning for the Relief Society's general conferences was rather informal. As secretary, Emmeline was responsible for arranging the use of the Assembly Hall and notifying the stake Relief Society presidents. She was invariably a speaker as well.

Emmeline was challenged even more by two developments in 1892. On the evening of January 5 of that year, the General Board met in Emmeline's parlor to consider the manner in which to celebrate the Jubilee anniversary

19. Isabella Horne was not only president of the Senior and Junior Women's Retrenchment Association, but also president of the Salt Lake Stake Relief Society, treasurer of the General Board of the Relief Society, president of the Women's Cooperative Mercantile and Manufacturing Institution, member of the Deseret Hospital committee, and counselor in the Deseret Silk Association. She was also the mother of fifteen children. See S. Madsen, "Mary Isabella Horne."

20. Z. Young, Diary, May 2–23, 1889.

of the founding of the Relief Society in Nauvoo in 1842. Emmeline was commissioned to send out letters and circulars to all branches of the Relief Society explaining the procedure for celebrating.[21] Much of the planning fell on her shoulders, since Zina Young was "much occupied" with her daughter Zina and children in Canada and in truth less a worker than an overseer. It was all the sixty-four-year-old Emmeline could do to find the time to implement the plans, and she reluctantly admitted that perhaps she was trying "to carry too much."[22] For the first two weeks in March, she was inundated with work, wanting to please "Aunt Zina" and meet her expectations in making a good impression at home and abroad. Counselor Joseph F. Smith's suggestion that all the material gathered for the Jubilee be compiled so that it could be a resource in the future, though an added burden, was an idea that caught Emmeline's fancy.[23]

Emmeline often found herself mediating the sometimes discordant views of the seven strong-willed leaders of the General Board who had lived through the entire fifty-year period since the Relief Society's inception in Nauvoo. Only Emmeline and Romania Pratt of the board had not been members of the original society. A consensus would be difficult, Emmeline knew. "Some are sure to be offended or disagreeable" over something, she anticipated. "We have met & counseled together over it [the Jubilee] and some of us try to conciliate & others are aggressive."[24] How a history of the organization should be prepared was one divisive issue.[25] The other was whether to hang Emma Smith's picture beside those of Eliza R. Snow and Zina Young, the first two her predecessors as president. This last issue so divided the board that Zina took it to President Woodruff for counsel. "Anyone who opposed it must be very narrow minded indeed," he responded, and so the matter was settled. Emma's portrait, alongside that of her husband, Joseph Smith, flanked by likenesses of Eliza R. Snow and Zina D. H. Young, was hung on the great pipes of the organ. Below the pictures was an eye-catching centerpiece, a three-foot key of white flowers and greenery depicting the key of knowledge that Joseph symbolically turned over to women. The rest of the tabernacle was transformed with flags, bunting, and flowers.

On the Jubilee day, the tabernacle was filled with loyal Relief Society

21. E. Wells, Diary, January 5, 8, 14, 30, 1892.

22. Ibid., February 5, 1892; see also March 2, 4, 7, 9, 1892.

23. Ibid., February 5 and March 11, 1892.

24. Ibid., March 11, 1892.

25. "Important to the Relief Society," *Woman's Exponent* 20 (April 1, 1892): 130. The committee appointed to compile the history included Sarah M. Kimball, Lula Greene Richards, Romania Pratt, Annie Wells Cannon, Augusta Joyce Crocheron, and Emmeline Wells. "Relief Society Conference," *Woman's Exponent* 20 (May 1, 1892): 157. The project was finally dropped. E. Wells, Diary, June 3, 1892.

women who listened to various segments of their organization's history given by Sarah M. Kimball and Isabella Horne. Emmeline then recounted the days following the closure of the Nauvoo Relief Society and its reorganization in Utah. She was also honored to give the final "sentiment" of the Jubilee celebration, in which she reaffirmed a conviction that had become her theme throughout her association with the Relief Society. It was read by Apostle Abraham H. Cannon. "What does this woman's Jubilee signify?" she asked. She then answered her question: "Not only that fifty years ago this organization was founded by a Prophet of God, but that woman is becoming emancipated from error and superstition and darkness. That light has come into the world, and the Gospel has made her free, that the key of knowledge has been turned, and she has drank [*sic*] inspiration at the divine fountain."[26] Emmeline deeply believed this. When Joseph Smith "turned the key to women"—the sweeping statement he made to the Nauvoo Relief Society in April 1842—the way was opened for women to develop "powers and attributes which had previously lain dormant and also [to claim] independence and freedom in civil[,] political and religious matters unheard of before."[27] It was a key to the future of women.

Besides the image-building effects of the Jubilee celebration, President Joseph F. Smith's suggestion for a woman's building excited the officers. "It would be an excellent thing to erect a building," he said in his talk at the Jubilee. He felt the sisters needed "a hall for the Society to meet" and, recognizing the women's fund-raising prowess, added, "which would be in a measure self-sustaining."[28] Individual wards had their own Relief Society halls; therefore, it seemed reasonable that the General Board should have one of its own. But it would be a long time in coming.

Even as the euphoria from the Jubilee lingered, Emmeline was thrown into orchestrating a major alteration in the structure of the Relief Society.

26. The entire proceedings were published as "Relief Society Jubilee," *Woman's Exponent* 20 (April 1, 1892): 140–44. See also "The Relief Society Jubilee: Interesting Exercises at the Fiftieth Anniversary of That Organization," *Deseret Evening News*, March 17, 1892, 4.

27. The complete phrase, as recorded by Eliza R. Snow in the original minutes, is, "I now turn the key to you in the name of God and this Society shall rejoice and knowledge and intelligence shall flow down from this time—this is the beginning of better days to this Society," from Record of the Organization and Proceedings of the Female Relief Society of Nauvoo, April 28, 1842, LDS Church History Library, Salt Lake City. See also E. Wells, Diary, March 14, 1892.

28. Joseph F. Smith's address was summarized in "Relief Society Jubilee," *Woman's Exponent* 20 (April 1, 1892): 143. The proposal for a woman's building was part of his address. He also endorsed the practice of women's exercise of the spiritual gifts, specifically the gifts of tongues, healing, and blessing. See Derr, Cannon, and Beecher, *Women of Covenant*, 142–43.

It was now to become a legally incorporated entity with a constitution and bylaws.[29] Because of the continual change of leaders in both the local and the general Relief Society, it was necessary to protect their personal liability against any financial problems incurred by the organization or its leaders.[30] Incorporation also enabled the Relief Society to exist in perpetuity despite the constant change of officers or variation in the duration of various units. Coincidentally, the National Council of Women was incorporating at that time and advised all of its associated members to do the same.

Just days after the Jubilee celebration, the church's attorney Franklin S. Richards, assisted by his father, Franklin D. Richards, acting as liaison with the Relief Society, along with Joseph F. Smith of the First Presidency, submitted to the General Board the Articles of Incorporation, which they had prepared for the organization. Zina Young was resistant to the idea of incorporation and expressed her fear that incorporation would take away the Relief Society's "spiritual character and make it only temporal."[31] Many board members also felt that incorporation secularized what was a divinely inspired organization. Though Joseph Smith had specifically counseled against writing a constitution and set of bylaws, incorporation required them. Presidents or representatives from the various stakes were to constitute a Board of Directors (including the seven-member General Board), each serving a five-year term, and the name of the society was now to be the National Woman's Relief Society, to which Zina particularly objected. The procedures dictated by the terms of incorporation were distasteful to most of the sisters, who felt that the Relief Society had functioned well just as Joseph Smith had organized it. But incorporating the Relief Society was not a negotiable issue, they learned, though it took time to be implemented.

At the Relief Society conference the following year, Franklin S. Richards explained the purpose and advantages of incorporating. "Be not afraid of the name, you have advanced a little," he assured them, "but it must not alter the spirit, but strengthen the work and add to instead of diminishing its influence.... This Society is of consequence now, it has a standing among other great organizations of the world."[32]

29. E. Wells, Diary, July 7, 1891.

30. At the time Zina Young became president in 1887, the Relief Society owned $56,236 worth of real estate, $19,246 in property, 37,493 bushels of wheat, and nearly $6,000 in cash, held in 302 Relief Society branches numbering approximately seventeen thousand members, a third of whom were considered to be "active," or contributing, members.

31. Ibid., March 21, October 2, 1892.

32. Minutes of the Semi-annual Conference of the Relief Society, October 4, 1893, in Minutes of the General Board of the Relief Society, October 4, 1893.

In time some of the doubts began to fade, and individual board members felt that when they fully understood its purposes, they would be able to see, as Jane Richards did, that the changes "were essential and for the progress of the work."[33] Apostle Richards promised that there was nothing wrong in incorporating: "How can it be wrong, the right to take your place among the great charitable institutions of the whole world? A woman or set of women, who have the sense and ability to acquire property should have it, and hold it, and control it; it is not wrong to do so."[34] For nearly a decade afterward, the task of explanation and reassurance fell primarily to L. John Nuttall, secretary to the First Presidency, and Emmeline as secretary of the Relief Society.

To meet the necessary organizational structure dictated by the terms of their newly incorporated status, Zina Young added a third vice president, Sarah M. Kimball, to serve in the presidency of the Relief Society, along with her counselors Jane S. Richards and Bathsheba W. Smith. Emmeline was promoted to general secretary. Isabella Horne continued as treasurer. Meetings of the Board of Directors, which soon became pro forma, were held before each general Relief Society conference, but the original General Board also met to handle most of the Relief Society business. It would take years to ease the discomfort caused by the prescriptive procedures dictated by rules of incorporation. However, requirements that a quorum of seven be gathered in order to transact business meant the original board could handle most administrative matters. Eventually, most of these structural requirements were quietly ignored or eliminated.

More than anything else, incorporation propelled Emmeline into a well-defined leadership role. She had already shown her talent as an organizer and facilitator. As general secretary she not only continued as the major contact with the various stake leaders of the society and with the officers of the national women's organizations, but was also keeper of the record, a conduit to the past that she loved, and source for all questions of precedent, policy, and procedure. Moreover, as a primary explicator of incorporation, she, in effect, ruled on the legal boundaries of proposed actions and supervised the parliamentary procedure required in the directors' meetings. As secretary, she influenced the affairs of the society almost as significantly as Zina Young, the president.

33. Special Business Meeting, National Woman's Relief Society Record, April 5, 1894.

34. Ibid. The subject is also treated in Derr, Cannon, and Beecher, *Women of Covenant*, 144–46, 307. The name was changed once again in 1945 to Relief Society of the Church of Jesus Christ of Latter-day Saints to indicate its attachment to the church.

CHAPTER 25

Dead Sea Apples
(1889–1891)

On the second day of 1889, Emmeline made one of her rare overnight stays at the "big house."[1] She sat up late into the night "talking with the girls [Susan and Lydia Ann] in the parlor." The visit was another reminder of the unappealing features of her current residence. "I see how very comfortable L. A. is in her cosy bedroom up stairs," Emmeline wrote, "much more so than I have ever been."[2] Before the month was over, however, Emmeline commiserated with Lydia Ann and Susan about their husband's decision to sell the "big house," which was to be razed for the construction of the multistory Templeton Hotel.[3] All three felt "low-spirited—and indignant, too" when advised of the move, but by the first week in February, Susan and Lydia Ann had packed and prepared to leave their longtime homes.[4] On March 4, the historic "big house" was on its way to archival memory after serving as a lively dwelling for nearly forty years. The loss of the big house underscored the sense of physical and emotional dislocation that Daniel's financial straits had imposed on his large family. "How I do wish we all had homes to settle down in and means for our support," Emmeline lamented. "But, alas," she was forced to acknowledge, "it is not so."[5]

1. At this time, only Susan and Lydia lived in the big house. Sometime earlier Martha and Hannah had moved into a duplex on First South in the Twelfth Ward.

2. E. Wells, Diary, January 2, 1889.

3. The Templeton Building, first a hotel and by 1893 an office building, occupied a prime location in downtown Salt Lake City. It stood until 1959, when it was razed, and the Kennecott Building took its place in 1965. It was remodeled as the Zions Bank Building and is currently called Gateway Tower East. See "Then and Now," *Deseret Morning News*, August 17, 2007, C1, C2.

4. E. Wells, Diary, January 22, 28, March 7, 1889.

5. Ibid., March 7, 1889.

In time, however, they were all ensconced in their own homes, with Susan and Lydia's residence at 323 Second Avenue, closest to Emmeline. She continued to visit them often and found it an easy trip once the electric streetcar line was available in 1890, which ran along South Temple to E Street and continued north to Third Avenue. The old adobe house with all its discomforts, however, remained home for Emmeline. To preserve her State Street home against an unknown future, she commissioned prominent photographer Charles R. Savage to photograph it before it was razed or remodeled.[6] She had earlier commissioned John William Clawson to do a painting of Louie from a photograph, as she had done for Emmie after her death.

She then turned her attention to her daughter Mell, now settled in Murray, Idaho. Mell had sent her money to make a visit, and Emmeline anticipated a reunion with her family. She left Salt Lake City on August 20, 1889, remarking on the destructive fires that had despoiled the area of Spokane and northern Idaho and poured continual smoke into the air. Though the mountain landscape made a stark contrast to the green hills of New England, she found it offered opportunity for long walks among the thick pines and hikes up the mountainsides, all of which offered lovely views of the narrow valley that enclosed the small mountain village of Murray. Tired at the end of each day's adventure, she felt "more than repaid for the exertion." Hillside picnics, luncheons, and teas with Mell's friends gave Emmeline the sociability she enjoyed while also introducing her to the "Gentile" world into which Mell and Will and the two girls had settled.[7] Mell had adopted a health regimen that included "many new ideas that are really better every way and I have great hopes of her in the future.... [N]either Mell or the girls use tea or coffee or any stimulant scarcely touch meat—Mell does not at all."[8] Emmeline also noticed how quickly Mell had assimilated the social protocol of the society in which she was now living and observed that the residents, even of the rough frontier mining town of Murray, "have a great idea of social etiquette and one must observe it or be ostracised."[9] Emmeline was intrigued with the operations of a quartz

6. Ibid., July 5, 1889.

7. See "Picnic in the Woods," *Woman's Exponent* 18 (September 15, 1889): 59. See also E. Wells, Diary, August 26, 27, 31, September 3, 1889.

8. Aunt Em [Wells], letter to Susa Young Gates, January 11, 1903, Gates Papers. Observance of the Word of Wisdom (Doctrine and Covenants 89), which advised against strong drink and stimulants and encouraged use of fruits in season and minimal use of meat, did not become an essential aspect of orthodoxy until the early part of the twentieth century.

9. E. Wells, Diary, September 3, 1889.

mill, information interesting enough to her to note in her diary.[10] She had a remarkable interest in technological advances and read almost as many books on the industrial developments of the age as on the literary subjects she enjoyed.

Then it was time to return to Utah, to her other daughters, to another chapter of "Hephzibah," to the ever-pressing publishing deadlines, to her uncomfortable house, and to more letters to Daniel in Manti. Only once does she report on what she wrote in those long letters. On the forty-seventh anniversary of her first wedding day, July 29, 1843, to James in Massachusetts, she decided to write some of her early life experiences for Daniel. "He knows so little of my life and what I have had to endure," she wrote. "Men scarcely realize when a young girl marries what a sacrifice she makes. It is indeed a new and trying ordeal." She hoped that the account would "amuse and interest him to say the least." She was on sure ground, however, since he had told her that "he likes to have me talk of these topics," and she thought he would "relish it in manuscript." As she wrote about that uncertain time in her youth, she recalled "how peculiar" were her sensations "in that great home on the Connecticutt river" where she lived after her marriage to James and how her heart "longed for something entirely different."[11] Her letters may have opened a wellspring of emotion in Daniel, for his letters to her were filled with "tender words and appreciation" and "tenderness and love for me."[12]

Though Emmeline was sorry to be separated again from Daniel so soon after his return from England, he had been a natural choice for president of the Manti temple because of his long service as supervisor of the Endowment House.[13] Moreover, he was a gentle, loving man and well loved and respected by church members. His tall frame and sculpted features made a dramatic contrast to the soft voice and kindly demeanor that were so often noted by others. This temple assignment was also a way of recognizing his position as an apostle with an important calling without bringing him into the Quorum of the Twelve Apostles, which inexplicably never happened. Emmeline often mused on this baffling situation. She knew that his undefined position irritated him, and he sometimes "complained to me of some of the apostles" and "felt very indignant" at their seeming indifference to his

10. Ibid., September 4, 1889.

11. Ibid., July 29, 1890. She is referring to the Harris home.

12. Ibid., June 4, 1889, and January 28, 1890.

13. After the 1877 dedication of the St. George temple, Daniel returned to Salt Lake City with Brigham Young, stopping in Manti to view a site where a proposed temple might be constructed. Before the Manti temple was built, the Logan temple was dedicated in 1884. The Manti temple became the third temple in Utah.

status. She ruefully noted that "once those men would have crawled to him," but she and Daniel agreed that there was "no accounting for the changes that come when there is another administration."[14]

His visits home from Manti and their clandestine meetings worried Emmeline. All transpired despite "the rigid enforcement of the law and the severe decisions of Judge [Charles Shuster] Zane."[15] Their meetings were usually brief trysts at her home, and his occasional overnights were fortunately never apprehended by federal agents.[16] Unlike the other four wives, Emmeline lived alone, and her home accommodated both an office as well as living quarters, making his visits there less conspicuous, since so many others came and went throughout the day.

Daniel also stayed with his other wives when he was in the city, sometimes having dinner with all of them together, and Hannah and Lydia Ann visited him in Manti on several occasions. There is less evidence of visits by Martha and Susan, but Daniel had a male companion who attended to both his personal and his administrative needs.

It was not just the convenience of Emmeline's home, however, that drew him to her. He obviously enjoyed staying with her, and she enthusiastically reciprocated the feeling. During one general conference visit when he dined with Susan, Lydia Ann, Martha, and Emmeline, he quietly took Emmeline aside to ask if he could stay the night with her. She had meetings scheduled that evening but indicated that she was willing to meet him later.[17] Frequently, without prior arrangements, she would find him awaiting her return from whatever activity took her away, often until midnight. Having been so long without him, she admitted to feeling "so satisfied to have him in the house," an experience she had never known on a daily basis.[18]

Their brief times together during his visits to the city were both stimulating and comforting. They talked about current events and read aloud their letters to one another. They discussed poetry and literature, talked over magazine and newspaper articles, reminisced of their early lives, and even perused a pictorial history of Rome, sitting side by side. One morning after breakfast, Emmeline showed him a letter from his first wife, Eliza Rebecca Robison, to Nehemiah Park Woods, Daniel's nephew, and also a lock of hair from Daniel's sister Catharine Chapin Wells Woods, the mother of Mell's husband. The lock of hair was "very precious to him from his manner,"

14. Ibid., August 12, 1889.

15. Ibid., July 18, 1889.

16. She seemed to be more nervous about their meetings than he was. Ibid., April 7, October 27, 28, 29, 1889.

17. Ibid., September 22, 1889.

18. Ibid., December 30, 1889.

and he was visibly moved, Emmeline observed.[19] Another time they talked "of poetry of songs of music of the Temple of love." Both retired on that particular evening, she wrote, "feeling at least I did that the time had been a season of delightful interchange of sentiment and poetic expression, one long to be remembered."[20] There were others. "This is the last day of the old year," she wrote in 1889, "and my husband said some very sweet things to me. Things I can never forget while I live—so pleasant to know after a life of care and woe." It was indeed strange to her, she pondered, "that after all my younger years have been past in comparative seclusion that when I am past three score even he should seem so devoted." Like so many others in plural marriages, she regretted that she was unable to keep all of his letters, for fear they would be confiscated by federal officers looking for evidence of their relationship.[21] Somehow she felt her diary was safe. But the pangs she had felt at the lack of such sweet words early in their life together were still vivid. "I scarcely dare acknowledge even to myself what declarations my husband made to me to night," she wrote in January 1890. "Had it happened years ago how different my life might have been. But Alas, it comes so late."[22]

Emmeline traveled again to Manti in March 1890. "O the joy of being once more in his dear presence," she effused when she met him. "His room is so nice and we are so cosy by the large grate and such a comfortable fire in it. We are more like lovers than husband and wife for we are so far removed from each other there is always the embarrassment of lovers and yet we have been married more than 37 years—how odd it seems I do not feel old neither does he—we are young to each other and that is well."[23] Age had no place in this rekindled love affair, though she was sixty-two and Daniel was nearly seventy-six. Each day they were together, she expressed the pleasure she felt in his company. "I am enjoying these few days most fully in my association with him," she wrote on one of those halcyon visits. She was entranced by an evening in the temple where "we were all alone together in that grand and solemn place. O, how perfect seemed the hours we spent together there, no sound but our own voices all so heavenly."[24]

Daniel was in Salt Lake City during the summer of 1890, and he and Emmeline continued with their secretive meetings, aware of the possibility of arrest. Always busy, Emmeline was often obliged to reject his requests to stay with her. As much as she relished his company, her life had taken on a new shape in the years without him, and she was too heavily invested to

19. Ibid., April 2, August 14, 15, October 28, December 28, 1890.
20. Ibid., April 1, 1890.
21. Ibid., April 9, 1890.
22. Ibid., January 2, 1890.
23. Ibid., March 13, 1890.
24. Ibid., March 14, 16, 1890.

relinquish the surrogate activities that had filled the void. Though thoughts of finding a different source of livelihood occasionally arose, she was not clear what it would be, and she loved her paper, despite its demands.[25] So she carried on. "I am no longer young," she wrote, "but that makes no difference whatever I must keep up under any and all circumstances however grievous they may be & preserve my composure and help others, and so I will if such a thing is possible, and for this I will ever pray."[26]

After the summer in Salt Lake, Daniel returned to Manti and sent another invitation for Emmeline to join him. "He said so many pleasant things, that in days past would have filled me with the most infinite pleasure," Emmeline lamented, "but now it is only like dead sea apples." But the sentiment was not entirely lost on her. "Yet to have the acknowledgemnt [*sic*] from him that he makes in that letter is something to be recorded in the tablets of memory. How strange that everything comes too late, when the desire to possess it has gone."[27] Only the letters they had exchanged while he was in England reflected their marital relationship during the past decade, but those letters had evidently laid the foundation for the revival of his affection. Though his newfound attraction for her was not too little—indeed, she was baffled by the intensity of it—it was nonetheless too late. His loving attention was inexorably bittersweet.

In September 1890, she once again accepted his invitation to Manti and was gratified that he made her "most welcome."[28] Combining her visit with Relief Society business, she spent the next two days in Mayfield attending a Relief Society conference and a session on woman suffrage. When her business was completed, she returned to Manti, "so glad to get back to my husband & be enfolded in his loving arms."[29]

25. Ibid., July 19, 1890.

26. Ibid., July 31, 1890.

27. Ibid., September 17, 1890. "Dead sea apples" are the large, green apple-shaped fruit that grows on trees most often seen in the vicinity of Israel's Dead Sea. While beautiful to see, they quickly dissolve into an ash-like substance when plucked. The phrase, as used by Emmeline, has a literary provenance, including Thomas More in "Lalla Rookh," pt. 5, which reads, "Like Dead Sea fruits, that tempt the eyes, / But turn to ashes on the lips." Lord Byron used the phrase in "Child Harold's Pilgrimage," canto 3, stanza 34: "but Life will suit/ Itself to Sorrow's most detested fruit, / Like to the apples on the Dead Sea's shore, All ashes to the taste." After visiting the Dead Sea, Mark Twain also referred to the apple in his book *The Innocents Abroad; or, The New Pilgrim's Progress*: "Nothing grows on the flat, burning desert around it but weeds and the Dead Sea apple the poets say is beautiful to the eye, but crumbles to ashes and dust when you break it." Twain, *Innocents Abroad* (Hartford: American, 1884), 446.

28. E. Wells, Diary, September 18, 1890.

29. Ibid., September 20, 1890.

The next day, Sunday, they arose "reluctantly" and breakfasted together in the hotel dining room. They risked driving together "in the same carriage" and spent the whole day together, enjoying their "social intercourse to the extreme," Emmeline recorded. They spent the evening singing and talking with the others in the hotel, and "finally when the great parlor was vacated—we had more close companionship with each other." When they visited the temple that evening, her romantic muse rose to the occasion. "The moon and stars held no vestal power—the Temple in the moon light was like a celestial Temple illuminated from on high." Emmeline was charmed by the love so effusively given her, and she gave way to all the emotions that she had tightly restrained for so long. "We had a most enchanted night," Emmeline told her diary, with "very little sleep but such exalted emotions & aspirations that we were lifted up to the regions beyond and soared as it were in the "realms of ^light^."[30] The transcendent feelings she described were all the more poignant because they had been suppressed for so long a time and now had full expression.

Daniel's entreaties persuaded her to remain for one more day. "I stayed over to see the Temple once more and be with him alone in that sweet communion we enjoy so closely together." The day was theirs to share alone. "After breakfast we drove to the magnificent building and wandered through its most beautiful rooms and gardens of enchantment. Then in his room the great elegant sleeping apartment we sat and conversed upon our most sacred themes. We read over again some of our correspondence and explained things to each other and we talked of the past the present and the future." In the completeness of their reawakened love, their "hearts were strung to the highest pitch of emotional excitement."[31]

Despite the vigor of their renewed romance, Emmeline was aware that her husband was aging rapidly and showing signs of uncharacteristic feebleness. She worried each time he made the arduous journey to and from Manti, especially during the stormy Christmas holiday that brought him back to Salt Lake City the winter of 1890. For several days before returning to Manti, he stayed with Emmeline. She gave him "an elegant book" for the temple and enjoyed their quiet visits, when they promised each other that there would be many more. Though she always had work waiting for her after their time together, she confessed that each time Daniel left for Manti, "all the first few days seem wearisome." She thought often about his situation there and wondered "how his health was and whether he was waited upon as he should be and [had] warm things prepared for him," all

30. Ibid., September 21, 1890.
31. Ibid., September 22, 1890.

the comforts, in other words, that his family provided for him when he was at home.[32]

After Daniel returned to Manti at the end of January 1891, Emmeline was preoccupied with the forthcoming triennial meeting of the National Council of Women and the annual convention of the National American Woman Suffrage Association in Washington, DC, directly afterward. Everyone expected her to attend, some saying that she could "represent the people better than most of the other ladies," but still wrapped in the aura of her reawakened love of Daniel, she admitted to herself that she would rather go to Manti than to Washington.[33] She finally relented to the constant urging by her sister suffragists, though a letter from her husband, "full of love and entreating [her] to come to him," almost dissuaded her from making the Washington trip. "O how much I should enjoy going there and doing some work for my dead and I feel it a positive duty to do so but cannot."[34] So she immersed herself in preparation for her trip to attend the two national conventions.

Since Jane Richards would attend as representative of the Relief Society, Emmeline joined several other women as delegates at large. A preliminary decision was whether to join the National Council of Women, if indeed they were invited, a discussion that frustrated Emmeline since she found it difficult "to get people to distinguish between this and the suffrage convention."[35] Finally, when the time came to leave Salt Lake City, the delegation comprised seven women: Emmeline, Jane Richards, Sarah Kimball, and Carrie Thomas of the Relief Society, and Phebe Beatie, Kate Thomas, and Electa Bullock of the YLMIA.[36] The morning after their arrival in Washington on February 20, 1891, they were summoned to the room of May Wright Sewall of the National Council of Women. The four Relief Society women presented their credentials to Sewall, who made "a clear statement of the case," acknowledging the strong opposition to Mormon membership, and then left the women to decide how they intended to proceed. After much discussion, Emmeline wrote out the final draft of their proposal for membership and carried it to Sewall, who presented it to the membership committee. After several hours of apprehension, the Utah women were relieved when Susan B. Anthony herself brought the women the good news

32. Ibid., January 6, 7, 8, 1891. During the winter of 1890 and 1891, Hannah and Martha moved into their own homes from the duplex they had shared since they left the "big house."

33. Ibid., January 22, 1891.

34. Ibid., January 27, 1891.

35. Ibid., February 4, 1891.

36. Ibid., February 16, 20, 23, 1891.

that Mormon women had been admitted to the National Council, "without a dissenting vote."[37] Once again their personal friendship with national leaders worked in their favor.

The next few days were filled with speeches, teas, receptions, sightseeing, and pleasant gatherings with other LDS people then in the capital. Bertha Honoré Palmer of Chicago, president of the Woman's Department of the World's Fair, "made her debut" before the group to incite interest in the forthcoming Columbian Exposition, a venture of much appeal to LDS women. Emmeline was invited to join more than four hundred press women at the Willard Hotel, where an International Woman's Press Association was announced. She was appointed one of seven women to prepare a constitution for the new association.[38] This organization inspired Emmeline to develop the literary interests of the women of Utah, and when she returned home, she organized a local Woman's Press Club. On the closing day of the council, Jane Richards, Carrie Thomas, and Emmeline all spoke before the large assemblage. The day was also the date on which she usually celebrated her birthday, but, she noted, "my time has been so occupied that it never occurred to me it was the day of my birth and I sixty three years old. But such it is."[39]

Most of the Utah women returned after the council meeting, but Phebe Beattie and Emmeline stayed to attend an executive meeting of the National American Woman Suffrage Association, after which they traveled to Philadelphia to meet with friends and then to New York to do some sightseeing. John W. Young willingly escorted them to plays (Sarah Bernhardt in *Camille*) and New York sites of interest.[40] Emmeline also visited her brother Hiram in Boston, where he was serving as a representative in the Massachusetts General Assembly, and made a quick trip to visit her sisters before returning home on March 19, after a month away.[41] No detail of this eventful trip had been too insignificant to be mentioned in her diary.[42]

37. Ibid., February 21, 1891.

38. Ibid., February 24, 1891.

39. Ibid., February 28, 1891.

40. They visited the graves of Phoebe and Alice Cary, popular poets of the time, and Fannie Fern, the pen name of Sarah Payson Willis Parton, who was one of the first woman newspaper columnists and the highest-paid woman writer of her time. Emmeline was familiar with the writings of all three of these authors. John Young was an apostle though not a member of the Quorum, like Daniel. This shared exclusion may have been a factor in the close affinity between Emmeline and John, who later resigned from the Quorum.

41. In Hiram's obituaries the term is either "Legislature" or "General Assembly." The official name of the legislature was the Massachusetts General Court, but that title does not appear in Emmeline's diary.

42. Whenever Emmeline traveled, she continued to write the editorials for her

After settling back into "my old Rookery the Owl's nest," Emmeline learned that Daniel had returned from Manti and was then lying very ill at Hannah's home on A Street. She was shocked to hear the news, and when Daniel's son Lewis informed her that his father "wanted to see me, and was very much disappointed that I had not been to see him," she was overcome with anxiety. "O, how I wanted to go then that very night, but what reason had I for going only impulse which we should sometimes follow. I restrained it and did not go as I ought to have done and lo, what were the feelings of my soul. That I must go—must fly to him."[43] The next morning she did just that and was alarmed to discover how sick he was. Though weak in body, Daniel was very lucid. He was eager to hear about her trip to Washington and learned that she had sent several letters to him, which he had evidently not yet seen. He then gave her two letters he had written to her but had not mailed. "He was more than delighted to see me," she joyfully discovered. "He could not restrain the expressions of his tenderness." His professions of love were nonetheless embarrassing to her, a feeling she always had when being feted or complimented, and she was not sure how to react to them with others nearby. She left after a short visit but returned to his bedside that afternoon. "I would not I could not leave him. I have never loved any one before as I love him, and I must stay whatever the consequences may be," she confided to her diary. Martha joined her in caring for him throughout the night.[44] Once, during the long hours, Daniel asked Emmeline if Martha was sleeping, but she was not. "I realized he has something to say to me, but wanted us to be alone.... [H]e seemed very disappointed!" His words remained unsaid, and Emmeline was left forever curious and disappointed.[45]

When she finally realized that Daniel would not recover, she sent an urgent message to Annie and then went to Ogden to help her bring the children to see their grandfather. They arrived in a dreary rainstorm that matched their already gray mood. Though many of the brethren administered to him with oil and the laying on of hands, promising him life, she could not understand their faith in doing so. "It did not seem to me that there was any promise of life."[46] Although she shrank from this thought, she was prepared for what she knew was inevitable.

---

paper, leaving Annie and various volunteers the logistics of putting it together and preparing the copies for mailing. She may also have left some poems or other articles for inclusion in the paper before she left home. Her travels, however, were certainly a factor in the persistent tardiness of the issues.

43. Ibid., March 20, 1891.

44. Ibid., March 21, 1891.

45. Ibid., March 22, 1891.

46. Ibid., March 23, 1891. At least seven others named general authorities and several unnamed individuals administered to him.

All five of Daniel's wives stayed with him his final night, answering his every need. "O, how sure I felt that the end was near, that my own darlings were there watching for him. O, my Louie I heard your angel-voice singing the grand anthem of release." Annie and John Q. came to him the next morning, and at Daniel's request John Q. administered to him, "the last one to perform this sacred ordinance." Finally, at one o'clock that afternoon, Daniel breathed his last "in peace and grandeur," Emmeline observed. Many were in the room with him during that transition. "Such a trying ordeal for us," Emmeline lamented, "but O, such a glorious entrance into the celestial world for him. It seems more like a dream than aught else."[47]

When she returned to her own home, she wanted desperately to be alone, but the visitors began arriving in droves. She could hardly find words. "I feel as though the most terrific storm would give some outward expression to my inward emotions," she wrote. The next day was also miserable for her. She chose not to go to the house where he lay in his coffin, preferring the solitude of her own place. Yet she wanted to be near him, even in death. "If he were only here, where I could even look upon his dead face, it would seem a comfort," she wrote, "but no, only memories, only the coming and going and parting at the door, the joy when he came the sorrow when he went as though all the light died out of my life." In so few poignant words, Emmeline summed up her life with Daniel and, unconsciously, the plight of every plural wife who loved her husband as Emmeline loved Daniel. The "coming and the going and parting at the door"—what a doleful reflection of the ebb and flow of emotion from an unnatural fusing of two people's lives. Love in polygamy? Oh, yes. But in its own time and season for Emmeline. She never fully assimilated the intensity of his late-blooming love for her. "Such a remarkable change from the long ago—when I needed him so much more, how peculiarly these things come about."[48]

A few days before the funeral, Emmeline went to the house where Daniel lay to spend a few moments alone with him. Again she mused over the irreversible incidents that had punctuated her life. "I am not prepared for all the changes that come into my life," she lamented, and admitted that "we do 'rebel and shrink,' when we ought to be submissive."[49] Wishing she could write all that was in her "heart of hearts," she for once could not. "My soul," she explained, "is in the depths of sorrow and I cannot lift up my head and heart as I ought and bear the great burden imposed upon me with the heroism I should like." But she would prove, as she had so often before, that

47. Ibid., March 24, 25, 1891. All of his surviving wives were with him at the last, as were several of his children and some friends.

48. Ibid., March 26, 1891.

49. Ibid., March 27, 1891.

she could indeed display the heroism that enabled her to avoid rebelling and shrinking from the burdens laid upon her. She had experienced loss after loss in her life, but she had not become weak or bitter. She attacked life with all her strength, and it yielded up small victories she did not always see during the emotional crises that beset her. As she looked on Daniel's mortal remains for the last time, she pondered the separation of his body and spirit, the spirit "gone to Joseph [Smith] & the loved ones behind the vail [*sic*]," and to those who remained it seemed to her that he was somehow still with them in the room where his body lay at rest.[50]

She tried to stay home that evening but discovered that she could "no longer keep within bounds" and "flew as it were to the house where he was, and joined the group assembled there. How cold and formal and dismal it all seemed. I longed to cry out in my anguish of spirit, 'come back, come back! and speak to me for a moment; tell me what you longed to when I came home give me the message you had for me, that you spoke of.'"[51]

The newspapers wrote extensively of Daniel's death and funeral, including a life sketch and a rehearsal of the funeral proceedings in the tabernacle. Family members sat directly across from the pure white casket mounted in silver. It was blanketed by a large bouquet of white flowers and surmounted by a snow-white dove. The hall was described as being "most imposing," without a single "vestige of black" anywhere to be seen. "The platform, stands and railings were hung in graceful draperies of white," made of delicate cashmere, and "great white folds were suspended between the pipes of the organ, separated near the bottom in curtain fashion," revealing a large portrait of Daniel, framed in white. The drapes were held back with white satin ribbon and edged with white tassels.[52] With white flowers stationed on the stand, the stairway, and every available setting, the tabernacle radiated the hope of the Resurrection—the funeral was held on Easter Sunday.

A solemn melody rose mournfully from the organ, which was surrounded by a profusion of Easter lilies. Counselor George Q. Cannon conducted the services, and church president Wilford Woodruff was the principal speaker, followed by several apostles. The tabernacle choir sang

50. Ibid., March 27, 28, 1891.

51. Ibid., March 28, 1891. See also March 26, 27, 29, 30, 1891.

52. "Daniel H. Wells," *Salt Lake Herald*, March 25, 1891 (Journal History, March 25, 1891, 5); "Daniel H. Wells," *Deseret Evening News*, March 28, 1891 (Journal History, March 28, 1891, 2–4); "A White Funeral," *Deseret Evening News*, March 28, 1891 (Journal History, March 30, 1892, 6); "Imposing Ceremonies," *Deseret Evening News*, March 29, 1891 (Journal History, March 30, 1891, 2–5); "Dust to Dust: Funeral of Daniel H. Wells," *Salt Lake Herald*, March 29, 1891 (Journal History, March 29, 1891, 8–9). Zina D.H. Young, Mary Isabella Horne, and Henry Dinwoodey were responsible for the decorations.

music that it had performed at Louie's funeral four years earlier. Emmeline listened numbly to the organ pealing its "requiem for the dead." This sudden deprivation, like the others before it, tried her stoic will to its limit. "The lessons are very hard ones sometimes," she well knew, "...and we are weak and frail & yield when we ought to be strong and invincible."[53] Accepting God's plan, which demanded submissiveness, ultimately conquered her weakness and fortified her at these critical times.

The long procession of carriages wended its way slowly in a pouring rain along the road from the tabernacle to the city cemetery. Emmeline, like many other mourners, stayed in her carriage instead of descending to stand at the graveside. A quartet sang, after which Apostle Francis M. Lyman dedicated the grave. Then it was over. A *Deseret Evening News* account of the services concluded with a long poetic tribute submitted to the paper the morning of the funeral. "It is a fitting termination to the account of the obsequies," the article noted. One verse, particularly, summarized the general character of Counselor Wells:

He worked for God, for truth, and humankind,
He gave his strength to this, his life, his all;
So Israel in their deepest heart enshrined,
And drowned with love this consecrated soul.[54]

The April 1 edition of the *Woman's Exponent* also printed the unsigned poetic tribute, entitled "The Departed Leader!," and identified the author as Henry W. Naisbitt, a local poet of some renown. It also carried poems by three women poets in tribute to Daniel: "A Tribute of Sympathy," by Emily H. Woodmansee; "Song of Triumph," by L. L. D. (Lucinda Lee Dalton); and "President Wells," by Lula (Louisa Greene Richards).[55] Emmeline published her own prose tribute on the editorial page, "In Memoriam," in which she echoed many of the sentiments expressed at the funeral while adding some of her own. "Language fails to give expression to the heart when such a man passes away," she wrote. "Many have been the sentiments of love, affection and esteem spoken and written of him since his death, faithful tributes to his memory, and he deserved them all. He was *beloved* by the people, and he loved *them* truly."[56]

Her private reflections indicated that this test of faith and acceptance had been "dreadful." But she found solace in knowing that "they have met,

53. E. Wells, Diary, March 27, 1891.

54. "Imposing Ceremonies," *Deseret Evening News*, March 30, 1891; Journal History, March 30, 1891, 5.

55. *Woman's Exponent* 19 (April 1, 1891): 145, 147.

56. Ibid., 148–50.

father and daughter. And to me," she added, "how significant must that meeting be." For herself she declared in a passion of grief and the abandonment of the hard-won reserve that had carried her through most of her marriage, "My whole soul was bound up in him. He possessed the key to the mysteries of my nature."[57]

It would be six months before Emmeline wrote her own poetic tribute to Daniel, though never mentioning his name. It appeared in the *Woman's Exponent* under the title "A Fragment," signed only with her initials. It was Emmeline's personal, poetic, and unapologetic testimony of her love for Daniel. Its setting is the night that Emmeline sat with Daniel before his death and expresses the thoughts that filled her mind in the silence of the room. It begins, "I only take my hand in thine, and all my pulses thrill to thee; / An indefinable, transporting joy, which lifts my soul in ecstacy." Then follow several long, descriptive verses of imagined scenes, swirling in her mind as she sat by his bedside:

Thus wrapt with silence as a mantle round my soul, thoughts come and go,
And answ'ring echoes from the distant past seem rippling soft and low;
And all the while I feel the magic touch
That brings such harmony of sight and sound.
And charity and love my bosom swell,
With that intensity no tongue can tell,
And thy bright presence vivifies the spell—
And I am treading on enchanted ground.

But then again, death takes away the source of her delight.

Thou'rt gone! the vision's fled, and moon and stars are dull, and sober night
Reigns all around in darken'd robes, and mocks as 'twere my lost delight;
And then some pitying angel softly speaks:
'Mortal 't was but a glimpse of love and heaven,
Back now to earth and thorny paths again,
Stern duty holds thee with a tightened rein,
Plod on and strive some vict'ry to obtain,
And love eternal will to thee be given.[58]

57. E. Wells, Diary, April 8, 1891. Emmeline also noted that this was the thirteenth anniversary of Emmie's death, which occurred almost at the same time of year as Daniel's.

58. "A Fragment," *Woman's Exponent* 20 (September 1, 1891): 35. The *Exponent* version uses "magic touch," while the *Musings and Memories* version uses "mystic touch." See E. Wells, *Musings and Memories*, 116–18. Another expression of a wife's love of her husband, presumably hers of Daniel, is "The Wife to Her Husband," undated but written before his death. See E. Wells, *Musings and Memories*, 270–71.

The words were plainspoken expressions of her life with and after Daniel. Her obeisance to duty, of her own and others' making, had become the pattern of her life. She would follow it still. With Daniel's death she had come to the end of a mercurial chapter in her life, and she mourned him deeply. "I have tried to be brave and keep above despondency & not be wholly useless in the midst of sorrow," she explained to her diary just weeks after the funeral.[59] This pronouncement would be one of the last expressions of sadness at this, her third marital loss. Few diary remembrances, few evocations of emotional turmoil, and few references to their life together would again grace her diary. Absent in person, Daniel would be absent in her daily chronicle. Affairs of the heart would give way to matters of the mind.

Emmeline lived thirty more years, a thrice-widowed woman at sixty-three, left in each instance on her own by three men designated by law, religion, and custom to be her "provider and protector" and one her eternal companion. She would recruit her resources and face those years with vigor, focus, and a determination to write the final chapter of her romance with new characters and story lines and an unforgettable ending.

59. E. Wells, Diary, April 9, 1891.

CHAPTER 26

Expanding Horizons
(1891–1893)

Daniel Wells had been the dominant focus of Emmeline's life for most of the thirty-nine years of their marriage. Their reunion during the last three years of their life together relieved much of the pain and resentment that had burdened Emmeline for so long. But it also added depth to her sorrow at his passing. "O," she wrote a few months after his death, "how can I hide my great grief always."[1] But she did not engage in repeated mournful expressions, as she had after the deaths of her daughters, having finally found a measure of peace in her oscillating relationship with Daniel.[2]

Though she was ever a defender of plural marriage, Emmeline was no stranger to its challenges. A few months after the 1887 Edmunds-Tucker antipolygamy law was passed, she foresaw its consequences. "O how hard it is for us all but especially for women in the order of plural marriage young and inexperienced how my heart aches for them."[3] While she herself had come to terms with the legal and familial effects of the new law, she worried for her daughter Belle and others of Belle's generation who had entered the practice. "The law places so many restrictions upon them and the social claim is very indistinct and indefinite," she observed. "Therefore," she believed, "the best way is to lay hold of whatever legitimate possession

1. E. Wells, Diary, August 31, 1891.

2. Only four entries in her diary contain references to Daniel after his death. During a visit to the Manti temple, she noted how the room they had shared in the Temple Hotel had been rearranged (ibid., February 24, 1892); she mentioned the one-year anniversary of her visit to him upon her return from the East shortly before his death (March 19, 1892) and a month later referred again to his passing: "One year ago and we had just been deprived of our loved one; how long ago it seems to me—such a tedious year it has been and some times I feel as though I could not submit to the separation" (April 1, 1892). Later that year, she noted details of their marriage forty years earlier in the adobe structure in which she was then living (October 10, 1892).

3. Ibid., August 4, 1887.

one may with propriety accept," an economically sound strategy that had eluded her for many years in her own marriage. "I hope the conditions of plural wives will be better ere long," she wrote. "Heaven help them and give grace and strength equal to our day."[4]

Emmeline kept herself well apprised of the numerous cases being litigated in the courts relating to the provisions of the Edmunds-Tucker Act and condemned the confiscation of church property and assets as injurious to an innocent people.[5] Wilford Woodruff's 1890 Manifesto had its own dramatic effect on church members, and Emmeline observed that within a month after the proclamation, people were "observing the law in its strictest sense and avoid[ing] prosecution," though some arrests were still being made. "This is the tendency of all the preaching nowadays," she noted, "and there can be no opportunity for married men to increase their families. All must remaein [*sic*] as they are." Being one of the earliest to engage in the practice, she was especially sensitive to the change and found the new order "peculiar" after living the principle for more than forty years.[6]

The Woman's Press Club became a satisfying redirection of her attention. She was astonished when the February 1892 meeting, only a few months after its organization, became a surprise birthday party for her sixty-fourth birthday. "I found poems, presents and refreshments had been brought and I received the greatest ovation of my whole life from the ladies present, and I was completely overwhelmed," Emmeline recounted afterward.[7] Determined to eradicate any undeserved pride over the unexpected tribute, she tried at church the next day to gain back "a balance of some sort" after the "great respect of the previous evening," hoping to receive guidance and protection from the "evil" of pride. "I tried to draw in the wanderings of my mind and center them upon divine subjects." After the church service she used poetry to express her resolve to store her "treasures in heaven" and "follow where Christ shall lead."[8] Her poetry was often a dialogue with

4. Ibid., March 7, 1890. The results of the Edmunds-Tucker Act were indeed severe on plural wives, who had no legal claims on their husbands' property or other possessions if their husbands died intestate. See C. Madsen, "'At Their Peril.'"

5. "The Church Property Question," *Woman's Exponent* 19 (June 15, 1890): 12. The editorial acknowledges the grievous condition of the Saints but promises that "in the Providence of God all will be made right, and those who endure will come off more than conquerers [*sic*] notwithstanding the severe ordeal they may have to pass through, for has He not said they shall be as gold seven times purified."

6. E. Wells, Diary, October 9, 1890.

7. Ibid., February 27, 1892.

8. "To Bereaved Mothers," *Woman's Exponent* 20 (May 1, 1892): 153, published as "A Bereaved Mother," in her *Musings and Memories*, 41–42.

herself, cajoling, reminding, encouraging, sympathizing, and promising that God rewarded the faithful.

One task she at last felt able to do was to select a marker for Louie's grave, five years after her death. She and John Q. chose "a pretty Italian marble scroll" with only her name inscribed on it. "It is the last we can do for her except to go and carry flowers as our heart's best tribute of love and memory," an errand Emmeline seldom neglected to do.[9] Later, she was asked to prepare the record Louie had kept while she was general secretary of the YLMIA for the organization's files and history. "It cost me a pang of grief to handle it and to pass it into other hands," she confessed. "My darling Louie's 'work.'"[10]

Her first good news after Daniel's death was the decision of Belle and Septimus to return to Salt Lake City after five years in San Francisco. They moved into a house on M Street in the Avenues that offered a fine view of the city from its second floor. With the spreading use of electricity, the city at night, Emmeline discovered as she viewed the scene from Belle's home, "looks like a fairy picture dotted all over with electric lights, etc."[11]

One issue clouded their homecoming, however. Septimus had earlier pledged to abide by the requirements of the Edmunds-Tucker Act and had lived only with Belle since then.[12] Upon his return from San Francisco, he and his first wife, Mary Ann Needham, made their separation permanent by divorce. Although Emmeline was upset by the necessity of another divorce in her family, she was eventually persuaded that it was best.[13] After the divorce was finalized, Septimus and Belle were married in Emmeline's home on April 11, 1892, by Bishop Nelson A. Empey "according to the law of the land," thus legalizing their marriage.[14] Septimus was soon employed by the

9. E. Wells, Diary, May 18, 1892.

10. Ibid., July 4, 1892.

11. Ibid., July 31, 1891. Electrical service had come to the largest cities in Utah in 1881, with businesses, streets, and public buildings among the first to be connected. Not until 1890, however, was electrical service stabilized enough to be constant and reliable.

12. James B. Allen, "'Good Guys' vs. 'Good Guys': Civil Disobedience in Nineteenth Century Utah."

13. E. Wells, Diary, March 5, 8, 24, 1892.

14. A plural wife could not assume the legality of a monogamous wife even if the first, or legal, wife was deceased, since plural marriages were not recognized as legal at the outset. While the church recognized the original polygamous marriage of Septimus and Belle, the court did not, and it was necessary for a licensed clergyman to perform the ceremony. For more information about the position of plural wives after the Edmunds-Tucker Act of 1887, see C. Madsen, "'At Their Peril.'"

Salt Lake Chamber of Commerce, for whom he traveled frequently. He was also elected to the legislature. Belle's return was of immense reassurance to Emmeline. "I have Belle near me to be a comfort," Emmeline wrote, "and she does everything in her power to help make my life more easy."[15] Their shared care of Louie had linked Belle and Emmeline in a distinctive mother-daughter way, and Belle had always been a dependable caregiver to her mother in a quiet, homely, mothering manner that was different from that of her efficient, busy, public-spirited sister Annie, who was so much more like her mother than Belle.

Mell's situation, however, was a different matter. Emmeline respected Mell for her decisiveness, her intelligence, her talents, and her ambitions, but her withdrawal from the church was a persistent ache. She and Mell often had spirited discussions about her disaffection, and though it strained their relationship, they remained constant in their attachment to and concern for one another. Emmeline's first visit to the rough mining towns of northern Idaho intrigued her and gave her a sense of Mell's life there, and three years after her first visit, she was ready to make another trip to Idaho. This time it would be to Wallace, which was now Mell's home. For a month, Emmeline basked in the company of her daughter and her family.[16]

As aspiring members of their community, Mell and Will attended the Episcopal Church, and Will became both an Elk and a Mason, while Mell was active in suffrage and literary circles. It was not long before they became leaders in the community. Active in politics as well as the law, Will was elected district judge in 1906, a position he retained until his death in 1920.

Before leaving Idaho, Emmeline learned of the death of her granddaughter Eleanor, the fifth of Annie's children. Now all of her married daughters had endured losses so familiar to her. Belle's first two children lay in graves as well as three of Mell's and three of their mother's and now one of Annie's. The cemetery held unfulfilled dreams of all four women.

About a year after Belle's return to Utah, Annie also returned from Ogden. In 1892, Orson F. Whitney requested help with his 1890 commission to write a history of Utah, which was to be published by George Q. Cannon and Sons, and Abraham Cannon arranged to assign John Q. to be Whitney's

15. E. Wells, Diary, May 16, 1892.

16. Emmeline recounts the visit day by day in her diary from August 19 to September 12, 1892. At the back of the 1892 diary, she includes a lengthy and detailed memorandum that lists her expenses for each month. See Cash Account, August, September, ibid., addendum, 1892. See also "Pines, Mines, and Stage Lines," *Woman's Exponent* 21 (September 15, 1892): 44–45, for a description of her travels.

assistant. This new opportunity necessitated his and Annie's return to Salt Lake City that fall.[17] The Cannons bought a house on the southeast corner of Third East and what is now Sherman Avenue (1320 South). "They will be near me, and I shall feel so much better," Emmeline wrote.[18] After a year in the Avenues, Belle and Septimus moved to the Waterloo area south of the city to a permanent residence that they named Thorndike House, the name of the town where Hiram lived in Massachusetts.

Emmeline did not expect to ever have another home of her own, but in the spring of 1893, it appeared that her years in the old adobe structure behind the wall were drawing to an end.[19] The thousand-dollar settlement from Daniel's will enabled her to hire an architect to build a home on property that had once been Squire Wells's farm, within a block of Belle's home in Waterloo and not far from Annie's. Construction continued throughout the summer and fall, and by November it was ready for occupancy.[20] "A new house all things different," Emmeline mused on her first night in her new home, "a new phase of life in some respects, and yet the old is ever present and hangs like a shroud around us go where we may." It would take time for the new house to develop the welcoming warmth of her first home. There would be far fewer events to store up as sweet memories in the new house, yet she was happy to be out of the dwelling that had stifled her longings for peace and solitary moments to rest, ponder, and write. Though removed from the center of town and all its activities, this new home would prove to be an effective antidote to the lingering resentment at the loss of her first home. Of most pleasure to Emmeline was the vista from her bedroom

17. A. H. Cannon, Diary, January 17, 18, 1892, in *Apostle's Record*, edited by Horne, 227–28.

18. E. Wells, Diary, October 2, 1892.

19. The previous December, evidently in anticipation of moving from the place that had been her home and workplace for seven years, Emmeline published an editorial reflecting on the historical value of the adobe house she would soon be leaving. It had seen much history making within its walls. The leading men of the church and community had made plans and decisions of long-lasting import there. Officers of the women's organizations had often met in its rooms, and visitors from across the country and abroad had been entertained in this simple pioneer structure. The "romance of this old place," Emmeline explained, "is greatly enhanced by the many poems and stories written here." "We all like to know not only what transpired in the past," Emmeline suggested, "but the feelings, affections and sentiments of those who took part in the affairs of the times in which they lived and flourished." The poetry written in that home, she asserted, provided the "history of the heart." "A Historic House," *Woman's Exponent* 21 (December 15, 1892): 92.

20. Emmeline's home was located at 429 Westminster Avenue between Fourth and Fifth East.

window on the second floor of the house. One section of the bay window opened to the southeast, giving an unobstructed view of the mountains and brought rays of sunlight into the small room. Often, as she awoke in the morning, she watched the sun rising over the mountains, "kissing the hilltops." "I do enjoy my sleeping room," she wrote; "it is a very handsome and comfortable chamber."[21]

In time, as her furnishings arrived, especially her piano, she welcomed their familiarity, and she looked forward to the dedication of her home by Ort, or "the Bishop," as she referred to Orson F. Whitney since his call as bishop of the Eighteenth Ward. The dedication took place on Saturday, February 10, 1894, a stormy day that kept some of her friends away. But neither their absence nor the weather dampened the spirit of the occasion. The bishop toured the house before offering the dedicatory prayer and then offered a blessing on each of its parts. Though some curtains had not yet been hung, Emmeline was pleased at how handsome her parlor appeared, with her piano, bookcase, music stand, and easel in place; her best pictures on the walls; and a large Japanese pitcher of red and white carnations on the desk. Following the dedication, refreshments were served, the bishop sang, and Emmie (Belle's daughter) played several pieces on the piano. That evening Emmeline recounted to her diary the blessings that the bishop promised to her in the prayer.[22] Amid her days of weariness and relentless melancholy, this was a day made bright with hope. Always a reader, Emmeline now added the practice of reading a chapter in the Bible before leaving her home each morning. "It gives me more courage for the day," she believed.[23] It had long been a source of many of her literary allusions.

Almost immediately after her move to her new home in Waterloo, the old adobe house and the familiar wall that ran in front of it were razed, and she was obliged to find a new office. She selected a second-story room in the Constitution Building on Main Street that would remain headquarters of the *Woman's Exponent* for four years. Fortunately, her new home was conveniently located near a trolley line, making it easy for her to travel to her office each day.

Emmeline's editorial work, her membership in the Pacific Coast and National Woman's Press Associations, and her organizing skills and success brought her to the attention of the planners of the National Editorial

21. E. Wells, Diary, February 1, March 3, 1894.
22. Ibid., February 10, 1894.
23. Ibid., February 21, 1894.

Association's convention, scheduled for May 1892 in San Francisco. She received a special invitation to a reception at the Hotel Pleasanton for "Ladies of the Press," which doubled her desire to attend the convention.

After acquiring the means to do so, Emmeline eagerly prepared for the forthcoming convention. When she was "set apart" by a priesthood blessing to do well whatever lay ahead for her, she felt fortified for this new experience.[24] Familiar with the spirited yet decorous conduct of women in the many conventions she had attended, she was disconcerted with the behavior of men in their shared meetings. "Such a hurrah as the men were making was something unusual for me, the shouting, cheering & applauding were terrific in the extreme." She found "the confusion was more than one wanted to hear."[25] But this distraction did not diminish the pleasure she felt at being with her professional peers. A large group of them visited Salt Lake City after the convention, arriving earlier than expected. Emmeline immediately filled in the extra time by arranging an organ recital on Temple Square and a walk around the outer parapet of the temple for a view of the city. So many wanted to visit her office that she had to arrange two different meetings. Being in the company of knowledgeable, experienced, and ambitious individuals always invigorated Emmeline.[26]

Even as she basked in the acceptance by her journalism peers, Emmeline became deeply involved in another extensive project that captured not only her time but also her interest: preparations for a display at the forthcoming Columbian Exposition planned for the summer of 1893 in Chicago. The creation of a Woman's Department within the administration of the exposition, with a separate Board of Lady Managers, ensured female representation at the grand celebration of Columbus's arrival in the New World and America's growth as a nation. Local Boards of Lady Managers were organized in every state and territory, with representatives from each

24. It was customary for those who had special assignments or responsibilities to ask for a priesthood "blessing," which involved the laying on of hands by someone holding priesthood authority. Emmeline always requested a blessing before attending national meetings. In this case, she was "set apart" by George Q. Cannon, meaning set apart for the role she would play on whatever level at the forthcoming convention. Ibid., May 19, 1892.

25. Ibid., May 26, 1892.

26. Ibid., May 18–June 3, 1892. Emmeline wrote about her experience in San Francisco in "In and about San Francisco," *Woman's Exponent* 20 (June 1, 1892): 172; "This, That, and the Other," *Woman's Exponent* 20 (June 15, 1892): 180; and "The Men and Women We Met in San Francisco," *Woman's Exponent* 20 (June 15, 1892): 180. Following the national convention, Emmeline met with the members of the Pacific Coast Woman's Press Association with whom she was well acquainted.

constituting the national board under the supervision of Bertha Honoré Palmer, a wealthy and prominent society leader in Chicago.[27]

To display the industrial, artistic, and domestic achievements of American women, the board commissioned a Woman's Building, designed by architect Sophia Hayden and decorated with paintings and statuary by women artists.[28] The Columbian Exposition, or World's Fair, as it came to be known, not only provided a showcase for women's industrial and artistic accomplishments but also offered an arena to demonstrate the connection between the public work of women and their social advancement. The message of the fair was that collective action gave women a larger share in the "work of the world" and a distinct role in shaping it.[29] This was of great appeal to Emmeline Wells.

Governor Arthur Thomas was enthusiastic about Utah's participation and appointed two non-LDS women to the national board: Alice J. Whalen of Ogden and Margaret Blaine Salisbury, niece of former secretary of state and presidential candidate James G. Blaine and a personal friend of Bertha Palmer. The governor also appointed Emily S. Richards to head the territorial Board of Lady Managers.[30]

27. Born in Louisville, Kentucky, in 1849, Bertha Honoré married Chicago millionaire Potter Palmer in 1871 and used her considerable wealth to advance women's interests. She was a well-known philanthropist and club woman in Chicago and used her position as president of the Board of Lady Managers to expand the presence and influence of women at the Columbian Exposition. Traveling to Europe, she interested many other influential women in the exposition, intending to make it a showpiece of women's achievements.

28. A complete account of women's role in the Columbian Exposition can be found in Jeanne Madeline Weimann, *The Fair Women*. See also Reid L. Neilson, *Exhibiting Mormonism: The Latter-day Saints and the 1893 Chicago World's Fair*; and Andrea G. Radke-Moss, "Mormon Women, Suffrage and Citizenship at the 1893 Chicago World's Fair." Months after the close of the exposition, Mell sent her mother an article for her paper entitled "Personal Impressions of Art at the Columbian Exposition," *Woman's Exponent* 22 (March 1, 1894): 97–99; and 22 (March 15, 1894): 105–7. Rather than identifying herself as author, Mell used the pen name "Edahoo," an easily construed play on the name of her home state, Idaho.

29. Gayle Gullett explores these ideas in "The Political Use of Public Space: The Women's Movement and Women's Participation at the Chicago Columbian Exposition, 1893." See also Gullett, "Our Great Opportunity: Organized Women Advance Women's Work at the World Columbian Exposition of 1893." A contemporary account is Enid Yandell's "To the Board of Lady Managers."

30. Margaret Salisbury appealed to the Utah Legislature for an appropriation of one hundred thousand dollars to ascertain "the condition of industrial women, their productions and earnings, whether in the studio, counting house, schoolroom, factory, mill, dairy, or the farm." She urged the legislature to allow Utah women the opportunity "to meet their sisters of the different States and Territories in a

Against her better judgment, Emmeline succumbed to the appeal of Margaret Salisbury and Emily Richards to head Salt Lake County's Board of Lady Managers. She had previously rebuffed the invitation, feeling that "it is right to refuse. It will be a great labor and I have already too much to do."[31] But in July 1892, Emmeline received a letter from Bertha Palmer, also requesting her help, and by September she was on board as chair of the Salt Lake County Board of Lady Managers. Almost immediately, Emmeline regretted her decision to take on this new responsibility. "One gets heaped up under the load and can scarcely extricate herself," she realized. "It is not good to undertake so much as I have undertaken."[32]

In her positions as secretary of the Relief Society and chair of the Salt Lake County Board of Lady Managers and editor of a semimonthly newspaper, Emmeline was truly inundated with work, either presiding over countless meetings and writing letters or making visits to various workers in the county. She was now experiencing the extent of the responsibilities she had agreed to bear. "I am always so busy," she lamented, "with so many committees to be looked after."[33] Nevertheless, she found the county meetings in the old federal courtrooms to be among the largest over which she had presided and discovered they were "not half so hard as being secretary for an Association."[34]

In addition to holding regular committee meetings of the county board throughout the early part of 1893, Emmeline was involved in editing a pamphlet, *Charities and Philanthropies: Women's Work in Utah*, and providing statistics for the National Board of Lady Managers relating to Utah women's employment, legal status, clubs and societies, reform and philanthropic work, and notable achievements.[35] She also edited a beautifully arranged, large coffee-table book of poetry by local poets, with accompanying pastel watercolor paintings by Edna Wells Sloan, *Songs and Flowers of the Wasatch*, which was dedicated to Margaret Salisbury. Emmeline assisted in preparing another volume, *World's Fair Ecclesiastical History of Utah*, consisting of contributions by representatives of all the religious denominations in Utah,

manner highly creditable to the energy, intelligence and talent which characterize the women of the West." Though "able," the appeal did not bring the desired results. "An Able Appeal: Women in the World's Fair," *Woman's Exponent* 20 (March 1, 1892): 125–26. See also "Women in the World's Fair," *Woman's Exponent* 20 (September 1, 1891): 36; and E. A. McDaniel, *Utah at the World's Columbian Exposition*, 73.

31. E. Wells, Diary, July 7, 1892.

32. Ibid., December 16, 1891.

33. Ibid., November 10, 1892.

34. Ibid., January 10, 1893.

35. Weimann, *The Fair Women*, 381; "Information Wanted, for the World's Fair," *Woman's Exponent* 21 (August 1, 1892): 24.

edited by Sarah M. Kimball. Twelve Utah women submitted their books to the library of women authors in the Woman's Building, including the anti-Mormon novels of Jennie Froiseth and Cornelia Paddock and several books by Eliza R. Snow and other Mormon poets.[36] Under Emmeline's direction, Columbian Clubs were organized throughout the county to enlist the help of talented women in preparing exhibits for both the Woman's and the Utah Buildings.

In April 1893, as the exposition was about to begin, a grand Columbia Ball was held in Salt Lake City to raise funds for the women's exhibits. Two of Belle's daughters, Dot and Lucile, attended with Emmeline. The proceeds helped the county meet the request to furnish curtains for the Woman's Building. County women made the pale-cream silk drapes, embroidered with sego lilies (later the state flower), that eventually graced the main hall of the building. All who passed under them, Emmeline mused, would likely be surprised that they were made by Utah women. Salt Lake County women also donated to the Utah Building elegant portieres made of Utah broadcloth lined with silk and embroidered with the sego lily.[37] With Margaret Salisbury's solicitation and persistence, Utah women were able to secure the funds to mount an exhibition in the Woman's Building of the entire silk-making process. Salisbury appointed Isabella Bennett to chair the project, with Emmeline as vice chair, assisted by Corinne Allen, Zina D. H. Young, and Margaret A. Caine as secretary.[38] With virtually no capital, only "the active energy and enterprise" of willing women, their contribution, all agreed, made "a creditable showing" of Utah products.

Of most importance to Emmeline was the weeklong Woman's Congress held at the beginning of the exposition.[39] Women's associations throughout the world were invited to participate, including the Relief Society and the Young Ladies' Mutual Improvement Association, both members of the International Council of Women, which sponsored the Woman's Congress.

36. The other authors were Hannah T. King, Augusta J. Crocheron, Mary Jane Tanner, Romania B. Pratt, Mrs. W. S. McCornick, Mary E. Almy, Emily B. Spencer, Hannah Cornaby, and Sarah E. Carmichael. "Editorial Notes," *Woman's Exponent* 21 (April 15–May 1, 1893): 156.

37. "Editorial Notes" and "The Silk Industry," *Woman's Exponent* 21 (April 1, 1893): 148. Both articles give a full description of the furnishings, and the materials of which they were made that adorned the Utah building and the names of the committee members. See also McDaniel, *Utah at the World's Columbian Exposition*, 88; and "The Silk Industry," *Woman's Exponent* 21 (April 1, 1893): 148.

38. "To the Women of Utah," Journal History, April 17, 1892, 4. See also in the Journal History "Conference of Charities," February 2, 1893, 8; "The Woman's Congress," April 3, 1893, 4; and "Woman's Great Work," May 25, 1893, 4, and October 3, 1893, 4.

39. "World's Congress Auxiliary of the World's Columbian Exposition."

As one of the representatives of the Relief Society, Emmeline was heavily engaged in preparing the paper she would deliver, assisting the printing of circulars, and selecting delegates. It was an exhausting but exhilarating time.[40]

After intensive months of preparation, Emmeline left Salt Lake City on May 10 for a month's stay in Chicago. Only weeks earlier, she had taken on the taxing task of moving her office from the adobe house on South Temple to the Constitution Building while also preparing an editorial relating to the April dedication of the Salt Lake Temple forty years in the making and dedicated only a month before the opening of the exposition.[41] Though exhausted when she arrived in Chicago, but realizing she was actually in the "great city of the World's Fair," she roused with the excitement of the grand celebration. Adding to her pleasure was her move from the visitors' dormitory to the Palmer House in downtown Chicago, the storied hotel owned by Bertha Palmer and her husband, Potter.[42]

Emmeline attended most of the weeklong meetings of the Woman's Congress and the teas and receptions offered by different women's organizations, all of which enabled her to add to her long list of acquaintances and correspondents, including May Wright Sewall, president of the National Council of Women, and Ellen M. Henrotin, a former president of the National Federation of Women's Clubs. She also met many foreign women representatives, whom she would see again at the next International Council of Women meeting in London.[43]

40. E. Wells, Diary, April 18, 1893.

41. "The Salt Lake Temple," *Woman's Exponent* 21 (March 1, 1893): 132; "Temple Dedication," *Woman's Exponent* 21 (April 15–May 1, 1893), 156.

42. E. Wells, Diary, May 12, 14, 1893.

43. Besides keeping her own personal daily account (May 8–June 16), Emmeline sent home editorials and articles on the people she met and events she attended at the exposition that provide a detailed account of her experiences there. Overviews of the congress from Emmeline's viewpoint are "World's Congress of Women," *Woman's Exponent* 21 (June 1, 1893): 172–73; "Editorial Notes: The Utah Room," *Woman's Exponent* 21 (April 1, 1893): 148; "Only a Glance," *Woman's Exponent* 21 (June 1, 1892): 173; and "Luncheon at the Richelieu," *Woman's Exponent* 21 (June 1, 1893): 173–74. Emmeline carefully noted many of the US and foreign women who attended the congress, some of whom are listed in "Noted Women at the Congress," *Woman's Exponent* 21 (June 15, 1893): 180; and also in "Editorial Notes," 21 (May 15, 1893): 164. See also "The World's Fair," *Ashtabula (OH) News Journal*, May 23, 1893, reprinted in *Woman's Exponent* 21 (June 15): 177–79. Two published volumes of the event are May Wright Sewall, ed., *The World's Congress of Representative Women*; and Mary Kavanaugh Oldham Eagle, ed., *The Congress of Women: Held in the Woman's Building, World's Columbian Exposition, Chicago, U.S.A., 1893*. Utah newspapers also included numerous write-ups of the impressive celebration, but the *Exponent* articles provide the essence of Emmeline's experience in Chicago.

Utah delegates from the Relief Society and Young Ladies' MIA conducted their meetings in the Art Institute, two of the many individual concurrent sessions that constituted the congress, along with daily plenary sessions featuring prominent national and international women leaders.[44] Zina Young and several members of the Relief Society board, including Emmeline, spoke at the Relief Society session. Emmeline's topics were Utah authors and journalists and the grain-saving mission.

To her immense surprise and pleasure, Emmeline was invited to preside over the "General Congress in the Hall of Columbus." She could not refrain from observing—to her diary—that it was "an honor never before accorded to a Mormon woman." Then she wryly added, "If one of our brethren had such a distinguished honor conferred upon them it would have been heralded the country over and thought a great achievement."[45]

At the conclusion of the Woman's Congress, Emmeline became one of thousands of tourists, walking among the buildings, statuary, art, and amusements of the White City, generally alone.[46] Many of the friends with whom she had traveled to Chicago had returned home, though she met others who were just beginning their tour of the exposition. She spent several days with Margaret Salisbury, who shared her interest in reviving the silk business when they returned to Utah.[47] Besides this reinvigorated desire to support sericulture, Emmeline's association with the national press women also energized her own journalistic work and provided her with new associates in the profession. Having taken a large supply of *Woman's Exponents* with her, she was able to share her editorial handiwork with her fellow editors.

Emmeline returned home fully refreshed and excited about her new contacts and what she had learned during her month away, all of which

44. E. Wells, Diary, May 19, 1893. Emmeline met many of her fellow journalists at a session for press women, including Dora Dartmoor of the *Golden Dawn*, published in San Francisco. She invited several of them to a small soiree in her room at the hotel. She also attended several business meetings of the National and International Councils of Women. She does not mention any LDS women who attended these meetings with her. Ibid., May 23–27, 1893.

45. Ibid., May 20, 1893.

46. Ibid., May 29–June 14, 1893. She had opportunity to dine with several prominent European visitors and joined the crowds to see the Infanta of Spain. She attended dedicatory services and other meetings held in the various state and territorial buildings that she visited, shaking hands and making acquaintance with many of the representatives. She was not shy in meeting the people she found interesting. Finally, she and Zina D. H. Young traveled home together, along with the Whalens and other friends from Utah. See "World's Fair Buildings."

47. E. Wells, Diary, December 8, 12, 30, 1893.

would prove valuable to her in later years. That women could subordinate their differences in preparing for this national exhibit gave Emmeline great hope for enduring female amity.[48] As a woman's advocate, she yearned for a union of women based on their common experiences and mutual efforts to overcome their shared civic disabilities, a womanhood in which differences enhanced the relationship of disparate women rather than alienating them. This idealistic hope was nurtured by the years of preparation for the exposition that, she believed, could establish "a more universal sisterhood" through the cooperation of this "vast army of [women] workers." For too long, she felt, they had let their differences prevent them from unitedly shouldering the work of community betterment and woman's advancement.[49] Utah women of faiths other than LDS also organized charitable societies, supported hospitals, and encouraged civic enterprises. However, they all functioned independently from one another. Preparation for the Columbian Exposition helped create a new sense of mutual interests and cooperation that would find its zenith during World War I.[50]

During this time, Emmeline labored on another long story. She had published her twenty-eighth and last chapter of "Hephzibah" in September 1890, along with several biographical sketches of various women for the *Exponent* and the *Young Woman's Journal*. She had also written several poems and short stories for the young men's journal the *Contributor*. Now she focused on a new story that was a romance, set in both America and England. She called it "In Rural England" and looked forward each day to writing another chapter, which intrigued her as much as "Hephzibah." It was as though she could remove herself from the pressures of her real life by losing herself in her imagined world. She seemed unable to conclude it, however, not for want of ideas but because of the emotional refuge it offered. She published it serially in the *Exponent* but did not sign her name to it. In this long story, she let her imagination truly run free, relishing the joy of letting the ideas and images flow without restraint. The story follows several generations of two British noble families, their intrigues, hidden secrets, ill-fated love affairs, untimely deaths, and the marriages that, for

48. Emmeline, like most other women involved in these national women's associations, was still exclusionary in her vision of uniting women. Most of the noted national movements were made up of white, middle-class, and personally well-funded women. Some minority groups had their own national organizations, but they, like working-class women, had causes of their own and few were engaged in the women's movement.

49. "Women and the World's Fair," *Woman's Exponent* 21 (December 1, 1892): 84. See also C. Madsen, "Decade of Detente."

50. C. Madsen, "Decade of Detente."

good or ill, entangled the two families. Emmeline concludes the story by noting in the last paragraph of the fiftieth and last chapter that a single descendant of these two star-crossed families accepts the "Ever lasting Gospel" and moves out west to be with its followers.[51] That is as close as the book comes to home literature.

Though Emmeline's editorial work continued to drain her energy and offered scant remuneration, she was taken by surprise when her stake president, Angus Cannon, suggested that she give up the paper and allow the church to support her. She was embarrassed at his suggestion and found it "perplexing," not sure of the underlying intent of his proposal. He was aware that the paper continually struggled for subscriptions and would never be financially rewarding, but he clearly had no hint of its meaning to Emmeline. He informed her that the First Presidency had agreed to pay the paper's indebtedness to the Deseret News Press, which printed it, leaving her free of debt.[52] This, of course, was a great financial relief to Emmeline, but did not affect her resolve to continue publishing it. Besides having been her primary source of income, it had become part of her identity, and she was loath to see it taken from her. Two months later, President Cannon approached her with the same suggestion. But her response was unchanged. "That seems such a queer proposal to me," she expressed to her diary. "I do not quite see how it would be. I fear I should get little to live upon in the way of delicacy and what about clothing who would furnish those." She was determined to retain her independence, whatever the cost to herself. "Not until I can no longer work will I do that certainly not but I do wish to do something literary more than I have done of late—I pray I may have the ability."[53]

So deeply caught up in the accelerated rhythm of city life, Emmeline returned with ever more frequency to memories of the simpler pace of her

51. The first chapter of the story was published in the *Woman's Exponent* 20 (September 1, 1891): 33–34, and it concluded with chapter 50 in *Woman's Exponent* 24 (December 1, 1895): 85–87.

52. E. Wells, Diary, January 25, 1892. There is nothing to indicate that the suggestion went beyond Angus Cannon's own initiative to relieve the financial burden of one of his stake members. Emmeline already received a stipend from the Relief Society for her secretarial work and rental payments for the use of her office for various women's meetings, so it was not unusual that he would suggest taking on some of that financial responsibility as a stake leader.

53. Ibid., March 30, 1892. Emmeline was astute enough to detect that Cannon's suggestion was a subtle way of terminating the paper. Since the church sponsored (though did not fund) the *Young Woman's Journal* and the *Contributor*, it is unlikely that there would be any reason to discontinue the influential woman's publication. Unlike the others, however, it was not supported by its auxiliary organization and was privately owned.

childhood in a small rural village. A brook, a hemlock tree, some peonies, ripe berries ready for plucking, and her notebook and pen were all she needed in this blissful utopia. "Memory," she poeticized, "thy peaceful mantle gently falls,"

Entrancing me in some lone, dreamy hour,
And its enchantment ev'ry sense enthrall,
And holds me spell-bound with its mystic pow'r.[54]

Memory was her anchor. It reinforced her primal identity so easily subverted by the realities she faced each day. But these she attacked with continually renewed determination to ride the waves of life's inconstancy. "I cannot half do what I have set my heart upon for myself or others but only keep on trying," she wrote after one long day.[55] Several of her poems reassert this strong will to resist succumbing to each new challenge. One of them reads, "And though we did not clearly understand / The voice that whispered, thrillingly, 'be still,'" she knew that there was "a guiding hand, / That buoyed us up life's duty to fulfill." When it was possible, the poem continues, to find a place

Where we might rest upon the great highway,
Then we have gathered courage, strength and grace,
To bear the burdens of another day.[56]

Embedded in a rocky present, always unsure of her future, she found respite in recalling the experiences of her past and expressing her deepest thoughts in poetic form. She noted that "many changes have taken place in the condition of women in this place in public and in private." As for herself, her extraordinary abilities had negated the usual deterrents to her sex, and she was called upon again and again to participate in positions usually reserved for men—as chair of committees; as speaker at socials, church meetings, and even funerals; and as an adviser to and occasional coworker with the First Presidency of the church on political, economic, and social issues. "How strange it seems in view of the past," she wrote at the beginning of 1892, "when I was just buried as it were in oblivion that I should ever speak in a public assembly, before the President of the Church."[57] She had also had interviews with two US presidents, spoken before the House and

54. E. Wells, "Memories," in her *Musings and Memories*, 195. The poem was not included in the first edition.

55. E. Wells, Diary, January 30, 1892.

56. E. Wells, "Trials and Happiness," in her *Musings and Memories*, 31. This poem was also printed in the *Millennial Star* 51 (1889): 16.

57. E. Wells, Diary, January 19, 1892.

Senate Judiciary Committees, and met many prominent writers, politicians, and educators who had visited Utah. These were experiences few women of her time enjoyed.

Though she did not speculate at length about the future, she was already primed for additional service in behalf of the women of her church. And through it all, she would manage to write the verses and romantic tales that crowded her mind. The year 1893 had already brought remarkable changes into her life. She once again had a home of her own, she had visited San Francisco to associate with her colleagues at the National Press Association convention, and she had prepared for and attended the Chicago Columbian Exposition, where she presented a paper to the World Congress of Women and conducted a plenary session. Her interest in politics brought her chairmanship of the women's political "silver meeting" in Salt Lake City and elicited her attendance at many sessions of the legislature. She also joined with others, Mormons and non-Mormons, in a newly formed committee on charities in Utah. In October 1893, she replaced Sarah M. Kimball as president of the Utah Territorial Woman Suffrage Association and traveled throughout the territory on behalf of the Relief Society and woman suffrage. The separation of her home and office offered a welcome surcease from the scores of visitors and interruptions at all hours of the day and night. Now she could steal a few uninterrupted moments alone for "reading and writing and meditating." At the end of the year, she could understandably proclaim that 1893 had been "one of the most eventful years within my memory."[58]

58. Ibid., December 29, 31, 1893.

CHAPTER 27

The Lure of Utah Politics
(1894–1895)

COMFORTABLY SITUATED in a new home and working in a new office in the Constitution Building, Emmeline Wells enjoyed the afterglow of Utah women's successful participation in the Chicago Columbian Exposition. Her desire to see a stronger sisterhood among women of all faiths, political persuasions, and backgrounds showed every evidence of becoming a reality in her own hometown, if not on the grand scale she envisioned. Moreover, Utah was rapidly moving toward statehood, nearly fifty years in the making, and she was guiding women's efforts to restore their voting privileges in the state's organic law. She continued to correspond with Susan B. Anthony and Rachel Foster Avery, secretary of the National Council of Women. She was unabashedly proud to have been made a patron of the NCW, "an honor which I should never have anticipated, and if any one had given me a quantity of gold I could not have been much more astonished."[1]

Emmeline's family life was generally stable. Susan and Lydia Ann Wells remained important fixtures, and they all continued to socialize together. "Went to lunch with Lydia Ann and Susan," she noted one day, and added, "to both of whom I am strongly attached."[2] Martha and Hannah appear less frequently in her diary, but there seemed to be genuine affection among Daniel's five widows. She enjoyed the conveniences and privacy of her own home, Annie and Belle were both back in Salt Lake City, and letters and visits kept her abreast of Mell's life. John Q. was working in his father's publishing company, and legislative activity kept Septimus Sears busy along with his job at the Chamber of Commerce. Belle's children were helping Emmeline with the *Exponent*, but she still carried most of the workload herself. "I have the tranquility and retirement here," she wrote of her new

1. E. Wells, Diary, January 25, 1894.
2. Ibid., March 13, 1894.

home, "but so much to do that seems imperative."[3] Not only her daily office work but the looming reality of statehood, bringing new perspectives on civic and religious life, swept Emmeline into the vortex of its formative challenges. Almost inadvertently, she was drawn into the volatile world of Utah politics.

Nothing prepared her, however, for the news that rent her life in 1893. She unexpectedly received a package from a cousin in New Salem. It contained a packet of letters, all addressed to Emmeline. She could hardly contain herself when she read the signer's name—James Harris. Written while he was at sea and little more than a teenager, they showed "all the confidence of boyish love." It was almost impossible for her to read them. "I can only read a word here and there. It is too trying," she exclaimed. At long last, she knew that he had not abandoned her completely and had written loving letters to her, though never receiving one in return. Reflecting the complexity of emotions that this startling event had evoked, Emmeline did not share it, even with her diary, until a year after receiving the letters.

Even more incomprehensible to her was that "his mother kept them while she lived notwithstanding I visited her she did not give them up."[4] Not knowing Emmeline's whereabouts, James had sent the letters to his mother, Lucy Harris Blackinton, years earlier, to be forwarded to Emmeline, but Lucy had never sent them on. Now she was dead and a cousin had come in possession of them. This level of vengeful withholding stunned Emmeline. "I must not look backward," she counseled herself. The "present demands my attention.... [L]et me not think of it."[5]

But she did. During her next visit to New Salem, Emmeline, with her sister Pallas and Pallas's daughter Lillian, went to the Blackinton home so that Emmeline could meet the current resident, Lucy's niece. After the visit, Emmeline asked Pallas to drive her to the cemetery, where the three women walked over to Lucy's grave. There, according to Lillian's eyewitness account, "that tiny but mighty old lady stood with her arms raised over the grave and she called down a curse upon her mother-in-law that made Mother tremble—and no doubt caused the wicked one to writhe in her shroud!"[6] Despite her usual self-containment and strength of will during

3. Ibid., March 24, 1894.

4. Ibid., July 29, 1894. The letters from James do not appear to have survived.

5. Ibid.

6. Geneva Kingkade (Lillian's daughter), letter to Carolyn Chouinard, August 24, 1970. Kingkade, in an earlier letter to her cousin Glenys Harris, June 10, 1967, described Emmeline as calling down "the curses of God on that conniving woman's soul" and explained that she "loved to hear my mother [Lillian] tell this story—

periods of crisis, on this occasion Emmeline unleashed years of pent-up anguish and an uncharacteristic desire for vengeance unparalleled in her life. This extraordinary visceral outburst was Emmeline's reflexive response to Lucy's callous cruelty.

Later, she also gave a more pensive account of receiving the letters in her long autobiographical poem "Faith and Fidelity":

And thus at last the mystery so long concealed....
These faded pages, worn to shreds, had now revealed....
Could she forgive the injury now that she knew
The story of her wrongs, alas, too late?
He loved her always, and he had been constant too—
This was some compensation for her fate.
What satisfaction could they ever bring?...
But "Dead Sea apples" seemed the offering.[7]

Another instance of love revealed too late.

As she had relished Sundays at Annie's Ogden home, so she did now in her own new home, enjoying a day's respite from the demands of her workdays. This gift of a few unscheduled hours gave her time to reflect, refresh, and regroup for the week ahead. Belle's breakfasts and Annie's dinners took care of her meals for the day, and a few hours were spent luxuriously reading and going through old manuscripts.[8] "I have read more books and magazines of late or during this year than for a long period heretofore," she happily reported in 1894.[9] Books appeared to be her favored extravagance.

Another diversion came in the form of the public birthday celebrations of prominent individuals. As general secretary of the Relief Society, Emmeline helped arrange a birthday tribute to the president, Zina D. H. Young, on her seventy-fifth birthday, January 31, 1896. She wrote articles

acting out Aunt Em's tragic fury—her little hands raised to heaven—eyes flashing all her pent up anger at that woman in her voice!" Photocopies of handwritten copies of both letters are in my possession, courtesy of Carolyn Chouinard of North New Salem.

7. E. Wells, "Faith and Fidelity," in her *Musings and Memories*, 227–28.

8. E. Wells, Diary, January 21, 1894.

9. Ibid., June 17, 1894. Among the books she read that year were several by British author Sarah Grand; *A Stranger Artist*, by Edith C. Kenyon; *Katharine Lauderdale*, by F. Marion Crawford; *Marcella*, by Mrs. Humphrey Ward; *In Varying Moods*, by Beatrice Harridon; an essay entitled "Sappho" and other articles from the *Atlantic Monthly*, by Thomas Wentworth Higginson; and George Eliot's Gothic novella *The Lifted Veil*. She clearly favored female authors and subjects. She also made careful notation of the books she bought for others.

about Zina for church magazines and the *Deseret News*, along with a sketch of Zina's life for the *Exponent*.[10] Concurrent celebrations were scheduled for Relief Societies throughout Utah. When a complaint over the "extravagance" of the celebration reached the First Presidency, Emmeline was summoned to their office a day before the event. When she arrived she saw at once "something very serious was wanted." Earlier that day, at the apostles' regular meeting in the temple, the men had discussed "the subject of the great stir throughout Utah in having a meeting on the 31st in honor of sister Young[s] birthday." Some felt it too extravagant, President Woodruff explained to Emmeline and noted that it was "setting an example not in wisdom throughout the Church."[11]

Emmeline was dumbfounded. Being admonished about the Relief Society's activities was new to her, and she felt the rebuke. "It was frightful and overwhelming," she wrote. Emmeline had always enjoyed an intimate and mutually respectful relationship with church leaders. This encounter was extremely disconcerting to her. In her mind, the men had given too much credence to such complaints, especially since so many similar celebrations for other church leaders had occurred. "I cannot imagine that men in high places could listen to such frivolous misconstructions and misrepresentations," she lamented. As the scapegoat, she had no choice but to submit "to such injustice which is nobler than to notice it."[12] Despite the caution, the party went on as planned and turned out to be a great success. George Q. Cannon of the First Presidency and Apostle Lorenzo Snow even attended and participated on the program.[13] Though there were few church-wide celebrations of birthdays after this event, there was no cessation of the number or extravagance of local birthday commemorations thereafter, including some of her own.

Besides private birthday and other celebratory parties, Emmeline and her friends found numerous opportunities to get together, many of their gatherings becoming spiritual feasts for the women. Mary Louisa Solomon, soon to give birth, invited several women, including Emmeline, Zina Young, and Bathsheba Smith, to give her a blessing preparatory to her confinement. Music, recitations, and remarks by the guests followed along with tasty refreshments. The gathering concluded after Mary Ann Hyde "spoke in the gift of tongues and Aunt Zina interpreted."[14] Emmeline valued those

10. E. Wells, Diary, January 9, 11, 24, 25, 1896.

11. Scott G. Kenney, ed., *Wilford Woodruff's Journal, 1833–1898*, 9:389.

12. E. Wells, Diary, January 30, 31, 1896. Actually, the account spills over to the page dated January 31, but the interview occurred on January 30.

13. Ibid., January 31, February 1, 1896.

14. Ibid., March 22, 1894.

occasions when she listened to "the glorious testimonies borne by Sister [Mary Isabella] Horne, and Sister Eliza Snow, and the rich history told by Sarah M. Kimball, Sarepta Heywood, Elizabeth Howard, and others; and the wonderful singing of Mother [Elizabeth Ann] Whitney, with it beautiful interpretation by Aunt Zina [D. H. Young]." These intimate women's gatherings spiritually energized Emmeline while reaffirming the sisterhood these first-generation Mormon women felt in each other's presence.[15]

Emmeline was herself the subject of such recognitions. The Utah Woman's Press Club and its companion club, the Reapers, organized by Emmeline a year after the Press Club for women who had not yet published their writings, began a tradition of honoring Emmeline each February. As many as forty women (all named in her diary) attended the commemoration of her sixty-sixth birthday.[16] Romania Pratt and Ellis Shipp, members of the Woman's Press Club, spearheaded many of these celebrations. The camaraderie expressed in these social events, which often brought Mormon and Gentile women together, complemented the cooperation they now exhibited in mutually fostering community development, a happy result of their participation in the Columbian Exposition. Several new organizations had even been created, composed of both Mormon and Gentile members, and Emmeline became involved in most of them, such as the General Relief Committee, the Committee on Charities, the Utah Kindergarten Association, and the Executive Committee of the 1894 Midwinter Fair held in California, a reduced replica of the Chicago Fair.

In 1893, another association that brought Mormon and Gentile women together was the Utah Federation of Women's Clubs, a local branch of the national federation. Emmeline enrolled her two literary clubs and participated in its annual conventions for several years.[17] The national club movement spurred the creation of many literary and culture clubs in Utah, some of which also became members of the Utah federation. Emmeline joined the Wasatch Chapter (so named by Emmeline) of the Daughters of

15. A. W. Cannon, "Mothers in Israel," 70. Romania Pratt also reminisced about the spiritual nature of many of these events, one occurring in Emmeline's home, where "each lady present spoke (not in tongues) by the power and spirit of the Holy Ghost and we truly had a time of feasting the soul and rejoicing." "Memoirs of Romania B. Pratt, M.D.," typescript copy, 10, 11, LDS Church History Library, Salt Lake City.

16. E. Wells, Diary, February 28, 1894.

17. Ruth May Fox, Emmeline's associate in the Republican Party, was an active member of both of Emmeline's clubs and represented them at many of the meetings of the Utah Federation of Women's Clubs. She remained active after Emmeline had dropped her membership. See Ruth May Fox, "Miscellaneous Activities," chapter 12, in her "My Story," ca. 1953, Special Collections, J. Willard Marriott Library, University of Utah, Salt Lake City.

the Revolution, organized by Susa Young Gates. Emmeline later became chaplain. With other LDS women Emmeline was an occasional guest of the Ladies Literary Club, a traditionally Gentile organization but moving toward accepting Mormon membership. She was honored to speak at a meeting of the Jewish women's society and also at a conference of the Lady Maccabees. Her cache of Gentile friends continually expanded. She had a deep respect for Margaret Salisbury and admired the influence she had in both Mormon and Gentile society. "She is really a sort of talisman towards the fulfillment of my hopes and aspirations," Emmeline wrote of her. "She is such a true friend in times of need."[18]

Every organization needs someone to do the basic arrangements for meetings, conventions, socials, and other business, and this job always fell to Emmeline. She was quick, efficient, and authoritative and knew the right people to help her get things done. "Some meeting every evening of my life," she unsurprisingly acknowledged.[19] Her friend Romania Pratt often brought lunch to her or invited her to dinner and in other small ways tried to help her, including wisely counseling her to resign from some of her commitments. Whatever drove her to take on so much additional work and to willingly assume the unheralded and often thankless tasks that others laid on her mystified her daughter Annie, who expressed her annoyance that her mother had so little time to be with her family. "I felt it [Annie's disapproval] very much indeed," Emmeline lamented, "but I feel that I must do some public duty and that will give me development in the direction of the pursuits I am working in as well as influence." Justifying her own sense of duty, she added, "One cannot work for the elevation and uplifting of humanity unless there is some public encouragement as well as personal

18. Utah's successful silk exhibit at the Chicago World's Fair ignited renewed efforts to interest the Utah Legislature in establishing a bounty on cocoons. Zina Young, Emmeline, and Margaret A. Caine represented Mormon women's interest, and non-Mormons Margaret Salisbury, Corinne Allen, and Isabella Bennett formed a lobbying committee that remained active for several years and eventually met success when the legislature established a Utah silk commission. See various entries in Emmeline Wells's diary for January 1894. This association was particularly useful in bringing Mormon and Gentile women together. E. Wells, Diary, January 18, 1895.

19. Ibid., July 31, 1894. In August 1894, she made all the arrangements for a fund-raising excursion to Saltair for the Relief Society, and for three weeks she was involved in one small detail or another. She was successful in obtaining the attendance of President George Q. Cannon of the First Presidency; Angus M. Cannon, president of the Salt Lake Stake; and other prominent leaders. She was often the liaison between her women's associations and church leaders. See ibid., August 9, 12, 22, 24, 1894.

effort."[20] She was adept at creating a useful symbiosis of her own ambitions with the demands of public service.

Her Gentile friendships played an important role in 1891 when Utahns adopted the national political parties prior to statehood. Most of these friends had strong political ties to the Republican Party, and Emmeline would be a good catch if she chose to join the party. However, the policy of the national suffrage movement, as well as the Utah association, was to remain politically neutral and to lobby both parties in behalf of woman suffrage, not knowing which would be the most supportive at any given time. But politics was in the air, and the women were as excited about the ultimate outcome of the changes that were occurring so rapidly as were the men involved in making them. At one of the meetings of her press club in 1893, Emmeline was obliged to set the limits of political discussion. "These meetings," she announced, "are strictly for literary improvement and devoted to the press and similar things, and not for the discussion of religion or politics as we can secure these things in other places. No subject should be presented here upon which we are likely to conflict or that will create unpleasantness."[21] Woman suffrage was exempt from the decree; their political focus was to be solely on regaining the vote.

Politics, however, did begin to make its divisive way into Emmeline's relationship with some of her friends and Relief Society associates. Exercising her new responsibility as president of the Utah Territorial Suffrage Association, Emmeline, with the help of Emily Richards, the new vice president, visited county associations and planned fund-raisers.[22] A newcomer on the political scene was Ruth May Fox, an eager, intelligent, and capable forty-year-old mother of eleven children excited to be involved in these historic events. In order to give the younger suffragist more public exposure, Emmeline intended to nominate Fox as chairman of the organizational meeting of the Salt Lake County suffrage association. Emmeline, however, was unable to attend the meeting, and Fox and Ella Hyde, another new member, decided that the forceful, well-known Dr. Ellen Ferguson "had

20. Ibid., January 12, 1894.

21. "Minutes of the Utah Women's Press Club," *Woman's Exponent* 22 (August 15, 1893): 21.

22. As a close worker with Sarah Kimball in both Relief Society and the suffrage association, Emmeline found her to be "something of a grand type of woman but hard & cold and haughty, not one to love as much as to reverence [crossed out and replaced with "bear"]." She recognized her, however, as being "one of the foremost leaders among women in the Church, not so much religiously as in Executive and political movements." E. Wells, Diary, December 29, 1895.

so much more experience in public affairs than we" that they decided to nominate her. She subsequently won the election as chair of the meeting and eventually became president of the county association. Ruth acknowledged that "this action did not please Sister Wells," who later characterized Dr. Ferguson as a "red-hot Democrat."[23]

Dr. Ferguson was keen on displacing Emmeline from her position as president of the territorial suffrage association and drafted a letter requesting a new territorial election for members to sign. Some members, including former UTWSA president Margaret N. Caine, expressed their disapproval of the letter. Emmeline chafed at it, seeing partisan politics at work in the suffrage camp. "No one," she was certain, "could misunderstand the spirit of envy and jealousy in the communication," a handy explanation for criticism.[24] But the undertone of politics was unquestionably evident in the move. Both Ferguson and Richards were vocal Democrats and openly expressed their political views, despite Susan Anthony's warning to remain politically neutral. While Emmeline maintained a friendly relationship with Emily Richards, this incident seemed to signal a clean break between Emmeline and Ellen Ferguson.[25] Nothing came of Ferguson's attempt to dislodge Emmeline as president, and the incident was soon passed over.[26]

After six efforts to gain statehood since 1849, the enabling act of 1894 set in motion the final push. A constitutional convention was scheduled to

23. Ruth May Fox, "My Story," ca. 1953, Special Collections, J. Willard Marriott Library, University of Utah, Salt Lake City, 25; E. Wells, Diary, March 12, 1894. Ruth May Fox became a protégée and close friend of Emmeline's. The account of the incident appears in Ruth May Fox, Diary, December 30, 31, 1894. In "My Story," Fox noted, "It is appropriate to acknowledge my great indebtedness to Emmeline B. Wells. No other woman had so great an influence as she in shaping my life. I became her devoted disciple and she in turn loved me as a daughter. I named after her my last child, Emmeline Blanche, born September 14, 1896, when Sister Wells was the center of my orbit of public activities. For many years subsequently she had much to do with my progress" (24).

24. E. Wells, Diary, December 31, 1894.

25. The source of Ellen and Emmeline's disagreements at this time is unclear. It may have resulted from some episode relating to the Deseret Hospital in which both were involved; it may have been their opposing political views; it may also have resulted from Ellen's gradual embrace of theosophy or spiritualism, which had made its way to Utah by the 1890s and was gaining converts, including Ellen, who began advocating the movement in 1896 and was excommunicated from the church in 1898. Or it may simply have been the desire for position and status. Dr. Ferguson's life is reviewed by Ann Gardner Stone in Burgess-Olson, *Sister Saints*, 325–39.

26. Emmeline and Ruth May Fox remained loyal friends. Emmeline recognized Ruth's leadership qualities and predicted a bright future for her. Ruth eventually became general president of the Young Ladies' Mutual Improvement Association. Emmeline B. Wells, letter to Ruth May Fox, circa 1910–11, in "My Story," 47.

convene in March 1895, followed by a ratification election in November. The Utah Territorial Woman Suffrage Association was eager to see the results of its intensive grassroots efforts to persuade delegates to reinstate woman suffrage. However, attempts to organize a separate suffrage league came to Emmeline's attention, and she felt it necessary to warn the counties about those heading the movement. Without naming them, she declared them to be "smart women and…very dangerous." They "have to be guided if they will submit, and if not then one must be on the watch for breakers."[27] After five years of careful groundwork in gaining support for woman suffrage, she was fearful that alternative and possibly more militant schemes would derail all their efforts. Her more pacific stance in the campaign to restore voting privileges was due to her personal acquaintance with many of the delegates to the constitutional convention, both Mormon and Gentile, and her sense that they were favorable to women's political rights. "I rather trust men than distrust them by far," she wrote in her letter. "Most of our leading brethren I believe think the woman element in politics at this present crisis will be a saving power."[28] The county associations all remained loyal to the territorial board.

The burden of these internal dissensions, however, was stressful. Emmeline often felt "out of sorts" when her ideas were challenged, and she preferred to be with those who gave her the leeway she desired. "There are some people who quite upset me and with whom I have no congeniality. I cannot work when they are near me, at any rate can do no mental labor," she complained. Fortunately, her frank admissions to her diary found verbal expression in less forthright ways. She chafed during a meeting of the Midwinter Fair Committee, "much annoyed at the way the matter is being conducted. There seems so little method and good judgment exercised," she complained, "but we can't have things as we like, so we must submit."[29] And she did, more often than her impatience and dismay at useless talk, wasted time, and alternative views would suggest. Her reputation as "strong-willed" and "even caustic" likely asserted itself in some form, however, during this volatile political period.

Utah women had voted for seventeen years, but the Territorial Suffrage Association nonetheless felt the necessity to elicit a promise from each of the convention delegates to put woman suffrage on their party platforms.

27. This letter also expresses Emmeline's hope that "there will be a feeling of unity" among the various workers. See Emmeline B. Wells to Mary A. White, January 13, 14, 1895, Beaver County Woman Suffrage Association Papers. See also E. Wells, Diary, February 11, 1894, for what Emmeline felt were efforts that would disunite their suffrage movement.

28. E. Wells, Diary, February 11, 1894.

29. Ibid., June 18, January 5, 1894.

The response to this grassroots effort seemed promising. But Susan B. Anthony was well versed in the unpredictability of partisan politics and sent Emmeline a message for Utah women: "Now in the formative period of your constitution is the time to establish justice and equality to all the people," she urged. "That adjective 'male' once admitted into your organic law, will remain there. Don't be cajoled into believing otherwise."[30] Emmeline added her own encouragement in an *Exponent* editorial. "Let all rejoice in the prospect statehood offers," she wrote, "more especially if it makes all citizens equal irrespective of sex. Only a simple act of justice to one half of the community who are taxed without representation, and who are as justly entitled to partake of the advantages and benefits arising from statehood as are their sons…or their brothers."[31]

A month later, when some delegates seemed to be hesitant about their support, Emmeline laid down the gauntlet in an *Exponent* editorial: "How will they consider the interests of the sex who have no representation save through them? Will their claims to citizenship be guaranteed to them through these great grand noble hearted sons of the soil? They must be trusted with this live question, it cannot be ignored for this is the woman's age of the world and now the imperative hour, is pending."[32] Who could resist such an appeal to their better nature? During the following months, the activities of the nineteen counties that had local suffrage associations were included in each issue of the *Exponent*, along with several editorials and many articles expressing the hope that the delegates would recognize the right of women to the franchise in the new state.

With the Utah Territorial Woman Suffrage Association carefully intact and strategies established for the pending constitutional convention, Emmeline turned her thoughts to the triennial meeting of the National Council of Women in Washington, of which she was still a patron, and the NAWSA convention preceding it in Atlanta.[33] Emmeline admitted that she was "full of the Convention and the Council in Washington," even as she lobbied for woman suffrage at home. In the meantime, she learned to her great delight that her suffragist daughter Melvina had recently debated the merits of woman suffrage with a lawyer—and she had won.[34]

30. "Susan B. Anthony's Letter," *Woman's Exponent* 23 (August 1–15, 1894): 169.

31. "Utah and Statehood," *Woman's Exponent* 23 (August 1–15, 1894): 172.

32. "The Need of the Hour," *Woman's Exponent* 23 (September 1, 1894): 180.

33. This southern city was selected in place of the usual Washington, DC, location in order to generate more southern interest in the suffrage movement and to support the suffrage workers already energized by membership in the National Council of Women.

34. E. Wells, Diary, December 12, 13, 1894.

Though Emmeline was in constant contact with planners of the suffrage convention and spent hours preparing Utah's part of the program, she was in no way certain of attending either convention. Convinced that she should go to the meeting of the NAWSA in her capacity as president of the Utah Territorial Woman Suffrage Association, she faced, as usual, the problem of financing the trip. "The Relief Society," she rather petulantly noted, "is a rich institution and ought to be ably represented as it deserves."[35] In point of fact, the Relief Society was a member of both national associations, and it was logical for the Relief Society to at least underwrite the attendance of its president, Zina D. H. Young, the official delegate to both of the conventions. In her absence, Emmeline made an effective alternate, since she was well known and highly regarded by the officers of both organizations and viewed as a key figure in the suffrage campaign in Utah. But no offer of funding from the Relief Society, the church, or her friends came her way.[36]

However, as often happened, the means to go suddenly materialized, and on January 26, 1895, Emmeline, Marilla John Daniels of Provo, and Aurelia Spencer Rogers of Farmington left for Atlanta. Upon arrival Emmeline was immediately caught up in the exciting whirl of meeting old friends and acquaintances, recounting the details of the personal encounters, socials, and meetings in both her diary and the *Woman's Exponent*. At the opening meeting of delegates, she received the signal honor of being seated next to Susan B. Anthony, a "very great compliment & I felt it very strongly," Emmeline acknowledged. At the plenary session she had ten minutes to report on Utah and was deeply moved when at her conclusion Susan Anthony embraced her after her talk and "made such an eloquent appeal that some of the ladies were moved to tears."[37]

35. Ibid., January 19, 1895.

36. When the First Presidency under Joseph F. Smith began to curtail the use of church moneys to fund attendance to the national conventions, Emmeline helped to instigate a program of dues from Relief Society members to support the attendance of women at these national conventions, a program that at first met some serious resistance as the value of membership was questioned.

37. Ibid., February 2, 1895. The article, "Convention in Atlanta," in the *Woman's Exponent* described the incident as it appeared in the *Atlanta Evening Journal*: "President Anthony came forward and putting her arm around her [Emmeline] gave her endorsement to the speaker. As she told of the work being done in Utah she kept her arms around the delegate and the audience was visibly affected at this exhibition of affection." *Woman's Exponent* 23 (February 1–15, 1895): 237. Aurelia Rogers kept a diary of her experiences at the convention, but it focuses more on the people and places she saw than on the content of the convention. See Rogers, *Life Sketches*, 301–22.

On February 6, Emmeline, Marilla, and Aurelia left Atlanta for Washington, DC, and the National Council of Women convention. Emmeline was appointed a member of the Resolutions Committee, after which she was invited to attend a luncheon in Philadelphia and an overnight stay in Somerton, the elegant home of Rachel Foster Avery, an officer of the national council.[38] Other guests were Louisa Barnum Robbins, the newly appointed corresponding secretary; the Reverend Anna Howard Shaw; Lucy Anthony, sister of Susan B. Anthony; and their hostess, Rachel Avery. Emmeline was overwhelmed by the opulence of the home the Averys called Milrae. She slept in the Anthony room, all of its furnishings decorated in bright yellow, the color of the suffrage movement, and was impressed that the home had thirty-two closets, a nursery for the youngest children, and a schoolroom with a full-time governess.[39] Avery was typical of the socioeconomic level of most of the workers in these national organizations, and Emmeline never ceased to be impressed with their lifestyles, which gave them the time and means to be involved in social causes.

Emmeline returned to Washington to attend the seventy-fifth birthday celebration of Susan B. Anthony, which occurred during the convention. Emmeline, representing the Relief Society, and Elmina Taylor, representing the YLMIA, were seated at the head table with Anthony, and both were invited to speak. Several other speakers praised the Utah women, and the Utah delegation received invitations to five additional receptions.[40] Almost as soon as the women appeared on the scene, they became objects of attention, Susa Gates, a member of the YLMIA board, noted. "They crowd around us and seem very anxious to vie with each other in the attention

38. The resolutions related to all aspects of women's lives, such as education, religion, dress reform, patriotism, capital and labor, and more. See *Woman's Exponent* 23 (April 1, 1895): 246–47.

39. E. Wells, Diary, March 5, 6, 1895. Many of the women who devoted time and money to national and international causes were affluent, leisured married women with help at home or single women devoted to the cause like Susan B. Anthony, who chose not to marry. They differed in religious and political views but were united in their zeal for women's advancement. See Susa Young Gates, "Utah Women at the National Council of Women," 396. Emmeline was not alone in noting the advantages that money gave to these workers.

40. The activities of the Utah delegation received much publicity. See Gates, "Utah Women at the National Council of Women," 392; "The Women's Councils," *Deseret News*, March 14, 1895, 5; "Addresses by Utah Women," *Salt Lake Tribune*, February 21, 1895, 2; and "Utah Women to the Fore," *Salt Lake Tribune*, February 22, 1895, 3. A national suffrage paper also noted their presence in "National Council in Washington," *Woman's Journal* (March 2, 1895): 65–72; and "National Council in Washington," *Woman's Journal* (March 9, 1895): 77.

we receive," she enthusiastically reported.[41] Much had changed since the uncertainty of their application for membership just four years earlier. Another honor was national council president May Wright Sewall's invitation to Emmeline to visit her home in Indianapolis on her way back to Utah. "Mrs. Sewall greeted me most cordially and welcomed me like a queen," Emmeline glowed, and added, "as she verily is queen of hearts."[42]

When she reached home, Emmeline immediately immersed herself in local politics and the policies that would form the governing law of the state-to-be. Of most concern to her, of course, was the status of woman suffrage. It no longer seemed as inevitable as it had before she left Utah a month earlier.

41. Susa Young Gates, letter to Family, February 17, 1895, Washington, DC, Gates Papers.

42. E. Wells, Diary, March 8, 1895.

CHAPTER 28

Partisan Politics
(1895–1897)

When the two national women's conventions adjourned in March 1895, Emmeline returned home to face an interview with a *Salt Lake Tribune* reporter to ascertain her views on the status of woman suffrage in Utah, which had become the subject of intense debate in the constitutional convention. She reminded her interviewer that Utah women had once been granted the vote by their territorial legislature, that they had exercised it responsibly for seventeen years, and that it had been taken from them as an expedient "political measure" by the antipolygamy Edmunds-Tucker Act. She skillfully cited the argument that "taxation without representation" was unjust—an issue that was now a personal matter for her. She further informed the reporter of the large number of Mormon women who had been made virtual heads of their families by congressional enactments (imprisonment of polygamists), while all Utah women who owned their own homes paid taxes, if only minimally.[1] None of these arguments, however, informed the debate then flaring up in the convention.

When Emily Richards and Nellie Little apprised Emmeline of their misgivings over the tepid loyalty of some of the convention delegates to their cause, Emmeline did not at first seem anxious. Nevertheless, she rallied her troops, and on March 18, seventy-five women accompanied Emily Richards to the convention with a well-prepared memorial to give to her husband, delegate Franklin S. Richards.[2] More memorials followed, inundating the delegates with appeals to honor their commitment to include woman suffrage in the new constitution, a promise made in the preconvention platforms of both parties. "The sensation of the hour," Democratic delegate

1. "Utah's Woman Suffragists," *Salt Lake Tribune*, March 15, 1895, 8.

2. "God Bless the Ladies," *Salt Lake Tribune*, March 19, 1895, 5. See also Fox, Diary, March 18, 1895.

Orson F. Whitney noted in his diary, as the issue began its two-week hold on the convention, "is the Woman Suffrage debate in the Constitutional Convention."[3] As a delegate, he observed that support for the measure was eroding as a result of the growing interest in presenting it separately to the voters in November. Woman suffrage was still a radical idea to most Americans, and some delegates were fearful that the constitution might not be ratified by Utah voters or approved by Congress if it allowed women to vote.

B. H. Roberts, a Democrat from Davis County and a member of the Quorum of the Seventy, the third-ranked group of general authorities, became chief spokesman for separate submission.[4] He delivered his speech to a packed house of delegates, suffragists, and the general public, all enthralled by his powers of persuasion.[5] He had long been opposed to the enfranchisement of women, and a second speech in the convention signaled his continuing bias against it.[6] He declared that for him, women's influence came not from public platforms but "from the fireside" and the political arena would do nothing but debase them. "You are the queens of the domestic kingdom," he declared, and if they became "embroiled in political agitation...the reverence that is paid you will disappear."[7]

Orson F. Whitney, a fellow Democrat and equally persuasive orator, felt differently about the issue. Thinking "to speak only about ten minutes" in rebuttal, Whitney "held for an hour," forcefully expressing his conviction that woman was made not "merely for a wife, a mother, a cook, and a housekeeper." While acknowledging the importance of these roles, he claimed that they "are not the sum of her capabilities." He regarded the women's

3. O. Whitney, Diary, April 6, 1895. The convention began March 4 and adjourned May 7, 1895. The ratification election took place November 5, 1895.

4. Reports of the idea of "separate submission" appear in "The Article on Elections," *Salt Lake Tribune*, March 23, 1895, 4; "Women and the Ballot," *Salt Lake Herald*, March 29, 1895, 1; "Woman Suffrage Again," *Deseret News*, April 5, 1895, 1; and "Created a Breeze," *Deseret News*, April 10, 1895, 1.

5. The *Salt Lake Herald*, an independent and influential Democratic publication, edited by Charles W. Penrose in 1895, wrote that "a stream of language, potent and pleasing, flowed from his lips and caught his listeners until even those who were most bitterly opposed to him were compelled to pay compliment to his power with rapturous applause." "Women and the Ballot," March 29, 1895, 1.

6. Preaching in the tabernacle in 1892, Roberts was so eloquent in his opposition that Emmeline feared he had "prejudiced many against the suffrage question and kept some back who believe in it from taking an active part." E. Wells, Diary, March 20, 1892.

7. As quoted in Jean Bickmore White, "Woman's Place Is in the Constitution: The Struggle for Equal Rights in Utah in 1895," 358. See also White, "Utah State Elections, 1895–1899."

movement to attain greater rights for women "as one of the great levers by which the Almighty is lifting up this fallen world, lifting it nearer to the throne of its Creator."[8]

Emmeline editorialized her disdain at Roberts's position. "It is pitiful to see how men opposed to woman suffrage try to make the women believe it is because they worship them so, and think them far too good," she wrote. "One would really think to hear those eloquent orators talk, that laws were all framed purposely to protect women in their rights, and men stood ready to defend them with their lives." She then cautioned, "We can only say they have been bold and must answer to their own consciences." She was certain that they would be convinced of the value of women's vote when they saw "the good that would follow," when "they and their children receive the benefit of what they could not discern in the future progress of the world."[9]

Encouraged by the favorable response to Whitney's argument, the suffragists were nonetheless aware of the growing sentiment for separate submission of the woman suffrage clause to the voters along with the proposed constitution. The idea of separating woman suffrage from the constitution, requiring a separate vote, appealed to various newspaper writers, non-LDS women's groups, and other non-Mormons.[10] With Roberts's endorsement, many delegates came to favor this compromise measure, putting woman suffrage as part of the new state constitution in serious jeopardy. Perceiving the women's apprehension over this new development, Joseph F. Smith of the First Presidency decided to meet with the Relief Society during its April conference, which coincidentally took place at the same time the debate was in progress. He delivered as forceful a speech on the rights of women as had probably ever been delivered during these years of struggle to regain the vote. He castigated those women who were "careless and indifferent to their rights" and who tended to "rest content and seek no changes, however much for the better a change might be." He regarded them as "enemies to

8. O. Whitney, Diary, April 6, 1895; White, "Woman's Place Is in the Constitution," 359. See also Utah Constitutional Convention, 1895, *Official Report of the Proceedings and Debates*, 1:459, 508. All of the local newspapers carried articles about the debate throughout March and early April.

9. "Woman Suffrage," *Woman's Exponent* 23 (April 1, 1895): 244.

10. The *Salt Lake Tribune* and the *Ogden Standard*, both Republican papers, and the Salt Lake Chamber of Commerce were strong supporters of separate submission. See C. Madsen, *Advocate for Women*, particularly 280–92. When the *Ogden Standard* became a Republican voice in 1891, Frank J. Cannon became editor, and its former editor John Q. Cannon moved to the Democratic paper, the *Ogden Commercial*, which the Democrats invited him to edit. See L. John Nuttall, Diary, February 24, 1891, 265.

society" but disdained even more those who prevented the progression of others. "Shall the male citizen have a voice in civil government because he is a male, and a female citizen be denied the same privilege simply because she is a female?...Why shall one enjoy civil rights and the other be denied them?" he continued. "Women may be found who seem to glory in their enthralled condition, and who caress and fondle the very chains and manacles which fetter and enslave them! Let those who love this helpless dependent condition and prefer to remain in it and enjoy it; but for conscience and for mercy's sake let them not stand in the way of those of their sisters who would be, and of right ought to be *free*."[11] This rousing declamation in favor of women's rights reassured the women, and they continued pressing their position through a continuing deluge of memorials and their attendance at the convention.

Finally, after the convention had debated the issue from all angles, on April 18 Emmeline and her coworkers heard the good news that the motion to include woman suffrage had passed and was now safely inscribed in the organic law of the state, awaiting only ratification by the voters of Utah. "A little bitterness was manifest from Roberts & [Charles S.] Varian also [William F.] James [delegates]," Emmeline observed, "but altogether it was smooth sailing." Though eager to show their exhilaration, the suffragists tactfully "kept very quiet and made no demonstration." She immediately sent a telegram to Susan B. Anthony to inform her of the good news.[12] Anthony promptly wrote back: "Hurrah for Utah, No. 3, State—that establishes a genuine 'Republican form of Government.'"[13] Both Anthony and Anna Howard Shaw were able to congratulate the suffragists in person at the Rocky Mountain convention of the NAWSA, held in May in Salt Lake City that year. Instrumental in planning and organizing the convention, Emmeline breathlessly commented, "One is puzzled to know how it is all to be done."

On the eve of statehood, Utah presented a different picture to Susan B. Anthony from what she had seen on her first visit twenty-five years earlier. Salt Lake City was now a thriving western city, complete with electricity, numerous commercial enterprises, hotels and beautiful brick homes, a system of public transportation, parks and libraries, and the newly completed Salt

11. "Relief Society Conference," *Woman's Exponent* 24 (August 15, 1895): 45–46; Minutes of the Relief Society Conference, April 5, 1895; Minutes of the General Board, April 5, 1895.

12. E. Wells, Diary, April 18, 1895.

13. "Equal Suffrage in the Constitution," *Woman's Exponent* 23 (May 1, 1895): 260. Utah followed Wyoming (1890) and Colorado (1893) in granting women the vote.

Lake temple, with its command of the city skyline. Emmeline arranged to use the convention hall in the City and County Building, recently vacated by the delegates to the constitutional convention, as a "neutral" meeting place for Mormon and Gentile attendees. She invited the governor and secretary of state (lieutenant governor) to address the conference, wrote articles for the newspapers, and sent out invitations to special guests, including Colorado suffragists Mary C. C. Bradford and Lyle Meredith Stansbury.

The two national leaders arrived early on Sunday morning, May 12, 1895. After breakfast at their hotel and a ride around the city in the "Utah Drag," a large omnibus that seated thirty, they proceeded to the tabernacle, filled with six thousand curious attendees. Both Mormon and non-Mormon suffragists sat on the stand, and the Reverend Anna Shaw, along with Susan B. Anthony, addressed the crowd, with Orson F. Whitney as the concluding speaker. Anna Shaw was clearly the star of the event whose major address in the tabernacle "carried the audience by storm." She spoke several times during the two-day conference and proved each time to be a favorite. The sessions were attended by a standing-room-only audience, requiring a move from the City and County Building to the more spacious Assembly Hall on Temple Square. As she often did for such visitors, Emily Richards opened her home to entertain three hundred guests at a formal reception. On the last day of the conference, a trip to Saltair, followed by well-attended meetings in the Assembly Hall, made a memorable conclusion.[14] Emmeline and her committee had done their best to include politicians, clerics, and suffragists from all persuasions to make the affair as ecumenical as possible. It turned out to be a triumph of goodwill and unity that had eluded Utah for nearly fifty years. Though exhausted from her responsibilities, Emmeline was sorry to see the conference draw to a close, and before the two visitors left, she invited them to her home for lunch with Margaret Salisbury, Belle, and Belle's daughter Lucile.[15]

The reclamation of woman suffrage was a major triumph for Emmeline Wells. Her participation in the suffrage movement brought her national

14. A preliminary notice of the conference is "The Coming of Miss Anthony: The National Conference," *Woman's Exponent* 23 (May 1, 1895): 260; a report of the conference is "The National Conference, National American W.S.A.," *Woman's Exponent* 23 (May 15, 1895): 268.

15. E. Wells, Diary, May 15, 13, 1895; "Coming of Miss Anthony." A biographical sketch is Eleanor Flexner, "Anna Howard Shaw." Anna Shaw's and Susan B. Anthony's talks along with that of Orson F. Whitney were published in the *Exponent*. See "Sermon by Rev. Anna H. Shaw in the Large Tabernacle in Salt Lake City," *Woman's Exponent* 24 (June 1, 1895): 1, 2; and "Bishop O. F. Whitney," *Woman's Exponent* 24 (June 15, 1895): 9, 10.

attention and acclaim for her abilities, especially given the unusual situation in Utah. It gave substance to her newspaper, which in turn gave opportunity to Utah women to become part of a national conversation on one of the major issues of their day in which they were major players. The federal intertwining of suffrage and polygamy highlighted ancillary issues of religious and marital rights and the extent of federal intervention in the life practices of individuals—questions introduced but neither fully addressed nor solved in her time. Emmeline was at the center of these questions both personally and professionally, and she did not shrink from expressing her position to anyone or in any setting. In the midst of the political drama that marked this significant year, she confidently asserted her belief that she did "as much work as seven other women" and then reiterated the purpose for such personal and exhaustive efforts: "I have desired with all my heart to do those things that would advance women in moral and spiritual as well as educational work and tend to the rolling on of the work of God upon the earth."[16] This particular endeavor brought her great satisfaction. Like Brigham Young, she saw little difference between her secular and religious pursuits.

If Emmeline felt her work in the political arena had been accomplished after the suffrage convention in May, she was wrong. She did not confide to her diary any aspirations for a future role in party politics, but she would soon be thrust into the midst of the decisive ratification election of November 1895, in which the officers of the new state would be elected. The question of the hour was whether the Enabling Act permitted women, who had been given the right to vote in the new constitution, to vote and be candidates at the November ratification election. The Democrats, hedging their bets, began courting women to their party and proudly announced that they planned to include women in their political societies, caucuses, and conventions. When Relief Society president Zina D. H. Young, her counselor Jane Richards, and Salt Lake Stake Relief Society president Isabella Horne all announced their allegiance to the Democratic Party, Democrats were elated. They could claim the "royalty" of Mormon women as members and eager campaigners. The Republicans were hesitant but galvanized into launching their own campaign to recruit women for fear their party would be "swamped" if women should be permitted to vote in November.[17]

At what point Emmeline decided to join the Republicans is not clear, but by July 3, after long political discussions with Isabella Bennett, Corinne Allen, Margaret Salisbury, and Judge James A. Miner, and visits from

16. E. Wells, Diary, August 1, 1895.

17. "The Political Arena," *Salt Lake Daily Herald*, June 21, 1895, 4.

Charles Bennett, Mrs. Isaac (Lydia White) Trumbo, Charles Crane, all Gentiles, as well as George M. Cannon, son of Angus Cannon, she was clearly convinced this was the party for her.[18] Though she had once stated that she had "turned from a Democrat to a Republican," Emmeline did not articulate her specific reasons for doing so. Without a living husband or son, she did not have the immediate political persuasion that the Richards women had to become Democrats. Moreover, her daughter Annie and her husband, John Q. Cannon, were Democrats (though his father became a Republican), while Septimus Sears and presumably Belle were ardent Republicans. Orson F. Whitney was a Democrat, but Daniel H. Wells had been considered "the father of Republicanism" in Utah, and his political influence may have lingered.[19] Perhaps the egalitarian views of Republican Joseph F. Smith might have persuaded her to his party. More likely, Emmeline calculated where she could do the most good, which political philosophy best supported her ideas, and where she would more likely realize personal opportunities. Emmeline's political work disappointed Annie, which dampened Emmeline's "ardor," but not her actions.[20]

Emmeline was not the only prominent Mormon woman to become a Republican. She was joined by Sarah M. Kimball; Elmina Taylor, president of the YLMIA; and two young women, Clarissa Young Williams and Ruth May Fox, both friends of Emmeline's. Fox's reason for becoming a Republican was probably unique. "When the women who had been ardently working for suffrage arrayed themselves for the political battle," she wrote, "most of them seemed to be Democrats while Aunt Em stood almost alone, a Republican. To even things up a bit, I joined hands with that great leader." They worked together in the campaign for state officers and traveled throughout the territory, organizing women's Republican clubs.[21]

Emmeline was assigned by the party to direct the effort to organize these clubs. Thus, with this new political responsibility she was eager to

18. E. Wells, Diary, July 2, 3, 5, 6, 1895.

19. Jesse N. Smith referred to Daniel H. Wells as in "the same party as Abraham Lincoln." Jesse N. Smith, "The Crowning Years of Pioneer Life," 1905, 455–56, L. Tom Perry Special Collections, Harold B. Lee Library, Brigham Young University, Provo, UT. The *Salt Lake Tribune* on January 7, 1896, referred to Wells as "that dear old man...still spoken of as the 'Father of Republicanism' in Utah," a dramatic reversal from its characterization of him years earlier as a "one-eyed pirate." See "City Jottings," *Salt Lake Tribune*, January 3, 1879, 4.

20. E. Wells, Diary, July 28, August 25, 1895. Ironically, though appalled at her mother's decision to become a Republican, Annie eventually joined the Republican Party and served in the state legislature from 1913 to 1915 and again in 1921.

21. Fox, "My Story," 26–27.

inform herself on all of the issues so she would "not be at a loss conversing with those who are up in everything" or "appear ridiculous" when she gave political speeches, which she was required to do "almost every evening."[22] Throughout the summer of 1895, she traveled, lectured, and organized while also answering derogatory newspaper articles deriding her efforts and those of the Republican Women's League, which she headed. While the publicity-generating political activities of the prominent Democratic women evoked concern by church leaders and an admonition for more moderation, Emmeline's work with the Republican Women's League escaped such censure.

Attending local, county, and territorial conventions, organizing Republican clubs, and then standing for office took Emmeline into a corner of the public realm that she found challenging and exciting. "We are all in commotion," she wrote shortly before the Republican territorial convention. "Scarcely know how to get through it all it has been very exciting for me and quite new too." "What an experience this has been for me," she concluded. "Really one could scarcely credit what I have done this year."[23]

In the meantime, the question of women's eligibility to vote at the ratification election had become an issue that required a judicial decision. The district court in Ogden, where the case originated, decided in the affirmative, but the decision was appealed to the Utah Supreme Court.[24] Emboldened by the lower court's ruling allowing women to vote in November and assuming the right to run for office was implicit in the ruling, the Republicans acted first this time by nominating three women: Lillie R. Pardee for the Senate, Emmeline for the House, and Emma J. McVicker for state superintendent of schools. Heber M. Wells was the Republican's choice for governor of the new state. However, just as the Democrats assembled for their own nominating convention shortly after the Republican convention, the Territorial Supreme Court overturned the lower court's decision and ruled that women were not eligible to vote in the forthcoming election.[25] Nothing was said, however, about the legality of their running for office since, the argument ran, women would not take office until after the constitution was ratified and Utah had obtained statehood. At first, the general assumption was that they could not be legal candidates, and the Democrats did not nominate any women, while the Republicans reluctantly recalled

22. E. Wells, Diary, September 9, 1895

23. Ibid., August 26, 1895.

24. Emmeline discussed the district court's decision in "The Opinion of the Court," *Woman's Exponent* 24 (August 15, 1895): 43.

25. See "Women May Not Vote," *Woman's Exponent* 24 (September 1–15, 1895): 49.

the women's names. When a shift in public opinion once again seemed to favor women's eligibility, the Republicans returned the women's names to the ballot.[26] Feeling confident of her candidacy, Emmeline continued her round of campaigning while at the same time arranging for a parade and a meeting of members of the Pacific Coast Women's Press Club, who were visiting Salt Lake City during the hectic August campaign.[27]

Emmeline's respite from these demands came from the quiet of her home, distanced from the bustle of the city. There she enjoyed the warmth of Indian summer and the brilliance of the early autumn nights from "thousands of stars" softened by moon and clouds, all of which stirred her poet's heart. "The feeling [is] indescribable that one has in gazing upon nature's beauties," she rhapsodized, especially "with the peculiar temperament I have."[28] In those quiet moments, Emmeline considered a political future that would be unthinkable to most women with whom she associated in the national suffrage movement. Utah women were clearly demonstrating that voting was merely an entry point to direct political influence. Making the laws that governed them was the real prize.

But this was not the year when Utah women would receive that prize. Public opinion as well as legal ruling shifted once again, which diminished party support, leaving the potential candidates without a base for their candidacy. In September, Emma J. McVicker withdrew her name, followed shortly thereafter by Lillie Pardee.[29] Emmeline remained adamant. She held on until she realized her backing had dissolved. "I suppose there is really no alternative but to withdraw," she concluded in mid-October. "I believe it is wrong.... I do not believe it would really affect the party or statehood or cut any figure in the matter whatever, and I think moreover I have a right to be elected to the Legislature—as also other women—I yield unwillingly to the pressure brought to bear against the name of women on the Ticket."[30] Emmeline did not run merely to further her own political interests, although she recognized the importance such an achievement would be in her dossier and the enviable platform that political office would provide in furthering her work for women. But she also deeply regretted the missed

26. C. Madsen, *Advocate for Women*, 321–26. See also Carol Cornwall Madsen, "Schism in the Sisterhood: Mormon Women and Partisan Politics, 1890–1900."

27. E. Wells, Diary, August 26, 27, 1895.

28. Ibid., September 8, 1895.

29. "Mrs. McVicker Withdraws," *Salt Lake Tribune*, September 15, 1895, 8; "Planned State Campaign," *Salt Lake Tribune*, September 12, 1895, 8. See also letter in "Withdrawal of Mrs. Pardee," *Salt Lake Tribune*, September 29, 1895, 4.

30. E. Wells, Diary, October 16, 17, 1895.

opportunity for the new state to include women among its first elected officials—and the possibility that she might have been one of them.[31]

With a resounding affirmative vote on the new constitution in November, Utah was prepared to celebrate, after nearly fifty years and seven tries, the achievement of statehood.[32] It was the Republicans' hour, and Emmeline was proud to say that Heber M. Wells, "one of our boys" (Martha's son), was swept into office as the first governor of the new state of Utah. On Saturday, January 4, she and Emily Richards telegraphed Susan B. Anthony to say that President Grover Cleveland had signed the statehood proclamation. "Women are full-fledged citizens," they reported. "Glory Hallelujah! Rejoice with us." Anthony responded, "We all rejoice with you that Utah is a State with her women free and enfranchised citizens."[33] Though united in the effort to achieve suffrage for women in the new state constitution, the truth of Isabella Horne's statement had already become evident: "Politics have divided us more than anything else that ever happened."[34]

While there was some celebrating on January 4, the actual date of statehood, the inaugural ceremonies were postponed until Monday, January 6. Nearly fifteen thousand excited spectators crowded into the tabernacle and surrounding grounds where the thirty-six-year-old governor was officially inaugurated. The hall was festooned with a large, illuminated replica of an American eagle surmounting the pipes of the organ, and an immense flag, 75 feet by 150 feet, covered the interior dome of the building. Guns were fired from Fort Douglas, a parade marched through the streets of the city, and the Tabernacle Choir sang Evan Stephens's newly composed song "Utah, We Love Thee." After the oaths of office were administered, Governor Wells gave a well-prepared accounting of the status of the new state and especially congratulated Utah women because now, he declared,

31. C. Madsen, *Advocate for Women*, 293–327; C. Madsen, "Schism in the Sisterhood."

32. The final tally was 31,305 votes in favor of the constitution and 7,687 opposed, with all of the state offices going to Republicans.

33. Emmeline B. Wells and Emily S. Richards, letter to Susan B. Anthony, and "Reply," *National Suffrage Bulletin* 2 (January 1896): 8. Elizabeth Cady Stanton and Susan B. Anthony Papers.

34. "Ladies Semi-monthly Meeting," *Woman's Exponent* 23 (February 1–15, 1895): 238. Ruth May Fox was similarly concerned about the antagonism that developed between party members in the Utah Territorial Woman Suffrage Association, of which she was now treasurer. "I do hope they will not engender bad feelings in their divisions on party lines," she wrote. "As for my part I care nothing for politics. It is Mormonism or nothing for me." Fox, Diary, July 14, 1895. See also E. Wells, Diary, January 16, 17, 1896.

"there is no abridgement of their rights; but on the contrary, they enter upon the domain of the citizen under Statehood as free and independent sovereigns."[35]

At the inaugural ball that evening, held in the Salt Lake Theatre, Emmeline sat in the governor's box with Heber's mother, Martha, and presumably the other sister-wives.[36] She noted that Martha "received very many demonstrations of her son's popularity—was introduced to hundreds." The ball turned out to be "a great success," she declared, "tho' over-crowded—and yet very enjoyable."[37]

Of equal interest to Emmeline, however, was NAWSA's planned recognition of Utah's achievement at its annual convention in Washington. Notices of the celebration were sent to all the suffrage associations announcing the admission of the third suffrage state into the Union, and Susan B. Anthony wrote Emmeline to ask for her suggestions as to the date and method of celebration. In response, Emmeline chose a day for the convention that coincided with the arrival of the newly elected Utah congressional team, adding to the luster of this significant celebration. It would certainly be the crowning achievement of her political work in behalf of women. Margherita Hamm, a correspondent for the *New York Mail and Express* and well known to suffragists, anticipated her welcome at the convention: "From far-off Utah will appear Mrs. Emmeline B. Wells, who has toiled thirty years for her principles, and now sees them triumphant in her own home. She will receive an ovation because long ago she foresaw and foretold what happened in the Great Basin last November. In fact, five years ago she laughingly said: 'Women will vote and hold office in my poor little mountain State before they do in the rich and powerful states of the seaboard.'"[38]

But the usual problem of funding loomed before Emmeline. "My impression has been all along that I should go, but how has not seemed to divulge itself," she worried. "I cannot borrow the money with no prospect of paying immediately and so I am in doubt."[39] Inexplicably, neither the church, the Relief Society, the Utah suffrage association, her family, nor

35. "The Inauguration," *Woman's Exponent* 24 (January 1–15, 1896): 100–101.

36. All of the newspapers carried details about the achievement of statehood and the celebratory events surrounding it. See Gustive O. Larson and Richard Poll, "The Forty-Fifth State," 395–97.

37. E. Wells, Diary, January 7, 1896.

38. "The Woman Suffragists," Journal History, January 23, 1896, 8, also available on *Selected Collections from the Archives of the Church of Jesus Christ of Latter-day Saints*, 2 vols. (Provo, UT: Brigham Young University Press, 2002), vol. 2, DVD 19, microfilm copy in Harold B. Lee Library, Brigham Young University, Provo, UT.

39. E. Wells, Diary, January 15, 1896.

Woman's Exponent.

VOL. I. SALT LAKE CITY, UTAH, JUNE 1, 1872. No. 1.

NEWS AND VIEWS.

Women are now admitted to fifty American colleges.

Rev. De Witt Talmage is pronounced a success as a sensation preacher.

Theodore Tilton says the best brains in northern New York are wearing white hats. They might wear chapeaux of a more objectionable color.

Daniel W. Voorhees in one day destroyed the political record of a life-time, and that was when he became henchman to a judge with an eclesiastical mission.

An Alabama editor writes "United State," and refuses to write "United States"—a straw to show how Southern sentiment runs. What a state he must be in?

The season of scattering intellectual filth has set in over the country. It occurs quadrennially in the United States, commencing a few months before the Presidential election.

Dr. Newman failed to become a Bishop at the Methodist General Conference, and Dr. Newman mourns this second great defeat. He has remembrances of Salt Lake in connection with the previous one.

Great outcry is raised against the much marrying of the Latter-day Saints. The tendency of the age is to disregard marriage altogether, but there seems no indication of a desire to have the race die out.

The "Alabama" muddle like "confusion worse confounded" becomes worse mixed the more it is stirred. It stretches itself over the path of time, and "like a wounded snake drags its slow length along." The country has become heartily sick of it.

Some Eastern journals head their Utah news with "Deseret." With keen appreciation of the coming and inevitable, they accept the mellifluous name chosen for the region wrested by that industry which "the honey bee" represents, from the barren wilds of nature.

George Francis Train sends us a bundle of Train Ligues. The compliment is appreciated, but the act is like sweetness wasted. We can vote, but not for "the next President of America." Utah has not become Deseret yet, nor can it participate in President making.

The last week of May, 1872, will be memorable in American annals as the first time since the first ordinance of secession was passed in the South, that both houses of Congress had their full list of members. Statesmanship can retain a complete Federal legislature, but the article has grown somewhat scarce.

To pardon the worst class of criminals on condition that they emigrate to the United States, is growing in favor with European monarchies. Germany and Greece so far have done the largest business in this line, the latest batch of villains thus disposed of being the Marathon murderers from Greece. Orders have been forwarded by President Grant to New Orleans, to which port it is understood they have been sent, to prevent their landing. They should be captured, ironed, returned to Athens with Uncle Samuel's compliments, and a bill for direct and "consequential" damages presented.

News comes from France that trailing dresses for street wear are going out of fashion. So many absurd and ridiculous fashions come from Paris that the wonder is thinking American women do not, with honest republican spirit, reject them entirely. This latter one, however, is so sensible that its immediate adoption will be an evidence of good sense wisely directed.

The anti-Mormon bill of Judge Bingham seems to have fared no better in the judiciary committee of the House of Representatives than the one to which Mr. Voorhees stood sponsor. It is gratifying to think that a majority of that committee yet respect the antiquated and once revered instrument still occasionally referred to as the Constitution.

Rev. James Freeman Clark claims "that if it is an advantage to vote, women ought to have it; if a disadvantage men ought not to be obliged to bear it alone." Speaking from experience we feel safe in affirming that the Rev. gentleman is right, and we hope for a time when this immunity may be universally enjoyed by our pure-minded and light-loving sisters. We don't presume that those belonging to the opposite class care anything about it.

Mrs. Carrie F. Young, editor of the "Pacific Journal of Health," has been lecturing in Idaho on Temperance and Woman Suffrage. The editor of the "Idaho World" was not present, but did not regret his absence. He says, "We feel a most decided repugnance to the exhibition of a woman upon the rostrum, advocating such degrading theories as 'woman suffrage' and other cognate subjects." He omits to state whether "Temperance" is one of the "degrading theories" to which he refers.

Force is ever the argument of a bad cause. The principles which cannot be overcome except by the exercise of physical power, present a front that arrests the attention of thinking minds. Where argument fails and force is employed to overcome an opponent, the power of the principles to which opposition is made is admitted. Will those who urge repressive legislation against the people of Utah think of it? Witness the Voorhees bill as an illustration.

A notable event, as a result of the late terrible Franco-German war, is the opening of the German University in Strasbourg, which takes place June 1st—to-day. That famous city on the Rhine, after a siege memorable in the annals of warfare, passed into the hands of the Germans, and now they take the surest means to permanently consolidate their power, by establishing there one of those seats of learning for which Germany has become enviably famous.

Miss Susan B. Anthony, it is said, declared before the Cincinnati Convention met, that if it gave her cause "the cold shoulder," she would go to Philadelphia and pledge the ballots of the women of America to U. S. Grant. As the women of America are yet without ballots, and as it is very questionable, if they had them, whether they would authorize any single individual to pledge them for any candidate, the supposition is fair that Miss Anthony possesses too much good sense to have made any such declaration.

Rev. Mr. Peirce, a Methodist clergyman who has made Salt Lake his headquarters for some time, in lecturing east proposed the extinction of polygamy by the introduction here of vast quantities of expensive millinery goods, and by inducing "Gentile" women to dress in gorgeous style that "Mormon" women might imitate them and run up such heavy dry goods bills that it would be impossible for a man to support more than one wife, if even one. Mr. Peirce, no doubt, preaches modesty and humility occasionally, by way of variety; now he recommends the encouragement of pride, vanity and extravagance to accomplish his "Christian" designs. The course he advises has been largely followed in many places, has tenanted brothels, aided to fill prisons, broken up families, hurled women of reputation and position down to degradation and infamy, and has met heavy denunciations from inspired men whom Mr. Peirce professes to revere. He would steal the livery of evil to serve religion in. There is not much of this reverend gentleman, and what little there is must be either very silly or very wicked.

The editor of "The Present Age" has been to a church and heard an orthodox sermon, in which the preacher took occasion to say that all religious "isms," including Mohammedanism, Mormonism and Spiritualism, rested their claims for being true "upon miracles." The "Age" is a Spiritualist and denies that his "ism" basis its claims to be true upon miracles. Latter-day Saints deny that Mormonism basis any claim for credence in it on miracles; the reverse is the truth. The "Age" defines a miracle to be "the setting aside for the time being of a natural law to meet an unexpected emergency." Had he said a miracle was the bringing into operation of certain natural laws not generally understood or comprehended, he would have been nearer correct. When somebody can tell how a natural law may be or can be set aside, except by the operation of some other natural law, his definition, which is the generally received one, may be entitled to more consideration. We imagine the working of the overland telegraph is as great a miracle to the Cheyenne Indians as any recorded miracle that the "Age" or the orthodox minister can quote.

Mrs. Laura De Force Gordon attended the Cincinnati Convention and claimed a seat as a delegate from California. Her claim was treated with hisses and laughter. She took a position in front of the stand and endeavored to speak, but her voice was drowned by a tumultuous discord. Her persistence in seeking to address an assemblage that treated her claim in such a manner was undignified; while the action of the Convention in receiving her with hisses and uproarious laughter, was disgraceful. The Liberal Republicans assembled in Cincinnati for a general work of purification and reform, evidently stood greatly in need of general reform themselves, in the matter of manners as well as in politics. Mrs. Gordon was as much entitled to a seat in that Convention as Carl Schurz himself, for we have yet to learn that the call for it specified that "male" Republicans only were admissable.

A new periodical in London is called "The Ladies."

FIGURE 22. First issue of the *Woman's Exponent*, June 1, 1872. Author's collection.

FIGURE 23. Emmeline B. Wells at work (1880; notice diary on desk). LDS Church History Library.

FIGURE 24. One of Emmeline's forty-seven diaries. Author's collection.

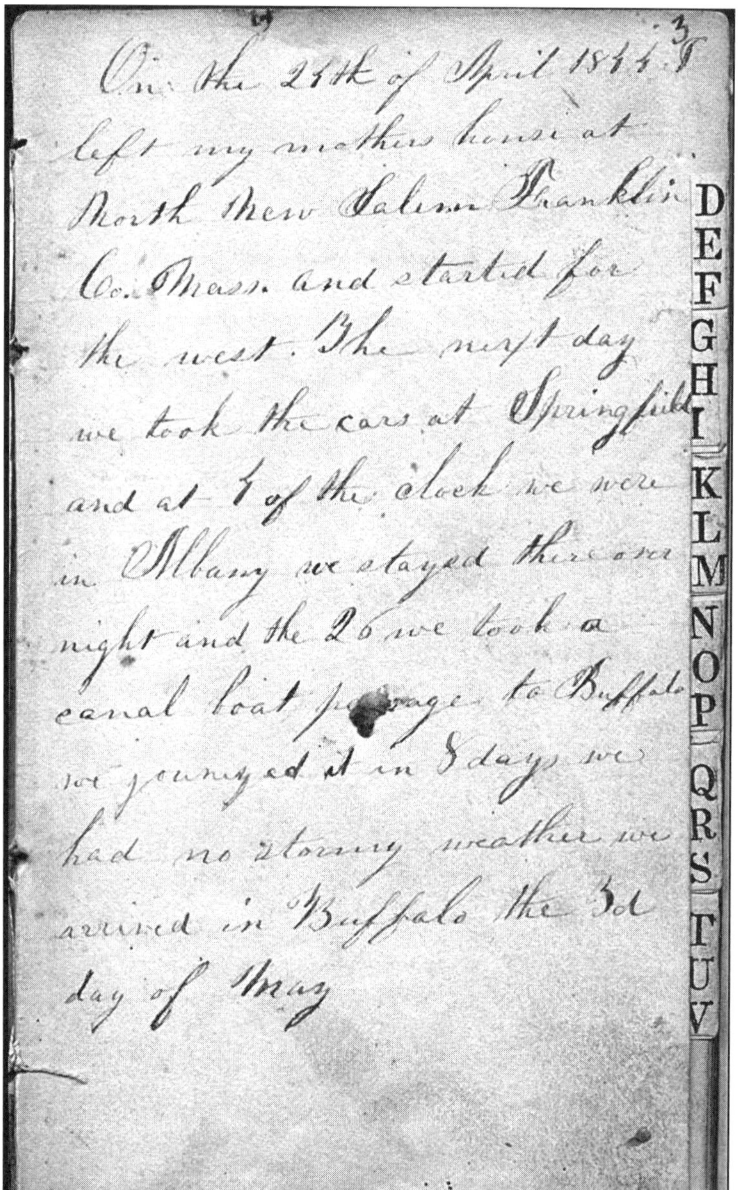

FIGURE 25. A page from Emmeline's diary. Author's collection.

FIGURE 26. *Musings and Memories*, Emmeline's book of poetry. Author's collection.

FIGURE 27. Thirteenth Ward Relief Society officers (*Emmeline is left on the second row*). LDS Church History Library.

FIGURE 28. Bishop's Building, 1910, north of the former Hotel Utah on Main Street. From *Young Woman's Journal* 21 (April 1910): 180.

FIGURE 29. Reception hall for three women's organizations, Bishop's Building, 1910. From *Young Woman's Journal* 21 (April 1910): 180.

FIGURE 30. General Board of the Relief Society, ca. 1914. LDS Church History Library.

FIGURE 31. Relief Society board going to conference, ca. 1920. LDS Church History Library.

FIGURE 32. Official Relief Society portrait of Emmeline by Lee Greene Richards. LDS Church History Library.

FIGURE 33. Three auxiliary presidents: Louie B. Felt, Primary; Emmeline B. Wells, Relief Society; and Martha Horne Tingey, Young Ladies' Mutual Improvement Association. LDS Church History Library.

FIGURE 34. Seagull Monument, which was unveiled by Emmeline B. Wells, 1913. Author's collection.

FIGURE 35. "Utah Women Celebrate National Suffrage Victory," *Salt Lake Tribune*, September 1, 1920. Emmeline Wells is at the center of the group.

FIGURE 36. Emmeline Wells at her eighty-eighth birthday celebration, 1916. Used by permission, Utah State Historical Society.

FIGURE 37. The aged Emmeline Wells near the Bishop's Building. Author's collection.

FIGURE 38. Bust of Emmeline B. Wells located in the Utah Capitol. Used by permission, Utah State Historical Society.

influential friends stepped up with the necessary funds. Emmeline would not attend the celebration geared to honor her, the woman who had led the effort to restore woman suffrage to Utah. What a twisted quirk of fate! In her place were Emily Richards and Sarah Boyer, a suffrage worker from Provo. "[I] can scarcely believe I am not going to Washington," Emmeline lamented to her diary the day Emily and Sarah left. "It don't seem true at all."[40] The expressions of regret proffered by ecclesiastical leaders were only salt in the wound. It is doubtful that President Woodruff realized how ironically painful his words were to Emmeline when he explained sometime after Emily and Sarah left that his preference had been for Zina Young and Emmeline to represent Utah. The absence of Zina Young, president of the Relief Society, which had been a consistent financial support and member of the national association for years, along with that of the president of Utah's Woman Suffrage Association (UWSA), deprived the event of the two women who were the most representative of this victory. After the exhilaration of achieving statehood with woman suffrage in its organic law, this unjust exclusion was one of the great disappointments of Emmeline's life.[41]

But as usual, she did not let it disable her. She prepared the credentials for Sarah and Emily, kept a running account of events in Washington for her paper, and accepted the regrets of those who felt a great injustice had been perpetrated. Emmeline had to content herself with a special tribute given to her in absentia which noted that her "influence had been paramount in securing the franchise for the women of Utah" and a telegram of congratulations from the national officers. Corinne Allen, Sarah Boyer, and Emily Richards all responded to the speeches of congratulation at the convention.[42] Emmeline suppressed her disappointment until some weeks later when her paper was too far behind and visitors too many in her office. "I have had many shocks that have unnerved me in a great measure, and I cannot be quite myself," she mused. "I have tried hard to control matters and to exercise great faith and to draw near to the Lord, but do as I will

40. Ibid., January 19, 1896.

41. Regrets from the "brethren" as well as her close Republican friends (almost any one of whom could have financed her way) perhaps eased her dismay at this unexpected circumstance. Ibid., January 11, 15, 19, 23, 1896. An extra thorn was admitting to making a mistake on Emily Richards's credentials and having to forward her a new document—"with an apology." Ibid., January 20, 1896.

42. Emily Richards's speech is included in Brian H. Stuy, comp. and ed., *Collected Discourses Delivered by Wilford Woodruff, His Two Counselors, the Twelve Apostles and Others, 1894–1896*, 4:419–23. Emily Richards made no mention of Emmeline Wells in her review of woman suffrage in Utah.

my heart is sad." Her continuing frustration at trying to accomplish what was important to her personally was discouraging. "I cannot seem to make things [happen] as I feel I ought to do, in consequence of opposition."[43]

Emmeline had little time to dwell on her disappointment, however. She immediately turned her attention to the new state legislature, lobbying for creation of a statewide silk commission, for public kindergartens, for more women in state agencies, for a raise in the age of consent, and for local libraries, all of which were eventually enacted. She was often alone in her legislative activities and had to "run about to try and get ladies to go to the Legislature with me," being successful in recruiting them only some of the time.[44] Of special interest was the proposal to legitimize all the children of polygamous marriages born before the 1890 Manifesto. The legislature moved the cutoff date to the year of statehood, 1896, which caused a ripple of anger among those who felt the decision represented a willful disregard for the Edmunds-Tucker Act of 1887 as well as President Woodruff's Manifesto.[45] Emmeline was dismayed to see that it awakened some of the "old prejudices."[46]

After the election Emmeline resumed her work with the women's Republican clubs, traveling and speaking for the party. By the summer of 1896, her party was once again willing to nominate women as candidates, and Emmeline was nominated as one of five at-large Republican candidates against five Democrats for five state senatorial seats. The top five vote getters from either party would be elected. She was the only woman of the five Republicans, and Martha Hughes Cannon was the only woman among the Democrats; Martha's husband, Angus Cannon, was one of the Republican candidates.

Surprisingly, Emmeline interrupted her campaign schedule to visit Mell. It seems incredulous that she would leave a month before Election Day, but leave she did. Her primary interest was the pending publication of a book of her poetry, which was then at press. She had been studiously gathering and arranging her poems for a projected volume, and before her departure for Idaho, she had prepared enough poems for the typesetters

43. E. Wells, Diary, February 13, 1896.

44. Ibid., February 5, 1896. Her lobbying was justified when she learned that had she and a few other ladies not been present when the bill relating to the age of consent was considered, it would not have been raised to eighteen from the traditional fourteen.

45. C. Madsen, "'At Their Peril'"; "Chance for the Exposition," *Salt Lake Tribune*, March 27, 1896, 5; "Evans Opposed the Bill," *Salt Lake Daily Herald*, March 27, 1896, 6; "Polygamous Issues," *Deseret Evening News*, March 28, 1896, 1.

46. E. Wells, Diary, March 27, 1896.

to begin work while she continued to gather, refine, or write additional poems. Idaho would give her the quiet time she needed to complete the collection.

As she did with many of her articles, Emmeline prefaced the book with a verse from a poem by a popular author of her day, the poet-priest Abram Ryan. The verse, taken from Ryan's poem "Song of the Mystic," prefigures the mood and message of the poetry that followed. It reads:

In the hush of the Valley of Silence,
I dream all the songs that I sing;
And the music floats down the dim Valley,
Till each finds a word for a wing,
That to hearts, like the Dove of the Deluge
A message of Peace they may bring.[47]

She also decided to change the title of the book from *Moods and Memories* to *Musings and Memories*. At Mell's she found the peace and freedom for which she constantly yearned and felt "as if I would like to be here some time for the quiet."[48]

Returning home on the night before the election and weary from travel, Emmeline was nervous but "determined to persever [*sic*]."[49] With women voting for the first time since 1887, the election drew much attention and public discussion. Emmeline felt the tension of candidacy. Unable to remain in her office on Election Day, she traveled back and forth to Republican headquarters, checking on the current results of the voting. By evening, she was weary of the confusion and contradictory reports and went home "tired out and half-sick," perhaps already aware of the returns, yet "hopeful of the result in my favor."[50]

But disappointingly, all five senate seats went to the slate of Democratic candidates. Though Martha Hughes Cannon garnered the fewest votes of the five (11,413), they were nearly 3,000 votes more than her Republican husband had received (8,742). The lowest number of votes of all ten candidates (7,064) went to Emmeline Wells.[51] It was a resounding defeat, and her empty diary pages for the following week indicate how devastating the loss was to her self-esteem. The thirty-nine-year-old Martha Hughes Cannon now had the distinction of being the first woman state senator in the United

47. Abram J. Ryan, *Father Ryan's Poems*, 9–10.
48. E. Wells, Diary, September 12, 1896.
49. Ibid., November 2, 1896.
50. Ibid., November 3, 1896.
51. Jean Bickmore White, "Gentle Persuaders: Utah's First Women Legislators."

States, not the sixty-seven-year-old Emmeline.[52] She partially relieved her feelings in a self-serving editorial in the *Exponent* that expressed her regret that "all the women [candidates] were not elected, for it would have been a much truer test of women's power had there been some women from each party." But, she optimistically stated, "women as well as men must content themselves as best they can until another election, when things may be different."[53]

Two years later, Emmeline was once again nominated by a party member to run for public office, but she did not win enough votes from the party to be its candidate. She had simply not lived up to its expectations. Political office was not to be hers. In her attempts to test the impact she might have had in politics, she had been rejected first by the law, then by the voters, and last by her own party. Terribly dejected, she was somewhat assuaged by the numerous congratulations that her name had been considered to represent her party and the deep-felt expressions of sympathy when she failed to win her party's nomination. Women, even from "the opposite party," thought it only right that she should be the Republicans' candidate.

Only in this single area—elective office—did Emmeline fall short of her own expectations, and being reconciled to that fact was difficult. "[I] have suffered tortures in my feelings," she wrote after the November election, cataloging the misery she felt elsewhere in her life. "I have such poignant grief over my family that it overburdens me even ordinarily and when added to that is the burden of debt it is too much for a delicate woman to endure."[54] Blinded by the demoralizing sense of failure, she lost sight of the esteem in which she was held by men and women both in- and outside her faith; of the constant calls on her knowledge, wisdom, and abilities by a diversity of individuals and groups; of the strength she exerted to successfully avoid surrendering to other losses and disappointments; and even of the feeble but persistent presence of her "little paper," all because of her unyielding resoluteness. But she was dispirited by this defeat, which she

52. This race became a cause célèbre in Utah and throughout the country. Not only was it unique for a woman to be running for political office, but to run against her husband and *win* was truly a novelty, and tradition has it that the event was noted in Ripley's *Believe It or Not* publication. In its November 1897 issue, *The Puritan: A Journal for Gentlewomen* published an article entitled "Women Lawmakers in the West," which read: "A political woman was no new thing, but a woman fighting for a woman was a novelty, and the spectacle of a woman running for office against her own husband, and defeating him, created a positive sensation, not only in Utah, but throughout the land" (50–51).

53. "Woman's Work and Duty," *Woman's Exponent* 25 (November 1, 15, 1896): 69.

54. E. Wells, Diary, November 11, 1896.

found especially humiliating because so many had held such high expectations for her success and she had let them down.

The two years following statehood were momentous. Statehood itself not only meant a new status for Utah and a reconciliation of the church and the federal government; it also marked some major achievements in Emmeline's life. She was not bound to the constraining provincialism that characterized many of her contemporaries. And statehood was symbolic of her personal embrace of the larger society to which Utah was now joined. She had heard the siren call of political office but would not taste its infectious power. Her failure in the political realm did not diminish her effectiveness elsewhere, and she was still the woman called on for counsel, conversation, ideas, sociability, and leadership.

CHAPTER 29

A Book of Her Own

(1896–1898)

EMMELINE'S DEJECTION over the election was soon superseded by her anticipation of the publication of her book of poetry. Preparations for the volume took more than a year, but finally she was nearing the realization of a long-held dream. Through the direction of Romania Pratt Penrose and Ellis Shipp, the Woman's Press Club and some friends raised sufficient funds for its publication. By the end of 1896, the drawing for the book cover was completed and sent off to New York for a printer's plate. Not until October 1897, however, did Emmeline finally have proofs in hand, which made her "tremble with excitement." The first few bound copies arrived on December 10, but her first examination of them brought disappointment rather than exhilaration, as she found them "not satisfactory."[1] But when the book was "fairly launched" with a special notice in the *Deseret News*, her mood brightened. "At last," she wrote, "after all these years of waiting it is an accomplished fact." Whether it would be a blessing to her and her family was yet to be determined, she acknowledged, but she knew she had succeeded in creating a legacy that gave promise of reaching an appreciative audience. "I do feel grateful for the privilege of making this contribution to the world and especially to my own people," she declared.[2]

The finished volume, measuring five inches by seven and a half, had on its cover a simple floral design in gold, with its title and Emmeline's name, also in gold print. Some volumes were issued in leather bindings, but most were in cloth of varied colors of Emmeline's choosing. Her dedication begins the volume followed by a short "introduction" written by M. C. W., likely Melvina Caroline Woods, Emmeline's daughter Mell. The volume includes 119 poems on 304 pages. Each member of her two literary clubs received a

1. E. Wells, Diary, December 10, 1897.

2. Ibid., December 11, 1897.

copy, and Emmeline gave away many others during the following months. The book was popular enough for a second edition in 1915 that included several additional poems and a preface by Annie Wells Cannon. It was a great personal triumph for Emmeline.

Musings and Memories was especially satisfying to Emmeline because she had always revered the poetic art and longed to be one of the poetic artists. For her, poetry was the surest medium through which she could publicly express her most intimate feelings, especially in her autobiographical poems in which she was usually the third-person narrator. In these writings, her life was truly a "romance," written by an offstage narrator a step removed from the events described, perhaps giving the poetic story more literary essence. The audience for poetry, she believed, would be those whose souls, like hers, "have a touch of this ideal sublimity inherent in them." They are the ones who would "appreciate the poetry of music, of motion, of nature most of all." Poetry, she explained, was "the extreme depth and minutest expression of sorrow, and the most ecstatic and exquisite joy."[3] Her colorfully embroidered and emotional style, popular in her time, was governed by her view of the purposes and elements of poetry. "If there was no sentiment in the world," she wrote, "there would be no poetry." Poetry is a "history of the heart," she wrote, and her own poetry confirmed it.[4] It is serious, reflective, and full of feeling. The light and dark of her own life are overriding themes. Again and again, whatever the subject, many of the bright poetic pictures she paints are ineluctably shadowed by unhappy memories, unexpected sorrows, deep-seated disappointments, and ominous forebodings.[5]

Yet these are all poems that give promise of hope and recompense at the end of one's struggles, reflecting her own faith in compensation. Without being doctrinaire, her poetry exudes religious sentiment, promising joy in a better world for steadfastness in this one.[6] "Disappointment cometh not in vain," she affirmed. "Life's richest treasures oft are bought with pain."[7] Her faith in this "talisman," as she called it, enabled her to push onward each time with a "brightness of hope" after adverse experiences.

3. Blanche Beechwood [Emmeline B. Wells], "Poetry, How Can We Define It?," *Woman's Exponent* 4 (August 1, 1875): 33.

4. "A Historic House," *Woman's Exponent* 21 (December 15, 1892): 92–93. See also "Editorial Notes," *Woman's Exponent* 24 (July 1, 1895): 20–21.

5. A typical example is E. Wells, "A Glance Backward," in her *Musings and Memories*, 167–71.

6. See, for example, "At Last," which counsels youth on the folly of wandering from truth and light and urges them not to turn aside but to be "diligent with constant care, / Stern duty for our motto, faith our guide, / Patience our helpmeet, and our watchword prayer." E. Wells, *Musings and Memories*, 69–71.

7. E. Wells, "A Glance Backward," in ibid., 167–71.

As an inveterate lover of the natural world, Emmeline used nature, especially the New England landscape, as the subject or principal imagery in much of her poetry. For her, nature emitted ethereal vibrations that resonated beauty, hope, and especially truth to the attentive listener. "The Dear Old Garden" was her homage to the garden she planted and nurtured at her State Street home that was the closest re-creation she could make of the lush landscape of her childhood home. But she knew nature could also wear a forbidding and dark visage, somberly affirmed in her poem "Memory of the Sea," written in the same throbbing meter as Coleridge's "Rime of the Ancient Mariner" or Poe's "The Raven." This particular poem ends not in anticipation of a surcease of sorrow and despair, as with many of her other poems, but in resignation to a fate that holds us captive.[8]

Another deeply personal poem, "Sorrow and Sympathy," reads like a confessional with obeisance to the axiom that pain begets understanding.

I know I oft have distant been and cold,
Because my sorrows seem'd to be so great;
But if perchance the wrongs I've felt were told
I would not murmur at my adverse fate;
May be I needed just such discipline,
To gain the prize I started out to win.[9]

Most revealing of her poetic writings is her long autobiographical poem "Faith and Fidelity." Written in the third person like "Hephzibah," it tells the story of Emmeline's loneliness after James's desertion until she is rescued by a noble stranger who comes by and listens to her tale of grief. She explains that from this kind and sensitive patriarch she learned

sacred truths, reveal'd from heaven;
And now she comprehends their purposes in part
For the great mission unto woman given.[10]

Then the strong man dies, and Emmeline adds another loss to her life, which leads her to write:

And so some lives go on in tragedies, each part
To be sustained by human effort grand;
Though 'neath the outward seeming lies the broken heart,
That only One above can understand.[11]

8. E. Wells, "Memory of the Sea," in ibid., 34–36.

9. E. Wells, "Sorrow and Sympathy," in ibid., 291.

10. These phrases quite obviously relate to Whitney's teaching her the principle of plural marriage and the importance of being sealed to a priesthood bearer.

11. E. Wells, *Musings and Memories*, 207–28.

Musings and Memories would be the only book of her own making that this prodigious writer ever published. She did not realize at the outset the necessary steps required in preparing a book for publication and thus felt justifiably proud when she finally achieved it. "I think it is a great thing accomplished that I have my book at last," she wrote at its publication. "I felt as if it was such an undertaking after I had it started I had not thought it would be so much actual hard work and anxiety."[12] She had edited a book of poetry and paintings, *Songs and Flowers of the Wasatch*, for the Columbian Exposition and compiled a pamphlet of the work of Utah's volunteer associations, *Charities and Philanthropies*, but *Musings and Memories* was the only published collection of her own writing. "My first book of my own," she wrote when it came off the press.[13] "I feel the Lord has blest me in giving me this after all my sorrows and grief."[14] Though elated at the literary recognition for which she always yearned, Emmeline again found the commendations and attention "fatiguing and embarrassing in the extreme, and sort of trying to say the least—an ordeal."[15]

The long-awaited publication of *Musings and Memories* in 1897 could not quite assuage Emmeline's frustration in failing to achieve similar recognition for her stories. No firm record of when each was written is easily discerned from her diaries, but she evidently had enough of them ready for publication by 1891 that she obtained a copyright. That same year, she began announcing in the *Woman's Exponent* her intention of issuing a compilation entitled "Aunt Em's Stories of the Long Ago" and indicated that the book would be "entirely a home production of stories from real life." They would contain "vivid descriptions of scenery and incidents of New England in the

12. E. Wells, Diary, December 19, 1897.

13. Though the book was not actually available until December 1897, the date of publication of the first edition is 1896.

14. Ibid., December 19, 1897. See also May 5, 1890.

15. Emmeline was honored for her accomplishment on her birthday two months after her book appeared. She was gifted with an autograph book that contained nearly a hundred pages with a poem, original or selected, from each of the guests, dedicated to Emmeline. Each page was also adorned with hand-painted floral pictures. The book, entitled "Soulful Thoughts of Loving Hearts," was a "unique and costly memento of the birth of her brain-child and also of the seventieth year of her life," wrote Romania Pratt a few months later in a report of the celebration sponsored by the Utah Woman's Press Club, of which Pratt was the outgoing president. E. Wells, Diary, February 26, 27, 1898; *Woman's Exponent* 27 (November 1–15, 1898): 59. Romania wrote the dedication: "Your life has been a busy one not for self alone but for all womankind whom you love and honor. This book of 'leaves' represents a few of those most indebted to you for help in the upward trend of the soul and many loving remembrances." "Soulful Thoughts of Loving Hearts," autograph book for Emmeline Wells, L. Tom Perry Special Collections, Harold B. Lee Library, Brigham Young University, Provo, UT.

earlier days, and also the New West." "Hephzibah," her semiautobiographical story, already serialized in the *Woman's Exponent*, would be the first story in the collection. Claiming the promised volume as "the first book of the kind published at home," she explained it was "a new venture in the field of 'home literature,'" helping to meet the demands for this "class of reading."[16]

Home literature was the Mormon response to the cheap dime novels and penny tabloids popular throughout the country decades earlier. In 1882, Elder George Q. Cannon, himself an editor and publisher, was "surprised as well as pained in our feelings to see trashy novels laid by the side of the Holy Bible on the front room table" as he visited homes throughout the church.[17] Calling the reading of such low-grade fiction "a species of dissipation," Elder Cannon was among other Mormon cultural arbiters who derided the banality and lack of truth and moral uplift in these widely popular novels and warned of their degrading influence on young readers.[18] Unable to successfully curb the enthusiasm with which Mormon readers consumed them, Cannon and other Mormon literary guardians reasoned that popular fiction could be turned to their own purposes and utilized as a vehicle for inculcating Mormon values rather than sermonizing against their unwholesome or frivolous stories.[19] Fiction could teach as well as entertain, it was reasoned, and the new genre of "home literature" was off to a solid start, drawing the talents of B. H. Roberts, Susa Young Gates, Orson F. Whitney, Josephine Spencer, Augusta Joyce Crocheron, and Nephi Anderson.[20] Though written at this same time, Emmeline's stories are not moralistic fables that reflect the intent of most of the home literature that followed Whitney's call to arms. Avoiding overt didacticism and even references to Mormonism, she concentrated instead on utilizing the conceits of a romance in her slim plots. More often, her romantic views of love and marriage, the principal themes of her stories, implicitly rather than explicitly accommodated Mormon values.[21]

Place was inordinately important to Emmeline. Though promising stories of the "New West," Emmeline actually set most of her stories in New

16. "A New Story Book," *Woman's Exponent* 20 (November 15, 1891): 76.

17. "Editorial Thoughts," *Juvenile Instructor* 18 (November 1, 1882): 328.

18. "Editorial Thoughts," *Juvenile Instructor* 19 (October 15, 1884): 312. A review of the development of home literature is Matthew Durrant and Neal E. Lambert, "From Foe to Friend: The Mormon Embrace of Fiction."

19. "Editorial Thoughts," *Juvenile Instructor* 17 (February 15, 1882): 56. Orson F. Whitney is credited with introducing the shift in policy in 1888, launching a major shift in Mormon literature.

20. Orson F. Whitney, "Home Literature."

21. For an early review of her writing, see Carol Cornwall Madsen, "A Blue Stocking in Zion: The Literary Life of Emmeline B. Wells."

England, and many are centered on events occurring during holidays, particularly Thanksgiving and Christmas. Incidents and people from her own life are everywhere evident, particularly from her early life in New England. Though Emmeline lived only sixteen of her ninety-three years in New England, it was dominant in her fiction. After reading popular author Sarah Grand's novel *The Beth Book*, Emmeline acknowledged that "so many sayings reminded me of myself—for instance taking leave of places instead of people—I have often felt condemned for this sort of sentiment. Even now it dominates me many and many a time."[22] Though she left most of her family behind when she moved west, it was the loss of place that infused her thoughts and writings most keenly. The homestead, the hemlocks and pines, the brooks and meadows, and the seasonal changes in her New England home—these are the principal elements in her New England memoirs and prominent features in her fiction and poetry.

Her brief life with James, including their young love, early marriage, their son's death, James's desertion, the undelivered letters, and his death in Bombay are truly the stuff of romantic fiction, and she made good use of it, framing these events in plots from her fruitful imagination. One of her stories that draws most directly on them, "He Cometh Not," was published a second time under a different but equally emotional title.[23] The two stories differ also in the names of the characters and in a few lines, but they are essentially duplicates, evoking her brief romance and life with James. When she published "He Cometh Not" again, ten years after its first publication, she gave it the title "Musty Leaves, Brown with Age." To this second version she attached a two-verse poetic epilogue. The short poem begins:

One day I searched an empty cabinet
And found a musty book—I have it yet;
A journal of the good year twenty-nine,
Kept by a long departed friend of mine;
And from its leaves, grown brown with age,
I take a story and a single page.

22. E. Wells, Diary, December 9, 1897. British author Sarah Grand (1854–1943), born Frances Bellenden Clarke, was a controversial but popular writer. Some of her books were considered radical for her notions of liberated womanhood. She is credited with having coined the phrase "the New Woman." *The Beth Book* (New York: D. Appleton, 1897), a semiautobiographical piece, was newly off the press when Emmeline read it in 1897.

23. "He Cometh Not," *Woman's Exponent* 23 (December 15, 1894): 217–19, 221–22. This was published a year after receiving James's letters. E. B. W., "Musty Leaves, Brown with Age," *Woman's Exponent* 33 (December 1904): 42–43, 46–48, concluded in 33 (January 1905): 54.

Wait! Wait! Love, I come,
Bless this dear day
That brings from far away Bombay—
These words to thee I say
Wait, love, I come.
In flowery, far away Bombay,
Died in December, twentieth day.[24]

While other stories also draw from her own life and experiences, none does so as explicitly as this one.[25]

In October 1902, still unsuccessful in publishing a compilation of her stories, Emmeline explained to her readers her eleven-year attempt to get the compiled stories in print. "Considering the many books of fiction bought by our people," a note of petulance creeping into her explanation, "it would be much better to encourage home talent and purchase those written by our own brethren or sisters, containing facts and good morals."[26] But her stories were not the ones they wanted. A month later, Emmeline was forced to admit to her *Exponent* readers that an insufficient number of subscriptions had been obtained and the book could therefore not be published at that time. "We are still hopeful," she nevertheless added, "as to the result of the undertaking, and will in our January number give an outline of what the book will contain."[27] Neither the outline nor any further announcements appeared in the *Woman's Exponent*. Instead of a collection, Emmeline published the stories singly in the *Woman's Exponent*, and some appeared in other church publications.

Neither Emmeline's poems nor her stories have much literary currency today, and in her own day, they held no truly distinctive quality or stature,

24. E. B. W., "Musty Leaves, Brown with Age," *Woman's Exponent* 33 (January 1905): 54. The number twenty-nine could relate to James's age rather than the year. He was born in December 1827 and died in December 1859 at age thirty-two. The words "Wait for me" seem to be James's, with the last two lines relating to his death. It is not an easily decipherable poem, as are most of her others.

25. "Aunt Esther's Sweetheart," "He Cometh Not," "Some Old Love Letters," and "Hephzibah" are just a few of the stories intended for the volume. All were published in the *Woman's Exponent*.

26. "A Book of the Holidays," *Woman's Exponent* 31 (October 1–15, 1902): 36; "Editorial Notes," *Woman's Exponent* 31 (November 1–15, 1902): 45.

27. "Editorial Notes," *Woman's Exponent* 31 (December 1–15, 1902): 52. She had planned to publish the book, entitled "Aunt Em's Stories of the Long Ago," as early as 1891 (E. Wells, Diary, December 2, 1891, and Memoranda for 1891) and had obtained a copyright, which she lost and later found in 1895 (E. Wells, Diary, May 29, June 2, 9, 23, 1895).

but as paths to finding the woman "'neath the outward seeming" they are invaluable. Ironically, her reputation as a writer rests far more on her editorials and articles in the *Woman's Exponent* than on her poetry or fiction. Her letters were a significant portion of her literary output, and had they been published, as she had hoped, they would have paralleled her diary in significant self-revelation. But these were all ancillary to her own choice of literary recognition. She wanted to be a poet's poet, recognized and lauded beyond the borders of her own Mormon circle. Even toward the end of her long life, she still seemed to feel that, had she been freer to write what she pleased and to express that voice dictated by a whispering muse, she might have secured a place in the broader field of American literature. As it was, *Musings and Memories* would be the single highlight of her literary aspirations.

Emmeline functioned as well as she did because of the female social network that supported her personally and professionally, including her daughters and their families. As Emmeline aged, they enfolded her and made her a focal point in their lives. She rejoiced at the birth of each new great grandchild, pleased to see her posterity growing. When Belle's daughter Dot had her first baby, Dot and her husband, Charles Bucholz, honored Emmeline by inviting her to give their daughter a name and a blessing. At the family gathering, she blessed and named the baby Marian. "I know I gave her a good blessing," Emmeline reflected, "and I remembered the promises of Joseph [Smith] to Bishop Whitney's posterity—I think she will live and be an honor in her day and generation."[28]

In contrast to the sweet feeling and hopeful tone of this experience was Emmeline's emotional and impulsive action on Louie's birthday eleven years after her death. The sentimental and record-keeping Emmeline inexplicably gathered together the letters written to and by Louie, including those from her stay in San Francisco, and burned them all. There were hundreds, many from Joe Sharp, Rob Sloan, her girlfriends, and Emmeline, John Q. and other family members. If this destructive gesture was meant to bring closure to the memory of the unhappy time surrounding Louie's death, it failed to do so. But she expressed little emotion as she performed this act, despite the enormity of its finality. She noted only the "weird feeling" she had "while burning Lou's letters with her looking down from the picture—into the grate."[29]

The many travelers who continued to find their way to Utah helped to counteract these emotional outbursts as Emmeline lost herself in their company. She relished acting as an unofficial hostess for guests to the city,

28. E. Wells, Diary, November 2, 1898.

29. Emmeline had large portraits painted from photographs following the deaths of Emmie and Louie. Ibid., August 28, 1898.

especially those from literary and cultural backgrounds. One intriguing visitor, who came to Salt Lake City in 1897 for a long visit, was the colorful Lydia Mary Olive Mamreov von Finkelstein Mountford, best known as Madame Mountford. Born in Palestine in 1848 to Russian emigrant parents of the Greek Orthodox faith, she created a career based on the American appetite for all things exotic. She presented a dramatic rendering of life in Palestine and the Middle East with costumes, actors, and artifacts, and her talks were all framed within the context of the life of Christ and the New Testament.[30] Her popularity led to a three-month stay in Utah, at which time Emmeline met her. A correspondence followed, with Emmeline hoping that her friendship with Madame Mountford "presages good for me, but perhaps nothing."[31] Long wishing for a trip to the Holy Land, she hoped that Madame Mountford might arrange it. To her disappointment, no invitation materialized.[32]

The late summer of 1898 brought the death of another church president, the fourth thus far in Emmeline's lifetime. Wilford Woodruff's death at age ninety-one ended his eleven-year tenure during which he had presided over some of the church's greatest challenges. Though never as close to him as she would be to Joseph F. Smith when he later became church president, Emmeline respected his quiet and "grandfatherly" manner. As usual, Emmeline was assigned to make the necessary arrangements for the Relief Society's participation in President Woodruff's funeral—buying flowers, engaging a carriage to drive the Relief Society officers to the funeral and cemetery, and distributing tickets for the funeral held on September 8. She reported on his funeral services with a brief tribute of her own in the *Woman's Exponent*, the third president she had eulogized.[33]

30. "Living Pictures of the Holy Land," *Woman's Exponent* 25 (February 15–March 1, 1897): 108. See also "Editorial Notes," *Woman's Exponent* 25 (April 1, 1897): 125 and 25 (April 15, 1897): 134; "Madame Von Finkelstein Mountford," *Woman's Exponent* 26 (January 1–15, 1898): 237. See also "The Jerusalem of Today"; and Richard C. Galbraith, "No Room at the Inn?"

31. E. Wells, Diary, April 21, 1898.

32. Several historians have speculated on the possibility of Madame Mountford's baptism into the church in February 1897 and subsequent sealing to President Wilford Woodruff off the shore of San Francisco in September of that year. Matthias Cowley, a nephew of Wilford Woodruff and one of his first biographers, met with Emmeline in 1909, the year the Woodruff biography was published. They talked "of Madame Mountford being baptized and sealed to President W. Woodruff etc." Ibid., August 4, 1909.

33. Ibid., September 2, 3, 5, 6, 8; "In Memoriam, President Wilford Woodruff," *Woman's Exponent* 27 (September 15, 1898): 44–45.

As other first-generation Mormons, such as Sarah Kimball, Emily Partridge Young, and Franklin D. Richards, left the scene soon afterward, Emmeline, at age seventy, knew that she would herself become one of the last of the generation to have known the Prophet Joseph Smith and to have experienced the turmoil leading to the exodus from Nauvoo, Illinois, and the settlement in Utah. In fact, in the last years of her life, she was invited to numerous gatherings of young people to review for them those dramatic events. With her faultless memory, total grasp of the church's history, and penchant for reminiscence, she made an able speaker at these events and repeatedly told the story of her first meeting with Joseph Smith.

The end of the century brought Emmeline into the midst of a large controversy that threatened to break the fragile bridge of détente that had been constructed over the chasm of religious differences between Mormon and Gentile women. Many organizations affiliated with the NAWSA and the NCW had long fought for the termination of Mormon polygamy. After the 1890 Manifesto and Utah's statehood six years later, the animus toward Mormons seemed to have softened, and Emmeline, her coworkers, and many other Mormon women looked toward a brighter future working on social issues in alliance with women in Utah and throughout the country. Deterrents to that hopeful ideal, however, manifested themselves just a few years after statehood with the election to the House of Representatives of B. H. Roberts, a foe of woman suffrage during the state constitutional debate in 1895. The women and their suffrage supporters had won that fight. Now, his candidacy as a Mormon general authority and a polygamist flared into instant and open opposition by the state's Gentile population, particularly agitated by women's groups and Protestant clergy. An immediate casualty was the newly achieved spirit of cooperation among the women of the state, the collapse of which became dramatically evident at the triennial meeting of the National Council of Women in February 1899 in Washington and the quinquennial meeting of the International Council of Women the following June in London. Emmeline was already familiar with the personal affronts of discrimination, the latest occurring at an executive meeting of the National Council of Women in Omaha in October 1898, three months before the NCW triennial.[34] The warm and friendly welcome she received from Susan B. Anthony, May Wright Sewall, and Louise Barnum Robbins, leaders of the council, contrasted with her experience at a dinner hosted by the local Council of Jewish Women about which Emmeline observed "one can easily comprehend the prejudice that

34. "Visit to Omaha," *Woman's Exponent* 27 (November 1–15, 1898): 60.

must be met when every one you meet wants to know directly if you are a Mormon, and would not think of asking a woman from any other state, what church she belonged to."[35]

At the NCW triennial in February, however, the opposition was far more public and harsh, ignited by the B. H. Roberts election. His first unsuccessful run for Congress in 1895 had brought no outside agitation over his church position or marital status, so he was surprised when his candidacy in 1898 evoked such a strong groundswell of opposition from both local and national individuals and groups. Ironically, his nomination this time caused a furor among LDS women as well, including some from his own party. Emmeline's office was flooded with "sisters coming to me with complaints and wanting to know what to do," all remembering his adamant opposition to woman suffrage. Moreover, two years earlier, the First Presidency had issued a "political manifesto" requiring those in high church positions to sign a document promising to gain permission from the First Presidency before seeking political office or other activity that might interfere with their church position. After considerable internal struggle, Roberts agreed to sign.[36] Thus, Emmeline decided to seek advice from the newly appointed church president, Lorenzo Snow, Woodruff's immediate successor, and his counselor George Q. Cannon, both of whom were also concerned about his nomination, fearing it would revive the long-standing split among church leaders over the church's activities in political affairs.[37] The First Presidency told her that "they were more than willing women should work against him—either privately or publicly." Their worries over Roberts's candidacy sharpened Emmeline's own feelings about it. "The idea that he should expect to be elected by women's votes after his anti-suffrage raid," she indignantly wrote.[38]

A persuasive orator, Roberts won the general election, which totally dismayed Emmeline, knowing that his election was aided by women's votes. "It is a great disappointment to me that Roberts was elected," she complained, and presciently predicted, "It cannot but be detrimental in every way. My

35. E. Wells, Diary, October 23, 24, 1898.

36. Apostle Moses Thatcher, who ran for the Senate, did not agree to the policy and refused to sign. He was subsequently released from his position in the Quorum of the Twelve.

37. Lorenzo Snow was ordained president of the church on September 13, 1898, just four days before Emmeline sought his advice over Roberts's nomination. He was sustained in that office by the membership of the church at the church's conference, October 9, 1898.

38. Ibid., September 17, 20, 1898.

heart is very sad. I cannot understand how the women of the State can be so unscrupulous as to vote for such a man."[39] For Emmeline, Roberts's election was a political defeat, but the public furor that erupted was based on Roberts's marital and church status, not his politics. It soon escalated into a national cry to prevent his taking his seat in Congress.[40]

Susan B. Anthony, concerned that he would use his oratorical skills to thwart the work of the national suffragists, advised Emmeline to extract a promise from Roberts that he would not oppose woman suffrage when he was in Congress, to which Roberts agreed. She also expressed the hope that Mormon and Gentile women "will banish sectarianism or partisanshipism and talk and work and vote only for good officials, regardless of church or party!" Anthony warned the women against what, she said, men have not learned "with a hundred and more years of practice," which is to be present "in the very first nominations [of candidates], for after the nominations are made it is so very difficult to persuade voters to stand there for any save their own party nominees." She urged the women to organize local women's councils to assess the candidates and educate the voters as an effective means of making their voices heard.[41]

In the months following Roberts's election, the opposition was extensive. National women's associations issued letters and resolutions against him. Petitions were sent to Congress with several million names attached. With the triennial convention of the National Council of Women in February 1899, just months after the election, Emmeline heard the voices predicting that she and the other Utah women planning to attend would have "a hard time in Washington with all the opposition."[42] Roberts's election had resurrected the dormant arguments against Mormon women's membership in national women's associations.

Ten women left Utah in early February, and almost upon arrival, in a blinding snowstorm, May Wright Sewall, the outgoing president of the

39. Ibid., November 10, 1898

40. Davis Bitton analyzed this episode in the life of B. H. Roberts in "The Exclusion of B. H. Roberts from Congress." It is to be noted that both President Snow and Apostle Cannon, though still apprehensive about the consequences of the furor that had erupted after his election, nonetheless supported the right for Roberts to be seated after he had been duly elected to Congress.

41. "Miss Anthony's Letter," *Woman's Exponent* 27 (January 1, 1899): 81. Anthony's purpose in organizing local councils is very similar to that of the League of Women Voters, organized after passage of the Nineteenth Amendment in 1920, giving all US women the vote.

42. E. Wells, Diary, January 24, 1899.

NCW, met Emmeline in her room for a confidential talk.[43] Pressured to produce a resolution against Roberts as many of its associate members had done, the National Council of Women was planning to make the composition and passage of its own resolution part of its agenda. For the Mormon women to side with the majority of the council against Roberts would increase the willingness of the associated members to accept Mormon women in the national council, she explained. "Mrs. Sewall had some talk with me... on the Anti-Roberts resolution," Emmeline noted. She "said we must vote for it, it would be our golden opportunity and used all her power of persuasion to convince me it was the only course to pursue."[44]

Emmeline made no mention of the conversation to her fellow Utahns and did not write about her decision or the debate over the resolution in her diary. But local papers and even the *New York Journal* found the debate and the speeches of the Utah representatives intriguing and wrote extensively about the proceedings.[45] Before any official announcement was made of the NCW's interest in the Roberts case, Elizabeth Grannis, president of the National League for the Promotion of Social Purity, twice expressed her desire that the NCW would produce a condemnatory resolution. Emmeline and Ann Mousley Cannon were on the Resolutions Committee, along with delegates from the Woman's Christian Temperance Union and other moral reform organizations. Sewall had forced Emmeline into a dilemma that would necessarily be played out in the meeting of the Resolutions Committee. But Emmeline had made her decision, with which Ann concurred. Despite their antipathy to Roberts's politics, their Mormon loyalty trumped the "golden opportunity" that Sewall promised. Four hours of deliberation in the committee meeting over the Roberts question pitted Emmeline and Ann Cannon against the strong voices of their opposition determined to

43. Of the ten women, Emmeline stood in for Zina D. H. Young, president of the Relief Society, and Martha Horne Tingey represented Young Ladies' MIA president Elmina Taylor. Others attending either as delegates or as guests were Zina Young Williams Card, Lucy B. Young, Lula Greene Richards, Mabel Snow, Minnie J. Snow, Susa Young Gates, Ann M. Cannon, and Hana Kaaepa, a Hawaiian who accompanied the group from Utah at May Wright Sewall's invitation. Emmeline was always disappointed when Relief Society president Zina D. H. Young did not attend herself and asked Zina Card to urge her mother to share her time more evenly between her temple ordinance work and her Relief Society presidency. Emmeline B. Wells, letter to Zina Y. Card and Zina D. H. Young, December 5, 1897, Zina Young Williams Card Collection.

44. E. Wells, Diary, February 11, 1899.

45. C. Madsen, *Advocate for Women*, 427–29nn4–23; "The Recent Triennial in Washington," *Young Woman's Journal* 10 (May 1899): 194–215.

issue a resolution condemnatory of Roberts. But Emmeline and Ann succeeded. By the end of the long debate, the committee agreed to formulate a majority resolution omitting Roberts's name or marital status and alluding only to preventing "law-breakers" from serving in "law-making" bodies. Insisting on a stronger condemnation of Roberts's lawbreaking status as a polygamist, the committee formulated a minority resolution as well in which Roberts's marital status was a major point of the resolution, though without his name.[46]

Both resolutions were reported to the delegates, who debated them for most of the day. The minority resolution was discussed first. After the opposing arguments of several Utah women and friends of the Mormons, such as Susan B. Anthony, Anna Garlin Spencer, and J. Ellen Foster, the minority resolution was defeated. The council then debated the majority resolution, presented by Emmeline and Ann Cannon. Just before voting began, Emmeline decided to speak. Explaining that she had been opposed to Roberts's election from the beginning, she described her efforts at trying to defeat him. But, she continued, he had been legally and properly elected by the citizens of Utah, there was no constitutional reason for refusing to seat him, and he should thus be allowed to take his seat in the House of Representatives. She concluded by expressing dismay that the "Mormon question" had taken up so much of the convention's time. Finally, the vote was taken. To the great relief of the Mormons, the delegates voted in favor of the majority resolution. A final vindication came in the form of a new resolution presented by Reverend Anna Garlin Spencer that restricted any future resolutions or petitions to matters affecting only the policy or work of the council and its relation as a body to other organizations.[47]

Emmeline traveled to New York after the convention, where she visited Elizabeth Cady Stanton, who declared that the protest against Roberts had been in "bad taste and wrong in principle," and she felt that women's groups

46. The minority resolution read: "Whereas As the passage of the Edmunds Bill (so-called) established the law of monogamic marriage as binding upon all citizens of the United States, therefore, Resolved, That no person shall be allowed to hold a place in a law-making body of the nation who is not in this, and in all other matters, a law-abiding citizen." The majority resolution stated: "Whereas the National Council of Women of the United States stands for the highest ideals of domestic and civic virtue, as well as for the observance of law in all the departments, both State and national; therefore Resolved, That no person should be allowed to hold a place in any law-making body of the nation who is not a law-abiding citizen." As quoted in Susa Young Gates, "The Recent Triennial in Washington."

47. "Women's Council Votes to Bar Out Roberts," *New York Journal*, February 18, 1899, 1.

would only make themselves look foolish by entering the debate.[48] Susan B. Anthony also defended Roberts's right to be seated, noting that it was not Congress's prerogative to prevent Roberts from taking his seat, and, like Stanton, she derided women's groups for becoming involved.[49] However, the press of public opinion and ambiguity of relevant policies resulted in the loss of his seat.

The friendships Emmeline had cultivated through her national visits and stream of letters would prove many times over their value to her personally and to the church. This was just the beginning of a decades-long effort to expel Mormon women from national organizations, paralleling a new crusade for a constitutional amendment outlawing polygamy in all states. It effectually ended the brief period of détente that LDS women had enjoyed with their Gentile sisters in Utah after the 1890 Woodruff Manifesto. Undaunted by the revitalized tide of anti-Mormonism, Emmeline pressed on in her effort to prove the merits of her religion and the integrity of Mormon women. But for now, the challenge that loomed largest was personal. How could she find funding to attend the quinquennial convention of the International Council of Women and its concurrent Congress of Women, scheduled for June in London? As second corresponding secretary, she was on the central board of the National Council of Women, and her presence would be expected. But expectations and realities were disparate poles in Emmeline's world.

48. E. Wells, Diary, February 26, 27, 1899.

49. Ida Husted Harper, *Life and Works of Susan B. Anthony*, 3:1150–53. See also "Miss Anthony on Roberts," *Woman's Exponent* 28 (November 15–December 1, 1899): 80.

CHAPTER 30

An Innocent Abroad

(1899)

Turn-of-the-century London, resplendent as a world center, not only in territory and wealth but in literature and drama, shone as a beckoning beam in Emmeline's eyes. Two of her favorite authors were British: George Eliot (Mary Ann Evans), whose literary artistry raised her to the status of a classic, and the contemporary novelist Marie Corelli, who barely outlived her popularity. The possibility of visiting their homes—number 1 Cheyne Walk in Chelsea for Eliot and Church Street in Stratford-upon-Avon for Corelli—was tantalizing to Emmeline. All, of course, depended on her ability to raise funds to attend the quinquennial of the International Council of Women in June 1899. Having already embarrassingly scrounged to acquire funds just four months earlier for the February meeting of the NCW, Emmeline was hesitant to repeat the process so soon afterward.

Her associate in garnering support among Relief Society women for the "council idea" was Susa Young Gates, who was adamant that funds should be found to send Emmeline to London. "Zion has never needed your wise help more than now," she assured her friend in January. Susa, who had worried about her own funding for the trip, was relieved when she was given financial support from the YLMIA, on whose board she served.[1] But as late as April, Emmeline was still in doubt about going "unless the Lord puts it into the hearts of some who have means to assist me."[2] With nothing more than hope, she proposed several sessions at which LDS women would present papers, similar to the format of the Woman's Congress in Chicago in 1893. But the arrangement for this convocation would be different, according to aspiring ICW president May Wright Sewall. Not only were there to be no

1. Susa Young Gates, letter to Emmeline B. Wells, January 23, 1899, Gates Papers.
2. Emmeline B. Wells, letter to Susa Young Gates, April 25, ibid.

department sessions from a single organization or delegation, but only one person from an organization was permitted to present a paper. Margaret A. Caine had already been selected to speak on sericulture in Utah, and Margaret Salisbury, an avid supporter of the industry, had loaned her the funds to attend.[3] As an alternative to presenting a paper, Susa proposed to Sewall that Emmeline be included as a discussant, to which Sewall agreed. Insulted by this belated invitation, Emmeline refused the offer. She was also irritated when Sewall invited Susa rather than the YLMIA president, Elmina Taylor, to present a paper as the representative of that organization. Though Sewall later apologized for the "pain" she had caused her, Emmeline was clearly chagrined. She had always presented a paper or addressed the delegates at every woman's convention she had attended.[4] It was not easy for her to be passed over.

Finally, in late May the Relief Society agreed to give Emmeline six hundred dollars to cover the two-month excursion with any unused money to go to Margaret Caine. Thus, on a rainy June 3, Emmeline left her family, and with the assurance of blessings for her safety and success from Bishop Orson F. Whitney and Rulon S. Wells, a member of the First Council of Seventy, she boarded the train for New York, where she met with the officers of the National Council of Women at the gracious home of NCW president Fanny Humphrey Gaffney. After another blessing from George Q. Cannon, then in the city, she was fortified to begin the long crossing of the Atlantic. Boarding the *Teutonic* on June 14, she shared passage with Fanny Gaffney and her family as well as Rudyard Kipling and his family. Engaging him in conversation, Emmeline found him "most courteous" and pleasant in recalling his visit to Salt Lake City in 1889, and he indicated he might visit again "by way of San Francisco."[5]

3. Margaret Caine, for whom sericulture was a primary interest, and Margaret Salisbury were coworkers with Emmeline and others in the movement to develop sericulture as a Utah industry, and Salisbury would be naturally interested in this opportunity for Margaret Caine to publicize the work of Utah women in this field.

4. Susa, as a member of the NCW Press Committee, also served as liaison for LDS women at the meeting. See May Wright Sewall, letters to Susa Young Gates, January 10, February 28, April 1, 24, 1899; Emmeline B. Wells, letter to Susa Young Gates, January 21, 1899; Susa Young Gates, letter to Emmeline B. Wells, January 23, 1899; and May Wright Sewall, letter to Susa Young Gates, April 1, 1899. Sewall's rejection of Emmeline as a presenter may also have related to the fact that Wells was a polygamous widow and a vocal defender of polygamy. The Roberts affair had thrust the controversial subject into the spotlight again just six months before the meetings were to begin, and Emmeline's feelings toward Roberts were well known. Gates was supportive of Roberts, but she had never participated in polygamy.

5. E. Wells, Diary, June 22, 1899.

Upon reaching the Mersey Docks in Liverpool, Emmeline recalled Daniel's residency there as European Mission president, first from 1864 to 1865 and later from 1884 to 1887. "Strange indeed it seemed to me, to be where my husband had been so often and remained continuously for months and years, and other dear ones. And where our people have had headquarters for more than half a century.... [A]t one time Louie fully expected to go there we made up our minds for it but things were ordered otherwise."[6]

Although Emmeline by no means slighted any of the official functions that she was expected to attend as the second corresponding secretary of the NCW, the magic of London descended on her almost upon arrival. Though the rains poured down, her first sight of the Houses of Parliament and Westminster Abbey "compensated for anything," she wrote. "Emotion, sentiment, every mental and spiritual sense awakened to its highest activity; tears as well as rain were streaming down, and it was well for the moment to be alone," she wrote of her introduction to that great city.[7] The abbey, which she revered as the last resting place of many of the nation's royalty and military, literary, scientific, and philosophical giants, "is the one place most sacred to me," the romantic Emmeline wrote, "and I know I am more emotional than I can express with others. I cannot endure all sorts of people when under special influence."[8] She promised herself she would return, though recognizing that being one of the large party of Utah women necessarily constrained her freedom. "It is terrible to be with a party who pull this way and that," the independent Emmeline complained.[9] "I know there are inward voices that affect certain temperaments that are destroyed or detracted from by outward elements or factors. These I have had in my time in sacred places such as groves[,] roads, on the sea, and by the shore and upon Mountain & hill tops." Such places spoke to her romantic temperament, and outer voices dispelled that private communion.[10]

On another day, she went again to Westminster Abbey, this time with Priscilla Jennings and her daughter May Farlowe and granddaughter Lucile. Once again, she was awed to be standing on "such consecrated ground and viewing the ancient archetectural [*sic*] grandeur as well as the sculpture & Arabic and other inscriptions and ornamentation and heraldry shields, swords, and accoutrements of war and of the crusades was overpowering and to one so full of the sentiment and romance of the days of troubadours and chivalry, the whole situation was most truly overwhelming and aroused all

6. Ibid., June 21, 22, 1899.
7. "Abroad in London," *Woman's Exponent* 28 (August 1, 1899): 36.
8. E. Wells, Diary, June 23, 1899.
9. Ibid., July 6, 1899
10. Ibid., June 23, 1899.

the sensibilities that find expression in emotional feeling."[11] Emmeline's fancies came dramatically to life in the artifacts and history that surrounded her.

Repercussions from the B. H. Roberts affair, still reverberating in the States, had reached England and made the welcome of the sixteen Mormon women tenuous at best. Six had some official status for either the meetings of the International Council of Women or the Congress of Women: Susa Young Gates and Margaret A. Caine were presenting papers at two of the congress's sessions; Elizabeth Claridge McCune, Lucy Bigelow Young (Susa's mother), and Jean Clara Holbrook were patrons of the NCW; and Emmeline was an officer and also a patron of the NCW.[12] NCW president Fanny Gaffney promised the Mormon women that she would put "her foot firmly on any attempt to discriminate against American women," especially the Mormons, knowing that many of the titled women of the International Council of Women looked down on their American counterparts. Elizabeth McCune also sensed the tension between women of Great Britain and the United States, and Susa Gates attributed the stiffness she perceived among the British women from their feeling that "it would be an insult for a plain American woman to be President over the heads of Countesses and titled women." Susa also heard that there was an effort made to deny Mormon women invitations to the social functions. However, according to Susa, they received "more offers than they could accept." Curiously, however, she contradictorily wrote to Elmina Taylor that "Aunt Em has suffered everything. No invitations, no notice, nothing but coldness."[13] Perhaps Emmeline's occasional forays away from the group suggested this idea to Susa, but she clearly did not know Emmeline's daily agenda. From the day Emmeline arrived, her diary gives minute details of meetings she attended, people she met, socials she attended, and her efforts to be alone to view some of the historic sites she had only read about. On her first day in London, besides the hours she spent as a first-time visitor, she attended a meeting of patrons of the ICW held in Susan B. Anthony's room at the St. Ermins hotel. The next morning she hurried to another meeting in Susan B. Anthony's room, where she met several distinguished guests from various countries, after which she attended an "At Home" hosted by ICW president Countess Aberdeen (Ishbel Marjoribanks or Marchbanks) at the

11. Ibid., June 26, 1899.

12. The other women who were visiting London and attended some of the sessions were Priscilla Paul Jennings and her daughter May Jennings Farlowe and granddaughter Lucile Jennings, Mrs. R. K. (Carrie) Thomas and her daughter Kate, Josephine Booth, Amanda McEwan Knight and her daughter Inez Knight Allen, Lydia Dunford Alder, and Emma Lucy Gates, Susa's daughter.

13. Susa Young Gates, letter to Elmina Taylor, June 19, 1899, Gates Papers.

council headquarters. The social included a number of titled ladies from England and other countries who were served "tea & coffee—cakes fruit & other delicacies," Emmeline noted.

The following day, Sunday, she had a private tour of the National Gallery and enjoyed a service in St. Paul's Cathedral with Madame Lydia de Mountford, then living in London, while Susa and the other LDS women attended a meeting at the LDS branch in the city.[14] Another day she visited headquarters of a well-known woman's publication, the *Englishwoman's Review*, where she met journalists from Canada and New Zealand. She attended Lady Warwick's "Hostel," a private reception, and then traveled to Reading, just outside of London, where she met several men and women connected with the college in that city. "Had a lovely time," she wrote at the end of the day.[15] Most of these activities did not include her Utah friends.

Emmeline attended the two sessions at which her friends spoke, noting that Susa's paper "The Scientific Treatment of Domestic Service" received "much applause," but was sorry to note that Margaret Caine "gave her address and made a failure."[16] Emmeline declined a last-minute request to participate in a session chaired by May Wright Sewall. She did, however, accept the unexpected request to act as a discussant in a session addressing the work of benevolent societies chaired by Beatrice Webb, widely known in Great Britain as well as the States as a socialist reformer.[17] The session was held in Convocation Hall in the Dean's Yard of Westminster Abbey, "the most select and noted of all the places of meeting," according to Susa Gates.[18] "There," Emmeline proudly noted in her diary, "I had the opportunity to speak and to explain our Relief Society fully its date of organization its thorough practical work its halls and buildings in this and other countries [and] its practical work for those needing assistance."[19] "She was listened to with marked attention," Susa Gates observed, "and the Chairman

14. E. Wells, Diary, June 26–July 4, 1899.

15. Ibid., July 5, 1899.

16. Ibid., June 28, July 3, 1899. Susa Gates's talk was summarized in "Report on International Council and Congress," *Woman's Tribune* 16 (September 1899): 65.

17. Beatrice and Sydney Webb had visited America, including Salt Lake City, the previous year, a visit that Beatrice recorded. She had been particularly interested in meeting Utah state senator Martha Hughes Cannon and noted in her journal Cannon's election victory in the open state senatorial contest that included her husband, Angus, and also Emmeline Wells. She was, therefore, acquainted at least with Emmeline's name and with Mormonism before the London meeting. See David A. Shannon, ed., *Beatrice Webb's American Diary, 1898*, 126–36.

18. Susa Young Gates, "International Council of Women," 443.

19. E. Wells, Diary, July 1, 1899. See also "Women in Social Life," in *The Transactions of the Social Section of the Congress of Women: Women in Social Life*, 7:192.

offered her an increase of the allotted time at the close of her remarks, which, however, was not accepted."[20] Though not an official "presenter," the seventy-one-year-old Emmeline presented all she would have said had she been one—and in one of the more distinguished sessions.

As an officer of the NCW, Emmeline attended a closed-door session discussing the merits of the candidates for president of the ICW. The experience exposed Emmeline to the political realities of assembling a group of well-placed international delegates under a single administrative umbrella. Universal sisterhood came face-to-face with nationalistic, political, and social boundaries. "There was much opposition to Mrs. Sewall's nomination," Emmeline observed, "and it seemed at one time that it would come to a conflict, many unpleasant things were brought up and wrangling was very annoying." But the outcome demonstrated the preeminence of qualifications. May Wright Sewall's superior organizational and managerial abilities overcame the social antipathy toward her "Americanism," and she was elected president.[21]

Most of the American women and certainly the Mormon women were captivated by the display of wealth and deference they encountered at the numerous receptions given by several British noblewomen and ICW officers. In addition, various British clubs and societies sponsored more than forty teas, luncheons, and receptions for individual groups of delegates and participants. Even journalists were impressed by the grand soirees held in London's elegant homes and establishments. This pageantry of British nobility introduced Emmeline to another source of female status and influence besides intelligence and ability. Her usual aplomb in unfamiliar social settings deserted her temporarily in the presence of such studied opulence and the deference it commanded. She could hardly believe that she was a peripheral partaker of such rarefied life. "It does seem remarkable," she mused, "that we should have such an opportunity given to us—from the very far away but we feel the Lord has done it."[22]

The first of these splendid social events occurred in the elegant Stafford House, hosted by the Duchess of Sutherland, the Countess of Aberdeen (the ICW's outgoing president), and the Countess of Warwick, who were attending together with others of the Utah delegation. The guests, a thousand of them, first encountered an imposing line of footmen who announced their names as the guests ascended the marble staircase, lit by oversized candelabra, toward the first landing, where the elegantly attired hostesses were waiting to receive their guests, acknowledging each guest with a few

20. Gates, "International Council of Women," 443.

21. E. Wells, Diary, June 29, 1899.

22. Ibid., June 28, 1899.

words of welcome. Charlotte Perkins Gilman, American feminist author and lecturer and special guest at the convention, arrived at the reception just after Emmeline and Susa, who were attending together. Drawing near the stairs, she recognized the two women, who were "plainly dressed and looking timidly up at the array of tiaras on the landing." Unintimidated by the regal panoply herself, she offered to introduce them to those she had met before. She and Susa ultimately became good friends, and she knew Emmeline from an earlier meeting in Des Moines, where Emmeline declared her to be "one of the brightest women of this nineteenth century" and one who "really seemed to take extra pains for some of our Utah party.[23]

Lady Battersea sent large cards of invitation to her reception at Drury House on Park Lane two days later. Emmeline was intrigued with the variety of costumes, Lady Battersea's collection of mementos from her travels, and the sparkling jewels that glittered throughout the reception hall. This prestigious event was followed a few days later by a garden reception at Fulham Palace, residence of the Lord Bishop of London and his wife, Mrs. Mandell (Louise) Creighton, one of the "ablest" women of the International Council of Women, who was largely responsible for the convention in London. No receptions, however, quite equaled that given by Lady Rothschild and her daughter-in-law Mrs. Leopold de Rothschild at Gunnersbury Park, their elegant residence and private park on the outskirts of London.[24] Twelve hundred invitations were sent, the number easily accommodated by the extensive grounds. Four bands, strolling magicians, trained dogs, and a circus ring with "lady performers" entertained the guests, who enjoyed delicacies of every kind served under the large colored tents that checkered the grounds. "The most magnificent gathering of all we have attended," Emmeline enthusiastically recounted. "Everything was on the grandest scale imaginable." "Beyond description; in mind and brain and heart forever engrafted."[25]

23. Charlotte Perkins Gilman, *The Living of Charlotte Perkins Gilman*, 263–64. See also "Home Again," *Woman's Exponent* 28 (August 15–September 1, 1899): 45. Distance evidently made Emmeline less intimidated by the titled ladies, and after returning home, she hoped to initiate a correspondence with the Duchess of Sutherland. She sent her a letter and a morocco-bound copy of *Musings and Memories* and was happy to receive a note of thanks and an accompanying picture of the duchess. E. Wells, Diary, August 28, September 4, October 10, 1899.

24. Mrs. Leopold (Maria) de Rothschild sold the estate in 1925 to the government for a local park, and the large mansion is currently a museum.

25. E. Wells, Diary, July 4, 1899; "Home Again," 45. For a full account of the convention, see E. Wells, Diary, June 24–July 4, 1899. For additional details, see "Home Again," 44–46; and Gilman, *Living of Charlotte Perkins Gilman*, 257–66. Brief accounts are given by Susan B. Anthony and Anna Howard Shaw in *History of Woman Suffrage*, edited by Anthony and Harper, 4:352–54.

The Countess of Aberdeen, outgoing president of the ICW, adjourned the grand assembly of women with a closing social held at the Royal Institute of Water Color. Throughout the conference Emmeline enjoyed many contacts with the countess. They had become more than obligatory acquaintances, and Emmeline featured her in her report of the conference in the *Woman's Exponent* when she returned home. "The women of the world are greatly indebted to the self-sacrifice of this philanthropic, heroic gentlewoman, who, without display or ceremony but with the true instinct of royalty, devoted her valuable time and magnificent talents to those who came from afar."[26]

Probably the pièce de résistance of the convention's social whirl occurred at Windsor Castle, where the convention's participants were invited to see Queen Victoria. After an exhausting tour of the Tower of London, Emmeline traveled to Windsor and joined the eager guests who lined both sides of the long drive leading from the castle. Then, at an arranged time, Queen Victoria appeared, seated in an open carriage, waving to the guests as she was driven from the castle to the grounds beyond. At her departure, the guests were invited into St. George's Hall for tea and refreshments and then given a tour of the state apartments. Thirteen of the sixteen Utah women attended that final and memorable social event.[27]

After the conclusion of the ICW meetings, Emmeline remained abroad for another month, most of the time sightseeing but also meeting members of the church in various cities. She was acquainted with most of the presiding officers of the church in England and many of the missionaries from Utah's cities and towns whom she had met in her Relief Society visits. She spoke in church meetings, discussed revitalization of a mordant Relief Society in London, and received invitations to speak at the Nottingham Conference and church meetings in Edinburgh. Back in London she attended a reception at the American Embassy for the ambassador, Joseph Hodges Choate of New York City, and his wife. Susan B. Anthony, May Wright Sewall, and several other convention delegates were among the guests, though Emmeline seemed to be the only Utahn among the fourteen women in attendance. Afterward, she visited Parliament with two of Sewall's guests, where they were given a tour by the representative from the Edinburgh district and treated to lunch on the terrace by Sir Phillip and Lady Fish.

With only her diary as companion for most of her travels, Emmeline negotiated train routes and schedules to visit the various cities on her itinerary. High on her list was Stratford-upon-Avon, where she was almost

26. "Home Again," 45. The Countess of Aberdeen presided over the International Council of Women for thirty-five of its first fifty years, at different intervals.

27. E. Wells, Diary, July 7, 1899.

as eager to see the home of popular novelist Marie Corelli as she was the Shakespeare sites that had been designated by Corelli for preservation. Corelli had recently moved to Stratford and was then in residence, so Emmeline sent a porter to her home at Mason Croft with her card, requesting a visit. She was delighted when Corelli agreed to see her, greeting Emmeline with a kiss and her own autographed card. Corelli offered her tea while they conversed, and all too soon the memorable interview was over, leaving Emmeline much elated. Emmeline returned to London by way of Birmingham, where she stopped to attend and address several LDS meetings. Back in London again, she visited number 1 Cheyne Walk in Chelsea, where George Eliot briefly lived before her death. Though not permitted to enter the privately owned dwelling, she was given a glimpse of the interior through the outside gate.[28]

Emmeline then traveled to Paris, where she took a Cook's tour through the city. During the tour, she met several travelers who took a special interest in her, buying her tickets to various sites, paying for her meals, and generally acting as her escort. One of them, James H. Osmer, a former congressman from Pennsylvania, did not "have any prejudice," Emmeline was grateful to discover.[29] Returning to England, she traveled to Liverpool, where she slept "in the old house at 42 Islington," headquarters of the European Mission when Daniel presided a decade earlier. In Glasgow she was shown the sights of the city by Elders David O. McKay and Joseph McMurrin, shortly before their return home.[30]

Finally, on August 4, she boarded her ship at the Mersey Docks in Liverpool, and Emmeline began the long voyage home. As she lay on her bunk during her seasick days, she wrote letters to the helpful people in Paris and to Louise Creighton, the wife of London's lord mayor, and to others whom she had met during her travels. She also had much time for reflection on the "past few weeks since leaving Utah. The many amusing incidents, the great fund of information[,] the stigma of Mormonism." She thought of the "stirring events" that had transpired during the previous years and could truly say, "My life seems wonderfully changed and developed. What further changes are yet to come I know not. Certainly a remarkable destiny and a most romantic life."[31]

28. Currently, there are bronze plaques on both Corelli's home in Stratford and Eliot's Chelsea home bearing the names of the famous writers who had once lived in them.

29. Ibid., July 26, 1899.

30. The detailed itinerary of her long stay in Europe following the ICW meetings is recounted in her diaries from July 7 to August 14, 1899, when she disembarked in New York.

31. Ibid., August 7, 8, 1899.

The large gathering of international women energized Emmeline and reinforced her enthusiasm regarding the value of women's associations. She was well satisfied with the two clubs she had organized nearly a decade earlier, the Woman's Press Club and Reapers, and the opportunity the *Exponent* gave members to publish their literary pieces. Emmeline felt almost as possessive and nurturing about her clubs as she did her paper. "It is one of my hobbies to organize," she had once declared, and she did not abandon the objects of her organization.[32] Emmeline headed both organizations during their formative years, opened her office for their meetings, and published the minutes and papers from their meetings, and she also wrote many of her own poems, stories, and articles for the two clubs before publishing them. She ushered both clubs into membership of the General Federation of Women's Clubs when a chapter was organized in Utah in 1893, not only as an instinctive outreach of association, but also as assurance that her clubs would have a place within the larger club movement of the time.[33] These two organizations flourished during her lifetime, and she counted them as successes in her efforts to broaden the knowledge and develop the talents of her Mormon sisters. Her experience at the recent ICW conference affirmed these organizing efforts.

Emmeline's travels for the last year of the decade were not yet over. She traveled north to Idaho again to attend the twenty-fifth wedding anniversary celebration for Mell and Will. Mell's home was decorated with a profusion of flowers, and the bay window in the parlor had a "yoke" of fabric hung across the top of the windows with "1874–1899" in silver letters, under which the couple greeted their guests. Invited to write a poem of tribute, Emmeline "never wrote anything under more difficult circumstances," she declared, but after finishing the "seven verses of six lines," which made up the poem, she felt "fairly well pleased with it."[34]

Wintertime in Idaho kept Emmeline indoors much of the time, writing letters to people at home and working on two new poems. Reading papers

32. Ibid., January 3, 1882; Linda Thatcher and John R. Sillito, "'Sisterhood and Sociability': The Utah Women's Press Club, 1891–1928"; Sharon Snow Carver, "Salt Lake City's Reapers Club."

33. The Utah Federation of Women Clubs Papers provide a historical overview of the club since its founding. See also Adelia Knudsen, "History of Utah Federation of Women's Clubs, 1893–1952," typescript copy, Utah State Historical Society, Salt Lake City. The end of the century saw a burgeoning of women's "culture clubs," as more women had the leisure time to give to them. A history of the club movement is provided in Karen Blair, *The Club Woman as Feminist: True Womanhood Redefined, 1868–1914*. A contemporary history is Jennie Cunningham Croly, *The History of the Woman's Club Movement in America.*

34. E. Wells, Diary, November 7, 1899.

from Spokane and San Francisco, she found them still "full of the Roberts affair," and lamented, "It has all been a fearful mistake, calling attention to matters that might have been quiet and making public, things that seem quite unnecessary—bringing on the old persecution, stirring up strife."[35] Her appraisal of the collateral damage of his election was borne out by the problems that followed, especially relating to Mormon women's affiliation with national associations.

Waking to a sunny day one morning, Emmeline set out from Mell's house on her own, walking as high up into the mountains as she could to "hear the pines singing." The day was quiet, she wrote, with only the sound of a bird piercing the thin, clear air, "singing so sweetly, it seemed a harbinger of good to me who have all my lifetime been so oppressed and forlorn until late years."[36] Though she was eager to return home and pick up the reins of her own life, the parting was difficult, and at the moment of separation, Mell's family was very "sober" at her leaving. She bade them all good-bye and returned to the world she knew best, always reluctant to leave them behind.[37] Her visits were refreshing respites in a life crowded to its margins with work.

With the rush to finish the Christmas edition of her paper that year, to prepare the annual "tea party" given by the members of the Daughters of the Revolution, to deliver lectures on her England trip to various social groups, to mail off copies of her book, and to keep up her correspondence, Emmeline faced a challenging holiday season. As usual, she spent Christmas Eve at Annie's, always amazed at the numerous gifts for the large family and appreciative of the gifts she received. Belle's home was the scene of Christmas dinner, and four days later the Sears family celebrated Dot's second wedding anniversary. Emmeline gave her Marie Corelli's book *Sorrows of Satan*, written, Emmeline noted, in the same room at the Falcon Hotel in Stratford in which she had stayed while visiting Corelli. A final social was the last meeting of the year of the Woman's Press Club, held at Andrew and Emma Jenson's home, decorated with curiosities from all parts of the world where he had traveled, collecting records of Mormon history. Knowing of Emmeline's interest in Palestine, he gave her a pebble that he had picked up on the Mount of Olives during his two-year world tour in 1895 and 1896.

35. Ibid., November 19, 1899.

36. Ibid., November 22, 1899.

37. Emmeline kept a daily account of her visit to Idaho in her diary from November 6 to December 5, 1899. She also wrote an account of the visit for her paper. See "Wayside Notes," *Woman's Exponent* 28 (November 15–December 1, 1899): 76–77, and a short account of two parties she attended in "Editorial Notes," *Woman's Exponent* 28 (November 15–December 1, 1899): 77.

Emmeline stayed at Annie's on the last night of the year 1899. She and her daughter talked late into the night of "all the wars and rumors of wars of Roberts and the Congress of the United States and of new books and old ones of great men in the Church and many other things." It had been a remarkable year for the seventy-one-year-old Emmeline, and the new day, new year, and new century that would all begin the next day were still a closed book. What lay in its pages, however, could wait. New Year's Eve was always a welcome restorative, a time to reflect, a time to wonder, and a time to muster her energy to meet the new challenges and old responsibilities of another year.

CHAPTER 31

The New Century
(1900–1901)

EMMELINE GREETED 1900 with a determination to follow each of the avenues that lay before her with both resolve and vigor. Of great importance to her was maintaining ties with her Woodward family. As busy as she was with her own children and grandchildren, she did not want to let distance or diverse interests separate her from her siblings and their families. By 1900, Hiram was the only one of Emmeline's three brothers still alive, and all six of the Woodward sisters were widows. Pallas and Cordelia had lived their entire lives in Massachusetts, Pallas dying in 1903 at the age of eighty-four and Cordelia in 1914 at ninety. Emmeline mused that Cordelia, like herself, had outlived three husbands. Though envying the devotion of her last husband, James Holden, and the comfort in which Cordelia lived, Emmeline was able to concede that her marriage to Daniel had been "a turning point" in her life. "There are days," she mused, "that prove almost epochs in one's history and this one forty-eight years ago was such an one to me." She concluded, "What a wonderful life I have had—the half could never be written."[1]

Her oldest living sister, Lucy, outlived both of her husbands and all but one of her six children, a series of losses that left her embittered and distant.[2] Talented and smart, she became a crusader for social causes, often visiting Utah and writing poems or articles for the *Exponent*.[3] Her disdain of the church and her bitterness strained her sisterly relationship with Emmeline. However, Emmeline welcomed and encouraged her popular contributions to the *Woman's Exponent*, which no doubt bridged some of their snappish

1. E. Wells, Diary, October 10, 1900.

2. "Lucy M. Hewlings," *Woman's Exponent* 29 (May 15, 1901): 105. Her husband, the Reverend George Robert Hewlings, died in Salt Lake City, where they had made their home for a short while.

3. "Temperance Lecturer," *Deseret Evening News*, September 26, 1879, 3.

moments. After living in several different cities after her second husband's death in 1877, Lucy returned to Salt Lake City and died there in April 1901. Emmeline, Ellen, and Adeline Maria were all with her at the end, and together they prepared her body for burial. Lucy was the first of the six surviving sisters to die, a sobering reminder that age was advancing on all of them.[4] Of all the sisters, Lucy most resembled Emmeline in her talents and ambitions and may well have been a spur to Emmeline's own activism and literary aspirations.

Adeline Maria, who had traveled west with Emmeline, Ellen, and Hiram in 1846, married Justus, or Jesse, Earl. A member of the Pony Express, Earl was killed on one of his rides by another rider who "was fooling with his revolver," but then "it went off killing Jesse Earl almost immediately." The gunman claimed it to be an accident, wrote Parley Hall, a rider with Jesse, "but we never believed it."[5] Public speculation, including an unconfirmed rumor that he was shot by order of Brigham Young, made the incident a cause célèbre. The rumors, accusations, and mystery about it left Adeline angry, embittered, and permanently estranged from the church. She eventually moved to California with her daughter's family and died there in 1919 at the age of ninety.[6]

Ellen remained in the church and married Elijah Knapp Fuller as his fourth wife, homesteading in Harrisburg, a small town northeast of St. George, Utah. In 1882, leaving her husband to his other wives, Ellen followed several of Knapp's sons, including some of her own, to Pine, Arizona, where she served as a midwife to help support herself and her boys and later opened a general store, which she managed until she was eighty-one.[7] She died in Arizona in 1915 at age eighty-four. At one time, Emmeline pondered the life of this beloved sister. Ellen had many children but "only one

4. Ibid., April 23, 24, 1901. The newspapers indicated that she would be buried in Hardwick, Massachusetts, near her husband, Henry Granger. Emmeline's diary indicated that Lucy's wish was to be cremated in Chicago, the home of her daughter Carrie's two sons, whom she helped to raise.

5. Jesse Earl was a well-known member of Salt Lake City society, and both his musical contributions and his unusual death received much publicity. Accounts of the accident (or murder in some records) are "Latest from the West," *Deseret News*, July 22, 1860, 165; and "Parley Hall, Utah and the Pony Express," in *Our Pioneer Heritage*, compiled by Carter, 3:382.

6. "Passing Events," *Improvement Era* 23, no. 3 (1920): 275.

7. Gerald R. Fuller and EKF Family Organization, comps., *Elijah Knapp Fuller Family Record*, 479–81; Dallas Coleman, *Elijah Knapp Fuller and His Ancestors*, 36–39; "Death Calls Aged Woman: Mrs. Fuller, Former Resident of Salt Lake, Passes Away in Arizona," *Salt Lake Herald-Republican*, January 19, 1915.

husband," Emmeline wrote in 1890, "which to me seems a great blessing, but we are not all constituted alike in this world and cannot judge each other."[8]

Hiram always held the deepest place in her affections. After a life of many achievements, at retirement he took up "motoring," indulging his love of cars. He died in 1923, age eighty-eight, as a devoted Congregationalist. His Masonic brothers served as pallbearers at his funeral.[9] Hiram, whose middle name was Eugene, the name Emmeline gave to her son, was the only member of the family who outlived her.

Emmeline visited her New England siblings nearly every time she traveled to the East. However satisfying New England life seemed to be, Emmeline never regretted her agreement to leave and follow a different course, though she carried thoughts of what might have been, even as a Latter-day Saint.[10] These New England visits not only satisfied Emmeline's nostalgic yearnings, but also gave her perspective on her subsequent choices and experiences. However placid and uncomplicated her siblings' lives seemed to be, Emmeline was content with her own choices, even though they had brought with them a surfeit of controversy, opprobrium, and hard work. But they had also brought her association with noted figures, adventure, and acclaim, which a quiet, poetry-writing life in New England could not have produced. Emmeline's conviction of Mormonism was steady and strong. Each visit to New England underscored the felicity in her conversion.

The new year also offered more opportunities for strengthening her national and international connections. As chaplain of the Salt Lake City chapter of the Daughters of the Revolution in May, she attended the 1900 annual convention in New York. While there she met with Fanny Gaffney, the current president of the National Council of Women. A leader whom she liked and admired, Gaffney lacked the level of leadership Emmeline found in other national leaders.[11] Reading an article by Gaffney in *Harper's Monthly*, Emmeline complained to her diary, "I am weary of so much nothingness, we are so far ahead of these women, in almost every respect except money."[12]

8. E. Wells, Diary, November 5, 1890.

9. "Passing of Captain Clark at 8:45 a.m.," *Palmer (MA) Journal*, December 6, 13, 1923. Thorndike, the location of Hiram's home, is within the environs of Palmer, where he worked.

10. Ibid., April 30, May 1, 1900.

11. Ibid., May 4, 1900.

12. Ibid., May 5, 6, 1900. While Emmeline maintained a warm friendship with Gaffney, she did not feel that for all her advantages, she had any larger gifts or abilities than LDS women.

November put her on the road again, this time to Minneapolis and a meeting of the National Council of Women. Her companion was the well-to-do Elizabeth Claridge McCune. Emmeline explained to her the workings of the National Council but despaired of making a true convert. "[Elizabeth] does not seem to care nor realize its benefits," Emmeline lamented. "We must try more than ever before to make our people understand the Council and appreciate what it means for them."[13] It was an uphill battle, however. Since the 1890 Manifesto, Mormon women had begun to settle into a lifestyle that was more compatible with their American sisters and felt less need to prove or defend themselves through national associations. Emmeline fought this developing ennui, using the *Exponent* and her speeches at Relief Society meetings and conferences to energize their interest.

While Emmeline had largely removed herself from participation in the ongoing movement for national woman suffrage, she joined with the Utah Council (replacement of the Utah Woman Suffrage Association) in sending one hundred dollars and a handbag made of Utah silk, embroidered with the sego lily, to Susan B. Anthony for her eightieth birthday. The Utah Silk Commission, to which Emmeline belonged, sent her a silk dress made by Adeline Barber from a length of black silk, cultivated and spun into fabric by Utah women.[14] Anthony praised the dress in her gracious response, "because," she wrote, "the silk worms—the mulberry trees were raised by Mormon women—the coloring—the spinning, the weaving, everything was done by the Mormon women in Utah." She wrote to each woman who had a part in its production and explained, "My pleasure in the rich brocaded silk is quadrupled because it was made by women politically equal to men."[15]

Inasmuch as 1900 was a presidential election year, politics also carved a large niche in Emmeline's schedule, especially the campaign to reelect Heber Wells as governor. As vice chair of the state Republican committee, Emmeline had the support of her daughter Annie, who had switched party loyalties and was now an active Republican. Emmeline's position in the local Republican party and with the Republican Women's League brought her into even more frequent contact with her non-Mormon friends than before, including the Siegel, Bamberger, and Salisbury families. Her friend Margaret Salisbury had earlier arranged a small salary for Emmeline as compensation for her work in the Republican Party.[16] Some of her Republi-

13. Ibid., November 10, 1900.

14. Ibid., January 6, 20, February 5, 1900, March 4, 1918.

15. The dress has been preserved and is on display at the Susan B. Anthony home in Rochester, New York. Barry, *Susan B. Anthony*, 342.

16. The three Siegel brothers were among a number of Jewish merchants who opened stores in Utah in the 1850s. Simon Bamberger was one of the most successful

can friends were now running for office. Both Emma McVicker and her husband, John, an assayer, had their eyes on public office, and O. J. Salisbury, Margaret's husband, was contemplating candidacy for a seat in the US Senate. Emmeline was included in the numerous socials these influential families hosted.[17] They perceived her as a valuable liaison with the LDS Church and its Republican members.[18]

As it turned out, Republicans were successful that year, and Heber M. Wells was returned to office, to Emmeline's delight. To herself she mused that had she been on the ticket, she might well have been elected.[19]

Once again she attended the inaugural activities. Her son-in-law John Q. Cannon had charge of the ceremonial, which took place in the Hall of Representatives.[20] A salute of seventeen guns followed the oath of office, and the band played "America."[21] Later, at the inaugural ball, held in the Salt Lake Theatre, Governor Wells, twice a widower, "led the grand march with his sister Edna Sloan," which Emmeline declared was "a brilliant affair, the most so of any."[22] She delighted in ceremonials.

Several candidates for the US Senate from Utah asked Emmeline to lobby for them among her friends in the Utah Senate, since state senates selected US senators at that time. She does not mention that she did so, but after twenty-two rounds of balloting, Thomas Kearns emerged the victor. Kearns's victory and Wells's reelection were not the only satisfying outcome of the election. Kearns invited Emmeline and Susa Young Gates to join his

---

Jewish entrepreneurs to settle in Utah, founding the Bamberger Railroad line and the Lagoon amusement park. He was an active Democrat, eventually serving as Utah's governor from 1916 to 1920. See Jack Goodman, "Jews in Zion."

17. E. Wells, Diary, July 19, 20, 22, 1900. See also September 18, October 26, and December 29, 1900.

18. Ibid., June 17–20, 1900.

19. Ibid., January 8, 1901. That observation was made directly after the Republican victory the previous fall. See ibid., November 6, 1900.

20. Ibid., January 3, 1901. She was probably referring to the Utah House of Representatives in the Salt Lake City and County Building, which was used as the state capitol until 1915 when the official state capitol was completed at the north end of State Street.

21. The song "America" ("My Country, 'Tis of Thee") was one of several songs used as the national anthem until "The Star-Spangled Banner" was officially declared the national anthem in 1931.

22. Edna Sloan did the paintings that were included in the book of poetry *Songs and Flowers of the Wasatch*, which Utah women presented to the Woman's Building at the Chicago Exposition in 1893. Heber Wells's first marriage, to Mary Elizabeth Beattie, ended at her death in 1888. Four years later, he married Theresa Clawson, who died in 1897. He did not marry again until 1901, when he married Emily Katz. He was between marriages during his second inauguration.

party for his swearing-in ceremony in Washington, DC, and to attend the inauguration of newly elected president William McKinley. Kearns paid all the expenses. With his partner, David Keith, Thomas Kearns, a Catholic, made a fortune in mining and railroads in Utah. His invitation to the two LDS women was a reward for their work in the party.

At the end of February 1901, with encouraging words from both LDS church president Lorenzo Snow and Governor Heber M. Wells, Emmeline and Susa Gates traveled to Washington with the Kearns family and their many guests. Prior to the outdoor inauguration, Senator Kearns's party viewed the procession of federal dignitaries from the gallery of the Senate chamber. There they witnessed the swearing in of new members of the Senate and Theodore Roosevelt as US vice president. Following that ceremony, the party adjourned to an outside platform to view the inauguration of President McKinley, impressive despite the pouring rain.[23] From an excellent vantage point, Kearns and his party also viewed the traditional parade that followed the inauguration. That night, the Utah party attended the inaugural ball in the new Pension Building, and throughout the following week, Emmeline and Susa enjoyed concerts, visits to Arlington Cemetery, luncheons, receptions, and dinner parties. Emmeline attended meetings with some of her Washington friends, including dinner at the Virginia home of Dr. Kate Waller Barrett, corresponding secretary of the National Council of Women and later its president.[24] This was Washington from a viewpoint that Emmeline had never experienced in her prior visits.[25] The only downside was the constant "stifling" company of Susa Gates. "She sort of absorbs me," Emmeline admitted, "and it is hard for me to endure her ways," but generously adding, "tho she is very capable."[26]

23. President McKinley's assassination a few months later was troubling to Emmeline, having seen him so recently at his inauguration. E. Wells, Diary, September 6, 14, 19, 1901.

24. Barrett's primary social contribution was as the founder and longtime leader of the Crittenton homes for unwed mothers. In later years, she became active in Democratic politics and the suffrage movement, while also serving as a Virginia regent of the Daughters of the American Revolution. Emmeline met her in Washington in 1895.

25. "In and about Washington," *Woman's Exponent* 29 (March 15–April 1, 1901): 90–91. In the same editorial describing their Washington visit, Emmeline lists the names of the women with whom she mingled at the various events. All of them were of national and even international stature, who welcomed and sought out Emmeline. Other details about the Kearns party in Washington are recorded in "Utah Contingent in Washington," *Deseret Evening News*, March 4, 1901, 1; "Utah at Inauguration," *Salt Lake Tribune*, March 5, 1901, 1; and E. Wells, Diary, February 24–March 10, 1901.

26. E. Wells, Diary, March 5, 1901.

When Emmeline's request for a visit with Vice President Roosevelt was granted, she gave him a note that "Liet. Col John Q. Cannon" had written to him, after which she was treated to his kind remarks about Utah. She found him "very genial" and he seemed delighted to speak with her, she happily reported, although she surmised he made everyone feel that way. He "spoke highly of Utah and of Liet Col Cannon and the Governor and of his visit," Emmeline noted, and despite her visits with Supreme Court justices, senators, and other Washington dignitaries over the years, this encounter added a certain panache to her entire Washington experience. Afterward, Senator Kearns introduced her to a number of the senators who had congregated in the Senate chamber, including the president pro tem of the Senate, William Frye, "who has just been re-elected," Emmeline noted. At their last meeting, Senator Kearns gave Emmeline eighty dollars to cover her return trip.[27]

After her socially demanding time in Washington, Emmeline went with Rachel Siegel to her Baltimore home, enjoying Rachel's hospitality and company in seeing the city's sights. She then made her way to New York to meet with Carrie Chapman Catt and Fanny Gaffney, presidents of the NAWSA and NCW, respectively. It had been a thrilling and informative month away for Emmeline, again thrust into the world of major political figures and women leaders. Now it was time to return to her own milieu.

When she arrived home, she learned that George Q. Cannon lay fatally ill while vacationing in Monterey, California. He died on April 1, and Emmeline's diary is silent for three weeks thereafter. She did, however, write for the *Woman's Exponent* a long biographical sketch of Cannon, one of the church's most prominent and effective leaders.[28] She had little time to mourn since she was obliged to make preparations for an unexpected visit from May Wright Sewall, president of the ICW, only a few months after returning from Washington.[29]

Sewall's trip to Utah was to revitalize the "council idea" and keep LDS dues-paying women active members of the National Council. Emmeline was obliged to make all of the arrangements for her visit, including lectures and socials. When the public festivities ended, Sewall and Emmeline spent a quiet evening alone discussing the many experiences they had shared—"a night I shall never forget," Emmeline wrote. "I gave her a good many

27. Ibid., March 9, 1901.

28. "In Memoriam," *Woman's Exponent* 29 (April 15–May 1, 1901): 98, 99.

29. May Wright Sewall, letter to Susa Young Gates, April 26, 1901, Gates Papers. Susa Gates, also a good friend of and coworker with May Sewall in the National and International Councils of Women, was then living in Provo and less able to assist Emmeline.

incidents in my life that were rather remarkable," she added.[30] "Needless to say," Emmeline wrote of their visit, "we considered it a 'red letter day'—a time we had both looked forward to for many years."[31] The visit underscored Sewall's continuing desire for Mormon membership in the two councils and her personal friendship with both Emmeline and Susa Gates.

Amid this flurry of activities that consumed so much of Emmeline's time, she faced the constant worry about her paper. She felt it needed invigorating with new ideas and format, and Sewall's visit helped Emmeline see some possibilities of putting "new ideas into the work," such as turning the *Exponent* into a "progressive woman's paper along all lines, and not confine[ing] itself to clubs or any one organization," that is, transcending the ideological limitations of the *Woman's Exponent*. She shared this idea with Susa Gates, her closest ally in the council movement, who jumped on it and immediately volunteered to help Emmeline expand the *Woman's Exponent*'s editorial scope.[32] Susa, in fact, asked Emmeline for permission to represent the *Exponent* as *her* magazine when she moved to New York with her husband for a yearlong mission and pointed out the advantages of Emmeline's mentioning Susa's name in connection with the *Exponent* whenever she met with Susa's friend and confidant Joseph F. Smith, recently ordained president of the church. Susa enthusiastically suggested that Emmeline move to New York and publish the *Woman's Exponent* from that setting.[33] Susa's eagerness for immediate engagement with the *Exponent* caused Emmeline to have second thoughts. For years, Susa had proposed, then pressed, and then persisted in "begging and pleading" to "take hold of the work of the *Exponent*." She presented herself as a devoted acolyte who only wished to ease some of Emmeline's burdens, but Emmeline was annoyed by Susa's obvious ambition and readiness to put her own stamp on the publication. Despite the help that the forty-four-year-old Susa would be, Emmeline was reluctant to create a journalistic partnership with her.[34] Lack of time, money, and energy impeded Emmeline's obvious desire for change. But Susa was not the answer.

In fact, the threat that her grinding schedule with the paper and her other commitments might only "grow worse" continually haunted her. "My time seems almost wholly occupied in giving advice to the Relief Society and other public work and interests of women," she complained. Yet this was exactly what she had proposed to do with her life many years earlier. It

30. Ibid., July 14, 1901.

31. "Mrs. Sewall's Visit," *Woman's Exponent* 30 (August 1, 1901): 20.

32. E. Wells, letter to Gates, September 20, 1901, Gates Papers.

33. Gates, letter to Wells, December 12, 1901, ibid.

34. E. Wells, Diary, December 4, 18, 1900.

was becoming clear to her, however, that achieving a balance between these goals and the paper that was her livelihood chained her to a schedule that meant "life is to be full of work."[35]

Her secretarial position in the general Relief Society, which gave her pleasure as a member of the General Board, assured her that her life would inevitably be "full of work." One of her new responsibilities was to head the Relief Society's "woman's building" committee. At the 1892 Relief Society jubilee, Joseph F. Smith had promised the Relief Society a building of its own, but not until 1900 were serious plans to construct a woman's building actually discussed.[36] Although the building was originally envisioned to house only the Relief Society, the expense of such a project soon argued for inclusion of the Young Ladies' Mutual Improvement Association and the Primary Association, both of which agreed to participate.[37]

In March 1901, Emmeline visited with church president Lorenzo Snow, "who was very gracious and talked lovely about the building—said we should have deed to the land as soon as we had twenty thousand dollars to begin with." The large amount to be raised overcame Emmeline's initial reluctance at including the other two organizations, and she was reconciled to the notion that it was now to be a woman's building in fact rather than just Relief Society headquarters. Two months later, she felt that "everything seemed favorable to the benefit of the Building."[38]

In August 1901, at a fund-raising event at Saltair just two months before his death, President Lorenzo Snow publicly announced that he would designate a parcel of land across from the temple for the erection of "a magnificent edifice" that would reflect credit on the women of the church.[39] As he had told Emmeline, he announced that he would give them a deed after they had raised twenty thousand dollars. Now, with this public announcement, Emmeline's work on the committee began in earnest.

Although only a few thousand dollars were raised during the first six months, the committee laid plans for a spring 1902 construction. The committee consulted architects and builders, but the project became entangled in problems of design, cost estimates, and contracts. Moreover, when spring came, church president Joseph F. Smith, Snow's successor and the originator of the idea of a woman's building, reminded the women of the condition set by President Snow: without the full twenty thousand dollars in hand,

35. Ibid., October 4, 6, November 28, 1900.

36. "Relief Society Conference," in Minutes of the General Board, April 5, 1892, October 3, 1896.

37. Ibid., October 2, 1900.

38. Ibid., March 26, June 27, 1901.

39. "President Snow's Address," *Woman's Exponent* 30 (August 1, 1901): 17.

he could not issue them a deed. It was evidently a nonnegotiable provision. With the church still struggling to regain some financial balance itself after the 1887 Edmunds-Tucker Act and recession of the 1890s, delaying such an expensive project may have been seen as simply a practical matter.

The prospect of raising money did not produce an abyss of despair, nor did the women complain about the extraordinary amount. The committee, backed by the officers of their respective organizations, launched another general fund-raising movement, continuing for six years, which brought just over fourteen thousand dollars into the building fund by 1908, still short of the required amount. It was an amazing achievement given how few financial resources most women commanded at that time. Obviously, more time was needed, but the women could be patient, and they trusted President Smith to reserve the desirable lot for their building until the money was raised. Moreover, the new building was envisioned not only as a convenient and comfortable headquarters for the officers and boards of the three organizations, but as an enduring symbol of women's position as partners with priesthood quorums and as a visible representation of their essential place within the church. The Relief Society, established by Joseph Smith, gave organizational identity to the women of the church and reinforced their sense of ownership of the work either assigned to or originated by them. For the women of the Relief Society, Joseph had implied an ecclesiastical partnership of the society with the priesthood quorums that was reinforced by subsequent church presidents within different contexts. Now there was to be a collaborative effort toward building the kingdom that would endure but would necessarily be realigned to meet the broad organizational changes occurring during this transitional period of Mormonism. Emmeline would be involved in the adaptations a new century demanded and the accommodations she would have to make in her own life.

CHAPTER 32

A New Generation

(1901–1904)

DURING THE SUMMER of 1901, Relief Society president Zina Young made a long visit to her daughter, Zina Card, in Cardston, Canada. In August, on the day she was to return to Utah, Zina fell seriously ill, and her daughter was obliged to accompany her home to Salt Lake City. She died on August 28, almost immediately after returning. Her death put fund-raising for the woman's building that she had longed to see materialize on indeterminate hold and also created an immense void for those who had known or worked with her. "It is hard for me," Emmeline wrote as she reflected on their experiences together. "We had been friends for so many years." She found it "very sad not to be able to commune with those who have been so closely associated for more than half-a-century."[1] Probably more than any other woman of that generation, Emmeline loved and admired Zina Young. Indeed, Zina was a beloved figure in the church, a healer of body and spirit, a soft, compassionate successor to the authoritative, efficient Eliza R. Snow. Both had left an indelible impact on the Relief Society, holding close to the original organization that Joseph Smith, to whom both were sealed as plural wives, had organized in Nauvoo. The organization's close relationship to the temple and its ordinances, a primary emphasis of Joseph's sermons to the society, was evident in the concurrent leadership roles in the Relief Society and over female temple ordinance workers that both Eliza and Zina had held. Emmeline occasionally fretted that Zina preferred to perform her temple duties than attend national women's conventions, but Emmeline knew the preeminence of the former to Zina. She also recognized Zina's strong desire to have the Relief Society represented at national meetings, selecting Emmeline herself most often as her proxy at the conventions. Few who met Zina did not feel the influence of her warm and inviting personality

1. E. Wells, Diary, August 28, 1901.

or come away from meeting her without sensing her quiet and unapologetic devotion to the church.[2] Now this compassionate, loving leader was gone.

Her Relief Society sisters dressed her body in a dress of fine lace, Emmeline noted, and then added a poignant detail, "but the sweet smile on her face was not there." For her funeral in the Assembly Hall, temple workers gave a bouquet of purple and white asters in the design of the temple, and the Relief Society board sent a floral design of the famous book *Gates Ajar*. A crown of white roses, a harp of "choice flowers," a sheaf of wheat, and a sickle of roses stood alongside a wreath of purple asters and white roses, tied with Utah silk, and presented by the Utah Silk Commission, of which Zina was president.[3] In all, these floral tributes were fitting and creative, communicating the links that each group had to this revered and cherished leader. Seats for the funeral had been reserved in the Assembly Hall for the Relief Society board with places on the stand designated for the officers. Zina's counselors, Jane Richards and Bathsheba Smith, and Emmeline, her corresponding secretary, were among the speakers.[4]

Zina's thirteen-year administration had been informal. Board meetings did not follow a regular schedule, the general board moving into action just before the semiannual general Relief Society conferences, which were instituted in 1889, two years after Zina took office. By 1902, the organizational structure of the Relief Society board imposed by incorporation had been largely modified.[5] The Board of Directors and the old Central Board became the General Board with a president, two counselors, a secretary, and a treasurer. References to incorporation had generally ceased.

Throughout Zina Young's tenure, Emmeline had served as more than corresponding secretary, her General Board title. She carried the burden of

2. Emmeline wrote a glowing tribute to Zina Young at her death, followed by an extensive history of her life. She felt particularly close to Zina, remembering the long talks the two of them had alone together at their homes. Zina had viewed Emmeline as an executive secretary and put many decisions and much of the daily work of the Relief Society on her shoulders. See "Our Beloved President, Zina D. H. Young," *Woman's Exponent* 30 (September 1901): 28–29; and "Impressive Funeral Services," *Woman's Exponent* 30 (October 1901): 36.

3. E. Wells, Diary, September 1, 1901; "Impressive Funeral Services," 36. *The Gates Ajar*, written in 1868 by Elizabeth Stuart Phelps, who dismissed Emmeline so rudely when they met in 1886, was a best-seller because of its depiction of the reconnection of loved ones after death in a heaven in which they retain their mortal appearances and personalities.

4. "Impressive Funeral Services," 36. Zina bequeathed her desk to Emmeline. The gift was made more memorable by being presented to Emmeline by Zina's daughter, Zina Young Williams Card, Emmeline's first associate at a national woman suffrage convention.

5. Derr, Cannon, and Beecher, *Women of Covenant*, 144–46.

meeting the requests of ward and stake Relief Societies for visitors to their conferences, arranging transportation, handling all the correspondence, and carrying responsibility for most of the business affairs of the Relief Society. She had also acted as a sub rosa counselor to Zina, reporting on the national conventions she attended on Zina's behalf and discussing national women's affairs with her. Emmeline and Zina were not only companions in their Relief Society work; they were also close friends and mutual admirers, each for her distinct qualities of leadership and personality. Zina's death left a great void in Emmeline's life.

For Zina's successor, the First Presidency passed over her first counselor, Jane Richards of Ogden, who was also serving as Weber Stake Relief Society president, and appointed Zina's second counselor, seventy-nine-year-old Bathsheba W. Smith, as the new president. She was the fourth Smith Relief Society president. The first three had all been wives of Joseph Smith. Bathsheba was the widow of Joseph's cousin George A. Smith. Emmeline thought Bathsheba was a good choice and found her to be quite "jubilant" at the honor. Reporters from the city's newspapers came to Emmeline to "get items from me" about the new presidency and reorganization of the Relief Society.

Though she clung tightly to tradition during her administration, Bathsheba selected two future-minded and much younger women as her counselors. Fifty-two-year-old Annie Taylor Hyde, first counselor, was the daughter of former church president John Taylor and Jane Ballantyne. She had attended the Deseret University, founded the Daughters of Utah Pioneers, and mothered eight children. Ida Smoot Dusenberry of Provo, Utah, second counselor, was a graduate of Brigham Young Academy and studied at Boston's Chauncey Hall College and Columbia University. She was a twenty-eight-year-old widow since the death of her husband, George A. Dusenberry, in 1898, which left her alone to parent two children. She devoted her career to childhood education and became principal of the Kindergarten Normal Training School at Provo's Brigham Young Academy in 1921. Emmeline, the only officer besides Bathsheba who had experienced Nauvoo, though not as a member of the Nauvoo Relief Society, was elevated to general secretary, and Clarissa S. Williams was appointed general treasurer.[6]

Bathsheba, widowed since 1875, did not try to equalize her attention between the two significant leadership positions she held. Becoming temple "matron" as well as Relief Society president after Zina's death, Bathsheba clearly made the temple her first priority. She had been involved in temple work, she said, since she was very young in Nauvoo and admitted that

6. Minutes of the General Board, October 6, 1902.

temple work was her "calling," or special mission, and therefore, she explained, she could not "visit very much among the sisters, as this is more my work than anything else."[7]

Two months after Zina Young's death in August 1901, eighty-seven-year-old church president Lorenzo Snow also died. He too had been well loved by his followers, and the two deaths left the Saints truly saddened. Since the semiannual church conference had concluded just shortly before his death in October, a special assembly of the church was convened in order to sustain Joseph F. Smith, President Snow's counselor and president of the Quorum of the Twelve Apostles, as his successor. The new officers of the Relief Society, in an unusual move, were voted upon in the same solemn assembly. Even though the need to reorganize the two presidencies was coincidental, Emmeline found this action to be a significant departure from precedent. "It was very gratifying to women interested in the advancement of the sisters," she wrote in the minutes, "to see the uplifted hands of all the several quorums of the Holy Priesthood raised to sustain them."[8] In an editorial, Emmeline expressed the same thoughts to her readers, wanting them to know that this had indeed been a "grand and imposing spectacle to witness, to see quorum after quorum of the holy priesthood and finally the whole congregation rise to their feet and raise the right hand as witness that they sustain the person or persons in the position to which they have been called," this time including the Relief Society officers and board members. Two years later, officers and boards of all the auxiliaries were named and sustained along with the general authorities at each general conference.[9]

Although Emmeline greatly admired both Joseph F. Smith and Bathsheba W. Smith, she also had concerns about the effect of the change of leadership on the Relief Society. "I doubt very much if Prest. [Joseph F.] Smith has as much confidence in what women can do, as Prest. Snow, or Prest. [George Q.] Cannon," Emmeline confided in a letter to Susa Gates. "There are so many things that need righting." President Snow had been

7. "The Relief Society Conference," *Woman's Exponent* 31 (October 1–15, 1902): 37–39.

8. The "Relief Society Record," containing minutes of the semiannual incorporated society, included in the Minutes of the General Board. This particular statement was recorded under "The Relief Society Record," November 10, 1901; and E. Wells, Diary, November 10, 1901. Unless noted otherwise, all board-meeting references will be referenced as Minutes of the General Board. Until this conference, only names of the presidency of the Young Men's Mutual Improvement Association were read for a sustaining vote at general conferences.

9. "Special Conference, Relief Society Reorganized," *Woman's Exponent* 30 (December 1901): 52. See also Relief Society Record, November 10, 1901; and Conference Reports, October 6, 1903, 85, LDS Church History Library, Salt Lake City.

supportive of women's political activities and alliance with national associations, and Zina's interest and support were of inestimable value. But, Emmeline lamented, "Bathsheba can't understand these matters, because it is all new to her."[10] Moreover, as the Relief Society began addressing issues that the new century raised, Emmeline discovered that there were also perceptual differences between the younger and older members of the board. Though she was supportive of Bathsheba's selection of counselors and board members, Emmeline found in time that generational differences created more diverse opinions and less deference than she had heretofore experienced, and she longed for "such women as Aunt Zina—Aunt Eliza [R. Snow], Mother [Elizabeth Ann] Whitney." "And Sister Isabella Horne," she added, "is worth a dozen of this younger lot." The unity and civility that had characterized Zina's board seemed to her to have diminished amid the strong-voiced opinions of the younger women. "How awful the change has been for the Society," she lamented one stressful day, "never peace or union scarcely at all. Vexation and annoyances all the time. Perhaps it is well for us to know the extremes."[11]

To Emmeline's surprise, just a few months into her administration, Bathsheba proposed that the secretary and treasurer each be paid ten dollars a month for their services. Emmeline responded that she had promised herself that if she served for ten years as secretary, only then would she be willing to accept remuneration for her service. The ten-year period would be up in three months, by October 1902. However, she explained to Bathsheba, the treasurer, Clarissa Williams, was under no such binding promise. The board responded by allocating money not only for Emmeline and Clarissa, but also for new carpet for the *Woman's Exponent* office, where they had met for years, as well as a cupboard in which to store papers, a lounge cover, three reclining chairs, and curtains.[12]

The first product of the new administration was a Relief Society handbook, planned during Zina's presidency but not completed and published until 1902. It was the first official guide of procedure from the General Board for the various stake and ward Relief Societies. Many of the policies and procedures had been instituted by Eliza R. Snow, who remained the primary procedural arbiter long after her death. The ninety-seven-page booklet included a history of the society, speeches by Relief Society officers and President Lorenzo Snow, and instructions to local Relief Societies.

10. E. Wells, letter to Gates, March 25, 1902, Gates Papers.

11. E. Wells, Diary, August 28, 1904.

12. Minutes of the General Board, July 4, 1902. To augment revenue from *Woman's Exponent* subscribers, Mell and Verona occasionally sent gifts of money, and sometimes Junius Wells also contributed to her welfare.

It also included a summary of projects the Relief Society then embraced, such as wheat storage and sericulture. It answered questions about stake quarterly conferences; the nurses' training program, begun under Zina's administration with the return of LDS women such as Ellis Shipp, Romania Pratt Penrose, and Martha Hughes Cannon from their medical training in the East; and mother education lessons, a program advanced by some board members to bring more young women into the organization. Also included was a paper Emmeline had written earlier entitled "The Age We Live In," which affirmed the Relief Society's forward look into the unique opportunities that a new century offered. "As sure as the scriptures are true, and they <u>are true</u>," she asserted at the end of the essay, "so sure woman must be instrumental in bringing about the restoration of that equality which existed when the world was created.... Perfect equality <u>then</u> and so it must be when all things are restored as they were in the beginning."[13] It was a bold assertion but reflected Emmeline's belief that women were indeed advancing in social and religious stature toward the day of true equality. The Relief Society was to be part of that affirmation of women's worth.

Establishing a training course for nurses by utilizing the services of trained women doctors drew much support from the board, but imposing a centralized course of study in mother education divided it. Emmeline had always supported self-direction by the Relief Society units and would continue to do so throughout her presidency, even though her efforts were in vain. In her many travels among the wards, she became convinced that wards and stakes were the best arbiters of the needs of their members. Counselor Annie T. Hyde, well educated and well traveled, and professional educator Ida Dusenberry favored adopting mother education courses as a uniform study program originating with the board. Both were in tune with the progressive mood of the age in wanting to apply scientific principles to the programs of the Relief Society. A standardized approach to course work written by qualified individuals, they believed, seemed a far better approach to Relief Society course work than a potpourri of lesson plans devised by each society.[14]

13. *The General Relief Society: Officers, Objects and Status*, 74–75. The full text also appears in the *Woman's Exponent* 30 (April 1902): 89–90. See also Derr, Cannon, and Beecher, *Women of Covenant*, 163–64.

14. Many of the wards or stakes that developed courses in mother education sent them to the General Board for approval, after which Emmeline usually published them in the *Woman's Exponent* as suggestions or guides for other ward Relief Societies that wanted to include "mother's work" in their lesson plans. Though opposed to standardized plans originating with the General Board, she was not against individual stakes writing their own or borrowing plans they felt suitable for their members.

Younger members of the board were generally more amenable to their idea, but the board as a whole was not yet ready to diverge too far from its traditional approach to either its educational or its charitable purposes.[15] Though a standardized course of study was never implemented throughout Bathsheba Smith's administration, Bathsheba was nevertheless interested in broadening the content of Relief Society meetings. Many wards that had adopted mother education lessons reported increased attendance, and she felt that anything "suitable for woman's work" could be properly utilized by the Relief Society. "Literature, sciences, nature, cooking, in fact, the whole field of domestic science, child study, nursing, home making, house furnishing" were all appropriate studies for Relief Society members, she explained in 1907, a dramatic addition to the usual testimony meetings, which characterized most Relief Society gatherings. Kindred subjects, Bathsheba added, such as "Ethics, Civics, Patriotism, Morals, Manners, the Gospel, the Virtues," were also "within the scope of the Relief Society." In urging the sisters to broaden their vision to include these and other subjects designed to enhance women's lives and responsibilities, she also admonished them "to be inspired to discover the greatest needs of your organization," suggesting that from all the possibilities for study, the individual Relief Societies should select those that met the needs of their own members.[16]

Emmeline never wavered from this latter point of view, though in 1913, during her own administration, the General Board, with new and younger members, began to centralize lesson topics. In respecting the autonomy of local leadership, she believed that the General Board was meant to be an aide to the local societies, not a manager. She did not resist the implementation of mother education or other topics in Relief Society meetings on their merits; she just wanted the individual wards and stakes to determine their own. She suggested that the Salt Lake Stake, under the highly regarded Isabella Horne, could "be an example in its plan for mothers' work, which was approved by the general board."[17] Emmeline expressed her philosophy best in a general Relief Society conference talk in 1910. Explaining "why the Relief Society did not have a general outline of Mother's work for the entire

15. Minutes of the General Board, October 19, 1906.

16. "The Officers of the Relief Society," *Woman's Exponent* 35 (May 1907): 68, some of which is quoted in Derr, Cannon, and Beecher, *Women of Covenant*, 161. Mother education lessons were part of the curriculum for ten years, beginning in 1903; standardized lessons were not implemented until 1913.

17. Minutes of the General Board of the Relief Society, February 6, 1903; March 6, 1903. Discussion on mothers' classes continued sporadically for several years. In December 1904, after little more than a year of mothers' education classes, the Salt Lake Stake requested that mothers' work be changed to a study of the Book of Mormon, a change approved by the General Board. Ibid., December 10, 1904.

society," she informed her audience that "it was to help educate and develop the sisters in their own locality by doing the thinking and studying of the subject required, which is all helpful to the mind and heart."[18] The Salt Lake Stake, she believed, could be an influential example of this approach.

The centralization and systematizing of the auxiliary programs, lessons, and procedures were, even then, however, on the church's drawing board, and within a few years, the issue became central to the board's planning as well as the Relief Society's relationship to the general church administration.[19] The new emphasis on standardization in all the auxiliaries affected the Relief Society's methods of fund-raising, wheat storage, writing and implementing curricula, and organizing quarterly conferences, but the board was ambivalent in defining its own role and the limits of its authority in relation to the local Relief Societies as well as to priesthood leaders. Thus, the early years of the new century became a testing period for the ability of the Relief Society to adapt to policies and procedures that would be correlated by a general church committee, resulting in a significant loss of autonomy.[20]

Another issue that the board continued to wrestle with was how—and whether—to fund the attendance of board members at national conventions. Even as many Relief Society members grew disenchanted with participation in national organizations and resented their ten-cent dues being used for representation at the annual meetings, board members' interest in affiliation increased. Both developments were problematic for Emmeline. The lack of support from among rank-and-file Relief Society members was disheartening after her long struggle to develop what she felt were valuable alliances with prominent national and international women leaders and associations. And the financial support of Relief Society members through their dues was essential to maintaining these connections. Unlike those who disavowed any need for national affiliations, the younger board members displayed a growing interest. Emmeline applauded their newly expressed desire for affiliation but chafed at the implication that she and her contemporaries on the board were no longer viable representatives and should be replaced. This notion compromised the value of all her years of nurturing

18. "General Relief Society Conference," *Woman's Exponent* 39 (June 1910): 6.

19. Derr, Cannon, and Beecher, *Women of Covenant*, 157–61. The thrust toward efficient and systematized homemaking and child rearing was addressed in 1828 by Lydia Maria Child, in *The American Frugal Housewife*, followed by Catherine Beecher's 1841 best seller, *A Treatise on Domestic Economy.*

20. For the consolidation of church programs and organizations, see J. Allen and Leonard, *Story of the Latter-day Saints*, 458–63. See also Derr, Cannon, and Beecher, *Women of Covenant*, 380.

those connections, both personal and institutional. "I have no heart to go on with the work I should like to take up because so much is being said—that hinders progress," she lamented on one discouraging day.[21] Emmeline was becoming ever more sensitive to the pain of her own redundancy.

The inevitable alterations from one generation to another were clearly playing out in the deliberations of the Relief Society General Board. Bathsheba, who had never shown interest in the national women's associations so dear to Emmeline, nevertheless felt some obligation to maintain these relationships, perhaps at Emmeline's urging. It probably did not seem untoward to Bathsheba to appoint her first counselor, Annie Taylor Hyde, to act in her stead for the forthcoming NAWSA and NCW meetings, rather than Emmeline. She had purposely called younger women to serve on the board, and it was prudent to give them the experience Emmeline had enjoyed for so long. Emmeline would at least be a delegate, along with Bathsheba's second counselor, Ida Dusenberry. But this was definitely a new and uncomfortable situation for Emmeline. She did not feel any better about it when counselor Annie Hyde, in a meeting attended by Bathsheba and Emmeline, had shown herself to be "very obstreperous" toward Bathsheba, and Emmeline felt that she had no "right or prerogative to domineer in that way." Though she did not identify the issue that elicited Annie's reaction, it was clear that Annie's assertiveness was new territory for Emmeline, and she did not know how she was "to bear it. [I] do not think that it is right—my whole soul rebels against it."[22] Emmeline had other reasons to be oversensitive. President Joseph F. Smith's growing lack of support for these affiliations and his immediate discomfort with the large delegation of women from the Relief Society and YLMIA preparing to attend the national convention disheartened her. Her effort at building bridges on behalf of the church seemed meaningless to her without the continuing support of the First Presidency.

More challenges to Emmeline's favored position lay ahead. Upon reaching Washington, she, Annie, and Ida went immediately to the Riggs House "to see some of the Suffrage people" who usually made their headquarters there during the annual woman suffrage conventions. This year, however, Emmeline had hoped to stay at the Fairfax Hotel, headquarters of the National Council of Women, where more of her current national associates, as well as Clara Barton, whom she almost venerated, would be housed. At earlier conferences, her choice would have been decisive, but this visit

21. E. Wells, Diary, January 30, 1902.

22. Ibid., January 31, 1902. Emmeline seldom mentioned names of her detractors or identified the "younger members" of the board. On this occasion, board members in attendance besides the three official Relief Society representatives were Phoebe Y. Beattie and Sarah J. Cannon.

was different. Annie Hyde and Ida Dusenberry, along with some of the other Utah attendees, insisted on staying at the legendary Riggs House and overruled Emmeline. "I was much opposed to it," Emmeline complained to her diary, "but was finally persuaded much against my will to yield to those of the party much younger & unexperienced." It was certainly a surprise to Emmeline to be outvoted, even in a matter as trivial as lodgings, and she later actually regretted having given in to the others. At the time, she may have seen her acquiescence as a model of cooperation, but later she felt that she had yielded a crucial element of her authority as a senior member of the delegation.[23] And she was not used to being countermanded. As usual, however, she made the best of the situation, confiding her sense of displacement only to her diary. But it was a straw in the wind that presaged more threatening adaptations ahead.

Rather than sulking over the situation, Emmeline turned it to her advantage, meeting and renewing relationships with her suffrage friends, some of whom she had known for more than twenty years. She was also mollified when invited to sit on the dais at the initial plenary session of the NAWSA convention, an invitation extended to her many times in the past. Sharing the platform were Carrie Chapman Catt, president of NAWSA; May Wright Sewall, president of the ICW; Clara Barton; Susan B. Anthony; the Reverend Anna Howard Shaw; and guest Madame Soffia Lenora Friedland of Russia, whom Emmeline had met in London.[24]

At the fourth triennial session of the National Council of Women, beginning shortly after the suffrage convention in February, Emmeline, the second corresponding secretary of the NCW, invited Annie Hyde, proxy for Bathsheba Smith, to read the report of the Relief Society, which Emmeline had prepared. At the evening session, Emmeline then read her own paper, "The Age We Live In."[25]

But the occasion was bittersweet for Emmeline. She was aware of the empty places at the suffrage convention once occupied by the earliest proponents of the women's movement, with whom she had shared the joy of small victories and the disappointments at defeat. Illness kept Elizabeth Stanton away, and she died a few months later. Susan B. Anthony, now in her eighties and more a bystander than an activist, died four years after Stanton. Others, like Sara Spencer, had left the suffrage movement and shifted their efforts on behalf of the goals of the National Council, much like Emmeline, or other causes. She was aware that many who were still

23. Ibid., February 9, 1902.

24. Ibid., February 12–20, 1902.

25. "The Age We Live In," in *General Relief Society*, 72–73. Also printed as "The Age We Live In," *Woman's Exponent* 30 (April 1902): 89–90.

active might not meet again, yielding to the toll of time, the exigencies of age, and other shifting circumstances. Indeed, this would be Emmeline's last attendance at a national woman suffrage convention.[26] Though she was chagrined at her loss of place among her Relief Society coworkers, at least Susa Young Gates, a member of the NCW press committee and representative of the YLMIA at the convention, praised Emmeline for what she had done for women over the years. "The party [of Utah women] was led by that gracious and great little woman," Susa wrote for the *Young Woman's Journal.* "Every Utah woman owes this indomitable soul a great debt of gratitude for the public work which she has so ably and untiringly performed these many years." With so many of Emmeline's fellow workers leaving the public scene, the time seemed propitious for Susa to acknowledge the service Emmeline had given to women's causes. "She was honored on this occasion," Susa explained, "not only by our own Utah women, but also by the great women of the nation convened in Washington."[27] As coworkers on the National Council during this period, Susa Gates and Emmeline collaborated in the effort to maintain connections with national associations and wrote extensively to one another about their concerns.[28]

Before returning home, Emmeline once again arranged a private meeting with Theodore Roosevelt, this time in his capacity as US president, the third with whom she had a private interview.[29]

The International Council of Women, scheduled to hold its quinquennial meeting in Berlin in 1904, became another divisive issue among members of the Relief Society board. The question of the hour was who would go to Berlin or whether anyone should go. Pivotal to the debate was a letter sent to the Relief Society by President Joseph F. Smith specifying that there would be no church money, evidently including Relief Society dues, available for attendance and only those who could pay their own way should be appointed delegates. Bathsheba Smith was very much "depressed...at the turn things had taken," wrote Emmeline, and they surmised that the decision had resulted from the "misrepresentation of envious and jealous

26. Details of the women who attended the conventions, their accomplishments, and, of course, their dress, as well as many of the social events, are found in "Happenings Here and There," *Woman's Exponent* 30 (March 1902): 84. See also "The National Council of Women," *Young Woman's Journal* 13 (June 1902): 246–51.

27. Ibid.

28. It is not always easy to discern Susa's motives in writing public laudatory comments about Emmeline while expressing demeaning comments elsewhere to others, with more of both in later years.

29. E. Wells, Diary, March 1, 1902. She noted that she wore the same dress to visit the president that she had worn when she visited Windsor Castle and saw Queen Victoria.

women."[30] Bathsheba Smith, as well as her granddaughter Alice Merrill Horne, a board member, was "grieved beyond what [Emmeline] imagined she would be, but Alice had counted on Relief Society money to pay her way to the conference as Bathsheba's proxy."[31] It seemed clear to Bathsheba that the directive was initiated "by the sisters who had been to President Joseph F. Smith against the use of the ten cent fund" to send board members to the Berlin convention. Counselor Annie Hyde was also against using the fund for this purpose.[32]

The directive, of course, affected Emmeline's own attendance at the Berlin meeting.[33] Certainly, Emmeline's acquaintance with many of the international delegates, her experience with the National and International Councils, and her position as second corresponding secretary of the NCW would seem to have made her a natural delegate. In expectation of her attendance, the NCW appointed her as an official American delegate and invited her to stop in Boston to speak at the national convention of the Daughters of the Revolution and in Paris to attend the executive committee meetings of the National Council. But all of Emmeline's efforts to find independent funding were futile. Even the pleadings of Rachel Siegel, Emmeline's Jewish friend, to Bathsheba Smith did not result in any help from the Relief Society, nor did Rachel volunteer any financial aid herself.[34] Hopeful of maintaining some dignity in her straitened circumstances, Emmeline could not allow herself to play the beggar before her financially able friends. Without any voluntary offers, Berlin faded from Emmeline's view. Alice Merrill Horne, however, attended as Bathsheba's proxy, and Lydia Alder, another bright, young member of the board, attended as delegate. Emmeline made no mention of the source of their funding but was pleased with both choices, despite her disappointment in not being one of them. Emily Richards and Ida Dusenberry traveled to Berlin on their own resources.

This had been a hard lesson for Emmeline. Experience, contacts, and ability were no longer primary qualifying criteria. While age was not a

30. Ibid., January 5, 1904.

31. Ibid., January 6, 7, 8, 1904.

32. When Annie Hyde expressed to the board her disapproval of this use of the ten-cent fund, Bathsheba then asked her "what use she would put it to." Annie felt it should be used primarily to visit the Relief Society sisters twice a year. Emmeline then explained that when the ten-cent dues were instigated during Zina's administration, the argument was that if all thirty-nine thousand members of the Relief Society paid a dime, all visits, within and outside the church, could be funded. Whether Annie Hyde was among those who took their complaints to President Smith is not recorded. See Minutes of the General Board, December 18, 1903. See also E. Wells, Diary, January 11, 1904.

33. E. Wells, Diary, January 14, 1904.

34. Ibid., April 27, 28, 1904.

deterrent in her mind, it was in the minds of the next generation of workers. Yielding to this reality was difficult. With a heavy heart, she prepared all of the necessary credentials and the statistical and financial report of the Relief Society for Alice. She also joined in a special prayer and blessing meeting for Alice in which five of the Relief Society officers each took a turn in giving her a blessing.[35]

When the day of Alice's departure arrived, Emmeline went to the depot and presented her with a bouquet of carnations as a departing gift. Once more she was obliged to hide her deep disappointment behind the well-practiced facade of cordiality. But later, she poured out her feelings. "Today I was to have spoken in the Woman's International Congress in Berlin—in Philharmonic Hall on Elementary Education and Co-education," she noted. "No one knows how disappointed I have felt over this affair. It makes me feel so bad that I am not good company for those around me.... The women who have caused the opposition do not value the Council as I do nor do they know how to estimate and appreciate its benefits—so cannot know how I feel."[36] It did not mitigate her disappointment to learn that Dr. Seymour B. Young, as well as Nelson Empey and T. G. Webber, all three her good friends, though men from whom she would have been embarrassed to solicit funding, would have provided the necessary money if they had known of her need. "All these offers came too late to do any good," she lamented, while wondering why she was "hindered & if it was best."[37]

Emmeline's disappointment over the Berlin conference and Alice's choice as Bathsheba Smith's proxy did not dilute their friendship. She and Bathsheba often met alone together to discuss Relief Society affairs, despite the fact that the board was now meeting biweekly and even more often in some months. They both attended the monthly fast meetings held on Sunday in the temple, and whenever she was invited to sit next to Bathsheba, Emmeline felt honored, since Bathsheba was "so highly esteemed by the First Presidency and was by the Prophet [Joseph] himself."[38] In December 1903, Bathsheba moved into the Beehive House, joining the Joseph F. Smith family who then occupied the home, and it became the place of the "ad hoc" meetings between Bathsheba and Emmeline.[39] It was a change from Bathsheba's small room in the church historian's office that had been her home while her husband was church historian and where she had lived for

35. General Officers Meeting, Minutes of the General Board, April 15, 1904.

36. E. Wells, Diary, April 18, June 14, 1904.

37. Ibid., June 4, July 20, 1904.

38. Ibid., September 6, 1903.

39. Bathsheba and Joseph F. Smith were kin. Bathsheba's husband, George A. Smith, was the first cousin of Hyrum Smith, who was Joseph F.'s father. Thus, by marriage, Joseph F. and Bathsheba were first cousins once removed.

so many years after his death. Emmeline discerned that her friend was lonely and had come to enjoy the loyalty and friendship that Emmeline, near her own age, provided.[40]

Emmeline was delighted when the board raised enough money to commission Lee Greene Richards, perhaps Utah's best-known portrait artist, to paint a life-size portrait of Bathsheba. Emmeline surveyed the results critically and adjudged the painting "beautiful in some respects quite masterly, but hardly satisfactory in the face."[41]

While relishing the broad number of acquaintances and friends who had entered her life, Emmeline felt that she could have been of more value in her public work had these contacts come earlier. "It does seem quite remarkable," she wrote, "that I should have had the attention of so many noted people & be sought after by those of our own faith as well after the obscurity in which I had lived during the time of raising my family & really when apparently it would have been more to my life and helped to awaken and develop ideas and sentiments to aid others."[42] Her long life offset her late start, however, and enabled her to integrate newly formed ideas and sentiments into her life while also broadening her perceptions and perspectives.

As if to make up for lost time, Emmeline, now seventy-three, participated in several new local associations, seemingly enthusiastic about any invitation to join. Of the number, only her own two clubs, the Reapers and the Woman's Press Club, could be considered "self-improvement" organizations. The Daughters of the Revolution, the Daughters of Utah Pioneers, the State Historical Society, the Kindergarten Association, the Mother's Congress (later Parent-Teachers Association), and the Utah Women's Council all directed their efforts to broader, more collective goals.[43] Besides her membership in these organizations, Emmeline served on various Relief Society subcommittees and assisted with Old Folks Day, holiday celebrations, and other occasional events and commemorative socials. Many of the meetings

40. Ibid., July 22, 1903.

41. Ibid., November 4, 1904. This would be but one of the portraits painted by Richards of the general Relief Society presidents. He also painted the portraits of Emma Smith, Emmeline Wells, Clarissa Williams, and Amy Brown Lyman. Emmeline's, unlike the others, is done in three-quarter-length profile. See fig. 32.

42. Ibid., August 3, 1901.

43. The Daughters of the Revolution is not to be confused with the Daughters of the American Revolution, which did not permit Mormon women to join until late in the twentieth century. Emmeline was the Utah state regent of the Utah chapter of the Daughters of the Revolution, organized in 1898; her friend Margaret Salisbury was the first Utah state regent of the Daughters of the American Revolution, organized in 1895.

of these groups were held in her office, now in the newly renovated Templeton Building, becoming so numerous they often overlapped.[44]

How did she do it all? Not without ruffling some feathers in her efforts to be efficient and timely in order to meet her many commitments. Constantly overworked, Emmeline undoubtedly showed flashes of irritability and impatience with people who did not always catch her vision or apply her methods. Some found her difficult to work with because of her persuasive will and penchant to get things done in as short a time as possible.[45] Her manner could be imperious as times, though her ability to accomplish every task laid before her commanded respect. She was a working woman living and associating primarily with relatively leisured, if not necessarily wealthy, Mormon and Gentile women, and her exasperation at their failure to see the value of her work "in their behalf" irritated and dismayed her. "No one will ever know how I have worked for the good of the Women of Zion, in a public way," she complained to her diary, "and the ingratitude of some who are envious is unbearable."[46] She repeatedly assumed that envy explained the lack of appreciation for her efforts, and this explanation served as an anodyne when dissension or conflicts arose. Her authority came from experience as much as ability, and she could not always relinquish that prerogative graciously.

But she was genuine in her belief of the good it would do her people to reach out to the non-Mormon world and build bridges and establish friendships. She was appalled to learn how many of her Mormon sisters knew so little about the associations to which the Relief Society belonged. "It seems hardly credible," she wrote shortly before a visit from May Wright Sewall, president of the International Council of Women, "that our sisters should not know that there are benefits to be derived from our connection with the Council."[47]

For every individual who failed to understand her vision or resented her imperious manner, there were those who admired, loved, and expressed their

44. Ibid., April 22, 1903. In January 1903, she accommodated a friend by trading offices with her, taking a larger room on the fifth floor of the Templeton, nearer the elevator. Ibid., January 2, 1903.

45. In 1902, Relief Society board member Elizabeth J. DuFresne and others bristled at Emmeline's insistence in adding her longtime friend Margaret Caine to the board rather than the popular choice of Elizabeth (Lizzie) Wilcox. Even Bathsheba was unable to persuade Emmeline to yield her choice to the majority, and Emmeline's "pathetic plea" won the day. DuFresne was "utterly astonished" that the board had succumbed so easily. Emmeline's "power of persuasion" was not something to be underestimated. Elizabeth J. DuFresne, Diary, October 5, 1902.

46. E. Wells, Diary, May 17, 1901.

47. Ibid., July 6, 1901.

loyalty in myriad ways. Ellis Shipp often met with Emmeline to talk over her own troubles and even assisted her in getting her paper mailed. When Romania Pratt, "one of my dearest true friends" and a fellow tenant when she had her office in the Constitution Building, moved her medical office to a newly purchased home on Ninth East, Emmeline was deeply saddened. "It will seem lonely," she wrote. "She has been near me so long and we have been very intimate." Emmeline wondered, however, that perhaps a separation of their workplaces might be good, "for one does not like to confide too much and yet one is apt to do so and perhaps regret it afterwards."[48] Few statements reveal so candidly how carefully Emmeline guarded the boundaries between her public and private lives.

A new blow to the family was the unexpected death of her fifty-nine-year-old son-in-law, Septimus Sears. He left Isabel not only with an inconsolable heartache but also with a large home and surrounding orchard and gardens to manage on her own. Septimus had been a well-known and successful businessman.[49] He was director of the board of the Deseret Agricultural and Mining Society at the time of his death. He was honored as an "intense, capable, industrious worker," who arose early to work in his garden. Remembered as being "generous and large hearted," he had also been a loyal and loving husband to Belle and a dutiful and considerate son-in-law to Emmeline.[50] His death was deeply felt by the whole family. But there were more.

Emmeline's sister Pallas died a few months later, and soon afterward came news of the suicide of Barry Hillard, the husband of Verona, Mell's daughter. "No doubt he was crazed with losses," Emmeline reasoned.[51] The year ended with the death of Elmina Taylor, general president of the Young Ladies' MIA. While these deaths reawakened the pain of her own losses, underscoring them all was the loss of Melvina's faith in the church to which her mother and father had given so much. "O how glad I should be to have all mine in full accord and harmony with the holy priesthood of God revealed in these last days. This is my greatest sorrow."[52]

One bright compensation during this saddened time was the birth of a new child for Annie, her twelfth. Anticipating that this would be the last of Annie's childbirths, Emmeline desired to prepare her daughter spiritually

48. Ibid., October 28, 1904. The home Romania purchased had originally been owned by Emmeline's sister Adeline Maria Earl, who had moved to California.

49. "S. W. Sears Claimed by Death," *Deseret Evening News*, April 5, 1903, 1; "The Life Work of S. W. Sears," *Deseret Evening News*, April 11, 1903, sec. 3, p. 1.

50. E. Wells, Diary, April 7, 1903.

51. Ibid., October 20, 1904.

52. Ibid., December 30, 1904.

and physically for the coming ordeal. A few days before the baby's birth, Emmeline, Bathsheba Smith, and Susan Grant rode to the Cannon farm, where they first enjoyed a tasty chicken luncheon with Annie. Afterward, they repaired to Annie's sitting room, made warm and inviting by "a lovely fire burning in the grate." Kneeling together beside Annie, the three women prayed, with Susan articulating their petition. Then Susan washed Annie preparatory to the anointing by Bathsheba, with all three women joining in "the confirmation of sealing the anointing."[53] They were engaged in a tradition that had been honored since the early days of the church. It would soon become expendable as priesthood blessings replaced it; while permissible, however, it proved to be a comforting, sacred ritual among the women of the church.[54] The healthy baby boy was born eight days later, only a few weeks after Annie and John Q. took possession of the large home on the Cannon farm, once the residence of George Q. Cannon.

Always prone to self-assessment, while writing an editorial for her paper one evening, Emmeline ruminated on her twenty-five years as editor, declaring that "the varied experience gained during that time cannot be told, but altogether it has been a labor of love." She added, significantly, that "no matter how arduous the work or how numerous the fault finders, never once has the writer been tempted to withdraw." She explained that "the work has been a solace in times of trouble and sorrow, something to turn to for relief, and, in a way, a pastime."[55] Its constancy was an essential and dependable cord holding together the pieces of Emmeline's fragmented life.

One summer evening in 1903, after a pleasant ride through Liberty Park with Belle, Emmeline took note of all the "stylish people" and felt compelled to take stock again of her own life. "I am truly grateful for every blessing of comfort and happiness I have had in the later years of my life," she acknowledged. "I have not had so many privileges as many of the sisters with whom I have been associated but I have enjoyed my own gifts of mind and heart and tried to make myself useful in spreading the truth."[56] The balance sheet unquestionably tilted in her favor.

53. Ibid., October 31, 1904.

54. For the exercise of this practice by women and its gradual loss, see Linda King Newell, "Gifts of the Spirit: Women's Share."

55. "Editorial Work," *Woman's Exponent* 31 (July 1–15, 1902): 12.

56. E. Wells, Diary, July 19, 1903.

CHAPTER 33

No Rest for the Weary
(1905–1908)

THE LAST TWO DECADES of Emmeline's life presented remarkable changes in the city that had been her home since 1848. After the turn of the nineteenth century, Salt Lake City had four daily newspapers, full-time police and fire departments, a sewer system, streetlights, and the beginning of paved roads. The Avenues had become a desirable residential area, attracting artisans, tradesmen, and city workers. Emmeline's sister-wives—Susan, Lydia Ann, Hannah, and Martha—made their homes in this area. In 1906, East Temple Street acknowledged the growing number of commercial properties springing up on both sides and was renamed Main Street. The population had grown to fifty-three thousand in 1900 and another decade would see it number more than ninety-two thousand.

The three decades following completion of the transcontinental railroad in 1869 had brought an accelerating flow of non-Mormon entrepreneurs, mining speculators, lawyers, and businessmen and their families, some of whom built large mansions on South Temple, then known as Brigham Street. Rows of tall poles and connecting wires traversed the length of Main Street and several other routes, transporting electric streetcars, which traveled from the Avenues to as far south as Sugar House, carrying as many as ten thousand people in a day. In 1910, twelve trains carried passengers for the hour ride north to Ogden, and several trains made the two-and-a-half-hour trip south to Payson daily. Public transportation made a remarkable difference for women like Emmeline, traveling without a male companion and without any other means of conveyance. These advances in transportation enabled Relief Society officers to visit outlying women's conferences more often and more conveniently. Emmeline also enjoyed the convenience of the telephone but never learned to use the typewriter.

Buildings in the north end of the city included four structures on Temple Square—the temple, the tabernacle, the Assembly Hall, and the Bureau of

Information, greeting tourists since its opening in 1902. The construction of the Hotel Utah in 1912, the nearly completed LDS Hospital high on Eighth Avenue, and the newly built Deseret News building and annex, along with historic ZCMI (Zion's Cooperative Mercantile Institution), buttressed the LDS Church's dominance of the north end of the city. But major new construction was also taking place at the south end. With the invention of the elevator, high-rise office buildings rose above the four or five stories that had been the maximum height several decades earlier. The completion of the Boston and Newhouse Buildings at ten stories each matched the height of buildings in many other cities. When the Walker Bank building was completed in 1912, at sixteen stories, it was one of the tallest buildings in the West.[1] O. J. Salisbury was responsible for the New York Hotel in 1906 and the Felt Building, completed in 1910. Several other hotels, including the beautifully furnished Newhouse Hotel, were constructed to meet the needs of the growing number of travelers to Utah. Auerbach's and Keith O'Brien's, popular department stores, competed with ZCMI for business, since ZCMI, which had served primarily Mormon customers, increased its patronage with the expiration of the cooperative movement before the turn of the century. In 1913, a "flickering," as it was called then, or silent movie, played to fascinated audiences at the American theater on Main Street, midway between the two sections of downtown Salt Lake City. It gave stiff competition to the live plays at the Salt Lake Theatre. The Hotel Utah on the north and the Hotel Newhouse on the south stood like twin pillars defining the outer edges of the commercial district and what had become a bona fide business section of the city. Restaurants, the Salt Lake Theatre, lecture halls, churches, saloons, and other diverse establishments occupied the streets verging from Main Street.[2]

Although Emmeline lived on the outskirts of the central city in Waterloo, most of her daily activities centered on the north end of town. The tabernacle and temple served her religious needs, and the five-story Templeton Building on the corner of South Temple and Main Street remained the central locale of her workdays. Her office still served on occasion as the meeting room for her two literary clubs, as well as for the Daughters of the Revolution and the women's auxiliary organizations. Visitors to her offices, large in number, still interrupted her work on the *Exponent*, but out-of-town travelers to the city, who inevitably found their way to her office, were

1. John S. McCormick, *Salt Lake City: The Gathering Place, an Illustrated History*; and Alan Barnett, *Seeing Salt Lake City: The Legacy of the Shipler Photographers*.

2. Thomas K. Hafen, "City of Saints, City of Sinners: The Development of Salt Lake City as a Tourist Attraction, 1869–1900"; Michael W. Homer, *On Their Way to Somewhere Else: European Sojourners in the Mormon West, 1834–1930*.

always welcome. In 1905, popular writer and lecturer Virginia Donaghe McClurg was one such visitor to the city and made a point of seeking out Emmeline. McClurg was noted for her efforts to save the Mesa Verde cliff dwellings and to promote the creation of the Mesa Verde National Park.[3]

Though her association with the National and International Councils of Women was mainly epistolary by this time, Emmeline briefly nursed the idea of attending the quinquennial meeting of the International Council of Women scheduled for Toronto, Canada, in June 1909. Her 1899 experience in London and failure to attend the Berlin conference only fed her desire to attend more of these large gatherings of women. As it turned out, the London conference would be her only international experience.[4] Though she included accounts of these conventions in the *Exponent*, they lacked the appealing details that once sparkled her firsthand reports of such meetings, particularly the personal portraits of the women attendees and their socials. She herself was not forgotten, however. At the 1906 Toledo, Ohio, executive meetings of the NCW, the delegates passed a resolution in honor of the contribution made by Emmeline Wells and Susa Young Gates, although both were absent. Of greater personal significance was Susan B. Anthony's bequeathal of a gold ring to Emmeline when Anthony died that same year. A note with the gift read, "In recognition of her esteem and love for Mrs. Emmeline B. Wells, Miss Anthony sent one of her gold rings on the day of her death to Mrs. Wells in Utah. The bond between these two women was very strong and the friendship had continued for nearly thirty years."[5]

Emmeline's primary focus now was her Relief Society assignment. She valued being an officer of an organization that had such historical significance, but record keeping was tedious at best, and the correspondence and errands heaped on her only increased over the years, particularly during the days immediately preceding the semiannual Relief Society conferences. "Though we have committees appointed," she ruefully noted, "the burden falls upon the secretary however much one tried to escape it."[6] As the

3. Virginia Donaghe McClurg, from New Jersey, made her home in Colorado after visiting the Mesa Verde cliff dwellings for the first time in 1889. She was a poet, writer, newspaperwoman, literary club enthusiast, and lecturer. See E. Wells, Diary, September 7, 1905.

4. Ibid., April 25, 1908.

5. The ring was accepted at a memorial service for Susan B. Anthony in Salt Lake City held on March 17, 1906, and noted in the report of the Annual Business Meeting of the National Woman's Relief Society, October 1, 1906, as contained in the National Woman's Relief Society Record, Third Record, May 1906–April 1911 (Incorporated Society Board Meetings Record). Most other quotations are taken from the Minutes of the General Board.

6. E. Wells, Diary, September 30, 1908.

organization's institutional memory and as the woman who knew—or knew about—virtually every officer in the wards and branches, she found herself serving as a source of information for all things relating to the Relief Society and other women's interests. She continually received requests to head a committee, write a letter, speak at a social or meeting, travel to Relief Society stake conferences, or write a poem for a birthday or other celebration. "One gets so weary of the questions and letters year after year," she bewailed. "It is tedious and wearisome."[7] But she soldiered on because she loved the organization and felt such perennial satisfaction in associating with the women who led it, particularly in the wards and stakes. Nevertheless, more than the pressure of her secretarial work, she deplored the tension that still ruled some of the board meetings, and after the first meeting of 1908, she pensively characterized it as "not exactly a battle of giants but strong-minded women."[8] She could not discount herself, although her name seldom appears in the minutes she wrote.

Emmeline's greatest recompense for meeting the persistent challenge to forbearance was her solidifying friendship with Bathsheba Smith. Early on, Bathsheba began to visit Emmeline's office after her work in the temple, resting on the lounge that had been placed there after Bathsheba became president of the Relief Society. The visits soon became almost daily, and when possible Bathsheba and Emmeline conversed at length. "I think she enjoys that old lounge and being here with me very much," Emmeline opined, "and I am deeply attached to her. In fact," she continued, "I feel the greatest reverence, and also sympathy for her as she really is lonely though surrounded with her own kindred."[9] The two of them often attended socials together, visited friends, gave blessings to women in need, and attended ward and stake Relief Society, YLMIA, and Primary functions together. On one such occasion the bishop called them "uncrowned queens." Their similar ideas about the Relief Society made them allies in many board meeting discussions, and partly because of Emmeline's unwavering support, Bathsheba was not reluctant to exert her will or cut off debate when she had heard enough. In the midst of a heated discussion over mother education outlines, the minutes reported that "the Pres. was weary and wanted to adjourn," and without further discussion or debate the meeting ended.[10]

This comfortable companionship could not have developed as easily between Bathsheba and either of her counselors. First Counselor Annie Taylor Hyde was nearly thirty years younger than Bathsheba and still had

7. Ibid., March 16, 1908.
8. Ibid., January 3, 1908.
9. Ibid., April 17, 1908.
10. Minutes of the General Board, October 19, 1906.

family responsibilities at home. Ida Dusenberry, a Provo educator, was even younger—only twenty-eight to Bathsheba's seventy-nine years when Ida joined the Relief Society General Board. Furthermore, in addition to the Relief Society, Ida had teaching responsibilities at the Normal Training School at BYU. In contrast, Emmeline and Bathsheba were of the same generation, with only six years' difference in their ages. Both had lived in Nauvoo and had known the Prophet Joseph Smith. Both had traveled over the long trail to Utah, had been early settlers in the city, and had been wives of important church leaders. Companionship naturally evolved through their association in the Relief Society. Both clung to its history and viewed the Nauvoo Relief Society, with its original purposes and procedures, as the cornerstone of the current organization, not just a quaint and brief opening chapter. They saw its meaning and purpose through a different lens than their Utah-born associates.

Besides the satisfaction she received from her position on the Relief Society General Board, Emmeline, at age seventy, had begun receiving recognition not only for her national work but also for her interest and involvement in local affairs. May Anderson of the Primary presidency, for instance, thought her "the most wonderful woman there has ever been in this Church," and Julia Brixon considered her "the best speaker in the Church of the women."[11] By this time, Emmeline was likely more well known for her position as Relief Society secretary than as editor of the *Woman's Exponent*, though both ensured impressive name recognition throughout the church and beyond. For years her name had conveyed the image of a woman broadly engaged in both community and church service, skilled at making friends and admirers in disparate groups, and exemplary in her desire to resist social categorization. Her presence graced so many socials and enlivened so many meetings that she was constantly sought after for both.

In appearance, as well as personality, Emmeline could not be ignored. She presented an antiquated picture that became ever more singular and part of her charm as fashions changed after the turn of the century. No sycophant of fads, she maintained her nineteenth-century appearance until she died: long dresses topped by chiffon scarves and softly colored batiste furbelows, a pocket watch attached to a gold chain hanging from her neck, and a purse, or "satchel," as she called it, which contained her diary, among other articles, always on her arm. But it was the essence of her presence that commanded attention, evoking an immediate impression that here was a woman whose intelligence and bearing belied the delicate image she presented at first meeting.

11. E. Wells, Diary, January 9, 28, February 4, April 15, December 6, 1908.

Of particular concern to both Bathsheba and Emmeline was turning talk of a woman's building into a reality. When the decision was made to have Lee Greene Richards, son of Levi Richards and Louisa Greene Richards, paint a portrait of Bathsheba, it was meant to grace a wall of the new building. Instead, it was temporarily placed in the temple where Bathsheba also presided as head of female temple workers, awaiting construction of the Relief Society headquarters. At the same time, in a glowing tribute to Emmeline, Emily Richards suggested that the artist also paint a similar portrait of Emmeline. According to the minutes, Emily "spoke earnestly of [Emmeline's] arduous labors and her faithfulness so many years and how they all come to her when anything was wanted; thought her services should be appreciated."[12] Both the verbal and the visual tributes were usually reserved for the president of an organization, not its secretary, but she had escalated the role of secretary in ways that were never quite matched. The two portraits were painted, with Emmeline's in profile, likely her decision. Both paintings became their official Relief Society presidential portraits. A more practical show of appreciation was a raise in Emmeline's monthly salary to twenty-five dollars.

When Emmeline presented her annual report to the board in 1906, there was little question that her workload deserved the additional pay. One year's secretarial duties consisted of writing 519 letters, producing 210 circulars, thirty-one copies of the Articles of Incorporation, and twenty-five copies of the bylaws of incorporation. She also wrote up the minutes of thirty-five stake conferences, twenty-nine board meetings, two general Relief Society conferences, a variety of special meetings, and reports of visits to the various Relief Society conferences by the Relief Society "missionaries."[13] An important notation indicated that neither she nor the president had missed a single board meeting that year.[14] In addition to all her secretarial labors, she wrote extensive accounts of the general Relief Society conferences for the *Woman's Exponent*.

By 1906, rumors accelerated regarding the promised woman's building when it became common knowledge that a new building would be constructed across from the temple on Main Street. Wanting information

12. Minutes of the General Board, November 3, 1905.

13. Relief Society missionaries, who formerly served as directors of the incorporated Relief Society, were primarily stake Relief Society presidents. They assisted in visiting stake Relief Society conferences throughout the territory. Emmeline's diary for 1907 consists of nothing but a listing of all the various stake Relief Societies that were visited that year, their dates, and the names of the visiting sisters from the Relief Society board and corps of missionaries.

14. Ibid., October 1, 1906.

about the building, the presidents of the three women's organizations wrote to the First Presidency in January 1907 and included a copy of Lorenzo Snow's 1901 letter promising construction of a woman's building. A month later, they received word that the new building was to contain the offices of the presiding bishop, the religion classes, and the general boards of the Relief Society, the Young Ladies' and Young Men's Mutual Improvement Associations, and the Primary Association. It was not to be the promised Relief Society building. The announcement was greeted with stunned disbelief. Moreover, it was to be known as the Bishop's Building. "Some felt very grieved over the way things stand," the minutes sadly reported, and Bathsheba Smith was said to have fainted at the unexpected news. The board was especially concerned about the feelings of the women who had contributed money over the years. The hope that the woman's building as originally envisioned, Emmeline wrote, "would be a monument to the women of Zion and show to the world that we had a memorial worthy [of] the cause we represent" now seemed dashed.[15] The First Presidency's request for a five-thousand-dollar contribution from the Relief Society for the new building only exacerbated the disappointment.[16] Utterly dismayed by the change of plans, the board could only acquiesce. Relief Society officers set the example for the disillusioned members. They would move forward and make the best of a situation in which they had no voice. Construction on the new building was soon under way. It seemed a propitious time for Emmeline to visit Mell.

For the first time, Emmeline traveled north to spend Christmas with the Woods family in Idaho. As always, it was a relaxing and joyful time for Emmeline. Several evenings, she and Mell read through a cache of letters once belonging to Will's mother, Catherine Wells Woods, Daniel's sister, which Will gave them to read. Eliza Robison, Daniel's first wife, had died just four months earlier in her Michigan home, which may have occasioned the reading of the letters. They provided "good insight into the life and circumstances" of Will's family and revealed things they had never known about Eliza. She had always made her home near her son Albert, a clergyman, who never married. Mell and Emmeline were certainly aware that Eliza had divorced Daniel in 1851, but were surprised to learn that she had once thought of marrying again.[17] "I do not think the Esquire knew about it,"

15. Ibid., March 2, 1907.

16. Ibid., October 1, 1907.

17. Eliza's complaint against Daniel is recorded April 23, 1851, in the Des Moines County, Iowa, District Court Records, Divorce Department, 1851, Apr.–Oct. She filed her petition for divorce in the Office of the Clerk on June 24, 1851. There is no evidence that Daniel contested the divorce, so it would have been granted. Eliza still

Emmeline noted. "He always spoke as if she could not do such a thing." The letters enabled Emmeline to see Eliza's "character differently than before," though she does not explain why. Catherine, they were happy to learn, adored Daniel "to the last" and agreed with other family members that he had simply been "deluded" in accepting Mormonism.[18]

As the *Woman's Exponent* increased in intrinsic value, it decreased in issues and subscriptions. As times changed, so did people's reading preferences, and new periodicals appeared on magazine stands. Even with the help of Emmeline's talented and hardworking daughter Annie, it was increasingly difficult to prepare each issue. Worse, it was becoming anachronistic and representative of a passing age and thus less appealing to younger readers. Less demand for subscriptions, of course, meant less revenue for Emmeline. Her response was to work harder to keep the paper afloat. Except for sick days or travel, Emmeline was in her office six days a week, often working until late hours to make the monthly deadline. "My paper worries me so much" was a familiar refrain, "and yet," she doggedly asserted, "I cannot and will not give it up."[19] But the years of hard work were slowly catching up with her.

Political activity was also a casualty of her waning energy. No longer as involved as during the heady days of statehood, Emmeline was still a loyal Republican and never failed to vote. She was disappointed that Heber Wells did not become the Republican candidate for a third term as governor and expressed her disappointment in the new governor, John C. Cutler, though she attended his inauguration in the City and County Building. He was a businessman, she disapprovingly noted, "whom we never would have thought of" as governor of Utah. A candidate for governor, she believed, should have "rendered some service or whose parents have in some way helped forward the community in civic or some public progress." He and the new secretary of state (lieutenant governor today), Charles S. Tingey, she complained, were of "very ordinary education and ability."[20]

The growing strength of the American Party also concerned her. It was fiercely anti-Mormon and had mobilized strength among many influential

lists herself as a Wells in the 1900 census for Traverse City, Michigan. Her death occurred in August 1905 in Alma, Gratiot County, Michigan, at the age of eighty-five.

18. E. Wells, Diary, December 12, 13, 15, 1908.

19. Ibid., January 26, 1905.

20. Ibid., January 2, 1905. A British convert to Mormonism, John Cutler, born in 1846, was eighteen when his family emigrated to Utah, where he became extremely successful in numerous business enterprises, namely, banking, and served as an officer or on the board of directors of prominent local companies. He was urged to run for governor by his business associates. He served only one term and at age eighty-two committed suicide.

Gentiles in the state as well as politically disgruntled Mormons. It charged the LDS Church with improper interference in politics and rallied enough support to be successful in local elections for several years. It was hopeful of winning state offices in the 1908 election. After losing his second bid for the US Senate, Thomas Kearns left the Republican Party and became a leading figure in the American Party.[21] Emmeline felt that its strong anti-Mormon base was "determined to ruin our people who have made the country what it is."[22] Both the Democrats and the Republicans hoped to garner enough votes to defeat the American Party. Emmeline, of course, supported the Republicans. "We are beginning to feel the need of an emergency call for help in securing the election of the Republican ticket," she wrote in 1908, a month before the election, and briefly reentered the political fray by preparing literature showing the dangers of electing American Party candidates.[23] She urged Republican women to register to vote, enlisting as many as possible to distribute campaign literature. She was encouraged to find that most of them were unexpectedly "quite pleased with the little episodes and occurrences they [met] with in going round." In her usual fatalistic way, she ultimately believed that only the Lord could help overcome the anti-Mormon influence of the American Party, "unless we need a scourging," she cautiously added.[24]

On Election Day, two of Emmeline's Cannon grandsons drove carriages to take Republican women to the polls while individual women kept watch over the polling places. Careful planning brought happy results. The Republicans won by a landslide, electing William Spry as governor and winning all but two seats in the Utah House of Representatives. Reed Smoot, a Republican, who had been successfully seated in the US Senate, was reelected by the 1909 legislature.[25] This was one of Emmeline's last political activities beyond voting.

With the death of Septimus Sears and the distant Idaho residence of William Woods, Emmeline had come to rely on John Q. Cannon for male assistance when needed. But her pleasure with his pleasing personality did not erase the worries she had over his financial problems as she learned

21. Thomas G. Alexander, "Political Patterns of Early Statehood, 1896–1919," in *Utah's History*, edited by Poll et al., 414–18. See also Thomas G. Alexander, *Mormonism in Transition: A History of the Latter-day Saints, 1890–1930*, 27–29.

22. E. Wells, Diary, July 29, 1908.

23. Ibid., October 8, 1908.

24. Ibid., October 28, 1908. At the temple fast meeting shortly before the election, Edna Lambson Smith, a wife of President Joseph F. Smith, urged Emmeline to speak, which Emmeline declined to do, and so Edna arose "and told them to vote the Republican ticket straight." Ibid., November 1, 1908.

25. Alexander, *Mormonism in Transition*, 29–34.

about them. Her concern was his many children who depended on him to feed, clothe, and educate them. His tendency to borrow or clandestinely use money not his own seemed to have become a life pattern, along with some other distasteful habits.[26] An incident in 1905 involving John's fiduciary irresponsibility that brought serious public and state censure deeply distressed Emmeline.[27] As bad as some of her own troubles were, she felt that "terrible indeed are the sorrows that come to our children, worse indeed than our own ten times over." The familiarity of such sorrow only doubled its burden and made it "almost beyond endurance." As the events relating to his misuse of public funds unfolded, Emmeline found it "very sad to be pitied and sympathized with," even by those who genuinely felt her misery. She consoled herself with her belief that "the darkest cloud has a silver lining and if we only wait and pray A brighter day may dawn."[28] In time John returned to his usual prominent place in Salt Lake society, his malfeasance paid for and forgotten.

Emmeline's visits to her Idaho daughter continued to give her respite from the troubles that plagued her at home. She was very proud of the accomplishments of Mell and her family and looked forward to spending another Christmas with them in 1908. This time they met in Spokane, where Verona and Daisy and their families were then living. Mell and Will stayed in a hotel to be with them all. It was a restful, delightful visit. Emmeline enjoyed preaching a little Mormonism to C. W. Betts, Verona's new husband, and commiserated with Will (even though he was a Democrat) for having lost his bid for the US Senate. She had many quiet conversations with her "very dignified" son-in-law, who had brought only honor to the family and seemed well suited to his position as a judge, she observed. He was cordial and open with Emmeline and made her feel that he enjoyed her company as much as she did his. She also became better acquainted with her four great-grandsons—Daisie's Marti and Tom and Verona's Barry and Robert.[29]

26. One fellow worker at the *Deseret News*, of which John Q. had become editor in 1892, cogently summarized his character, describing him as "a charming conversationalist, a wit of no small boundary, a good friend to young men, and a splendid boss." He also astutely noted that John Q. "was no paragon of virtue" and "never set himself up as one." And John Q. did indeed seem to skirt the edges of propriety without fear of consequences. His pleasure-loving and often risky activities actually endeared him to many. See Les Goates, "Time Out for the Colonel," *Deseret News*, January 15, 1931, sec. 2, p. 2, as quoted in Kenneth L. Cannon II, "Wives and Other Women: Love, Sex, and Marriage in the Lives of John Q. Cannon, Frank J. Cannon, and Abraham H. Cannon."

27. For information on the incident, see "Committee Report."

28. E. Wells, Diary, February 15, 17, April 3, September 1, 1905.

29. Ibid., December 14, 19, 20, 1908.

When gifts were exchanged, Emmeline observed that "Christmas is the season when people buy things they can't afford to give to people who don't want them."[30] With music from Daisie and Mell ringing in her ears, long and satisfying conversations with them all, and warm feelings destined to linger long in her memory, Emmeline made her way home.

Though privately bruised by personal and family troubles, Emmeline maintained her usual public demeanor. She followed her own formula for living, expressed in a poem written decades before:

'Twere better if we never turned aside
But labored diligent with constant care,
Stern duty for our motto, faith our guide,
Patience our helpmeet, and our watchword prayer.[31]

30. Ibid., December 23, 1908.
31. E. Wells, "At Last," in her *Musings and Memories*, 69–71.

CHAPTER 34

The Elect Lady

(1908–1911)

In 1909, Emmeline watched from her office window in room 567 of the Templeton Building the razing of the old Tithing Office and Deseret News Building, both giving way to the grand new Hotel Utah. Meanwhile, the Bishop's Building had taken the place of the area presently occupied by the gardens just north of the site of the new hotel.[1] The old adobe home on that same block, which held so many varied memories, was long gone. Though Emmeline felt there was no need to mourn the changes that were occurring, "to me," she nostalgically wrote, "who has seen it all built up and watched it year after year and lived behind the dear old wall and had so many tender recollections of the familiar places—it brings to mind such vivid pictures of the past that it strikes deep into the innermost crevices of my being." Yet even seeing family members and friends, many from Nauvoo days, now slipping off the scene one by one, she felt that "one cannot go mourning over lost hopes or even friends who are gone however dear but one must act in the living present and go on as best they may."[2]

How much better for her if only she could have heeded her own counsel. She turned eighty in 1908, and her diary recounts a continual round of silent mourning, depressed spirits, nostalgic evocations of a time long gone, and the birth and death dates of friends and family that kept her rooted in the past. "I am so weary and yet I try to persevere and do much more than I am able," she repeatedly confessed—though only to her diary. On

1. The Tithing Office and Deseret Store had occupied the first floor of the adobe brick building on the corner of Main and South Temple Streets, while the *Deseret News* had occupied the second and third floors. The area was fronted by a cobblestone wall, so often mentioned in Emmeline's journal when she lived in the adjacent adobe house. The Hotel Utah is now known as the Joseph Smith Memorial Building.

2. E. Wells, Diary, June 19, 1909.

one unpleasant day, she admitted that she was "not as well as the folks think," and on another she believed that she was "grieving beyond what is apparent outwardly."[3] Her ever-increasing fainting spells, dizziness, fatigue, and "nervousness" were as much a result of her unchecked emotions as her overwrought body. She seldom had a full night's sleep, and she never passed a day without writing letter after letter, editorials, and copy for her paper or transcribing notes to her minute book and skipping meals. Six short words encompassed her general frame of mind that had settled on her like a permanent shroud: "O, so tired and most unhappy."[4]

The rigid secrecy with which Emmeline guarded her inner life meant that she could not ask others to share her burdens or even to be a sympathetic presence that would allow her to vent her tensions and melancholy. Her unyielding work and social schedule drained her diminished physical resources, but she would not, could not, even at this point in her life, give up her paper. Too much of her life was contingent on its existence. Payment for her secretarial services to the Relief Society and for use of her office for board meetings boosted her financial status, but she continued to depend on family and friends for anything beyond frugal living.

Her hard work did not go wholly uncompensated. At her advanced age, she took some pride that she was still sought after for advice, for consultation, for the influence she was able to exert from her long experience in public affairs, and for her exceptional memory and extensive knowledge. While the constant claims by others on her time were wearying and sometimes annoying, she was gracious and forthcoming in meeting those requests. "Her room is a Mecca," wrote May Booth Talmage, a writer, member of the YLMIA General Board, and wife of Apostle James E. Talmage, "to which come pilgrims who desire advice or encouragement or information concerning things literary or otherwise, and to each she endeavors to supply the need." It is remarkable, Talmage wrote, that in the midst of all her public activities, Emmeline has been able "to attend to the minor things that so many fail or forget to do who have no duties outside their own little world."[5]

In February 1908, Utah governor John C. Cutler asked for Emmeline's help in selecting delegates to an International Congress of Mothers. In April, she received an invitation to attend the International Conference on Woman Suffrage to be held later that year in Amsterdam, and Lillian M. Hollister, corresponding secretary of the National Council of Women,

3. Ibid., August 9, September 7, 1909.

4. Ibid., August 25, 1909.

5. May Booth Talmage, "Coronets of Age," 182.

invited Emmeline and Bathsheba Smith to assist with an international Peace Conference to be held in London in July.[6] The two aged women deferred to Relief Society workers living near the sites of these conferences, a more practical policy, but it was not easy to turn down such prestigious invitations. Emmeline reluctantly acknowledged that her days of active participation in such events were behind her, but she was gratified to be invited.

Family affairs also kept Emmeline rooted at home. Since the death of her sister-wife Martha in 1908, only four of Daniel's widows were still living. Then in August 1908, eighty-one-year-old Lydia Ann (Alley) also died, depriving Emmeline of one of her closest friends and sister-wives. Lydia Ann and Susan, who lived together, had provided Emmeline with a warm and welcoming home whenever she visited and were ever solicitous of her well-being.

Besides the *Exponent*, Emmeline was also loath to give up her affiliation with either of her two clubs or the local and national associations in which she still maintained membership. Correspondence, however, was now her means of connection, and her first action upon reaching her office each day was to read through the mail, always disappointed when "nothing of interest" appeared.

Despite their own troubles, her daughters were moving on with their lives. Belle, a widow for six years, was deeply engaged in temple service and acted as proxy for many of their Woodward relatives. She was also active in the Daughters of Utah Pioneers, as was her mother, but she did not share Emmeline's interest in politics or other civic affairs. Annie, on the other hand, increased her public activities. Now a Republican, she was active in the party, belonged to several service or literary clubs, served as president of her stake Relief Society, and twice served on the General Board of the Relief Society. She assisted her mother in writing for and editing the *Woman's Exponent* and somehow raised her eleven living children on a penurious income. Although John Q. edited the *Deseret News* while also working at his father's publishing business, neither job was particularly lucrative, and Emmeline felt that Annie could have been more productive outside her home had the family been more financially secure. She saw her daughter's talents and abilities as well as ambition unable to find release "thro' untoward circumstances that seemingly cannot be overcome unless the Lord intervenes & overrules."[7]

Another visit to Idaho awaited Emmeline in the summer of 1909. This time, she would travel to the two-story summer cottage Mell and Will

6. Lillian Hollister later became president of the International Council of Women.

7. E. Wells, Diary, July 28, 1910.

had built on the shore of the lake at Coeur d'Alene, Idaho. Taking one of Annie's daughters, twelve-year-old Katherine, with her, she headed north to spend several weeks on the lakeshore. From Spokane, she and Katherine traveled by "electric train" to Coeur d'Alene City, where Will met them with his launch. They crossed the lake to the bungalow, which enchanted Emmeline. There followed days of boat rides, swimming, walking in the woods surrounding the lake, partying, and picnicking on the shore, with excursions to friends' lakeside cottages and always music and reminiscing. Emmeline reveled in this new kind of communion with nature, so different from their home in Wallace or her own home in Utah. It was clear to her that Will and Mell were content in their Idaho life.

Emmeline returned home to her usual schedule, which included an increased workload of Relief Society activity. For nearly nine years of Bathsheba Smith's presidency, Emmeline had watched her position on the board slowly erode as younger newcomers energetically dismantled the rule of tradition that had governed the Relief Society for so long. While Bathsheba and Emmeline spoke often and at length over Relief Society affairs, Emmeline felt the surge of energy that was moving her offstage. The tension between the older and younger members emerged as they expressed their divergent ideas during board meetings. "There are so many who criticize and find fault and who want to control matters beyond all reason," she complained.[8] While she openly expressed her feelings about board meetings to her diary, the absence of her name in the minutes suggests her public silence on matters of personal concern to her or simply her decision not to record her comments. Though she was still acclaimed in national circles, and her insights, experience, and administrative skills were still utilized in local cultural and civic activities, those qualities were often dismissed by the louder claims and newer visions of the younger Relief Society Board members.

In March 1909, First Counselor Annie Taylor Hyde unexpectedly died. Bathsheba, herself ailing, with the acquiescence of the board relinquished control of the meetings to second counselor Ida Dusenberry.[9] Young, well educated, and eager to make a mark, Ida became influential in clarifying and establishing policies of the general board. She reinforced the decision that stake Relief Society presidents should not simultaneously serve on the board. She also gave instructions to improve coordination and efficiency: questions asked of the Relief Society aids ("missionaries") or board

8. Ibid., June 18, 1909.

9. After the death of Annie Taylor Hyde, Ida remained the only counselor until a new presidency was installed following Bathsheba Smith's death the following year.

members when they visited stake conferences were to be collected and the answers correlated to maintain uniformity; meetings should follow her newly outlined agenda; the General Board should "guide" the discussion of subjects at stake Relief Society conferences; and only the executive board, not board members, should authorize changes in dates for stake conferences once the stakes had set a date. Other systemic procedures followed, all of which tended toward more uniformity, continuity, and efficiency.[10] She also proposed that the secretary's salary be raised to thirty-five dollars a month.[11]

While Ida's attention to standardized procedure and centralized authority brought order to the board and more direction to their deliberations, her proposals, like many prior developments, added to Emmeline's secretarial duties. After nearly twenty years as secretary, Emmeline began to weary of the weight of that position. Repetitious questions, especially about the Bishop's Building and the Relief Society funds, exhausted her. "Getting sisters off to visit the Stakes" was particularly difficult, she wrote to Susa Gates, as there were "so few to choose from because they are away summering or sick or someone in the family is ailing etc." And then, she added, "there are always business letters to answer giving advice etc." She resented the fact that she was burdened with these additional assignments "because of petty things that other people might do even better only they will not see it."[12] Rather than the honor she originally felt when becoming a member of the Central Board of the Relief Society, she now felt that she had become the board's lackey, to do all the little jobs members did not want to do. This relegation of responsibilities to her, along with the disputations that so often characterized board meetings, disillusioned Emmeline. "These days are full of pain to me," she lamented. "There appears to be a spirit of jealousy rampant among the younger sisters that is very apparent to me in feeling tho' nothing is said," she wrote in late 1909.[13] While competition and ambition may have generated jealousy among board members, Emmeline could not deny her growing feeling of obsolescence, her experience and pathbreaking work no longer valued.

When the time arrived to select delegates to the 1909 meeting of the International Council in Toronto, the board selected Emily Richards and

10. Minutes of the General Board, February 9, March 6, April 3, April 8, April 16, 1909. Dates for stake women's conferences were not yet systematized and seem to have been casually arranged to suit both stake and assigned board visitors' schedules.

11. Ibid., March 9, 1909.

12. Emmeline B. Wells, letter to Susa Young Gates, July 19, 1910, Gates Papers.

13. E. Wells, Diary, November 22, 1909.

Ida Dusenberry. Both could afford to pay their own way.[14] Alice Merrill Horne and Elizabeth S. Wilcox, two other younger board members, were appointed to attend the triennial meeting of the National Council in Seattle.[15] Emmeline found herself once again preparing the credentials for delegates to conventions she would not attend. When Bathsheba later insisted that Emmeline accompany the two delegates to the Seattle meetings, she declined, hurt at being an afterthought. She preferred to go to Toronto, but "I was not encouraged," she complained, "and now when others have been named I am not going to be forced into it when others are ready." Besides, she petulantly added, "it requires clothes and much thought and I am not in the mood."[16]

Despite Emmeline's absence at the ICW meeting, Lillian Hollister of the National Council asked her to head a reception committee for a number of delegates from the Toronto convention who would be traveling through Utah on their way to California. The Relief Society and all other member clubs in Utah were to assist.[17] With a hundred international visitors expected in July, Emmeline spent the early summer preparing for the event.

When the visitors arrived on July 16, Emmeline and other members of the committee escorted the visitors to the tabernacle for an organ recital followed by a tour of Temple Square. Then they all boarded the train for Saltair, where they experienced the buoyant water of the lake before attending the luncheon prepared for the guests and their hosts.[18] Members of the committee were invited to bring their husbands and also their individual "head ministers." Joseph F. Smith, president of the LDS Church, was thus invited as Emmeline's ecclesiastical leader. Upon learning that he would be in attendance, Corinne Allen, a member of the committee and also an avid antipolygamist, refused to attend the Saltair festivities, drawing away the other non-LDS committee members with her.[19] "It was most unpleasant,"

14. Emmeline wrote several articles for the *Woman's Exponent* preceding and following the quinquennial in Toronto. See "International Council Quinquennial" 37 (May 1909): 59; "International Council Delegates" 38 (August 1909): 12–13, which describes their visit to Salt Lake City; and "Triennial Report of the National Woman's Relief Society" 38 (August 1909): 14–15. This report, written by Emmeline, was presented at the triennial meeting.

15. Minutes of the General Board, June 4, 1909.

16. E. Wells, Diary, June 26, 1909,

17. The Utah clubs that had membership in the council included the Maccabees, the Woman's Relief Corps, the Jewish Council, the Woman Suffrage (Utah) Council, the National Christian League, the LDS Relief Society, and the Young Ladies' Mutual Improvement Association.

18. "Prominent Women to Be in City Today," *Salt Lake Tribune*, July 16, 1909, 1.

19. President Smith had been a principal defense witness in the Reed Smoot

Emmeline wrote. "However it was unavoidable on my part as in no case would I leave out Joseph F. Smith." Ironically, President Smith made only a brief appearance before returning to the city. The program featured talks from the presidents of various national councils from Europe, several local women, and a special greeting from Rabbi Charles Freund of the B'nai Israel Congregation of Salt Lake City. Though not on the program, Charlotte Perkins Gilman was publicly recognized as one of the guests.[20]

The newspapers made great sport of Corinne Allen's dramatic last-minute boycott of the premier event at Saltair. The *Salt Lake Tribune* faulted Mormon women for filling the guests with Mormonism during their tour of Temple Square and, like Allen, focused its criticism on Joseph F. Smith's inclusion at the luncheon. It also printed the letter that Corinne Allen wrote to Emmeline Wells, citing her reasons for refusing to attend.[21] The *Deseret News* rose in defense of the committee and the decision to invite various ministers of committee members, noting that President Smith was only a guest, not an honoree, and wondered why Corinne Allen had waited until the last moment to lodge her complaint.[22]

Emmeline put the episode behind her and turned her attention to entertaining Charlotte Gilman, probably the most avid and influential feminist of the late nineteenth and early twentieth centuries. "Many of her ideas are not new to us as women nor even as a people," she concluded, but she admired her courage to commence a newspaper, the *Forerunner*. "She is to

---

hearings of several years earlier and had thus drawn the personal ire of many anti-polygamy women. Corinne Allen was particularly hostile to the church and the women who practiced plural marriage, though many had once been her coworkers, including Emmeline, in various civic projects and the Federation of Women's Clubs. While most of the country found polygamy a tiresome issue by this time, Corinne Allen was unable to let it go and continued for several years to agitate for a constitutional amendment barring the practice throughout the country.

20. Minutes of the General Board, July 16, 1909.

21. Besides outlining her dissatisfaction with the planned luncheon program, Corinne Allen used the published letter to announce her determination to cancel Mormon membership in the International Council of Women and noted that Lillian Hollister, president of the National Council, "will prove that Mormons cannot affiliate with us." She contended that May Wright Sewall "betrayed her trust and disgraced pure womanhood by dealing with the Mormons" and announced that "we are now in the majority, so they must get out." She also noted that Emmeline Wells and Susa Young Gates, both patrons of the ICW, "would never go to Europe again as delegates from the NCW." See "Salt Lake City Visited by Distinguished Women," *Salt Lake Tribune*, July 17, 1909, 1–2.

22. "Mrs. Allen Criticized," *Deseret Evening News*, July 17, 1909, 1. Emmeline's *Woman's Exponent* editorial on the event also rebutted the *Tribune*. See "International Council Delegates," *Woman's Exponent* 38 (August 1909): 12.

write it all by herself," Emmeline noted, "which is decidedly new for man or woman." Who would know better than Emmeline the difficulty of implementing such a lofty but precarious goal?[23] A long, private conversation at the end of Gilman's visit drew Emmeline into the more intimate circle of this woman whose advocacy of woman's advancement she had so long admired.

In the restless hours of the night, Emmeline fretted about the passing of time and her own waning energies, berating herself for failing to produce more literary pieces. "There are so many things I want to do," she wrote, "and now my allotted time seems so short that I can never do all." Again, when looking back on her life, she counted her blessings "such as I never expected," though she admitted they were not all "the ones I so much desired." She felt that she had one more book in her, possibly her book of stories, and had saved money for its publication, "but the money goes and time too."[24] Age and energy were formidable deterrents.

By December 1909, the Relief Society offices in the new Bishop's Building were ready for occupancy. It was another emotional time for Emmeline. On the one hand, she dreaded the first board meeting that would be held there "more than ever before." She had grown weary, she wrote, and "very moody almost melancholy, thinking how dreary it will be."[25] When she finally took possession of the secretary's room in the new headquarters, she became nostalgic about the block where it resided, remembering Belle's birth in the Whitney wagon on that block and the adobe house that had been her home and office for so many years. Added to her reminiscences were memories of the "big house" that had once occupied the site of the new Templeton Building and the office in that building that she was now vacating. "I loved the place where the Wells house stood," she reflected, "because of President Wells more particularly, than of the family."[26]

By the beginning of 1910, after just a few weeks in her new office in the Bishop's Building, Emmeline was surprised at how pleasant it was. "I am enjoying the new building and do feel quite at home here," she wrote, "as if it all belonged to me." She was not sure why the suite of rooms so appealed to her, but she hoped she would have "much pleasure and inspiration while sojourning in this beautiful place."[27] Undoubtedly more comfortable than

23. E. Wells, Diary, July 19, 1909. The first issue of Gilman's magazine appeared in November of that year. She remained the sole editor and writer of the publication until its demise in 1916. It expressed her feminist ideas in both essays and fiction and had as many as fifteen hundred subscribers, which were evidently enough to keep it going for seven years.

24. Ibid., August 21, 1909.

25. Ibid., December 1, 1909.

26. Ibid., December 2, 1909.

27. Ibid., January 5, 1910.

any of her former offices, the rooms assigned to the Relief Society on the second floor of the building offered a new, spacious, and well-furbished office for her secretarial responsibilities, receiving visitors, editing her paper, and hosting association meetings. A bed was even installed for Emmeline's use.

Although Bathsheba and Emmeline unexpectedly basked in the spacious rooms allotted to the Relief Society in the new building, many Relief Society members were disappointed and even resentful that in the end, eight thousand dollars of the money that had been raised for the woman's building had been utilized to construct the Bishop's Building. Martha Hammond of Moab gave Emmeline "a good idea of the way the sisters feel about the Building," reporting that "they are not at all satisfied." Emmeline was certainly sympathetic, responding that she "did not imagine that they would be." She explained that "we are powerless in the matter ourselves—here in the City just as much as those at a distance. We must abide by the counsel of the priesthood, those whom we ourselves pray for to be rulers in Zion—the Lord is over all and will maintain his own work in the way that is best for his people."[28] Nor were all board members as pleased with their headquarters as Bathsheba and Emmeline. One of them suggested that the loss of the woman's building was due to "the times when women's importance in the Church was diminishing." She was not a little sarcastic in describing the building as providing "an upstairs meeting room and a back door entrance for the women's organizations."

The Bishop's Building represented more than a physical consolidation of the auxiliary organizations of the church. It also represented the beginning of centralization of church administrative units under priesthood leadership that would express itself more fully with the organization of a correlation committee in 1913. While the church president's office had existed in a variety of buildings or homes, in 1917 the impressive Church Administration Building on South Temple was completed. It housed the First Presidency, the Quorum of the Twelve, the Seven Presidents of Seventy, and other general church priesthood leaders. Other church buildings, constructed during the early years of the twentieth century, filled the rest of the block, directly east of Temple Square, known as the Church Administration Block. The LDS University was a major occupant, consisting of a semicircle of buildings including Barratt Hall, the Brigham Young Building, the Joseph F. Smith Building, the LDS Business College, and the Deseret Gymnasium. The impressive Genealogical Building had a prominent place on the block, which also accommodated a Mission Home for missionary preparation.

28. Ibid., May 26, 1910. On January 25, 1910, Bathsheba Smith received approval from the board to give three thousand dollars in addition to the original five thousand dollars the Relief Society had given to the construction of the Bishop's Building.

Both the Lion and the Beehive Houses remained intact during this flurry of building.[29] In her new quarters, Emmeline was surrounded by evidence of the growth and centralization of church administration and the place of the auxiliaries, now housed in a church building, as part of the church's administrative family.[30] The Bishop's Building was a prominent feature of this consolidation.

In 1910, Emmeline enjoyed more than a new office. While she often paid honor to her own generation and those who went before for their sacrifices and contributions to building the kingdom, she was heralded in her own lifetime for being one of them.[31] Her eighty-second birthday in February 1910 indicated the esteem in which she was held. After an afternoon dinner at Belle's with some of her close friends, there followed a public reception in the Bishop's Building at which six hundred people enjoyed lemonade and cake. The reception room was handsomely decorated with flowers and potted plants. Against this background stood the diminutive and fragile Emmeline, dressed in pale-blue silk of Utah weave, greeting each of the guests. At a private reception afterward, such dignitaries as B. H. Roberts, Heber J. Grant, Rulon and Joseph Wells, President Anthon Lund, and Francis Lyman of the Council of Twelve, as well as the wives of each, joined both Whitney and Wells family members for the occasion. When the eighty-two candles on the birthday cake were all extinguished, the guests listened to brief tributes recognizing the accomplishments of the honoree.[32]

29. All of these buildings, except Brigham Young's two homes, the former Hotel Utah, and the Relief Society Building, built in 1956, succumbed in 1962 to the wrecking ball in order to make space for the new Church Office Building and its plaza and gardens. In 1984, the Relief Society Building became headquarters for the Primary and Young Women in addition to the Relief Society.

30. It also meant a change in the boundaries of the Relief Society's autonomy. In a conference address in April 1913, Joseph F. Smith made clear that the Relief Society was one of the "auxiliaries," which it had never considered itself, and that none of the auxiliaries existed "independently." All of them functioned only under priesthood leadership. See *Official Report of the General Conference of the Church of Jesus Christ of Latter-day Saints (1898–2013)*, April 4, 1913, 4, LDS Church History Library, Salt Lake City. This was also a time when restrictive conditions were placed on women in utilizing the gifts of healing and the washing and anointing of women prior to childbirth. Newell, "Gifts of the Spirit."

31. As one young friend observed, "Her devotion to the sisters who have stood at the head of women's work in our Church is beautiful to witness." The memory of these great ladies is "to her most sacred." Talmage, "Coronets of Age."

32. E. Wells, Diary, February 28, 1910 (one of three overlapping 1910 diaries). See also Minutes of the General Board, February 28, 1910; and "Public Reception," *Woman's Exponent* 38 (March 1910): 61–62.

Emmeline was surprised at the presence of B. H. Roberts. But their past political differences were no longer relevant. He had been selected to honor Emmeline and her accomplishments. She was touched by his words and wrote him a letter in her usual extravagant literary style, explaining that she resolved to personally thank him for the bouquet of white roses, her favorite flowers, and especially for his "eloquent tribute," coming from one "who knew me so distantly." She, and many others, she told him, declared his words "the gem of the evening's entertainment." Her hope was that someday she might converse with him "to exchange, or interchange thoughts with one of superior intelligence," which would be "a luxury in this barren world of cold communication."[33] Unfortunately, that meeting never occurred.

These events that drew important church leaders as guests caused Emmeline to reflect on her associations with church leaders in her early years. "I realize more and more what opportunities I had in my young life of that kind," Emmeline considered, "in the society of Bishop Newel K. Whitney & Brigham Young & Heber C. Kimball and others of the foremost men of the Church." Nor did she ignore the women "whose names stand for good works on the rolls of fame—chosen of God in these latter days to fill important positions and whose destiny is to be waymarks for others to follow."[34] Her marriage to Newel K. Whitney in Nauvoo so many years before had set her on the path to such associations, and for fifty years she had been in company with men and women on the highest levels of church leadership.

As the board members prepared for the April 1910 Relief Society conference in the Assembly Hall, they little suspected that this would be Bathsheba's last. She presided at the two-day conference, but gave little more than a welcome on the first day. She attended her last board meeting two months later, missing only the final meeting on July 1 before the board adjourned for summer recess. Throughout the summer, Bathsheba's health deteriorated, and Emmeline consistently visited her bedside to keep her abreast of Relief Society matters and at Bathsheba's request gave her a blessing. In a letter to Susa Gates, Emmeline noted that "Aunt Bathsheba has a very great tenacity for life. I want her to live," she added, "but I am not desirous to have her live, if she cannot walk.... She could not be submissive, and patient as some would be."[35] By the end of summer, it became clear that Bathsheba would not recover, and when Emmeline received word of her death on September 20, she was saddened but not unprepared. She took

33. Emmeline B. Wells, letter to B. H. Roberts, March 20, 1910, B. H. Roberts Papers.
34. E. Wells, Diary, July 2, 1910.
35. Emmeline B. Wells, letter to Susa Young Gates, July 19, 1910, Gates Papers.

seven white roses to place on the casket and viewed Bathsheba for the last time shortly before the funeral, held in the tabernacle on Sunday, September 25, in place of its usual Sunday services.

Bathsheba's was the first funeral of a woman held in the tabernacle, and Emmeline and Ida Dusenberry were the only women on the program. Having known Bathsheba for sixty-six years, Emmeline found it difficult, she said, to sift through her thoughts as to what to say about this great woman. But she was part of the generation of women whom Emmeline venerated, and she spoke of Bathsheba as one of the greatest. She mentioned that Bathsheba was a charter member of the Nauvoo Relief Society and remarked on her leadership of more than forty thousand current members. She also noted her longtime and "magnificent" work in the temple. Bathsheba, Emmeline said, "belongs to that great galaxy of noble women that I seem to see in vision before me...who laid everything on the altar of their faith" and "made no reserve."[36]

For days afterward, Emmeline was obliged to meet visitors wanting to talk about the former president and speculate about her successor. Ida Dusenberry, a very close friend of Emmeline's for many years, was certainly a logical choice. Emmeline thought of Ida as "very like my own" and claimed that Ida's daughter Margaret was "the dearest girl in Provo." She even wrote a poem to "my well-beloved Ida," in which she counseled her to

Remember thou art favor'd more,
Than many women of thy age,
And study well life's lesson o'er;
Yes, write thy name on history's page.[37]

Ida had given exceptional service in conducting board meetings and systematizing procedures. She was well educated and would bring youth and vision and vitality to the society in the new century as its president. Emmeline admired her abilities, her experiences, and her character. She would be an excellent choice. And she was not the only capable candidate. Several other board members and Relief Society stake presidents had already proved themselves to be women of talent and leadership. The choices were many.

36. Ibid., September 20, 21, 25, 1910. Her entire speech was printed as "Fitting Tributes Paid to Noble Woman's Life," *Deseret Evening News,* October 1, 1910, 31. In her tribute she listed the names of the "noble women" of the past, twelve in number. Her talk appears to have been extemporaneous, and so the names were likely recalled from memory.

37. Emmeline B. Wells, letter to Ida Dusenberry, October 28, 1908. The poem is from an autograph book dated February 29, 1902, in Ida Smoot Dusenberry Papers.

Four days after Bathsheba's funeral, Emmeline received a message from the First Presidency's office to call a board meeting on Saturday, October 1.[38] "Of course, it means a new Presidency and goodness knows who," Emmeline wondered.[39] The next day she admitted to being in a "state of anxiety wondering how it will be tomorrow and what would be done." Her tension was heightened by a flood of inquiries from others who were similarly curious. Nineteen board members attended the Saturday meeting. President Joseph F. Smith, who was unwell, sent his counselors Anthon Lund and John Henry Smith, to direct the meeting. President Lund instructed the women to write on slips of paper the names of their first and second choices for president of the Relief Society and then collected the papers and scheduled a second meeting for the following Monday.[40]

On Sunday, Emmeline, as usual, attended the fast meeting in the temple and at President Lund's request met with him directly after the meeting. She was stunned when he took her aside and "in a few simple words told me I had been selected by President Joseph F. Smith to preside over the Relief Society." She found the moment awkward, even "embarrassing," and for a few moments, she was unable to speak. After finding her voice, she requested them to select her counselors, while leaving the choice of secretary to her.[41]

After a sleepless night, she attended the scheduled Monday meeting, where President Lund announced the selection of Emmeline Wells as the new president, the first choice of the board and a unanimous choice of the First Presidency. He then announced that board members Clarissa Smith Williams and Julina Lambson Smith would be her first and second counselors, respectively, the two of them receiving the next-highest number of votes.[42] It would be several months before she selected a secretary.

38. Because Ida Dusenberry lived in Provo, Emmeline, as secretary, served as the primary contact for the Relief Society with church leaders.

39. E. Wells, Diary, September 29, 1910.

40. Minutes of the General Board, October 1, 1910; E. Wells, Diary, October 1, 1910.

41. E. Wells, Diary, October 2, 1910.

42. Ibid., October 3, 1910; Minutes of the General Board, October 3, 1910. Clarissa was the daughter of Bathsheba Smith's husband, George A. Smith, and his seventh wife, Susan Elizabeth West. Julina became the first wife of church president Joseph F. Smith after his first marriage dissolved in divorce. She was a niece of Bathsheba Smith since her mother, Melissa Jane Bigler Lambson, was a sister to Bathsheba. At this same meeting, President Lund released five board members who also served as stake Relief Society presidents, including Annie Wells Cannon. The minutes for this meeting were the last taken by Emmeline Wells. Annie Cannon served as interim secretary for several meetings following her release from the board.

Possibly the only blot on Emmeline's new calling was that her friend Ida Dusenberry had acted "strange," perhaps feeling that her contributions to the orderly functioning of the Relief Society board during the prior two years had been unrecognized and unappreciated by her fellow board members. She retained her position on the board, but her behavior confused Emmeline, who privately remonstrated seven months after her appointment, "It is not my fault that she is not in office."[43] Their friendship, however, remained undiminished.

The October Relief Society conference, two weeks after Bathsheba's death and only days after Emmeline's appointment, was the first over which she presided. In her short maiden address, she admonished secretaries to keep accurate records and recommended collecting books and manuscripts for Relief Society libraries in each of the wards. She also urged unity among the sisters of the society and a determination to promote the society's efforts "in the cause of humanity."[44]

When the names of the new Relief Society presidency were read to the congregation assembled for General Conference on October 6, Emmeline began to realize the extent of the responsibilities that lay before her as the new "elect lady," the honored title Joseph Smith gave to his wife when she became the Relief Society president in Nauvoo. "I hope and pray I may be worthy the calling and be wise and prudent in all matters pertaining to the position. I do realize it will require prayer and great humility and intelligence from the highest source—may our Father in heaven help me to carry out the counsel of those in authority and may those associated with the <u>three</u> presiding officers, be willing to assist in carrying out the counsel they may give from time to time," clearly a hope for unity in the presidency and among the members.[45] To have risen to the highest level of female leadership in the LDS Church crowned her faith in the ultimate personal value of the organization she had come to love. The Relief Society radiates "the spirit of love and magnanimous charity that unites us in a fellowship grander and holier than the highest educational organizations among the cultured and learned women of the world," she wrote to her friend Amy Brown Lyman in 1909.[46] This conviction imbued the society with a significance for Emmeline that underscored the honor of her new calling.

By the end of the day, the local newspapers were already trumpeting the news of Emmeline's appointment and that of her counselors. Declaring

43. E. Wells, Diary, May 5, 1911.

44. "The General Relief Society Conference," *Woman's Exponent* 39 (October 1910): 26. See also Minutes of the General Board, October 4, 1910.

45. E. Wells, Diary, October 6, 1910.

46. Emmeline B. Wells, letter to Amy Brown Lyman, October 6, 1909, Amy Brown Lyman Papers.

her to have been "unanimously elected" by the board, the *Deseret Evening News* claimed the choice to have been "peculiarly appropriate, rounding out, as it does, for the esteemed lady, a long life spent in Relief Society work and in the cause of woman generally."[47] The *Herald-Republican* included a two-column picture of Emmeline and stated that "the first presidency and board of the society made a choice that will not only be approved but applauded by members of the church throughout the world, for the activities of this most estimable woman and indefatigable worker have, like those of her beloved predecessor, Mrs. Bathsheba W. Smith, been such that is known and revered wherever Mormons congregate."[48] Calling her "a loving link... between the heroic beginnings and the glorious present of this latter-day dispensation," the *Deseret News* opined that "it is difficult to conceive of an appointment that would be more *appropriate* or that would be received with more general delight than that of Mrs. Emmeline B. Wells."[49] The *Salt Lake Tribune* managed to give a twelve-line spot at the bottom of page 16 to announce the new presidency.[50] Portraits of the three new members of the Relief Society presidency headed the first page of the October *Woman's Exponent*, under which Annie Wells Cannon wrote an article summarizing the qualities and experience of each one.[51]

Emmeline and her counselors were set apart by the First Presidency of the church in the Beehive House, home of President Joseph F. Smith. Emmeline's appointment was in effect an honorarium for a life of service on behalf of women. "Surely the Lord has greatly blessed me in the honors shown and showered upon me," she shared with her diary.[52] At age eighty-two, Emmeline could not be expected to exert the kind of energy and vision that she might have done years earlier.[53] Also, as the choice of the board,

47. "Emmeline B. Wells," *Deseret Evening News*, October 3, 1910, 1. The church periodical the *Improvement Era* 14 (November 1910): 69 gave the news a full page, dominated by a portrait of Emmeline.

48. "'Aunt' Emmeline Chosen President," *Salt Lake Herald-Republican*, October 4, 1910, 12. The picture used in both this paper and the *Deseret News* article is the three-quarter-length profile painted by Lee Greene Richards some years before Emmeline became president. It is now her official portrait as one of the general presidents of the Relief Society.

49. "President of Relief Society," *Deseret News*, October 8, 1910, 4.

50. "Mrs. Wells Honored," *Salt Lake Tribune*, October 4, 1910, 16.

51. Annie Wells Cannon, "The New President and Counselors of the Relief Society," *Woman's Exponent* 39 (October 1910): 25.

52. E. Wells, Diary, February 23, 1911.

53. In 1868, when Brigham Young called Eliza R. Snow to assist in reorganizing the Relief Society in the wards throughout the church, she was sixty-three. When she became general president, she was seventy-five. Zina Young was sixty-seven when called to the presidency, and Bathsheba Smith was seventy-eight.

Emmeline could well have supposed that she had been given a mandate to continue in the tradition of the past. But unlike her predecessors, what she brought to the office were a wealth of experience and an understanding of the internal dynamics of women's organizational work that none of her precursors enjoyed. She had been preparing for this honor all of her life and was not overburdened with self-doubt. Six months before her appointment, she felt comfortable in declaring to her diary, after a worrisome but ultimately satisfying meeting with members of the Ladies of the Maccabees, "I really feel myself most unlike the generality of people[.] I do not belong in the ordinary category. I am quite sure of that."[54] She was gifted in qualities and experiences that she believed set her apart from many other women of her time and place and had always looked for ways to use them. In the next eleven years, though subject to the infirmities of age, she was nonetheless determined to maintain that self-confidence and fulfill the trust placed in her as the fifth elect lady. She committed herself to fulfilling the expectations that Joseph Smith outlined for the officers of the Nauvoo Relief Society. They would serve only as long as they did so, he said, "during good behavior or so long as they shall continue to fill the office with dignity &c. like the first Presidency of the church."[55] This she intended to do.

In May 1911, reflecting on the outcome of her first board meeting as president, Emmeline was thankful to be able to reveal to her diary, "I had great anxiety over the matter but after all it passed off fairly well.... I maintained fairly good order—and things passed off without any friction," certainly an encouraging sign for the future of her administration.[56]

54. Ibid., April 20, 1910.
55. Minutes of the Nauvoo Relief Society, March 17, 1842.
56. Minutes of the General Board, May 25, 1911; E. Wells, Diary, May 25, 1911.

CHAPTER 35

End of an Era

(1911–1914)

As Emmeline Wells entered what would be the last decade of her long life, she had been a westerner for sixty-two years. Remarkable changes had taken place in the city during that time. With its "skyscrapers," widespread electricity, telephones, and even automobiles, it was following the lead of other western cities. All had become accessible by 1910.[1]

The electricity-fueled streetcar was a necessity for Emmeline's commuting schedule. Never an owner of a carriage and certainly not an automobile, she had long depended on walking or using various forms of public transportation. Those who sported an automobile, fortunately for her, were eager to share its pleasures and convenience, and she was frequently the passenger in traveling to a meeting or social or just cruising the city. The material changes in which she was most emotionally vested, however, were in the three homes that had sheltered her during those sixty-two years. They were more than domiciles. To Emmeline, they were shrines to life-giving and life-altering events.

The Mormon-Gentile geographic divisions, evident in Salt Lake's cityscape, reflected a tenacious social division, though mitigated since statehood. In her own life, Emmeline had tried to breach the chasm that divided Salt Lake City society and valued the friendships she had developed among Gentile residents. With few exceptions, now largely in the past, they were respectful and supportive of her with a gradual melting of the *Salt Lake Tribune*'s former icy barbs.

The twenty-one years Emmeline gave to the Relief Society as secretary resulted in three leather-bound volumes of handwritten minutes, carefully copied from notes scribbled in her diaries, notebooks, and temporary

1. "Utah Population in Urban Areas, 1860–1970," in *Utah's History*, edited by Poll et al., 687.

minute books. She wrote often late into the night and in 1896 asserted that "those who never do these things know very little about it—the anxiety and thought and actual work of recording."[2] She often noted how little respect "brain work" garnered. But her position as secretary also resulted in a more public way—name recognition that came from her constant contact, written and personal, with Relief Society workers throughout the church. The *Deseret News* noted this unexpected renown when she was appointed president. "As general secretary of the Relief Society," the article read, Emmeline Wells was "the best known and best loved of all its corps of willing workers."[3]

Now she had inherited the position once held by three of the most admired women in the church, two of them her close friends and associates. As with Zina Young's death, Emmeline mourned the loss of her friend and coworker when Bathsheba Smith died. "My love for her," she wrote shortly before her passing, "has been past all one could imagine almost."[4] And now she had taken on the responsibility to lead the Relief Society and affect the lives of all the women in the church. As a known bridge builder, she would find many opportunities to utilize that skill in her new calling, but this time it was between age and youth. Her officers were all much younger: First Counselor Clarissa Young was fifty-one, Second Counselor Julina Smith was sixty-one, Secretary Olive Derbidge Christensen was forty, Assistant Secretary Amy Brown Lyman was thirty-eight, and the treasurer, Emma Empey, was fifty. Her board also included two and later four single women, a novelty then, with the youngest only twenty-eight. Most of the board members served for ten of Emmeline's eleven-year tenure, the average number of board members being twenty-three. With Julina Smith, wife of the president of the church, as a counselor and Rebecca Nibley, wife of the presiding bishop, as a member, there existed an informal connection with "the brethren" that would be very useful.[5]

The new board reflected Emmeline's allegiance to tradition and her respect for progress. She would preside over a Relief Society that was growing beyond a provincial woman's association to a worldwide, broad-based

2. E. Wells, Diary, February 15, 1896.

3. Journal History, October 3, 1910.

4. E. Wells, Diary, July 22, 1910.

5. Holdovers from Bathsheba's administration were Sarah Jenne Cannon, Romania Pratt Penrose, Emily S. Richards, Julia P. M. Farnsworth, Phebe Young Beattie, Ida S. Dusenberry, Carrie S. Thomas, Alice Merrill Horne, Priscilla P. Jennings, Elizabeth S. Wilcox, and Rebecca N. Nibley. New members were Elizabeth C. McCune, Susa Young Gates, Edna May Davis, Sarah McLelland, and Elizabeth C. Crismon.

woman's organization marked by a corps of talented and efficient workers whose view was to the future. Emmeline would help them recognize that the Relief Society, grounded in a past of vision and spiritual power, could be the source of personal and social possibilities through a consortium of ward and stake organizations. Incorporation had helped professionalize the society, and the new century brought women into leadership more in tune with their own time than with the past. Emmeline was an unmistakable symbol of the Relief Society's origins, which she hoped would continue to define the distinctiveness of the organization.

Her board was composed of strong women with distinct points of view that Emmeline hoped would result in constructive creativity rather than dissension. The primary divisive issues were the implementation of centralization and standardization, promoted by the church's Social Advisory and Correlation Committees. The agenda of the Correlation Committee included adoption of uniform lessons, uniform meeting schedules, uniform business and accounting records and other procedures, all originating on the general level. The controversy that did indeed develop was the offspring not only of new church directives but also of generational experience.

If the Relief Society under Bathsheba Smith's presidency had started to shape itself to the new patterns of organizational structure influenced by the rise of progressivism then being established within the church, the pace accelerated during Emmeline's tenure. She was an active, decisive leader for much of that time, and the board broadened its purview to keep step with the growing diversity of social problems. By the end of her first year, she raised membership dues from ten cents to twenty-five cents to cover its multiplying expenses. The Relief Society revitalized the nurses' training program, which was constantly modified to be consistent with new training methods and treatment. The board made plans for a Relief Society home for single women and lent assistance to "rescue work" by supporting the kindergarten movement, the Neighborhood House for youths, the juvenile court, and protective legislation for women and children. Emmeline also supported expansion of the Relief Society's employment bureau and the one remaining woman's commission store, along with the decision to provide temporary shelter for immigrants. Under her administration, the Relief Society was assigned responsibility to head a burial and temple clothing department, which brought in needed revenue. She also instigated a program of statistical compilations of hours of charity work that she called "organized charity." "So much has been told to the public of the dinners and assistance during the holiday season given through other organizations," she explained, that she felt the Relief Society should tally its own charitable contributions.[6] She was pleased that President Smith endorsed a burial and school insurance program for women and children. She was not adverse to the proposal to raise her monthly salary to seventy-five dollars for her service as president, although this action, the minutes cautiously noted, was not intended to set a precedent.

Despite the disappointment in losing the woman's building, Relief Society members valued the support of Joseph F. Smith, who affirmed his opinion that "the Relief Society organization is one of the most important organizations in the Church.... Its objects and purposes are among the greatest that affect the well-being, happiness and prosperity of the human family." To Emmeline's satisfaction, he added, "We cannot do without each other; mother and father, brother and sister, are equally essential to building up Zion."[7]

Emmeline enjoyed a congenial relationship with President Smith and his wife, Julina, her second counselor, joining them for automobile rides and social and cultural events. Though sharing neighboring offices and institutional objectives with Presiding Bishop Charles W. Nibley, Emmeline still turned to the First Presidency as her priesthood contact, which all her predecessors had done.[8] In 1919, after the death of Joseph F. Smith, the Relief Society presidency visited the new First Presidency, headed by Heber J. Grant, and affirmed that "the Relief Society had always received special attention from the First Presidency." The women added their hope that "this would be the case under the new administration."[9] In time, however, the personal ecclesiastical relationship Emmeline enjoyed with members of the First Presidency would yield to a working relationship with the presiding bishopric in much the way that ward Relief Societies functioned with their bishoprics. Their common responsibility for the material welfare of the members made the alliance a natural one, but it also reinforced the position of the Relief Society as an auxiliary, which it had long resisted. Traditionally perceiving a parallel partnership with the priesthood quorums, some board members felt that as an auxiliary, the Relief Society lost much of its prestige. Emmeline would try to restore it.

6. "Organized Charity," *Woman's Exponent* 40 (February [Midwinter Number] 1912): 45–46.

7. Report of Relief Society General Conference, April 3, 4, 1912, Minutes of the General Board, April 1912.

8. While her diary is replete with references to Joseph F. Smith, Bishop Nibley's name is seldom mentioned. However, a month before her appointment, she had a long, friendly conversation with Bishop Nibley and noted that it seemed strange to her that "he has taken such an interest in me, not having known me much in former times." E. Wells, Diary, September 8, 1910.

9. Minutes of the General Board, January 9, 1919.

Besides the growing ascendancy of the presiding bishopric as the Relief Society's priesthood partner, the church's Correlation Committee, under the direction of Apostle David O. McKay, and later the Social Advisory Committee, under the direction of Apostle Stephen L. Richards, also intervened in the Relief Society's direct relationship to the First Presidency.[10] The directives of these new agencies underscored the efficiency of a more systematized structure with central leadership and standardized procedures, a move pleasing to the progressive-minded women on the Relief Society board. While Emmeline liked order and efficiency, her primary concern was what she felt was a usurpation of local and general Relief Society autonomy. "She did not feel to exercise too much authority over the stakes in this regard," the minutes stated, "as they knew their own conditions best." For Emmeline, the stakes were the vital nerve centers of the church, and she respected both their individuality and their authority. While subscribing to the idea of uniform meetings and records, she held inviolate the right of stakes to implement and innovate according to their specific needs and resources. She was receptive to new educational theories, administrative efficiency, and the development of organized social services, but she believed that the stakes could implement these progressive ideas as they saw fit in their own situations. As part of her ongoing resistance, she reminded the board that "the dominant feature of the Relief Society is charity," but even that would be subject to a "scientific" reordering of its implementation and not without controversy.[11] Not surprisingly, the Relief Society was the last auxiliary to adapt its program to these new procedures, including prescribed lesson topics, a dictum issued by the Correlation Committee. Emmeline saw the wisdom in some of these changes, such as uniform record or minute books, but wrestled with the dilemma that Correlation had imposed on her organizational philosophy. The General Board, she maintained, was to assist, not direct, the ward and stake Relief Societies. She very reluctantly accepted measures that gave the Correlation Committee authority to issue uniform programs and practices to wards and stakes. On one small point she was able to stand her ground. When the recommendation was made to change all board meetings from Thursday to some other day of the week, she refused. The board had always met on Thursdays, the day the general authorities met in the temple, she pointed out. Moreover, Thursday had once been the monthly "fast day" for the church, and it had

10. Correlation efforts began in 1907, but the committee was not formed until 1908 under the direction of Apostle David O. McKay. J. Allen and Leonard, *Story of the Latter-day Saints*, 458–65, 475–80, 498–501. Most of the uniform measures prescribed by the committee took effect in 1913 and thereafter in the Relief Society.

11. Minutes of the General Board, January 16, 1913.

become "almost sacred," Emmeline argued. For a while, at least, board meetings remained on Thursday.[12] Withal, she generally demonstrated forbearance and restraint, acknowledging her minority status regarding correlation and centralization.

With the Correlation Committee's authority to shape curriculum and procedure, the Relief Society was obliged to adopt uniform lesson plans for the weekly meetings. In 1913, the committee on lesson outlines announced completion of a course of study of six topics, one of which, genealogy, was required. Relief Societies could select from the others: home ethics, home gardening, health education, and art, literature, and architecture. The secular nature of the lessons reflected the influence of popular women's clubs to which many members belonged. Variations of these topics would occur over the years, but all were designed to make the Relief Society more relevant to a younger generation of Mormon women and make Relief Society a viable alternative to culture clubs. Emmeline was uncomfortable with introducing such a heavy secular component to the local weekly meetings and warned that "in these outlines we are getting too far away from the spiritual side of our great work, and from the thought that inspired the first organization of the Relief Society." She reminded the sisters that the Relief Society "stands first for spirituality and then for charity and mercy."[13] But this lesson format endured for nearly a half century because of its popularity with the members.

While Emmeline felt that this new Relief Society calling was the capstone to her work for women, her tenure was a long lesson in reconciling the differing expectations of the older and younger members of her board and her own organizational ideals with the insistent demands for conformity and central planning. She eventually found it not only expedient but also beneficial to yield some of her own predilections to the will of her board. Moreover, during these early years of her administration, she was learning a new corporate style. As centralization of policies and procedures steadily increased, subcommittees proliferated and community involvement deepened. Many of these outreach programs coincided with Emmeline's agenda on behalf of women. She organized a legislative committee to follow and support legislation relating to women and children, such as guardianship

12. Noted in ibid., October 12, 1917.

13. Ibid., December 10, 1913. A year earlier, in an *Exponent* editorial, Emmeline suggested that "the subjects discussed in clubs, social and literary, might be introduced in their proper place in the Relief Society...if care is taken to keep a balance of spiritual growth in the ascendancy." "Suggestive Thoughts," *Woman's Exponent* 41 (December 1912): 28.

rights, juvenile courts, and minimum wages.[14] Community welfare programs such as the Relief Society's home for women and its employment bureau expanded the reach of the board's charitable service. Increased dues gave Emmeline latitude to provide social services beyond the personal charity that had long been women's province, and she welcomed associating with other local charitable organizations, never fearing that the Relief Society would lose its unique character among the many other benevolent institutions.

Another principal question that arose related to the membership of Relief Society women in literary and social clubs and the affiliation of the Relief Society with the National and International Councils of Women. Members had frequently asked about the propriety of joining clubs, and Emily Richards brought the question to the board after hearing a discussion about it during her visit to the Tooele Relief Society in 1913. The board had been reluctant to take a position on the question, since so many of its members were affiliated with various literary and social clubs.[15] No policy was agreed upon, but at the Relief Society's seventy-second birthday anniversary the following year, President Smith answered the question for them. "I want it distinctly emphasized," he told the assembled women, "that the Relief Societies of the Church of Jesus Christ of Latter-day Saints cannot afford to yield their prerogative to stand at the head of any other self-made, self-constituted female or male organization in the world." He felt the women of the church might lose their own personal and collective identities by "mixing up with these woman-made organizations."[16] This was a startling announcement. As the organizer of two literary groups created as a means of developing the intellect and talents of women, Emmeline long supported association with culture clubs, seeing a complementary relationship of their purposes on behalf of women with the Relief Society. When the Utah Federation of Women's Clubs held its first convention in 1894, Emmeline had written that such groups are for the "development of home talent—its higher cultivation" and serve to "bring out the most and best of one's possibilities for mutual helpfulness and interchange of ideas," a sentiment hardly incompatible with the goals of the Relief Society but effected through different channels.[17] But President Smith was emphatic in

14. In February 1921, church leaders instructed the Relief Society to rescind this practice and correct the impression that it had "attempted to interfere in matters of state." Minutes of the General Board, February 5, 10, 1921.

15. Ibid., June 22, 1911.

16. Ibid., March 17, 1914.

17. "A Few Thoughts," *Woman's Exponent* (May 15, 1894): 132.

his advice to the sisters. "You are the head and not the tail," he declared to the sisters. "Maintain your own [organization], stand by your own, defend your own. Make it first, make it foremost, make it the highest, the best and the deepest of any organization in existence in the world."[18] No sister remembering the empowering words of Eliza R. Snow as she encouraged membership in the Relief Society could argue with such counsel. However, while some women thereafter resisted the appeal of social organizations, they continued to thrive, and many LDS women found a place for both in their lives.[19]

Continuing affiliation with the National Council, however, was of immediate concern, since it involved using Relief Society funds for representation at several meetings already on the horizon. Support for the National Council had declined nationwide, which prompted May Wright Sewall once again to visit Salt Lake City in April 1913 to reinvigorate interest. She met with Emmeline, Susa Gates, and President Smith, explaining to President Smith that the participation of Emmeline and other Mormon women had "done much to create the good feelings now existing toward our women." Sewall also hoped to have a bust of Emmeline included in a proposed Hall of Statues of "great women of the United States." "President Wells," Sewall explained, "was the connection between the women of the Council and the women of the Church."[20] Such an appeal could hardly be ignored, and President Smith evidently gave his support to Mormon representation at these conventions.

These alliances, Emmeline already had seen, brought benefits to all. For Mormon women, "the influence gained in the world by association with women of note and ability who devote their lives to causes of humanity" was invaluable. But she also felt that "Latter-day Saint women yield an influence that is beneficial to others." Senator Reed Smoot, a speaker at the October 1913 Relief Society conference, six months after Sewall's visit, affirmed that national affiliations had engendered "undying friendship… between our women and the prominent women of the world" and reminded the sisters that "nearly all noted women knew Mrs. Wells, and always asked after her." His hope was that "the association with the eastern women in their mammoth conventions would not be given up, but continued with unabated vigor, for the educational value was incomparable."[21]

18. Minutes of the General Board, March 17, 1914.

19. Jill Mulvay Derr, "'Strength in Our Union': The Making of Mormon Sisterhood," esp. 181–86.

20. Report of Susa Y. Gates in Minutes of the General Board, April 17, 1913.

21. Minutes of the General Board, October 3, 1913. This was a generous sentiment

With the triennial meeting of the National Council scheduled for that same month in Port Huron, Michigan, the executive meeting of the NCW, which was planned for November in New York, and the quinquennial meeting of the ICW scheduled for the following year in Rome, Sewall was particularly eager to have a full representation of the National Council's member organizations at all of these meetings.[22] With no dissenting word from President Smith, representatives were chosen to attend the NCW as well as the ICW meetings in Rome in 1914. To the many requests for her presence at the 1914 New York executive meeting of the National Council, the eighty-six-year-old Emmeline finally acquiesced.[23]

Emmeline was "welcomed with open arms" at the National Council meeting. The Utah delegates were given front-row seats at the meetings, and Emmeline was chosen to introduce the presidents of the newly affiliated associations. Clarissa Williams, nominated by Emmeline, was selected one of the national delegates to the Rome meeting.[24] They were definitely being courted by the NCW officers, who were successful in keeping the Mormon organizations aboard.

Concerned about President Smith's publicly expressed feelings about "woman-made organizations," the General Board asked President Smith specifically whether the Relief Society should continue its membership in the two councils. Having enjoyed the support of church leaders in maintaining membership since 1891, the board hoped an official statement of continuing support would allay the discontent of any members still opposed.[25] The response, however, was ambiguous. Not wishing to interfere with the "corporate life" of the Relief Society, the First Presidency recommended that the society should "remain as it is for the present, at least." But, as Emmeline had surmised, the First Presidency also felt that the affiliation was merely "a passing incident in the life of the Society, an incident which may be terminated at any time without affecting in any way

---

on the part of Senator Smoot, whose seating in the US Senate had been broadly challenged by these same women's groups.

22. Ibid., September 4, 1913. While some of the board members felt that the cost was the main deterrent to attendance at national meetings, Emmeline believed that much of the lack of support was due to the diminished belief of church leaders in the necessity for such affiliation.

23. Ibid., April 10, 1913.

24. Ibid., December 4, 1913; "The National Council," *Woman's Exponent* 41 (December 1913): 84. Emmeline appointed Susa Gates to accompany Clarissa Williams to Rome and allocated one thousand dollars for their trip, remembering her own difficulty in finding funding for prior overseas trips.

25. Minutes of the General Board, January 14, 1914.

the Society itself." This was not happy news to Emmeline, who had given so much effort in maintaining national ties for what she believed was in the best interest of her LDS sisters. Asserting the preeminence of the Relief Society "to everything else connected with it, or which may hereafter be connected with it," the First Presidency made clear the distinctive character of the Relief Society. Emmeline could not disagree with that assertion and endorsed their concluding words that Relief Society meetings should be "conducted in the spirit of a religious organization, as though no affiliation at all with the National organization had been entered into."[26] She knew, however, that voicing such thoughts diminished much of the rationale for incorporating the society to align it in legal and national status with other national women's organizations. Though their words created a degree of tension between the First Presidency and the Relief Society, their tentativeness allowed the General Board to support continuing membership during Emmeline's administration.

With a decade of conjoint effort in obtaining and maintaining representation in prestigious national women's groups, Susa Gates and Emmeline had developed a cooperative but ambiguous relationship. They admired each other's strengths and created a large and revealing correspondence while Susa was either in New York or in Provo. Susa often wrote complimentary descriptions of Emmeline in various publications, but they were often undermined by Susa's privately expressed comments. In turn, Emmeline admired Susa's literary abilities and organizational capabilities, but remained wary of her calculated ambition and trustworthiness. They worked together, however, to alter negative ideas about Mormon women, and together and individually they created many personal relationships with the prominent women leaders of their time. Emmeline needed Susa's abilities and contacts and, despite some misgivings, appointed Susa to the board in June 1911. Inexplicably, just six months later, Susa wrote an extremely injurious letter about Emmeline to President Joseph F. Smith, a close personal friend of Susa's.[27] Susa evidently felt secure in confiding her views to him of Emmeline's initial leadership of the Relief Society. "There is no order, no real liberty [of] speech allowed, and there is but one woman on the board who does things, and she only does what she wants to, and when she wants to," Susa complained to President Smith. "That woman is Emmeline B. Wells." Then follows a litany of complaints, such as Emmeline's

26. Ibid., February 13, 1914.

27. They appeared to be very fond of each other. In one of many such letters, Joseph F. Smith writes that he "cherishes the kind and sisterly expressions" she writes to him and prizes "your friendship and pure sisterly love more than I can tell." Smith, letter to Susa Young Gates, June 30, 1906, Gates Papers, courtesy of Lisa Tait.

retention of making stake conference assignments, the slipshod way Susa felt they were managed, and the requirement that board members manage their own travel arrangements and "attend to our own works of preparation."[28] Susa had other complaints, including the silence or disregard that stung her whenever she voiced an opinion contrary to the president's.[29] She particularly complained of the position taken by Emmeline and "some of her old members" against initiating outlines of study for the individual societies.[30] Of most concern to Susa, however, was her feeling that Emmeline made the *Exponent* of "more and graver importance than the interests of all the fifty thousand women in the Relief Society," even though women throughout the church, she explained, wanted the Relief Society to have a magazine of its own. However, when rumors reached Susa that she and Julina Smith, Clarissa Williams, or Alice Merrill Horne were trying to get "Em's paper" for either Susa herself or Alice to run, she informed President Smith that she considered such speculation to be "a disgrace to women" and expressed her feelings to the board. "Whereat," she reported in her letter, "pandemonium reigned." The minutes make no mention of the unprecedented uproar, so the board's response was not officially recorded, but Susa's mention of an official magazine had ominous undertones. Finally, at the end of her declaration of grievances, Susa asked advice on the two options she felt available to her. Either she could "keep perfectly quiet, allowing Aunt Em to have her own way unchecked and unhampered," or she could "resign and let her go her own way without having me there as a reminder."[31] That no responsive

28. Emmeline had earlier expressed the difficulties to Susa of this particular responsibility. Wells, letter to Gates, July 19, 1910, Gates Papers.

29. That Emmeline was definitely strong-willed and often felt that her way was the only way was tactfully noted in some of the otherwise eulogistic write-ups Susa did about Emmeline. At the board meeting two months earlier, Susa had "made quite a sensation introducing Resolutions that were very unwise," Emmeline confided to her diary. "It was very hurtful to me and indeed made confusion and division." E. Wells, Diary, October 7, 1912. The minutes state simply that "resolutions to live better lives [were] made and agreed to by Susa Y. Gates," hardly a resolution that would make "quite a sensation," unless it was a compromise resolution that did not please her. The secretary, Olive D. Christensen, was evidently exercising her own judgment in what to record.

30. Minutes of the General Board, October 19, 1911. Sixty-three-year-old board member Carrie Thomas verbally expressed her agreement with Emmeline, finding that the stakes that developed their own courses of study expressed much more satisfaction in their work than those that did not.

31. Susa Young Gates, letter to Joseph F. Smith, December 22, 1911, Gates Papers. I have not yet found evidence that it was ever sent or if President Smith responded if, indeed, he received it. Because President Smith appointed Emmeline president of the Relief Society, he probably felt some obligation to support her in that calling.

letter appears in Susa's papers among the many other letters from President Smith suggests that she likely did not send the letter or that President Smith did not respond to it or that Susa did not preserve his response. Whatever the ultimate disposition of the letter, her thoughts are perplexing and inordinately harsh. They also suggest Susa's thwarted expectation of being a dominant voice as a member of the board. Whatever the disposition of the letter, Susa remained a member of the board throughout Emmeline's tenure, and the board, with Emmeline's concurrence, elected her as corresponding secretary in 1913.[32] It is safe to say that Emmeline never learned of Susa's sentiments, and Susa either overcame or masked them and their inexplicable relationship endured.

Besides the significant challenges in the first years of her administration, Emmeline also confronted a debate over guardianship of the original Nauvoo Relief Society minutes. The record had been in Bathsheba W. Smith's possession, after resting in a variety of places following the death of its original caretaker, Eliza R. Snow. Bathsheba's daughter Bathsheba Smith Merrill and Merrill's daughter Alice Merrill Horne had both desired to give it to Emmeline Wells after she became president, but Apostle John Henry Smith, son of George A. Smith and his plural wife Sarah Libby Smith, felt it should be placed in the historian's office. President Joseph F. Smith agreed, and the book was thus put in the care of church historian Anthon H. Lund. Later, John Henry Smith felt that Emmeline Wells was right in claiming it for the Relief Society.[33] However, the Relief Society did not regain possession of it, so Emmeline utilized her own handwritten copy of the Nauvoo minutes for 1842 to 1844, as she continued to reprint the minutes of various meetings in the *Exponent*.[34]

Emmeline's eighty-fourth birthday in 1912 occurred on the actual date of her birth, February 29. Several dinners and programs celebrated the milestone, bringing a host of people to honor her on that important day. The last of the events, held in the auditorium of the Bishop's Building, brought an array of special guests, including church and state officials as well as members of the Wells and Whitney families. Former governor Heber M. Wells was the master of ceremonies, and speakers included President Lund

32. Emmeline, however, asked that she "initiate and approve all correspondence" written by Gates. Minutes of the General Board, September 25, 1913.

33. Ibid., July 6, 1911.

34. Her copy is filled with underlines and sidebars. An account of the provenance and significance of the Nauvoo Minute Book is Jill Mulvay Derr and Carol Cornwall Madsen, "Preserving the Record and Memory of the Female Relief Society of Nauvoo, 1842–1892."

and President Penrose of the First Presidency and J. Golden Kimball of the Quorum of the Seventy, along with Horace G. Whitney and Apostle Orson F. Whitney. Horace Whitney noted that Aunt Em was the link between the Whitney and Wells families and then read a short ditty he had written about Emmeline's relationship to the Whitneys:

Proud Wellses, tho' you claim Aunt Em,
Your title is the worst,
Your mortgage is a second one,
The Whitneys hold the first.
So while we're willing you should share
Our claim—and won't oppose it;
Please keep that mortgage well in mind,
Lest some day we foreclose it.

Not to be outdone, Rulon S. Wells spontaneously provided a rebuttal:

The Whitneys claim a prior right
And threaten to foreclose,
The adjudication of this case
We'll leave to Him who knows;
But this I know and do maintain,
That you are ours pro tem,
And in the great eternity
You'll always be "Aunt Em."[35]

The major feature of the evening, however, was the bestowal of an honorary doctor of literature degree upon Emmeline by President Joseph F. Smith in behalf of Brigham Young University. As the first woman in the state to be so honored, and the first honorary degree recipient from that institution, after Karl G. Maeser, Emmeline could not have been more deservedly honored, the speakers agreed.[36] Her response was typical: "She expressed her deep feeling at the honor accorded her," the report read, "and said that it meant much to her not only as a personal tribute, but as a matter of honor to her sex. It had always been a matter of regret to her that great educational institutions had withheld this distinction from women, and she hoped that this would have its influence in showing that Utah withheld

35. "Emmeline B. Wells, Lit.D.," *Woman's Exponent* 40 (March 1912): 49–51, 54–55.

36. A petition sent to the church's Board of Education from "a number of leading ladies of the city" to present Emmeline Wells with an honorary degree was referred to the Board of Trustees of Brigham Young University, who acted favorably on the suggestion. Church Board of Education Minute Book, February 1912.

nothing from the women of the state."[37] It was a memorable moment for the aged Emmeline and surely helped to fulfill her long-held desire that her literary efforts were worthy of such recognition.[38]

The next year, Emmeline received an additional honor when she was invited to unveil the newly sculpted monument to the seagulls by Utah sculptor Mahonri M. Young. A crowd of five thousand gathered on Temple Square on a sunny, crisp day in October 1913 to witness an event that brought vivid memories to some and recollections of the oft-told story to others. A band played, the Tabernacle Choir sang, and then Presiding Bishop Charles W. Nibley introduced Emmeline "as one of the pioneers of 1848 who had witnessed the ravishes of the crickets and deliverance of the crops from destruction by the gulls." In response, Emmeline described that perilous time and then made a novel analogy: "It is a poetic coincidence that our idea of national freedom from oppression, and our idea of state deliverance from starvation, should be represented by birds," she noted. "The eagle, majestic monarch of the air, is represented on shield, and coin, and tablet of bronze, all over the broad land. The gentle gull, humble habitant of the shores of our Great Salt Sea, has found shrine heretofore only in the grateful memories of this valley's pioneers and descendants. My heart swells with thanksgiving that we are now to preserve in sculptured art the miraculous incident we all know so well." She then pulled the cords that released the two American flags veiling the monument, and cheers rose up from

37. Writing to Joseph F. Smith about the occasion, Susa Gates remarked that she had been told that Emmeline would have preferred a degree from the University of Utah and that even "dear old Bro. Maeser" cared little for the "so-called honorary degree" awarded him from BYU, a less prestigious honor when awarded by a church school rather that a state institution. It is hard to discern whether it is "sour grapes" on Susa's part or a true rendering of Emmeline's feelings, though there is nothing in Emmeline's writings to suggest as much. Susa went on to say that she had once made a sarcastic remark "about the old ladies clinging on to their honors when they were unable to do the work" and had been reminded that she would likely do the same. She then explained that she did not go to the birthday celebration, "for I know she [Emmeline] would enjoy it better without me there. She has an uneasy feeling about me and my actions and I do really love her for the much good she has done in this world, and for her priceless integrity." Gates, letter to Smith, February 29, 1912, Gates Papers.

38. Heber M. Wells, "Aunt Em's Birthday Party," *Young Woman's Journal* 23 (April 1912): 208–12; "Many Tributes to Mrs. E. B. Wells," *Deseret News*, March 1, 1912, 1; "Emmeline B. Wells, Lit.D.," *Deseret News*, March 2, 1912, 5. The second article carried an arresting picture of Emmeline in cap and gown with her "diploma" in hand. BYU's school paper also noted the occasion in "Emmeline B. Wells Honored," *White and Blue* 15 (March 5, 1912): 1.

the huge assemblage.[39] In her diary Emmeline, whose eyesight had begun to fade, scrawled across the page in almost unreadable text her feelings on that occasion. "I cannot describe the sensations that thrilled my soul as I stood in the midst of that vast multitude assembled on that memorable occasion, one that helps to make history and—so in my later life much that seemed impossible has come to pass and the gift of foretelling events has been verified in what has really transpired in these later years." Once again she could feel that she had indeed become what others had anticipated. "When a very little girl the village people seemed to understand that I was to be a child of destiny," she concluded.[40] And so she was.

In October 1914, a long-lost member of the Wells family made an unexpected visit to Utah. Albert Wells, Daniel's only child with his first wife, Eliza Robison, traveled to Utah to celebrate the one hundredth anniversary of his father's birth. He had never married and served as a minister in his church. Emmeline was much impressed with his appearance, but probably not as impressed as Albert was at meeting the huge number of "step"brothers and -sisters, cousins, aunts, and uncles. Raised as an only child, this was a remarkable revelation to him. He stayed for several days, visiting his father's grave and spending a day with Emmeline and her daughter Annie. Though he was royally treated by his extended family, he never returned to Utah.[41]

As a counterpoint to the unexpected honors she had recently received, Emmeline was shortly to experience a devastating but inevitable loss. A newly conceived Relief Society guide and a monthly bulletin, edited by Susa Gates, made their initial appearance in January 1914. The guide was the first publication of the unified plan for Relief Society work. Among other policies and instructions, it provided the lesson outlines for the weekly Relief Society meetings as well as procedures concerning charity and business affairs. It clearly superseded the *Woman's Exponent* as a Relief Society organ. It was only wishful thinking that prompted Emmeline to place on the paper's masthead "The Organ of the Latter-day Saints' Woman's Relief Society" for its last fourteen issues. Only she made that claim. The new guide met an enthusiastic response.

When talk of a guide had surfaced two years earlier, in April 1912, Emmeline hoped that she could transfer the *Woman's Exponent* to the

39. "The Gull Monument"; Benjamin Goddard, "The Sea-Gull Monument," *Young Woman's Journal* 24 (November 1913): 667–74; "The Monument to the Gulls," *Woman's Exponent* 41 (November 1913): 76–77.

40. E. Wells, Diary, October 1, 1913.

41. Ibid., October 26, 27, 28, November 9, 1914.

Relief Society as its official organ. It would be an unencumbered gift, with Emmeline retaining her position as editor and her daughter Annie remaining as assistant editor. A business manager would be appointed later. However, the lesson committee was then focused on preparing a guide, and no action was taken on her proposal. A few months later, she explained to the board that after making her April offer, several board members had advised her not to give her paper to the Relief Society, and so she did not pursue the matter. However, she said, the *Exponent* would eventually become the property of the Relief Society, since she had always considered it to be the organ of the society, and it would be "turned over to it free from debt."[42] As "editor, managing editor, business manager, publisher, and owner," according to the editorial page, and without any bondholders, mortgages, or other security holders, she was indeed in a position to transfer the paper by her own volition and without encumbrance.[43]

The question of the *Exponent* remained unresolved, however. In April 1913, at a special bulletin advisory committee meeting, which Emmeline did not attend, Julina Smith recounted a visit she had had with Emmeline shortly before the death of Bathsheba Smith. Julina had suggested at that time that Emmeline immediately turn over the *Woman's Exponent* to the Relief Society, explaining that "Aunt Bathsheba might die and she wanted the paper to have her name," though Emmeline could remain as editor. "It struck me to the heart—so flippantly was it all said," Emmeline recorded and of course refused the offer.[44] Now, three years later, the question of the disposition of the *Exponent* was again under discussion. Based on Emmeline's earlier refusal, Julina Smith said that the paper belonged to "Aunt Em. It is just like her own child, and the Relief Society would not care to ask her to give it up, nor to ask for any change in the matter."[45] Julina's words were convincing, and once again, no decision was made. The question lay dormant for nearly another year. But Emmeline learned in January 1914 that the advisory committee had again met to discuss the *Exponent* without her presence or knowledge beforehand. "So much unpleasantness has transpired," Emmeline recounted to her diary, "that it seems almost unbearable and no telling what dark schemes are yet to be met & borne."[46] Deeply concerned, she and Annie met with Bishop Nibley and President Smith, but Emmeline did not record what advice they gave her. She felt

42. Ibid., August 1, 1912.

43. "Statement of Ownership," *Woman's Exponent* 41 (December 1912): 28.

44. E. Wells, Diary, May 20, 1910. This conversation was not recorded in the other two diaries.

45. Minutes of the General Board, April 5, 1913.

46. E. Wells, Diary, January 8, 1914.

certain, however, that decisions had been made to undermine her plans for the *Woman's Exponent*. With all these new developments occurring without Emmeline's knowledge or concurrence, she had some reason to be apprehensive.

Before the regularly scheduled January 14 board meeting, Emmeline underwent days of reflection and soul-searching. Anticipating that her proposal would be denied and unwilling to suffer the indignity of her paper's irrelevance, Emmeline finally reached a momentous life decision. After calling the meeting to order, she began by speaking of a "permanent publication by the Relief Society and of the *Woman's Exponent*," the secretary recorded. She then made the startling declaration that "it was her present intention to discontinue the *Woman's Exponent* with the February number." She explained that it had been her desire to give "the good will of her paper and the name to the Society" and had also desired "that her name continue to be used as editor of the Relief Society organ. These privileges had been denied her, and she had given up the paper, the name of the paper, and the idea of having her name used as editor." However inevitable this decision was, the emotion transmitted in that surreal moment must have resonated with every board member. Those who knew Emmeline best understood what depths she had to plumb to sever such a vital part of her being. Only silence greeted her announcement. Nothing could match this moment as the nadir of her presidency.[47]

During a long, sleepless night, Emmeline reflected on the emotional meeting. "Ambitious and aspiring woman seems to be destitute of fine feelings I have never received so terrible a blow as she has brought about I do not see how she would stoop to do so mean a thing," she wrote, her thoughts flowing into each other without pause or break. Who had made her feel so betrayed? She ached at the thought that it was a single voice that had influenced the board and wreaked so much pain. Not privy to any of the discussions, she had only her wild thoughts to feed her speculations.

Emmeline's last editorial for the *Woman's Exponent*, entitled "Heartfelt Farewell," appearing the following month, noted that "the *Exponent*

47. Minutes of the General Board, January 14, 1914. The General Board, Annie Cannon believed, had planned events to "compel the discontinuance of the Exponent." Annie and Belle felt that the "underhanded and cruel way it was brought about nearly killed our mother," and they would not soon forget "the unkindness and injustice of those who so offended." Fortunately, Emmeline felt the continuing friendship and support of her friend President Penrose as well as that of President Lund, counselors to Joseph F. Smith, and several members of the Twelve who made their sympathetic feelings known to her. Margaret Cannon Clayton, "Our Mother: Biography of Elizabeth Anne Wells Cannon," typescript copy, 10, 11, L. Tom Perry Collection, Harold B. Lee Library, Brigham Young University, Provo, UT.

has striven more than anything else to be the organ of the Relief Society," and "its numbers contain sketches of the lives of Relief Society workers and notices of their death." For women, Emmeline noted, the paper had always stood as a "standard bearer, proclaiming their worth and just claims throughout the long years of its existence." With admirable restraint and considerable understatement, she concluded, "To lay aside the editorial pen, even after so many long years, seems a hard task, but though the pen may be idle, the mind will ever gratefully remember all the associations which this little paper has been instrumental in creating."[48]

Finally, on September 24, the board resolved the long and difficult issue. Clarissa Williams reported that the Relief Society advisory committee recommended that the society publish a monthly magazine to be known as the *Relief Society Magazine* and that Susa Gates was to be its editor. The recommendation was immediately accepted. That the plan had been decided upon well before it came before the board without Emmeline's knowledge or approval and that the board would accept it without her approval were obvious by the detailed format Susa outlined for the first issue, which she read to the members. The new magazine would be issued in 1915 and take the place of both the guide and the bulletin.[49]

When Emmeline went home that September night, she was a broken woman. "At our General Board Meeting today," she told her diary, "many things were done hurtful to me. I can scarcely imagine how I sat under the ignominy heaped upon me, but I am sure the Lord restrained me, and I shall eventually come off victorious that has been revealed to me and made manifest."[50] It is unlikely that any termination of her paper could have been free of regret and disappointment, but matters could have been arranged more amicably "had we been allowed a hearing," Annie told her daughter Margaret. Then "all this might have been taken care of without any heartaches."

On the first page of the final edition of the *Woman's Exponent* appeared the first two verses of a poem that Emmeline wrote years before, entitled "Sorrow and Tears." It seemed appropriate now:

Out of my sorrow and mourning,
Out of its grief and its pain;
Its sighing, and sobbing, and moaning,
The deepest and wildest refrain
Swells forth with a melody pleading
For the heart that is stricken and bleeding.

48. "Heartfelt Farewell," *Woman's Exponent* 41 (February 1914): 100.
49. Minutes of the General Board, September 24, 1914.
50. E. Wells, Diary, September 24, 1914.

Regrets for past promises waiting
And prophecies yet unfulfill'd;
The tears, and the voice that is wailing,
The strength of strong passions distill'd;
The agony past self-containing,
The grief that o'ermasters restraining.[51]

With her eyesight failing, her poetic muse slipping away, and her voice for women silenced, Emmeline moved into a new—and the last—phase of her long, productive life.

51. "Sorrow and Tears," *Woman's Exponent* 41 (February 1914): 97. Also in E. Wells, *Musings and Memories*, 272.

CHAPTER 36

Winding Down
(1915–1918)

In the eighty-eighth year of her life, now free from the exacting toll of maintaining a monthly publication, Emmeline was in the throes of confronting other irreversible conditions in her life: her diminishing energy, her growing anachronism, and her dimming eyesight. "I suffer so because of my eyes," she lamented at the close of one difficult day in 1916. "I long to be able to see again," she wrote on another. "If I could see," she wrote in explanation of her sorrowful mood, "I am sure I should be more content."[1] Books had always been her most constant and dependable companions, but now she could not make out the words, and a satisfying and comforting pastime was over. Her usual flow of editorials, stories, and poems had virtually ceased, though ideas still thronged her mind as busily as they had in the past. An occasional article for the *Deseret News*, the *Relief Society Magazine*, or the *Young Woman's Journal* along with an abbreviated correspondence gave voice to some of her thoughts, though the words had to be written by her daughters. To the end, however, her mind remained sharp and retentive. It was of immeasurable satisfaction that in December 1915, a second enlarged and revised edition of *Musings and Memories* was issued. An endorsement and glowing review of the new volume appeared in the January 1916 issue of the *Relief Society Magazine*, which explained that the cost of publication was once again borne by the Utah Woman's Press Club.[2]

Though her literary life was now curtailed, Emmeline could not give up her diary, and after 1916, the last year in which she was the penman, she dictated her entries to Annie. Rather than drawing the reader into her rich world of heartfelt minisoliloquies on people, places, and events, she created a record that was little more than a jotting of daily activities and names of

1. E. Wells, Diary, January 17, 24, May 15, 1916.
2. "Poems by Emmeline B. Wells."

people encountered.[3] Gone were the enticing musings that once flowed so freely from her mind, now locked there without their usual route of escape. Belle and Annie and two or three of her granddaughters read to her daily from the newspaper, from her favorite scriptures—the Psalms—from current novels, and from poetry, especially Longfellow and Tennyson. Many times over she requested a reading of Longfellow's "Hiawatha" because she found the meter soothing and pleasing to her ear.[4]

Sometime in 1916, Emmeline left her home to the care of her grandson George Q. Cannon, Annie's son, and his young family and moved to room 834 of the Hotel Utah, only steps away from the Bishop's Building, eliminating the long streetcar rides to and from her home in Waterloo.[5] Like the windows in her room in her Waterloo home, the windows in her hotel room opened up to an unobstructed eastern view. The move proved to be convenient for her family as well. Belle had become a scheduled temple worker, and she often visited her mother between her assigned sessions. Annie, living some distance away at the Cannon farm, was often in town to attend to the many civic and church affairs in which she was now involved. Both daughters gave their mother remarkable attention and companionship day and night during Emmeline's last years.

Mell's open invitation to visit enticed Emmeline to make one last trip to the cottage on the lake at Coeur d'Alene in the fall of 1916. Her granddaughter nineteen-year-old Katherine was again her companion. She wrote very little of this final visit, but it did not go unnoticed by the local Idaho papers.[6] The *Press* of Coeur d'Alene noted her visit to the Woodses' lakeside cottage, and the magazine *Sunset*'s report on "interesting westerners" described Emmeline as a woman "slight of figure but powerful in influence," adding a brief biographical account.[7]

As her public activities diminished, Emmeline flourished even more than usual in the family circle and rejoiced at the number of great-grandchildren coming into the family. "My posterity is increasing I shall soon be up with

3. Emmeline's 1915 and 1916 diaries are fairly lengthy and difficult to read. The only other diaries from this last decade are brief accounts in 1917, 1918, and the last, 1920, written for her or at her dictation by Annie.

4. E. Wells, Diary, October 30, 1917. See also August 14, October 14, 24, and November 1, 3, 1917.

5. Originally, she had asked the presiding bishop if she could rent a room merely through the winter months. Room 834, however, became her year-round residence. Ibid., January 18, 1916.

6. Ibid., September 17–21, 1916.

7. The two Idaho reports were mentioned in the *Salt Lake Tribune*, September 22, 1916.

all the great tribe of mothers I have many children grandchildren and great grandchildren I have much to be grateful for," she exulted.[8] But she also lamented the loss of those in the larger Wells family who left the church or put it on the periphery of their lives. "The next generation," she despaired, "will not be as brave in respect to religion as the children of such a man as Gen. Wells and they will not have so great a man as father as he was."[9]

When she was past ninety, Emmeline was invited to speak to the students of the LDS high school in Barratt Hall about her experiences with the Prophet Joseph Smith. Years later, Ethel Newman (Lund), one of the two young women sent to accompany her to the hall, recounted Emmeline's explanation of a vision she had received when attending the Salt Lake temple some years earlier. She said that she had had "a compulsion to press her [temple] clothes the night before and see that everything was in order," Ethel remembered. At the temple the next day, Emmeline told her, she put on her freshly pressed white dress, and walking to the creation room, she had a special vision. "'I'm going to tell you girls this,'" Ethel recalled her saying, "'because some day you'll go to the temple' and she wanted us always to remember that the temple is 'a sacred place.' Emmeline then declared, 'I saw the Savior.'" It was a startling announcement, Ethel said, but absolutely convincing in its detail. "When you go up that little ramp into the temple proper and you go to turn into this first room, just before you turn to go in the first room, the Savior came toward me," Emmeline told the girls. "He was dressed in a white robe, standing above the floor... He spoke only one sentence: 'Emeline, how beautiful you are in your beautiful dress.'" Emmeline's statements, filtered by retelling through Ethel's memory, had made such a strong impression on Ethel that she always kept her temple clothes in proper condition, she said, and never stepped on the spot where Emmeline said she had seen the Savior. Ethel concluded her recollection by saying, "This isn't a figment of my imagination. She told [us] that, but I don't know that it wasn't a figment of her imagination, but I believed her."[10] Though Emmeline experienced many meaningful dreams in her later years, which she often recorded, this experience did not find a place in her diary.

Besides the numerous invitations to speak on church history, she continued to be invited to the meetings of the National Council of Women,

8. E. Wells, Diary, March 20, 1916.

9. Ibid., April 13, 1916.

10. Ethel Cecelia Newman Lund, oral interview by Davis Bitton, May 17, 1987, LDS Church History Library, Salt Lake City. Ethel Lund was herself ninety years old at the time of the interview. She remembered her friend as being Alene Margetts. Ethel's memory of exact dates are somewhat skewed, but Emmeline's account of her experience and the places, the lecture, and the other people involved was clear in Ethel's mind.

though she no longer attended them. "We need women like you who are fearless in expressing themselves and who believe in the Council idea," wrote Emma Bower, the first vice president, in October 1915.[11] Emmeline missed her direct association with the council and was thus pleased when the Countess of Aberdeen, once again president of the International Council of Women, agreed to stop in Utah on her philanthropic lecture tour with her husband in December. Susa Gates, in charge of their visit, scheduled them to speak in four Utah cities. Emmeline was in charge of the reception for the two guests and introduced them at two of the meetings at which they spoke. After Emmeline's introduction at the second lecture, held in the Salt Lake Theatre, the countess "kissed the brilliant little lady's hand and replied, 'It is seldom that one has the honor of being introduced twice in one day by a queen, but that honor has come to me today. For in my brief visit here I have quickly observed that "Aunt Em" is the Queen of Utah.'"[12]

Though Emmeline could—and did—rise to the occasion when events like this presented themselves, she struggled increasingly with the infirmities of old age. Dr. George Middleton was not only a friend but also a willing medical adviser, along with Dr. Seymour B. Young, both ready to attend her at any hour of any day. Illness had become her nemesis, and it truly stalked her during these later years. But as debilitating as it was, she enjoyed the attention and visits each flare-up brought, truly an example of finding silver linings in the dark clouds so heavy upon her. When she fell seriously ill in January 1917, just before her eighty-ninth birthday, she was confined to her hotel room for more than six weeks. Belle and Annie attended to her day and night, with visits from Dr. Middleton at each relapse. His diagnosis of her illness is not recorded, but her bouts of extreme headaches and neuralgia, along with back pain and swelling in her feet, required occasional doses of morphine. That her friends and Relief Society associates calculated that this might be the frail Emmeline's final illness is not surprising given her age and condition. She was thus inundated with visitors who brought gifts of food and flowers as well as bottles of wine, a daily sip of which Dr. Young prescribed as a tonic, and Emmeline refused.

11. Emma Bower to Emmeline B. Wells, October 15, 1915, E. Wells Papers, LDS Church History Library. The Relief Society continued to affiliate with the National Council of Women, sending various board members and officers to its meetings. It maintained membership through the administration of Relief Society president Belle Spafford, who served nearly thirty years as Relief Society president, from 1945 until 1974. Twice she served as president of the National Council of Women.

12. "Prominent Woman Approaches Majority—'Aunt Em' Wells Nears Important Event," *Salt Lake Tribune*, January 9, 1916, 10; Susa Young Gates to Joseph F. Smith and Counselors, December 19, 1915, Relief Society Executive Papers. See also "Lord and Lady Aberdeen in Utah"; and Journal History, January 9, 1916, 7.

She remained the inveterate chronicler, even when ill, making certain that Annie recorded the visitors' names as well as the gifts she received while she was recovering. If rest and quiet were prescriptions for a return to health, it is little wonder that her illness claimed so much recovery time. Never fewer than five and as many as forty-seven visitors came to her room in a day, their names recorded in compliance with Emmeline's insistence that "every one who comes is to come in and speak with me."[13] An interesting duo of callers on the same day was her son-in-law John Q. Cannon and Robert Sloan, who was once a suitor of her daughter Louie.[14] Rachel Siegel visited and left a jar of custard. Many others sent get-well cards.[15] The gifts were as profuse as the visitors, with flowers adorning every available surface in room 834. Food came to her in abundance, including fried chicken with brown parsnips and jelly, chicken and gravy, fresh strawberries, ham and milk gravy, grape juice, quince juice, baked apples, jars of marmalade, and plum and raspberry jelly.[16] The gifts she most appreciated, however, were the comfort and healing blessings given to her, sometimes several in a single day, by the numerous church leaders who visited her, as well as family members and friends. While they may have been overtaxing and repetitious to those who gave them, for Emmeline the blessings were reassuring and effective. To everyone's surprise, she recovered.

Emmeline's daily life continued to be bound up in her responsibilities as Relief Society president. She attended to them with as much assiduousness as she had given her paper. The mercurial Susa Gates noted that "each morning when the office force at headquarters gather about their duties and daily toils, they watch with deep affection for the Morning Miracle. She comes—our little, delicate, great-minded President, walking softly, yet with fierce independence into the rooms, and the Miracle is born again for the new day."[17] Emmeline loved the buzz of people working at their various tasks throughout the building and bemoaned the fact that Saturdays, which had always been a workday for her, left her a lonely occupant of the building. She still looked to the board meetings, however, with a mixture of anxiety and anticipation.[18] She liked observing the discussions and hearing the ideas from the energetic and innovative board members, but they were

13. Journal History, January 8, 12, 1917.

14. Ibid., February 9, 1917.

15. Margaret Salisbury, still a close friend to Emmeline, traveled extensively and thus did not appear as often in Emmeline's diary. The Bambergers were also solicitous.

16. The accounts of her visitors and the gifts she received are included in diary entries between January 3 and February 15, 1917.

17. Susa Young Gates, "Our Lovely Human Heritage: President Emmeline B. Wells."

18. See, for example, E. Wells, Diary, January 13, 17, February 3, March 3, and April 3, 1916.

often irritating and divisive.[19] "Today there has been very much confusion and annoyances and I am so weary of it all," she wrote after one fractious meeting. "The sisters are too persistent in having new measures...which would be injurious to the work at present." Emmeline believed in cautious progress and warned: "We must be wise in voting in new measures."[20] One new measure, however, was a resolution in which board members pledged "to set an example of courtesy to each other and to speakers."[21] Evidently, the meetings were vexatious not only to Emmeline.

For her part, Emmeline became inordinately sensitive to small actions that seemed to distance the board from past precedents and was particularly annoyed over a simple decision to divide among the board members all the old dishes and cutlery that had been purchased over the years and held sentimental memories for Emmeline. She felt that this little task could have been done after she was gone.[22] A discussion on the release of an aged and ill stake Relief Society president was also disconcerting. Susa Gates entered the conversation with a proposal to create a new policy that would affect all such situations. "If a woman is incapable, either through age or inability, to do the work for which she has been appointed," the sixty-one-year-old Susa proposed, "she should be willing to slip out and let some one who is able take it up." She then suggested that seventy be the age limit for active service and that when women reached that age, "it is probably wise for them and beneficial to the society to resign the work to younger and more active women."[23] Though Emmeline was familiar with Susa's lack of tact and had long worked around it, she could hardly avoid taking this proposal personally. She was, after all, eighty-two when she had been appointed president. Resigning from her position had no precedent, and Emmeline's calling to this high office rested on the First Presidency's confidence, as well as the board's, that she had the ability to guide the Relief Society at this juncture in its history and in hers. Susa's motion did not pass.

Emmeline's frustration with Susa over the years did not diminish her respect for her capabilities. In 1910, before becoming Relief Society general president, she urged Susa "not to neglect [her] temple work or risk losing [her] place there" and announced to her on one occasion that "when it comes <u>your time</u> to preside [over the Relief Society] always have a hymn sung." Emmeline reminded her that "Eliza [R. Snow] was president of the Endowment House and Pres. of the Relief Society. And so was Aunt Zina

19. Ibid., January 13, March 23, 1916.
20. Ibid., April 3, 1916.
21. Minutes of the General Board, October 12, 1917.
22. Ibid., September 20, 21, 22, 27, 1917.
23. Ibid., May 3, 1917.

[D. H. Young]!" Emmeline felt Susa capable of holding both positions concurrently, as they had done.[24] "Comparing you with other Mormon women of your generation," Emmeline wrote, "you stand high."[25] Susa could reciprocate. The "*Woman's Exponent*," she asserted in a board meeting years later, "was a gigantic monument to the women of the Church, also the women of the world. The greatness and importance of the work of its editor, President Emmeline B. Wells, had risen constantly to greater heights in the vision of the speaker."[26] While Emmeline did not wholly trust Susa's motives or methods, Susa could be a strong ally in causes they both supported.

Despite the sometimes rancorous meetings and her concern over the rapid expansion of the Relief Society's purview and secularization, Emmeline was invigorated by the verve and energy that sparked many of the meetings and relished being at the head of such productive activity. Though she often felt sidelined by the fast pace of the decision making, the authority of the subcommittees, and the growing encroachment of general church committees with oversight of the auxiliaries, she remained an engaged and respected leader, as much by what she was as what she did.[27] Simple victories, such as the board's approval of her proposal to adopt as a motto "Charity Never Faileth" and a sheaf of wheat, rather than the long-used sego lily, as an emblem of the society, were important to her.[28] Always striving to keep a strong connection with the Relief Society's roots, Emmeline often used Joseph Smith's instructions to the Nauvoo Society as her themes at the annual Relief Society conferences.[29] She was also diligent in marking the anniversary of the Relief Society each March, which was generally commemorated quietly among board members and individual wards, since the First Presidency had discouraged larger public commemo-

24. Susa Young Gates, Diary, March 9, April 8, 1916.

25. Emmeline B. Wells, letter to Susa Young Gates, July 19, 1910, Gates Papers. She addressed it to "My Own Darling Susa" and ended it, "Good Night Very Lovingly Aunt Emm Wells." The letter was written before the fiasco of the *Woman's Exponent* in 1914.

26. Minutes of the General Board, February 15, 1919.

27. E. Wells, Diary, August 2, 1916. Despite the leveling effect of the Correlation Committee's directives, general Primary president Louie Felt acknowledged what most Relief Society members already believed, that "the Relief Society... is the mother of all the auxiliary organizations of the Church." "General Conference of the Relief Society," 529.

28. Minutes of the General Board, May 17, 1917.

29. Invitations to speak about Joseph Smith greatly increased over the next few years. See, for example, E. Wells, Diary, March 4, April 24, May 16, June 17, October 20, and December 16, 23, 1917. See also her general Relief Society conference talks recorded in the minutes, October 2, 3, 1918, April 4, 5, and also on June 4, 5, 1919.

rations. When March 17 fell on a Sunday in 1918, she requested that the Sunday service in the tabernacle be devoted to the founding of the Relief Society. Her request was denied, but all of the wards were encouraged to make their Sunday service a commemoration.[30]

Emmeline keenly felt her place as liaison with the spirit as well as the potential of the Nauvoo Relief Society, the "loving link," as the *Deseret News* earlier observed. Though appreciative of the accomplishments of the board, she did not hesitate to express her hope that "the members of the General Board would see to it that the organization of the Relief Society shall preserve its originality and that if any changes are to be made they will not interfere in any way with the original design of the work."[31]

The Nauvoo Relief Society minutes were sacrosanct to Emmeline, and she believed Joseph Smith's words to the women of the church were divinely inspired. They were her guide throughout her administration. In 1895, she wrote a long sketch of the history of the Relief Society for the *Exponent* and was currently updating it for *Appleton's History*, a national publication that had invited the submission. She was naturally upset when Rebecca Nibley nominated Susa Gates as general historian of the board with a commission to write a history.[32] When Emmeline noted that she was already writing one for *Appleton's History*, Susa quietly asked her diary, "Why does the poor little soul do such ill advised & secret things. No one knew it, it was not authorized."[33] This small episode simply emphasized the need for Emmeline to accept the constraints of an organization whose will often superseded her own. She acceded to the board's proposal, and Susa wrote an extensive and creditable history for the board.

America's entry into World War I had a long-lasting effect on the work of the Relief Society and brought to the fore the impact of progressivism on humanitarian service. Clarissa Williams and Amy Brown Lyman spearheaded the society's wartime activities. Both were devotees of the new methods of social welfare. Clarissa worked through her position as head of the Utah Council of National Defense Woman's Committee, and Amy coordinated the social welfare efforts of the Relief Society with the Red

30. E. Wells, Diary, March 17, 1918. See also "Relief Society to Observe Anniversary," *Salt Lake Tribune*, March 17, 1918, 14.

31. "President of the Relief Society," *Deseret News*, October 8, 1910, 74–75; Minutes of the General Board, October 23, 1919.

32. Minutes of the General Board, March 25, 1915.

33. Gates, Diary, March 25, 1915. None of Emmeline's public writings had ever needed "authorization" before. She would have been surprised at Susa's comment, if she had known of it. If Susa meant authorization from the Relief Society board, Emmeline herself was the highest source of that "authorization."

Cross and other local humanitarian associations. The society rapidly mobilized to meet the emergency. The Relief Society joined with numerous other agencies involved in civil defense, emergency preparation, and food conservation. As the largest of the local relief agencies, the Relief Society assumed a major humanitarian presence in the community. It joined the government program in providing funds and workers for a milk depot for new mothers and young children, and even before the rumblings of war reached American shores, it had agreed to adopt lessons from the Agricultural College in Logan relating to home gardens and food preservation.[34] The declaration of America's entry into the war in April 1917 made the lessons even more imperative. This topic also became a theme for Emmeline at the semiannual Relief Society conferences, since she viewed the national food conservation movement as a replication of the grain-saving mission she had supervised at Brigham Young's request and now directed as Relief Society president.

As early as 1915, with the war raging in Europe, the *Relief Society Magazine* devoted an issue to the history of the grain-saving movement, and the following year Emmeline urged the women "to be especially diligent in performing this important duty of the organization."[35] She appointed a conservation committee from the board that arranged for demonstrations of food conservation and preservation, and individual Relief Society members took extension courses from the Agricultural College in Logan in emergency measures and attended the yearly "Housekeepers Convention and Round-up" sponsored by the college. As the war progressed, Emmeline encouraged cooperation with such groups as the Community Kitchen, the State Conservation Commission, the Child Clinic, and the State Council of Defense in community preparedness. Though Emmeline attended many of the conjoint meetings and studied their programs, she deferred to Clarissa Williams and Amy Lyman to manage the Relief Society's participation.

Throughout the war, because of their large numbers and church-wide network, Relief Society workers became a mainstay of the Red Cross activity in Utah, with ward Relief Society presidents organizing Red Cross units in their communities. The large kitchen in the Bishop's Building was transformed into a beehive of activity as women met to make bandages and sew clothing for the war effort. "In no time in the history of Utah," Emmeline joyfully observed, "has there been presented such a wonderful opportunity for the women to unite in the interest and welfare of the people at large."[36]

34. Minutes of the General Board, May 18, 1916, March 8, 1917.

35. Ibid., October 4, 5, 1916.

36. Ibid., March 8, 1917.

She refused invitations to serve as honorary chairman or vice chairman of various volunteer organizations, but often attended their meetings to keep abreast of women's part in the war effort.

This close association with the Red Cross was the impetus for the Relief Society to develop a more "scientific" mode of providing welfare service to individual families. President Joseph F. Smith was an early convert and believed that "modern family welfare methods could be advantageously adopted throughout the church." He commissioned Amy Brown Lyman to implement these new methods through the Relief Society, as the minutes attest: "Amy Brown Lyman is to devote herself to a study of family welfare work with a view of helping improve the LDS charity work."[37] Through her work at Jane Addams Hull House and the training she received from the Red Cross, its national training sessions, and other social work conventions, most of her expenses borne by the church, Amy was in the obvious position to implement the new department.

In order to retain control of the church's social work program, the Relief Society indicated that it would not use Red Cross workers to investigate the needs of Mormon families, since its training was "as good as anyone's," Clarissa Williams declared. Nor would it be subordinate to the Red Cross or any other organization with which it might be associated. Moreover, the Relief Society reserved the right to maintain its independence in determining the allocation of funds.[38]

The Social Advisory Committee, converted to organized social work, also urged the Relief Society "to be at the forefront in social welfare work and in touch with all that is being done."[39] With more enthusiasm than tact, Clarissa Williams, herself caught up in the vision of the new approach to social welfare, announced the need for additional board members, especially "young, progressive women." Then, evidently remembering that there were older women among those to whom she made the appeal, she hastily added, there was also "a need for the older sisters who are already members of the board...who could not be spared from the work, that their splendid lives,

37. Ibid., January 31, March 28, 1918.

38. Ibid., September 20, 1917. Emmeline made frequent mention of the various meetings and activities in which the Relief Society and Red Cross cooperated throughout 1917. See, for example, E. Wells, Diary, May 29, June 7, September 19, October 9, 22, November 5, 6, 16, and December 6, 20, 21, 27, 1917. Amy Brown Lyman explained the relationship of the Red Cross and Relief Society and also President Smith's decision to adopt a social service department for the church in Minutes of the General Board, January 31, 1918.

39. The Relief Society Social Service Department was officially established in January 1919.

their wisdom and spirituality and their standing in the community are assets that could not well be foregone."[40] (The role of "figurehead" had been well defined.) Under the ambitious and dedicated supervision of Amy Brown Lyman, along with the endorsement and funding of the church, the Social Services Department became a major feature of the Relief Society for four decades.[41]

Emmeline's wariness toward the rapid pace of program development began to diminish during her final years, as she recognized the capabilities of her board members in meeting the challenges of their generation. But she hoped to find some relevance of Relief Society activities of the past. Memories of the penny fund, sustained by Relief Society women in Nauvoo to buy nails and glass for the Nauvoo temple, inspired her to inaugurate a similar fund to buy supplies for the Hawaiian and Canadian temples then nearing completion or under construction. The board graciously acted on her suggestion after she explained that it was, for her, the fulfillment of a recent dream in which she was given a golden lock with a silver key and two large rolls of manuscript with names on them, presumably donors to the fund. Though halfheartedly endorsed by the First Presidency, the fund netted more than seven thousand dollars.[42] The Relief Society had become a large-scale organization and could raise workers and funds almost immediately upon request. By 1917, it numbered 43,895 members in 1,191 branches throughout the church. It held 315,393 bushels of wheat, and its financial resources, including wheat, real estate, and investments, totaled $604,027.59.[43] Through its activities in the war effort, its network of willing workers, and its ability to raise money and goods, the Relief Society was a welcome church and community asset, recognized for its efficiency and productivity.

Knowing that her position at the head of LDS women would be the culmination to her life's work on behalf of women, Emmeline reluctantly gave way to the deficiencies of her age. Her retreats into the past had served as nostalgic excursions that strengthened her when she returned to take up present-day burdens, but now they tended to add to her general malaise as she remembered the joys of her youth but also the tragedies that intervened. She attributed the hold of the past to "my extreme age," yet she recognized that it was necessary "to face these terrible calamities in life with what courage possible." She may have indulged herself in doleful nostalgia, but

40. Ibid., March 6, 1919.

41. Brown's contributions to Relief Society social work are noted in David Hall, *A Faded Legacy: Amy Brown Lyman and Mormon Women's Activism, 1872–1959*.

42. Minutes of the General Board, March 30, April 27, 1916, September 20, 1917.

43. Ibid., April 5, 1917.

she was always quick to acknowledge the good days that brought "many blessings and comforts while still here on the dear old Earth" with "loving and trusted friends and other comforts & joys."[44] Her conversational skills and agile mind, as well as her robust memory, did not abate with the diminution of her other faculties. It was always a delight, one friend noted some years earlier, "to listen to her bright conversation and repartee." "Just to converse with her," one account observed, "is to get a start toward a liberal education."[45] An early assessment of her central place in so many relationships stayed with her to the very end. Though her administrative skills diminished along with her physical stamina, she remained, if only symbolically, as "the very heart of the public life of the women of Utah... answering everybody's questions, listening to everybody's tale of woe, and furnishing information to everybody on every subject under the sun."[46]

Yet almost in defiance of the many friends, the opportunities still coming to her, and the multiplying honors, she seemed compelled to assert that "there [is] still grief."[47] Her obsessive embrace of sorrow was almost pathological, but it was not debilitating like symptoms of depression, and she continued to draw on the animating spirit that drove her to be deserving of the accolades heaped upon her.

Birthdays were annual reminders that she was successful in this effort. The Relief Society General Board now consistently celebrated the important day with a luncheon for board members followed by a public reception, another burden borne by possibly resentful overworked board members. But for Emmeline, more than the personal honor of such occasions was her pleasure in seeing old friends and new who attended the public receptions. Since only once in four years did the celebration occur on the actual day of her birth, her "twenty-first" birthday in 1916 was a cause célèbre for the newspapers. The *Salt Lake Tribune* anticipated the celebration with a long article and pictures featured in the January 9 Sunday edition. "Prominent Woman Approaches Majority" headlined the article announcing that this was only the twenty-first time the eighty-eight-year-old Emmeline celebrated her birthday on the actual date of her birth. Recounting her accomplishments, the article also noted that "though bent with the weight of many years and their tremendous responsibilities, she can only be thought of as an energetic, capable business woman, who is always to be reckoned with in many important phases of the city's and state's life."[48] The *Deseret Evening*

44. E. Wells, Diary, April 10, 12, 1916.
45. Journal History, February 29, 1916, 2.
46. "With the Editor," *Young Woman's Journal* 9 (March 1898): 334–336.
47. E. Wells, Diary, April 11, 1916.
48. "Prominent Woman Approaches Majority."

News was similarly eulogistic, and telegrams and letters acknowledged the event. Congratulatory telegrams came from the Countess of Aberdeen in New York, the Bambergers in Havanna, Joseph F. Smith in Hawaii, and Mabel Vernon, woman suffrage leader in Idaho.

These late-life tributes acknowledged the laborious effort Emmeline exerted to accomplish something of worth for the women of the church. They caught not only the intensity of her commitment but also its breadth. As one tribute read, "She has traveled far in the interests of her sex...and has been the personification of mental industry, frail in body, but inflexible in will."[49] These tributes, written in the effusive prose of the time, showed that Emmeline had moved into a special status as a public figure, one to be admired, cherished, and feted. Despite her tiny frame, many agreed, she effused power wherever she went. "No 'Mormon' woman has been more widely known within and without the Church and probably no woman has been entrusted with more responsible commissions by the leaders of the Church," noted a later tribute that could hardly be disputed.[50] For any woman of this time to be acknowledged as a trusted emissary of and coworker with the First Presidency of the church was indeed noteworthy. News writers vied in their expressions of regard for this "familiar figure on the streets of Salt Lake." As one writer observed, "It is seldom that a day passes when Mrs. Wells cannot be seen attending to her business and social interests downtown."[51] Indeed, the whole of downtown Salt Lake City had been her "village."

Even as her vitality waned, Emmeline approached each new year with determination to make the most of every day. At age eighty-eight, she continued to walk the short distance to her office north of the Hotel Utah each morning, and she attended the fast meetings held in the temple each month. She often attended Sunday-afternoon stake conferences held in the tabernacle and visited Primary and Young Ladies' MIA meetings. She occasionally turned up at Daughters of Utah Pioneers and Daughters of the Revolution meetings and still traveled to stake Relief Society conferences. She spoke long and forcefully at the semiannual Relief Society general conferences, even as she approached ninety, and her talks were evocations of the organization's beginnings and Joseph Smith's prescience in establishing it. She usually attended all sessions of the church's general conferences, sitting at the front of the tabernacle with other auxiliary officers.

A fall into the hotel's elevator shaft and fortunate rescue by Belle as well as a brush by a streetcar a few months after the fall left her shaken, bruised,

49. "'Aunt Em' Wells—Aged 88," *Deseret Evening News*, February 29, 1916, 7.

50. "President Emmeline B. Wells."

51. "Prominent Woman Approaches Majority."

and in pain in both instances, but with a few days of rehabilitation, she was back at work.[52] Habits die hard.

Eight hundred guests attended Emmeline's ninetieth birthday celebration in 1918. Gifts poured in, and visitors came to her hotel room early on the morning of February 28. The board hosted a luncheon for its members, after which photographers arrived with their "machines" and took Emmeline's picture. There she stands for posterity, slightly stooped, arrayed in a long old-fashioned white and lightly floral-printed dress with a long shawl about her shoulders and a ruffle around her neck, holding her "satchel" by a chain in her hand. She looks tiny, frail, and very old, but her appearance was deceiving. She greeted each one of the eight hundred guests who attended the reception and musical, lasting four hours.[53] More festivities occupied a second day, at the end of which Emmeline noted, "My 90th anniversary has been much remembered."[54] Not to be outdone by any other tribute, the *Improvement Era* identified her as "one of the most remarkable women in the world."[55]

By the time she was ninety, Emmeline could see the success of one of the major commissions given to her—heading the grain-saving program for the church. World War I had brought a resurgent interest in saving grain as an emergency measure. Newspapers and the *Relief Society Magazine* invited public attention to the Relief Society's faithful stewardship of the assignment.[56] In 1880, President John Taylor had instructed bishops that the wheat was to be used or sold only under the direction to the Relief Society.[57] Over the years, some ward Relief Societies had built granaries

52. E. Wells, Diary, February 20, 21, 22, 25, 26, 1918.

53. "Ninety Candles Adorn Big Cake: Birthday of 'Aunt Em,'" *Deseret Evening News*, February 28, 1918, 1.

54. E. Wells, Diary, February 25, 26, 28, March 1, 1918.

55. "Noted Anniversaries."

56. Emmeline always considered this assignment as the fulfillment of a blessing she had received from Eliza R. Snow in Nauvoo that promised her she would live to fulfill a mission that no other woman had ever performed before. Reported in "The Mission of Saving Grain." President John Taylor indicated that the mission of saving grain by the women of the church "will be one of the greatest acts of statesmanship that could occur" (55).

57. Annie Wells Cannon, "Grain Saving in the Relief Society"; E. Cecil McGavin, "Grain Storage among the Latter-day Saints"; Olga W. Snell, comp., "The Story of Wheat," photocopy in my possession; various accounts of the grain mission in Priscilla Livingston Evans files, typescript; Jessie L. Embry, "Grain Storage: The Balance of Power between Priesthood Authority and Relief Society Autonomy." The association of the Relief Society with the Red Cross during World War I and the selling of the wheat to the government are noted in "Red Cross Workers Give Wheat Stores to Nation," *Nauvoo (IL) Independent*, November 9, 1918; and Journal History, November 9, 1918, 10.

to store the wheat, but by 1910, many Relief Societies had abandoned their granaries in favor of more efficient storage facilities in Salt Lake City, receiving monetary credit for and continued ownership of the wheat that was stored. Unresolved questions over supervision of the wheat plagued the relationship of the Relief Society and bishops, including the presiding bishopric, for many years.[58] In 1915, however, Emmeline modified this dictum. Urging cooperation with bishops and stake presidents, she advised that "wheat is stored under the direction of the Presiding Authority of the Church, and everything connected with its distribution is to be done under his direction."[59] In effect, the wheat was now under joint ownership.

By 1917, in accordance with a general confiscation policy by the government regarding commercial wheat, federal agents, along with Utah's congressional representative Milton H. Welling, had repeatedly approached the presiding bishop, requesting the Relief Society wheat for the war effort. Bishop Nibley, with the concurrence of the Relief Society, persistently explained that the Relief Society wheat was stored not for commercial use but for charitable purposes. However, in May 1918, the government finally demanded the wheat, indicating that the scarcity at that moment was acute. In his haste to comply, Bishop Nibley drafted a letter and with the approval of the First Presidency sent it to all ward Relief Societies, asking for their compliance. The letter was sent out above the names of the presiding bishopric and the Relief Society general presidency. However, the Relief Society presidency had not been consulted in the matter, and though Emmeline was in total support of selling the wheat to the government, she was distressed to learn that the Relief Society presidency had had no voice in the decision.

The breach of trust occasioned a personal visit of Bishop Nibley to the Relief Society General Board meeting the following week to make amends. "We are very properly subject to criticism for the haste in which the matter was handled," he began. "Now I am here to apologize. We probably could have waited a day or two or made the Government wait a day or two, but the exigency seemed great." He promised that the sisters would get their money for the sale and then concluded, "What more can I say. We acted hastily because we thought we had to and we should not have done it. We should have waited." Emmeline's response was that "the sisters were not adverse to selling their wheat to the Government but that she could not help but feel very much hurt personally that such an important action had been

58. An example is in Minutes of the General Board, October 2, 3, 1918.
59. Ibid., February 4, 1915.

taken without consulting the General Board." Adding to his contriteness, Bishop Nibley willingly accepted responsibility for the insensitive action. "I back you up in anything you say and will ask you to lay it on me and Bishop Smith more than anybody else. I am to blame more than anybody. Wish you would give me 'Thunder.'"[60] The sisters declined this invitation and graciously, if somewhat begrudgingly, accepted his apology. This was a personal, not official, act of contrition, an act of respect for the Relief Society board.

When news of the sale of wheat was sent on to Washington, the House of Representatives stopped its proceedings in a round of applause for the Relief Society's contribution, which was to be sent to Europe for the use of the military. Representative Welling took the occasion to express the appreciation of Herbert Hoover, head of the US Food Administration, for "this service by the women of the Relief Society who had thus tendered over two hundred thousand bushels of first-class milling wheat to the United States for the cause of human liberty, and for the saving of the lives of thousands who might suffer for the lack of bread to eat."[61] It may not have initiated the sale, but the Relief Society felt justified in accepting the words of appreciation for this final use of the wheat that had been under its stewardship for more than forty years.[62]

Perhaps only Emmeline could fully appreciate the irony of President Woodrow Wilson's private visit to her in 1919, when he and his wife sat at her bedside in her room in the Hotel Utah. Visiting Utah on a national tour to promote the League of Nations, the ailing president and his wife, Edith, were housed in the Presidential Suite of Hotel Utah, on the same floor as Emmeline's room. He declined to grant any interviews but indicated that he wanted to make just one private visit while in Utah, and that was to the woman who had sold the wheat to the government the year before. He sent his assistant to ask permission to visit her, and fifteen minutes later, he and his wife knocked on her door. Emmeline, recovering from her own illness, was still confined to her bed. Her daughter Belle and Belle's daughter-in-law

60. Ibid., May 23, 1918.

61. "Recognition of Noble Work"; "Mormon Women Praised in Congress," *Deseret Evening News*, June 19, 1918, 4; Minutes of the General Board, June 20, 1918.

62. This unexpected action triggered a change in the long-held tradition of storing wheat by the Relief Society. No more granaries were to be built, and no more grain was to be gathered. The money from the sale of the wheat to the government was placed in a trust fund for the Relief Society to be used for maternity and child welfare work at the close of the war. The final disposition of the grain mission did not occur until after Emmeline's death.

and grandson were the only other persons in the room and were visibly flustered by these unexpected visitors.[63] President Wilson thanked her for the generosity of the Relief Society in turning over the stored grain to the nation "in its hour of need." He complimented her on her work for woman suffrage and other public actions and especially the contributions of the Relief Society during the war. He then asked her to write him a letter (which she surely did) and spoke of the beauties of the valley. Edith Wilson was warmly gracious and indicated she had known much about "Mrs. Wells of Utah" for some time.[64] Then the brief visit was over.

President Wilson was the last of six US presidents with whom Emmeline had personal interaction. Her first had occurred forty years earlier, in 1879, when she met with Rutherford B. Hayes in Washington, followed by a visit with Grover Cleveland in 1886, and later Theodore Roosevelt in 1902. She had also entertained James A. Garfield during his visit to Utah in 1872, before he became president, and had briefly met President Ulysses S. Grant when he visited Utah in 1875. This time the president visited her.

By coincidence, Emmeline also numbered six LDS presidents among her personal associates during her public years. The longest association was with Joseph F. Smith, from 1901, when he succeeded Lorenzo Snow as church president, until his death in 1918. She had shared the Nauvoo and exodus experience with all but one of them (Heber J. Grant was born in Utah), a bond that united all of the pioneers in a unique way. President Smith's death in November 1918 was a sad day for Emmeline, and the dreary, rainy day of his funeral may have contributed to Emmeline's feeling that "the funeral was not at all satisfactory." Susa Gates invited Emmeline to write a tribute to President Smith for the *Relief Society Magazine*, but after reading Emmeline's piece, she declined to print it. Susa, daughter of Brigham Young, felt that in some way the article diminished the preeminence of her own father. But eventually it did appear in the magazine.[65]

The death of Joseph F. Smith closed an era, both for Emmeline and the church. Joseph F. Smith was the last church president to have known the

63. Annie and her husband, John Q., were official members of the welcoming committee, stationed at the tabernacle, and among descriptions of their duties Annie merely notes in her diary that the "Pres called on mother in hotel." A. W. Cannon, Diary, September 23, 1919.

64. "President and Mrs. Wilson Make Informal Call on Aged Leader, 'Aunt Em' Wells," Journal History, September 23, 1919, 17; Minutes of the General Board, September 25, 1919.

65. E. Wells, Diary, December 1, 6, 1918; "Appreciation from the Three Leading Ladies of the Church: A Tribute," 14. The offending sentence may have been, "Surely no greater man [than Joseph F. Smith] has lived in this dispensation, save it were his uncle, the Prophet Joseph Smith."

Prophet Joseph Smith, his uncle, and to have experienced, even though a small boy, life in Nauvoo. And Emmeline would be the last Relief Society president to have known the prophet. She would now serve with "one of the boys" who had frequented her home as a member of the Wasatch Literary Association nearly fifty years earlier.

Heber J. Grant was the only child of his mother, Rachel Ridgeway Ivins Grant. Rachel was sealed to the Prophet Joseph and married for time to Jedediah M. Grant as his last plural wife. Heber would be the first church president born in Utah. His father, Jedediah, died ten days after Heber's birth in 1856, and he was raised alone by his mother, who had been Emmeline's Relief Society president when she served as secretary in the Thirteenth Ward many years earlier. President Grant had further endeared himself to Emmeline when he married one of the Wells girls, Emily, the daughter of Emmeline's sister-wife Martha. Emmeline and her counselors wrote him a congratulatory letter upon his ascendancy to president of the church, expressing her hope that "the special attention" that the Relief Society had always received "from the First Presidency of the Church in the past" would be continued under the new administration. She received a warm and encouraging response.[66] Though she was now ninety years old, she was obliged to adjust to a new church administration more synchronized with her young board members than the previous church president had been and more centered on the future than what was rapidly becoming a "distant past." History had replaced memory.

66. Minutes of the General Board, January 9, 1919.

CHAPTER 37

The True Light

(1919–1921)

If in our way some shadows in the years,
Darkened our path and hid the light from view,
Now looking back through mists of bitter tears,
We know whose Hand has brought us safely through.[1]

EMMELINE PENNED a perfect coda to her long life. From her childhood, she felt she was in the hands of a superior power, and her place was to accept its rule in patience, faith, and anticipation that it would lead her "safely through" the dark shadows that so often beset her. Moreover, she relied on her belief that "If our faith fail not and we endure, / Then all our Father's promises are sure."[2] Unlike many of her Mormon peers, she spent much of her working life in a secular world in which misunderstanding and ridicule of her Mormon beliefs were ever present. She never equivocated, however, on her loyalty to what she believed were spiritual truths and gained respect, and even admiration for so doing. When struggling with the emotional tides of plural marriage as a young woman, she had eventually reached a point of reconciliation with its challenges and could announce to her diary, "I have risen triumphant."[3] A woman of many dimensions, her life experiences plucked every emotional string. Her dual life—the public and the private—gave evidence of how she was able to sublimate a perpetual melancholia in a public demeanor that exuded strength and self-confidence and brought her accolades from all parts of her extensive world.

Emmeline had relinquished much of her Relief Society responsibility to Clarissa Williams during and after the war, but she still tried to constrain

1. Emmeline B. Wells, "Twilight Reveries," in her *Musings and Memories*, 47–49.
2. Emmeline B. "Sorrow and Sympathy," in ibid., 291–92.
3. E. Wells, Diary, October 10, 1881 (her twenty-ninth wedding anniversary to Daniel H. Wells).

the Relief Society's far-reaching engagement in aspects of community life that she felt exceeded the society's mandate. She also continued to attend to office duties as often as possible, proving that she was still at the helm and fulfilling the calling to which she had been appointed. Under her presidency the Relief Society had broadened its stewardship to include cooperative community humanitarian work, nurse training, modern methods of social service, genealogical study, the publication of an official monthly magazine, and a variety of civic-oriented committees. Many of these programs were of her initiative and others implemented without her full support, but she could look back and feel she had met the expectations of her calling.

From the time she had served as secretary in the newly organized Thirteenth Ward Relief Society, Emmeline had seen the society develop into a worldwide organization with more than fifty thousand members over which she now presided. From the personal, authoritative, and organized mode of Eliza R. Snow's presidency, the Relief Society General Board now functioned in the style of a corporate association, with weekly meetings, reports from fifteen different subcommittees, a regulated schedule of stake conference visits, and a preplanned agenda for the general Relief Society conferences. It controlled several different funds and considerable property.[4] Meetings were generally more lively than cantankerous, with more respectful exchanges. Occasionally, Emmeline's retreats into the past intruded on the realities of the present, resulting in a spontaneous reminiscence or word of caution.[5]

Despite these reminiscent diversions, Emmeline was very much alert to the conversation about Relief Society headquarters when the board learned that the Relief Society would no longer be required to pay rent for its rooms in the Bishop's Building. She wanted to make clear, the minutes reported, that the board understood "once more that the land upon which the Bishop's Building is built is owned by the Relief Society and she said that it had been expected by President Bathsheba W. Smith and her associates that the building erected thereon would be a woman's building."[6]

A few months later, the subject of a separate woman's building was again discussed when the First Presidency of the church accepted Alfred and Elizabeth McCune's gift to the church of their beautiful mansion, a few blocks north of the city center. The First Presidency in turn offered it to the Relief

4. By 1920 the Relief Society numbered 4,171 units, enrolling 54,314 members with financial resources amounting to $850,068. Relief Society Annual Report for 1920, Minutes of the General Board.

5. Minutes of the General Board, February 6, 1919, February 26, 1920.

6. Ibid., February 18, 1920.

Society for its long-awaited headquarters.[7] Still anticipating a building of its own on the Church Administration Block, neither Emmeline nor the board was in favor of moving from the Bishop's Building, recognizing the expense of remodeling the mansion and the inconvenience of its location up a steep hill from the more accessible Bishop's Building. In a letter to the First Presidency, dated November 11, 1920, Emmeline expressed appreciation for the gift and explained the board's reluctance to leave its present offices, asking only that a front entrance to their present headquarters be made available with a sign placed above the door saying "Woman's Building." Ever the astute business manager, she also asked that the rental fees for the lower offices in the Bishop's Building be assigned to the Relief Society. As for the McCunes' offer, which was accepted by the church for other purposes, she claimed a financial interest in the home since it was initially offered to the Relief Society, explaining, "Now that another opportunity has offered for us to obtain some valuable holdings in this, the headquarters of our Church, we hesitate to relinquish all claim to such property."[8] Reminding the brethren that although Relief Society units throughout the church had their own halls, the General Board had not yet obtained "a permanent abiding place in Zion." Having one would surely signify the permanence and importance of the Relief Society. A woman's building was still in the future, but the negotiations around the McCune offer demonstrated that Emmeline, at ninety-two, was still a business-minded woman, qualities developed from years of managing a home and a business by herself.

While Emmeline could still authoritatively voice her thoughts, time was ineluctably conquering her body. Afraid of being alone, she constantly sought the company of family members and friends. She tended toward hypochondria, and every pain or faintness required immediate medical help. Her worn and aged body had been overtaxed for long years and could no longer meet the demands of her irrepressible spirit. Though no longer a familiar figure walking the streets of the city, she did venture on occasion to walk across South Temple Street from the hotel or her office to have lunch at the Tea Room in the ZCMI department store. It offered not only a pleasing lunch but also many friends with whom to visit. One windy day, however, when her tiny frame could not withstand the force of the wind, which had increased by the time her lunch was over, the ever-resourceful and independent ninety-two-year-old Emmeline called a taxi to take her across the street to her office.[9]

7. Ibid., November 4, 1920.
8. Ibid., November 11, 1920.
9. E. Wells, Diary, June 16, 1920.

Occasionally, during various bouts of ailments, Emmeline moved to Annie's home for recuperation. Even these temporary removals from the center of the city did not deter visitors.[10] Board members, grandchildren, and friends found their way to Annie's, where Emmeline basked in their visits. Though once annoyed by the interruption to her work by well-meaning visitors to her *Exponent* office, she now viewed the number of them as a weather vane of continuing friendship. There is no question that she loved people, and being with them lifted her spirits. She enjoyed meeting them, conversing with them, socializing with them, learning from them, and noting their names in her diary.[11] In response, few who met her, even casually, failed to acknowledge her warmth, her spirited conversation, her focused attention, and her remarkable memory and intelligence. "She always has time to pause and would make it appear by her humble attitude that you are bestowing the favor rather than she," one admirer observed.[12] Noting the enduring acuity of her mind, one effusive writer described her as "the personification of mental industry, frail in body, but inflexible in will. From a mind richly stored with treasures of knowledge she has been, and still is, able at any moment to draw forth gems of intelligence and experience."[13] Even her voice elicited compliments. Though she was tiny, wrote one admiring woman after attending a Relief Society meeting, "her voice reached out as if coming from delicate organ music. There was power in that small frame."[14] Moreover, she exuded a charisma that only deepened as she aged.

As had become customary, the board made plans for celebrating Emmeline's ninety-second birthday in 1920, once again on the actual date of her birth, February 29. The reception was to be small this time, the board decided, with a birthday cake for Emmeline and small wrapped pieces for the guests. About six hundred were expected. A thousand came. Travelers in the hotel asked to attend and meet "the distinguished Mrs. Wells of whom they had heard," and one entire family came from Uintah County, it was reported at the following board meeting. Ida Dusenberry felt "that Mrs. Wells is the only one woman who could draw so many people together" and spoke

10. The Cannon farm was located on Eighth West (Ninth West today) and Thirteenth South. Annie and John Q. were by this time living in the original George Q. Cannon home on the farm.

11. A bibliography of names mentioned in her diary numbers in the several hundreds.

12. Edith R. Lovesy, "A Tribute."

13. "Mrs. Emmeline B. Wells Celebrates Birthday as Guest of General Board," *Deseret Evening News*, February 29, 1916, 6.

14. Maybell Cazier Palmer, as quoted in Derr, Cannon, and Beecher, *Women of Covenant*, 199.

of her wonderful personality. Annie, once again a board member, noted that fifteen telegrams and hundreds of letters and cards, along with numerous floral arrangements, had been sent to her mother.[15] It was another ebullient response to Emmeline's long life of service. These public celebrations were validations of her years of work for women, and she did not shy away from the honor they represented.

When the party was over, she went back to her room "fatigued and lame from the fall" she had sustained just before the reception, but buoyed once again to have seen so many friends.[16] The newspapers were effusive in their praise. "In social services, literature, politics, her power has been outstanding in the West, and her acquaintanceship and influence have spread, literally, to the great nations of the world, and the ends of the earth," lauded the *Deseret Evening News*. Describing her as "delightfully eccentric," it also noted her "saving sense of humor." The *Salt Lake Tribune* described her "dainty dress of white brocaded satin, with a light wrap thrown around her frail body" and noted the bouquet of ninety-two carnations with a red rose in the center given to her by the First Presidency of the church. "You stand on the height of your eminence as a representative of all that is good and of eternal importance," the accompanying note said, "honored by all who meet you and crowned with a fullness of benisons from the Church and people to whom you belong with blessings and a glory which shall endure through the endless ages of eternity."[17]

Invigorated once again by the unsolicited words of appreciation, Emmeline was thrust back into family affairs when she learned in December of the death of Melvina's husband, William Woods, at age seventy-nine. Though she regretted his lack of interest in the church, Emmeline had known only his kindness and respect, and she in turn respected him, not only for his accomplishments but also for his love of her daughter. His death was prominently noted in both Idaho and Utah newspapers because of his distinguished service as a major in the Civil War, as an attorney in a number of prominent mining cases, and as a longtime district judge of Idaho. A funeral was held in his hometown of Wallace and another in Spokane, where he had spent many of his working years. Emmeline would not have been happy with either service, had she been able to attend, since the first was conducted by the Masons in Wallace and the other by the Elks Club in

15. Minutes of the General Board, March 4, 1920.

16. E. Wells, Diary, February 28, 1920.

17. See "Aunt Em Wells at Ninety Two" and "Big Reception for Aunt Em," *Deseret News*, February 29, 1920, 1; "Hundreds Greet 'Aunt Em' for Birthday," *Deseret Evening News*, March 1, 1920, 7; and "'Aunt Em' Observes Birthday, Attains Ninety-Second Year," *Salt Lake Tribune*, March 1, 1920, 24.

Spokane, after which Woods's body was cremated.[18] Mother and daughter never met thereafter. Melvina lived another twenty years, making her home in California, where both Verona and Daisie now lived.[19]

On a happier note for Emmeline, the year also marked the successful conclusion of the long struggle for woman suffrage. Though Utah women had enjoyed the use of the ballot continuously since 1896, woman suffrage was not then the law of the land. When the amendment granting the right to vote to all women in the country finally passed Congress and had been sent to the states for ratification, in 1920, the National American Woman Suffrage Association, in anticipation of its ratification, held a victory celebration in Chicago in February. The goal now met, this fifty-first convention would be its last. This was an occasion "to rejoice that their struggle was over, their aim achieved."[20] Donnette Kesler and Susa Gates represented the Relief Society at the gathering. Though invited, neither Emmeline nor Emily Richards attended the historic event, where they were each awarded a gold pin for being pioneers in the movement.[21]

When the Nineteenth Amendment was finally ratified later that year, forty-one years after Emmeline's official inauguration into the cause, she exclaimed, "I rejoice and am exceedingly glad that the battle is over and the women of our nation have at last received their enfranchisement." The Relief Society sent a letter of congratulations to Carrie Chapman Catt, the current—and last—president of NAWSA, probably composed by corresponding secretary Susa Young Gates: "Utah's hive of busy workers, some of whom have exercised their voting privileges for fifty years, join the song of victory which rises from every enfranchised woman in these United States of America today. As women wing their triumphant passage into every avenue of public and private endeavor may they bring back to their

18. "Judge Woods Is Dead after Long Illness," *Wallace (ID) Press Times*, November 11, 1920, 1; "Judge Woods Is at Final Rest," *Wallace (ID) Press Times*, November 13 1920, 8; "Taps Sound for Veteran and Jurist," *Wallace (ID) Press Times*, November 13, 1920; editorial, *Wallace (ID) Press Times*, November 13, 1920; "Prominent Former Utahn Dies in Idaho," *Deseret News*, November 11, 1920, sec. 2, p. 1; "Former Jurist of Utah Dies," *Salt Lake Tribune*, November 12, 1920, 11. The final sentence of the *Wallace (ID) Press Times* editorial notes that Judge Woods was "an honorable and upright man, and to that nothing can be added for it is a most precious legacy." His courtliness, gentlemanly qualities, and utter devotion to his wife were themes of the many eulogies.

19. "Mrs. Woods Dies on Coast," *Deseret News*, April 22, 1940, 9; "Native Utahn Dies at 89 in Coast City," *Salt Lake Tribune*, April 23, 1940, 17.

20. Donnette Smith Kesler, "Three Important Conventions."

21. Ibid. See also Susa Young Gates, "Suffrage Won by the Mothers of the United States."

home lives only the rich essence of a sex purified and glorified by the fruit of life which shares liberty and the pursuit of happiness with every male voter in the land." After Emmeline's name was added the phrase, "Utah's Queen Bee."[22]

The state of Utah was also ready to celebrate. On the appointed day, a parade of happy celebrants marched up State Street, stopping at the steps of the state capitol, where city and state officials waited, including Governor Simon Bamberger and former governor Heber M. Wells. Emily Richards and other veteran suffragists spoke of the long struggle to gain the vote, and members of the newly organized League of Women Voters urged the large gathering to value the precious privilege of citizenship. Emmeline Wells, the honored guest, was described as "the most impressive figure on the platform." She did not address the crowd but was praised as one who had worked and waited for this moment for a half century. "What those dim eyes had seen of history in the making, what those old ears had heard and what that clear brain had conceived and carried out only her close associates knew," Susa Gates observed. "She was the incarnate figure of tender, delicate, eternally determined womanhood, arrived and triumphant."[23] Indeed she was. She had truly tamed her inner demons sufficiently throughout her long life to reach the destiny that had been expected for her.

Emmeline continued to preside over an organization that was rapidly moving beyond her grasp. She began the year 1921 in reasonably good health and conducted the first two board meetings of the year, but in February and March, her attendance faltered. Altogether, she attended six of the weekly board meetings until the end of March that year. Only a luncheon was planned to celebrate her ninety-third birthday, but she opted for another reception. Held at the Hotel Utah, it again brought many well-wishers to greet the venerable president. Looking like "a fragile Dresden figure in her pale silks, white laces, and trailing flowers," according to one account, she was nevertheless "very much alive and enjoyed every moment of the afternoon's greetings, music, compliments, gifts of flowers as well as the telegrams and congratulations which poured in upon her."[24] Clarissa Williams declared it "one of the most remarkable receptions the board has ever given." Special guests were descendants of early church leaders as well as current leaders.[25] An editorial from the *Relief Society Magazine* caught the essence of what had been the focus of Emmeline's Relief Society stewardship.

22. Minutes of the General Board, August 19, 1920.
23. Susa Young Gates, "Utah."
24. "Birthday Reception for President Emmeline B. Wells," 235–36.
25. Minutes of the General Board, March 3, 1921.

"President Emmeline B. Wells has been extremely careful . . . to protect and carefully preserve the original genius and spirit of this great, and glorious society," it noted. "She has been willing always that improvements shall be made in non-essentials, glad to permit old truths to be dressed up in new phraseology, and old forms modified to meet changing conditions." But, the tribute continued, she has "constantly refused to permit changes which would disintegrate and finally, perhaps, destroy the institution itself, founded under the revelation of God, by the Prophet Joseph Smith." According to the editorial, "it is this particular service for which our gratitude should extend toward this wise leader and faithful officer."[26]

Each of these public birthday celebrations shored up Emmeline's sense of relevance. She would not be relegated to obsolescence, which age so often imposes and against which she constantly struggled. These events honored her position as general Relief Society president and validated her claim to that title. Not since Eliza R. Snow had a woman received such adulation in the church and, for Emmeline, well beyond the borders of Mormondom. She was a formidable female face in a sea of male leadership, and her community of Mormons and Gentiles alike channeled their appreciation of her service in the multiple honors they bestowed.

Emmeline had been steadfast in her pledge to advance the status of women and to gain respect for the women of her faith. "She has done more than any woman in the state to dispel prejudice and unite the varying elements of social and religious life in her native country," read one admiring life sketch.[27] These had been reassuring words to Emmeline, and they retained their currency to the end of her long life. She had presented Mormon women in their best lights and catalyzed a relationship reconnecting them with the female society from which they had long stood apart. In the remarkable celebrations of her birthday, Mormons coalesced around one of their own—a woman no less—whose name brought honor to them as well as to those whom she served outside their own circle. Each celebration in her honor was theirs to share. They did not withhold their pleasure in having a celebrity in their midst.

At age ninety-three, she was honored for her accomplishments of the past. The present called for vigorous visionary leadership that Emmeline could no longer muster. In the highly charged corporate system of the Relief Society in 1921, lack of such strong leadership was truly debilitating. Rumblings among board members were constant and pervasive. While many felt that a release "would kill her," others decried the lack of direction and

26. "Birthday of President Emmeline B. Wells."

27. *Biographical Record of Salt Lake City and Vicinity*, 377–79.

vigorous leadership that such an organization required. The Relief Society had begun to feel the ennui of an enervating plateau, which deterred innovation and forward movement in meeting the challenges of a worldwide membership. Against the women who would regret her release were those who were quietly agitating for it.

At the board meeting on March 23, the minutes noted that though "President Emmeline B. Wells was not well and was very feeble, she presided at this meeting. This was the last time she presided over a meeting of the General Board of the Relief Society." It was also the end of her residence at the Hotel Utah. After frequent stays at Annie's to recover from a series of ailments, she had permanently moved to the Cannon farm. A week after her last board meeting, Annie and Belle's daughter Dot packed up Emmeline's belongings and gave up the "little room 834 where," Annie wrote, her mother "has had so much comfort and pleasure receiving friends and distinguished people."[28]

Despite her disabling weakness, Emmeline was determined to attend the annual Relief Society conference scheduled a few days later on April 1, 1921. However, nothing could have fully prepared her for what occurred. Plans for a change of the Relief Society board had begun three years earlier when Heber J. Grant became president of the church. He and his counselors, with members of the Quorum of the Twelve Apostles, had discussed the possibility of reorganizing the Relief Society board, but no action was taken at that time.[29] Two years later, several Relief Society board members urged President Grant to release the ailing Emmeline. "I plead with them," President Grant wrote to a friend, "to give her one more year's trial, believing that in all probability she might pass away," so the year's trial was granted. He was very reluctant to impose this decision on Emmeline, to whom he was so closely tied. He had admired her work on behalf of the church over the years, and he was unsure of the effect a release from her position would have on her. But when the year was over, and she still lived, he explained that "it was one of the most disagreeable and painful tasks of my life to ask her to resign."[30]

On April 1, the first day of the conference that Emmeline reluctantly missed, eight board members were released, and the meeting consisted

28. A. W. Cannon, Diary, March 31, 1921. In 1919, among the distinguished visitors besides President Woodrow Wilson were the king of Belgium and other lesser members of royalty and European upper classes.

29. Family lore suggests that when Emmeline was approached by President Grant with this proposal at that time, her response was that she would certainly die if he did so, a fair-enough reason for him to delay.

30. Heber J. Grant, letter to Isaac K. Russell, February 17, 1922, Heber J. Grant Papers.

mainly of their farewell messages. Afterward, Annie gave Emmeline's message of love to the sisters and returned home with a heavy heart.[31] It is not clear whether Annie knew that her mother was to be released as well, but she was aware that any proposed change of the board without her mother's approval or knowledge would be upsetting to her. "I dread very much the effect on her when she learns of the changes to be made," Annie confided to her diary.[32] That Emmeline had not been advised well before action was taken is baffling, since her release was now at hand.

The next morning, prior to the opening of the second day of the Relief Society conference scheduled for that afternoon, President Grant and his counselor Anthony W. Ivins called on Annie and Emmeline in the Cannon home. President Grant explained his intention to release Emmeline that afternoon and appoint her counselor Clarissa Williams in her place. "We had a very painful interview," Annie reported. While Annie admitted to being quite hysterical at the news, her mother remained "calm but courageous." But that calm exterior hid the humiliation and even betrayal that she was feeling. Joseph Smith, she knew by heart, and explained to President Grant, had indicated that the officers of the Relief Society were "to preside as long as they shall continue to fill the office with dignity &C. like the First presidency of the Church."[33] Except for Emma Smith, all of the general Relief Society presidents had served until their deaths, despite long illnesses beforehand, just as general church leaders did. Emmeline may well have felt that in some way she had failed to meet this final test of worthiness. She was utterly crushed. With her own death clearly not far off, it seemed unnecessarily insensitive—both to her and to those who loved her—to rob her of this final dignity, and with only hours' notice. It had been a tense and uncomfortable meeting, leaving all of the participants shaken and upset.

In consideration of the historical precedents Emmeline recited when she was released, President Grant felt obliged to explain at the conference that "there is not a single word of condemnation or criticism from any of the authorities on the labors that 'Aunt Em' has performed as the President of this Society." In noting her long service to the organization, he wanted all to

31. A.W. Cannon, Diary, April 1, 1921. The women were Julina Smith, Romania Penrose, Sarah J. Cannon, Julia Farnsworth, Rebecca Nibley, Lizzie Wilcox, Emily Richards, and Donnette Kesler. Some had asked to be released.

32. Ibid., March 31, 1921. At the conclusion of the first day of the conference, President Grant consulted with Clarissa Williams for two hours regarding the release of all of the board members and reconstituting it after a new presidency assumed office. Grant, Diary, April 1, 1921, Grant Papers.

33. Record of the Organization and Proceedings of the Female Relief Society of Nauvoo, March 17, 1842, LDS Church History Library, Salt Lake City.

know that "she has been ever faithful, ever true."[34] But words could not assuage the pain or undo this untoward break in precedent. The mortification was too great. Emmeline could not be reconciled. She could find no silver lining in this cloud, no purpose in this unforeseen blow. Within days of the interview, she retreated to her room at Annie's, unable to withhold the emotions that overcame her at this final heartbreak. She wept continuously, tears that had been withheld over a lifetime of disappointment and sorrow, spilling over her worn cheeks. Even the sympathy and solicitations of her many visitors could not revive her spirit as in the past. "I can never in all the world think this change is right nor feel other than hurt beyond words for the anguish of my darling mother," Annie lamented.[35] This last shock no doubt hastened the inevitable. As her grieving became deeper, Emmeline grew weaker, and Annie sorrowfully dismantled Emmeline's office, in the Bishop's Building, retrieving all of her papers and personal effects. "It is like putting away things after one has died," she wrote.[36]

When learning the news, Emmeline's friends visited Emmeline at the Cannon farm, where Emmeline rallied enough to greet them. Members of the Siegel, Bamberger, and Rosenbaum families proved their loyalty to the last. Clarissa Williams also came by and spent an hour with Emmeline. "Mother was very composed while she was here," Annie observed, "and talked of different things but kept clear of relief society subjects." When alone, Emmeline wept helplessly. When Annie asked her why she cried, she answered with her usual forthrightness, "I should think I would cry when they have taken away my position."[37]

President Grant was unprepared for the agitated response he received when announcing Emmeline's release to Annie and her mother. Unnerved, he made no attempt to visit them again, expecting only more of Annie's recriminations. Annie finally wrote to him on April 17, asking him why he had not visited and explaining how much her mother wanted to see him. After reminding him of the great service Emmeline had rendered the church throughout her long life, Annie chided him. "Surely," she wrote, "as our great leader, you would at least give her the consideration of your thoughts, unless you have wonderfully changed since a few weeks ago." She admitted that "it would certainly give me some satisfaction to have her feel a little more reconciled to your recent action, if that were possible, before she meets her dear ones on the other side."[38] Even faced with this

34. "General Conference of Relief Society," 338–39.

35. A. W. Cannon, Diary, April 5, 1921.

36. Ibid., April 5, 1921.

37. Ibid., April 17, 19, 1921.

38. A. W. Cannon, letter to Heber J. Grant, April 17, 1921, Grant Papers.

direct plea, President Grant could not bring himself to answer for another week. Then he confessed that he had mentally outlined at least ten letters to Annie, explaining that he would gladly have visited Emmeline and given her a blessing "had I thought this could have been done without a repetition of the painful scene at your home the day Brother Ivins and I called." He had hoped that Annie and her mother might have been reconciled to the release, he wrote, but he did not see evidence in her letter that this was the case and doubted that "any words of mine, judging from our former visit, would have the least impression on your mind." He concluded by expressing his hope that Annie and Belle "might become converted to the wisdom of the changes made in the Relief Society, and after this happened then I felt that with the blessings of the Lord and your aid that I could reconcile [your mother]."[39]

A month later, he explained to his daughter Frances, then studying in the East, another reason for her release besides Emmeline's infirmities. He first recounted the sorrow he felt in releasing her and her emotional reaction. "I am sure," he added, "had we known that our dearly beloved Aunt Em was going to pass away so soon we would have perhaps let the matter go over." Then he noted what became a firm policy in the church thereafter. Still, he argued, "I am half inclined to think that it was the best thing that could have happened, and that it has destroyed the precedent that has existed in the Church, namely that the Presidents of the Relief Society stay president until their death no matter how aged she was or how incapable she was of performing the duties devolving upon her."[40] If there had been any question before, it was now clear that the Relief Society was not in the same category as the First Presidency and Quorum of the Twelve Apostles, and its officers served at the pleasure of the brethren. Meanwhile, in their distress over Emmeline's release, Annie and several Wells family members surmised that the convergence of several circumstances and the "fine hand" of a particular woman, whose identity was not revealed, had actually maneuvered the release. Though unable to do anything to change matters, Annie was left to declare, "Wo[e] to them who have done this thing."[41] It is ironic that four years earlier, President Grant

39. H. Grant, letter to A. W. Cannon, April 25, 1921, ibid.

40. H. Grant, letter to Frances Grant, May 18, 1921, ibid. Presumably, this policy was extended at the time to include other auxiliary presidents. Clarissa Williams, however, resigned from her position after seven years as president, but her successors were subject to the new policy.

41. A. W. Cannon, Diary, May 4, 1921. As with the loss of the *Woman's Exponent*, it seemed to the family that someone had agitated for a change in Relief Society leadership.

had blessed Emmeline with the promise that she would "live to fulfill the desires of my heart," and now he was the instrument for cutting short that promise.[42]

Emmeline continued to decline, and toward the end she slipped in and out of consciousness. Annie gave her mother a beautiful white handkerchief, a simple gift, which evoked the last words Emmeline ever spoke to her daughter, "Oh you are too good."[43] Later that day, Susa Gates visited and assured Emmeline that "everybody loves you." Again, the ever-candid Emmeline replied, "I hope they do if they dont I cant help it."[44] To assist with her mother's care, Belle had moved in with Annie, and they took turns sitting by their mother at night. By April 22, it was obvious that Emmeline was near death, "and we are all heart broken," Annie wrote. "Dear little soul to die so sorrowful when all on earth she wanted was to give happiness."[45] On the twenty-fourth, the blessings given to her that day all dedicated her to the Lord, a final acknowledgment that death was imminent. Annie notified Melvina of her mother's condition, but Melvina's health and recent loss of Will kept her at home.

Belle sat with her mother throughout the night of Sunday, the twenty-fourth of April, and on the beautiful spring morning that followed, she aroused Annie and John Q. to inform them that Emmeline had "passed into the great beyond without a struggle." "Beautiful tender, little mother," Annie wrote, "the world will never be the same to me again."[46]

Following a long Relief Society tradition, the services of an undertaker were not used. Belle and Annie assisted in washing and preparing the body, while Julina Smith, Emmeline's counselor, and Rebecca Nibley, a board member, both released with Emmeline, dressed her in her temple clothes. On April 28, the casket was placed in the parlor of Annie's home, surrounded by a garden of floral offerings from friends near and far. In the next few days, hundreds of people visited to take their final view of Emmeline, and letters and messages poured into the home.[47]

On the day of the funeral, April 29, the officers and members of the Relief Society board met at the Cannon home and with the family proceeded in a long parade of automobiles to the tabernacle where Emmeline's body lay in state from 12:00 to 2:00 PM. On Bishop Nibley's instructions

42. E. Wells, Diary, January 4, 1917.
43. A. W. Cannon, Diary, April 20, 1921.
44. Ibid., April 15, 1921.
45. Ibid., April 20, 1921.
46. Ibid., April 25, 1921.
47. Ibid., April 28, 1921.

and with the concurrence of hundreds of church workers, the flags on all church buildings, including the Hotel Utah, had flown at half-mast since her death.[48] Thousands walked past the casket, and six thousand mourners filled the tabernacle for the services, which were under the direction of Junius Wells and John Q. Cannon, while President Grant presided. The pulpit and railings throughout the building were decorated in white, forming a background for the exquisite floral offerings that filled the hall. The casket itself was overlaid with roses, lilies, carnations, and ferns. An outstanding floral tribute was a wreath of wheat and roses with letters in violets, representing the Relief Society's official emblem.[49]

Besides the flowers, Emmeline would have loved the music, provided by a Relief Society choir at the beginning and end of the service and the vocal and violin solos performed by dear friends. A special male quartet sang at both the funeral and the interment. Clarissa Williams, the first to speak, briefly rehearsed the many areas in which Emmeline attempted to better the lives of women and carry the message of the Relief Society, noting at the end that one of Emmeline's unfulfilled wishes was to fly in an airplane. Both of her doctors spoke at the service. Bishop Nibley declared Aunt Em to be "one of the finest products of 'Mormonism'" and believed that "she had the mental force which caused her to be a pillar of strength perhaps more than has been given to any other woman of her day." Charles W. Penrose of the First Presidency claimed her to be "bright, keen, quick, and capable to understand the truth" and believed that "her name would be remembered, forever." Orson F. Whitney honored her as a mother to him and noted that she was not only a poet but an executive and also a saint. President Heber J. Grant, who had known Emmeline since his youth, commented on the significance of the large congregation, which was one of the largest he had ever witnessed at a funeral in the tabernacle on a day other than Sunday. "No other woman in the Church," he said, "has had so many prominent people call on her as our dear departed sister," and he noted that she could express herself forcefully by both tongue and pen but was most impressed by "her loving desire to help others," which, he felt, was "above all others of her characteristics," a feature noted by all of the speakers.

48. "Flags on Church Edifices at Half Mast in Honor of Mrs. Emmeline B. Wells," *Deseret News*, April 25, 1921, 2.

49. The elaborate funeral plans were announced in the Minutes of the General Board for April 27, 1921, while a review of the funeral service was included in the April 29, 1921, minutes. See also "Plans Complete for Funeral Rites for Mrs. Wells," *Deseret News*, April 27, 1921, 1; and "Program Announced for Funeral Services for Mrs. Emmeline B. Wells," *Deseret Evening News*, April 28, 1921, 2.

Following the services, a large cortege proceeded to the city cemetery. Gathered several rows deep around the grave site were members of her board, the pallbearers, her family, the general authorities of the church, officers and members of the auxiliary organizations, and friends. After one last musical number, Rulon S. Wells dedicated the grave, encircled by a wide array of floral tributes.[50] Emmeline was buried next to Daniel and near the graves of Emmie and Louie.[51] Only the participation of Orson F. Whitney, now an apostle, and the presence of Belle and her family gave evidence that she was also a Whitney.

Newspaper accounts relating her life and accomplishments were long and effusive in their praise. The *Deseret Evening News* noted that she was "known, admired and beloved to a degree and with a universality that has fallen to the lot of few of her sex in this or any other country or time." It characterized her as being as "unyielding as the granite of her native New England in her devotion to that which she considered her duty."[52] "Life's book of experience was a 'well-thumbed' one to 'Aunt Em,'" the *Salt Lake Tribune* noted.[53]

Emmeline's mental acumen and association with people of the world were pervasive themes. "Her remarkable recollection of important events connected with the early history of the Church and of the state, and her intellectual attainments and charming personality," the *Deseret News* explained, "ever made the little woman a personage of much interest to prominent persons from all parts of the world." Her office was "the Mecca of distinguished visitors, statesmen, soldiers, authors, publicists, writers, to say nothing of thousands of admiring friends."[54] Public gatherings of

50. These details are in the Minutes of the General Board, April 27, 29, 1921. The June issue of the *Relief Society Magazine* was given over to her life and death and service to the organization. Her death was also noted in the *New York Times*. See "Mrs. Wells, Suffragist, Dies at 93," April 27, 1921, 17. The notice identified her as "Utah's grand old lady."

51. Accounts of the funeral and burial services were printed in all the local newspapers and publications. For a few of them, see "Glowing Tribute Paid at Bier of Beloved Woman," *Deseret News*, April 30, 1921, 10; "Final Respects Paid Mrs. Wells," *Salt Lake Tribune*, April 30, 1921, 23; "Funeral Services of President Emmeline B. Wells"; "Funeral of 'Aunt Em'"; and "Notice." The choice of her burial site raises interesting questions, since Newel K. Whitney, buried in the Kimball-Whitney private cemetery, was her husband for eternity. How Belle and Mell perceived the choice of burial in the Wells plot is unknown.

52. "Mrs. Emmeline B. Wells," *Deseret Evening News*, April 25, 1921, 4.

53. "Early Settler of the State Dead," *Salt Lake Tribune*, April 26, 1921, 20.

54. "Life of Emmeline B. Wells Comes Peacefully to Close," *Deseret News*, April 25, 1921, 1, 2.

importance were never complete without her presence, it concluded. The *Young Woman's Journal* opined, "No 'Mormon' woman has been more widely known both within and without the Church and probably no woman has been entrusted with more responsible commissions by the leaders of the Church," certainly an unusual relationship for most Mormon women.[55] Junius F. Wells, writing an editorial tribute for the *Millennial Star*, gave an apt summary: "She will be remembered by many travelers and people of distinction, whom she met and impressed with the charm of her intellectual personality and the sweet influences of her vivacious conversation, rich in reminiscence of people, places, and incidents of interest concerning the Church, of which she became the most widely known woman representative in the world."[56]

The effusiveness of these tributes was not mere hyperbole. No other Mormon woman of the nineteenth and early twentieth centuries quite achieved the notoriety, high regard, respect, and genuine love of such a wide range of admirers as did Emmeline Wells. Nor was anyone feted quite so much over such a long period of her life. She did not experience the anonymity of old age.

When the eulogies ended, the realities of dismantling Emmeline's material life took over. In Melvina's absence, Annie and Belle shared the task. Their cooperation in attending to their mother's last days slowly slipped away, however, as they tried to determine what Emmeline's unstated wishes might have been. Physically exhausted, emotionally depleted, and without the guidance of a will, the two sisters descended into a strained and tense relationship that had tugged at them for years. Promises were the only evidence of Emmeline's desire for the distribution of her personal effects, and they were few and overlapping. Determining the disposition of her Waterloo home was a major cause of tension. Annie asserted it was given to her, but both Belle and Melvina objected, and so when the home was sold, Annie distributed shares of the assets to her sisters. These and other disputes left the sisters inescapably at odds with each other.

But it was Emmeline's papers that required the most time and negotiation in deciding how to sort them and what to preserve or destroy. Emmeline was a keeper, and her two daughters worked long hours for many days going through multiple boxes of her letters, writings, manuscripts, and other papers. Somehow they managed to finish the daunting task together, but not without friction or unfortunate irreversible decisions. They did not have a historian's eye to help them recognize the tremendous value

55. "President Emmeline B. Wells."

56. Junius F. Wells, "Funeral of 'Aunt Em.'"

of the papers of a chronicler like Emmeline. They evidently selected what they each wanted from the store of writings before them or what they felt had value for the family, perhaps reserving some for the historian's office or Relief Society records. Then they burned the rest. It was a precipitous and irreparable error. Originals of her literary works, hundreds of letters, *Exponent* records and correspondence, organizational records, and the collection of miscellany that accrues over time—all were sifted through and most of it evidently destroyed. Decisions were made in the midst of intense emotional stress that calmer minds might have governed. Only a small portion of the great treasury of her handwritten writings was left. The diaries remained with Annie.

The rift between Emmeline's daughters left scars, and there were few contacts with one another thereafter.[57] Annie followed her mother into public life, becoming an active Republican worker, member of the state legislature, and a twenty-year member of the Relief Society General Board. Ironically, within two weeks of her mother's death, she was writing to "my dear brother Heber" about pending and future Relief Society affairs, clearly putting past affronts behind her.[58] Belle, who had moved several times, eventually bought a home in the Avenues and continued her work in the temple until she moved to Newport, Kentucky, in 1930 to live with her daughter Lucile and her son Eugene and his family. In 1941, ninety-three-year-old Belle died and was buried in Kentucky. Mell died in California in 1940. There was little contact between the sisters after Emmeline's death. Had Emmeline known of the schism between her three daughters over something as ephemeral as her material effects, this would surely have been for her "the most unkindest cut" of all.[59]

Though sorrow can't be quantified or compared, Emmeline was a woman of deep, intense, and enduring sorrow. All the plaudits, honors, and opportunities that came to her never had the strength to abrogate the melancholy that always lay just beneath the surface. She leaned heavily on her Mormon faith and believed deeply in the worth and equality of women. The framework of her life rested on three foundational points: her sense of personal destiny, the guiding hand of Providence, and her desire to win the race of life, despite its hurdles.

57. This and previous comments about the growing apart of the sisters during this emotional time are from Annie Wells Cannon's diary, May through December 1921. The tension between them began even before their mother's death. See, for example, A. W. Cannon, Diary, April 6, May 2, 1919, and June 4, 1921.

58. A. W. Cannon, letter to Grant, May 6, 1921, Grant Papers. Annie was at that time a member of the Relief Society board.

59. Shakespeare, "Julius Caesar," act 3, scene 2.

She had been a strong and forceful link, connecting the present with the past and the women of her church with their American sisters. Outreach, inclusion, and promotion of women were her primary objectives, and she stepped over religious, economic, and social barriers time and again to create bonds of respect, understanding, and friendship. Her honors came early and multiplied with each passing year. All were honestly earned. The last one came to her posthumously on the centenary of her birth, February 29, 1928.

In late 1927, Dr. Jane Skolfield and representatives from women's groups throughout the state made plans to celebrate the hundredth anniversary of Emmeline's birth the following year. "The plan was to reach all the women of the state," the committee explained, "regardless of position in life, religion or any other condition." Many stories emerged of Emmeline's personal though unheralded acts of service and kindness to individual women as well as organizations, and response to the celebration was positive and immediate. The committee commissioned Utah sculptor Cyrus Dallin to sculpt a bust of Emmeline, and state officials agreed to place it in the rotunda of the state capitol.[60] The ceremony took place in the capitol rotunda, attended by Governor George H. Dern and other state officials. Mrs. C. W. Maw, president of the State Federation of Women's Clubs, presided, and President Heber J. Grant offered the invocation. The national flag stood near the veiled sculpture, and the state flag was draped behind the speaker's platform. Emmeline's familiar paisley shawl adorned the piano. The curtains that veiled the statue were the same silk portieres made by Utah women for the Woman's Building at the Chicago World's Fair in 1893.

Dr. Skolfield made the presentation of the statue and verbally painted Emmeline as a "frail, slight, almost ethereal figure in soft silks and pastel shades, threading her way among friends with all the grace and dignity of a queen." The honor of unveiling the artistic rendering was given to Emmeline's namesake granddaughter, Emmeline Cannon Martineau. When in full view, the marble likeness evoked "an intense and breathless moment."[61] In a most felicitous tribute, the citation inscribed across the pedestal on which her marble likeness rested read, "A Fine Soul Who Served Us."

When all expenses for the memorial were finally paid, there was a surplus of $885. The committee designated it as a student loan in Emmeline's name to be established at the University of Utah for the benefit of women desiring

60. "Dr. Emmeline B. Wells Memorial."

61. Ibid. As usual, the newspapers made much of the occasion. See "Noted Woman's Statue Ready for Unveiling," *Salt Lake Tribune*, February 29, 1928, 22; "'Aunt Em' Statue Unveiled during Capitol Program," *Deseret News*, February 29, 1928, 1; "Statue of Noted Woman Unveiled at State Capitol," *Salt Lake Tribune*, March 1, 1928, 20; and "State Accepts 'Aunt Em' Gift," *Deseret News*, March 1, 1928, 8.

to complete their studies. Making it an even $1,000, Ernest Bamberger wrote a check in behalf of his friend Emmeline.[62]

The Memorial Committee agreed that three goals had been attained in this successful commemoration. The members recognized that the statue was the first to be placed in "Utah's pantheon" of achieving individuals, that it was in honor of a woman, and that they had been responsible for this amazing accomplishment.[63] The sculptor, Cyrus Dallin, requested that the plaster cast of the Wells statue be given to the Art Association of Springville, Utah, his home, to which the board readily assented. Finally, they were delighted to have had the means to establish the Emmeline B. Wells Memorial Fund at the University of Utah, all lasting mementos of the woman they deemed to honor.[64]

Emmeline once characterized herself as "the last leaf on the tree," having outlived most of her contemporaries. She was one of the few first-generation suffragists to see victory crown their effort, to witness the entry of women into colleges and professions so long closed to them, and to be part of a worldwide consortium united in addressing issues of social welfare and women's advancement. Within the religion she had embraced, she prized her acquaintance with its founding prophet and her association with a generation of stalwarts who gave so much of themselves to establish it.

Utah had been Emmeline's home for seventy-seven years, but the engrafted westerner could never quite free herself from her New England beginnings. "How brightly 'soever the present may seem," she poetically mused, "The scenes of one's childhood will linger alway."[65] Her western experience bred strength, initiative, perseverance, and self-reliance while also giving her the opportunity to use all her faculties in influencing epochal

62. Report of the Emmeline B. Wells Memorial Committee, LDS Church History Library, Salt Lake City. Ernest Bamberger's wife was a member of the executive committee, as were Rachel Siegel, Emily Richards, Amy Brown Lyman, Mary Kelly Pye, and Mrs. E. O. Howard, with Dr. Jane Skolfield as chair. That year, the Relief Society General Board announced a similar fund to be established at Brigham Young University in Emmeline's name to assist in the education of women students. It was known as the Emmeline B. Wells Relief Society Memorial Loan Fund. See Amy Brown Lyman, Relief Society Memorial and Honor Funds for General Presidents, September 10, 1943, LDS Church History Library, Salt Lake City; "An Emmeline B. Wells Memorial Fund Is Started"; and "Emmeline B. Wells' Memorial Fund."

63. It remained the only one of a woman until 1997, when a full-length statue of Martha Hughes Cannon, the country's first woman state senator, was placed in a nearby niche in the rotunda. Both statues have since been removed from the rotunda and are located elsewhere in the capitol.

64. Report of the Emmeline B. Wells Memorial Committee.

65. Emmeline B. Wells, "Memory's Dream," in her *Musings and Memories*, 20.

events. But New England gave birth to the sensitive, soulful, and meditative lover of nature, and the impressionable years during which it was her home bound her to a time and place that also shaped the woman she became. Those early scenes of childhood created the "romantic fantasies" in which so much of her life was expressed, but it was the tangible realities of that life that brought her the well-deserved eulogies. The child of destiny had indeed become a woman of achievement. Her largely female world had been her greatest support. But she set herself apart from the expectations of that world by her own inimitable individuality, the strength of her drive to achieve something of importance, the power of her personality, and her unyielding hold on the principles that guided her life.

With all the honors, tributes, eulogies, and life sketches that continued long after her death, Emmeline best penned her own epitaph: "I have not followed anyone else," she declared, "but I hope I have stayed within the radius of the true light."[66]

66. Emmeline B. Wells, letter to Susa Young Gates, September 1, 1909, Gates Papers.

APPENDIX

The Family of Emmeline B. Wells

Grandparents
Elisha Woodward
Born November 2, 1754, Taunton, Bristol, Massachusetts
Died May 2, 1842, Petersham, Worcester, Massachusetts

Lucy Manson Woodward
Born 1762, Taunton, Bristol, Massachusetts
Died June 9, 1791, Petersham, Worcester, Massachusetts

John Hare (Hair, Haire) Jr.
Born 1766, Brookfield, Massachusetts
Died ?

Sarah Morgan Hair
Born 1773, Brookfield, Massachusetts
Died ?

Parents
David Woodward
Born October 22, 1781, Petersham, Worcester, Massachusetts
Died November 1832, Petersham, Worcester, Massachusetts

Deiadama (Diadama) Hare
Born December 26, 1794 or 1795, Worcester, Massachusetts
Died October 1846, Iowa

Siblings
Adaline Emily Woodward (1816–29)
Lucy Minerva Woodward Granger Hewlings (1817–1901)
Pallas Eliza Woodward Clark (1818–1903)
Manson Jessie Woodward (1821–97)
James Woodward (1824–81)
Cordelia Maria Woodward Hinckley Fuller Holden (1824–1914)
Adeline Maria Woodward Earl (1829–1919)
Ellen Celeste Woodward Fuller (1831–1915)
Hiram Eugene Woodward Clark (1835–1923)

Husbands

James Harvey Harris
Born December 24, 1827, Wendell, Franklin, Massachusetts
Married Emeline Blanche Woodward, July 29, 1843, Vernon, Vermont
Abandoned Emmeline, November 1844
Died July 29, 1859, Calcutta (or Bombay), East India

Newel Kimball Whitney
Born February 5, 1795, Marlborough, Wyndham, Vermont
Married Emeline Blanche Woodward Harris, February 14, 1845, Nauvoo, Illinois
Died September 23, 1850, Salt Lake City

Daniel Hanmer Wells
Born October 27, 1814, Trenton, Oneida, New York
Married Emeline Blanche Woodward Harris Whitney, October 10, 1852, Salt Lake City
Died March 24, 1891, Salt Lake City

Sister-Wives

Elizabeth Ann Smith Whitney (1800–1882)
Olive Marie Bishop Whitney (1807–74)
Anne Houston Whitney (1821–48)
Louisa Free Wells (1824–86)
Elizabeth Mahala Moore [More] Whitney (1826–?)
Elizabeth Almira Pond Whitney (Bainbridge, Lewis) (1827–99)
Abigail Augusta Pond Whitney (1828–46)
Henrietta Keys Whitney (Hales) (1828–1901)
Lydia Ann Alley Wells (1829–1909)
Hannah Corilla Free Wells (1829–1913)
Susan Hannah Alley Wells (1830–1924)
Martha Givens Harris Wells (1832–1908)

Children

Eugene Henri Harris (1844–44)
Isabel Modalena "Belle" Whitney (Sears) (1848–1941)
Melvina Caroline Blanche "Mell" Whitney (Dunford, Woods) (1850–1940)
Emmeline Whitney "Emmie" Wells (1853–78)
Elizabeth Ann "Annie" Wells (Cannon) (1859–1942)
Louisa Martha "Louie" Wells (Cannon) (1862–87)

Grandchildren

Isabel Whitney and Septimus Sears

Sidney Whitney Sears (1870–70)
Herbert Whitney Sears (1871–72)
Seraph Isabel Sears (Buchholz) (1872–96)
Septimus Whitney Sears (1874–1922)
Laura O. Lucile Sears (1876–1949)
Emma W. Sears (Roberts) (1878–99)
Eugene S. Sears (1882–1950)

Edward Benton (Brenton) Sears (1885–?)

Melvina Whitney and William Dunford

Daisie Dean Dunford Allen (1868–1950)
Verona May Dunford Hillard Betts (1869–1942)
Leslie Alma Dunford (1872–82)

Melvina Whitney Dunford and William Wells Woods

Winnifred Isabelle Woods (1875–79)
William Percival Woods (1878–87)

Elizabeth Ann Wells and John Q. Cannon

George Quayle Cannon (1881–1967)
Louise Blanche Cannon Andrew (1884–1967)
Margaret Cannon Clayton (1886–1977)
Daniel Hoagland Cannon (1889–1954)
Eleanor Addy Cannon (1891–92)
Emmeline Cannon Martineau (1893–1972)
Cavendish Wells Cannon (1895–1962)
Katherine Cannon McKay (1897–1947)
Abraham Hoagland Cannon (1899–1992)
David Woodward Cannon (1899–1973)
John Quayle Cannon Jr. (1901–80)
Theodore Lincoln (1904–66)

Bibliography

Manuscripts and Archival Sources

Aiken, Samuel R. Papers. LDS Church History Library, Salt Lake City.

Beaver County Woman Suffrage Association. Papers. L. Tom Perry Special Collections, Harold B. Lee Library, Brigham Young University, Provo, UT.

A Book of Records Containing the Proceedings of the Female Relief Society of Nauvoo. LDS Church History Library, Salt Lake City.

Brown, Zina Card. Papers. LDS Church History Library, Salt Lake City.

Cannon, Abraham H. Diary, 1889–1895. L. Tom Perry Special Collections, Harold B. Lee Library, Brigham Young University, Provo, UT.

Cannon, Angus M. Collection. LDS Church History Library, Salt Lake City.

———. Diary. L. Tom Perry Special Collections, Harold B. Lee Library, Brigham Young University, Provo, UT.

Cannon, Annie Wells. Diary, 1877–1942. L. Tom Perry Special Collections, Harold B. Lee Library, Brigham Young University, Provo, UT.

Cannon, George Q. Letterbook. LDS Church History Library, Salt Lake City.

Cannon, John Q. Diary, 1881. John Quayle Cannon Collection, L. Tom Perry Special Collections, Harold B. Lee Library, Brigham Young University, Provo, UT.

Canon, L., Diary. In author's possession.

Card, Zina Young Williams. Collection. L. Tom Perry Special Collections, Harold B. Lee Library, Brigham Young University, Provo, UT.

Church Board of Education Minute Book, 1903–18. LDS Church History Library, Salt Lake City.

Co-operative Retrenchment Society. Minutes of Meetings. LDS Church History Library, Salt Lake City.

Crosby, Jonathan and Caroline. Papers. Utah State Historical Society, Salt Lake City.

Daughters of Utah Pioneers History Department. Salt Lake City.

Davis, Daniel. Diary, 1856–92. Holograph, LDS Church History Library, Salt Lake City.

DuFresne, Elizabeth J. Diary. Matthew and Claire Noall Collection. Special Collections, J. Willard Marriott Library, University of Utah, Salt Lake City.

Dusenberry, Ida Smoot. Papers. L. Tom Perry Special Collections, Harold B. Lee Library, Brigham Young University, Provo, UT.

Eastern States Mission History, 1830–1870. Electronic Records. LDS Church History Library, Salt Lake City.

Evans, Priscillia Livingston, Files. LDS Church History Library, Salt Lake City.

Evans, Priscilla Merriman. Autobiography, ca. 1914. LDS Church History Library, Salt Lake City.

——. Files. LDS Church History Library, Salt Lake City.

Fox, Ruth May. Diary, 1894–1932. Photocopy of typescript. Special Collections, J. Willard Marriott Library, University of Utah, Salt Lake City.

——. "My Story," ca. 1953. Special Collections, J. Willard Marriott Library, University of Utah, Salt Lake City.

Franklin County Registry of Deeds. Franklin County Court House, Greenfield, MA.

Freeze, Lillie Tuckett. Papers. LDS Church History Library, Salt Lake City.

Gates, Susa Young. Diary, 1915–1925. LDS Church History Library, Salt Lake City.

——. Papers, 1870–1933. LDS Church History Library, Salt Lake City.

Grant, Heber J. Papers. LDS Church History Library, Salt Lake City.

Gunnison Ward, Gunnison Stake. Gunnison Ward Relief Society Minutes and Records, 1872–1949. LDS Church History Library, Salt Lake City.

Gunnison Ward Relief Society, Gunnison Stake. Minutes. Vol. 1, 1872–77. LDS Church History Library, Salt Lake City.

Hale, Alma Helaman. Diaries, 1889–1909. Holographs. LDS Church History Library, Salt Lake City.

Hovey, Ross. Hovey Family History, ca. 1933. LDS Church History Library, Salt Lake City.

Illinois Public Domain Land Tract Sales http://www.cyberdriveillinois.com /departments /archives/databases/data_lan.html

Journal History of the Church of Jesus Christ of Latterday Saints (chronological scrapbook of typed entries and newspaper clippings, 1830–present). LDS Church History Library, Salt Lake City.

Kimball, Vilate. Papers. LDS Church History Library, Salt Lake City.

Life History of Nancy Naomi Alexander Tracy Written by Herself. L. Tom Perry Special Collections, Harold B. Lee Library, Brigham Young University, Provo, UT.

Lyman, Amy Brown. Papers. L. Tom Perry Special Collections, Harold B. Lee Library, Brigham Young University, Provo, UT.

——. Relief Society Memorial and Honor Funds for General Presidents. LDS Church History Library, Salt Lake City.

Maughan, Peter Weston. Family Association Collection. LDS Church History Library, Salt Lake City.

Mayer, George. Journal, 1805–96. Holograph. LDS Church History Library, Salt Lake City.

Memoirs of Romania B. Pratt, M.D., typescript copy. LDS Church History Library, Salt Lake City.

Minutes for Relief Society Conference, April 5, 1895. In "National Woman's Relief Society Board Record." Vol. 1 (Corporate Board Meeting Minutes). LDS Church History Library, Salt Lake City.

Minutes of the Eighth Meeting of the Fourteenth Ward Relief Society, February 16, 1869. In "A Book of Records Containing Minutes of the Meetings and Proceedings of the Quorum of Teachers of the Female Relief Society in the 14th Ward." LDS Church History Library, Salt Lake City.

Minutes of the General Board of the Relief Society. LDS Church History Library, Salt Lake City.

Minutes of the Nauvoo Relief Society. LDS Church History Library, Salt Lake City.

Mountain Meadows Massacre Research File. LDS Church History Library, Salt Lake City.

National Woman's Relief Society Record. LDS Church History Library, Salt Lake City.

Nauvoo Temple Endowment Register, 1845–46. Typescript copy. LDS Church History Library, Salt Lake City.

New Salem Vital Records up to 1850. LDS Church History Library, Salt Lake City.

Nuttall, L. John. Diary, 1876–89. Typescript copy. LDS Church History Library, Salt Lake City.

Official Report of the General Conference of the Church of Jesus Christ of Latter-day Saints (1898–2013), April 4, 1913. LDS Church History Library, Salt Lake City.

Pearce, Jean Rio Griffiths Baker. Journal, January 1851–March 1852 and September 1869–May 1880. Typescript. LDS Church History Library, Salt Lake City.

Record of the Organization and Proceedings of the Female Relief Society of Nauvoo. LDS Church History Library, Salt Lake City.

Relief Society Executive Papers. LDS Church History Library, Salt Lake City.

Relief Society Record and Minutes, Thirteenth Ward, Ensign Stake, 1849–1908. LDS Church History Library, Salt Lake City.

Rich, Sarah De Armon Pea. Reminiscences, 1885–93. Typescript copy. LDS Church History Library, Salt Lake City.

Richards, Franklin D. Diary. LDS Church History Library, Salt Lake City.

———. Journals, 1844–99. LDS Church History Library, Salt Lake City.

Roberts, B. H. Papers. Special Collections, J. Willard Marriott Library, University of Utah, Salt Lake City.

Sessions, Patty. Diary, 1846–88. LDS Church History Library, Salt Lake City. Published diaries are printed in *Mormon Midwife: The 1846–1888 Diaries of Patty Bartlett Sessions*, edited by Donna Toland Smart. Logan: Utah State University Press, 1997.

Smith, George Albert. Journal, September 27 to October 25, 1857. Journal History of the Church, October 25, 1857, 16. LDS Church History Library, Salt Lake City.

Smith, Jesse N. "The Crowning Years of a Pioneer Life," 1905. L. Tom Perry Special Collections, Harold B. Lee Library, Brigham Young University, Provo, UT.

"Soulful Thoughts of Loving Hearts," autograph book for Emmeline Wells. L. Tom Perry Special Collections, Harold B. Lee Library, Brigham Young University, Provo, UT.

Special Collections, San Francisco Public Library, San Francisco.

Stanton, Elizabeth Cady, and Susan B. Anthony. Papers. Manuscript Division, Library of Congress, Washington, DC.

Taylor, John. Family Collection. Special Collections, J. Willard Marriott Library, University of Utah, Salt Lake City.

Taylor, John. Family Papers. LDS Church History Library, Salt Lake City.

United States Federal Census Records. www.census.gov.

Utah Federation of Women Clubs. Papers. L. Tom Perry Special Collections, Harold B. Lee Library, Brigham Young University, Provo, UT.

Weber Stake Relief Society. Minutes. LDS Church History Library, Salt Lake City.

Wells, Daniel H. Papers. LDS Church History Library, Salt Lake City.
Wells, Emmeline B., Diaries 1844–1919. Original in L. Tom Perry Special Collections, Harold B. Lee Library, Brigham Young University, Provo, UT.
———. "My Trip East," typescript of Emmeline Wells's diary from 16 December 1885–29 January 1886. L. Tom Perry Special Collections, Harold B. Lee Library, Brigham Young University, Provo, UT.
———. Papers. L. Tom Perry Special Collections, Harold B. Lee Library, Brigham Young University, Provo, UT.
———. Papers. LDS Church History Library, Salt Lake City.
Wells, Hannah Corilla Free. Papers, 1856–85. LDS Church History Library, Salt Lake City.
Whitney, Newel K. File. Nauvoo Land Records Office, Nauvoo, IL.
———. Papers. L. Tom Perry Special Collections, Harold B. Lee Library, Brigham Young University, Provo, UT.
Whitney, Orson F. Collection. LDS Church History Library, Salt Lake City.
———. Diary, 1877–1931. L. Tom Perry Special Collections, Harold B. Lee Library, Brigham Young University, Provo, UT.
Williams, Zina Young. Diary, January–March 1879. Zina Card Brown Papers. LDS Church History Library, Salt Lake City.
Young, Brigham. Papers. LDS Church History Library, Salt Lake City.
Young, Zina Diantha Huntington. Collection. LDS Church History Library, Salt Lake City.
———. Diary, 1844–45, 1848–50, 1886, 1889. LDS Church History Library, Salt Lake City.

Newspapers, Magazines, and Periodicals

Ashtabula (OH) News Journal
The Ballot Box (Toledo, OH)
Deseret Evening News
Deseret Morning News (Salt Lake City, UT)
Deseret News
Deseret News Semi-Weekly
Deseret News Weekly
Deseret Weekly News
Farmer's Gazette (Barre, MA)
Franklin Democrat (Greenfield, MA)
Greenfield (MA) Gazette and Franklin Herald
Improvement Era
Juvenile Instructor
Millennial Star (Liverpool, UK)
The National Citizen and Ballot Box (Syracuse, NY)
Nauvoo (IL) Independent
Nauvoo (IL) Neighbor
New York Journal
New York Times
Orange (MA) Journal

Palmer (MA) Journal
Philadelphia Press
The Puritan: A Journal for Gentlewomen
Relief Society Magazine
Revolution
The Revolution (New York City)
Salt Lake Daily Herald
Salt Lake Daily Tribune
Salt Lake Herald
Salt Lake Herald-Republican
Salt Lake Tribune
Times and Seasons (Nauvoo, Il)
Tullidge's Quarterly
Wallace (ID) Press Times
Woman's Exponent
Young Woman's Journal

Other Sources

"The Aaronic Priesthood." *Contributor* 6 (January 1885): 129–30.

"The Age We Live In." In *The General Relief Society: Officers, Objects and Status*, 72–73. Salt Lake City: General Board of the Relief Society, 1902. Also published in *Woman's Exponent* 30 (April 1902): 89–90.

Agnew, Theodore. "Angelia Louise French Thurston Kilgore Newman." In *Notable American Women: A Biographical Dictionary*, edited by Edward T. James, Janet Wilson James, and Paul S. Boyer, 2:620–22. Cambridge, MA: Belknap Press of Harvard University Press, 1971.

Ahlstrom, Sydney E. *A Religious History of the American People*. 2 vols. Garden City, NY: Image Books, 1975.

Alexander, Thomas G. "An Experiment in Progressive Legislation: The Granting of Woman Suffrage in Utah in 1870." *Utah Historical Quarterly* 38, no. 1 (1970): 20–30.

———. *Mormonism in Transition: A History of the Latter-day Saints, 1890–1930*. Urbana: University of Illinois Press, 1996.

———. *Utah: The Right Place*. Salt Lake City: Gibbs Smith, 1996.

Allen, James B. "'Good Guys' vs. 'Good Guys': Civil Disobedience in Nineteenth Century Utah." *Utah Historical Quarterly* 48 (Spring 1980): 148–74.

Allen, James B., Jessie L. Embry, and Kahlile B. Mehr. *Hearts Turned to the Fathers: A History of the Genealogical Society of Utah, 1894–1994*. Provo, UT: BYU Studies, 1995.

Allen, James B., and Glen M. Leonard. *The Story of the Latter-day Saints*. Salt Lake City: Deseret Book, 1976.

Allen, James B., Ronald W. Walker, and David J. Whittaker, eds. *Studies in Mormon History, 1830–1997: An Indexed Bibliography*. Urbana: University of Illinois Press, 2000.

Allen, Margaret Vanderhaar. *The Achievement of Margaret Fuller*. University Park: Pennsylvania State University Press, 1979.

Anderson, Clara Hedges. "Daniel H. Wells' Experience." In *Heart Throbs of the West*, compiled by Kate B. Carter, 5:456–57. Salt Lake City: Daughters of Utah Pioneers, 1940.

Anderson, Lavina Fielding, ed. *Lucy's Book: A Critical Edition of Lucy Mack Smith's Family Memoir*. Salt Lake City: Signature Books, 2001.

Anthony, Susan B., and Ida Husted Harper. *History of Woman Suffrage*. Vol. 4. Rochester, NY: Susan B. Anthony, 1902.

"Appreciation from the Three Leading Ladies of the Church: A Tribute." *Relief Society Magazine* 6 (January 1919): 14–15.

Arrington, Chris Rigby. "The Finest of Fabrics: Mormon Women and the Silk Industry in Early Utah." *Utah Historical Quarterly* 46, no. 4 (1978): 378–96.

Arrington, Leonard J. "The Economic Role of Pioneer Mormon Women." *Western Humanities Review* 9 (Spring 1955): 145–64.

———. *From Quaker to Latter-day Saint: Bishop Edwin D. Woolley*. Salt Lake City: Deseret Book, 1976.

———. *Great Basin Kingdom: An Economic History of the Latter-day Saints, 1830–1900*. 1958. Reprint, Lincoln: University of Nebraska Press, 1966.

Arrington, Leonard J., and Davis Bitton. *The Mormon Experience: A History of the Latter-day Saints*. New York: Alfred A. Knopf, 1979.

Aunt Em. "Early Christmas Reminiscences." *Young Woman's Journal* 12 (December 1901): 539–42.

"Aunt Em." *Young Woman's Journal* 26, no. 3 (1915): 138–42.

Babcock, Barbara Allen. "Reconstructing the Person: The Case of Clara Shortridge Foltz." *Biography* 12, no. 1 (1989): 5–16.

———. *Woman Lawyer: The Trials of Clara Foltz*. Stanford, CA: Stanford University Press, 2011.

Backman, Milton V., Jr. *People and Power of Nauvoo*. Salt Lake City: Greg Kofford Books, 2002.

Bagley, Will. "One Long Funeral March: A Revisionist's View of the Mormon Handcart Disasters." *Journal of Mormon History* 35 (Winter 2009): 50–115.

Baker, Julia A. "Mispah." In *A Little Archive of Poetry*. N.p., 1890.

Bancroft, Hubert Howe. *History of Utah*. San Francisco: History, 1890.

Barnett, Alan. *Seeing Salt Lake City: The Legacy of the Shipler Photographers*. Salt Lake City: Signature Books, 2000.

Barry, Kathleen. *Susan B. Anthony: A Biography of a Singular Feminist*. New York: New York University Press, 1988.

Bartholomew, Rebecca Cornwall, and Leonard J. Arrington. *Rescue of the 1856 Handcart Companies*. Salt Lake City: Signature Books, 1993.

Baskin, Robert N. *Reminiscences of Early Utah*. Salt Lake City: Robert Baskin, 1914.

Beecher, Maureen Ursenbach, ed. "'All Things Move in Order in the City': The Nauvoo Diary of Zina Diantha Jacobs." *BYU Studies* 19 (Spring 1979): 285–320.

———. "The 'Leading Sisters': A Female Hierarchy in Nineteenth-Century Mormon Society." In *Eliza and Her Sisters*, edited by Maureen Ursenbach Beecher, 129–47. Salt Lake City: Aspen Books, 1991.

———, ed. "Letters from the Frontier: Commerce, Nauvoo, and Salt Lake City." *Journal of Mormon History* 2 (1975): 35–51.

———, ed. *The Personal Writings of Eliza R. Snow*. Salt Lake City: University of Utah Press, 1995.

———. "Women at Winter Quarters." *Sunstone* 8 (July–August 1982): 11–19. Reprinted in *Eliza and Her Sisters*, 89–92. Salt Lake City: Aspen Press, 1991.

Bennett, Richard E. "Adoption, Law of." In *Encyclopedia of Latter-day Saint History*. Salt Lake City: Deseret Book, 2000.

———. "'Dadda, I Wish We Were Out of This Country': The Nauvoo Poor Camps in Iowa, Fall 1846." In *The Iowa Mormon Trail: Legacy of Faith and Courage*, edited by Susan Easton Black and William G. Hartley, 155–70. Orem, UT: Helix, 1997.

———. "Eastward to Eden: The Nauvoo Rescue Missions." *Dialogue: A Journal of Mormon Thought* 19 (Winter 1986): 100–108.

———. *Mormons at the Missouri, 1846–1852: "And Should We Die."* Norman: University of Oklahoma Press, 1987.

———. "Winter Quarters." In *Encyclopedia of Mormonism*, 4:1568–69. New York: Macmillan, 1992.

Bennett, Richard E., Susan Easton Black, and Don Q. Cannon. *The Nauvoo Legion: A History of the Mormon Militia in Illinois, 1841–1846*. Norman, OK: Arthur H. Clark, 2010.

Bennett, Richard E., and Rachel Cope. "'A City on a Hill': Chartering the City of Nauvoo." *John Whitmer Historical Journal* (Nauvoo Conference Special Edition, 2002): 17–41.

Bennion, Sherilyn Cox. "Enterprising Ladies: Utah's Nineteenth Century Women Editors." *Utah Historical Quarterly* 49 (Summer 1981): 291–304.

Berrett, Lamar C. "Adam-ondi-Ahman." In *Encyclopedia of Mormonism*, 1:19–20. New York: Macmillan, 1992.

Bigler, David L. "'A Lion in the Path': Genesis of the Utah War, 1857–1858." *Utah Historical Quarterly* 76 (Winter 2008): 4–21.

Biographical Record of Salt Lake City and Vicinity. Chicago: National Historical Record, 1902.

"Birthday Celebration of Our Honored President." *Relief Society Magazine* 4 (April 1917): 200–201.

"Birthday of President Emmeline B. Wells." *Relief Society Magazine* 8 (February 1921): 113.

"Birthday Reception for President Emmeline B. Wells" (editorial). *Relief Society Magazine* 8 (April 1921): 227–36.

Bishop, M. Guy, Vincent Lacey, and Richard Wixon. "Death at Mormon Nauvoo." *Western Illinois Regional Studies* 19 (Fall 1986): 70–83.

Bitton, Davis. "The B. H. Roberts Case, 1898–1900." *Utah Historical Quarterly* 25 (January 1957): 27–46. Revised version in Davis Bitton, *The Ritualization of Mormon History, and Other Essays*, 150–70. Urbana: University of Illinois Press, 1994.

———. "The Exclusion of B. H. Roberts from Congress." In *The Ritualization of Mormon History, and Other Essays*, by Davis Bitton, 150–70. Urbana: University of Illinois Press, 1994.

———. *George Q. Cannon: A Biography*. Salt Lake City: Deseret Book, 1999.

Black, Susan Easton, comp. *Membership of the Church of Jesus Christ of Latter-day Saints, 1830–1848*. 50 vols. Provo, UT: BYU Religious Studies Center, 1998.

Black, Susan Easton, and William G. Hartley, eds. *The Iowa Mormon Trail: Legacy of Faith and Courage*. Orem, UT: Helix, 1997.

Blair, Karen. *The Club Woman as Feminist: True Womanhood Redefined, 1868–1914*. New York: Holmes and Meier, 1980.

Blanchard, Paula. *Margaret Fuller: From Transcendentalism to Revolution*. Cambridge, MA: Delacorte Press / Seymour Lawrence, 1978.

Blatch, Harriot Stanton, and Theodore Stanton, eds. *Elizabeth Cady Stanton as Revealed in Her Letters, Diary, and Reminiscences*. 2 vols. New York: Harper and Brothers, 1922.

Boyer, Paul S. "Howe, Julia Ward." In *Notable American Women: A Biographical Dictionary*, edited by Edward T. James, Janet Wilson James, and Paul S. Boyer, 2:225–29. Cambridge, MA: Belknap Press of Harvard University Press, 1971.

"The Brand of the Slave." *National Citizen and Ballot Box* 4 (May 1879): 2.

Brennan, James F. "Talk on Mormonism." Men's Club, All Saints Church, Episcopal Parsonage, January 11, 1925, Church of Jesus Christ of Latter-day Saints Collection in Peterborough Historical Society, Peterborough, NH, as quoted in Ronald O. Barney, "Joseph Smith's Wentworth Letter and the Forgotten Eli P. Maginn." Paper delivered at the 2005 meeting of the Mormon History Association, Killington, VT.

Brooks, Juanita. *John Doyle Lee: Zealot—Pioneer Builder—Scapegoat*. Glendale, CA: Arthur H. Clark, 1964.

Brooks, Van Wyck. *The Flowering of New England*. Boston: Houghton Mifflin, 1936.

Brown, Samuel M. "Early Mormon Adoption Theology and the Mechanics of Salvation." *Journal of Mormon History* 37, no. 3 (2011): 1–52.

Bullard, Eugene. "Historical Address." In *New Salem Sesqui-centennial*. Athol, MA: Transcript Book and Job Print, Exchange Street, 1904.

Bullock, Thomas. "Glorious News from Salt Lake." *Millennial Star* 10 (December 15, 1848): 370.

Burgess-Olson, Vicky, ed. *Sister Saints*. Provo, UT: Brigham Young University Press, 1978.

Burton, Alma P. "Endowment." In *Encyclopedia of Mormonism*, 2:454–56. New York: Macmillan, 1992.

Bushman, Richard Lyman. *Joseph Smith: Rough Stone Rolling*. New York: Alfred A. Knopf, 2005.

Cannon, Annie Wells. "Grain Saving in the Relief Society." *Relief Society Magazine* 2 (February 1915): 50–58.

———. "Mothers in Israel." *Relief Society Magazine* 3 (February 1916): 63–71.

Cannon, George Q. *The Life of Joseph Smith the Prophet*. Salt Lake City: Deseret News, 1888.

Cannon, Kenneth L., II. "The Tragic Matter of Louie Wells and John Q. Cannon." *Journal of Mormon History* 35, no. 2 (2009): 126–90.

———. "Wives and Other Women: Love, Sex, and Marriage in the Lives of John Q. Cannon, Frank J. Cannon, and Abraham H. Cannon." *Dialogue: A Journal of Mormon Thought* 43 (Winter 2010): 71–130.

Carter, Kate B. "Emmeline B. Wells." In *Our Pioneer Heritage*, compiled by Kate B. Carter, 20:295–97. Salt Lake City: Daughters of Utah Pioneers, 1957.

———, comp. *Heart Throbs of the West*. 12 vols. Salt Lake City: Daughters of Utah Pioneers, 1939–51.

———, comp. *Our Pioneer Heritage*. 20 vols. Salt Lake City: Daughters of Utah Pioneers, 1958–77.

Carver, Sharon Snow. "Salt Lake City's Reapers Club." *Utah Historical Quarterly* 64 (Spring 1996): 108–20.

A Centenary of Relief Society, 1842–1942. Salt Lake City: General Board of the Relief Society, 1942.

Christian, Lewis Clark. "Mormon Foreknowledge of the West." *Brigham Young University Studies* 21 (Fall 1981): 403–15.

———. "A Study of Mormon Knowledge of the American Far West prior to the Exodus (1830–February 1846)." Master's thesis, Brigham Young University, 1972.

Christy, Howard A. "Handcart Companies." In *Encyclopedia of Mormonism*, 2:571–73. New York: Macmillan, 1992.

Chronicles of Courage. 8 vols. Salt Lake City: International Society of Daughters of Utah Pioneers, 1990–94.

Clark, Elizabeth. *Religion, Rights, and Difference: The Origins of American Feminism, 1848–1860*. Legal History Program, Working Papers, ser. 2. Madison: University of Wisconsin Law School, Institute for Legal Studies, 1987.

Clarke, Frances Elizabeth Bellenden [Sarah Grand]. *The Beth Book*. New York. D. Appleton, 1897.

Cleveland, Rose. *George Eliot's Poetry, and Other Studies*. New York: Funk and Wagnalls, 1885.

Coleman, Dallas. *Elijah Knapp Fuller and His Ancestors*. Sacramento: Dallas Coleman and Gerald R. Fuller, 1985.

Colvin, Don F. "Nauvoo Temple." In *Encyclopedia of Mormonism*, 3:1001–3. New York: Macmillan, 1992.

"Committee Report." In *House Journal*, March 9, 1905, 758–66. Salt Lake City: Utah State House of Representatives.

Compton, Todd. *In Sacred Loneliness: The Plural Wives of Joseph Smith*. Salt Lake City: Signature Books, 2001.

Conrad, Susan P. *Perish the Thought: Intellectual Women in Romantic America, 1830–1860*. Secaucus, NJ: Citadel Press, 1976.

Cook, Lyndon W. *Joseph C. Kingsbury: A Biography*. Provo, UT: Grandin Book, 1985.

Cook, Lyndon W., and Milton V. Backman Jr., eds. *Kirtland Elders Quorum Records, 1836–1841*. Provo, UT: Grandin Books, 1985.

Coolidge, Mabel Cook. *The History of Petersham, Massachusetts*. Petersham, MA: Petersham Historical Society, 1948.

Cornaby, Hannah Last. *Autobiography and Poems*. Salt Lake City: J. C. Graham, 1881.

Costin, M. Georgia. "Mother M. Augusta (Anderson): Doing What Needs Doing." In *Worth Their Salt: Notable but Often Unnoted Women of Utah*, edited by Colleen Whitley, 32–42. Logan: Utah State University Press, 1996.

Cott, Nancy. *The Grounding of Modern Feminism*. New Haven, CT: Yale University Press, 1987.

Craik, Dina Maria Mulock. *A Life for a Life*. N.p., 1859.

Crocheron, Augusta Joyce. "Dedication." In *Wild Flowers of Deseret*. Salt Lake City: Juvenile Instructor Office, 1881.

———. *Representative Women of Deseret*. Salt Lake City: J. C. Graham, 1884.

Croly, Jennie Cunningham. *The History of the Woman's Club Movement in America*. New York: Henry G. Allen, 1898.

Dahl, Paul E. "'All Is Well…': The Story of 'the Hymn That Went around the World.'" *BYU Studies* 21 (Fall 1981): 515–27.

"Daniel H. Wells and His Wives." In *Our Pioneer Heritage*, compiled by Kate B. Carter, 8:179–201. Salt Lake City: Daughters of Utah Pioneers, 1965.

Daynes, Kathryn M. *More Wives than One: Transformation of the Mormon Marriage System, 1840–1910*. Urbana: University of Illinois Press, 2001.

Derr, Jill Mulvay. "'Strength in Our Union': The Making of Mormon Sisterhood." In *Sisters in Spirit: Mormon Women in Historical and Cultural Perspective*, edited by Maureen Ursenbach Beecher and Lavina Fielding Anderson, 153–207. Urbana: University of Illinois Press, 1987.

Derr, Jill Mulvay, Janath Russell Cannon, and Maureen Ursenbach Beecher. *Women of Covenant: The Story of Relief Society*. Salt Lake City: Deseret Book, 1992.

Derr, Jill Mulvay, and Karen Lynn Davidson, comps. and eds. *Eliza R. Snow: The Complete Poetry*. Provo, UT: Brigham Young University Press; Salt Lake City: University of Utah Press, 2009.

Derr, Jill Mulvay, and Carol Cornwall Madsen. "Preserving the Record and Memory of the Female Relief Society of Nauvoo, 1842–1892." *Journal of Mormon History* 35, no. 3 (2009): 89–117.

———. "'Something Better' for the Sisters: Joseph Smith and the Female Relief Society of Nauvoo." In *Joseph Smith and the Doctrinal Restoration: The 34th Annual Sidney B. Sperry Symposium*, 123–43. Provo, UT: BYU Religious Studies Center; Salt Lake City: Deseret Book, 2005.

Deseret News. *2011 LDS Church Almanac*. Salt Lake City: Church News / Deseret News, 2011.

Deseret Sunday School Union Music Book. Salt Lake City: Juvenile Instructor Office, 1884.

"Dr. Emmeline B. Wells Memorial." *Relief Society Magazine* 15 (April 28): 199–202.

DuBois, Ellen Carol. *Feminism and Suffrage: The Emergence of an Independent Woman's Movement in America, 1848–1869*. Ithaca, NY: Cornell University Press, 1978.

Durrant, Matthew, and Neal E. Lambert. "From Foe to Friend: The Mormon Embrace of Fiction." *Utah Historical Quarterly* 50 (Fall 1982): 325–39.

Eagle, Mary Kavanaugh Oldham, ed. *The Congress of Women: Held in the Woman's Building, World's Columbian Exposition, Chicago, U.S.A., 1893*. Chicago: Monarch Book, 1894.

Ehat, Andrew F. "Joseph Smith's Introduction of Temple Ordinances and the 1844 Mormon Succession Question." Master's thesis, Brigham Young University, 1982.

Ehat, Andrew F., and Lyndon W. Cook, eds. *The Words of Joseph Smith*. Salt Lake City: Bookcraft, 1980.

"Elizabeth Ann Whitney." In *Latter-day Saint Biographical Encyclopedia*, edited by Andrew Jenson, 3:563–64. Salt Lake City: Andrew Jenson History, 1920.

Ellsworth, S. George, ed. *The History of Louisa Barnes Pratt, Mormon Missionary Widow and Pioneer*. Logan: Utah State University Press, 1998.

Embry, Jessie L. "Grain Storage: The Balance of Power between Priesthood Authority and Relief Society Autonomy." *Dialogue: A Journal of Mormon Thought* 15 (Winter 1982): 59–66.

"Emmeline B. Wells." *Improvement Era* 14 (November 1910): 69

"Emmeline B. Wells." *Improvement Era* 20 (February 1917): 370.

"Emmeline B. Wells." In *Chronicles of Courage*, 2:182–86. Salt Lake City: Daughters of Utah Pioneers, 1991.

"Emmeline B. Wells." In *Representative Women of Deseret*, edited by Augusta Joyce Crocheron, 62–71. Salt Lake City: J. C. Graham, 1884.

"Emmeline B. Wells." *Relief Society Magazine* 8 (July 1921): 416–17.

"Emmeline B. Wells." *Tullidge's Quarterly Magazine* 1 (January 1881): 251–53.

"Emmeline B. Wells Honored." *White and Blue* (BYU student paper), March 5, 1912, 1.

"Emmeline B. Wells' Memorial Fund." *Millennial Star* 83 (November 3, 1921): 693–94.

"An Emmeline B. Wells Memorial Fund Is Started." *Improvement Era* 25 (December 1921): 187.

"Emmeline B. Woodward Wells." In *History of Utah*, by Orson F. Whitney, 4:586–90. Salt Lake City: George Q. Cannon and Sons, 1904.

"Emmeline Blanche Wells." In *Chronicles of Courage*, compiled by Daughters of Utah Pioneers Lesson Committee, 5:147–54. Salt Lake City: International Society of Daughters of Utah Pioneers, 1993.

Esplin, Ronald K. "The Emergence of Brigham Young and the Twelve to Mormon Leadership, 1830–1841." PhD diss., Brigham Young University, 1981.

———. "'A Place Prepared': Joseph, Brigham and the Quest for Promised Refuge in the West." *Journal of Mormon History* 9 (1982): 85–111.

Esshom, Frank. *Pioneers and Prominent Men of Utah*. Salt Lake City: Utah Pioneers, 1913.

———. "Utah Wheat." *Tullidge's Quarterly Magazine* 1 (July 1881): 575–82.

"Extracts from the Journal of Henry W. Bigler." In *Chronicles of Courage*, compiled by Daughters of Utah Pioneers Lesson Committee, 5:134. Salt Lake City: Daughters of Utah Pioneers, 1993.

"F. L. Woodward Tells of Aspinwall and Nemaha City." In "Stories of Early Nemaha County Settlers." Special issue, *Nebraska History and Record of Pioneer Days* 1, nos. 3–4 (1918): 4.

Fales, Susan, and Chad Flake, comps. *Mormons and Mormonism in U.S. Government Documents*, Salt Lake City: University of Utah Press, 1989.

Ferry, Jeanette. *Industrial Christian Home Association of Utah*. Salt Lake City: n.p., 1893.

"The Five General Presidents of the Relief Society." *Relief Society Magazine* 7 (March 1920): 126–37.

Flake, Kathleen. *The Politics of American Religious Identity: The Seating of Senator Reed Smoot, Mormon Apostle*. Chapel Hill: University of North Carolina Press, 2004.

Flammer, Philip M. "Nauvoo Legion." In *Encyclopedia of Mormonism*, 3:997–99. New York: Macmillan, 1992.

Flanders, Robert Bruce. *Nauvoo: Kingdom on the Mississippi*. Urbana: University of Illinois Press, 1965.

Flexner, Eleanor. "Anna Howard Shaw." In *Notable American Women: A Biographical Dictionary*, edited by Edward T. James, Janet Wilson James, and Paul S. Boyer, 3:274–77. Cambridge, MA: Belknap Press of Harvard University Press, 1971.

———. "Carrie Chapman Catt." In *Notable American Women: A Biographical Dictionary*, edited by Edward T. James, Janet Wilson James, and Paul S. Boyer, 1:309–13. Cambridge, MA: Belknap Press of Harvard University Press, 1971.

———. *A Century of Struggle: The Woman's Rights Movement in America*. New York: Atheneum, 1974.

Fox, Ruth May. "Emmeline B. Wells, a Tribute." *Young Woman's Journal* 32, no. 6 (1921): 344–46.

Fuller, Gerald R., and EKF Family Organization, comps. *Elijah Knapp Fuller Family Record*. Bountiful, UT: Family History, 1889.

"Funeral of 'Aunt Em.'" *Millennial Star* 83 (May 26, 1921): 329–30.

"Funeral Services of President Emmeline B. Wells." *Relief Society Magazine* 8 (June 1921): 355–57.

Galbraith, Richard C. "No Room at the Inn?" *This People* (Winter 1995): 41–45.

Gates, Susa Young. "Emmeline B. Wells." In *History of the Young Ladies Mutual Improvement Association*, 45–53. Salt Lake City: Deseret News, 1911.

———. *History of the Young Ladies Mutual Improvement Association*. Salt Lake City: Deseret News, 1911.

———. "Utah." In *History of Woman Suffrage*, edited by Ida Husted Harper, 6:644–50. New York: National American Woman Suffrage Association, 1922.

———. "The Young Woman's Journal." In *History of the Young Ladies Mutual Improvement Association*, 101–21. Salt Lake City: Deseret News, 1911.

"The Genealogical Society of Utah at the International Congress of Genealogy." *Utah Genealogical and Historical Magazine* 7 (January 1916): 1–7.

"General Conference of Relief Society." *Relief Society Magazine* 8 (June 1921): 319–54.

"General Conference of the Relief Society." *Relief Society Magazine* 2 (December 1915): 526–33.

The General Relief Society: Officers, Objects and Status. Salt Lake City: Relief Society General Board, 1902.

Gilman, Charlotte Perkins. *The Living of Charlotte Perkins Gilman*. New York: D. Appleton–Century, 1935.

Godfrey, Kenneth W. "Winter Quarters: Glimmering Glimpses into Mormon Religious and Social Life." In *The Eighth Annual Sperry Symposium: A Sesquicentennial Look at Church History*, 149–61. Provo, UT: Brigham Young University Press, 1980.

Goodman, Jack. "Jews in Zion." In *Peoples of Utah*, edited by Helen Z. Papanikolas, 187–220. Salt Lake City: Utah State Historical Society, 1976.

Gordon, Ann D. "The Young Ladies Academy of Philadelphia." In *Women of America: A History*, edited by Carol Ruth Berkin and Mary Beth Norton, 68–91. Boston: Houghton Mifflin, 1979.

Gordon, Sarah Barringer. *The Mormon Question: Polygamy and Constitutional Conflict in Nineteenth Century America*. Chapel Hill: University of North Carolina Press, 2002.

Grover, David H. *Debaters and Dynamiters: The Story of the Heyburn Trial*. Corvallis: Oregon State University Press, 1964.

Gullett, Gayle. "Our Great Opportunity: Organized Women Advance Women's Work at the World Columbian Exposition of 1893." *Illinois Historical Journal* 87 (Winter 1994): 259–76.

Gurko, Miriam. *The Ladies of Seneca Falls: The Birth of the Woman's Rights Movement*. New York: Schocken Books, 1976.

Hafen, LeRoy R., and Ann W. Hafen. *Handcarts to Zion: The Story of a Unique Western Migration*. 1960. Reprint, Glendale: Arthur H. Clark, 1981.

Hafen, Thomas K. "City of Saints, City of Sinners: The Development of Salt Lake City as a Tourist Attraction, 1869–1900." *Western Historical Quarterly* 28 (Autumn 1997): 343–77.

Hale, Sarah Josepha. *Northwood: A Tale of New England*. Boston: Bowles and Dearborn, 1827.

Hall, David. *A Faded Legacy: Amy Brown Lyman and Mormon Women's Activism, 1872–1959*. Salt Lake City: University of Utah Press, 2015.

Hall, Parley. "Utah and the Pony Express." In *Our Pioneer Heritage*, compiled by Kate B. Carter, 3:333–420. Salt Lake City: Daughter of Utah Pioneers, 1960.

Hansen, Karen V. *A Very Social Time: Crafting Community in Antebellum New England*. Berkeley: University of California Press, 1994.

Harmon, Nicholas D., Michael S. Huefner, and Shauna C. Anderson Young. "Almon W. Babbitt, Joseph E. Johnson, and the *Western Bugle*: An LDS Frontier Newspaper at Kanesville." *Journal of Mormon History* 3, no. 3 (2013): 163–97.

Harper, Ida Husted. *Life and Works of Susan B. Anthony*. 3 vols. Indianapolis: Hollenbeck, 1908.

Harper, Reid L. "The Mantle of Joseph: Creation of a Mormon Miracle." *Journal of Mormon History* 22 (Fall 1996): 35–71.

Harris, Mark W. *Among the Dry Bones: Liberal Religion in New Salem, Massachusetts*. N.p.: Historical Information Project of the Connecticut Valley District, 1881.

Hartley, William G. "Common People: Church Activity during the Brigham Young Era." In *Nearly Everything Imaginable: The Everyday Life of Utah's Mormon Pioneers*, edited by Ronald W. Walker and Doris R. Dant, 249–95. Provo, UT: BYU Press, 1999.

———. "From Men to Boys: LDS Aaronic Priesthood Offices, 1829–1996." *Journal of Mormon History* 22, no. 1 (1996): 80–136.

———. "Mormons, Crickets, and Gulls: A New Look at an Old Story." *Utah Historical Quarterly* 38 (Summer 1970): 224–39. Reprinted in *The New Mormon History*, edited by D. Michael Quinn, 137–51. Salt Lake City: Signature Press, 1992.

———. "Spring Exodus from Nauvoo: Act Two in the 1846 Mormon Evacuation Drama." In *The Iowa Mormon Trail: Legacy of Faith and Courage*, edited by Susan Easton Black and William G. Hartley, 61–83. Provo, UT: Helix, 1997.

———. "Winter Exodus from Nauvoo: Brigham Young's Camp of Israel, 1846." In *The Iowa Mormon Trail: Legacy of Faith and Courage*, edited by Susan Easton Black and William G. Hartley, xiii–xxxii. Provo, UT: Helix, 1997.

Hatch, Charles M., and Todd M. Compton, eds. *A Widow's Tale: The 1884–1896 Diary of Helen Mar Kimball Whitney*. Logan: Utah State University Press, 2003.

Heads of Families, First Census of the U.S., 1790, State of Massachusetts. Washington, DC: Government Printing Office, 1908.

Heath, Harvard, ed. *In the World: The Diaries of Reed Smoot*. Salt Lake City: Signature Books, 1997.

Hedges, Andrew H., Alex D. Smith, and Richard Lloyd Anderson, eds. *Journals*. Vol. 2, *December 1841–April 1843*. Salt Lake City: Church Historian's Press, 2011. In Joseph Smith Papers, edited by Dean C. Jessee, Ronald K. Esplin, and Richard Lyman Bushman. Salt Lake City: Church Historian's Press, 2011.

Henretta, James A., et al. *America's History*. Chicago: Dorsey Press, 1987.

Herringshaw, Thomas William, ed. *Local and National Poets of America: With*

Interesting Biographical Sketches and Choice Selections from over One Thousand Living American Poets. Chicago: American Publishers Association, 1890.

Hinckley, Bryant S. *Daniel Hanmer Wells and Events of His Time*. Salt Lake City: Deseret News Press, 1942.

"History of Joseph Smith." *Millennial Star* 15, no. 35 (1853): 567–68.

History of New Salem, Massachusetts, 1753–1953, Prepared for the Celebration of the 200th Anniversary, August 7, 8, 9, 1953. Amherst, MA: Hamilton I. Newell, 1953.

The History of Winnebago County, Illinois. Chicago: H. F. Kett, 1877.

Hobson, George C., ed. *Gems of Thought and History of Shoshone County*. Kellogg, ID: Kellogg Evening News Press, 1940.

Holland, J. G. *The Bay Path: A Tale of New England Colonial Life*. New York: Scribner's and Sons, 1857.

Holzapfel, Jeni Broberg, and Richard Neitzel Holzapfel, eds. *A Woman's View: Helen Mar Whitney's Reminiscences of Early Church History*. Provo, UT: Brigham Young University, Religious Studies Center, 1997.

Homer, Michael W. *On Their Way to Somewhere Else: European Sojourners in the Mormon West, 1834–1930*. Spokane, WA: Arthur H. Clark, 2006.

Horne, Dennis B., ed. *An Apostle's Record: The Journals of Abraham H. Cannon*. Clearfield, UT: Gnolaum Books, 2004.

Horr, George W. "Petersham." In *History of Worcester County, Massachusetts*, 2:199–214. Boston: C. F. Jewett, 1879.

Hyer, Paul V. "Temple Sealings." In *Encyclopedia of Mormonism*, 3:1289–90. New York: Macmillan, 1992.

Hymns and Sacred Songs, Designed for the Use of the Children of the Latter-day Saints. Salt Lake City: Juvenile Instructor Office, 1888.

Hymns of the Church of Jesus Christ of Latter-day Saints. Salt Lake City: Church of Jesus Christ of Latter-day Saints, 1985.

Illinois Public Land Purchase Records, 1813–1909. Database online. Provo, UT: Ancestry.com Operatives.

Irving, Gordon. "The Law of Adoption: One Phase of the Development of the Mormon Concept of Salvation, 1830–1900." *BYU Studies* 14 (Spring 1974): 291–314.

Iversen, Joan Smyth. "Feminist Implications of Mormon Polygyny." *Feminist Studies* 10, no. 3 (1984): 505–22.

Jensen, Richard L. "Forgotten Relief Societies, 1844–1867." *Dialogue: A Journal of Mormon Thought* 16 (Spring 1983): 105–25.

"The Jerusalem of Today." *Relief Society Magazine* 8 (February 1921): 71–77.

Jorgensen, Lynne Watkins. "The Mantle of the Prophet Joseph Passes to Brother Brigham: One Hundred Twenty-One Testimonies of a Collective Spiritual Witness." In *Opening the Heavens: Accounts of Divine Manifestations, 1820–1844*, edited by John W. Welch and Erick B. Carlson, 373–480. Provo, UT: Brigham Young University Press; Salt Lake City: Deseret Book, 2005.

Jorgensen, Lynne Watkins, and *BYU Studies* Staff. "The Mantle of the Prophet Joseph Passes to Brother Brigham: A Collective Spiritual Witness." *BYU Studies* 36, no. 4 (1996–97): 125–204.

"Joseph Smith, the Prophet." *Young Woman's Journal* 16 (December 1905): 554–56.

"Junius Free Wells." In *Latter-day Saint Biographical Encyclopedia*, by Andrew Jenson, 4:249. Reprint, Salt Lake City: Western Epics, 1941.

Kane, Elizabeth Wood. *Twelve Mormon Homes Visited in Succession on a Journey through Utah to Arizona*. Salt Lake City: Tanner Trust Fund, University of Utah Library, 1974.

Kenney, Scott G., ed. *Wilford Woodruff's Journal, 1833–1898*. Bound typescript. 9 vols. Midvale, UT: Signature Books, 1983–85.

Kesler, Donnette Smith. "Three Important Conventions." *Young Woman's Journal* 31 (May 1920): 271–76.

Kimball, Sarah M. *Woman Suffrage Leaflet*. Salt Lake City: n.p., January 1892.

Kimball, Stanley B. *Heber C. Kimball: Mormon Patriarch and Pioneer*. Urbana: University of Illinois Press, 1981.

———. *Historic Resource Study: Mormon Pioneer National Historic Trail*. Washington, DC: US Department of the Interior, National Park Service, 1991.

Langley's San Francisco Directory, 1887, 1888, 1889. San Francisco City Library.

Larson, Gustive O. *Outline History of Territorial Utah*. 3rd ed. 1965. Reprint, Provo, UT: Brigham Young University Press, 1972.

Larson, Gustive O., and Richard Poll. "The Forty-Fifth State." In *Utah's History*, edited by Richard D. Poll, Thomas G. Alexander, Eugene E. Campbell, and David E. Miller, 387–404. Provo, UT: Brigham Young University Press, 1978.

Larson, Stan, ed. "The King Follett Discourse: A Newly Amalgamated Text." *BYU Studies* 18 (Winter 1978): 193–208.

Latter-day Saints' Psalmody. 2nd ed. Salt Lake City: Deseret News, 1896.

Leonard, Glen M. "Nauvoo." In *Encyclopedia of Mormonism*, 3:987–93. New York: Macmillan, 1992.

———. *Nauvoo: A Place of Peace, a People of Promise*. Salt Lake City: Deseret Book / Provo, UT: Brigham Young University Press, 2002.

"Letters from the Camp of Israel." *Millennial Star* 10 (October 15, 1848).

"Letters of a Proselyte: The Hascall-Pomeroy Correspondence." *Utah Historical Quarterly* 25 (July 1847): 237–40. There are twenty-four letters written between May 1845 and August 1854, with an introduction in the first installment. Pts. 1–4. *Utah Historical Quarterly* 25 (January 1957): 53–70; (April 1957): 133–51; (July 1957): 237–57; (December 1957): 339–57.

Lieber, Constance L., and John Sillito, eds. *Letters from Exile: The Correspondence of Martha Hughes Cannon and Angus M. Cannon, 1886–1888*. Salt Lake City: Signature Books, 1989.

Lisonbee, Janet. *Obituaries and Life Sketches of the Early Saints Who Died in the Kirtland, Ohio, Area*. Kirtland, OH: Lake County Historical Society, 2003.

"Livestock Industry in Utah." In *Heart Throbs of the West*, compiled by Kate B. Carter, 1:210–15. Salt Lake City: Daughters of Utah Pioneers, 1947.

Lockwood, Jeffrey. *Locust: The Devastating Rise and Mysterious Disappearance of the Insect That Shaped the American Frontier*. New York: Basic Books, 2001.

"Lucy M. Hewlings." *Magazine of Poetry: A Quarterly Review, 1889–1895*, edited by Charles Wells Moulton (Buffalo, NY) 3 (1891): 436.

Ludlow, Daniel H., ed. *Latter-day Prophets Speak*. Salt Lake City: Bookcraft, 1948.

Lutz, Alma. *Susan B. Anthony: Rebel, Crusader, Humanitarian*. Boston: Beacon Press, 1959.

Lyman, Edward Leo. *Political Deliverance: The Mormon Quest for Utah Statehood*. Urbana: University of Illinois Press, 1986.

Lyman, Josephine Wells. "Daniel H. Wells." In *Bruce Hales Lyman and Josephine Wells Lyman*, filmed by Genealogical Society of Utah. Salt Lake City: Family History Library, 1888.

MacKinnon, William P. "'And the War Came': James Buchanan, the Utah Expedition, and the Decision to Intervene." *Utah Historical Quarterly* 76 (Winter 2008): 22–37.

———. "At Sword's Point, Part 1: A Documentary History of the Utah War to 1858." In vol. 10 of *Kingdom of the West: The Mormons and the American Frontier*. Norman: Arthur H. Clark, an imprint of the University of Oklahoma Press, 2008.

Madsen, Carol Cornwall. *An Advocate for Women: The Public Life of Emmeline B. Wells, 1870–1920*. Provo, UT: Brigham Young University Press; Salt Lake City: Deseret Book, 2006.

———. "'At Their Peril': Utah Law and the Case of Plural Wives, 1850–1900." *Western Historical Quarterly* 21 (November 1990): 425–40.

———, ed. *Battle for the Ballot: Essays on Woman Suffrage in Utah, 1870–1896*. Logan: Utah State University Press, 1997.

———. "A Blue Stocking in Zion: The Literary Life of Emmeline B. Wells." *Dialogue: A Journal of Mormon Thought* 16 (Spring 1983): 125–40.

———. "Decade of Detente: The Mormon-Gentile Female Relationship in Nineteenth-Century Utah." *Utah Historical Quarterly* 63 (Fall 1995): 298–319.

———, ed. *In Their Own Words: Women and the Story of Nauvoo*. 1994. Reprint, Salt Lake City: Deseret Book, 2002.

———. *Journey to Zion: Voices from the Mormon Trail*. Salt Lake City: Deseret Book, 1997.

———. "A Legacy of Faith." In *A Heritage of Faith: Talks Selected from the BYU Women's Conferences*, edited by Mary E. Stovall and Carol Cornwall Madsen, 113–20. Salt Lake City: Deseret Book, 1988.

———. "Remember the Women of Zion: A Study of the Editorial Content of the *Woman's Exponent*, a Mormon Woman's Journal." Master's thesis, University of Utah, 1977.

———. "Retrenchment Association." In *Encyclopedia of Mormonism*, 3:1223–25. New York: Macmillan, 1992.

———. "Schism in the Sisterhood: Mormon Women and Partisan Politics, 1890–1900." In *New Views of Mormon History: A Collection of Essays in Honor of Leonard J. Arrington*, edited by Davis Bitton and Maureen Ursenbach Beecher, 212–41. Salt Lake City: University of Utah Press, 1987.

———. "Telling the Untold Story: Emmeline B. Wells as Historian." In *Telling the Story of Mormon History: Proceedings of the 2002 Symposium of the Joseph Fielding Institute for Latter-day Saint History at Brigham Young University*, edited by William G. Hartley, 17–22. Provo, UT: Joseph Fielding Smith Institute for Latter-day Saint History, 2004.

Madsen, Carol Cornwall, and Susan Staker Oman. *Sisters and Little Saints: One Hundred Years of Primary*. Salt Lake City: Deseret Book, 1979.

Madsen, Gordon A., Jeffrey N. Walker, and John W. Welch. *Sustaining the Law: Joseph Smith's Legal Encounters*. Provo, UT: BYU Studies, 2014.

Madsen, Susan Arrington. "Mary Isabella Horne." In *Encyclopedia of Mormonism*, 2:657–59. New York: Macmillan, 1992.

Magnuson, Richard G. *Coeur d'Alene Diary: The First Ten Years of Hardrock Mining in North Idaho*. Portland, OR: Binford and Mort, 1968.

Marlowe, George Francis. *The Old Bay Paths: Their Villages and Byways and Their Stories*. New York: Hastings House, 1942.

Matteson, John. *The Lives of Margaret Fuller*. New York: W. W. Norton, 2012.

McCormick, John S. *Salt Lake City: The Gathering Place, an Illustrated History*. Woodland Hills, CA: Windsor, 1980.

McDaniel, E. A. *Utah at the World's Columbian Exposition*. Salt Lake City: Salt Lake Lithographing, 1894.

———. *Nauvoo the Beautiful*. Salt Lake City: Stevens and Wallis, 1946.

Melder, Keith E. *Beginnings of Sisterhood: The American Woman's Rights Movement, 1800–1850*. New York: Schocken Books, 1977.

Miller, David E., and Della S. Miller. *Nauvoo: The City of Joseph*. 2nd ed. Bountiful, UT: Utah History Atlas, 1996.

"The Mission of Saving Grain." *Relief Society Magazine* 2, no. 2 (1915): 47–58.

"Mormonism." *Times and Seasons* 4, no. 13 (1843): 206.

"Mormon Women before the House Judiciary Committee." *National Citizen and Ballot Box* 3 (February 1879): 11.

Mortensen, Joann Follett. *The Man behind the Discourse: A Biography of King Follett*. Salt Lake City: Greg Kofford Books, 2011.

Moulton, Charles Wells. "Tears." *Magazine of Poetry and Literary Review* 4 (1892): 382.

Myerson, Joel, ed. *Critical Essays on Margaret Fuller*. Boston: G. K. Hall, 1980.

"The National Council of Women." *Young Woman's Journal* 13 (June 1902): 246–51.

Neff, Andrew Love. *History of Utah, 1847–1869*. Salt Lake City: Deseret News Press, 1940.

Neilson, Reid L. *Exhibiting Mormonism: The Latter-day Saints and the 1893 Chicago World's Fair*. New York: Oxford University Press, 2011.

Newell, Linda King. "Gifts of the Spirit: Women's Share." In *Sisters in Spirit: Mormon Women in Historical and Cultural Perspective*, edited by Maureen Ursenbach Beecher and Lavina Fielding Anderson, 111–50. Urbana: University of Illinois Press, 1987.

Newell, Linda King, and Valeen Tippetts Avery. *Mormon Enigma: Emma Hale Smith*. 2nd ed. Urbana: University of Illinois Press, 1994.

Nylander, Jane C. *Our Own Snug Fireside: Images of the New England Home, 1760–1860*. New Haven, CT: Yale University Press, 1994.

Packard, Rev. Theophilus, Jr. *A History of the Churches & Ministers, and of Franklin Association in Franklin County, Mass*. Boston: S. K. Whipple, 1854.

Paige, Lucius R. *History of Hardwick, Mass., with a Genealogical Register*. Boston: Houghton Mifflin, 1883.

Parker, Scott. "Deseret Hospital." In *Encyclopedia of Mormonism*, 1:374–75. New York: Macmillan, 1992.

Pascoe, Peggy. *Relations of Rescue: The Search for Female Moral Authority in the American West, 1874–1939*. New York: New York University Press, 1970.

"Passing Events." *Improvement Era* 23 (January 1920): 274–77.

Pearson, Lisa Madsen, and Carol Cornwall Madsen. "Innovation and Accommodation: The Legal Status of Women in Territorial Utah, 1850–1896." In *Women in Utah History: Paradigm or Paradox*, edited by Patricia Lyn Scott and Linda Thatcher, 36–81. Logan: Utah State University Press, 2005.

Peirce, Elizabeth. "New Salem Revisited." In *The Lost Towns of the Quabbin Valley*, by Elizabeth Peirce, 105–22. Portsmouth, NH: Arcadia, 2003.

"Petersham History." In *200th Anniversary, Petersham, Mass., 1754–1954*. Pamphlet, n.d. Copy in my possession.

"Petitions." *National Citizen and Ballot Box* 2 (March 1878): 3.

Phelps, William W. "History of Joseph Smith." *Times and Seasons* 5, no. 16 (1844): 624–27.

"Poems by Emmeline B. Wells." *Relief Society Magazine* 3 (December 1916): 46.

Poll, Richard D., Thomas G. Alexander, Eugene E. Campbell, and David E. Miller, eds. *Utah's History*. Provo, UT: Brigham Young University Press, 1978.

Pomeroy, Thomas C. "Emmeline B. Wells." Chapter 14 in *The Gospel in Action*, 250–55. Salt Lake City: Deseret Sunday School Union Board, 1949. Printed for use in the Gospel Doctrine Department of the Sunday Schools of the Church of Jesus Christ of Latter-day Saints.

"Private Burial Grounds." In *Heart Throbs of the West*, compiled by Kate B. Carter, 6:334–35. Salt Lake City: Daughters of Utah Pioneers, 1945.

Radke-Moss, Andrea G. "Mormon Women, Suffrage and Citizenship at the 1893 Chicago World's Fair." In *Gendering the Fair: Histories of Women at World's Fairs*, edited by T. J. Boisseau and Abigail M. Markwyn, 97–112. Urbana: University of Illinois Press, 2010.

"Report on the International Council and Congress of Women." *Woman's Tribune* 16 (September 1899): 65.

"Resolutions Passed at the National Council of Women." *Woman's Tribune* 16 (February 25, 1899): 4.

Richards, Lula Greene. "How the *Exponent* Was Started." *Relief Society Magazine* 14 (December 1928): 604–7.

Robbins, Louise Barnum, ed. *History and Minutes of the National Council of Women of the United States*. Boston: E. B. Stillings, 1898.

Roberts, B. H. *A Comprehensive History of the Church of Jesus Christ of Latter-day Saints, Century I*. 6 vols. 1930. Reprint, Provo, UT: Brigham Young University Press, 1965.

———. *John Taylor, Third President of the Church of Jesus Christ of Latter-day Saints*. Salt Lake City: George Q. Cannon and Sons, 1892.

Roberts, David. *Devils Gate: Brigham Young and the Great Mormon Handcart Tragedy*. New York: Simon and Schuster, 2008.

Rogers, Aurelia Spencer. *Life Sketches of Orson Spencer and Others and History of Primary Work*. Salt Lake City: George Q. Cannon and Sons, 1898.

Ryan, Abram J. *Father Ryan's Poems*. Mobile, AL: Jno. L. Rapier, 1879.

Scott, Anne Firor. *Natural Allies: Women's Associations in American History*. Urbana: University of Illinois Press, 1991.

Scott, Patricia Lyn. "Jennie Anderson Froiseth and the Blue Tea (a Gentile Women's Literary Club)." *Utah Historical Quarterly* 71 (Winter 2003): 20–35.

Sewall, May Wright, ed. *The World's Congress of Representative Women*. Chicago: Rand McNally, 1894.

Shannon, David A., ed. *Beatrice Webb's American Diary, 1898*. Madison: University of Wisconsin Press, 1963.

"Sixteenth Amendment Workers." *National Citizen and Ballot Box* 3 (April 1878): 2.

Smart, Donna Toland, ed. *Mormon Midwife: The 1846–1888 Diaries of Patty Bartlett Sessions*. Logan: Utah State University Press, 1997.

Smith, George Albert. "Address to the Members of the Relief Society General Conference, October 1945." *Relief Society Magazine* 32 (December 1945): 714–21, 783.

Smith, Joseph, Jr., et al. *History of the Church of Jesus Christ of Latter-day Saints*. Edited by B. H. Roberts. 2nd ed. 6 vols., 1902–12; vol. 7, 1932. Reprint, Salt Lake City: Deseret Book, 1949.

Smith, Lucy E. W. "Sister Emmeline B. Wells." *Millennial Star* 83 (May 19, 1921): 315–16.

Smith, Nola Diane. "Reading across the Lines: Mormon Theatrical Formations in Nineteenth Century Nauvoo." PhD diss., Brigham Young University, 2001.

Snell, Thomas. *A Sermon Containing a Brief History of the Town, and Especially of the Church and Parish of North Brookfield, from 1798 to the Present Time*. Brookfield, MA: L. Merriam, 1838.

Snow, Florence L. "Mispah." In *Poetry of Kansas*, 100–101. Topeka: Crane, 1900.

Solomon, Martha M. *A Voice of Their Own: The Woman Suffrage Press, 1840–1910*. Tuscaloosa: University of Alabama Press, 1991.

Staker, Mark Lyman. *Hearken, O Ye People: The Historical Setting of Joseph Smith's Ohio Revelations*. Salt Lake City: Greg Kofford Books, 2009.

———. "Thou Art the Man: Newel K. Whitney in Ohio." *BYU Studies* 42, no. 1 (2003): 74–138.

Stanton, Elizabeth Cady, Susan B. Anthony, Matilda Joslyn Gage, and Ida Husted Harper, eds. *History of Woman Suffrage*. 6 vols. New York: National American Woman Suffrage Association, 1876–1920.

Stapley, Jonathan A. "Adoptive Sealing Ritual in Mormonism." *Journal of Mormon History* 37, no. 3 (2011): 53–118.

Stoll, William T. *Silver Strike: The True Story of Silver Mining in the Coeur d'Alenes*. Idaho Yesterdays. 1932. Reprint, Moscow: University of Idaho Press, 1991.

Stowe, Harriet Beecher. *Oldtown Folks*. Boston: Fields, Osgood, 1869.

Stuy, Brian H., comp. and ed. *Collected Discourses Delivered by Wilford Woodruff, His Two Counselors, the Twelve Apostles and Others, 1894–1896*. 4 vols. Burbank, CA: B. H. S., 1991.

Tait, Lisa Olsen. "Between Two Economies: The Business Development of the *Young Woman's Journal*, 1889–1900." *Journal of Mormon History* 38, no. 4 (2012): 1–54.

Talmage, May Booth. "Coronets of Age." *Young Woman's Journal* 19 (April 1908): 177–82.

Taylor, John. "Address to the Saints." *Millennial Star* 10 (November 1, 1848): 325–26.

Temple, Josiah Howard. *History of North Brookfield, Massachusetts*. North Brookfield, MA: n.p., 1887. Reprint, Salem, MA: Higginson Book, n.d.

Thatcher, Linda, and John R. Sillito. "'Sisterhood and Sociability': The Utah Women's Press Club, 1891–1928." *Utah Historical Quarterly* 53 (Spring 1985): 144–56.

Theriot, Nancy M. "Mary Wollstonecraft and Margaret Fuller: A Theoretical Comparison." *International Journal of Women's Studies* 2, no. 6 (1979): 560–74.

"Told by Emmeline B. Wells." In the section "Pioneer Love Stories." In *Our Pioneer Heritage*, compiled by Kate B. Carter, 14:534–36. Salt Lake City: Daughters of Utah Pioneers, 1960.

Tougias, Michael J. *Quiet Places of Massachusetts*. Edison, NJ: Hunter, 1996.

The Transactions of the Social Section of the Congress of Women: Women in Social Life. 7 vols. London: Congress of Women, July 1899.

"Treasurer's Report." *National Citizen and Ballot Box* 5 (August 1878): 3.

Tullidge, Edward W. *History of Salt Lake City and Its Founders*. Salt Lake City: Star, 1886.

———. *The Women of Mormondom*. New York: Tullidge and Crandall, 1877; lithograph reprint, Salt Lake City, 1975.

Turley, Richard E., Jr., ed. *Selected Collections from the Archives of the Church of Jesus Christ of Latter-day Saints*. Provo, UT: Brigham Young University Press, 2002.

US Census. Illinois, Ogle County, Flagg. June 8, 1860, 40.

———. Nebraska, Nemaha County, Aspinwall. August 18, 1870, 250.

Utah Constitutional Convention, 1895. *Official Report of the Proceedings and Debates*. 2 vols. Salt Lake City, 1898.

Van Wagenen, Lola. "Sister-Wives and Suffragists: Polygamy and the Politics of Woman Suffrage, 1870–1896." PhD diss., New York University, 1994.

Van Wagoner, Richard S. "The Making of a Mormon Myth: The 1844 Transfiguration of Brigham Young." *Dialogue: A Journal of Mormon Thought* 28 (Winter 1995): 1–24.

Waldo, Dorothy. "Story of the Academy from Its Earliest Days." *New Salem Academy Reunion Banner* (1938): 45–54. Copy in my possession.

Walker, Ronald W. "'Going to Meeting' in Salt Lake City's Thirteenth Ward, 1849–1881: A Microanalysis." In *New Views of Mormon History: A Collection of Essays in Honor of Leonard J. Arrington*, edited by Davis Bitton and Maureen Ursenbach Beecher, 138–61. Salt Lake City: University of Utah Press, 1987.

———. "Grant's Watershed: Succession in the Presidency." In "Qualities That Count: Heber J. Grant as Businessman, Missionary, and Apostle," edited by Ronald W. Walker. Special issue, *BYU Studies* 43, no. 1 (2004): 195–229.

———. "Growing Up in Early Zion: The Wasatch Literary Association, 1874–1878." *Sunstone* 6 (November–December 1981): 44–51.

———. *Wayward Saints: The Godbeites and Brigham Young*. Urbana: University of Illinois Press, 1998.

Walker, Ronald W., Richard Neitzel Holzapfel, and James S. Lambert. "Salt Lake Interior Photograph, Sabbath School Union Jubilee, July 1875." *BYU Studies* 42, no. 2 (2003): 65–74.

Ward, Maureen C., ed., *Winter Quarters: The 1846–48 Life Writings of Mary Parker Haskins Richards*. Logan: Utah State University Press, 1996.

Weimann, Jeanne Madeline. *The Fair Women*. Chicago: Academy Chicago, 1981.

Welch, John W., and Erick B. Carlson, eds. *Opening the Heavens: Accounts of Divine Manifestations, 1820–1844*. Provo, UT: Brigham Young University Press; Salt Lake City: Deseret Book, 2005.

Wells, Daniel H. "Daniel H. Wells' [first person] Narrative." *Utah State Historical Quarterly* 6 (October 1933): 124–32.

Wells, Emmeline B. "Biography of Emmeline B. Wells," ca. 1902. Written for inclusion in *History of Utah*, edited by Orson F. Whitney, 4:586–90. Salt Lake City: George Q. Cannon and Sons, 1904.

———. "Heroines of the Church: Biography of Mary Ann Angell Young." Pts. 1 and 2. *Juvenile Instructor* 26 (January 1, 1891): 16–20; (January 15, 1891): 94–96.

———. "Home Industries in Utah." *Woman's Words* 1 (August 1877): 67.

———. "Louisa Greene Richards." *Young Woman's Journal* 3 (December 1891): 97–99.

———. "Lucy Bigelow Young." *Young Woman's Journal* 3 (January 1892): 145–47.

———. "Martha Jane Horne Tingey." *Young Woman's Journal* 2 (January 1891): 145–52.

———. "Memories." In *Musings and Memories*, by Emmeline B. Wells, 195. 2nd ed. Salt Lake City: George Q. Cannon and Sons, 1915.

———. "Memory of the Sea." In *Musings and Memories*, by Emmeline B. Wells, 34–36. Salt Lake City: George Q. Cannon and Sons, 1896.

———. *Musings and Memories*. 2nd ed. Salt Lake City: George Q. Cannon and Sons, 1915.

———. "The Prophet Joseph." *Young Woman's Journal* 23 (August 1912): 435–38.

———. "Retrenchment Associations." *Woman's Words* 1 (October 1877): 101–2.

———. "Trials and Happiness." In *Musings and Memories*, by Emmeline B. Wells, 31. Salt Lake City: George Q. Cannon and Sons, 1896. Reprinted in *Millennial Star* 51 (1889): 16.

———. "'Twas on the Mount of Calvary." In *Hymns and Sacred Songs, Designed for the Use of the Children of the Latter-day Saints*. Salt Lake City: Juvenile Instructor Office, 1888.

———. "Utah." In *History of Woman Suffrage*, edited by Susan B. Anthony and Ida Husted Harper, 4:936–56. Rochester, NY: Susan B. Anthony, 1902.

———. "Vilate Murray Kimball." Pts. 1–5. *Juvenile Instructor* (July 15, 1891): 447–50; (August 15, 1891): 506–8; (September 1, 1891): 540–42; (September 15, 1891): 561–63; (November 15, 1891): 682–85.

———. "The Young People of Utah." *Woman's Words* 1 (July 1877): 53.

Wells, Junius F. "Funeral of 'Aunt Em'" (editorial). *Millennial Star* 83 (May 19, 1921): 312–15.

———. "A Manner School." In *Our Pioneer Heritage*, compiled by Kate B. Carter, 15:134–36. Salt Lake City: Daughters of Utah Pioneers, 1972.

Wells, Louie. "In Memoriam." *Contributor* 3 (February 1882): 156–58.

Welter, Barbara. "Mystical Feminist, Margaret Fuller: A Woman of the Nineteenth Century." In *Dimity Convictions: The American Woman in the Nineteenth Century*. Athens: Ohio University Press, 1976.

Wheeler, Leslie, ed. *Loving Warriors: Selected Letters of Lucy Stone and Henry B. Blackwell, 1853–1893*. New York: Dial Press, 1981.

White, Jean Bickmore. "Gentle Persuaders: Utah's First Women Legislators." *Utah Historical Quarterly* 38 (Winter 1970): 31–49.

———. "Utah State Elections, 1895–1899." PhD diss., University of Utah, 1968.

———. "Woman's Place Is in the Constitution: The Struggle for Equal Rights in Utah in 1895." *Utah Historical Quarterly* 42 (Fall 1974): 344–69.

Whitney, Helen Mar Kimball. "Scenes and Incidents at Winter Quarters." In *A Woman's View: Helen Mar Whitney's Reminiscences of Early Church History*, edited by Jeni Broberg Holzapfel and Richard Neitzel Holzapfel, 411–79. Provo, UT: BYU Religious Studies Center, 1997.

———. "Scenes in Nauvoo, and Incidents from H. C. Kimball's Journal." In *A Woman's View: Helen Mar Whitney's Reminiscences of Early Church History*, edited by Jeni Broberg Holzapfel and Richard Neitzel Holzapfel, 269–325. Provo, UT: BYU Religious Studies Center, 1997.

"Whitney, Newel Kimball." *Utah Genealogical and Historical Magazine* 28 (April 1937): 64–68.

Whitney, Orson F. "Daniel Hanmer Wells." In *History of Utah*, 4:175–79. Salt Lake City: George Q. Cannon and Sons, 1904.

———. "Emmeline B. Woodward Wells." In *History of Utah*, 4:586–90. Salt Lake City: George Q. Cannon and Sons, 1904.

———. *History of Utah*. 4 vols. Salt Lake City: George Q. Cannon and Sons, 1892–1904.

———. "Home Literature." *Contributor* 9 (June 1888): 297–302. Reprinted in *A Believing People: Literature of the Latter-day Saints*, edited by Richard H. Cracroft and Neal E. Lambert, 203–7. Provo, UT: Brigham Young University Press, 1974.

———. "Newel K. Whitney." *Contributor* 6 (January 1885): 123–132.

———. *Through Memory's Halls: The Life Story of Orson F. Whitney*. Independence, MO: Press of Zion's Printing and Publishing, 1930.

———. "The Wasatch Literary Association." *Improvement Era* 28 (September 1925): 1017–24.

———. "Woman's Work and 'Mormonism.'" *Young Woman's Journal* 17 (July 1906): 293–296.

Wickham, Gertrude Van Rensselaer. *Memorial to the Pioneer Women of the Western Reserve*. Cleveland, OH: Women's Department of the Cleveland Centennial Commission, 1896.

Widtsoe, Leah D. "Alma Bailey Dunford." In *Treasures of Pioneer History*, compiled by Kate B. Carter, 5:85–88. Salt Lake City: Daughters of Utah Pioneers, 1956.

Wilder, Charles K., comp. *Sketches of Petersham Natives and Adopted Citizens by J. B. Howe*. N.p., 1915. Pamphlet in my possession.

Wirthlin, Joseph B. "Newel K. Whitney: Faithful Steward, Steadfast Saint." In *Heroes of the Restoration*, 194–210. Salt Lake City: Bookcraft, 1997.

Woloch, Nancy. *Women and the American Experience*. 3rd ed. Boston: McGraw-Hill, 2000.

Woodruff, Wilford. "The Law of Adoption." *Utah Genealogical and Historical Magazine* (October 1922): 145–50.

Woodward, Harold Edward, comp. *Some Descendants of Nathaniel Woodward Who Came from England to Boston about 1630*. Boston: New England Genealogical Society, 1984.

"World's Congress Auxiliary of the World's Columbian Exposition." *Young Woman's Journal* 4 (October 1892): 19, 43–45.

"World's Fair Buildings." Pts. 1 and 2. *Young Woman's Journal* 4 (February 1893): 193–201; (May 1893) 337–44.

Yandell, Enid. "To the Board of Lady Managers." In *Three Girls in a Flat*, edited by Enid Yandell, Jean Loughborough, and Laura Hayes, 53–82. Chicago: Knight, Leonard, 1892.

Yarn, David H. "Sealing." In *Encyclopedia of Mormonism*, 3:1288–89. New York: Macmillan, 1992.

Yurtinus, John F. "A Ram in the Thicket: The Mormon Battalion in the Mexican War." 2 vols. PhD diss., Brigham Young University, 1975.

Index

Entries in *italics* and followed by *F* (i.e. *1F, 2F, etc.*) refer to unpaginated photographic inserts. The abbreviation E.B.W. is used in place of the full name of Emmeline B. Wells.